NINETY NINE DEAD BABOONS
AND
OTHER TALL TALES
(FURTHER ADVENTURES AND DISCOVERIES)

BY KEVIN SCOTT

This book is dedicated to my mother and late father who allowed me to be free thinking and see the world in a different light.

TABLE OF CONTENTS

Foreword	5
Bedbugs And Chopsticks	9
Baksheesh, Guns And Plugholes	85
Carthage Has Been Destroyed	213
The Rain In Spain Drains Mainly Through My Undies	273
That Place Over There	337
Jesus Christ My Part In His Downfall	407
Riding The Dirty Dog	519

FOREWORD

This book was supposed to have come out a couple of years ago, however the whole COVID nonsense somewhat scuppered everything. Trips to Turin, South Africa and India were all cancelled. The Indian one four times, however if everything goes to plan, it has been rescheduled for late 2023.

This edition includes pre pandemic trips to China, Egypt, and Tunisia. Post Lockdown trips are to Spain, South Africa, and Israel whilst there is a long lost diary that I found from my trip across the United States of America and Canada, way back in 1991.

I always approach travel with an open mind and am generally fascinated by a country's history and archaeology. Hopefully this comes across in these travelogues, as does my general view of a world that takes itself far too seriously.

The Chinese trip was an eye opener in a number of ways and was unlike any other country I have visited. It is totally different to what we are told in the Western news and rather than oppressed, the Chinese seemed very happy and getting used being lifted out of poverty. The issue in China was the fact that much of their history was destroyed under Mao and the concern there is that the ever expanding New China will eliminate what little remains of it's past.

My third visit to Egypt was by far my most ambitious and rather than book a tour, I made my own itinerary and found a guide to drive me from Cairo down to Luxor, so that I could see parts of the country that I had previously only crossed in an aeroplane. By setting my own agenda, I could spend more time where I wanted and dig into the archaeology a little deeper.

The great Phoenician city of Carthage was my inspiration for going to Tunisia. But whereas this played a role in this trip, Tunisia has some of the finest Roman remains in the world and is a fascinating country in its own right. Being home to the Berbers, who were the original Barbarians.

In a way, my trip to Spain was partly down to the fact that post COVID, there weren't many more countries in the world that would let the British in. But the region of Andalucía has some amazing Moorish and Islamic history as well as Roman remains and having played a leading role in Spain's Golden Age. The cities of Seville, Granada and Cordoba were equally fascinating.

South Africa was my homage to The British Empire. I would love to say that I went there to find out more about Nelson Mandela and the modern country, but my inspiration was the 1960's movie "Zulu". Rorke's Drift and Isandlwana were two sites that I really wanted to experience, and I had no problem with a few days on safari too.

All the above-mentioned trips were undertaken with a view to writing about them afterwards. The Israel and Palestine trip was a book that I had wanted to write for a long time on the subject of religion. I may well have written the book whether I went there or not, but last year I decided that I needed to experience these so called holy sites in order to see what history, if any, could back up the stories. It was an amazing trip, which although not really changing my views on the world, certainly left a few marks.

The final trip is a bit of an added bonus and is the diary I wrote in 1991, whilst crossing America on a Greyhound bus with a friend. It was my first real adventure abroad and although my writing tyle may have changed over the years, I think the same bewilderment in the world is still there to see. The first Gulf War was raging at the time, and it was a fascinating time to go coast to coast. It was also an age before mobile phones, laptops, and other things we take for granted in the 21st century.

A third volume is in the pipeline, with trips to Southern India and Jordan already planned. Further trips To Cambodia, Morocco and another Indian Adventure are also further on the horizon and I am sure other destinations will surface along the way.

I hope you enjoy reading this book as much as I enjoyed travelling for it!

BEDBUGS AND CHOPSTICKS
CHINA 2017

1. Hutong Tiddle Eye Po   10
2. The Chinese Cresta Run   20
3. Dumpling Overdose   29
4. Off With It's Head   38
5. Light And Buddha   47
6. Time For Tea   56
7. Boris Johnson Joins The Teletubbies   66
8. Is That A Sword In Your Suitcase   75

1   HUTONG TIDDLE EYE PO

China was an interesting choice of destination in that I was going totally into the unknown. With my trips to Egypt, Rome, Greece, and Mexico, I knew that each and every day would be full of amazing archaeological and historic wonders. With the exception of The Great Wall and the Terracotta Warriors, China was going to be more of a cultural experience than a three-week history lesson. If only because Chairman Mao's Red Guard destroyed the vast majority of the country's history during the Cultural Revolution. I'm not really sure what I was expecting. The romantic image of hundreds of Chinese on bicycles, all dressed the same juxtaposed with the severity and dourness of what we in the west are supposed to believe about living under a communist regime. The reality was to be somewhat different, but let's start from the beginning.

For once there weren't any crazy airport stories as things went very smoothly on the way to Heathrow. I don't think I have ever managed to get there any quicker. I was twenty minutes too early and had to hang around for a bit before I could drop off my suitcase.

The flight left on time and was quite full, but no screaming babies thankfully. Considering it was British Airways, there were a few complaints about the quality of service. No glass of water or orange juice before take-off and no wine with dinner. The main meal was ok, considering it was airline food, but my scrambled eggs for breakfast were green. I tried to convince myself it was a blue cheese omelette but couldn't stomach it. Having said that, three movies and two documentaries after leaving Heathrow, we were 20 minutes from Beijing.

Despite what you see on the news and read in the papers there was no smog to greet me. Supposedly it can get worse than Victorian London in Beijing with daytime visibility down to a minimum. There was a bit of dust in the air as the wind was blowing straight in from The Gobi Desert. But this wind, which was quite pleasant, making the temperatures a bearable high twenties, had blown the smog away.
Beijing airport is enormous. It is so big that you have to take a train between passport control and baggage reclaim. Thankfully it was all pretty easy, and all the signs were in Chinese and English. After a slight mix up I found my guide and the other three people who were on the same flight in the arrival's hall. It turned out that the tour group is 13 strong, 12 Brits and one American.

A car was waiting for us outside and we set off into the Beijing traffic. Not the wall to wall bicycles I had foreseen but modern motorways gridlocked with traffic. It was pretty crazy, and I likened the chaos to Mumbai with the mute button on. The driving was still as suicidal, but everyone was far too polite to honk their horns.
The airport is about 25km outside of the city and it took a good hour to get to the hotel. First impressions of the city were not great. The parts I saw were a cross between the blandest parts of New York and East Croydon. Rows upon rows of nameless concrete tower blocks, which according to our guide are mostly inhabited by Korean immigrants of which there are far too many. In fact. our guide, Willow, was a Chinese version of Nigel Farage and loves the Koreans about as much as Farage likes the Germans or the French. Funnily enough, this made me warm to him slightly.

The one pleasant part of the journey into the city were the rows and rows of wild roses along the roadside. The rose is the flower of Beijing and most of the roads were awash with pinks, reds, and yellows of some of the most exotic roses you'll ever see.

The Guangxi Plaza Hotel was about as good as I expected. The room was a bit smoky, but adequate in size. All rooms had their very own computer to use. This would have been great if it hadn't had been all in Chinese and needed a Chinese password to access it. This was a bit too much of an ask, having only had a few hours in the country.

After an hour in my room, I decided it was time to venture out for a wander and was immediately struck by how Western everything was. Realistically I didn't really foresee men on bicycles with funny hats and wall to wall rickshaws. What I wasn't prepared for was men driving Ford Mustangs in shorts and with baseball caps on back to front. If this is communism, I don't know what the yanks are worried about.

In an attempt to see some more of the authentic China, I headed off down the road to the Panjiyuan antique market, which was about 750 yards from the hotel. To be fair it would have been busier at weekends, but it really wasn't great. The antiques, most of which were not as old as I am, were more minging than Ming and the precious stones looked more jaded than jade.

One stall was doing a brisk trade in decorated walnuts, something I couldn't see the attraction of personally, but most of the antiques were fake, including bad fake pottery, jade that wasn't jade and a few reproduction magazines from the Mao era, which admittedly were interesting to look at, but certainly not worth buying. Certainly, there was nothing to tempt me to get my Yuan out of my wallet. Not even the life-sized Terracotta Warrior which would have been fun carrying around for three weeks.

I had at least hoped for some decent street food. But having purposefully walked past the local donkey meat restaurant, there was nothing, or at least nothing I was brave enough to ask for. Our guide had suggested a supermarket across the street from the hotel to get supplies, so I went there looking for something tasty for lunch and for a few cans of beer. Well, you have all heard of the pub with no beer, but I bet nobody has been to the supermarket with no food. In fact, beer, well Budweiser and Heineken, was all it had. All the other shelves were empty. A further shop across the road seemed to specialize in only Chinese sweets and Chinese medicinal herbs.

So, as it was day one, I played it safe and went back to the hotel without lunch and had a couple of cold ones in the bar, before having a couple hours of sleep. Prior to lying down I went to the bathroom and was somewhat amused by the sign above the toilet. A danger sign, showed a man going head over heels, having slipped up. The English translation on the sign read "Be Careful of Landslide." I presumed this was aimed at anyone who had braved the donkey meat restaurant and then had to run to the loo.

At 6pm, all 13 of us met and walked to the Xin Jiang Tourist restaurant for dinner. It was only five minutes from the hotel and first impressions were that it was more brothel than restaurant. A strict looking madam saw you in and each group had a table in their own private room with a burly bouncer on the door in case you complained.
I had sort of expected fairly bland food but was pleasantly surprised. Some of it was quite spicy, especially when you added the Szechuan peppercorns provided. Nobody is allowed knives and forks, so its chopsticks or starve. Thankfully I am fairly adept with them, but for others this could have proved to be the diet they had been looking for.

There were two gripes with dinner. Firstly, the beer. Eight of us asked for beer and slowly bottles started to arrive. Being polite, I passed them around the table, only to discover we were only getting six bottles and were supposed to share, leaving me and another person without one. Not that you could drink much with the shot glasses provided. I did finally get a thimbleful of beer and at the end of the meal and felt slightly better as I saw the percentage of it was only 2.5%. I wouldn't normally touch that with a barge pole. Rather interestingly, and civilized is that evidently beer is classified as a soft drink in China. At 2.5% this is hardly a surprise.

The second gripe was that, as is typical with Chinese meals. A number of dishes are placed in the middle of the table, which revolves. You are supposed to then take your share of each dish and pass things on. Now, when you have a group of thirteen, and thirteen dumplings are put on the table, it doesn't take a great mathematician to work out that if you help yourself to more than one, somebody else will go without. A couple of the group clearly failed math's at school. There was one boy who had autism who would only eat the rice and his brother who kept asking for chips. One guy took one of the dishes and kept it for himself and funnily enough, the bowl of steamed cabbage sat there untouched all evening.

Still, it was a chance to bond with the group, which all in all seemed a good bunch. As it had been a long day, I returned to the hotel and was in bed by 10. Technically I had gone 48 hours without sleep, allowing for the eight-hour time difference. It didn't take long to pass out.

The following morning, my body clock was totally out of synch. I woke up around 4am, having gone to sleep at 10. I couldn't get back to sleep and as a result of being awake I was one of the first to get to breakfast, which was pretty good with a few alarming overtones. Breakfast overseas can always be a little worrying. The thought of the Full Chinese could have offal from anything that moved in it, but you have to be brave and try something new.

The positives were the spring onion and celery pancakes and steamed buns, but these were overshadowed by more green eggs and some sort of pickled insect. My guess was scorpion or caterpillar. I was brave enough to put it on my plate, if only for the rest of the group to think how brave, or insane, I was. I was not brave enough to eat it.

Our coach left around 8.30 into the crazy Beijing traffic. It took half an hour to go three miles. But still, it seemed a lot more bearable than it had done in India. There did at least seem to be some rules being observed and more importantly, there weren't any stray cows ambling down the motorway.

Our first stop was The Temple of Heaven which was where emperors would come each year and pray for good harvests and to maintain the harmony between the cosmos, the earth, and the Chinese people. It is set in a massive park which was full of locals doing anything from exercise to gambling.

The first thing I noticed was a group of men sitting on the lawn on small wooden stalls, seemingly picking blades of grass one by one. I have no idea whether this was some sort of
Government full employment scheme or whether they simply couldn't afford lawn mowers, but nevertheless, they were going to be there for a very long time.

We walked along a beautiful, covered walkway, aptly named The Long Corridor. The ceiling was a beautiful floral pattern of pastel green and blue. Sitting below were many elderly Chinese people playing cards, backgammon or Mah Jong and gambling away their pensions. It was a bit like an al fresco Ladbrokes really.
On the lawns that weren't being hand mown, other elderly people were participating in their early morning ritual of tai chi, which our guide described as pretending to sit on a horse whilst holding an imaginary moving ball. It was fairly interesting to see. Other activities included dancing, shuttlecock (played with feet rather than racquets) and one corner was reserved for desperate parents to find suitable matches for their offspring, where they place photographs and large sums of money on the ground trying to spark some interest.

The temple itself was beautiful and a vibrant blue and green. It was built during the Ming Dynasty in 1420 and its official title is The Hall of Prayer for Good Harvests. It is 38 metres high and from the top gives a great view across the park with The Forbidden City in the far distance.

I managed to annoy the guide here, not for the first time. He was gloating how the temple was one of the largest purely wooden buildings in the world and that no metal nails or the like were used in its construction. Something to do with wood being natural and metal being what weapons are made of. Anyway, I pointed out that I had some furniture like that and did the temple come flat packed from Ikea with a few wooden plugs and an allen key. So that was me ignored for a while. This was a shame, because somebody asked what card games the locals were playing and our guide replied "puker" I was sorely tempted to ask if that was the game where they could hold, fold, and throw up, but decided not to.

You cannot enter the Temple, only walk around the base. It stands on a circular white stone platform. Projecting out of the base are numerous stone dragon heads which looked remarkably similar to those I had seen in Mexico, especially at Chichen Itza. To be fair, I don't see any possible connection, however the resemblance was staggering.

The new Beijing rose market is in the grounds and as a result, the temple was decked with roses of many colours. I must admit to a modicum of jealousy here. I have tried to grow roses of various colours on my balcony for a number of years, only to be thwarted by the gale force winds and accompanying sand blasting of salt from The English Channel. These rose bushes and trees were truly staggering.

Across from the Rose Market is the beautifully decorated Pavilion of Longevity. Only constructed in 1700, and only moved to this location in 1975 from Zhongnanhai, it has some of the most intricate artwork you could imagine. It would be the perfect place to contemplate life and the world in general, if it was not surrounded by hordes of Chinese hacking up phlegm and partaking in what is loosely described as singing.

We went back to the bus and headed into the city centre. As I gazed out of the window, it struck me how much Beijing was like Berlin. Those communists certainly loved concrete.

I also spotted a Wu Mart which looked remarkably like Walmart, and I kid you not, a fried chicken shop that had a picture of Michael Portillo in the window. Probably one of the last people I saw threatening Colonel Sanders at KFC but there you go.

We parked the minibus opposite the very impressive Beijing Railway Museum, which is housed in the city's original railway station. We then proceeded to descend into a pedestrian subway where we had to go through numerous metal detectors, show ID and undergo virtually everything apart from a full body search.

As you climb up from the subway, the first thing that strikes you are the last remains of the original city walls and the imposing Zhengyangmen Gatehouse. Built in 1451, this was the tallest gate of the city walls and would have been the final security gate for the Imperial City. Just south of the gatehouse is the equally imposing Arrow tower, where archers would deal with those who were not welcome in the city.

I had really wanted to go and see Mao, who has been pickled and on display here since his death in 1976. This was not possible, mainly due to the length of time it took to get through the six security checks. However, the enormous Chairman Mao Memorial Hall is pretty impressive as mausoleum's go. An impressive frieze showing the history of Mao's revolution is carved outside and I took a few minutes to admire the artwork.
In the middle of the square stands the Monument to the People's Heroes. This is a 38-metre-tall cenotaph honouring China's dead from The Opium Wars through to the Revolution of 1949. Behind the Monument stands the imposing Great Hall of The People, a 10,000-seat meeting place for the National Congress of The Communist Party. On the opposite side is the equally imposing National Museum of China.

At the far Northern end of the Square, Mao's giant portrait gazes down from The Gate of Heavenly Peace, the entrance to The Forbidden City, where we were to head that afternoon.

I could have stayed longer here, but we were rushed off because one old lady in our group had decided she wanted a cheap pair of glasses. Effectively I missed out on seeing Mao, because of her myopia.

I swear the whole group, minus yours truly, spent more time in the optician's than they did at The Temple of Heaven. And then we had to go and have lunch, a rather bland affair, before finally heading off for The Forbidden City.

In order to enter The Forbidden City, you have to circumnavigate a rather smelly, algae infested, moat. This was the enormous complex where the Emperor would have lived. Our guide said that there were 9,999 and a half rooms. Obviously 10,000 is far too many and I was annoyed we never saw the half room.

We entered through The Meridian Gate, where the Emperor would sit in the tower, watching his, hopefully, victorious troops return from battle. Entering The First Courtyard it was clear that for every one of the 9999 rooms there were at least twenty tourists here. It was swamped. Beijing has an amazing 24 million inhabitants. You don't get a quiet moment here.

Five ornate bridges take the Imperial pathway over a stream and continue to The Gate of Supreme Harmony where Emperors would hold court sessions with their officials. Two impressive bronze lions guard the gate, only allowing those worthy enough to enter The Outer Courtyard. This is the largest Courtyard in the city, and as a result, the busiest. As was the case at The Temple of Heaven, large dragon heads were on each wall, and it transpired that these were actually drinking fountains. Also dotted around the courtyard are enormous metal water vats. This was not drinking water. As the entire structure was made from wood, fire was a major concern, hence large vats of water were kept as a precaution.

At the end of the courtyard is The Hall of Supreme Harmony. I would love to know what it looked like but there were too many people. No amount of elbowing would get you to the entrance to look inside.

Beyond the Hall of Preserving Harmony, you finally reach the Inner Courtyards. Emperors rarely walked around their palace, instead being transported by carriage, and intricately carved ramps in front of each gate and hall, allowed for easy passage as his minions carried him on his way.

To make this, 16-metre-long carriageway was carved from a single piece of stone that was quarried in the city's southwestern Fangshan district, before being remarkably transported in the depths of Beijing winter, taking 28 days to be slid along a 30-kilometre man-made ice path.

In the Inner Court is the Palace of Heavenly Purity, the imperial bedroom for the Emperors and the Grand Hall of Union which are both beautiful, but overshadowed by the Palace of Earthly Tranquility, the Emperor's day quarters.

By now it was late, and we were behind schedule. There are numerous museums within the Forbidden City, but we just managed a brisk walk back through The Imperial Garden in order to get back to the bus.

Next stop was the Hutong area of Beijing where we were to take a rickshaw ride around the sights. It was billed as a bohemian and traditional part of the city but was little more than a slum. Albeit not quite to the level of the Mumbai slums. The Highlights were The Time Travel Bookshop, which I am guessing was like the fancy dress shop that Mr. Benn used to go to, and you could read a book and be transported off in time for an adventure. Secondly, the local primary school had the unfortunate name of fensitting and hopefully isn't developing a generation of people unable to make a decision. On the plus side there was a craft beer bar which allegedly sold the best burgers in Beijing, but my rickshaw driver didn't understand my protestations as we rode past. Probably more concerned about getting to the end of the route and dropping this overweight foreigner off and be able to go back to peddling around lighter locals.

Yes, it was time for another meal which was quite ropey. The positive was that the guide served ten bottles of beer between eight people, six of whom weren't drinking. It was tough, but I got the job done. Although I probably looked like a typical English oik walking into a theatre still trying to finish bottle number eight.
We went to see a Kung Fu show this evening which was very touristy. The others seemed to enjoy it, but funnily enough I was more concerned about it finishing and being able to get to the toilet.

2   THE CHINESE CRESTA RUN

My body clock was slowly adjusting to Chinese time, and I managed to sleep until 6am, which was a vast improvement on the previous night. Also, somewhat surprisingly, I hadn't been running to the loo all night, having consumed 8 bottles of watery lager.

As I strolled into the breakfast room, I was met by the onrushing sound of jackboots as a coach load of well-fed looking Germans marched out. The scene of desolation and the ransacked breakfast buffet was probably more akin to that caused by the Mongolian hordes in these parts. From what little was left, there was still one new food that was positively frightening. Sausages generally look quite appealing and let's face it, the German's aren't referred to as sausage munchers for no reason, but even they turned away this sausage which was grey/blue in colour. All but decomposing. I tried to make it more palatable by reasoning that The Clangers eat blue string pudding, therefore these must be blue string sausages. Not sure I'd try them again though. Pretty tasteless to be honest. Funnily enough, the pickled insects from yesterday, remained untouched and were clearly even beyond the rigours of a German's constitution.

We left the hotel around 8.30 and headed into the traffic through the modern business district of Beijing. As we crawled past the CCTV building (China's version of the BBC), our guide made a very interesting statement, "Chinese people always want to tell the truth, but sometimes the truth doesn't help." Quite refreshingly honest in a strange way. The Western media peddle their own agenda and make news up, but you will never hear them admit it.

Our guide also gave the Chinese view on why google is banned in China and as a result causes most westerners, including myself, untold problems staying in touch. Basically, according to our guide, the Chinese government wanted no access to pornography in China, but Google refused to block it. So, China blocked Google and solved the problem.

Having said that, this doesn't actually explain why you can't access the BBC website or any other UK news site. Even more bizarre when you realise that BBC world is available on the hotel tv. Chinese road signs are quite funny. My favourite being the no heavy loads one that shows an elephant on the back of a motorised rickshaw with a big line through it. Also, as per the look out for landslides sign in my hotel room, the English translation signs are a constant source of amusement. The local motor racing circuit is signposted as "Racist Park", whilst the Disabled toilet at the service station we stopped at was named The Deformed Man Toilet.
As we left the service station, it became very apparent that shopping for supplies in China was proving dangerous for some of the group. One guy was just about to swig from his bottle this morning when a look of horror came across our guide's face. Rather than water, the guy had been sold a bottle of screen wash fluid and was about to drink it down. I'm sticking to beer. Even though it is only 2.5%
After about two hours we got to The Great Wall. For something that you can supposedly see from space, I have to report that you can't see it from the ground. Partly because it is so high, but mostly because of the rows upon rows of Starbucks, Burger Kings, and Michael Portillo Fried Chicken shops.

To see it you must take your life in your hands on a rickety old chair lift on which you really don't want to look down. Not so much for the hundred-foot drop, but for the fact that you can see how you have to get back down, but I'll get to that.

The wall stretches for over 13,000 miles and is over 2,300 years old. Started by the Zhou Dynasty in 770BC, it was originally designed to keep out warring states to the North. It was the Qin Dynasty that expanded the wall in 221BC, and it was continually extended, right up to 1644AD when its primary function was to protect trade along the Silk Road.

At its highest the wall is 26 feet high. Which is not that impressive until you realise that most of it sits atop extremely high mountains. Every five hundred metres there are towers which were used by archers to guard against attack.

Today, 30% of the wall has disappeared, due to a combination of erosion and more likely, human damage. Much of which survives is not structurally sound, therefore there are only certain sections that are open to the public.

We visited the Mutianyu section which has the longest stretch of fully restored wall which you can stroll along, taking in several watchtowers.

I don't want to say that I was underwhelmed by the wall, it really is an amazing feat of engineering and design. I did think it would be taller but if it had had been, climbing up the steep steps and slopes would have been even harder. Not helped by the thirty-degree heat, which meant the intermittent fortification towers, offered some welcome shade. Once we reached the top, we were given two choices. We could climb up an extremely steep section to a watchtower or walk the longer section, taking in a few smaller towers. I decided to walk the longer section, about 2km each way, which took in Five smaller turrets and had less fierce climbs, but still some pretty challenging sections. The view is beautiful, but after an hour and a half of the same view, you have had enough. But I am glad I walked the entire length of the section that was open as the view back of the long section of wall, snaking over the mountains, was amazing.

Just as the pyramids have a Pizza Hut, I can confirm that a branch of Burger King has been built into a section of the wall whilst a Subway has been earmarked for another bit.

Whilst wandering along the wall, I stopped and chatted to the one American who was on our tour. He had saved up for this trip for months but was now totally out of his depth. Like most American's he was overweight, something that would soon get treated as he was complaining about having to use chop sticks and refusing to eat until they brought him a knife and fork. He was trying to gain favour amongst the group for us all to go to MacDonald's for lunch. But I fear all our meals are pre-booked in Chinese restaurants and his self-imposed starvation would seemingly continue.

So now for the descent. Steps weren't an option as we were about 700 feet up. So, you build a chairlift, right? Not the Chinese. They build a toboggan and their own version of the Cresta Run. You queue, with hordes of terrified tourists, all frantically checking their travel insurance policies. Finally, you get close to the front of the line and see your travel companions unceremoniously hurled down the mountain with very little chance of stopping.
All too soon it was my turn, and a loud Chinese gentleman beckoned me over, waving a large tray in his hand. I did think to myself that had the British not stopped selling opium to the Chinese, we might all fix this without a problem. He could go off and pass out somewhere and I could find some steps or a lift. I was manhandled and made to sit on a tea tray with a dodgy bit of string, which was supposedly the brake.

Suddenly a psychopathic glint came over the Chinese gentleman and I was pushed down the mountain, gaining speed on the metal switchbacks and praying that the person in front of me wasn't going so slow that I rear ended them, or even worse, the person behind, didn't smack into me at high speed. I gripped the rather flimsy brake, uttered three of four hail Mary's, shut my eyes, and the Chinese psycho yelled something in Mandarin as I was launched down the shoot.

Thankfully I wasn't rear ended, but I did end up tail gating the old bloke in front who was out for a Sunday drive. To be fair it was great fun, and if it didn't involve climbing 700 feet back up the hill, I might have had another go.

From here we went to what was a rather rushed lunch. Typical, as the food was actually very nice, and I was about to partake in my second beer of the day when lunch was curtailed abruptly by our guide forcing us all back on the bus and our driver sped off at great speed. What was the rush I thought? Maybe they had found the only knife and fork in Beijing for our American friend. Evidently it was because the president of China was bringing his guest, the president of Vietnam for a private trip to the Great Wall. When something like this happens, all roads within a ten-mile radius are shut for four hours. Basically, our bus had to get back to the main road before the President left it, or we would be stranded.

This was quite imperative, as if we had not got to the junction before The President, we would be missing our Peking Duck dinner. And in the immortal words of Elmer Fudd. I Do so like a duck dinner.
We made it to the junction of the main road with five minutes to spare. We had to wait in a small village for the motorcade to pass, which was quite interesting. Soldiers were on guard every hundred yards along the route and villagers didn't really seem to care. One thing I did notice were the recreational amenities that the Chinese government supply for even the smallest villages. They all seemed to have pagodas which would be used for early morning Tai Chi or singing, and more impressively, along the side of the road, gym equipment is provided so that the people can stay fit.

On the way back into the city we had a photo stop at The Birds Nest stadium, where the 2008 Olympics were held. It is a very impressive stadium and a far better legacy than the cheap and cheerful stadium we built four years later, and the crumbling remains of the Athens stadium from the 2000 Olympic Games.
The Cube, the Olympic Aquatic centre was equally impressive and the entire Olympic village, dominated by the towering structure where the Olympic flame was lit, has been transformed into a modern business district.

Our next stop was supposed to be billed as a traditional Chinese tea ceremony. I am always slightly wary of these sorts of claims, especially as we had yet to be taken to any special shops, as chosen by the Travel company. This turned out to be a big sales push at a tea store. We tried six teas, mostly bland, but the one with lychees was quite pleasant. Not pleasant enough to pay 275 yuan for a packet though. The highlight was the boy with autism asking for PG Tips. I wanted to but didn't have the nerve.

So, we went back to the hotel for an hour in order to psych ourselves up for our grand duck dinner. What little I had was very nice but there were still certain members of the group who were hogging the food. We got dishes to share and quite often there wasn't enough to go around. There are 13 in the group. This evening we got a dish of sweet and sour chicken with 13 pieces of chicken. So how someone can justify taking three for themselves is beyond me. At least there was enough beer again.

The following morning, we left Our Beijing hotel around 8.30 and headed to what is known as The Summer Palace. This is somewhat misleading as there isn't a palace in sight, only a beautiful park and numerous attractive pavilions.
Up until 1860 though, there was a Palace, and the fact that it is no longer here has been the reason for the Chinese bearing a rather large grudge against the British ever since. Central to all of this is one Lord Elgin. Not the one who destroyed The Parthenon in Athens, but his son, who it would appear was a complete chip off the old block. Elgin was leading a joint Anglo-French expeditionary force during the Second Opium War. In an act of insane Victorian arrogance, rather than go and meet the Crown Prince, the Emperor's son, himself, Elgin sent the Chief Reporter from The Times to negotiate the Chinese surrender. Legend has it, that the Prince was asked to bow down to a cardboard cutout of Queen Victoria, which he refused. Whether this is true is perhaps irrelevant, as British, and French troops ransacked and looted the Palace, stealing a fortune in priceless Chinese relics, most of which have never been returned and can be found scattered around 47 museums in Western Europe and America.

The journalist from The Times was captured and tortured by The Chinese and rather than negotiate, Elgin, in an act his father would be proud of, burned The Emperor's palace to the ground. Relations between China and Britain have never been the same since and whereas very few people in Britain would have heard of this incident, in China, it is still raw and there are many TV dramas, portraying Elgin as the evil villain and the British as vicious thugs and thieves.

To this day, The Chinese still describe The Park where the palace once resided as their very own Ground Zero. Whereas the Emperor would mainly reside in The Forbidden City, it would have been here that he would entertain foreign dignitaries.

Today there is a beautiful lake, bridges, pagodas, and a beautiful opera house in which foreign royalty, including the Queen, have watched performances. The boats that sail on Kunming Lake are replicas of the dragon boat that would transport the emperor to the Pavilions on the other side.

The boats carry around fifty passengers, are a bright red, yellow and green and have a bright yellow dragon's head at the front. The lake is some six kilometres in circumference, so we too took a dragon boat across the lake, passing the amazing Seventeen Arch Bridge which connects to The South Lake Island and is 150 metres long, lined by hundreds of lion statues.

The remaining Pavilions are beautiful, especially The Hall of Benevolence and Longevity. A giant dragon guards the brightly painted building, which was built in 1889, as part of the rebuilding works after the British had cleared off home. Inside, the hall's centrepiece is an ostentatious throne surrounded by a series of peacock statues and golden ornaments and backed by a mirrored screen.

Next to the Hall is the Garden of Virtue and Harmony, which houses the current Opera House. This was being refurbished, so we were unable to go in.

Along the shores of the Lake is a boardwalk that is interspersed by a number of lakeside pavilions. We stopped for a bottle of water in the shade of The Heralding Spring Pavilion. From here the views across the lake and back towards the city are stunning and despite the hordes of people, it is surprisingly tranquil.

As we made our way to the Northern exit, we passed the gorgeous Jade Belt Bridge, a dramatically steep and arching marble bridge, that thankfully you don't need to climb.

One of the main highlights here was The Long Corridor. It is a 728-metre-long covered walkway built in 1750, adorned with over 14,000 intricate paintings, depicting Chinese legends, historical battles, landscapes, and wildlife. No portrait of Lord Elgin though!

The park is wonderfully landscaped around perfectly picturesque canals, weeping willow trees and intricate temples and shrines. Too many to describe in full but one last structure that deserves a mention is the Marble Boat. Not particularly sea worthy and a reproduction, as Elgin managed to sink the original, So distraught was The Emperor in 1893, that his marble boat pavilion had been destroyed, that he diverted funds from the Chinese Navy, in other words from boats that could actually float, to pay for his new marble one which he used to have an evening snifter on board watching the sun go down.

We spent a pleasant couple of hours here before heading to the airport. En route we passed an amazing rockery that specialized in life size dinosaurs. I would have loved to have bought a life size Tyrannosaurus Rex or Brontosaurus for my balcony. Well to be honest, the brontosaurus would take up four balconies but, in any case, how on earth do you ship a dinosaur?

Our American friend on the tour was not doing anything to improve anyone's views on his strange nation. He managed to insult Chinese medicine after our guide tried to help him. He was complaining of various aches and pains and wanted some pain killers. So, everything in the airport grinds to a halt whilst we wait for a doctor to turn up in his white coat to examine him. He is offered numerous Chinese remedies but refuses all of them, insisting he only wanted American medicines. As there wasn't any Western medicine available, he continued to moan about his aches and pains. At least we got rid of him for a while as there was a MacDonald's at Beijing Airport, and he rushed off to catch up on two days' worth of missed meals. To make matters worse, on returning from MacDonald's, he complained he had a cough, so we had to wait again, as two paramedics and two security officers turned up, took his blood pressure, and checked his pulse.

They offered him some Chinese medicine at which point he went off on one demanding some American brand name cough tablet. Obviously, this was not available, so he went off to sulk. Only to return wearing a face mask and looking like a very fat version of the Green Hornet. Why do they leave America?

By this stage I had wished I had joined the three members of our group who had arranged to travel to Xian via Bullet train. I would be using the train later in the trip, so I wasn't missing out, but if it meant losing the yank, it might have been a good idea.

The flight to Xian was just under two hours. We were met by a new guide, and it took about an hour to drive into the city. On the way into town, we could see the pyramid mounds where the Han Dynasty emperors were buried. It is a shame that we wouldn't get to see these, but to be fair, they are not open to the public.

Despite rumours of overwhelming riches and rivers of mercury with diamond encrusted ceilings, the Chinese have a deep respect for their ancestors, and it would never occur to them to disturb the deceased. It was still amazing to see pyramids here, and once again more proof that society used to be global.
The centre of Xian was amazing. It is the only city in China which still has its complete city walls. They stretch for thirteen kilometres around the city, and you still enter through the imposing main gates. Inside the walls, the original bell and drum towers are still intact. The latter was surrounded by a vibrant carpet of purple, yellow and pink flowers. The bell towers were used in the morning and the drums signaled the evening curfew.

Dinner was at a theatre where we are seeing a show the following night. We were greeted outside by a youth dressed in traditional Chinese armour, banging a large drum. The coachloads of Americans were queuing up to have their pictures taken with him, which was a shame as the Chinese tourists don't bother queuing and just barge in front.

It all seemed a bit tacky to be honest and the less said about that the dinner the better, apart from the unlimited beer. I'd had two bottles before we got to our table. The two words "unlimited" and "beer" rarely get uttered together, therefore one must make the effort to comply. To be honest I took one look at the food and decided on a liquid dinner. Everybody else was overly excited because they had chips on the menu. Need I say more.
It was unfortunate that our dumpling banquets the following night would be prepared by the same place. Supposedly, the emperor would have a dumpling banquet of over 120 different dumplings. Now I like dumplings, but 120 might even challenge me. Unless we could have golden syrup on some. Supposedly we only got 13 courses.

The hotel in Xian was much nicer, although the kettle took an hour to boil. I had actually fallen asleep and forgotten I had put it on by the time it sprang to life. The traffic was a bit noisy but wasn't bad enough for me to not go to sleep and dream about dumplings.

3 DUMPLING OVERDOSE

Despite the fact that this hotel was ten times better than the one in Beijing, it could still have done with some double glazing as the noise from the 24-hour traffic kept me awake for much of the night. On opening the blinds, my first-time view of downtown Xian was one of a large, traffic filled metropolis. In hindsight, this could be said for every Chinese city I visited.

Breakfast was pretty good with no nasty surprises and a pleasant discovery in pumpkin cake, which was yummy.

At the rear of the hotel is a towering statue of the first Chinese Emperor Qin and a pond full of some of the largest goldfish you could imagine. You can't escape Qin here. This was his capital city and the heart of China during the early dynasties.

After breakfast we were informed that our American companion would not be joining us because he still had a cough. I don't know about anyone else, but having travelled all the way to China, and to Xian, to not make the effort to see The Terracotta Warriors, was insane in my eyes. We left the hotel around 9am and headed towards the site of the First Emperors tomb and the Terracotta Army. The roads were busy and wet. Not because of any excess rain, but because the local authorities wet the road every day to stop dust settling. This may well work in the summer, albeit leaving motorists massive car cleaning bills every week, but they still do it in winter when temperatures frequently plunge to minus ten and as a result the roads become an ice rink. Supposedly car insurance is not particularly cheap here as a result.

Much of Chinese culture seems very alien to the average Western visitor. Our guide was talking about population control this morning which on the face of it seems wrong.

China has recently changed from only allowing one child per family to two. But when you consider the unique issues faced by the Chinese you do have some sympathy. With a population this large it is hard to house, employ and feed everybody. Western culture is based on greed and the desire to have more. This by default leaves many without, and a small minority with nearly everything.

The Chinese system allows everyone to have a house, food, and healthcare, as long as they work. The thinking behind the one child policy that they used was that if families were allowed to have as many babies as they wanted, and the Government still promised to feed, house, and look after everyone, the country would either be bankrupt or suffer extreme poverty.

Nevertheless, in Chinese society, the younger generations are expected to support the older ones and with extended life expectancy, this has meant certain people having to support up to three generations of their family all by themselves. This is the thinking behind allowing families to have two children so as to lighten the burden of caring for the elderly. It sort of makes sense, but as with all systems, things can and do go wrong.

Our first port of call was the factory where they are restoring the terracotta warriors and make replicas of various sizes. Although a life size terracotta warrior with a real crossbow would look good on my balcony, once more I had to decline. Although we were certainly getting nearer to the mark after the life-sized dinosaurs from the previous day.

As well as every conceivable size of terracotta warrior, there were also some amazing bronze statues of dragons and mythical creatures and a workshop that was producing traditional Chinese lacquered furniture such as tables, screens, and an amazing four poster bed. These were beautiful but the prices were equally astronomical.

You can see the large untouched pyramid mound of the first emperor for miles. It is enormous. There are pits all over the area and it is believed that the underground city of tombs and burial pits stretches for an area larger than Manhattan.

A notable Han Dynasty Historian wrote of Qin's tomb that the tomb is huge. The coffin of Qin Shi Huang was cast in bronze. The Underground Palace was a gem-studded replica of imperial housing above ground. Moreover, booby traps with automatic-shooting arrows were installed to deter would-be tomb robbers.

Heaven and earth were represented in the central chamber of the tomb and the ceiling shaped into sun, moon and stars by inlaying pearls and gems symbolizing the sky and the ground was an accumulation point of rivers, lakes, and seas. It is said that the underground palace was brightly lit by whale oil lamps for eternity. Another giant statue of The Emperor greets you at the entrance as you prepare to see one of the most amazing archaeological discoveries ever made. Unfortunately, in order to get to China's past, you must circum navigate China's present and run the labyrinth of Pizza Huts, Subways and Starbucks.

The four pits that are open to the public are just a taster of what is buried around here. But a combination of superstition and respect for the ancestors means it is very unlikely to ever be dug up.
Pit one was the first we saw, and it is by far the biggest. It is hard to describe the size of it. Larger than two football fields and a building larger than an aircraft hangar for a Jumbo Jet. There are row after row of soldiers and horses, 6.000 in all and all different. It really is a jaw dropping moment to see it for the first time and archaeologists are still working here. It is easy to forget that this was only discovered in 1974 and it is very much still a live dig.
All soldiers and horses face east in a rectangular array, each one either armed with long spear, dagger, or halberd. The vanguard appears to be three rows of infantry who stand at the easternmost end of the army. Close behind is the main force of armoured soldiers holding weapons, accompanied by 38 horse-driven chariots.

Every figure differs in facial features and expression, clothing, hairstyle, and gestures, providing abundant and detailed artefacts for the study of the military, cultural, and economic history of that period. To the sides of the pit, there are a few warriors that are being painstakingly restored.

Pit three was next and is a small show pit split into two. The first half to show the condition that they found many of the warriors in, broken and in pieces due to the wooden roof collapsing at some point over the past 2200 years and then a recreation of what it would have looked like with the soldiers reconstructed. There are only 68 soldiers in this pit, and it is assumed this was a command post as all of the warriors appear to be officers.

At this point we headed for lunch, which was awful and not made any better by the local firewater. One woman and I were brave enough to try the saffron and the pomegranate wine which may well have been used by the Chinese Moon mission to launch their rocket. It was strong to say the least. Nobody was brave enough to try the frog wine. And I don't mean a cheap Bordeaux, this was a large vat of neat alcohol with a dead frog floating in it.

On to pit 2 which archaeologists have decided to keep intact. They have managed to protect the petrified wooden beams and left the warriors in their original state. All you can see are the roofs of the various rows of warriors. Partly this has been done to protect the warriors as exposure to the air makes them lose their colour in a few years, and partly to give future generations of archaeologists the chance to explore, maybe with better techniques.

The final pit contained two bronze chariots and horses, plus a museum of some of the finer statues. The two bronze carriages displayed in the hall were discovered 20 meters from the west side of the Tomb of Qin Shihuang in December 1980 and were elaborately restored before exhibition.

The carriages have about 3,400 parts each and were driven by four horses. They were mainly made of bronze, but there were 1,720 pieces of golden and silver ornaments, weighing 7 kg, on each carriage. The carriages were so well-made, and so vivid, that they boast being the best-preserved and having the highest rank among the earliest known bronze relics in China. These chariots are the biggest pieces of ancient bronzeware ever found in the world.
One of the most remarkable things about the Terracotta Warriors is that many carried real weapons, such as bronze swords, longbows, arrows, spears, axes, and crossbows. The weapons were treated to make them resistant to rust and corrosion, so that even after being buried for over 2,000 years, they are in remarkable condition and still razor sharp. Even more remarkable was a chrome plated sword. Chrome plating was supposedly invented by The Germans in 1937, well that was until the Americans invented it in 1950. Yet here was a two-thousand-year-old sword that used the same technology. Which begs the same old question. Are we evolving or devolving?

We must have spent 4 hours there and it was well worth it. We were told that we had to walk back to the bus via a row of market stalls and shops. I had envisaged lots of local market traders, but these shops were once again MacDonald's, Subway, Burger King, and another branch of Michael Portillo fried chicken.

We drove back to Xian and stopped at The Small Wild Goose Pagoda which dates to the Tang Dynasty and 960AD. It is one of the holiest sites in Chinese Buddhist beliefs and the Monastery where Buddhism was first brought to China from India. Originally named the Jianfu Temple Pagoda, after the adjoining temple, it was erected by Emperor Zhongzong in order to store the sutras that the monk Yi Jing had brought from India.

The Small Wild Goose Pagoda was built of blue bricks. Originally, it had 15 stories, and measured about 148 feet in height. Because of numerous violent storms and earthquakes, the two upper stories were destroyed. The existing 13-storey pagoda measures 142.4 feet in height.

The base of the pagoda is square. Beneath the pagoda there is an underground palace. The multi-eaves are made of overlapping bricks. The ground story has two doors facing south and north respectively and other stories have exquisite windows. The pagoda looks like a rectangular pyramid, with a beautiful design and perfect proportions.

In 1487, a violent earthquake occurred and caused the Small Wild Goose Pagoda to crack in the middle. The crack was over a foot long. In another violent earthquake in 1521, the crack disappeared, and the two parts of the pagoda magically combined with each other overnight.

The mystery was revealed during the restoration after 1949. The reason why the Small Wild Goose Pagoda can withstand dozens of earthquakes is that ancient craftsmen have formed its foundation as a hemisphere of rammed earth. In this way, pressure can be distributed evenly when an earthquake happens.
It is set in a very pretty park which was a pleasant thirty-minute stroll. Lots of flower gardens, small temples, and a large bell that you could pay a few Yuan in order to ring it.

After this we were corralled into a room for a Chinese calligraphy lesson. All of course in the attempt to make us buy some overpriced souvenir. I didn't. My attempt at calligraphy was equally pointless. We were supposed to write our names, but heaven knows what I wrote. The teacher was certainly less than impressed.

All of this, even The Terracotta Warriors, were of course nothing more than a prelude to the highlight of the day. The dumpling banquet. The word disappointment doesn't do the evening justice. The less said the better, especially the one that looked like a brussels sprout and was filled with cabbage. There was one that was made in the shape of a duck which was quite tasty, but we all felt that the dumplings didn't meet the expectations of the hype. Worse was to come in the shape of The Tang Dynasty Show.

Earlier in the day, one of the group asked if it was going to be like a Chinese Riverdance. I quipped at the time "yes, it's called Liverdance". This of course got the normal bemused response. The surrounding theatre was amazing and totally over the top. This unfortunately was where the positivity ends. I know I am being a Philistine here and this was possibly a very accurate representation of Chinese Art and Dance from well over a thousand years ago, but at the end of the day, I had dumpling envy and was no number of Chinese acrobats, dancers or singers were going to rectify this. As I endured the show, hoping that they would sing the only Chinese song I know, Ying Tong Tiddle Eye Po by The Goons, I was comforted by the fact that there was someone even more underwhelmed by the whole experience than me.

A woman was loudly snoring behind me, and I would have joined her if I hadn't been so transfixed by the leading lady who looked like she was sucking on a pickled egg all night. If there was a highlight, it would be the man in traditional Tang Dynasty costumes who managed to create an entire act out of making duck noises.

Thankfully it was over in an hour. Call me a philistine, I don't care.

The following morning saw another relatively early start with a visit to Xian city walls. There was the option to cycle around, the walls are 13km in length and we only had 90 minutes, and I did consider this for a while, however, those that did book this option looked horrified. When we climbed to the top of the steps, we saw that the whole length of the path was cobblestones. There were some very sore bottoms amongst our group that night and I would hazard to guess, sales in piles cream went up upon our return.

The fact is that whilst they were all messing around getting their bikes, I got a massive head start and actually saw as much if not more of the walls than they did. I walked from the east gate to the South Gate, slightly over 3km and then back, making it over 6km, and still made it back before a couple of the cyclists. It was a bit of a route march in 32-degree heat with no shade, but worth it. The south gate still has its original drawbridge and was worth the hike. The walls are 40 feet high and nearly 50 feet thick, covering 8 and a half miles around the ancient city. A deep moat surrounds the walls, upon which you can hire boats and sail around. Every 120 metres there are ramparts which extend out from the main wall, each of which has a sentry building.

The only entrances to the city were the four main gates which were situated North, South, East and West. The South Gate has been restored and has a working drawbridge which leads to the magnificent Royal Square. As I approached the Gate Tower, a group of soldiers dressed in period costumes, golden armour with bright red feathers on their helmets marched past. It is quite strange really. As you look back along the walls from the South Gate to the East, the soldiers almost march back in time. To the left and inside the walls, the world is thrown back 1500 years, whilst across the moat on the right, the modern skyscrapers of twenty first century Xian dominate.

The water and air conditioning on the coach was very welcoming as we headed to the Shaanxi History Museum. En route we passed the Large Wild Goose Pagoda, which was not as pretty as the smaller one we had seen the day before.

The museum had some interesting exhibits, notably from the Terracotta Warriors and also some impressive Tang and Han Dynasty relics. Most interesting was the mini–Terracotta Warriors that a later Emperor had commissioned. A similar number of troops but only about six inches high. Still impressive but not quite so space taking.

Lunch was truly appalling and was back to the same old theatre where we had endured the previous night's performance. One of the boys in our group had nine cheap beef burgers and chips from the buffet and claimed it was the best food he had had in China. When you have people like that on the tour what hope do you have of eating proper Chinese food.

Talking of people out of their depth, news came through that the American had flown back home because he developed a cough and refused to treat it with Chinese medicine. I tried explaining that most western medicines are just synthetic versions of Chinese herbal ones, but he had looked back blankly.

After lunch we went to the local Muslim market and finally saw some real life. Deep Fried crabs on sticks that looked like something out of Doctor Who, boiled goats' feet and Chinese meat pie (I'm not that brave). But I did have the most amazing lamb kebab doused in chili. The rest of the group just looked on in horror as firstly I approached the stall that had a large goat's skull dangling in front of it, and then even more so when I ordered a kebab and ate it.

The street is about 500 metres in length and although not authentic, the houses are modelled on Qing and Ming Dynasty styles. It is said that in olden days, foreign diplomatic envoys and merchants lived here and then they married and had children, so gradually the population increased. Today, most of the inhabitants here are the descendants of those immigrants and all of them are Muslim.

At the end of the street is the imposing Drum Tower. Originally built in 1380 during the Ming Dynasty, it stands at 112 feet high. As was the case with The Temple of Heaven in Beijing, it is a wooden structure that has no metal nails to hold it together. I thought about the Ikea joke again, but as it didn't get a laugh the first time, decided against it. The tower now boasts what the locals claim to be the biggest drum in China, which allegedly, if you are unlucky enough, is wheeled out for concerts occasionally.

By now it was time to head to the airport for our flight to Guilin. Xian airport is enormous and proved to be entertaining for a few hours. Inside the terminal there were little pods inside the departure areas called sleep fis. About the size of a small skip, simply pull back the lid to reveal a pillow and duvet, climb in, pull the lid back down and doze off whilst waiting for your plane, in the hope that it's not bin day in Xian. Cheaper than a hotel, I guess.

In stark contrast, the baggage for the flight was brought across the terminal by a man on a push bike. China really is a country of bizarre contrasts.

It was nearly 9 o clock before we landed in Guilin and ten before we got to the hotel. Guilin is a very modern city, and everything is lit up, almost to the extent of Las Vegas. The reason everything is new is because Guilin is China's version of Dresden or Coventry. The Japanese completely bombed the old city into extinction during the second Sino Japanese War.

4 OFF WITH IT'S HEAD

The hotel in Guilin was by far the most comfortable in the entire trip, which would have been a wonderful opportunity to have a lie in if it wasn't for the pre-arranged wakeup call at 7am. So, I staggered down to breakfast and lo and behold, three more busloads of Germans had annexed the hotel and were proceeding to devour most of the food like a swarm of locusts. It was all western food this morning as for some reason, the hotel decided that western guests would want this, whilst Chinese guests had their own breakfast room. Never could the two meet. This was disappointing; however, I was not sure I was game enough for the local breakfast delicacy which was Guilin Noodles which is noodles and horse meat. Still playing it safe, I still stayed well clear of the hot dogs just in case. All that was left after the breakfast Blitzkrieg were bacon and beans and to make things worse, when I sat on the sofa behind the table, it was so low I nearly cracked my chin on the table. At least that way I couldn't spill any of the beans down my shirt. Giving up on breakfast, I went for a short walk through the park outside of our Guilin hotel.

There is a beautiful lake next to the hotel and some peaceful gardens where you can stroll and forget about the traffic. Early morning in China is a sight to behold, the various pavilions around the lake were filled with old women doing Tai Chi or singing. Younger men were practicing more challenging martial arts, whilst others simply sat either contemplating the serenity, or practiced yoga. In one pavilion, a group of elderly ladies seemed to be dancing to what can only be compared to a Chinese version of the Birdie Song. I was sorely tempted to join in, but the clock was ticking, and I had to return to the hotel.

Guilin is surrounded by lakes and two rivers which are all shrouded with striking, tree clad peaks. It would have been nice to have had a morning to relax and enjoy the serenity.

Our coach left at 9 and set off for the wharf where we were to catch our boat down the Li River to Yangzhou. What we thought was going to be, and was in fact described as, a quiet relaxing day on the river was far from that as there were hundreds of people waiting to board a convoy of at least 20 boats.

Nevertheless, I elbowed my way to the front of the boat and stayed there for the entire voyage, ensuring a good view of the amazing scenery. This was to be the one real chance to see a glimpse of the China, away from the big urban sprawls.

The cruise departed from the town of Daxu and lasted for four hours before the hordes descended on the poor town of Yangzhou, all but seemingly doubling its 30,000 population.

The scenery from the ship will stay with me for a very long time. As we left Daxu, there were a few hills, but no clue as to what is to come. Village life goes on along the riverbank, locals paddle out to fish on what were described as bamboo rafts, but they looked more like fibre glass to me, and the occasional water buffalo comes to the shore to drink the water.

About 45 minutes into the journey, you come to Ox Gorge and the full majesty of the Li River hits you. The karst mountains soar up from places that they seemingly have no right to and their rounded summits, covered in lush green trees, loom mightily overhead. Each peak seems to be named, with the better ones being Dragons Playing The Water and Five Tigers Catch A Goat. Makes Ben Nevis pretty dull really.

Each peak has its own distinct shape and small villages appear intermittently between the lush bamboo groves. Finally, if it wasn't for the other 49 boats we were in convoy with, I was in the real China.

Our guide pointed out a ragged cliff face which was called Mural Hill. The rock has stratified and is multi coloured and it is claimed that nine horses can be made out on the rock face. Any person who can find all nine is considered smart. I think I made one out, so I guess I'm still bottom of the class.

From Mural Hill onwards, the mountains get higher, and the river gets wider, it is of little surprise that this vista is the most painted by artists in the whole of China and can in fact be found on the back of the 20 Yuan bank note.

The four hours passed very quickly and soon we were approaching Yangzhou, where we would stay the night.

Unlike Beijing and Xian, we were now into more rural China and as a result not everything was so tightly controlled. Suddenly there were beggars on the streets, some deformed, some just old and destitute. There seems to be no help here for those unable to work. This was the major issue I had with the Chinese culture to be honest. The full employment ideals were great in that if you were healthy and could work, you were well paid, given a house and plenty of pre-paid leisure opportunities.

The old are traditionally taken care of by their descendants, which is sort of OK, but the problems lie with the disabled and those who suffer work injuries. Health and safety is non-existent here and I am not talking about the bonkers system in the UK where if you can't lift more than two pieces of paper at a time for fear of suffering a repetitive strain injury and opening an insurance claim against your employer. Here people lose limbs because there is no control over safety. No goggles, no gloves, maybe a crash helmet if you are lucky. If you lose an arm or a leg, tough luck. You are out of work and on your own. It's ruthless, and despite sorting of understanding the strict economics and what they would describe as logical thinking behind it, there doesn't seem to be any room for sentiment or compassion in Chinese Social Policy.

We walked along West Street, the main tourist street, which was just wall to wall tourist rubbish. Thankfully we were going to our hotel, but some boats only cater for day trips and I'm sure the tourists are fleeced left, right and centre. I'm sure the Luftwaffe were on one boat and would soon be pillaging the shops in due course.

What our guide said would be a five-minute walk to our hotel proved to be a 15-minute route march with luggage, through loads of people. We did finally get to our hotel, which was underwhelming to say the least. No air conditioning, nor double glazing for that matter. Oh, for the comfort and soft bed at Guilin.

After an hour's rest, I set out on a mission. Yangzhou is famous for three culinary dishes. Snail noodles, snail porridge and fish cooked in beer. Snail porridge was maybe a step too far for even my adventurous appetite and despite a plethora of snail noodle bars, I went on a hunt for Beer Fish, a local delicacy which isn't even available in Guilin. This was my one chance to try real Chinese food. I wandered back to West Street and ventured down a few side alleys before plumping for a family run restaurant. No English spoken, but I pointed to a picture of a large fish drowning in a bottle of lager, and everything seemed fine.

The chef came out holding two red chilies. I gave a thumbs up, as for once I didn't want food aimed at westerners. The chef then proceeded to plonk a large bottle of beer in front of me and leave the restaurant, walking off towards the river.

Before I could pour myself a glass of beer, she was back and holding a carrier bag under my nose with a massive live carp wriggling around in it. Another thumbs up and the chef returned to the kitchen.

There then followed a loud thud, which I am guessing was curtains for the carp and into the wok it went, head, tail, you name it, with beer, soy sauce, chilies, green pepper, spring onion, tomato, and grated ginger. It was all thrown onto a plate, fish head and all, and placed in front of me. It was quite possibly the best meal I have had in years. I even got the meat from the fish's head out with my chopsticks!

Suitably full I could enjoy a stroll back to the hotel along West Street. The street has a history of over 1400 years, not that you would know it from the plethora of mobile phone shops and MacDonald's, rather aptly, locals call it Foreigners Street, as tourists rarely venture any further and outnumber the locals during the day. It is quite sad that for most tourists, they will see this as being as close to the authentic China you can get, whilst for the locals they feel like they are in a foreign country.

The few shops selling local delicacies are always fascinating as you have to try and guess what on earth they are. Thankfully, due to the tourists, many items had English subtitles. Having said that, Horse Hoof Cake didn't sound particularly appetising. Thankfully I later found out this wasn't as bad as first feared and is named due to its shape rather than its contents which are simply red beans. Dog meat is also popular here and although I didn't come across any, Dog Meat Dry Pot is a type of Balti that would never find in an RSPCA canteen.

At the end of the street, sitting on the ground was something I had hoped I wouldn't see, but was nevertheless there. An old woman, clearly suffering from leprosy, was begging, and being ignored by locals and tourists alike. Again, this is the brutal side of Chinese culture, and it is as though the whole country, Government, and people alike, have embraced capitalism and managed to make the search for profit as inhumane as possible. No prisoners are taken and those unable to join in are discarded like rubbish.

At the end of West Street is a footbridge that crosses the main road. I thought I could get a good photograph of the street from the top; however, this was impossible without getting an enormous KFC and smiling Colonel Sanders sign in the way. Welcome to 21st Century China. Away from the tourists, I walked back along the river in the direction of our hotel where everyone else was meeting for another bland dinner. I gave this a wide berth but did try the dessert, Tarrow Root which was as near as damn it to suet pudding with golden syrup on it.

After dinner we boarded the coach to see a spectacular show which takes place every night on the Li River and is directed by the man who created the opening ceremony for the 2008 Beijing Olympics. The old adage goes, never act with animals or children. Only the Chinese could conceivably attempt to choreograph over 600 performers, including local fishermen a host of cormorants, school children, local ethnic people and two water buffalos, whilst illuminating the karst mountains and river as a natural backdrop for an amazing spectacle.

The story is in six acts and tells the tale of Sanjie Liu, a mythical fairy singer from the legends of the local Zhuang people. I couldn't understand a word of it, but it was visually stunning.

After a surprisingly good night's sleep, it was time to get back on the bus and head back to Guilin. Coming down to this part of the world is all about sailing up the Li River, which we had done the day before. We needed to have a second day here and as a result what followed was a bit of a filler and pointless day with our guide getting excited about second-rate attractions.

We set off from Yangzhou by coach at 9.30 and drove back to Guilin which took around 90 minutes. It was probably quite scenic, but I dozed off.

Back in the city, we first visited Elephant Trunk Hill Park. Supposedly the hill there looks like an elephant having a drink. It has allegedly been a tourist destination since the Tang Dynasty and is said to be the embodiment of a God elephant who used to be the mount of the Emperor of Heaven. It was separated from the Emperor in a war and stranded in Guilin with severe wounds, A local couple saved its life and took care of it and as a result the elephant fell in love with Guilin and decided not to return to Heaven. When it died, it turned to stone but will supposedly come to life and protect the people. Personally, I thought it looked like a large pair of boxer shorts and in any case, the elephant didn't wake up when the Japanese raised Guilin to the ground.

In the surrounding park and botanical garden there is a poor elephant that is forced to kick a football around all day, much to the amusement of the locals and an eighty-year-old tortoise who gets whacked on the shell about twice a minute for good luck. Not exactly a nation of animal lovers are the Chinese. If they can't eat it, they abuse it. It is commonly said about the Chinese that they will eat anything with legs except for the table.

A highlight for me, but not for anybody else, was what must be the world's most hideous theme park. Any photographs would not do this travesty any justice whatsoever. And to make matters worse, our guide was waxing lyrical about it. There were papier mâché models of various movie characters that got lit up by cheap and tacky fairy lights at night. None of them were flattering to their subject matter. Whether it be the Dirty Dancing statue of Patrick Swayze that looked more like Frankenstein, Clark Gable and Scarlett O Hara impersonating The Woodentops rather than Gone With The Wind or my personal favourite, The Titanic with a big hole in it, with Leonardo Di Caprio and The Angel of The North statue taking the place of Kate Winslet, bringing the whole meaning of wooden acting to a new pinnacle.

Lunch included a glass of Osmanthus (the local flower along with azalea) wine, which was very nice, unlike the snake wine which had three dead snakes fermenting in a vat, which for some reason, nobody fancied trying. It was also notable because we got to try the local delicacy, well at least I did, the chips and burger brigade were still moaning, the Guilin Chili sauce, which is an age-old recipe of the Zhuang people and made from fresh chili, garlic, and fermented soya beans.

The centre of Guilin, where we had lunch looked fascinating, and as we rushed off to the bus, we passed an amazing Drum Tower which I would have loved to wander around and there was also a house where Sun Yat Sen lived when he set up the headquarters here for his Northern Expeditionary Army in 1921. But no, we had to rush off to Fubo Hill or as it is also known Wave Subduing Hill. Now had this been called Febo Hill, after the bland, potato croquet style snacks you can pick up in Amsterdam, I may have been more excited.

To be fair, it was quite scenic, but having experienced the karst peaks of the Li River a mere 24 hours earlier, I was somewhat underwhelmed. There were some intricate ancient Buddhist carvings in caves beneath the hill. In typical Chinese exaggeration, The Thousand Buddha Cave has a mere 239 statues. Still impressive, but well short of what was advertised. No amount of renaming an impressive stalagmite as Sword Testing Rock or building giant golden teapots was really going to improve matters.

Having declined to climb the precarious looking steps to the top of the hill, we returned to the bus for our final port of call for the afternoon. Reed Flute Caves, so named because of the abundance of reeds picked near the caves from which the locals used to make flutes. Definitely it was what it said on the tin.

As far as caves go it was spectacular and extremely artistically lit. As with all Chinese attractions, every second piece of rock or cavern had a wonderous name such as Tower Shaped Pine. Underneath this supposed pine was a rock that somebody once likened to a snowman. The rather unfortunately named Crystal Palace, a brightly lit cavern, was equally uninspiring.

It may sound as though I really didn't want to be there, but this was certainly not the case. In fact, the highlight of the day was actually situated at Reed Flute Caves. No stalagmite or Stalactite in the shape of a cow, no brightly lit cavern, or glass like underground lake, but China's first and only six-star urinal.

A couple of years earlier, The Guangxi Tourist Board, for reasons only known to themselves, decided to rate every toilet at every tourist location in the state. The ones at Reed Flute Caves were the only ones to be awarded six stars as they were deemed too good to only get the best rating of five.

To be fair they were impressive. The clear glass walls peer over a mountain ledge and give you an amazing view of the valley whilst you are going about your business. Having said that, they were out of loo roll so that should have lost them a star.

From here we went to a pearl factory for the obligatory hard sell where it always fascinates me how some people are more concerned about spending money than experiencing the country. Finally, we went back to our hotel for a couple of hours.
In the evening we travelled back to the river to see a demonstration by local fishermen of how they use cormorants to help catch the fish.

Cormorant fishing is only native to Southern China and Japan. It dates to the Tang Dynasty which ruled between 618 and 907AD, coincidently a period where there were close relations between the two countries.

The fishermen, on bamboo rafts, each have four cormorants, that have had their wings clipped. The birds then have a noose tied around their neck so that they don't swallow any fish they catch. The locals will try and argue that this is not cruel, but it must be said, I was not convinced. At the end of each raft is a lantern which shines on to the water. This supposedly attracts the fish to the surface for the waiting cormorants. For daytime fishing, several rafts would form a circle and the fishermen would beat the water with their oars in order to attract the fish.

The fishermen push the birds off the raft and into the river where they dive down and catch fish, returning to the boat where due to the noose around their neck, they either surrender the fish or choke. Even if they choose the latter option, they still have to fight the fisherman who will try and wrestle the fish from the bird's beak. For roughly every third or fourth fish that a cormorant tries to swallow, the fisherman unties the noose enough so that the bird can gulp down its hard-earned catch. The locals argue that because the fish get to swallow every fourth fish they catch, that it is not cruel. But without the noose, the cormorants could eat as much as they wanted to.

Mind you, we send packs of dogs after foxes, so who are we to preach about it.

After a quick drink in the hotel bar, it was an early night and a chance to enjoy the comfort of the Guilin hotel again before another early morning wake up call.

5 LIGHT AND BUDDHA

Another 6 am wakeup call, and I drew back the curtains to see the rain was lashing down in Guilin. My first thought was that you had to feel sorry for those people who were destined to do their cruise down the Li River that day. A quick breakfast was consumed, followed by check out of the hotel and then a bus ride to the airport. Our flight left Guilin at 10.15 and took 90 minutes to get to Chengdu, which is in the mid-west of the country. Thankfully this was far enough to leave the driving rain behind, and we were met with dry, muggy, and overcast weather. We were all met in the arrivals lounge and marched off to the awaiting coach.

The first thing you notice about Chengdu is that the road network is the craziest you will have ever seen anywhere in the world. If you think of Mumbai on acid combined and then throw that into a system that makes spaghetti junction or Los Angeles look simple, you would still be unable to comprehend the insanity Lanes veer off in various directions, there are up to four layers of roads on top of each other, with no way seemingly to get from one layer to another. Add into the mix, that buses and taxis can seemingly do a u turn whenever they want to change direction and you have absolute carnage.

After half an hour of traffic jams and what appeared to be driving around in circles we were taken for lunch. To be honest, this was a bit annoying. The traffic was bad, it would take quite a bit longer to get to our hotel and I still wanted a few hours to explore the centre of the city. Nevertheless, as Sichuan is famous for its spicy food, I had been looking forward to trying some.

Finally, the food seemed a little more authentic which resulted in numerous complaints from the rest of the group. I had a word with our local guide and wangled that I could get my own personal Sichuan pepper and chili oil to douse the food in. At least this way we are all happy. Lunch here was really good and I had an amazing Sichuan fish.

As with all cities here, Chengdu is a modern metropolis. Hence getting through the traffic took forever and we didn't get to the hotel until around 3 o clock. Thankfully we checked in fairly quickly and whereas most of the group went for a lie down, I could make my escape for a couple of hours.

We were not far from Tianfu Square, the centre of the city. A large statue of Chairman Mao peers down on the square and I found it strange that there aren't many more statues of him around. I had expected one in every city.

According to the guidebooks, Tianfu Square was Chengdu's equivalent of Tiananmen Square. I really couldn't see the connection. Tiananmen Square had checkpoints at every turn and armed guards. And although there were a number of police present at Tianfu Square, the fact that they whizzed around on Segway's made the whole thing seem a bit Toytown. Furthermore, whereas Tiananmen Square is a vast open space for military parades, Tianfu is nothing of the sort, a green park, surrounded by skyscrapers, with Mao pointing at you from one end and a giant modern art structure entitled the Golden Sun Bird in the centre.

All of the major city centre sights encircle the Square. The Science and Technological Museum, The Art Palace, The Imperial Mosque, and several shopping malls. I only had a few hours, so headed straight for the modern and recently constructed Chengdu Museum. In the past couple of years, they have found a couple of civilisations near here that seem more advanced than they should be, and the statues look totally different to anything else. Both the villages of Jinsha and Sanxingdui are near to Chengdu and although most of the finds are to be seen at the relevant sites, some relics are on show at Chengdu Museum.

Some of the remains and artefacts from Sanxingdui are believed to date back to at least 7000 BC. They were only discovered in 1986 and have completely shattered the previously conceived origins of the Chinese people.

It is now thought possible that the Mythical land of Shu, actually existed and both Sanxingdui and Jinsha were major settlements. The bronze statues found here, one of which was on display at the Chengdu Museum, have been described by the Oriental History expert from the British Museum, as a more important find than The Terracotta Warriors. The level of bronze working is far more advanced than anything found anywhere else in the World at the time' It would have been wonderful to have been able to get to see the actual site, but I am glad that I saw a few highlights at this museum.
In fact, the area's history, right up to the communist revolution was covered over six floors, whilst there was also an interesting display on Traditional Chinese Shadow puppets. All in all, I probably spent a good hour and a half there.

The museum is housed in a totally state of the art, modern structure. So, it comes as a bit of a shock when you leave via the back entrance and end up in the local meat market, with carcasses of every conceivable animal being hung up and the smell of meat being grilled by street hawkers. But this was the real China I wanted to see, which makes me ashamed in hindsight, that I passed this by and went to Starbucks for an iced coffee.

There had been the option to go and watch Sichuan Opera that evening, but every one of us declined. Instead, we went out for yet another meal at a local restaurant. Our guide led us through a maze of streets, ensured I had my little bowl of chili oil and peppers, but then announced she had to leave, and we would have to find our own way back to the hotel. Not thinking anything more of it, I tucked into an extremely spicy Kung Pao Chicken and drank a couple of beers.

By the time we left, it was dark, and I for one didn't have a clue where we were. The same could be said for almost all of our group, but cometh the hour and all that, step forward the autistic kid. He may not say much, he may ask for chips all the time, but evidently, he has a sense of direction like a bloodhound. Show him once and he can retrace any route. I admit, a few of us were skeptical, but he got us back without a problem and in plenty of time for a quick pit stop in the bar before bedtime.

It was another 7 am wakeup call and march down to breakfast. You know it is going to be one of those days when the first thing you see on offer at the breakfast buffet is labelled "rotten meat". To be fair, it was a Chinese version of bubble and squeak, but I think that got lost somewhere in translation.

The itinerary that was planned for today left me with pretty low expectations and I fear in hindsight, even they were not reached. Chengdu is one massive construction project. Roads are being built, houses are being constructed and as a result chaos abounds. The traffic this morning was just ridiculous, and we took hours to get to Leshan, which was only about 75 miles south.
Towering over the city of Leshan is Mount Emei, one of the four holy mountains of Chinese Buddhist beliefs. It was on the mountain where the first Buddhist temple was built in China in the 1st Century AD. The temple here evolved into the Guang Xiang Temple, receiving its present royal name of Huazang in 1614. The addition of more than 30 other temples including the Wannian Temple founded in the 4th century containing the 7.85m high Puxian bronze Buddha of the 10th century, and garden temples including the Qingyin Pavilion complex of pavilions, towers and platforms dating from the early 6th century; the early 17th century Baoguo Temple and the Ligou Garden (Fuhu Temple) turned the mountain into one of Buddhism's holiest sites.

We were not here to climb the mountain though, we had come to see the world's tallest Buddha, standing at 71m, and carved into the rock. Carved in the 8th century CE on the hillside of Xijuo Peak overlooking the confluence of three rivers, it is the largest Buddhist sculpture in the world. First, we took a boat trip to see it from the river, which was fine apart from one Chinese woman who could shout louder than anyone I have ever heard before. The plan was to then, according to our guide, climb up the steps to the top. Our guide was somewhat surprised that none of us wanted to do this. It was really hot and humid today and the thought of climbing a hill, mobbed by shouting locals was not appealing.

It was a remarkable piece of sculpture. A monk called Hai Tong initiated the project. His concern was for the safety of the long-suffering people who earned their living around the confluence of the three rivers. Tempestuous waters ensured that boat accidents were numerous, and the simple people put the disaster down to the presence of a water spirit rather than a lack of health and safety procedures.

So, Hai Tong decided to carve a statue beside the river thinking that the Buddha would bring the water spirit under control. Besides, the fallen stones dropped during the carving would reduce the water force there. After 20 years' begging alms, he finally accumulated enough money for the plan. When some local government officials tried to tax the money from Hai Tong, the monk said that they could get his eyeball but not the money raised for the Buddha. After Hai Tong dug out his eyeball, these officials ran away scared. The project was half done when Hai Tong passed away, probably from an eye infection, and two of his disciples continued the work. After a total of 90 years' hard work, the project was finally completed.

What we didn't realise was that the backup option to climbing the Buddha was even worse. On the way back to the bus we passed The Buddha Pub, which I suggested we all went into for a pint of light and buddha. I know they get worse.

Back on the bus, it was another three hours in traffic back to Chengdu to see Huang Longxi Ancient Village. We had hoped that this was going to make up for six hours on a bus to see a buddha, but no. If you can imagine what Disney would do to Bourton on The Water, you would only be a quarter of the way to realising what a monstrosity this place was. The buildings may well have been ancient, but they were all transformed into shops selling crap which seemingly, the entire population of Chengdu couldn't get enough of on a Saturday afternoon. There were thousands, no, millions of them in one street. So much so that some poor bugger had to walk their dog in the river because there wasn't room on the footpath. Maybe on a weekday it may have been more bearable. The town itself dates to around 200 BC and was of great military importance to the Western Han Dynasty.

The brochure said there were seven ancient streets. Unfortunately, all seven were full of mobile phone shops and candy floss stalls. What I think was the ancient Ming Dynasty Temple, was now a restaurant selling Peking Duck. I tried walking down a side street and to be fair, it was a little bit more authentic away from the swarms of screaming adults and wailing children. This is still billed as an archaeological site; however, it could not have been more about the consumerism of modern-day China.

Once again, we couldn't wait to leave and get back to the traffic jams, which proved so bad, we didn't have time to go back to the hotel to freshen up before dinner. Instead, we headed straight for Jinli Street which is an original street dating back to the Qing Dynasty. Still shops and restaurants but much more tasteful than what we saw earlier at Huang Longxi. To get there, we passed the impressive Wuhou Temple originally built to house Shu Emperor Liu Bei's remains in 221BC. This was the heart of Chengdu's Tibetan quarter, and lots of shaven headed monks in their bright orange robes were walking along the street.

In the days of the Qing Dynasty, Jinli Street was the place to head for baldachin, a rich, ornate cloth, native to this area. It is known as the First Street of The Shu Kingdom and was restored to its former glory in 2004. It was quite cool after dark with impromptu Sichuan opera singers, shadow puppet displays and traditional street food, intermixed with the mobile phone shops and inevitable Starbucks. The latter is situated next door to a traditional Chinese tea house, which I thought was an interesting juxtaposition. Some of the ornate local lacquerware was beautiful and it was a pleasant contrast to our earlier nightmare. I couldn't help thinking that a bit longer here, a visit to the Wuhan Temple and to either Jinsha or Sanxingdui would have been far better.

I'm not sure why, but I was quite miffed that rotten meat wasn't on the menu for a second morning. We checked out of our Chengdu hotel and set off for the main reason that people come to this part of China.

The weather was a bit drizzly but very humid for most of the morning, which we spent at The Chengdu Panda Base, which is the world's leading giant panda breeding centre. Starting with only 6 pandas, they now have over 130. The whole reserve has been created to imitate the natural habitat of the pandas to give them the best possible environment to breed.

Giant pandas are only native to three states in China, of which Sichuan is one. A wooden walkway takes you through the lush bamboo and natural hillside.

After initial concerns that my panda safari would be about as successful as my tiger one in India a few years ago, we came across quite a few of them. Mostly fast asleep, but totally unaware of the hordes taking pictures. Apparently, the giant pandas wake up and go on a bamboo feeding frenzy around 8 am and gorge themselves. By 10 am they are so full they just pass out for the rest of the day. This of course is why they are so scarce. Any predator simply has to wait until after ten and then attack whilst they are out cold. We arrived around 10.30 and most were asleep or at the very least looking for somewhere comfortable to get their head down.

There was very little action apart from one really chilled out Panda who managed to take an enormous dump whilst fast asleep on a tree branch. You would need to be pretty relaxed to manage that.

Apart from giant pandas, they also have the less scarce red panda which resembles a rather large racoon and seems a lot more agile and partial to sweet potatoes. Even though they were more active and easier to locate, they really are second class citizens here as everyone wants to see the Giant Pandas.

We spent all morning there and also had a very nice lunch at the restaurant. And I know that I should be waxing lyrical about the fluffy pandas and not returning to age old subjects, but the panda base had the best toilet ever. No view like the one in Guilin, but heated seats that you could regulate yourself, four different types of water jet to clean up afterwards, soothing music or the sound of running water to help you on your way plus a jet of warm air to dry things off at the end. If I hadn't had to catch a train, I could have sat there playing all day.

But this was the parting of the ways for a while. The two boys and their parents were flying off to Hong Kong, I was off to Chongqing by train and the other four, who I would catch up with in Shanghai, were heading off to Lijiang.

I was dropped off at Chengdu East railway station to catch the bullet train to Chongqing. Southern Railways should send all their employees to China to see how a proper train service should be run. On time, clean, personal live tv screens on the back of seats, all messages in English and Chinese, waitress service and a train that does 300 kilometres per hour. Southern have enough trouble getting from Seaford to Brighton.

I was met at Chongqing by a guide who drove me to a restaurant for dinner before I boarded my cruise ship which was to take me down the Yangtze River for three days. En route he asked me what I knew about Chongqing. Firstly, I said that I knew it was the largest city in the world, with a current population of over 32 million.

He was impressed by this and I continued that I was aware that it was the home of Hotpot, Chinese not Lancashire, that was supposed to be the spiciest dish in China, He must have thought by now that I was well informed but unfortunately this was completely shattered by the third thing I knew about Chongqing, which was that it boasts the world's largest urinal called The Porcelain Palace.

My guide confirmed this was true and said it was interesting to see which parts of information make it to the west. I tried to explain that I probably wasn't a typical example of a tourist, but he told me that there were over 1000 urinals which were open 24 hours a day, some of which are shaped like crocodile heads whilst others are shaped like the Virgin Mary. Now I was really annoyed I couldn't get there.

Despite not managing to get to The Porcelain Palace, I did get to experience the food. As it was just me, I convinced the guide to let me eat the local food rather than the tourist rubbish that everyone else gets. So, whilst other tourists were eating bland old sweet and sour pork, I tucked into chillied rabbit, duck, fish and water buffalo and some extremely fiery prawns. After dinner, the guide took me to a local supermarket where I stocked up on some beers for the cruise.

It was about 7pm when I boarded the boat and was shown to my fairly large cabin, which had a private balcony. Chongqing looked amazing lit up at night, with the lights of the skyscrapers reflecting in the waters of The Yangtze. The problem was that the river was so low that we couldn't leave on time and had to wait for a few hours until the levels rose again.

If we left too late, it would affect where we would stop the following day, as the boat has to moor at set points along the river. I was hopeful that we would embark at some stage later that night, if not early morning. I wasn't that bothered really. As long as I got to where I was supposed to be at the end of it all. I planned to treat the next few days like a proper holiday, have a few beers and watch the world go by from my balcony.
The passengers on the ship were split into four distinct groups. The Chinese who were extremely loud and annoying. It comes natural to them. The Americans who were equally loud and annoying, which comes natural to them too, a coachload of Indians, who weren't very loud but had no sense of direction and bumped into everyone and everything. And then there was me.

Whilst the cultural chaos exploded around me, I wandered down to the main bar, took a stool and introduced myself to the barmaid, ensuring personal service throughout the trip. There then followed a safety meeting, which was pointless as if we were sinking the Americans and Chinese would shout very loudly whilst the Indians crashed into everyone and knocked them overboard,
I had another beer and retired to my room where a rather delicious looking bowl of Chinese Pears had been left for me.

6 TIME FOR TEA

I think we finally left Chongqing around 2am, around five hours late. I woke up to a miserable rainy day. The clouds were hugging the riverside hills and the drizzle occasionally made way for driving rain.

As a result of our late departure, the scheduled mid-morning stop at Fengdu was cancelled and we carried on down river until 3pm. This was a shame as Fengdu sounded quite interesting as it was an abandoned town known as Ghost City full of statues portraying the Chinese beliefs in the afterlife. It sounded a bit like a Halloween theme park, but the problem was that you had to climb six hundred steps up a mountain to reach it and I'm not sure that would be very pleasant in driving rain.

The food on board seemed to be seriously disappointing. Breakfast was very bland; the lunch buffet wasn't good, and the evening meal was so salty you couldn't taste it. So, with no onshore excursions, there wasn't really much else to do but drink and watch the world go by. At least I got some laundry done. The view from the balcony was a contrasting one of industry and countryside. The Yangtze is the third largest river in the world and winds across China for 3,964 miles and is one of the economic lifelines of the country. In ancient times much of the traffic on the water would carry grain from the fertile lands to the big cities. These days the large ships carry anything from cars to livestock. Factories, whether they be cement works or electronics factories grace the riverbanks and load their goods on to ships, mostly destined for Chongqing upstream or Shanghai, downstream. Derelict ships that have run aground are frequently seen sitting redundant on the shore and then for a few miles you may get a section of unspoilt countryside with water buffalo drinking from the river.

I did go down to the main deck for a lecture on Chinese medicine in the morning but the large group of elderly Americans, large both in quantity and girth, were just too embarrassing to be around. When one of them tried to start a hokey cokey during a lecture on herbal remedies for back pain and then performed the birdie song dance, I decided it was time to retire back to the beers in my fridge.

Thankfully there were a couple of Australians onboard, and we spent a couple of hours drinking beer and insulting the other guests.

It was mid-afternoon before we moored at our only stop of the day, which was to the small town of Shibaozhai, which roughly translated, means Precious Stone Fortress. It is on a 720-foot hill and is crowned with an amazing pagoda and temple.

The rain was lashing down at this point and 300 umbrellas walking around a temple was difficult, if not dangerous. I nearly had my eyes poked by umbrellas several times. We had to walk through a small market which was notable for someone selling live snakes in a bucket. I declined and prayed that the ship's chef stayed on board and did the same. Having said that, maybe not in hindsight after what he served up for dinner.

The most dangerous part of this shore excursion was the rickety bridge that connected the little island the temple was on to the mainland. It was swaying all over the place, like an ice rink due to the wet conditions and full of tourists. There is no such thing as health and safety in this country and one old Indian woman nearly ended up in the Yangtze.

Built in the Ming Dynasty, Shibaozhai consists of a gate, a pavilion, and a temple. The gate is caved with some vivid reliefs. Within the gate is the 184 feet high 12-storey wooden pavilion. It is the tallest specimen of ancient architecture with the most stories in China and regarded as one of the finest examples of this type of architecture in the world.

Inside the pavilion, there are steles and inscriptions of past dynasties on each floor. The view of the river, albeit through the rain and mist and between umbrellas, was spectacular. The temple at the top could only be reached by a path hewn in the rock with an iron chain to hold on to. In the driving rain this appeared impossible. Few tried, none succeeded.

At the top of the pavilion is a small hole that is known as the Rice Flowing Hole. According to legend, rice once flowed from the hole every day after the temple was built. A greedy monk wanting more rice to flow from the hole made it larger and from that day no more rice appeared. It was interesting but by this point I was so wet and the thought of going clip clop over the rickety, and very slippery bridge meant all I could think about was the warmth and dry of my cabin.

Back to the subject of health and safety. As we left Shibaozhai we passed under a large bridge where some men were welding in the middle of a downpour and a lightning storm.

That evening, after what was billed as a banquet, but in reality, was inedible, the crew put on a fashion show in the ship's main bar. This unfortunately scuppered my plans of a quiet drink and resulted in an early night.

The following morning saw more grey skies, but it was thankfully dry and there was no mist. The ship had moored overnight at Finjie, and we had to have an early breakfast before our first shore excursion of the day, which was to Baidi, also known as The White Emperor City.

Very few people opted to go on this tour due to the inclement conditions of the previous day, but I took the view that I would be unlikely to come back here, so I may as well see it.

It is said that in the late Han Dynasty, Gongsun Shu, a general, set up a separatist regime by force in Sichuan. He claimed himself the King of Shu. Because he saw white fog rising from the well of the mountain, which was like a white dragon, he called himself the White Emperor. And he made it the capital city and gave the city the name of White Emperor City.

To be honest there is nothing authentic here. What time hasn't destroyed, Mao and his revolutionary Red Guard did. What is there now is a type of Disney type monstrosity with caricatured statues and fake period buildings. The fresh air was nice, as was the view of the Yangtze, but in hindsight, a morning in bed may have been better.

A few miles after sailing away from Finjie, we came to the highlight of the cruise, an area known as The Three Gorges. The first gorge, named Qutang Gorge, was only 5 miles long but spectacular. The river stares up at two majestic mountains, Mount Baiyan and Mount Chijia. Together, the two peaks almost form a gateway that the river has to go through.

After clearing Qutang Gorge we were summoned for another, slightly more palatable lunch. By the time we had finished eating the boat had reached the second and longest of the Gorges, Wu Gorge, which is over thirty miles long. I spent the first ten miles with my feet hanging over the edge of the boat, drinking cold beer and watching the scenery go past.

Halfway down Wu Gorge we pulled over and filed off the boat for a tour along a small tributary of the Yangtze called the Goddess Stream, so called because the daunting looking peak overhanging it is named Goddess Mountain. The water is too shallow for the main ship along this part, so we all boarded a flotilla of small boats with a guide.

This small tributary is 15 kilometres long and because of the close proximity of the mountains and the rushing rapids, it is probably the most breath-taking section of the river. According to the local legend, the twelve daughters of the Heavenly Queen were lured from heaven by the magnificent scenery of Wushan Mountain and used to descend to the stream to swim and have fun. The stream they swam in was named the Goddess Stream and the twelve goddesses became the twin peaks near the stream to protect it.

Unfortunately, I was unable to concentrate on the stunning scenery. This was because our guide resembled a cross between Spike Milligan and Benny Hill doing a fake Chinese accent. I couldn't understand a word he said but was killing myself laughing, under my breath. It all culminated in him starting a sing song which the yanks loved. There was a chorus where they were supposed to sing something along the lines of "Hong Tai" but most Americans seemed to be singing "oy vey" instead.

After we all got back on the boat, we continued down the rest of Wu gorge and then proceeded slowly overnight to Mao Peng, where we would disembark the following morning to go through the lock at The Three Gorges Dam. Or at least that was the plan.

At dinner we were told that as long it wasn't raining and there was not too much wind, we would be catching a smaller boat and travelling through the new boat lift on The Three Gorges Dam first thing this morning. All was looking good at 6 am when I opened my curtains to reveal a sunny, still morning. A bunch of bleary-eyed passengers got to breakfast at 6.30 and it was here that it was announced that the boat lift had broken down. Not only did this scupper going through the lift, but also the chance to sail through the third gorge. We were informed that they were frantically organising buses to get us to where we needed to be.

The buses finally showed up at 9.30, some three hours after being woken up.

We disembarked and made our way to the awaiting buses that along with tour guides would take us to the dam. Or at least that's what we believed. Unfortunately, this wasn't a trip to see the dam, just to a viewpoint where we could see it and take photos.

In fact, we got more of a tour of the town we docked in, Mao Peng. The town had been completely rebuilt when the dam was built, the original village being some 70 metres under water now. The town had been full of farmers prior to the dam, but the Chinese state rehoused them and gave them jobs in three exciting new projects for the twenty first century. Solar energy, modern pharmaceuticals and wait for it, underpants made from bamboo fibre. I could have done with a pair of those in Chengdu on Sunday. It may have woken some of the pandas up. Having said that, I reckon I would have been glad I packed some Germoline.

The actual dam was completed in 1997, however the surrounding project was not finished until 2009. It is impressive but we didn't get inside it as I thought we were. At the end of the day, it is 607 feet high wall of concrete and hydroelectric power station. Travelling through the boat lift would have been impressive, unfortunately there was no way that they could wrap up this contingency plan and after an hour, we were put on a bus and sent to Yichang to meet our tour guides for our onward journeys.

At least we saw the third gorge from the bus.

I arrived in Yichang around 1 pm. Got taken for an appalling lunch of rice and potatoes and was unceremoniously dumped at the airport at 2pm for a 5pm flight.

The flight arrived in Hangzhou around 6.45 and it was dark before I left the terminal, so I didn't see too much. My guide got me to the hotel and was taken to dinner in the hotel restaurant which consisted of green beans and anchovies with mushrooms (weird). The highlight of the day came when my guide told me that I didn't need to be up until 10 am the following morning. I thought this was a good thing at the time, but by the time I strolled down to breakfast at 9am, all that was left was a cold fried egg and a banana fritter.

My guide met me at 10 and greeted me by saying "Welcome to Paradise." To be fair I did question this at the time because all I could see was a traffic jam and a building site, but nevertheless I took his word for it. An old Chinese saying says that there are the heavens and then there is the earth. In the middle lie Hangzhou and Suzhou. I couldn't comment on Suzhou until I go there later in the week, but having spent a day in Hangzhou, I can see where the saying comes from. Marco Polo came here in the 12th century and described the city as heaven on earth, yet my guide said only ten percent of western visitors to China come here. For the Chinese, Hangzhou is the most popular tourist destination.

We started our tour at Xi Hue, otherwise known as the West Lake. The lake is over 3km long and was the inspiration for the Summer Palace in Beijing. The Emperor came to Hangzhou and loved it so much that he recreated a mini version in his city. The lake is beautiful and surrounded by a labyrinth of footpaths, weeping willows, smaller ponds, colourful gardens and exquisite bridges.

Legend has it that Bai Suzhen was a white snake spirit and Xu Xi'an was a mortal man. They fell in love with each other when they first met on a boat on the West Lake and got married very soon. But the evil monk Fa Hai attempted to separate the couple by imprisoning Xu Xi'an. Bai Suzhen fought against Fa Hai and tried her best to rescue his husband. But she failed and was imprisoned under the Leifeng Pagoda by the lake. Years later the couple was rescued by Xiao Qing, the sister of Baisuzhen. From then on, Bai Suzhen and Xu Xi'an lived together happily. Because of the moving story, the lake becomes an ideal place for dating.

You could walk around it for three days and never see anything twice. After all of the concrete and tower blocks in the other cities, the chance to see some greenery and even better, to not have hordes of people coming from all directions, was quite pleasant. We boarded a small boat in order see all of the lake, which took around 40 minutes. Around the lake are a collection of pavilions and pagodas and only at the far end is the illusion dampened when you can see the high-rise tower blocks of modern Hangzhou.

Artists are drawn to The West Lake, whether it is to paint the full moon glowing in the water, snow on the perfect arched bridges or the amazing pool of red carp that is surrounded by a colourful bed of peonies. The Peony Pavilion and its zig zagging bridge are a wonderful place to sit and contemplate the peacefulness.

Our next stop was Lingyin Temple and Feilai Feng. The temple is one of the largest Buddhist complexes in China. Feilai Feng roughly translates as The Hill That Flew Here. The story goes that a visiting monk from India, and one of the founders of Chinese Buddhism, was so convinced that this hill was the same as one he knew in India, he convinced himself it had flown there. Funnily enough, it hasn't flown back yet.

I was speaking to my guide about religion in China and technically it is still illegal. Buddhism is ok on a technicality; in that it is seen as a philosophy rather than a religion. That said, whereas individual belief is accepted, as soon as two people get together and start preaching, it becomes illegal.

Lingyin is roughly translated as the place where the soul retreats. In its heyday, Temple of Soul's Retreat comprised nine buildings, eighteen pavilions, seventy-seven palaces and halls with over thirteen hundred rooms providing accommodation for around three thousand monks. The main building that can be seen today is a result of the restoration that was carried out in 1974 following the ten-year Chinese Cultural Revolution.

We then drove into the country for a home cooked lunch. Beef and green chilies, rice, and aubergines. Very nice too. The view from the restaurant window was amazing. We were in the village of Longjing, which is where everyone agrees the best tea in China is grown. The hills were full of row upon row of green tea bushes and after lunch we went to the local tea plantation. Longjing means Dragon Well and Chinese legend states that the local spring is protected by a dragon, appointed by the emperor, as he loved Longjing tea so much he kept it all for himself. The village has been growing tea, especially for the rich and famous for 1200 years now. The wall of the plantation shows pictures of various dignitaries who have come here for a cuppa, so it made sense to sit down in the idyllic surroundings and enjoy a brew. There is something special about drinking tea from leaves that were picked about 100 yards from where you are sitting. I did buy some to bring home but not sure it will taste the same on Seaford seafront.

I wandered around the museum and once again, it was all very peaceful. Supposedly, there is a temple nearby where the original eighteen tea trees, owned by Emperor Qianlong 250 years ago, are held in high reverence.

From here we went back to the city, driving through the new commercial district, which seemed far more laid back than any other I had encountered over here and finally to Qi Feng Street which is Hangzhou's ancient street market full of frightening food and things you would never dream of buying. As with other Chinese towns, very little of the past remains, and seems to be restricted to one street which is reconstructed to appear as it would have done around a thousand years ago if you ignore all the mobile phone shops.

To be fair, there are a few notable stores along this street that are, at least to my western eye, fairly authentic. The Baohetang Pharmacy is a traditional Chinese herbal remedy shop which has been on this street for over a thousand years in one shape or another. It provides free healthcare for the poor which is certainly commendable. The Longquan Royal Kiln has been selling traditional porcelain since 960 AD, whilst the Zhang Xiaoquan Scissor Shop supposedly sell the best scissors in China. The Wang Xing Ji Fan store, although only established in 1875 is renowned as producing one of the three wonders of Hangzhou. These being Dragon Well Tea, Silk, and Wang Xing Ji Fans.

Despite all of this, my eyes are always drawn toward some of the tasty looking and certainly the less tasty looking street food on offer. Today's food you thought you would never see prize was christened quack gazey pie. Not a star gazey pie with fish heads peering out, no, this one had duck heads sticking out. A special mention should also go to The Sheep Soup Restaurant, that had numerous broths with some rather unappetising parts of the sheep in them.

This of course did not put me off dinner which tonight wasn't included. So, I had to brave the hotel restaurant without any help from a translator. Thankfully there was a picture menu which was on an iPad. This was fine until you pressed the wrong button and got the settings menu. Beer and special fried rice were easy to point out, but the rest was difficult.

It could have been worse, the barbecued spareribs that I thought was going to be sweet and sour pork was fine, but I really don't know what the other dish I ordered was. It was green beans, red chilies and a mystery meat that may well have been fish. Lots of bones, but edible.

Highlight of dinner was four Germans coming into the restaurant demanding to know where the bar was. Very few people speak English here, let alone German. But it was hilarious watching Germans demanding that a Chinese person spoke English. I don't think things got any better, as when one of the waitresses finally thought she had worked out what they wanted, she led them to the coffee bar. The Germans looked very angry, which made me smile even more. They will no doubt be furious when they do get a bottle of beer, only to find it is a mere 2.5%. No doubt they will take their revenge by blitzkrieging the breakfast buffet in the morning before I get up.

I had planned to have a whole day wandering around Hangzhou the next day but was informed that rather than catching a train at 7.30 pm the following evening, I was now booked on the 1.30 pm instead.

7 BORIS JOHNSON JOINS THE TELETUBBIES

For once I had a morning to myself which allowed me to sleep in, avoid the rather unappetizing hotel breakfast and simply explore Hangzhou at my own pace.

The thought of cold fried eggs and banana fritters was enough to make me want to see if I could find anything more tempting in the local shops. And this was something I tend to like to do abroad but hadn't really had a chance to. To explore the everyday supermarkets and stores that the locals use. If all else failed, there seemed to be a MacDonald's or Starbucks on every other street, but I was hoping for better.

Turning right out of the hotel, I crossed the Grand Canal. A remarkable piece of engineering that the First emperor built to connect Beijing with Hangzhou. Remarkable because it was built at least a thousand years before Europeans invented canals. It is still in use today, transporting goods from the capital to towns in Southern China.

After passing the inevitable MacDonald's and KFC, I came to a massive supermarket, and it was here that I managed to get some breakfast, as well as lunch and dinner. Food wasn't included today, so this proved to be an excellent find. I picked up a rotisserie duck (just like you get chickens at home), some amazing eel and salmon sushi, some fresh melon, a couple of iced coffees and a selection of savoury buns from the bakery. It all cost about £10 and lasted me all day.

Overall, the Chinese supermarket wasn't that dissimilar to a UK one, with one major difference. The vast majority of the meat was still alive. Baby ducklings, turtles, all sorts of fish and some very cute bunny rabbits. Larger animals were already dead and skinned, but you could point to which part of its anatomy you fancied throwing in your wok and a butcher would hack it off there and then. I think I would have to go vegetarian if Waitrose sold live bunny rabbits.
So, it was back to the hotel for breakfast and a couple of hours in my room. A leisurely checkout and getting a lift to the railway station to catch the 1.35 bullet train to Shanghai. Once again, I cannot over emphasise the cleanliness and orderly fashion that these enormous stations are operated in.

Considering the vast number of passengers, the fact that everything is run like clockwork, and everybody follows the simple instructions, means that you can easily get from a to b, very quickly and with the least possible hassle. The train got in around 3.2, exactly as scheduled, but it was at least 5 before I got to the hotel. Shanghai station must be the most enormous I have ever seen. You could drop London Victoria into it five times, including all the passengers. There were almost 40 platforms where I arrived and that was just one level. As a result, finding my guide was slightly problematic. Thankfully my tour company had provided a phone number with English speaking operatives, and with a little outside help, my guide found me.

In China it seems that railway stations, especially the ones where the bullet trains depart, are similar to airports, in that they can be 30 km outside of the city centre. As a result, I saw very little of downtown Shanghai en route to the hotel. Despite being 20km from the railway station, our hotel was still a good 10km from the city centre. You could see the skyscrapers in the distance but that was about as good as it got for that evening.

The hotel was quite nice apart from the bar. It had very expensive beer and excessively loud dance music blaring out. I wouldn't have minded if people were enjoying it, but I was the only person in there. It is hard to tolerate loud music when the alcohol you are drinking is only 2.4 per cent, rising to 3.4.

One slightly disturbing aspect of my hotel room was that on opening the wardrobe, I noticed a large package on one of the shelves. On closer inspection, it was a gas mask to be used in the event of a chemical warfare attack. I hadn't seen much news for the past couple of weeks, but I felt fairly sure I would have heard of any impending chemical attacks on China. I quickly scanned through my travel insurance to see if I was covered against Sarin or Mustard Gas.

The following morning was really hot. Around 34 degrees with no wind, which made sightseeing in a busy city quite arduous at times.

Breakfast was nothing special, apart from the lychees, and was dominated by a large group of fat Russian women who seemingly complained about everything. They still consumed most of the buffet though.

My guide met me at 8.45 and we headed off into the Shanghai rush hour. It was a bank holiday weekend for the Dragon Boat Festival. The holiday was actually on the Tuesday, but many people were working this Saturday so that they could have a three-day holiday. As a result, traffic was busy.

Our first stop was The Shanghai Museum. As is the case with many buildings in Shanghai, this building has fairly unique architecture in that is built to resemble a traditional Chinese Ding cooking vessel, with its circular roof having three concrete handles. The museum was built in 1952 and has an interesting collection of historical and cultural items.

The collection is divided into nine sections, Bronze, jade, ceramics, paintings, calligraphy, sculpture, coins, seals, and costumes. We didn't really have time to do the whole museum justice, so I concentrated on a couple of these.

The sculpture section had some quite interesting historical artefacts, the highlight probably being The Head of Kashyapa, a wooden bust dating back 1500 years and one of the oldest Buddhist sculptures in China. Another stele with a thousand small carvings of Buddha, was impressive.

Some of the calligraphy and art was quite beautiful whilst some of the bronzes dated back nearly 4,000 years. Some of the furniture was ornate and beautiful whilst the ethnic costumes, included those of the Miao people, which I was sorry to see didn't wear Hello Kitty pyjamas, rather than plumping for something a bit more traditional. Back on the street, you notice that the skyline of Shanghai is a mixture of the weird and astounding. It is as if all the most adventurous buildings of tomorrow, dreamed up in the 1950's, were constructed here. Some have flying saucers on top, others have other geometric shapes, it is an architect's heaven.

Having said that, our next stop was the traditional Chinatown area (yes, even Chinese cities have a Chinatown) called Yu Yuan. This was by far the biggest and most authentic of these areas I have come across. It was here that we stopped for a quick cold drink, and I discovered my favourite new thirst quencher, Iced Passion Fruit and Green Tea. It was so good I had to have two.

Yu Yuan is a mixture of tacky tourism, the inevitable mobile phone shops, and traditional Chinese stores. In the middle of the square was a brightly coloured Dragon Boat that was going to be racing the following Tuesday. The Dragon Boat Festival dates back to 278 BC where legend states Qu Yuan, a famous poet and distinguished Minister, drowned himself in the Huangpu River whilst protesting against the occupation of the area by the state of Qin. Legend has it that hundreds of locals set sail in their boats to try and find Qu Yuan, and over the centuries, this has evolved into Dragon Boat races, where brightly coloured rowing boats, some up to 100 feet in length, are raced along the river.

In the middle of Yu Yuan, is the Huxinting Tea House, which dates back to The Ming Dynasty, originally as a private house, but since 1855. Has been a public tea house. The tea house is reached via The Bridge of Nine Turnings, which zig zags over the pond, the reason being that evil spirits travel in a straight line and by zig zagging, people can evade them. Prior to becoming a tea house, the British occupied the building during the First Opium War in 1842. In light of this, we should be thankful it wasn't burned to the ground.

The bridge was packed with locals and tourists alike, however, despite the crowds there is a little piece of sanctuary amongst the hordes which is the Yu Yuan Garden. Dating back to 1559, this is quite possibly the most perfect example of an ornate Chinese Garden anywhere in the world. It is a virtual maze of gardens, pavilions, lakes, rockeries, bridges, dragon walls, gardens, and traditional buildings. The highlight for me was in the Inner Garden where there was a very beautiful gold covered opera stage.

Although not as old, this is Shanghai's version of The Globe Theatre and was very interesting.

After lunch, of which the less said the better (boiled cabbage and tinned Heinz spaghetti Bolognese I reckon) we crossed the Huangpu River and headed for the World Financial Centre which has the world's highest observation deck at over 425 metres high and then a further viewing area at 600 metres in the air. It is the second highest building in the world, behind the Burj Khalifa in Dubai, however the observation deck here is higher.

The view was stunning. In fact, the first thing I saw was someone waving outside the window as the window cleaners were in. Sod that.

The glass floor was probably not needed. Some people seemed terrified to look down, but if you could open your eyes, the view down and upriver was amazing. The Thunderbirdesque Pearl Tower dominates the skyline but that is just one of numerous amazing things to see. The weirdest thing to see here was in the gift shop where there was a quite hideous cuddly toy for sale. There is no perfect description of it, other than a bright pink Teletubby with the face of Boris Johnson. Very weird.

Back on terra ferma we crossed back to the other side of the river to stroll along The Bund. Similar to Victoria Embankment or the path along the East River in Brooklyn, people like to stroll along here to watch the boats on the river and take in the views of the skyline.

Across the road, the buildings of The Bund were all constructed by The British in the 19th century and were built to control the import of opium, the export of tea and to control all goods coming in and out of the harbour. The world's first global bank, HSBC, has its original branch here and today, most of the other buildings have been taken over by other financial institutions or upmarket hotels. It is perhaps a monument to the complete and utter mess that the world finds itself in today.

It is very British, and one must remember that Shanghai was not a major city until The British East India Company were barred by The Chinese from landing their opium at Chinese ports. The British, not taking no for an answer, built their own ports at Shanghai, Hong Kong, Guangzhou amongst others.

Whilst the locals got more and more out of it and dependent on opium, the British took all the tea and made a fortune selling it back at home. The British ruled their part (concession of Shanghai) between 1845 and 1863 at which point the city became an international concern, with the French, Americans and Portuguese, all staking claims to parts of the city.

The city was transformed into the richest city in China, something it still is today. International rule ended abruptly though in 1941, when the Japanese invaded and all British and foreign privileges were revoked.

Final stop of the day was to The Jade Buddha Temple. Buddhist temples are starting to get like churches did in Mexico, but this was slightly more interesting as monks still lived there, despite it being in the middle of a building site. Yes, the buddha was made of jade but no, I wasn't impressed.

After an hour freshening up at the hotel my guide took me to a local restaurant for dinner. After weeks of pleading for spicy food I finally got my wish. A molten hot beef broth, with chilies swimming in it, a pork chili and onion stir fry and green beans and spring onion with more chilies. The poor old guide who ate with me was suffering and sweating like anything. I think the waitresses were expecting me to choke on the chilies, but it was the local guide they were laughing at. I felt that I had ticked that box now, allowing me to investigate more local cuisine in the next couple of days. Shanghai food is a lot sweeter than anywhere else, and hopefully I could find some tasty delicacies.

The following morning, the band was back together, as five of the group I had left behind in Chengdu had flown in the night before and were already tucking into breakfast when I went down to the dining room.

I had high hopes for Suzhou, where we were headed to, as it is always described in the same breath as Hangzhou, which I found to be beautiful. It has been described as the Venice of the East and poets have waxed lyrical about it for centuries. Around 100 AD, it was probably amongst the ten largest cities in the world and right up to 1860, it would have been the largest, non-capital city in the world. Yet, wait for it, it all started to go wrong when the British arrived and with the rise of Shanghai, Suzhou's importance began to decline. Many describe Suzhou as the Venice of the East, yet after a few hours there, I felt like I had been on a day trip to Reading.

Suzhou is renowned, worldwide, for its abundance of beautiful Chinese Gardens. In fact, our first stop here was the rather long winded titled The Garden of The Master of the Fishing Nets. It dates back to 1140 and was the private garden of an administrator who had nothing to do with fishing. Despite being the smallest of the many gardens in the city, it is regarded as the finest example of a Chinese Garden, anywhere in the world. As with all traditional Chinese gardens it is a labyrinth of footpaths, pavilions, ponds, and bridges, with weeping willows, rock carvings and goldfish in the ponds. One pavilion, named the Pavilion for The Advent of The Moon and The Wind, is allegedly the most romantic spot in the world to sit and watch the moon reflect in a pond. Unfortunately, it was midday, so I can't comment any further. It was pretty, but personally, I didn't find it as amazing as the Yu Yuan Garden in Shanghai.

After lunch we went to the Pan Men District which boasts a beautiful pagoda, remains of the cities original walled defences and a few sideshow stalls, all in a beautiful garden setting.

Dominating the garden is the Ruiguang Pagoda, standing at 176 feet tall. It is the oldest pagoda in Suzhou and dates to around 247 BC, having been constructed by Sun Quan, a famous King, out of respect for his mother.

The surrounding gardens are quite peaceful as you wind yourself towards the Pan men City Gate, which dates back to about 500BC, although the current structure is only from 1333 AD. This gate is unique as it is the only surviving land and water city gate in the world, allowing both boats and land vehicles through separate entrances. There is a watchtower and battlements above the gate and about 300 metres of restored city wall that you can walk along to get the perfect picture.

Across from the gate was a small fairground with the most dangerous sideshow I have ever seen. I was well aware that health and safety was all but non-existent in China, however this took the classic fairground coconut shy to a whole new level.
They all looked like an accident waiting to happen. Firstly, there was a bow and arrow shoot, but with real bows and real arrows, none of these rubber tipped health and safety arrows. But highlight was the shooting at targets with a gun. No pretend rifles either, there was a fully-fledged mounted machine gun to fire. I am quite glad we didn't hang around too long.

The gardens eventually join up with The Grand Canal, where the famous Wumen Bridge traverses it. Built in 1084, it is 36 feet high and 72 yards long. Originally it consisted of three separate bridges, but due to various accidents, wars, and acts of vandalism, it is now just one singular bridge. There are 50 steps on each side leading up the steep arch, and the view from the top would have been quite pleasant had we not been caught amid five coachloads of Chinese tourists elbowing their way to the other side very loudly.
Back below the Pan men Gate, we boarded a boat for a cruise along the Grand Canal. This was the same canal that I had seen in Hangzhou, where it originates, cutting through Suzhou en route to Beijing. Whereas in the UK, canals are seen as a thing of the past, there are still over 6,000 active boats on this canal, many transporting goods to and from the capital.

The boat trip lasted about an hour but was fairly underwhelming. As I said earlier, it felt as though as I was taking a trip on The Thames at Reading. It wasn't quite as nice as a trip on the Thames at Maidenhead.

We all went back to the minibus, and I don't think any of us were particularly enamoured with Suzhou. We had all read the glowing reports and read the beautiful poetry about it. Maybe it was because we had all seen so many other amazing things in China over past few weeks, but at the end of the day, Suzhou was a disappointment. On the drive back to Shanghai, it was decided, as the rest of the group had not actually been to the city centre yet, that we should go there for some dinner and then take an evening cruise along the Huangpu River.

The city centre of Shanghai is very similar to the city centres of other great metropolis cities around the world. Tall buildings, shopping malls, neon signs and crazy taxi drivers. Dinner was eaten in a restaurant in a shopping mall before we were marched down to the river to board our boat.

The Huangpu River is the best place to appreciate Shanghai from. One side of the river you have the Imperialist and Victorian splendour of The Bund, with its former majestic banking buildings having been turned into exclusive hotels that only rich bankers can afford. On the other side is a sci fi fantasy scene with neon lit skyscrapers, flashing advertisements being played on other buildings and the centrepiece being the Shanghai Pearl TV Tower, illuminated in purple neon, resembling man's first rocket to Mars. And whilst most of the tourists were taking pictures of the amazing scenery, it became increasingly obvious, that a certain percentage of the younger Chinese passengers were more interested in their own image than that of what was around them. A group of young girls took three quarters of an hour getting their make up right, and staring into mirrors, just so that they could get a perfect picture of themselves in front of the Shanghai skyline. If this is what social media has turned humanity into, even more vain and clueless, I want nothing to do with it.

It had been a long day, so when we finally made it back to the hotel, it was an early night and time to recharge the batteries for the last couple of days.

8 IS THAT A SWORD IN YOUR SUITCASE OR ARE YOU JUST PLEASED TO SEE ME?

Whilst the rest of the tour group went off to do the same Shanghai tour that I did a couple of days earlier, I had hired a private guide to take me around to see some of the places that I wanted to get to. Despite the fact that I had a screaming child in the next room all night which was very close to being murdered, I managed to get through the day without incident.

My guide met me at 10 am and we decided the best route into the city was via a taxi. We would have got the metro, but the travel company had managed to find a hotel that is over 2 miles from the nearest metro station, despite there being 18 lines and well over 200 stations. There would be numerous complaints about this when we get back.

Our first stop was Peoples or Renmin Park which was near the museum that I had visited on Saturday. Here, at the "marriage market", desperate parents put adverts on opened umbrellas for children that can't find a spouse. I had seen something similar in Beijing, near The Temple of Heaven, however, was unable to ask questions or investigate further. Although you hear about arranged marriages in India, the Chinese version of this is less well publicised. As they get older, parents get gradually more concerned, as in Chinese society, there is no state pension, and younger generations pay for their upkeep in their old age. Therefore, marriage and grandchildren are vital if you do not want to become destitute. I did ask how long it generally took them to find a wife there, and the answer was anything up to ten years. Oh well, my visa was only for 60 days.

Generally, the adverts aren't there too long, but in the international corner, my guide pointed out a guy who was in New Zealand, earned 140,000 New Zealand dollars per year and had a big house, yet his parents couldn't find him a wife. I Tried pointing out that he was probably gay, but that didn't seem to register with my guide. In any case, if the guy is earning that much money, what do they have to worry about.

In fact, my guide steered me away from the area, as next to it is what has become known as English corner, where local language students accost tourists and force their less than perfect English on them.

In the middle of the park is the giant bronze Memorial to the May Thirtieth Movement, an anti-imperialist group and precursor the Chinese Communist Party. Nearby is The Antarctic Stone, which is exactly what it says on the tin. A stone from the Antarctic, brought back by the first Chinese Exploration team to head there in 1982. The prettiest area of the park is the Lotus Pond, a typically well landscaped garden area, full of lotus flowers bamboo pavilions and picture-perfect bridges.

The reason for crossing the park was to reach the Site of the First National Congress of The Communist Party of China. Despite the puzzled looks from locals, as to why on earth I wanted to visit this place, it was somewhere that I really wanted to see and was surprised that very few westerners were interested in it. Even the guards there seemed bewildered that I would want to visit such a place, but it is extremely integral to the modern history of China.

Today it lies in the fashionable Xintiandi district of Shanghai. Mao Zedong famously joined 12 other leaders here from July 23 to August 2, 1921, to lay out communist plans to revitalize a nation that continued to struggle after the fall of the Qing Dynasty in 1911. Although he had yet to become the life of the party, Mao represented the Changsha region where he took radical action and opened a bookstore to disseminate the flowering communist philosophy, hoping to assert a new approach to government. At the time of the First National Congress, there were 50 members of the Communist Party. The museum has eight exhibition rooms divided into three sections that focus on the formation of the party, the history of the party in Shanghai, and the civil war that began in 1927.

The First National Congress actually met in the basement, which has been restored to its 1921 appearance and is protected almost as a shrine, such that not even photographs are permitted. The rest of the museum contains authentic items from the period and features life-sized dioramas including a wax Mao preaching to his audience.

From here we wandered through The French Concession and stopped for a coffee at one of many street side cafes. This is the most international area of modern Shanghai and home to most expats in the city. Unlike anywhere else in China, you can get international food and more importantly, beer stronger than 3%.
As with the British areas of Shanghai, this part is visibly French and there are times where you feel you could have been daydreaming all along and find yourself on the streets of Montmartre in Paris. The French were granted the land here in 1849 but didn't start transforming it until 1899. French trees were imported and houses more suited to Marseille were constructed.

By the 1920's, the area had become the most fashionable area of the city, swelled by the influx of wealthy white Russians, fleeing the Bolshevik Revolution.

This all came to a crashing end in 1941 when the Japanese invaded and effectively used the area as a prison camp and through the early years of Communist rule it was generally ignored and seen as an unfortunate legacy of China's imperialist past. Thankfully, from 1980 onwards, the area has seen a regeneration and developers have been keen to keep the French feel to the area, resulting in an ideal neighbourhood to relax and people watch.

From here we went in search of some antique shops as I had a few items I had been asked to seek out. We headed for the Dongtai Road Antique Market, which ten years earlier would have been a bustling and vibrant street. Today it is more of an epitaph to what used to be and an example of what commercial developers are doing to downtown Shanghai. In the old days there would have been over 100 stalls selling "antiques" of all shapes and sizes. The vast majority are fake, but the fakes here are perhaps of a slightly higher quality than elsewhere. Today there were only six or seven stalls open, but fascinating, nevertheless.

Many of the dealers have been removed to a large indoor flea market on Shanghai's main shopping street, Nanjing Road. At three and a half miles long, it wasn't really viable in the 34-degree heat, the wander along all of it, but we headed for the main flea market and then around a few gift stores and traditional Chinese medicine stores.

By 3 o clock I decided that shopping was over, and we took a cab, firstly to a shop called Madame Mao's Dowry where I picked up three Chairman Mao alarm clocks for £20, and then to the Shanghai Poster Propaganda Museum, where I spent more money than I should have done on original cultural revolution posters.
The museum is fascinating if you are interested in poster art and propaganda imagery. It is almost impossible to find, I would never have located it without my guide, and can be found in the basement of a nondescript tower block.

The owner has lovingly restored hundreds of original Chinese Communist Party propaganda posters which he displays and sells if the price is right. There are original revolutionary posters from the 1940's and 1950's and then the more dynamic ones relating to The Cultural Revolution, with joyful soldiers, chubby children, and happy ruddy-faced peasants in the field with an abundance of food in their baskets. Naturally, Chairman Mao's apple cheeked face, which would be hung in every household gaze down from every wall.
In 1979, posters were abolished and destroyed, which explains why originals are hard to find today.

Money spent there was only one place to head to and that was the pub. We went to The Boxing Cat Brewery where I tried everything on offer from the Sucker Punch Pale Ale through to the TKO IPA, before having five pints of something called Glasgow Kiss. It was a mere 6.4 per cent, slightly up on the local rubbish.

On returning to the hotel, the other members of the tour group were in the bar, and I joined them for a night cap. They were somewhat alarmed by the antique sword I had bought for a friend, but I assured them it was fake and very blunt and would be kept in my hold luggage. Thinking no more of it I retired to bed.
As I had got everything done that I had wanted to as far as shopping was concerned, plus the fact that our tour guide had said we could catch the Maglev train back to the airport on the way home, I told my private guide to have the day off and enjoy the Dragon Boat Races. The rest of the group were going to a local water town which included lunch and dinner and for a small charge I could join them, which seemed reasonable.

Shanghai is surrounded by several so-called water towns. Suzhou being the main one, but there are numerous others. These are basically towns that grew up along the banks of the busy canals and to this day, have waterways rather than roads along their main drag.

The tour was to the town of Zhujiajiao, some 48 kilometres west of Shanghai. Whereas Suzhou was known as The Venice of The East, Zhujiajiao is bizarrely known as the Venice of Shanghai. Maybe the East stops at Suzhou?

The town dates back 1700 years and probably hasn't changed that much over the years.

I am glad that I went as the town turned out to be everything that I had thought Suzhou was going to be on Sunday. Winding canals, men in pointy hats punting along on bamboo rafts, arching bridges, and a distinct smell of sewers.

In fact, as long as you tried to forget the wafting fumes from the sewers, this was a very pretty town built around a network of small canals. There were some pretty stone bridges, another large, landscaped garden that we wandered around and then a short boat trip along the canal.

Our final Chinese meal was the first stop of the day, and it was no more memorable than any other. Tourists seem to be served the same food everywhere, and the plate of steaming boiled cabbage sits in the middle of the table, untouched, getting colder and colder. From the restaurant, our guide marched us through several alleyways and then we came across the majestic Fangsheng Bridge, which traverses the Caogang River. Although older, the current bridge dates from 1571. It is the symbolic heart of Zhujiajiao Ancient Town. The bridge is known as the number one bridge in Shanghai as it is the longest, largest, tallest bridge in the world with five arches. The name Fangsheng comes from the tradition of releasing animals on the first and the fifteenth day of every lunar month. To this day, monks and Buddhists will gather here to release animals.

Unlike Suzhou, we were able to pause for photographs without being elbowed by the locals. The view from the pinnacle of the bridge, with the white Ming and Qing Dynasty houses along the riverbank, and the traditional boats paddling up the river, was much more authentic and picturesque than what we had seen before.

We walked along the canal where women in bright, traditional costumes posed for tourists, and hopeful men with traditional pointy hats, pestered you for the chance to punt you up to the bridge and back. The waterside shops were mostly arts and crafts based, aimed at tourists, but not as crass and in your face as elsewhere. This was traditional craft rather than tourist tat.

We crossed a picturesque little bridge and entered the Kezhi Garden, another well landscaped Chinese Garden, and a typical Jiangnan style garden, native to this area. The former owner was Ma Weiqi whose family were salt merchants for generations, hence being one of the richest men in Zhujiajiao Ancient Town. Built in 1912, the owner spent 300,000 taels of silver and 15 years in building the garden. The architecture in the garden is a combination of the Chinese traditional and the Western styles, rarely found in the country. The garden is divided into 2 parts: the Ke Garden and the Zhi Garden. "Ke" in Chinese means "study" and "Zhi" means "farming", implying that people should study and farm to keep a good house.

Although we didn't go into it, the end of the canal was dominated by the Yuanjin Buddhist Temple. A Yuan Dynasty temple, dating back 600 years which enhanced the picture book panorama perfectly. The North Street of Zhujiajiao is the most well-preserved Qing Ming Dynasty Street in the area. It is full of traditional stores, tea houses, art galleries and restaurants. Having said that, some of the local street food stalls were quite frightening. The local delicacies are pig thighs and meatballs, which with enough gravy could be palatable. However, there were some more alarming things on offer such being deep fried centipedes and scorpions on sticks for that tasty take away snack.

One local gift store caught my eye with its rather diverse range of fridge magnets which included the rather interesting trio of Prince Philip, Saddam Hussein and Osama Bin Laden. Am not quite sure which of those is most offensive, but kudos to the shop owner for trying a diverse market.

Our final port of call was The Qing Dynasty traditional Post Office. Our guide said this was a special treat. I am guessing he collected stamps as a child, and probably still does. Although this Post Office dates back to only 1903, the Chinese postal service dates back around a thousand years. There was an interesting collection of Qing Dynasty postcards here, but much of the display was only in Chinese, so was lost on us all.

That evening the group went back to The French Concession area of Shanghai for a few beers in a pleasant roadside bar and burger and chips! I like rice and noodles, but after three weeks it was time for some western cuisine again.

We took taxis back to our hotel and started packing, as we had a mid-morning flight the following day back to London.

With everything packed, there was to be one last rushed breakfast before heading off into the early morning Shanghai traffic. The Holiday weekend was well and truly over, and gridlock returned to the roads. It took well over an hour to cover the ten kilometres into the city centre and then over the Huangpu River, allowing one final glimpse of the amazing skyline, albeit shrouded in grey clouds that morning.

Our driver dropped us off at what appeared to be a shopping mall in Longyang Road. Around the back of the mall was the station for the SMT, or to give it its full name, The Shanghai Maglev Train.
It was here that the problems started. To enter the station, we had to clear security and the x ray managed to flag up the small bronze fake antique sword in my suitcase. Everybody waited politely whilst they searched for anything more dangerous, but I was cleared and allowed to get to the escalator which led up to the platform. At the top of the escalator was another security check and once more my underpants and everything else were on display for all and sundry. As a result, we missed the first train, but they ran every 15 minutes, so it wasn't a major issue.

As the small, box-like train slowly pulled into the station, there really is no clue as to what you are about to experience. The Maglev, an abbreviation of Magnetic Levitation, was opened in 2002 and was the first, and still is the only, commercialized maglev train in operation.
It shuttles passengers to and from Pudong International Airport which is 19 miles away. It manages to do this in a mere 8 minutes with a top speed of 430 kilometres per hour, which is 267 miles per hour. Not that you travel at that speed for long, as it takes two minutes to reach top speed and then another two to slow down. A display at the end of each carriage shows the speed that the train has reached.

It is all very smooth until you pass the other train heading back to Shanghai which is also doing 267 miles per hour. At this point there is a very loud bang and the whole train starts to shake. Thankfully it is all over very quickly and at the end of it all, you sort of realise why the line has never been extended.

As we exited the train, my heart sank as I saw another security check. In fact, there were another three before we even entered the airport. Each one rummaged through my suitcase and by this point, the rest of the group had left me behind, presumably thinking I was going to end up rotting in some dank Chinese prison cell charged with terrorist offences.

I finally got to check in and handed my suitcase over to the airline. Only for them to return it and ask me into a small room to explain why I was carrying a sword. Finally, I was allowed to go to the departures gate, thankfully with enough time to reach my flight.
It was a long flight home, followed by a long drive through the rush hour traffic on the M25.

China was an amazing trip. Much of their antiquities have been destroyed and they have to rely on the few remaining showstoppers, to remind them of a long and fantastic history. Some of the recreations, and faux historical sites are quite alien for Western tourists, but for the Chinese themselves, it is all they have that links them to the past.

The culture and the scenery were amazing and highlights such as the sled down the Great Wall, The Terra Cotta Warriors, The Li River and Beer Fish in Yangzhou will stay with me forever.

BAKSHEESH, GUNS, AND PLUGHOLES

EGYPT 2018

1. Foreword   86
2. The Oasis Nobody wants To Go To   92
3. The Fat Lady Is Singing, So Why Isn't It Over   106
4. The Ancient Egyptian Rod Hull and Emu   115
5. 99 Dead Baboons   125
6. Egyptian Gridlock   137
7. Tours By Von Smallhousen   145
8. Japanese Camera Torture   156
9. The Goddess of Destruction   171
10. A Town Called Alex   180
11. Pyramids   191
12. A Day In The Delta   203

FOREWORD

This was going to be my third trip to Egypt and by far my most ambitious. Previous trips had seen me based in one city, Luxor, or taking a cruise down the Nile on an organised tour. This time I was able to set my own itinerary, have my own personal guide and hopefully do what I wanted to do at my own pace. Well, that was the plan at least.

Of course, there were going to be loads of exciting new tombs and Dynastic treasures to explore. But one thing I was really excited about looking into was a new theory regarding a number of the pyramids. I have never believed that the Egyptian pyramids were built as tombs, but on the other hand, the theory that they were built by aliens as electrical generators or the like, seems equally unlikely. Prior to getting into the story of the trip, it is probably prudent to explain some of the science and theory behind what I was looking for. Despite still being taught in schools, the idea that man suddenly decided to give up the hunter gatherer lifestyle and move into cities around 3000BC and manage to invent writing, the wheel, mathematics, astronomy, and irrigation almost overnight, has been thoroughly discredited. The discovery of Gobekli Tepi in Turkey, pushed human history back to at least 10,500 BC and the subsequent discovery of Gudang Padang in Indonesia, pushes it way back to between 20,000 and 28,000BC. Ever since the mass acceptance of Darwin's theory of Evolution, there has been a uniform acceptance that human evolution and history has been one long smooth upward curve. All of this, despite the fact we happily accept that dinosaurs were wiped out by some cosmic cataclysm. The fact is, and the evidence is there to suggest, that humanity has faced similar near extinction events, The discovery of a comet impact crater under the Greenland ice, dating back 12,500 years, could easily be the evidence to prove a catastrophe of biblical or Atlantean proportions that would have hurled humanity back into the stone age. Such a comet would have evaporated the entire Northern ice caps and sent tsunamis across the globe.

Similarly, between 3500BC and 3100BC it appears that the Earth annually passed through the tail of Comet Enki. This still happens today and is known as the Torrid meteor shower and is nothing more than a pretty light show. Due to the closeness of the Earth and the comet between 3500 and 3100, things would have been far more dangerous. Every year, there would be a period of weeks where fireballs and large meteorites smashed into the Earth. This almost certainly explains some of the underground cities that exist in the Middle East.

We have no records of the damage caused, but what we do have is the recorded history of many major civilisations at this time. The Mayan Calendar starts in 3114BC, pottery from the Yang Shao culture in China dates back to 3100 BC, Kali Yuga, the first great age of the Indus Valley people starts at 3100BC, and Newgrange in Ireland also has been dated to 3100BC. Pottery from Ecuador and Japan can also be dated from this time.

All of these civilisations had tales of fiery chariots, ancient wars of the Gods. Rather than going down the alien route, this simple explanation does seem the most likely. It is possible that the earth would be hit at the same time each year by a swarm of meteors which would result in mass migration and destruction of established civilisations.

At this time, the onset of desertification began in North Africa. What had been a fertile land full of flora and fauna, visibly died before the population's eyes. Sumerian legend tells of a great King named Itana of Kish, who stabilised the lands and brought water back to the Fertile Crescent.

So, what of Egypt? What was happening in 3100BC? Well, it just so happens, that the first King, or Pharaoh of Egypt, appeared out of nowhere in 3100BC. Narmer was the first ruler of the Horus Kings of the First Dynasty of Egypt, uniting both Upper and Lower Egypt. All of his Royal seals and contemporary artwork on relics traced back to this era, show a clear Mesopotamian influence and it is highly probable that the Gerzean culture, as it was known, invaded Lower Egypt from Sumer or one of its provinces.

Narmer was known as the Pharaoh of water management and it makes sense that anyone who could irrigate the land, at a time when the desert was seemingly claiming the entirety of Egypt, would wield a lot of power.

And so, we get to the theories about the function of the pyramids. I now believe that they were part of a major irrigation project. And this is not as bizarre as it seems. 1980's carbon dating of organic matter in cement in between blocks of The Great Pyramid points to c. 3100 BC. In fact, even the Solar Boat, which Egyptologists claim was a funerary boat for Khufu, despite having no sails or a rudder, has been dated between 3800 and 2800BC. Well before the reign of Khufu.

The Great Pyramid subterranean chamber clearly held water. This is undisputed and there is even a well shaft and a natural spring beneath it. There was an enclosure wall around the pyramid in antiquity, with the entrance to the pyramid, below the height of the wall. The theory is that water would fill the moat around the pyramid and fill the underground chamber. As the Western Nile is higher than the Giza Plateau, a simple series of aqueducts, would supply the water to the moat.

No mummies, treasures or writing have been found in the Great Pyramid. What they have found is dissolved limestone and traces of gas. Both of which would have been instrumental in creating a compression chamber. There are two output tunnels from the subterranean chamber. One leading back towards the Nile, the other connecting to a vast network of underground tunnels, some natural, some man made, that stretch to Saqqara and beyond. A well shaft connects the subterranean chamber to the Grand Gallery which leads to the Kings and Queens Chamber.

These chambers are made of rose granite which resonates creating a certain frequency. A Compression wave from the subterranean chamber would create a specific sound making the granite resonate and vibrate. Physicists agree this creates a small electrical field. The sort of field that modern scientists agree can promote plant growth. Hence the pyramid deflects small electrical waves into the surrounding fields and stimulating growth on the newly watered land.

But if the pyramid was pumping all of this water, where did it come out?

North of Giza is a site called Abu Rawash. Directly south, is another site called Zawyet El Aryan. According to mainstream Egyptology, these are both unfinished pyramids. Others claim that they were pyramids, but they exploded in antiquity. Both ideas are utterly ridiculous. If the pyramid had exploded, there would be rubble. There isn't any and a 200-metre-based pyramid would create a lot of rubble. Abu Rawash is built on top of a steep hill. We do not understand how giant granite blocks were lifted on to a pyramid at ground level. Here they would need to be hauled up a massive hill first. Furthermore, the base of the structures are made from Aswan granite. Aswan being some 550 miles away.

Zawyet El Aryan has been off limits since 1964 and is currently in the middle of a military base. This is very convenient for Egyptologists as it creates more questions than it answers. A 105-metre corridor leading down from ground level into a chamber or pit. This is carved out of limestone, but the floor is carved from giant pink granite blocks of 30 – 40 tons. These blocks are well polished to the point of reflection. At the western end of the chamber is an oval tub cut into one block. Obviously, Egyptologists call this a "sarcophagus" but the lid was still intact and empty apart from a black residue when Italian archaeologist Alexandre Barsanti opened it in the 1920's. Remarkably, the granite comes from the same quarry as that found in the chambers of The Great Pyramid. Unfortunately, much of the site was destroyed by Barsanti who insisted on continuing his treasure hunt long after it was clear that nothing was to be found. He cut through 22 cubic metres of granite before a massive storm resulted in 3 metres of water and 380 cubic metres of flood water filling the chamber. Remarkably, it disappeared instantly. He finally removed the lid from the tub to find a cavernous shaft. Around the top of the shaft was a 10cm black band. It is my guess this was charcoal.

Abu Rawash is identical. Same oval tub with fitted lid, which is claimed to be a sarcophagus, but in reality, is a very deep shaft.

Both sites had perimeter walls and "causeways" leading away. These causeways were almost certainly canals, and it is highly likely that both Abu Rawash and Zawyet El Aryan were reservoirs for the water pumped from the Giza plateau. The fact that there were perimeter walls would certainly suggest these projects were finished and not unfinished pyramids, which the mainstream claim. The charcoal found in the tubs would have been used for water purification, hence these would be similar to the step wells in ancient India, where locals could come and get fresh drinking water. It is not as though this would be a unique thing to Egypt. In Persia, they had beehive shaped pyramids called yakhchal's which were designed to keep water and ice cool. There are still some villages in Iran that use them today. India is scattered with massive step wells, especially through the Rajasthan area, which were large communal reservoirs to provide clean water.

The site that really fascinated me was Abu Ghorab, which was south of Zawyet El Aryan and just North of the Abu Sir Pyramids. As with Abu Rawash, I had to get special permission to go to Abu Ghorab and Abu Sir. My guides had said all was sorted so this was going to be a highlight of the trip.

Known as The Great Sun Temple of Ra, the remains of Abu Ghorab are bizarre. The remains of the largest obelisk to stand in Egypt and a massive quartz "altar". In the middle of this is a massive round granite stone acting as a plug. Once again, a giant shaft of 180 feet has been plugged with a massive chunk of granite. The shaft goes to the depth of the ground water.

Most interesting are around twenty, identical stone hand basins. Nobody really has a clue what they are. All are perfectly rounded and smooth and have a circular hole in the base of the bowl to allow some form of liquid to pour out.

Egyptologists claim these were used in animal sacrifice and the holes allowed blood to pour away. This is the most bizarre explanation of all, as blood would stain the perfectly white bowls. Others claim that gold was produced here but the truth seems to be obvious. You have a deep well that has been plugged and my guess is that these bowls were used for cleansing either on a personal or ritual basis.

The fact is that Abu Ghorab, Abu Rawash and Zawyet El Aryan had all had their shafts plugged and sealed off. It is my guess that by the time of the 4th Dynasty, and the so-called pyramid builders, some 400 years later, The Nile had receded, and these once functional structures were transformed into temples, and even possibly tombs in certain cases.

Khufu certainly had something to do with The Great Pyramid, but it is my hunch, that he merely repaired and modified an older structure. This makes much more sense when you come to the Pharaoh Sneferu, who allegedly built three pyramids in his 24-year reign. Even if they were tombs, he could only be buried in one. Doesn't it make more sense that he restored three older pyramids?

So back to this trip. The itinerary I had arranged saw me getting to Abu Rawash, Abu Sir and Abu Ghorab on my first day. This was followed with days at Saqqara and then Dashur. From here it was off to what is known as The Valley of The Whales and on to the Meidum Pyramids. Then driving through the desert to Minya, Asyut and Abydos before getting to Luxor. I would stay there for a couple of nights before flying back to Cairo, where I would spend some time on The Giza Plateau and have a day trip to Alexandria.

Well, that was the plan.

1. The Oasis Nobody Wants To Go To

I just about got to Heathrow despite the traffic on the M25 and for once getting through airport security was a breeze.

The problems only started in attempting to board the plane. You may recall my insistence on the need for sheepdogs to shepherd fat old Islamic women through airports. Unfortunately, my pleas have seemingly fallen on deaf ears. She was in front of me in the queue to board the plane. Despite the fact there was only one way to go, and everybody in front of her had got on board without issue, it was beyond her. Twice she stopped and looked confused. Trying to help, I pointed her in the right direction. This unfortunately had a negative effect as she then put her bags down in a heap and started wailing. This blocked the queue for at least five minutes until someone who could speak her language calmed her down. She then proceeded to the front desk, bent down and blocked the rest of us again. We did think this was the end of it, but we were sadly wrong. The best was still to come.

As a result, the flight left 15 minutes late, around 5.15. Rather bizarrely, before take-off there was an Islamic prayer. I had flown Egyptian Airlines before without the need for Allah's intervention. I presume this was to put off any jihadist nutters and show that the plane and all onboard were still on their side. The rest of the flight consisted of two children impersonating an air raid siren, only interrupted by chicken or beef. Despite having a window seat, I didn't really see much as my head was in a book for most of the time, but I did notice lots of snow over Slovenia and Greece when we flew over.

Cairo traffic is legendary for being awful and I can report that it looks just as bad from 10,000 feet. I had hoped to see the pyramids from the air, but I think they were on the other side of the plane.

So, we landed around 9pm local time., I got my hand luggage from the overhead locker and got my passport ready for immigration, joining the queue to get off the plane. There was then a crash and a loud scream, and the same bloody woman came bowling down the aisle, against the traffic, like a runaway train. Bags and documents flew everywhere in her wake and the stewards couldn't do a thing. As a result, my prepaid visa got lost under a seat somewhere and I was forced to buy another one at immigration.

My guide met me at the gate and after about an hour we got into the delightful Cairo traffic. It took about 45 mins to get to the hotel, which on the face of it, seemed OK. But appearances can be deceptive. I hoped it would seem better in daylight.

It was in the car to the hotel that the guide dropped the bombshells, that despite all of their assurances, prior to me arriving, that they would get permissions for the sites I wanted to see, they didn't manage to get them. As a result, I had overnight to dream up a new route, although I was told that the following morning we would head to Saqqara, which seemed OK with me. Abu Ghorab and Abu Rawash were now shut indefinitely due to locals taking pot shots at tourists in The Western Desert, whilst there was still a chance I could get to Abu Sir, but it would not be until later in the week, providing we could get permission from an ongoing archaeological dig.

After a long journey I had a quick beer in the hotel bar, The Thirsty Camel, which was empty apart from a cat playing with a sheesha pipe.

Although it was gone midnight, I still wasn't ready to go to sleep when there was a power cut, and we were plunged into darkness. I scrambled into bed, only to be woken up two hours later with all the lights coming back on and then two hours later when reception decided to give me someone's 5.30 wake up call. I maybe managed 5 hours sleep.

Having said that, those five hours were fairly fruitful for the local mosquito population as I woke up smothered in bites. The Oasis Hotel was really not of the standard I have become used to. Breakfast, or the lack of it, only made this assumption worse. I only wanted some fruit. There wasn't anything apart from stale croissants and rather unappetising eggs. I made a note to skip breakfast for the next few days which at least should help the diet.

I was picked up at 8.30 by my guide for the next few days. Evidently, he is the fourth choice as the other three saw what I wanted to do and backed out. Having said that, Sami, the guide is an Egyptology graduate and trained under the legendary Dr Hawass. This of course means he sticks to the party line and is not at all open to alternative theories, but he did seem to know a lot and I thought we would get on.

I'm not sure if he was trying to pull a fast one, but Sami stated that his normal tour of Saqqara took about 90 minutes. Unfortunately for him, I made him stay there for seven, which was hard work climbing through the sand with temperatures in the mid-thirties. We Still didn't see everything, but even I was exhausted at this point. To be fair, the previous tour I had made to Saqqara was probably no more than 90 minutes with a quick look at the Step Pyramid and a chance to explore a couple of tombs.

The route to Saqqara from Giza is not exactly scenic. Pollution infested canals with icebergs of plastic bottles. Cars zigzagging through the chaos which resulted in a collision between a tuk tuk and a donkey. The donkey seemed fine, much to the annoyance of his driver who seemingly would have preferred him to be limping so he could claim damages.

Getting into the Saqqara site was much harder than it had been four years ago. There were now sniffer dogs, police with machine guns and steel bollards. It is a sad reflection on humanity that it has come to this.

We started at The Valley Temple of the Pharaoh Unas, which was interesting, and then followed the ancient causeway to the Imhotep Museum. Imhotep being the supposed architect of the large Step Pyramid here. As you enter the museum you are confronted with a large statue of Djoser, the pharaoh accredited with ordering the construction of the pyramid. There is also an incredible statue of Imhotep and some other quality statues and funerary treasures found throughout the Saqqara Necropolis.

Interestingly Imhotep was more renowned for being a physician and healer and was deified like Asclepios in Greece. Having visited an Asklepion in Turkey, which was a healing centre, I have to say there were remarkable similarities to what is thought to be the mortuary temple of the pharaoh Djoser. The architecture is most unlike any other Egyptian building and resembles Mesopotamian architecture, such as the ziggurats. My guide was having none of this but there is a theory that this building was a sonic healing centre and it does have many openings which supposedly you could put your head into and feel the resonating of the natural rock. I am not totally convinced by that theory; however, it is certainly as valid as saying it was built in the Third Dynasty. If we accept that Narmer and the Horus Kings of the First Dynasty invaded from Mesopotamia, this is far more likely a good 500 years older than generally believed.

The single entrance to the enclosure is the southernmost doorway on the eastern side of the wall and leads to the entrance colonnade. 20 pairs of columns, resembling bundles of reeds line the corridor. The roof of the entrance colonnade was constructed to represent whole tree trunks. What strikes you is the stonework and precise cutting and the polished effect of the outer walls. Something I haven't seen anywhere else in Egypt.

My guide then pointed out Djoser's heb sed court. The heb sed was along the lines of a jubilee. Every 15 years or so, the pharaoh would celebrate the heb sed. This involved him running around four pillars screaming and shouting that he was the heir of the sun god Ra. This was performed in front of dignitaries and priests. I can't help thinking that the British royal family should adopt this and allow us all to watch the spectacle of Liz running around screaming that she is the rightful heir to the throne whilst the pm and archbishops look on.

On the north-eastern corner of the pyramid is a court which contains a small structure known as a 'serdab'. Inside this tiny, sealed chamber, which is tilted upwards at an angle of 30 degrees, a life-sized painted statue of the King sat on his throne and gazed out through a peephole towards the northern stars and the land of Osiris. Today the original statue can be seen in Cairo Museum, but you can peep into the serdab and see a replica statue of Djoser, disconcertingly staring back you.

All over the Saqqara site are ridiculously deep shafts and tunnels. Now I am inclined to believe that these were constructed to take water around Egypt and help irrigate the fields. The official line is of course that they are tombs. I pointed out a big pipe going down one of the deepest shafts and was told that they had to pump water out when they found it. Did they find any tombs down there? No, but they were probably robbed in antiquity. Closed minds everywhere.

Which brings us to the Step Pyramid, regarded as the oldest and first pyramid of Egypt. Even the most conservative of Egyptologists accept that the structure was constructed in a number of stages.

Starting as a one platform structure, moving on to be a three-layered pyramid and finally to the six layers that survive today. The problem is that most will have you believe that the first layer was a simple mastaba tomb. Yet this cannot be the case, as a forty-metre-deep shaft extends through the centre of the structure which, had the structure ever been only one layer high, would have been open to the elements. Despite the sheer 40 metre drop, this is regarded as a burial shaft. You would think that had Djoser taken so much time in constructing an entire pyramid, he wouldn't then want his sarcophagus dropped from such a great height.

From the bottom of the shaft, there extends three and a half miles of tunnels and caves, some natural and some not so. To the east of the pyramid, there are eleven identical shafts, 32 metres in depth, leading to horizontal tunnels. None of which connect to the central, supposed, burial chamber and shaft. The Egyptologists answer here is that they were a repository for grave goods. To be fair, a lot of pottery has been found in the shafts, but mostly jugs and drinking vessels from the First Dynasty, dating from around 3100BC. Maybe Djoser wanted to start early and had people drop grave goods into his tomb five hundred years before he was born!

At the bottom of the central "burial shaft" is what is known as the sarcophagus of Djoser. Firstly, it looks nothing like any sarcophagus I have ever seen and as per usual, nobody has ever been found. The usual tale of grave robbers just doesn't work here because this so-called sarcophagus is made up of giant granite blocks, in the middle of which is a 3.5-ton, round, granite plug. Did Djoser really want his royal body squeezed into his final resting place through a plughole? And following on the official line, did grave robbers manage to remove it and then replace the 3.5-ton plug?
The fact is, that if you take away the upper levels of the pyramid, you have platform with a 40-metre shaft with a sarcophagus at bottom. When the plug was removed in modern times, traces of charcoal were found. This surely points to the fact that the structure was originally used as a source for drinking water. Charcoal would purify and sweeten it against the natural magnesium from the bedrock.

As if this isn't proof enough, there is an identical shaft to the South of the structure which has a steep descending staircase. Halfway down is a gallery, in which was found hundreds of identical jars. These would be water carriers and this shaft was probably used for non-drinking water.

The final nail in the Egyptologists coffin comes when you go back to the original Khmetian language. Egypt was only referred to as Egypt after the Greeks invaded in the 4th Century BC, Egypt stemming from the Greek Aegyptus. The actual Egyptians knew their land as KMT or Khemit.

The Step Pyramid is known as KBHW NTRW. This translated as Drink Offering of the Gods, and it is possible that priests added honey, fruit, herbs, and grains to the water here in later times to produce a true drink of Gods. There is actually one theory that Djoser charged one block of stone per drink, in order to finance the rest of the pyramid, but that is pure speculation.

Around the enclosure is what has become known as The Great Trench. Passed by Egyptologists as either an outer wall or defences, there is another clear problem. The trench does not line up on the southern side. It measures 130 feet in width and is 2360 feet long. Did Imhotep make a mistake? The trench would be useless as defences as any enemy could walk through the gap. Looking at aerial photography, this is clearly a canal. If you extend the trench, it would go directly through 5th Dynasty pyramid of Unas and into the desert. Clearly an earlier design from a time when water was more abundant. This water must have dried out by the time of Unas, who reigned between 2345 and 2315BC.

Despite all of this, there are images of the Pharaoh Djoser within the pyramid. Furthermore, sarcophagi of Djoser's daughters have been found inside. Therefore, I believe that Djoser inherited the large platform and first layer of the pyramid, restored it, and then added the top five layers, creating the pyramid shape.

Following the Great Trench, we came to the pyramid of Unas. Many people would not recognise this as a pyramid at all and to the naked eye it is little more than a pile of rubble. Many of the later pyramids were made from mud brick rather than limestone and granite. As a result, they have not survived the centuries as well. There is however an underground tomb that can be accessed, and I managed to crawl in. This is the first pyramid that has writing in it. As a result, Egyptologists believe that as this was a tomb, all pyramids were built as tombs. I think we can now safely say that the oldest, original structures were not tombs at all, but maybe converted into them, whilst those built from 2300 onwards were tombs but poor, cheap imitations.

I tried to put my point across to my Egyptologist guide but was told that Pharaohs didn't need to write anything in their tombs because they were so impressive. To which I replied, then how did my guide know which pyramid belonged to which pharaoh? I didn't get an answer.

After crawling down into the bedrock for about forty feet you come to two large burial chambers. On the walls are what have become known as The Pyramid Texts. These are spells for the King to use in the afterlife. Although these are just simple hieroglyphs, this evolved into what we see in the spectacular tombs in The Valley of The Kings. Much of what is written on the walls here evolved into The Egyptian Book of The Dead.

The 283 spells in Unas's pyramid constitute the oldest, and best-preserved form of religious writing from the Old Kingdom. Their function was to guide the ruler through to eternal life and ensure his continued survival even if the funerary cult ceased to function. Whilst underground, the lights suddenly went out. It's somewhat alarming what goes through your mind in an ancient tomb with the lights out. Having said that, I took it slightly better than some who started screaming. I did think about doing a quick Boris Karloff impression, but prudence won the day. With many scurrying back up the shaft to get to the light, I patiently waited for the lights to come on and managed to enjoy them in a more peaceful situation. Moving on from the Unas pyramid, a wooden boardwalk extends off into the desert. We followed this for a few minutes and came to a number of New Kingdom Mastaba tombs.

We explored three tombs, all fascinating for varying reasons. Firstly, was the tomb of Horemheb. Horemheb was a general in Tutankhamun's Army, who suddenly found himself as Pharaoh in 1306BC, reigning to 1292BC. As a result, he was buried in The Valley of The Kings, but he had previously had this tomb constructed. As a result, his two wives Mutnedjmet and Amenia were buried within the structure.

Only excavated in 1979, the tomb has three clear stages of design, getting grander as Horemheb's status rose. Military scenes were carved on the original court and scenes showing Horemheb's duties in office on the walls of the later, first open court including one where he deputised for Tutankhamun on the north wall. On the North wall are scenes from the funeral, showing kiosks with smash pots and mourners.

Next was the tomb of Meryneith, a priest from 1350BC, the Amarna period. The style of artwork was totally different and fascinating. The well-known Egyptian Gods replaced by the one sun god The Aten, with its rays stretching down with hands on the end of each ray. His official title, Scribe of The Temple of Aten is written on the wall in hieroglyphs.

He died during the reign of Tutankhamun and also has a tomb at Amarna. It is believed that the Amarna tomb was unused and Meryneith returned to Memphis (Saqqara) after Akhenaten was banished. Considering this it is fascinating to see that the Amarna style artwork was still used.

Up and down more steps, we came to the tomb of Maya, another tomb dating back to the reign of Tutankhamun. Maya had numerous wonderful job titles, including fan bearer on the King's right hand, overseer of the treasury, chief of the works in the necropolis, and leader of the festival of Amun in Karnak.

Maya is known to have lived until at least the eighth year of Horemheb's reign as an inscription mentions he was charged with tax collection for the entire country. So clearly the most unpopular man in Egypt.

The tomb has impressive reliefs with an open courtyard having a colonnade on its west side and doors leading to three vaulted ceilings. An inner courtyard has reliefs of very fine quality and a statue of Maya and his wife. The underground burial chambers are paved with limestone and decorated with reliefs showing Maya and his wife in front of the gods.

Some have claimed that the Maya tomb is actually the tomb of a Mayan traveler from Mexico. As much as I like a good conspiracy theory, I wasn't sold by that one. It seemed authentic Egyptian to me.

Although I was more than happy to continue, Sami was flagging due to only used to being in Saqqara for 90 minutes. We retired to a local restaurant for lunch which was some sort of Egyptian set menu of bread, dips, rice, and potatoes. I tried to explain I was avoiding carbohydrates to no avail.

After lunch, Mohammad drove us to the Northern car park, where we could explore more of the site.

First stop after lunch was the tomb of Ptahhotep dating back to 2400BC. For a long time, it was believed by many scholars that Ptahhotep wrote the first book in history. His book was entitled The Maxims of Ptahhotep. As the Vizier, he wrote on several topics in his book that were derived from the central concept of Egyptian wisdom and literature which came from the goddess Maat. Ptahhotep's instruction was written as advice to his people in the hopes of maintaining this said, "social order". He wrote perspicacious advice covering topics from table manners and proper conduct for success in court circles to handy hints to the husband for preserving his wife's beauty. Ptahhotep also wrote more social instructions such as ways to avoid argumentative persons and cultivate self-control. You could he was to the Egyptians, What Confucius was to The Chinese.

The entrance to his mastaba is decorated with two pillars. It follows a room with two further rooms on each side. The middle of the complex is occupied by a court with ten pillars. Going further north, several other rooms follow with one containing the false door of Ptahhotep and an offering table in front of it. Most walls of the mastaba are decorated with reliefs, but mostly only the lower parts of the scenes are preserved. They are mainly showing offerings bearers. The only family member preserved in the tomb decoration is his son Akhhotep.

Across the way from the mastaba of Ptahhotep is an innocuous staircase leading underground. This for me was to be the highlight of the day. The Serapeum.

The official line states that this was the chamber of underground tombs of the sacred Apis bulls. A theory and nothing more as not a single remain of any part of a bull has been found there. The name cannot be correct anyway, as Serapis was a bull deity introduced to Egypt by the Ptolemaic Greek Pharaohs, who only arrived in Egypt in the 4th Century AD.

The tunnel dug directly into the rock was originally approached by an avenue of sphinxes. These predated Ptolemy I by at least 1,000 years if not a few thousand more.

Twenty-four side chambers each hold enormous, 100-ton granite boxes, sealed with lids weighing a further 15 tons. The craftmanship on these boxes is so perfect that the right angles are correct to the nearest millimetre on both the outside and inside of the boxes. Furthermore, the sheen on the granite is still perfect enough to see a reflection in.

If we believe the history books, these massive boxes all contained mummified bulls. Grave robbers have since managed to remove all the lids, steal the bulls, and then replace the lids once more. Personally, I find this unlikely.

In the Nineteenth century, an Egyptologist tried to remove one of the boxes, but only managed to move it a few feet before even attempting to raise it above ground level. Even modern cranes are unable to access the boxes due to them being underground.

There are hieroglyphs on a couple of the sarcophagi, but it looks very childish and not anything a pharaoh or even High Priest would be liable for. This really is one of history's greatest mysteries. What was it used for and more importantly how did they get these 100-ton blocks of granite, all identical and perfectly square and smooth, into place?

We do know that the son of Ramses II, Prince Khaemweset, spent a lot of time here. So much so that some actually claim he was responsible for building it. It is probable that Khaemweset was responsible for the inscriptions on two of the boxes, and texts from the time of Ramses II claim that the prince was working to re-establish true traditions of Egyptian worship. He lived underground in the Serapeum and became known as the first Egyptologist. He accumulated a huge library about sacred traditions and medicine and founded the library of Ramesseum in Thebes. Could the Serapeum have been an ancient healing centre? It is doubtful we will ever know, or at least be allowed to know.

The French archaeologist, Auguste Mariette, discovered the Serapeum in the 1860's and compiled a full report of what he found. This report has disappeared without trace. Meanwhile, dozens of openings within The Serapeum have been sealed off by authorities with no reason given. Other areas are off limits with armed guards protecting them. Make of this what you will, but there is certainly something that we are not likely to find out about down there and I very much doubt it is a mummified bull.

One thing we are allowed to know about the discoveries of Mariette is that he found a mummy with a golden mask. This was presumably Khaemweset, however this mummy has also vanished into thin air. Some texts now state that what Mariette found was a mummified bull made to look like a human. Maybe Khaemweset was the first pantomime cow.
As we left the cool of the underground Serapeum, we had to tread through more sand in what was becoming a very hot afternoon. Sami did state that he could have done four of his 90-minute tours by this point, but deaf eared, I carried on marching.

Next stop was the Mastaba of Ti. A well-preserved tomb with some equally stunning reliefs. Ti held the title of Overseer of the Pyramids of Niuserre, an obscure Pharaoh from the 25th Century BC. What I did find interesting was that he was responsible, not for the building of, but the restoration of pyramids and also of the Sun Temple at Abu Ghorab. A clear indication, in my opinion, that the pyramid structures were maintained and restored by, but not necessarily built by the Pharaohs that history has gifted them to.

This mastaba was discovered by Mariette, just like the Serapeum. Funnily enough, his reports on this one have survived. Ti's mastaba is generally regarded as one of the most beautifully decorated tombs discovered from the Old Kingdom.

Reliefs show Ti in a variety of agricultural and daily scenes. There are statues of his son and of his wife, both in remarkably good condition. One wall contains a depiction of the entire Egyptian brewing process, which I found particularly fascinating. Other walls showed metalwork, boat building and dancing.

There is a statue of Ti in what is called the serdab. A serdab was a sealed off chamber with a small peep hole. Statues representing the deceased were put inside so that they could view the outside. These days you can stare back at Ti through the hole. It was amazing to think he has been staring out of that hole for 4500 years.
The main wall of the burial chamber has a fantastic relief, showing Ti on a boat, hunting a hippopotamus, who shares the Nile with crocodiles and a multitude of fish.

Across from the mastaba was the Pyramid of Teti, the first Pharaoh of the Sixth Dynasty. By this stage even I couldn't handle clambering on my hands and knees down a 40-foot shaft and then back up again. Instead, we moved on to the impressive tombs of Ankhmahur and Mereruka, both senior officials to the Pharaoh Teti.

Ankmahur's Mastaba is known as The Physician's Tomb. Not that Ankhmahur was a physician, he was a vizier, but the wall reliefs are some of the most complete records of Old Kingdom medicinal and surgical practices.

Mereruka was Teti's right-hand man and the second most powerful man in the kingdom. His tomb is the largest tomb in Saqqara for a non-Royal, consisting of a staggering 33 rooms. He was married to Teti's daughter, Princess Seshseshet Waatetkhethor, who was also buried here. In fact, it is a relief of her, playing with her three dogs and pet monkey, that was by far the most stunning aspect of the tomb.

Another spectacular scene shows Mereruka hunting. But it is not Mereruka who is the star of the scene, it is the exquisite wildlife paintings. Nesting lapwings are depicted protecting their young from a marauding mongoose, by either "spreading their wings over their chicks or by mobbing the intruder." In the Nile River, one adult hippopotamus is shown seizing and killing a basking crocodile, "while behind it another crocodile turns the tables, waiting to devour a newborn hippopotamus."

By now Sami was almost begging to go home and I finally relented. We staggered back to the car and through the Cairo traffic. After a cold beer I went to bed for a few hours and then for an unmemorable dinner. I went for the dinner buffet which was awful. Pickled salad, followed by thrice boiled vegetables and bones, loosely labelled as chicken. Apart from water and beer I really haven't consumed much and wasn't hopeful that it would improve until leaving The Oasis Hotel.

2.   The Fat Lady Is Singing, So Why Isn't It Over?

It was one of those mornings. I woke up covered in mosquito bites, my ankle was swollen after turning it slightly at Saqqara the previous day and I skipped breakfast as it really wasn't very appetising the morning before. Furthermore, hundreds of schoolkids had descended on to The Oasis Hotel for some sort of pageant. I locked myself in my room until it was time to go.

I met Sami and Mohammad at reception, and we set off around 9 to go to Dashur, some 30km south of Cairo. Opposite the hotel, is the building site for the new Grand Egyptian Museum, which will be amazing when it is finally opened. Allegedly this will happen in 2020, but four years earlier, they were saying something similar.

You never get tired of driving past the Giza pyramids. Well as a passenger at least. I wouldn't fancy it as a driver with the chaotic traffic, donkeys and people aimlessly walking across the road. As it was, Mohammad tried to take a short cut and ended up in the middle of a slum, negotiating a herd of goats.

Having never been to Dashur before, I was quite excited to see the three main pyramids that were built there. One day I will actually find some pyramids that are adrift and alone in the desert. Whereas Giza is in the heart of Cairo and can be seen from Pizza Hut, and Saqqara is surrounded by soldiers, the first thing you notice about Dashur is an oil refinery and loads of thick black smoke billowing out.

There are three main pyramids at Dashur in various states of ruin. As per usual, the older they are, the better condition they are seemingly in.

The newest, The Black Pyramid, dates from 1790BC and is a shadow of its former self. By this stage the builders were using mud bricks rather than stone and only the core is still standing. As a result, it is unsafe to get too close. In fact, we didn't get within half a mile of it.

According to Sami, it was known as the Black Pyramid for the colour of the bricks used on the interior structure, but I must admit, much of the black covering on it these days is probably due to the emissions of the oil refinery which is seemingly downwind from it.
The pyramid was supposedly built by Amenemhat III who ruled between 1860 and 1815BC and as is the case with the later, less well-built structures, it was used as a tomb, with both Amenemhat and his Queen buried within.

The pyramid was originally about 75 metres tall with a base 105 metres long and an incline of 57°. Typical for pyramids of the Middle Kingdom, the Black Pyramid, although encased in limestone, is made of mud brick and clay instead of stone.

The core of the pyramid was made of mud brick alone with no internal walls. The pyramid was built on clay that was unable to support the weight and began to sink and somewhat revealingly, this pyramid was built nearer to The Nile than any other which would account for the soft ground.

The pyramid was abandoned after it began to crush the underground chambers. The builders had hastily installed supporting beams and mud brick walls to stop the sinking caused by water from the Nile seeping in, but it was too little, too late, and the pyramid was abandoned, leaving a timeless monument to bad planning, and promoting Amenemhat III as a prime candidate to be the patron saint of dodgy builders.

It was clearly left in ruin and by the 13th dynasty, (1803 – 1649BC) the lack of security meant that locals had already usurped the Valley Temple and were using it as a granary and the first breach of the pyramid happened at about that time too. There is some evidence of attempts at restoration work perhaps 100 years later, when King Auibre Hor was buried in two of the ten shaft tombs on the northern side of the outer enclosure, but for what The Great Pyramid at Giza is to perfection and symmetry, The Black Pyramid is unfortunately the polar opposite.

The Bent Pyramid is far more interesting. There are numerous theories about why it is the shape it is ranging from explosions, earthquakes through to architectural miscalculation. The fact is that if the builders had continued building the pyramid at the angle they had started with, it would have been enormous, standing at over 200 feet high. Had this been the case it would also have been structurally unsound. So halfway up, the angle of the pyramid changes, giving it a weird shape.
Strangely, according to mainstream Egyptology, the Pharaoh Sneferu still chose to be buried in this pyramid, despite having two other ones that were seemingly perfect. This claim, however, is rather dubious. The other striking thing about the bent pyramid is the fact that the casing stones are mostly intact, and you can get up close and see how amazingly accurately they were supposedly cut.

I say supposedly, as the traditional view taken from the great Cecil B De Mille epics, of Hebrew slaves carting massive 10-ton granite blocks, up wooden ramps whilst being whipped by their Egyptian overlords doesn't really hold sway anymore. Firstly, no slaves were ever used in Egyptian construction projects. The Pharaoh would bring in the finest craftsmen in the land to build their grand pyramids or tombs.

Secondly, the fact that the enormous casing stones are seemingly cut so precisely and all but melt into each other, with miniscule joins, has baffled archaeologists for centuries. Thankfully new technologies are beginning to come up with the answers, despite most mainstream Egyptologists still sticking to their copper chisels and Hebrew slaves.

Tests have been made on some of the casing stones at The Bent Pyramid. Rather than being pure limestone, their makeup is crushed limestone, silica, kaolinite and naturally occurring natron salts. Stir all these up with a little bit of Nile water and you get a perfect geopolymer or cement.

So, all the builders had to do was create wooden moulds, place them adjacent to the previous land casing stone and pour in the mixture. Come back the next morning and you have a perfectly encased pyramid. Historians will still swear blind that the Romans invented cement. Well maybe they did invent that precise formula, but it is clear that Old Kingdom Egypt had a similar, if not more advanced technique.

A 2011 nuclear magnetic spectra test on the stones showed without doubt that the grains of limestone came from the local Tura Quarry, however these were cemented together with an amorphous calcium silicate gel which could only have been manmade.

So, if that solves the mystery of how they built the pyramid, it still doesn't solve the problem of why the bottom half ascends at an angle of 54 degrees and then halfway up changes to 43 degrees. According to the mainstream, Sneferu built the pyramid in one go around 2600BC, making it predate the official date for the Great Pyramid. This, however, seems more to do with maintaining their linear view of history and a smooth curve in the evolution of pyramid building. First there was the Step Pyramid at Saqqara, then the pyramid at Meidum that collapsed, then the Bent pyramid, then the Red Pyramid before finally getting it right at Giza. Officially the architect got his angles all wrong and as a result the internal masonry of the pyramid collapsed under the weight.

This story is fine as long as nobody goes inside the pyramid and finds that there is no falling masonry, and everything seems perfectly secure.

As with Saqqara, this seems to suggest two stages of construction. All of the internal workings of the pyramid descend directly into the bedrock. The "burial chamber" contained no human remains or even a sarcophagus.

Strangely, the authorities have filled a number of round holes in the antechamber in modern times, however a deep vertical shaft is still there and goes very deep. In 1948, archaeologists attempted to descend to the bottom of the pit but didn't have a long enough rope. Nobody has tried since. Leading up from the antechamber is what some have called a chimney. The chimney contains two, remarkably advanced stone portcullises, which clearly were in place to stop something getting out or in as the case maybe.

To me this again says waterworks. A deep well with water being pushed to the top of the platform. The portcullises being used to stop water overflowing during the Nile floods.

I totally believe that Sneferu built the top half of this pyramid. It is a solid structure with no chambers. He would also have had to encase the structure. But he realised that to make a perfect pyramid from the base of the existing structure would never have worked and would have brought the entire complex crashing to the ground.
As we walked around the base of the pyramid, taking in the ruined mortuary temple, there were suddenly loud sirens, and three heavily armed soldiers went running into the desert. An unsuspecting tourist had wandered a little too far and I would hazard a guess that three soldiers in full combat gear pointing machine guns at them would deter them from doing it again.
The "mortuary temple" is quite small compared to the grander ones at Giza and very little remains of it. Adjacent to the pyramid is a small 26-metre-high pyramid, believed to be the tomb of Sneferu's wife, Queen Hetepheres. This is unique in that it is the only other pyramid in Egypt to have a similar interior to that of The Great Pyramid, which would indicate that this may have been the pump for the well at the Bent pyramid.

About half a mile across the desert is The Red Pyramid. Thankfully Mohammad drove us there.

Unfortunately, it isn't very red anymore, its red tinted stones blackened in recent years by the oil refinery that billows out smoke a few hundred yards away. You can enter this pyramid, which involves 75 steps up the outside, 175 metres on your hands and knees down the shaft, 175 metres on your hands and knees back up the shaft and 75 steps back down. I decided that neither my knees nor ankles were up for that.

It is the third largest pyramid in Egypt after the two main pyramids at Giza. It is seen by the mainstream as the first true pyramid and the prototype for its more famous successors. Locally it is referred to as The Bat Pyramid, but that probably relates to a mummified bat that was found in it which only dates to Ptolemaic times from 330BC.

The Red Pyramid was not always red. It used to be cased with white Tura limestone, but only a few of these stones now remain at the pyramid's base, at the corner. During the Middle Ages much of the white Tura limestone was taken for buildings in Cairo, revealing the red limestone beneath.

According to official lines, this pyramid was third time lucky for Sneferu, having supposedly cocked up the Bent Pyramid and the one at Meidum which I would be seeing the following day.
Walking around the base of the pyramid you come to a simple mortuary temple and also what is claimed to be the original capstone of the pyramid is on a plinth here. The problem with this however is that the capstone has a far steeper angle than the actual pyramid, which would have looked weird.
The plan from here was to go to the Southern Saqqara pyramids or Abu Sir pyramids but it turns out you need 48 hours' notice and approval from the Supreme Council of Antiquities. We put in an application and hoped for the best.

Furthermore, we had hoped to get to what is known as The Valley of The Whales which is in The Western Desert. Here you can find fossilised whale skeletons in the middle of the desert, going back 40 million years when there was a bit more water in these parts. Unfortunately, the locals were getting a bit restless again and threatening to take pot shots at tourists. As a result, I would now have an extra night in Luxor.

During my research for this trip and endeavouring to find a way to get to Abu Sir and Abu Ghorab, I stumbled across The Saqqara Country Club and Spa who supposedly hire out quad bikes and organize guided tours around the desert surrounding Abu Sir.
The guide who met me at the Airport and Sami both denied its existence. So, imagine my annoyance as we drove past it on the way back to Cairo. There are times when I feel I know more than the guides.

We stopped for lunch somewhere between Dashur and Cairo. For once it was edible but off putting in a number of ways. Firstly because of a duo dressed like Tommy Cooper and managing to play the violin like Les Dawson played the piano. And secondly because of a poor camel being dragged along by a string attached through its nostril, being forced to give children rides. For the record, lunch was more chicken, more houmous and more bread.

The ride back to Cairo was eventful. There was a large wedding procession heading south, involving numerous trucks, tractors, donkeys, tuk tuks, you name it. As a result, other vehicles heading south decided to do so on the northbound section. This of course resulted in the inevitable standoff, as a lorry and tuk tuk faced each other. The southbound lorry was insistent that the tuk tuk go around him. All well and good until you realise that there was a canal full of heaven knows what, waiting to greet the tuk tuk with open arms.

Despite getting stuck in the mud twice, the tuk tuk got past, and then we were next. Thankfully our driver sounds quite menacing when he swears at other drivers, and finally got the lorry to reverse half a mile back down the road to where it could re-join the correct lane. I had insisted on no shopping stops on this trip and was quite annoyed when our guide stopped at a place he said was where we could learn about meditation and ancient healing. This turned out to be a shop selling oils and fake perfume. The talk was literally that there were seven sacred oils, we can dab some on your forehead, shut our eyes for five minutes and sell you 100ml of each for a total of £280. UK pounds not Egyptian. This got rather nasty on all sides, and I ended up giving money for something I didn't want, just to get out of the shop. What I was sold went straight down the toilet and I made an official complaint about it to the tour company. I told Sami that if they tried to pull anything else like this that I would refuse to get out of the car.

I got back to the hotel around three o'clock in a bad mood after this incident. When I got to my room I was shivering. I wasn't sure whether this was due to malnutrition, from having no breakfast, malaria, from the mosquito bites, anger from being fleeced for something I didn't want or that the cleaner had turned the air conditioning to extra cold. Thankfully it was the latter and a hot cup of tea cured the problem.

I really don't know why I decided to do it. I like pyramids and occasionally listen to the odd Vivaldi concerto but booking tickets for a full-blown production of Verdi's Aida at The Giza Plateau was possibly a step, or maybe even a ten-mile walk, too far. I wouldn't be seen dead at Glyndebourne unless there was a beer festival there. Why couldn't Pink Floyd have been playing. Hell, even The Spice Girls would have been preferable. Marginally.

Admittedly, if you are going to see Aida anywhere, adjacent to The Sphinx and The Great Pyramid is probably as good as it gets. Isma'il Pasha, Khedive of Egypt, commissioned Verdi to write an opera for performance to celebrate the opening of the Khedivial Opera House, paying him 150,000 francs, but the premiere was delayed because of the Siege of Paris (1870–71), during the Franco-Prussian War, when the scenery and costumes were stuck in the French capital, and Verdi's Rigoletto was performed instead. Aida eventually premiered in Cairo in late 1871.

I started to get ready for the opera and came across a major stumbling block. The jacket and tie were ok, trousers fine, but my ankle was still swollen and wouldn't fit into the shoes. So, I ended up going to my first opera in Danger Mouse socks and trainers. The trainers came in useful as due to the Cairo traffic, my minibus was running late and all the occupants were told to disembark and run 100 yards down the road, through the filth that is the Cairo street system, and jump on another minibus that was further up the queue. The poor women in their designer high heels weren't too impressed, but I was fine in my grubby old trainers. Luckily it was dark, and nobody noticed them.

I got the impression that going to the opera was more about being seen to have done so, rather than any appreciation of the performance. The levels of arrogance of self-importance in the refreshments area were way off the scale.

Finally, we went to our seats and awaited proceedings to start.

Set in the court of the Pharaoh, the synopsis of Aida is that the Egyptians have captured and enslaved Aida, an Ethiopian princess. An Egyptian military commander, Radames, struggles to choose between his love for her and his loyalty to the King of Egypt. To complicate the story further, the King's daughter Amneris is in love with Radames, although he does not return her feelings. It all sounds wonderful, and the setting of the illuminated Sphinx and Pyramids was out of this world.

What can I say about opera? The experience was probably like going to the dentist and having teeth pulled through your backside. In fact, the latter sounds more fun and much quicker. As we had arrived at the performance area, the sunset call to prayer was wailing out over Cairo and in hindsight, listening to that for four hours would have been more enjoyable.

It was bad enough that they started late. It was bad enough that I was right at the back and could see little more than heads. It was bad enough that I was surrounded by enough Germans to resurrect Bomber Harris back into action. But then the singing started.

They say it isn't over until the fat lady sings, so I guess you know you are in for a long night when she warbles the first note. After about an hour of singing and looking at the backs of people's heads, it all stopped, and I thought to myself it must be half time and after a quick pie and a pint we could get through the second half quite quickly. How wrong I was. That was Act 1. There were three more to come.
To be fair I did stand up for Act 2 and got some good pictures of the pyramids and sphinx lit up. But then I sat back down, and it was gone midnight before they shut up. I think Aida's body was still warm as I darted out of the arena to the courtesy bus. My ears hurt and even worse I was freezing. The desert gets bloody cold at night. Especially in a shirt and tie.

When I got back to the hotel, I was cold, starving and in need of a beer. I called room service for a hot drink and a burger. The latter was a grave error as I spent much of the night on the toilet getting rid of it in one form or another. I set my alarm to 7am and tried to get 4 hours sleep.

3. The Egyptian Rod Hull and Emu

After 4 and a half hours' sleep and my bowels regretting the decision to call room service at 1am, I thankfully said goodbye to The Oasis Hotel at 7.30, hopefully never to return.

Today was the day when the best part of the holiday would begin, albeit slightly truncated due to our being unable to go to The Valley of The Whales. A three-day road trip from Cairo, through the desert, to Luxor, stopping at numerous archaeological sites en route.

It was good to get out of Cairo, but even better to know that when I came back later in the week, I would be staying at what is regarded as the best hotel in Egypt.

It is strange, but despite the roads in the cities being little more than rubble tracks, the motorways and main roads across the desert are as good as anything we have at home. As a result, it only took an hour and a half to travel the 100km south to Meidum.

Once you get away from the centres of Cairo and Luxor, the archaeological sites are deserted, and you get the place to yourself. This is brilliant, because you can take all the time you want to take it all in and not get hustled and bustled by anybody.

The pyramid is in the middle of nowhere and can be seen for miles as you approach it. Mohammad seemingly had trouble finding a parking space in a very large empty car park, but when we did finally get out of the car and take it all in, you saw what a unique structure this pyramid is.

This is another pyramid that is accredited to Sneferu. This was supposedly his first attempt at a pyramid, before he went to Dashur, messed up the Bent Pyramid and finally got it right with the Red Pyramid.

What we see today is the core of the pyramid which sits atop a massive pile of rubble. Originally an eight-step pyramid covered in casing stones, but today only the top three steps can be seen rising from the debris.

What you first notice is the remarkable similarity to a Mesopotamian ziggurat, which if the theories about Narmer invading from that area are correct, makes perfect sense. The pyramid at Meidum is thought to be just the second pyramid built after Djoser's at Saqqara and may have been originally built for Huni, the last pharaoh of the Third Dynasty, and continued or restored by Sneferu.

It seems bizarre that the core of the pyramid is built with immaculate precision, yet the outer casing was just thrown on in a hap hazard fashion and collapsed, seemingly within a few years of it being built. In fact, this makes no sense at all, and I would suggest that the internal core of the structure is many hundreds of years older than the outer casing.

After chickening out the previous day at the Red Pyramid, I did go inside this one. It was about 40 metres up the sandy bank to the entrance and then down a 75-metre shaft, about 4 feet in height at a fairly steep descent. This leads to an empty chamber from where there were a series of ladders leading to the burial chamber.

Once again, the term "burial chamber" is misleading. No human remains or even sarcophagus have been found inside the pyramid. The inside of the structure is very crude and hardly somewhere that a King would want to spend eternity. It screams out that the structure is functional rather than ceremonial.

I called it a day here and settled for the steep 75 metre climb, crouched down, back up the shaft. As I got back to daylight, the guardian invited us over to his little shack for a mint tea, the mint being picked straight from his little patch outside. As we sipped our tea, three coach loads of kids turned up and I breathed a sigh of relief that they weren't ten minutes earlier and trying to get past me huffing and puffing up the pyramid shaft.

Sitting and admiring the view, we discussed the structure further. The original eight step pyramid was built on bedrock, however when Sneferu, who I have already dubbed the Patron Saint of dodgy builders, came along, his extended outer layers were constructed on sand. Furthermore, clearly Huni, or whoever built the eight-step structure, had no intention of turning it into a true pyramid, thus the outer surface was polished, and the platforms of the steps were not horizontal, but fell off to the outside. This severely compromised the stability and is likely to have caused the collapse of the Meidum Pyramid in a downpour while the building was still under construction.

The absence of a Valley temple at Meidum would suggest that the whole thing came crashing down to the ground before the project was finished. There was a mortuary temple, but this was found under the rubble and there is no way of telling whether it was completed or not.

By the time it was investigated by Napoleon's Expedition in 1799 the Meidum Pyramid had its present three steps. It is commonly assumed the pyramid still had five steps in the fifteenth century and was gradually falling further into ruin, because al-Maqrizi described it as looking like a five-stepped mountain.

After our cup of mint tea, and the marauding hordes of Egyptian schoolchildren had left, we wandered over to another structure which is adjacent to the pyramid. Known by the rather boring title of Mastaba 17, this is one of the more fascinating structures in Egypt, although entry is forbidden these days.

Mastaba 16, which is Northeast of the pyramid, holds the remains of Sneferu's son. A tomb that has seen two stages of enlargement. Mastaba 17 is far larger, grander, and built all in one go. Which raises the question, who was more important to Sneferu than his son? And if Sneferu had two empty pyramids, why wasn't his son given one of those?

The outer casing of the collapsed pyramid is identical to the casing of Mastaba 17, therefore Sneferu clearly restored it. A black granite pavement surrounds the structure, similar to the one that surrounds The Great Pyramid. This is something that isn't found anywhere else in the country.

Unlike most mastabas, this one does not have a shaft that connects it to the outside world. This would suggest that either this was very different to a normal Egyptian burial, or it dates to a time before funerary rituals of The Old Kingdom became commonplace.

Unlike the pyramid, this Mastaba contains a large red granite sarcophagus which is three times thicker than the one found inside The Great Pyramid. The sarcophagus weighs 8.5 tons and is topped with a 3.5-ton lid.

When it was opened there contained the remains of a man holding two crooks and a wooden mace. Bizarrely, the remains of a large bird were buried with him. It did cross my mind that this could have been an Egyptian version of Rod Hull and Emu, but then again, why would they deserve such a grand burial.

Before the body was laid to rest, it had been defleshed, and each bone wrapped individually. Some skin on the skull showed that the man was black and hair curly. Hence an African origin. The burial practice was unlike anything ever found in Egypt.

The skin was taken for carbon dating, but you guessed it. It mysteriously got lost in transit and the establishment's tale of Egypt remained intact. The official line is that the occupant was an unknown son of Sneferu who died prior to pyramid building. Strange because his favourite son, got a meagre tomb half a mile away.

The occupant of the tomb was clearly as important in death as in life. Maybe he was responsible for phase 1 of the pyramid?
One theory is that it is the tomb of Andjety. A real Pre-Dynastic King who became deified and was the precursor of Osiris. As a King he was known for draining swamps and making land arable. Once again, we have references to water next to a pyramidical structure.

Furthermore, Andjety, the God, is shown with a crown with two crooks and a mace and was known as the son of vultures. Another "coincidence" is that Sneferu is the first Egyptian Pharaoh ever to be seen wearing the Lower Egyptian crown of Andjety.

From Meidum we were given our own escort of four police officers armed with machine guns. This was allegedly for our protection as a tourist was shot somewhere in the area in the 1990's. However, as the day progressed it became increasingly obvious that it was not so much about my protection but a protection racket. First, we had a police car. Then a jeep and then believe it or not an armoured car with a cannon, before finally a soldier came in the car with us. Each and every one of them demanded money.

Anyway, back to the day. Stop two, and another 45 minutes down the road was the mud brick pyramid of Hawara, accredited to Sneferu's main rival for constructing the dodgiest pyramids, Amenemhat III who ruled around 1900bc and is also given the dubious honour of building The Black Pyramid at Dashur. It is believed that Amenemhat was interred here, but as per usual there have been no remains or sarcophagus found. Modern day Hawara is slightly south of the ancient city of Shedyt or latterly Crocodilopolis, cult centre of the crocodile god, Sobek.

In common with the Middle Kingdom pyramids constructed after Amenemhat II, it was built of mudbrick round a core of limestone passages and burial chambers and faced with limestone.
Most of the facing stone was later pillaged for use in other buildings and today the pyramid is little more than an eroded, vaguely pyramidal mountain of mud brick, and of the once magnificent mortuary temple precinct formerly enclosed by a wall there is little left beyond the foundation bed of compacted sand and chips and shards of limestone.

From the pyramid entrance a sloping passageway with steps runs down to a small room and a further short horizontal passage. In the roof of this horizontal passage there was a concealed sliding trapdoor weighing 20 tons. If this was found and opened a robber would find himself confronted by an empty passage at a right angle to the passage below, closed by wooden doors, or by a passage parallel to the passage below, carefully filled with mud and stone blocking. He would assume that the blocking concealed the entrance and wasted time removing it (thereby increasing the likelihood of detection by the pyramid guardians).

In fact, there was a second 20-ton trapdoor in the roof of the empty passage, giving onto a second empty passage, also at a right angle to the first. This too had a 20-ton trapdoor giving onto a passage at a right angle to its predecessor (thus the interior of the pyramid was circled by these passages). However, this passage ended in a large area of mud and stone blocking that presumably concealed the burial chamber.

This, however, was a blind and merely filled a wide but shallow alcove. Two blind shafts in the floor, carefully filled with cut stone blocks, further wasted the robbers' time, for the real entrance to the burial chamber was even more carefully concealed and lay between the blind shafts and opposite the alcove.

Despite these elaborate protective measures, famous British archaeologist Flinders Petrie found that none of the trapdoors had been slid into place and the wooden doors were open. Whether this indicated negligence on the part of the burial party, an intention to return and place further burials in the pyramid (when found there were two sarcophagi in the quartzite monolith described below and room for at least two more), or a deliberate action to facilitate robbery of the tomb, we cannot know.

The burial chamber was made from a single quartzite monolith which was lowered into a larger chamber lined with limestone. This monolithic slab weighed an estimated 110 tons according to Petrie. A course of brick was placed on the chamber to raise the ceiling then the chamber was covered with 3 quartzite slabs (estimated weight 45 tons each). Above the burial chamber were 2 relieving chambers. This was topped with 50-ton limestone slabs forming a pointed roof. Then an enormous arch of brick 3 feet thick was built over the pointed roof to support the core of the pyramid.

We could only go ten metres into the pyramid because of flooding. This is a fairly recent event as Petrie managed to get to the burial chamber in the nineteenth century. A canal was dug here in the early 20th century and has flooded all of the underground passages. Around the pyramid they have found graves of hundreds of mummified crocodiles. There are so many that you can see and pick up crocodile jaws lying in the sand.

Whilst the pyramid is an impressive site, even though the outer casing has collapsed, the most interesting thing here was the site of The Labyrinth described by Herodotus in Greek times as having 3000 rooms. Excavations have only just started but there is an enormous column top that gives some idea of the size.
Herodotus, writing in the 5th Century BC and other Greek and Roman writers described a magnificent labyrinth in Egypt, containing three thousand rooms on two levels. Pliny the Elder (first century A.D.) related that the Egyptian labyrinth was already 3600 years old in his time.

Herodotus wrote: -
"The Labyrinth has 12 covered courts -six in a row facing north, six south. Inside, the building is of two stories and contains 3,000 rooms, of which half are underground, and the other half directly above them. I was taken through the rooms in the upper story, so what I shall say of them is from my own observation, but the underground ones I can speak of only from report, because the Egyptians in charge refused to let me see them, as they contain the tombs of the kings who built the Labyrinth and also the tombs of the sacred crocodiles. The upper rooms, on the contrary I did actually see, and it is hard to believe that they are the work of men; the baffling and intricate passages from room to room and from court to court were an endless wonder to me, as we passed from a courtyard into rooms, from rooms into galleries, from galleries into more rooms, and thence into yet more courtyards. The roof of every chamber, courtyard and gallery is, like the walls, of stone. The walls are covered with carved figures, and each court is exquisitely built of white marble and surrounded by a colonnade."

He went on to say "It is beyond my power to describe. It must have cost more in labour and money than all public works of the Greeks put together – though no one would deny that the temples of Ephesus and Samos are remarkable buildings. The Pyramids too are astonishing structures, each one of them equal to many of the most ambitious works of Greece; but the Labyrinth surpasses them."

In 2008 the 'Mataha Expedition' discovered amazing proof of the Labyrinth's existence. Using GPS instruments, the team found "the presence of a colossal archaeological feature below the labyrinth 'foundation' zone of Petrie's record, which has to be reconsidered as the roof of the still existing labyrinth."

Researchers are using space-based technology to penetrate the Hawara complex for underground anomalies. What they have found is mind-boggling. Multiple levels of huge chambers and what looks like a complex of either an underground city or perhaps an ancient storage bunker.

The actual building was destroyed by The Romans but hopefully a lot more can be recovered.

In the distance, behind Hawara stands Lake Moeris, Egypt's only saltwater lake. Interestingly, when they tested water down a shaft near the Great Pyramid in 2016, they found it to be saltwater. This could only have come from the Mediterranean or Lake Moeris. Just as interesting is that in Early dynastic times, there were two pyramids built that stood side by side in the lake. The lake has dried up since ancient times, and the pyramids are now on dry land, but they are out of bounds for archaeologists and tourists alike.

In prehistory it was once a freshwater lake, with an area estimated to vary between 490 – 656 miles. Today it is a smaller saltwater lake called Birket Qarun. The lake's surface is 140 feet (43 meters) below sea-level and covers about 78 square miles (202 sq. km). It is unknown when Lake Moeris turned from freshwater to seawater, or the cause.

What's interesting about Lake Moeris and Hawara is that it shows a massive network of tunnels and underground waterways as well.

The Greek historian Herodotus wrote about the "pathways" between the Labyrinth of Hawara and the Giza Plateau being linked, much like an ancient underground subway system.

From here we went to see the last great pyramid ever built at El Lahun. Built for Sesostris 2nd around 1816BC this is the largest pyramid in area, but not the highest due to the less severe angle upwards. Once covered in limestone and gold, it is today a sad mound of mud bricks.

Here again there are signs that the structure originally had another purpose. The ancient name for the structure translates as Opening of the Canal. And as at Saqqara, there were numerous seemingly bottomless shafts, leading to a network of underground tunnels. The other striking similarity is that the Pyramid stands on an artificial terrace which almost certainly predates the main structure.

On the north side eight rectangular blocks of stone were left to serve as mastabas, probably for the burial of personages associated with the royal court. In front of each mastaba is a narrow shaft leading down to the burial chamber underneath. Also, on the north side is the Queen's Pyramid or subsidiary pyramid.

The most remarkable discovery was that of the village of the workers who both constructed the pyramid and then served the funerary cult of the king. The village, conventionally known as Kahun, is about 800 meters from the pyramid and lies in the desert a short distance from the edge of cultivation. When found, many of the buildings were extant up to roof height, and Petrie confirmed that the true arch was known and used by the workmen in the village. However, all the buildings found were demolished in the process of excavation, which proceeded in long strips down the length of the village. When the first strip had been cleared, mapped, and drawn, the next strip was excavated, and the spoil dumped in the previous strip. As a result, there is very little to be seen on the site today.

Among the curiosities found there were wooden boxes buried beneath the floors of many of the houses. When opened they were found to contain the skeletons of infants, sometimes two or three in a box, and aged only a few months at death. Petrie reburied these human remains in the desert.

That was it for sightseeing, but we still had a two-hour drive to the town of El Minya, some 152 miles South of Cairo, where we stayed for the night. The hotel seemed much better than The Oasis Hotel and had a pleasant view of the Nile from the balcony.

El Minya is a modern university town which has several claims to fame. It is the alleged birthplace of Khufu, alleged builder of The Great Pyramid and is the centre of the lucrative Egyptian cotton industry.

After a quick lunch, followed by a lie down, Sami, Mohammad and I decided to go into the town to look around. This proved problematic. Firstly, we didn't realise that the armed guards were still on duty and they literally demanded money to allow me to leave the hotel.

Having coughed up the baksheesh, we strolled along the Nile and then sat outside at a coffee shop on a main street. Sami recommended I tried the house speciality which was boiled apple juice with a whole cinnamon stick in it. It was like liquid apple pie and amazing.

Our evening was rudely brought to a halt when the tourist police, clearly having been tipped off by the guard at the hotel, turned up at the cafe and fined the owner for serving a tourist without telling them. It really is a complete racket.

As we couldn't afford any more bribes, we walked back to the hotel and had some dinner before turning in for the night.

4. 99 Dead Baboons

I slept relatively well, considering I was woken up by the sound of gunshots at 2am and then again at 4.30 when the wailing mullah wakes all and sundry up to go pray to Allah.

Breakfast was very basic with nothing cooked. I avoided the salad but in hindsight the orange juice was a bad move as it was watered down with tap water. I probably lost half a stone throughout the day. The combination of climbing over 700 steps in 35-degree heat, interspersed by sprinting to each and every available toilet to squirt out the orange juice. Why does more come out than you put in?

We left the hotel at 8am and a new tourist policeman was grinning as he had been selected to travel with us and get his slice of pie. As we drove through rural villages, by passing the donkeys and sheep, there was a stark contrast in scenery. To the right was green fertile land leading to the Nile, whilst to the left were barren brown mountains and desert.

Our first stop was Beni Hasan, 30 minutes south of Minya, where there are 25 Middle Kingdom tombs of local officials who oversaw the Oryx District. Only four are open to the public and to get to them you must climb 250 steps up the mountain. Thankfully my ankle had stopped hurting, but by the end of the day, my thighs were killing me from all of the climbing.

Just to show what a scam the tourist police were, our armed protector looked at the steps and decided to have a cup of tea and wait for us at ground level. So, Sami and I started the ascent, in the knowledge that if there were any armed terrorists in the area, we were on our own. Thankfully halfway up there were a few seats where you could sit down and take the view of The Nile Valley below.

Onwards and upwards we reached the summit, and the guardian unlocked the first tomb. In a way it was nice to be back to simple Egyptian history. No question marks as to why something was built, who built it and what its purpose was. Here we had an amazing selection of Middle Kingdom tombs, decorated with reliefs of everyday life.

The first tomb belonged to Baqet III, who was an official and Great Chief of the Oryx Nome during the 11th Dynasty in the 21st century BC. Apart from the position of governor of the entire Nome, Baqet III also held the titles haty-a, treasurer of the king of Lower Egypt, confidential friend, true royal acquaintance, and mayor of Nekheb. Despite all of this grandeur, Baqet' s tomb is known as The Wrestling Tomb. Although not as large as some of the tombs at Saqqara, this was still a fairly elaborate last resting space, comprised of a cult chapel and an inner burial chamber.
The northern wall depicts Baqet and his wife in their daily life, the hunting of various animals and various artisans whilst working. Most notably weaving, which is still very much a local tradition.

The south wall mainly shows Baqet' s funeral, but also some people playing senet. There are also reliefs of pygmies dancing for the entertainment of Baqet and his friends and families. Pygmy slaves were seen similar to court jesters in Medieval England.

The eastern wall is split into two, with half showing a fortress garrisoned by Egyptians and besieged by a mixed army composed of Egyptians infantry, Nubian bowmen, and maybe Libyan slingers, likely representing a Theban offensive. The other half depicts an impressive number of wrestling positions and techniques. I am no expert, but the holds they used then seem very similar to those used today and had he been alive today, I am sure Baqet would have been a keen fan of the WWE.

A couple of doors along from Baqet is the tomb of his son, Khety who assumed his father's political duties. As a result, the tomb's basic design and layout is very similar. Six lotus shaped columns and its rectangular shape, the same as that of Baqet, with the northern wall showing Khety on hunting trips in the desert.

There are also some scenes of Khety, accompanied by his wife, and supervising the activities taking place in the province they were ruling. This included some scenes of women singing and dancing. The eastern wall of the tomb has some scenes of soldiers practicing participating in battles. The ancient Egyptian artist who brilliantly created this wall showed the movement of the soldiers wonderfully by using different shades to show how each soldier moved during his training. Khety clearly wasn't a wrestling fan however, and this part of the wall showed women practicing some form of yoga.

The wall located in the southern section of the tomb shows Khety supervising the process of making wine and there are some burial rituals displayed in this section as well.

The second set of tombs belonged to another pair of overseers, but from the 12th dynasty. The tombs of Amenemhat and Khnumhotep both had columns at the entrance to the tomb and six columns inside. Amenhotep seemed like a good bloke. His colourful tomb shows some wonderful reliefs of birds and animals, as well as the traditional hunting scenes. His tomb is unique as he left his own epitaph which reads "to those who love life and hate death, I grant thousands of bread and beer." What a nice man.

Amenemhat oversaw the district during the reign of Senusret I in the 20th Century BC. He accompanied the pharaoh in a military expedition to Kush; though the date is unknown, it's likely the same, known expedition of Year 18 of Senusret I.

In another expedition Amenemhat escorted the "king's son Ameny" – very likely the future pharaoh Amenemhat II – with 400 men to collect gold from an unknown Nubian location. Amenemhat was also sent to Coptos along with the vizier Senusret in order to bring other gold. These expeditions suggest that Amenemhat was a very important official who usually accompanied high dignitaries and even members of the royal family. All of these journeys are depicted on the walls of the tomb.

The tomb's main room is richly painted with more scenes of wrestling and on the south wall, Amenemhet himself and his wife Hetepet are depicted with a large amount of offerings. The room's ceiling was divided into three decorated naves. A small cult niche was made in the east side of the main room, probably meant to host a statue group of the tomb owner, traces of which have been found. The final tomb, that of Khnumhotep, is unique in that he had his biography written on the wall. He was another Governor of the area, serving under both Amenemhat II and Senusret II.

In ancient times, the tomb would have been approached via a path that was distinguishable by dark brown boulders on either side; the path extended from the open outer court down the hill to the edge of the cultivated land.

On the wall are also depicted Khnumhotep's most notable officials and employees at his local court, which somewhat resemble a downscaled version of the royal court with a local treasurer and many stewards and overseers.

Khnumhotep's biography is in the main chamber. It begins to the left of the entrance to the shrine and runs counterclockwise around the walls of the main chamber, ending to the right of the doorway leading to the shrine. The main types of information included are about the actions Khnumhotep II performed during his lifetime, his family, and their lives, as well as the close relationship of his family to the royal house, Khnumhotep's excellent character, and his request to visitors that offerings are made to him.

On the eastern end of the north wall there is a large-scale standing figure of Khnumhotep receiving offerings primarily of several types of animals and birds. What makes this tomb stand out among the 39 large rock-cut tombs at Beni Hasan is the well-known scene of the Aamu group, Asiatic nomadic traders who are sometimes considered Hyksos or at least their forerunners; the group, led by a man called Absha, was bringing offerings to the deceased.

The west end of the wall has another large-scale figure of Khnumhotep only here he is facing right and using a bow to hunt in the desert which is on the edge of the Egyptian world, the boundary between order and chaos. It has been interpreted that in this scene Khnumhotep is assuming the role of the king dominating over the chaotic power of the desert.

The east wall houses the entrance to the shrine, as well as two large depictions of Khnumhotep hunting in the marshes, one on the north side and the other on the south side. To the south he is harpooning two fishes and to the north he is fowling with a throwing stick.

The south wall was dedicated to the celebration of the cult meal of Khnumhotep and his wife Khety. The east end of the wall features the deceased seated in front of an offering table covered with offerings holding a flail, traditionally seen as a symbol of royalty or divinity, in his right hand. At the west end of the wall there is an illustration of Khety sitting in front of a full offering table. She is facing left and participating in her husband's meal presented by his cult. The shrine portrays a smaller version of the offering cult and in many ways can be seen as an expansion from the false door of the Old Kingdom, where a statue inside a niche could have been integrated. The placing of statues in the chapel itself is a new funerary art style that appeared in the Middle Kingdom tombs.

At this point we heard a vague rumbling sound. 500 jackbooted German tourists were marching up the steps like mountain goats. So much for our mate with the gun, I thought to myself. He could at least have held them off and actually earned his tip.

In any case, the dodgy orange juice was beginning to take effect and I can attest that going back down the steps was a lot faster than climbing up.

So, we retreated and hoped the sausage munching hordes wouldn't follow us to our next stop, Amarna. This was always going to be one of the highlights of the trip to see a pile of rubble that only stood for 40 years in the 14th century BC. It may have been only 40 years but there is enough evidence to suggest that the heretic Pharaoh Akhenaten and possibly his brother, crown prince Tuthmosis are the founders of Judaism, Christianity, and Islam. The priests of Amun at Karnak won the battle, Amarna was destroyed, and the followers of The Aten kicked out of Egypt. The biblical exodus and we know where that ended.

Construction of Amarna started around 1346 BC and was probably completed around 1341 BC. To speed up construction of the city most of the buildings were constructed out of mudbrick, and whitewashed. The most important buildings were faced with local stone. This reason alone would explain why there isn't much left here, but the fact is that once Akhenaten was driven out, the Theban Priests attempted to have the entire city raised to the ground. Clearly this didn't happen straight away, as a shrine to Horemheb has been found and he was not Pharaoh for a further fifteen years.

The city was enormous, spanning some eight kilometres. Akhenaten built 14 steles on the surrounding mountains showing the boundaries of the city. Only one is still in situ and it was another tough climb up a mountain but had to be seen.

Giant statues of Akhenaten and Nefertiti carved into the rock face with a proclamation that this land was granted to the people of the Aten (promised land anyone?) and that the Pharaoh was a God on Earth, completely eliminating the priesthood.

This was technically the problem. One Pharaoh against thousands of unemployed priests who had enjoyed total control over the former capital Thebes and the minds of the sheep. There was only going to be one result.

The boundary stelae preserve an account of Akhenaten's foundation of this city. The document records the pharaoh's wish to have several temples of the Aten to be erected here, for several royal tombs to be created in the eastern hills of Amarna for himself, his chief wife Nefertiti, and his eldest daughter Meritaten as well as his explicit command that when he was dead, he would be brought back to Amarna for burial.

Akhenaten's body has never been found in Egypt (in other words, he left with his followers), but his royal tomb at Amarna is still there to be seen. There was a slight delay at this point as we pulled up to a checkpoint where an armed soldier and the guardian of the tomb had to join us to drive the two miles to the tomb. We had four spaces in the car, all taken by myself, my guide, the driver, and our money grabbing tourist policeman. 6 people in four seats is not possible so an argument began between the other three as to who was more important. We gave the policeman another few pounds to go and sit under a tree. The soldier with a machine gun got in the car and the guardian set off on a moped to a little hut. That can't be the royal tomb I thought to myself. I know they thought Akhenaten was a heretic, but surely, he wasn't buried in a shed. It turns out that this was a generator and the guardian had to put 50p in the meter to get the electric working.
The interior of the tomb was amazing and unlike anything you would find in the valley of the kings. No Egyptian gods towering over the mortals, just a giant relief of Akhenaten and Nefertiti getting the rays from the Aten and blessing the tiny minions. One mummy was found in this tomb that is believed to have been a princess and daughter of Akhenaten and Nefertiti. Sadly, she was the only member of the royal family to die there.

A flight of twenty steps, with a central inclined plane leads to the door and a long straight descending corridor. Halfway down this corridor there is a suite of unfinished rooms (perhaps intended for Nefertiti). The main corridor continues to descend, and to the right again a second suite of rooms branches off.

The corridor then descends via steps into an antechamber, and then to the pillared burial chamber where the granite sarcophagus sat in a slight dip in the floor. It was decorated by carvings of Nefertiti acting as a protective goddess, and by the ever-present sun-disks of the Aten.

The second suite of three chambers are believed to be used for the burial of Meketaten, Akhenaten's second daughter. Two of the chambers are decorated and depict very similar scenes: in one chamber Akhenaten and Nefertiti bend over the inert body of a woman, weeping and gripping each other's arms for support.

Nearby a nurse stands with a baby in her arms, accompanied by a fan-bearer, which indicates the baby's royal status.

The names in the scene have been hacked out. In the other chamber a very similar scene is shown; here the hieroglyphs identify the dead young woman as Meketaten.

In the same chamber another scene shows Meketaten standing under a canopy which is usually associated with childbirth but can also interpreted as representing the rebirth of the princess. In front of her, amongst courtiers, stand Akhenaten, Nefertiti and their three remaining daughters, Meritaten, Ankhesenpaaten and Neferneferuaten Tasherit. The presence of a royal baby causes many to believe the young princess died in childbirth.
Next stop, and up another few hundred steps, was the tomb of Meryre, High Priest of the Aten. Some amazing colours in the reliefs and notable for the first known depiction of a rainbow. The sepulchre is the largest and most elaborate of the noble tombs of Amarna.

The tomb was found in relatively good condition compared to the other tombs of Amarna. After the end of Akhenaten's rule, depictions of his reign and religion were destroyed because they were considered to be heretical. In Meryra's tomb, Akhenaten and Nefertiti's features have been consistently erased.

The desecration is confined to these individuals, and the names and figures of the princesses remain untouched. The tomb consists of four sections: the antechamber, the hall of columns, a second hall, and the shrine. The entrance to the tomb was originally decorated with inscriptions to the Amarna Royal family and the deity Aten.

These decorations have either been destroyed or are hidden by the modern doors protecting the tomb entrance. The antechamber itself shows Meryre offering prayers to the Akhenaten, and the cartouches of the king, Nefertiti and the Aten. The door jambs are inscribed with funerary prayers for Akhenaten and the Aten. The entrance from the antechamber to the outer hall is decorated with the Short Hymn to the Aten, which is identical to Psalm 104, and shows Meryre's wife Tenre making offerings to the sun-disc.

Akhenaten and Nefertiti are depicted paying a visit to Meryre at the temple. It is uncertain if Meryre is included in this image and the description of the scene has been destroyed. It is speculated that the scene either shows Akhenaten on his way to the temple to appoint Meryre as the High Priest of Aten, or it is simply as example of Meryre honoured with the presence of the King and Queen at the temple and exercising his office for them. Either situation serves to promote the role and importance of Meryre, even though the scene seems to be immediately focused upon Akhenaten.

In the immediately preceding scene, Akhenaten officially declares Meryre as the High Priest of Aten. Despite being the High Priest of Aten, Meryre was not recognized with the power to access the Aten, an exclusive ability of Akhenaten. In the text of this relief, Akhenaten addresses Meryre with the proclamation, "Behold, I am attaching you to myself, to be the Greatest of Seers of the Aten, in the House of Aten, in Ahket-aten." In this statement, the reliance on Akhenaten in Atenism is referred to in a physical sense, as Akhenaten pledges to "attach" Meryre to him. This is similar to the contact the royal family has with the Aten, which is furnished with hands, or ankhs extending from its rays. One purpose of the ankhs is to literally fill the recipient through bodily orifices with the life and prosperity of the Aten. Similar to what a cross signifies in Christianity.

The tomb of Ay was next. I have seen his actual tomb in the Valley of the Kings, which was originally going to be the tomb of Tutankhamun, or Tutankhaten as he was known in Amarna. This is another well preserved tomb and from the writings of the wall it is believed that he may actually have been the father of Nefertiti.
He had the title of God's father in Amarna. We know Akhenaten's father was Amenhotep 3rd, so the only other god was Nefertiti. Whether this is right or wrong, Aye was a very powerful vizier to three pharaohs before finally claiming the throne after Tutankhamun's death. The tomb is notable for the scenes of Ay and his wife Tiyi receiving gifts from Akhenaten and Nefertiti. The tomb is unfinished but contains many of the more recognisable reliefs from the Amarna period.

Final stop at Amarna were the remains of the only building that that really survives in any state or form, The Small Temple of The Aten.

The Great Temple lies buried beneath the sand somewhere and to be honest there is little left of this apart from one and a half columns and a few foundations. But it was amazing to be there.

There are brick pylons at the entrance, and others which subdivided the interior of the temple building. In the back of the temple stood the sanctuary originally built of limestone and sandstone.

This temple had a foundation layer of gypsum that is now covered over by sand. However, modern stone blocks have been laid atop the sand in order to provide the basic outlines of this temple.
As there were no toilet facilities here. In fact, there are no real tourist facilities at Amarna at all, which is sad, we moved on to our final stop of the day which was Tuna el Gabel, formerly known as Heliopolis and cult centre of the god Toth, God of wisdom and knowledge. Toth is generally portrayed as an Ibis, but here he was also shown as a baboon.

There are a few remains of the actual temple but there are three major sites to see here. Actually, make that four. Sami was also now feeling the effects of the watered-down orange juice, but I pulled rank, as I had the roll of toilet paper in my rucksack and made a beeline for the loo.

The first site here was the tomb of Petosiris, High priest of Toth around 300BC. Suddenly we found ourselves 1300 years ahead of the Amarna period and the tomb was very Ptolemaic and Greek in its feel. The reliefs are beautiful but show a distinct Greek bias already, only 30 years after Alexander conquered Egypt. Egyptian clothing is replaced by Greek outfits, people are pale with beards, yet it is also has a very Egyptian theme and honoured the Egyptian god Toth, although by this point, he had been joined with Greek god Hermes.

The small memorial tomb is constructed in a way that makes it look like a very small version of the Temple of Hathor at Dendera, one of the major Temples of the period. We saw a major change from the mastabas from the Old Kingdom we had seen at Saqqara and Meidum.

The other tomb here that is open is that of a young girl called Isadora. This is a later tomb from 138 AD, long after Cleopatra, the last Pharaoh had died and when the Romans were ruling Egypt. It is the tomb of a young girl who died trying to swim across the Nile to see her secret lover.

She fell in love with a young soldier from Antinoöpolis, and they wanted to get married. However, her father refused, so the young couple decided to elope. Unfortunately, Isadora drowned while crossing the Nile. Her body was mummified, and her father built an elaborate tomb for her, featuring a poem of 10 lines inscribed in Greek elegiac couplets. At some time after her death, a cult developed around her tomb. Isadora's mummified remains are still present, encased in glass, in her mausoleum.
The final port of call were the catacombs of the Toth temple. This was amazing and had over 3km of tunnels, all full of tiny coffins containing mummified birds and baboons.

Hermopolis, "the City of Hermes", was known in Egyptian as "Khemenu", and was a major city in antiquity, located near the boundary between Lower and Upper Egypt.

A black siltstone obelisk of King Nectanebo II, now residing in The British Museum, stood at the doorway of the sanctuary of Thoth. Most of the ibis mummies have been destroyed by robbers over the centuries, and only one of the baboons has survived. This belongs to the best-preserved part of the catacombs, the shrine close to the entrance.

From here it was a ninety-minute drive, without the need for an armed escort, to the Cement Works Hotel in Asyut, which was, you guessed it, in a cement works. In fact, Asyut, formerly Lycopolis, the only place where mummified wolves have been found, is now a small town built around the cement works.

Surprisingly, for a hotel with such an uninviting name, it wasn't too bad, although there was no alcohol on sale anywhere and it was cold Pepsi max all round.

Having said that, we looked at the Hotel Lunch menu and decided against it, instead deciding to venture into Asyut itself to find better.

This was an experience. Dust, filth, tractors, donkeys and hundreds of cement trucks trundling up and down the only road as we sat on the pavement at a roadside café eating freshly grilled chicken. It was an interesting shop. Half a dead goat was hanging up in the entrance whilst another goat, presumably next to be put on the grill was bleating in the back of the shop. Worryingly, the bleating had stopped before we left. The toilet was al fresco and a simple hole in the ground. One bloke simply dropped his trousers and went for it in full view of us eating our chicken and rice. I always seem to end up in the best places.

5. Egyptian Gridlock

Another awful 7am breakfast with the cement workers which was easily rushed, and we were on the road by 8am, leaving Asyut behind. All went well for about ninety minutes as we made good time heading south on the main road through the desert. The rest of the day however, turned out to be more about modern day Egypt than the ancient Egypt which was on the itinerary.

Our first stop was the small town of Akhmim, formerly known as Panopolis or Khentmin, and site of the cult of Min, the fertility goddess. Unfortunately, neither the driver, nor my guide, quite knew where Akhmim was exactly. We stopped and asked people. Some of whom pointed one way, and others would then point back to where we came from. I learned a few new Arabic words from our driver, the rough translation of one being "I would get more sense from your donkey."

It took at least 40 minutes to actually find the town, and then the real fun started. Akhmim was full of tuk tuks and donkeys, presumably all ready to show us how to get to where we wanted, if only we could talk to them. We were directed down this tiny alleyway, only to be confronted with an articulated lorry reversing towards us, which did not stop the swarm of tuk tuks heading straight for it.

We reversed back on to the main street and drove around a bit more. Finally, I spotted a statue and shouted out. It's a bit much when you hire a guide and a driver and find the place yourself.

Anyway, the statue is really all that is left of the temple. Having said that, it is a magnificent work of art. It is of Ramses 2nd's second wife and fourth daughter Meret Amun and stands 11 metres high, making it the highest known statue of any Egyptian queen.

Another large statue of Ramses II is sitting towards the rear of the Temple enclosure but is not as impressive as that of his Queen. There are records of some sort of ancient games recorded here. Herodotus wrote on a trip to the city that there were Egyptians, Nubians and people from the Kingdom of Punt clambering up poles before the God Min and the winners would receive prizes.

Min was especially a god of the desert routes on the east of Egypt, and the trading tribes are likely to have gathered to his festivals for business and pleasure at Coptos (which was really near Neapolis) even more than at Akhmim. Strabo mentions linen-weaving and stone-cutting as ancient industries of Panopolis, and it is not altogether a coincidence that the cemetery of Akhmim is one of the chief sources of the beautiful textiles of Roman and Christian age, that are brought from Egypt.

At the beginning of the harvest season, Min's image was taken out of the temple and brought to the fields in the festival of the departure of Min, when they blessed the harvest, and played games naked in his honour, the most important of these being the climbing of a huge pole. This four day festival is evident from the great festivals list at the temple of Ramses III at Medinet Habu in Luxor.

There are records of the Temple standing here up to and including the Thirteenth Century however it, and much of the ancient city was dismantled and their material reused in the later Middle Ages. There are ancient burial sites within the city, but as yet these remain unexplored and even the giant statue of Merit Amun was only unearthed in 1981.

Returning from the temple we found Mohammad, our driver, still shaking his fists at tuk tuk drivers. Unfortunately for him the real fun had yet to begin. To get to Abydos from Akhmim, we had to get to the Nile at Sohag and then follow the river west. Simple. Or at least it would have been had the road not been dug up.

We found ourselves in donkey and tuk tuk gridlock. Beeping horns and eye ores filled the air as we went nowhere. There were no road signs, no diversions and when you actually needed a policeman, there wasn't one to be found. We even tried dangling money out of the window to see if that would help find one. We tried one road, then tried another. Asked people who would shrug their shoulders or point back to the road that was shut. After an hour, with the temperature on the inside of the car a lot hotter than the outside, we stumbled across a policeman sitting on a chair watching the chaos.

Now I have discovered, often to my cost, that there is no such thing as an overreaction in Egypt. The policeman made a phone call and ten minutes later, a four-star general from the Egyptian army turns up in a police jeep, with four heavily armed soldiers. They then escorted us, blue lights flashing and sirens wailing, all of the 30 miles to Abydos. For a small fee of course.

It was lunchtime by this point, and we were massively behind schedule. Sami's plan was to go to Dendera after Abydos, but I said I was happy to leave this out if it meant we could spend more time here. I had been to the Hathor Temple at Dendera twice and had no real desire to go there again on this trip. We were hungry, so went to the only hotel in town for a meal. Unfortunately, what was served was raw chicken and was returned to the chef. My innards have only just survived so far, and raw chicken was not the answer.

Cooked chicken was not returned from the kitchen as the chef by this point realised, he was never going to get a tip, so buggered off. Briefly, the madness of the day was interrupted by some sightseeing. The temple of Seti 1st at Abydos is probably the most colourful and best preserved of all the temples that still stand. The artwork is vivid and depicts the pharaoh paying homage to seven gods, each of whom have their own sanctuary within the temple. Considered one of the most important archaeological sites in Egypt, the sacred city of Abydos was the site of many ancient temples, including Umm el-Qa'ab, a royal necropolis where early pharaohs were entombed. These tombs began to be seen as extremely significant burials and in later times it became desirable to be buried in the area, leading to the growth of the town's importance as a cult site.

The Great Temple of Osiris and most of the ancient town are buried under the modern buildings to the north of the Seti temple. Many of the original structures and the artefacts within them are considered irretrievable and lost; many may have been destroyed by the new construction.

Abydos was occupied by the rulers of the Predynastic period, whose town, temple, and tombs have been found there. The temple and town continued to be rebuilt at intervals down to the times of the Thirtieth Dynasty, and the cemetery was in continuous use.

The pharaohs of the First Dynasty were buried in Abydos, including Narmer, who is regarded as the founder of the First Dynasty, and his successor, Aha. Some pharaohs of the Second Dynasty were also buried in Abydos. The temple was renewed and enlarged by these pharaohs as well. Funerary enclosures, misinterpreted in modern times as great 'forts', were built on the desert behind the town by three kings of the Second Dynasty; the most complete is that of Khasekhemwy.

The Seti I temple is famous for what is known as the King's list. A list of all Dynastic rulers of Egypt, starting with Narmer and ending with Seti himself. Covering the period from 3100 BC through to 1279 BC. 76 Kings are listed; however, the list is not exactly complete.

The Rulers from the Hyksos invasion between 1650 BC and 1545 BC, the Amarna Kings, Akhenaten, Smenkhare, Tutankhamun and Ay and the female Pharaoh Hatshepsut are all missing.

The temple is clearly built upon the foundations of an earlier construction however this is not believed to have been the Great Temple of Osiris which dates back to the First Dynasty.

There were seven chapels within the temple, built for the worship of the pharaoh and principal deities. These included three chapels for the "state" deities Ptah, Re-Horakhty, and Amun-Re and for the triad of Osiris, Isis, and Horus. The rites recorded in the deity chapels represent the first complete form known of the Daily Ritual, which was performed daily in temples across Egypt throughout the pharaonic period.

Seti's temple was mainly built of limestone, though parts of it were constructed with sandstone. Although work began under Seti, the temple was only completed during the reign of his son, Ramesses II. This is visible in some of the temple's reliefs depicting Ramesses slaying Asiatics and worshipping Osiris.

Although Ramesses II completed the temple, most scholars believe that the best artwork at the site was created during Seti I's lifetime. Seti had artists depict him with many of the gods presented in the temple and Ramesses added in some scenes with him and his father as well as representations of his successful military campaigns.

Like the temples of his predecessors, Seti's temple was dedicated to Osiris, and consisted of a pylon, two open courts, two hypostyle halls, seven shrines, each to an important Egyptian deity and one to Seti himself, a chapel dedicated to the different forms of the god Osiris, and several chambers to the south.

The Temple of Seti played an important role in his family's claim as a legitimate royal household. Prior to the ascension to the throne by Seti's father, Ramesses I, Seti's ancestors were merely warriors, generals at most. Without royal blood in his veins, Seti had to consolidate his position, and one of the ways to do so was to build temples.

As Akhenaten's religious reforms did away will the old gods, Seti's dedication of his temple to Osiris and other important Egyptian deities symbolized a return to the traditional way of life, thus allowing himself to be seen as a restorer of order.

Things here were a little rushed, but understandably as we still had a two-hour drive to Luxor and wanted to get there by sunset. As I had seen this temple before, I took a few pictures and then moved outside to what I really came to see. Last time I was here, the Osirion was flooded, and you couldn't get near it.

This time it was accessible, however cordoned off. Regular tourists don't get access to it, but if you have a big enough bribe for the guardian, gates open and entrances are unlocked. I spent about five minutes in the actual structure. It is one of the most remarkable places I have ever seen. It cannot be dynastic Egyptian. For starters it is some 15 feet lower than the Seti temple that dates to 1300 BC. The stones used are enormous and must way around a hundred tons each. The stonework is reminiscent of that found in Peru or Bolivia, where giant lumps of granite seem to melt into each other.

Supposedly, the Valley temple at Giza is similar, something I could confirm later in the week. And just when you think that you have seen everything, there is what is known as the flower of life. Even if it is as mainstream archaeologists say, and is around 4000 years old, it is still incredible. It is a geometric pattern, carved perfectly into the granite. A sort of 2-foot-high spirograph, but 4000 years old and supposedly done with copper chisels. There is no possible answer as to how it was designed so accurately. There are those who dare to say that the symbol seems as if it was engraved with some sort of laser. Of course, there isn't actually evidence to support this claim, other than the fact that 'it looks like that'.

The traditional view and that held by my Guide was that it was built by Seti I, but I just don't see it. The architecture is so different. Some counter this by saying it was actually built to look like an older structure but that is just bizarre.

Firstly, there are no other structures of this period that have such a high level of craftmanship. Secondly, the structure floods on a regular basis and despite protestations that it was always meant to be part filled with water. This would mean that staircases would have had to have been built to descend to underwater chambers. The biggest reason that goes against the conventional dating of this structure is the architectural context. The New Kingdom architecture of the ancient Egyptians is incredibly different in its style and form, and although each temple of the New Kingdom is unique, there is a multiplicity of stylistic coherence between their designs.

Whether Seti knew that the Osirion was there before starting his temple, perhaps we will never know, but upon finding the structure in the path of his new temple, he turned his new temple to the left. It is the only temple in Egypt that makes an 'L' turn.

According to Strabo, the Greek geographer, philosopher, and historian, who travelled to the Osirion in the first century BC it was built by Ismandes, or Mandes (Amenemhet III), the same builder as the Labyrinth at Hawara. There is no proof of this, but it is nice to see that the Ancient Greeks didn't believe the Egyptologists either. The fact is that it may not have been a temple at all. Nobody has ever come up with a watertight theory.

We left the Osirion and started walking across the sand to the little known about Temple of Ramses II. Busloads of tourists come to Abydos every day, yet none seem to walk the 400 yards across the sand to the other temple that is standing there. Having said that, we had only walked one hundred yards when an armed soldier on a quad bike came racing towards us. He escorted us to the temple and once we had paid him enough, we were allowed to ask the Temple Guardian to unlock the door, which he did for a slightly smaller fee.

This temple is slightly smaller and in slightly more of a state of ruin than its illustrious neighbour. My guide says that nobody ever comes to see it, which is a shame because entry is included in the price for the main temple. Most bus trips rush people around and shepherd them back on the bus, telling them that they have seen everything. Sadly, most tourists accept everything they are told. Sami, to his chagrin, was finding out this wasn't always the case. The walls of the temple still have some fine reliefs, and as is the case with most of Ramses II's temples, they boast about his military achievements and show what a great military leader he was. The outside of the temple has scenes from The Battle of Kadesh against The Hittites and there used to be a second Kings List, updated with Ramses on it. This however was plundered by the British and is now in The British Museum.

We got back to the car around 3.30 and set off for Luxor. Unfortunately, we only got around 300 yards before a soldier jumped out of a sentry box with a gun and made us pull over. The general who escorted us earlier had taken it upon himself to arrange an armed escort all the way back to Luxor. Mohammad's face dropped as he realised what this meant. It was not one truck escorting us all the way, it was a relay of four soldiers doing ten miles each, so all of them could get a slice of the pie. And it wasn't even like a proper relay where you simply handed over the baton, or bribe in this case, and moved on. If the next truck wasn't waiting for us, we would have to wait for them to turn up, get paid, count their money, and drive off. The only light relief was that on certain stages of the route, they were assisted by a private security firm who had a truck like Corporal Jones in Dads Army. Three holes down each side for rifles. We tried to escape once, only to be tracked down by an armoured car.

So that we didn't try and escape again, they confiscated Mohammad's driving licence and told him he could have it back in Luxor. And then when you think things can't get any worse. We were now in a convoy which included a load of geriatric Americans on a coach with no toilet. We had to stop and wait for them on a few occasions. Supposedly a few of them had tried to make the bus stop so that they could go to the toilet in the desert, however the soldiers stopped them getting off at gunpoint. By all accounts there were some very angry people on that bus.

At one point, where we had pulled up waiting for the yanks to catch us up, we saw two dead camels by the roadside. I pointed out to my guide that I had always wanted to spend an evening in the desert to watch the stars and it was very kind of his company to provide the meat for the barbecue. The problem was nobody was laughing anymore. This whole charade turned a 90-minute journey into a four-and-a-half-hour pantomime.

We got to Luxor at 8 o clock, but then had to wait for the army to release Mohammad's driving licence. To make matters worse for Sami and Mohammad, they had to drive straight back to Cairo that night as the tour company had a job for them. For once I hoped for their sake it was nothing more than a 90-minute trip around Saqqara. They couldn't even stay over for the night.

This whole ridiculousness is all about money. I could have left my Luxor hotel in the evening and walked around the town without the need for an armed escort.

The fact was that I was completely shattered and my original plans to visit the curry house I had eaten at in Luxor before disappeared out of the window.

On a positive note, I was back in The Novotel Hotel, which I stayed in during my first trip to Egypt. And once again had a high balcony overlooking The Nile. I decided to have the dinner buffet at the hotel, which was more than acceptable. I followed this with three of the amazing fresh dates that I haven't found anywhere else in the world apart from this hotel, a couple of cold beers and an early night.

6.   Tours By Von Smallhousen

There are moments in your life you can look back and think I was genuinely happy there. These sometimes can over the years get viewed with rose tinted spectacles, but sitting on this balcony, watching the balloons skim the Theban Hills, whilst the Nile shimmers with the early morning sun, has lost nothing of its magic. It is a place I could sit for hours, content with my lot and my surroundings.

The balloons didn't disappoint this morning. The red one still brushes against the treetops and crashes first whilst the stripy one goes higher than the others. By 7am the entertainment was over, but it was worth waking up at 6.15 and enjoying a cup of tea whilst watching them. And what better way to round this off than a breakfast of a freshly made omelette, fresh orange juice and a handful of the best dates known to man!

The hotel seems to be full of French people. This isn't too bad as they are less high maintenance than the Germans. They are too aloof and ignore you rather than trample right through you.

As I met my guide for the next few days, I spared a thought for Sami and Mohammad, my previous guide and driver, who had probably just about got back to Cairo and were being forced to set off for Saqqara. The new guide seemed friendly enough, but he was quite old. This proved to be a bit of an issue later in the day.

A driver was waiting outside, and we headed off to the West Bank of the Nile. There are 10 sites I want to see there, so the plan was to do five each day.

I still get a buzz when I first see the two statues of the falcon god Horus that guard the bridge that connects the East and West Bank of the Nile. As you move away from the dusty city into lush fields of sugar cane, donkeys trotting down the road and farmers tending to their fields, almost oblivious to the wonders that lie a matter of minutes away.

First stop was The Valley of The Queens. I had been here twice before, but this time things had changed. The tomb of Nefertari, first queen of Ramses 2nd, is renowned as being the most spectacular tomb in all of Egypt. For many years, entrance was by invite from the Antiquities Department or Government who occasionally held parties down there.

When I was here last, groups of ten people were allowed to book the tomb at a cost of 20,000 Egyptian pounds each. A little out of my league. But for the past year, anyone can enter the tomb for 1000 Egyptian Pounds. Sounds expensive, but with the favourable exchange rate, it worked out to be a mere £45. This was affordable and really had to be done.

Unfortunately, you can't take pictures, but the imagery was so magnificent that it will stay with me forever. The artwork is amazing, and the colours are so vibrant and fresh that it could have been painted yesterday. You are only allowed ten minutes in the tomb, and I ensured that I got my money's worth.

A flight of steps cut out of the rock leads down to the antechamber, which is decorated with paintings based on The Book of The Dead. An astronomical ceiling represents the heavens and is painted in dark blue, with a myriad of golden five-pointed stars. The east wall of the antechamber is dominated by large representations of Osiris and Anubis. This in turn leads to the side chamber, decorated with offering scenes, preceded by a vestibule in which the paintings portray Nefertari being presented to the gods who welcome her.

On the north wall of the antechamber is the stairway that goes down to the burial chamber. This covers a surface area of about 90 square meters having a similar astronomical ceiling, supported by four pillars entirely covered with decoration. Originally, the queen's red granite sarcophagus lay in the middle of this chamber.

The tomb itself is primarily focused on the Queen's life and on her death. One wall is a portrayal of Nefertari playing the game of Senet. A whole entire wall was dedicated to show the Queen at play, demonstrating the importance of the game of Senet. Nefertari lived an elegant life on earth, and she is also promised an elegant afterlife. Chapter 17 of the Book of the Dead, which tells a spell for the Queen, is inscribed on the tomb. This spell is supposed to guide Nefertari on how to transform into a bird. For Nefertari to become a bird in the afterlife, it is promised freedom to move around.

Ramses' affection for his wife, as written on her tomb's walls, shows clearly that Egyptian queens were not simply marriages of convenience or marriages designed to accumulate greater power and alliances, but, in some cases at least, were based around some kind of emotional attachment. Also, poetry written by Ramesses about his dead wife is featured on some of the walls of her burial chamber. "My love is unique — no one can rival her, for she is the most beautiful woman alive. Just by passing, she has stolen away my heart.".

For anybody who has dreamed of an Ancient Egyptian tomb or tried to picture one in their mind, this is it. It is so colourful and appears as though it was painted yesterday. My ten minutes flew past, and I could easily have stayed down there longer. But the guardians are quite strict as people breathing affects the artwork.

We also went to the other tombs in the valley that are always open, where now you take pictures, So I took that opportunity. As we climbed the hill to the third tomb, my guide was clearly struggling. It wasn't even 9 o clock in the morning at this stage and I was a little concerned he may not last the pace. I am glad I didn't have him for the first stage of the trip as we would have got nothing done.

We left the Valley and headed to Medinet Habu, the mortuary temple and palace of Ramses 3rd. I had visited before but had to see his toilet again. In fact, I missed one last time as I didn't realise his bedroom was en suite.

The colours in the temple are vivid in places and you can't believe they have stayed so bright for 3500 years. After a brief tour, the guide went to find some shade and have a rest, leaving me to my own devices. It was at this point that I realised who he reminded me of. He is the Egyptian version of Von Smallhousen, from 'Allo 'Allo. This at least gave me something to laugh about, albeit not to his face. I made a mental note to try a clandestine Herr Flick impersonation the following day. Especially if there were Germans nearby.

The temple walls are some of the best preserved in Luxor and it is surrounded by a massive mudbrick enclosure, which may well have been fortified. The original entrance is through a fortified gatehouse, known as a Migdal which was a common architectural feature of Asiatic fortresses of the time.

Just inside the enclosure, to the south, are chapels of Amenirdis I, Shepenupet II and Nitiqret, all of whom had the title of Divine Adoratrice of Amun.

The first pylon leads into an open courtyard, lined with colossal statues of Ramesses III as Osiris on one side, and uncarved columns on the other. The second pylon leads into a peristyle hall, again featuring columns in the shape of Ramesses.

The third pylon is reached by continuing up a ramp that leads through a columned portico and then opens into a large hypostyle hall (which has lost its roof). Reliefs and actual heads of foreign captives were also found placed within the temple, perhaps in an attempt to symbolise the king's control over Syria and Nubia.

The most famous reliefs in the temple refer to Ramses III and his battle with the Sea Peoples. The texts and reliefs that deal with the Sea Peoples date to year eight of the pharaoh's reign, approximately 1190 B.C. The significance of these texts is that they provide an account of Egypt's campaign against the "coalition of the sea" from an Egyptian point of view.

The Medinet Habu inscriptions are also significant for their artistic depictions of the Sea Peoples. This provides valuable information about the appearance and accoutrements of the various groups and can lend clues towards deciphering their ethnic backgrounds.

But this was not the first attempted invasion by the Sea Peoples, the first attempt was against King Merenptah.

The Peleset and Tjeker (Minoans) of Crete, they would later be known as the "Philistines" after they had settled in Southern Canaan. Over time, this area became known by a form of their name "Palestine". The Lukka who may have come from the Lycian region of Anatolia, The Ekwesh and Denen who seem to be identified with the original (Black) Greeks, The Shardana (Sherden) who may be associated with Sardinia, The Teresh (Tursha or Tyrshenoi), the Tyrrhenians - the Greek name for the Etruscans, and The Shekelesh.

From the textual evidence on the temple walls, it appears that the Peleset and the Tjeker made up the majority of the Sea Peoples involved in the year 8 invasion. In the artistic depictions, both types are depicted wearing a fillet (a ribbon used as a headband), from which protrudes a floppy plume and a protective piece down the nape of the neck.

Their armament included long swords, spears, and circular shields, and they are occasionally shown wearing body armour. Other groups, such as the Shekelesh and Teresh, are shown wearing cloth headdresses and a medallion upon their breasts. The weaponry that they carried consisted of two spears and a simple round shield. The Shardana soldiers are most obviously armoured in the artistic depictions, due to the thick horned helmets that adorn their heads.

The land battle and sea battle scenes provide a wealth of information on the military styles of the Sea Peoples. The reliefs depicting the land battle show Egyptian troops, chariots and auxiliaries fighting the enemy, who also used chariots, very similar in design to Egyptian chariots.

Although the chariots used by the Sea Peoples are very similar to those used by the Egyptians, both being pulled by two horses and using wheels with six spokes, the Sea Peoples had three soldiers per chariot, whereas the Egyptians only had one, or occasionally two.

The land battle scenes also give the observer some sense of the Sea Peoples' military organization. According to the artistic representations, the Philistine warriors were each armed with a pair of long spears, and their infantry was divided into small groups consisting of four men each. Three of those men carried long, straight swords and spears, while the fourth man only carried a sword. The relief depicting the land battle is a massive jumble of figures and very chaotic in appearance, but this was probably a stylistic convention employed by the Egyptians to convey a sense of chaos. Other evidence suggests that the Sea Peoples had a high level of organization and military strategy.

A striking feature of the land battle scene is the imagery of ox-pulled carts carrying women and children in the midst of a battle. These carts seem to represent a people on the move.

The other famous relief at Medinet Habu regarding the Sea Peoples is of the sea battle. This scene is also shown in a disorganized mass, but as was mentioned earlier, was meant to represent chaos, again contradicting the Egyptians' descriptions of the military success and organization of the Sea Peoples. The sea battle scene is valuable for its depictions of the Sea Peoples' ships and their armaments.

The Egyptians and the Sea Peoples both used sails as their main means of naval locomotion. However, interestingly, the Sea Peoples' ships appear to have no oars, which could indicate new navigation techniques. Another interesting feature of the Sea Peoples' ships is that all the prows are carved in the shape of bird heads, which has caused many scholars to speculate an Aegean origin for these groups.

In the Greco-Roman and Byzantine period, there was a church inside the temple structure, which has thankfully since been removed. Some of the carvings in the main wall of the temple have been defaced by Christian carvings.

I also found The Medinet Habu king list which mentions the festival of Min, where I had been the previous day, with the names of nine pharaohs. It can be found on the upper register of the eastern wall in the second courtyard.

Whilst I was looking around the temple, my guide had found the guardian for the rarely visited temple of Thoth, which is in the adjoining village of Qasr El Aguz. There are very temples of Thoth left and the reliefs in this one, albeit mostly Greek and Roman, are very clear.

It was a five-minute walk from Medinet Habu, but the Guardian said I was the first person to visit his temple in over a month. This is a shame as despite its small stature, it is quite fascinating.

It was constructed by Ptolemy VIII (163 BC) and was also dedicated to the ancestors of the Ptolemaic pharaoh. The structure is very simple, consisting of a small forecourt leading to three chambers. There is little to be seen in the first hall, but the entrance door to the second hall depicts the titles of Ptolemy and Cleopatra II. Scenes in the second hall show the king offering before various deities. The sanctuary behind also shows the king before deities although much of the decoration is difficult to make out. The reliefs here depict Ptolemy making offerings to some of his ancestors, Ptolemy V and Ptolemy IV with their queens. Ptolemy VIII can also be seen receiving the heb-sed symbol from Thoth. The northern wall of the sanctuary depicts the king opening a shrine containing Thoth and the rear wall shows him making offerings of ritual objects to many different (and some lesser known) deities. The ceiling shows the goddesses of the north and south, Nekhbet and Buto as vultures.

We stopped for a cold drink here, at the request of the guide who was worn out. This allowed our driver to find us and give us a lift to the Mortuary Temple of Ramses II, otherwise known as The Ramesseum. Evidently the one we saw in Abydos was only a pretend one and this was the real one. The statues here would have been the tallest in Egypt. An enormous fallen head blocks the front entrance, having succumbed to an earthquake in ancient times. The Italian treasure hunter Belzoni (I can't call him an Egyptologist or archaeologist as all he did was steal things to order and break into things), failed to move the head in the nineteenth century after a French buyer had wanted it for his collection. It could not be moved. Which asks the question, how did they erect it in the first place.

Belzoni did make his mark here. He chiseled his name into one of the pylons along with other nineteenth century vandals.

Ramesses II modified, usurped, or constructed many buildings from the ground up, and the most splendid of these, in accordance with New Kingdom royal burial practices, would have been his memorial temple: a place of worship dedicated to pharaoh, God on earth, where his memory would have been kept alive after his death. Surviving records indicate that work on the project began shortly after the start of his reign and continued for 20 years.

An enormous pylon stood before the first court, with the royal palace at the left and the gigantic statue of the king looming up at the back.

As was customary, the pylons and outer walls were decorated with scenes commemorating the pharaoh's military victories and leaving due record of his dedication to, and kinship with, the gods. In Ramesses's case, much importance is placed on the Battle of Kadesh (ca. 1274 BC); more intriguingly, however, one block atop the first pylon records his pillaging, in the eighth year of his reign, a city called "Shalem", which may or may not have been Jerusalem.

Only fragments of the base and torso remain of the syenite statue of the enthroned pharaoh, 19 m (62 ft) high and weighing more than 1000 tons. This was alleged to have been transported 170 mi (270 km) over land. This is the largest remaining colossal statue (except statues done in situ) in the world. However, fragments of four granite colossi of Ramesses were found in Tanis with an estimated height of 69 to 92 feet (21 to 28 meters). Like four of the six colossi of Amenhotep III (Colossi of Memnon), there are no longer complete remains, so the heights are based on unconfirmed estimates.

Scenes of war and the rout of the Hittites at Kadesh are repeated on the walls. In the upper registers, are shown a feast in honour of the phallic god Min, God of fertility.

On the opposite side of the court the few Osiride pillars and columns still left furnish an idea of the original grandeur. Scattered remains of the two statues of the seated king which once flanked the entrance to the temple can also be seen, one in pink granite and the other in black granite. The head of one of these has been removed to the British Museum. Thirty-nine out of the forty-eight columns in the great hypostyle hall still stand in the central rows. They are decorated with the usual scenes of the king before various gods. Part of the ceiling, decorated with gold stars on a blue, ground has also been preserved. The sons and daughters of Ramesses appear in the procession on the few walls left.

Adjacent to the north of the hypostyle hall was a smaller temple; this was dedicated to Ramesses's mother, Tuya, and to his beloved chief wife, Nefertari. To the south of the first courtyard stood the temple palace. The complex was surrounded by various storerooms, granaries, workshops, and other ancillary buildings, some built as late as Roman times.

Unlike the massive stone temples that Ramesses ordered carved from the face of the Nubian mountains at Abu Simbel, the inexorable passage of three millennia was not kind to his "temple of a million years" at Thebes. This was mostly due to its location on the very edge of the Nile floodplain, with the annual inundation gradually undermining the foundations of this temple and its neighbours. Neglect and the arrival of new faiths also took their toll: for example, in the early years of the Christian Era, the temple was put into service as a Christian church.

 A joint French-Egyptian team has been exploring and restoring the Ramesseum and its environs since 1991. Among their discoveries during excavations include kitchens, bakeries, and supply rooms for the temple to the south, and a school where boys were taught to be scribes to the southeast. Some of the challenges in preserving the area have been the control of modern Egyptian farmers using the area for farming and encroaching on the ruins.

Having said that, I find that to be part of The Ramesseum' s charm. What was once the Temple of a Thousand Ages, belonging to the greatest Pharaoh of all time, is now shared with buffalo and farmers carrying sugar cane.

We stopped for lunch after this at a restaurant across the car park. It was blisteringly hot but sitting enjoying a plate of chicken and chips with a couple of cold beers whilst overlooking The Ramesseum, was a wonderful experience. In any case, I felt I was owed a few beers after the middle of Egypt was alcohol free.

The final stop of the day was the mortuary temple of Merenptah, one I hadn't visited before. It is a fairly standard New Kingdom Mortuary Temple. There were two pylons and courts, and it seems that the original building was changed and enlarged replacing the mudbrick pylons with stone and adding statues of the living king to its pillars. In the first court a huge stela of Amenhotep III was found which had inscribed texts for Merenptah on the reverse side telling of his victories in the Libyan War and making peace with the Hittites.

Merenptah was the son and successor of Rameses II. His temple has long been destroyed, probably due to its position close to the Nile flood plain and the rising water which also destroyed the temple of Amenhotep III. Merenptah used many blocks from Amenhotep's temple and from other nearby temples in the construction of his own monument. There is nothing more than foundations, but there is a famous stele here that has the only mention of the nation of Israel that is known in ancient times. The dates of this would again tie in with Akhenaten leaving Amarna some 80/90 years earlier.

Unfortunately, a road now goes through what was a major part of the temple and the village of Qurnet Murai is on the other side of it. Adjacent to Merenptah's Temple is that of Amenhotep III. Famous for the two Colossi of Memnon, which were way in the distance at the other end of the temple structure.

Recently, however, they have re-erected two further colossal statues of Amenhotep and the other end of the temple and I managed to scramble over a wall to get a couple of pictures.

And with that it was back to the car. We did a quick detour into central Luxor so that I could buy a few cans of beer for the hotel fridge. Buying beer in Luxor is not easy. The only licensed liquor store can be found down a back alley and you have to knock on a window to get served. Beer or other booze is dispensed in brown paper bags, and you sheepishly sneak back to your car and disappear.

It was really hot here by 2 o clock, and all I could think about was sitting back on my balcony, cold drink in hand, watching the boats sail down The Nile, followed by a siesta.

I woke up in time to see a beautiful sunset and discovered that my feet and legs ached too much to go out again. Once again it was the dinner buffet at the hotel and a plateful of the dates of The Gods.

7.   Japanese Camera Torture

Today was to be a tiring one. Up at 6.15 to watch the balloons with a cup of tea on the balcony, breakfast at 7, which was another omelette and loads of dates and then back on the road by 8, followed by eight hours of walking across sand, climbing, and scrambling up and down things in ridiculous temperatures under a baking sun.

It was back to The West Bank again today, so past the statues of Horus, across the bridge and past The Colossi of Memnon and into the world's best archaeological theme park.

First stop was The Valley of The Kings. Apart from the tomb of Seti I, there was nothing open that I hadn't seen before.

However, in the past year or so, for 300 Egyptian pounds (less than £10) you have been able to buy a camera pass which allows you to take pictures where previously you could not. So, I picked three and got some amazing photographs. I also think I picked the three longest and three deepest ones too. The descent was generally treacherous, the climb back up steep and arduous.

My guide quickly found some shade and put his feet up whilst I wandered around the Valley. As was the case with the tomb of Nefertari the previous day, there was a charge of 1000 Egyptian pounds to enter the tomb of Seti I. I have to say it was worth it and thankfully not many other tourists, on their organised coach tours, seemed to be prepared to splash out the cash for it, preferring to queue in the sun for Tutankhamun and his tiny little tomb across the way.

Officially, the Tomb of Seti I is known as KV17, but it is also by the name "Belzoni's tomb" after the Italian who rediscovered it. It is one of the best decorated tombs in the valley. Belzoni first discovered it on 16 October 1817. When he first entered the tomb, he found the wall paintings in excellent condition with the paint on the walls still looking fresh and some of the artist's paints and brushes still on the floor.

Belzoni was a circus strong man who originally came to Egypt to market an irrigation pump he had designed in England. The project fell through, but he arranged the successful transportation of the colossal head of Ramses II from the Ramesseum to the British Museum in London, and by the standards of the day he was forthwith an archaeologist! He turned his energies to the Valley of the Kings and made this remarkable find just one year later.

The longest tomb in the valley, at 137.19 meters (450.10 feet), it contains very well-preserved reliefs in all but two of its eleven chambers and side rooms. One of the back chambers is decorated with the Ritual of the Opening of the Mouth, which stated that the mummy's eating and drinking organs were properly functioning. Believing in the need for these functions in the afterlife, this was a very important ritual.

The sarcophagus removed on behalf of the British consul Henry Salt is since 1824 in the Sir John Soane's Museum in London. KV17 was damaged when Jean-François Champollion, translator of the Rosetta Stone, removed a wall panel of 2.26 x 1.05 m (7.41 x 3.44 ft) in a corridor with mirror-image scenes during his 1828-29 expedition. Other elements were removed by his companion Rossellini or the German expedition of 1845. The scenes are now in the collections of the Louvre, the museums of Florence and Berlin. The tomb also became known as the "Apis tomb" because when Giovanni Belzoni found the tomb a mummified bull was found in a side room off the burial hall.

A steep flight of stairs leads to the entrance of Seti's tomb which is covered with sacred texts along its full length from the highest reaches down to the bed rock. The first corridor is carved in high relief. On the left-hand wall the sun-disc bearing a scarab, and the ram-headed Sun-God can be seen between a serpent, a crocodile and two cows' heads. The texts which start on the left are continued to the right. The roof is painted with flying vultures.

From the third corridor onwards the quality of the colour on the reliefs is superb. A combination of the Pharaoh, the full pantheon of Egyptian Gods and mythical and not so mythical beasts. This all builds up to the burial chamber which is truly magnificent.
The chamber is decorated with the gods of the dead including Anubis, Isis, Hathor, Harsiesis and Osiris. It comprises two portions.

The front portion has pillars and the rear portion a vaulted ceiling. It was in the rear section that the alabaster sarcophagus of the Pharaoh stood when the tomb was discovered. It was made from a single piece of alabaster, carved to a thickness of two inches and with exquisite reliefs filled in with blue paste.

This magnificent piece is comparable only to the alabaster vase found in Tutankhamun's tomb which is today in the Cairo Museum. The mummy, which was one of those found at Deir el Bahri, is in the same museum. The sarcophagus lies in the Soane Museum in London. When Belzoni effected its transportation to England, the Trustees of the British Museum considered the price set too high and the treasure was without a buyer until 1824 when Sir John Soane paid Henry Salt £2,000 for it.

The decorations on the walls of the pillared portion of the hall show the journey through the first region of the underworld on the left entrance-wall and through the fourth region of the underworld on the left-hand wall. In a small recess at the end of this wall is a beautiful representation of Anubis performing the opening-of-the-mouth ceremony before Osiris. On the right-hand entrance wall and the right-hand wall are representations of the journey through the second region of the underworld.

The vaulted ceiling has been painted with astrological figures. From early times, of course, the Egyptians had mapped out heavens, identified some of the fixed stars and were able to determine the positions of others. This ceiling is unusual in that it has not been painted in the familiar balanced, repetitive form and is astrologically accurate.

Entering the square chamber with four pillars on which the Pharaoh is shown before the various deities: Isis and Nephthys the sister-wife and the sister of Osiris, Hathor, Selket the goddess to whom the scorpion was sacred, Horus the national Sun-God, and Harsiesis and Harmaches who were special forms of Horus; also of course Anubis, the jackal-God of embalming. The walls, especially those at the sides, have marvelous representations of the sun travelling through the fourth region of the underworld. On the rear wall Osiris is enthroned before Hathor while the Pharaoh is led into his presence by the hawk-headed Horus. This is a superb mural with intricate detail and rich colour. Near the corner of the left-hand wall the four chief races of men known at the time stand before Horus: these are Egyptians, Asiatics with pointed beards and coloured aprons, four negroes and four Libyans with feathers on their heads and tattooed bodies.

Climbing back to the surface, I decided on which three other tombs to go and explore and take photographs of. The tomb of Ramses III has some fine reliefs, and this was my first choice. Forgetting at the time that, behind the tomb of Seti I, this was the second deepest and longest tomb in the Valley.

The most memorable moment here was that I entered the tomb whilst a coach load of Japanese tourists were in there. None of them had a photo pass and it must have been torture for them to see me snapping away and them not being able to.

Although the wall decorations in this tomb may not be considered of the best artistic quality, their variety and richness are certainly unsurpassed. The entrance door is at the foot of a flight of steps. On each side are small pillars with bulls' heads. Over the door is a representation of Isis and Nephthys worshipping the sun-disc. Along the first corridor are figures of Maat, goddess of integrity and truth, kneeling and sheltering with her wings the deceased Pharaoh as his body enters the tomb. On the walls are Praises of Ra. The pharaoh himself can be seen on the left-hand wall before Harmaches (one of the forms of the Sun-God), followed by the familiar sacred serpent, crocodile and two gazelles' heads.

There are five chambers on the right-hand side of the corridor. The first contains a double row of sailing ships: those in the upper row ready to set sail and those in the lower with sails furled. The second chamber is the Pharaoh's armoury. The walls have representations of all the royal weapons and standards. At the top of the left-hand wall are standards with heads of sacred animals. At the top of the right-hand wall are standards with gods' heads. On the rear wall are a multitude of bows, arrows, and quivers. The third chamber is particularly interesting if we remember that this was a very wealthy Pharaoh, for it contains his treasury. On the walls are representations of furniture and ornaments, utensils and jewelry, elaborate headrests, cushioned benches, and comfortable couches that are attained by steps. The fourth chamber contains rural scenes. The Pharaoh sails along a canal watching ploughing, sowing, and reaping. In the fields are sacred animals. The last on the right-hand side is notable for its twelve different forms of Osiris, the god of the underworld.

The burial chamber itself is a bit of an anti-climax. It is a long oblong room with four pillars on each side and an extra chamber at each of the four corners. The actual sarcophagus is now in the Louvre, its lid is in Cambridge.

The Pharaoh's mummy, amongst those taken from the shaft at Deir el Bahri, is now in the Cairo Museum. Much of the reliefs have been damaged.

Nearby was my next choice of tomb. That of the Pharaoh Merenptah. The tomb design, although large, is simpler than many in the Valley. A staircase and two descending corridors were decorated and although the paintings were badly damaged by flooding there are some very beautiful painted reliefs in the first corridor.

In the entrance on the outer lintel a sun disc flanked by the goddesses Isis and Nephthys contain the ram-headed god Khnum and the Kheper beetle. The first corridor depicts inscribed passages from sacred burial texts, one with an interesting disc similar to that on the lintel, but with the crocodile god Sobek, a serpent and horned creature, enemies of the gods, around it.

The King's actual burial chamber has a magnificent, restored sarcophagus, carved from red granite in the shape of a cartouche and the lid shows the recumbent deceased king holding his crook and flail. There are four small annexes to the north and south of the burial chamber and shown on the upper register of the south wall is a scene relating to the 'Book of Caverns'. There are also scenes from the 'Book of Gates' and an astronomical ceiling with the barque of Ra carrying the gods through the night.

My final choice was the combined tomb of Ramses V and Ramses VI. This tomb was started by Ramses V and was usurped by his successor. It has three entrance halls, two chambers, a further two corridors, an antechamber, and the tomb chamber. The standard of craftsmanship is not high but the tomb chamber itself has one of the most important ceilings in the Valley of the Kings.

Dark blue and gold predominate in the tomb chamber. Across the vaulted ceiling the goddess Nut is twice represented along its entire length, in a graceful semi-circle with backs touching.

This represents the morning and evening skies. Her elongated body curves to touch the earth with finger and toe, head to the west, loins to the east.

Despite the sarcophagus being smashed in antiquity, the burial chamber is beautiful, representing texts from The Book of The Dead.

My guide needed oxygen before heading back to the car, and he wasn't even allowed to climb down the tombs with me. He needed to sit down back in the car more than I did.

Next stop was Howard Carter's house. I had to get a photo taken sitting at his desk, where all his plans for excavating Tutankhamun's tomb were. I wasn't allowed to have a picture taken on his toilet though, much to my annoyance. I had planned to do that whilst reading a copy of my guidebook.

Though his home was left to decay for many decades following his departure from Egypt in 1939, the Egyptian government eventually restored it completely and subsequently opened it for public tours.

It is more than just a set of empty rooms as it has been restored using many of Carter's actual possessions he used in his daily life whilst working in Egypt. Interestingly, his original photo lab has been restored and you can see his cameras and other photography equipment. His original desk is likewise still in the house, as is the library he kept.

There is a small display about the discovery of the Tomb of Tutankhamun and a short audio-visual display.

It was nice to sit and have a cup of tea in his garden, where the guardian told us we were the first tourists he had seen in ages. Luxor is full of French, Chinese, Germans, and Americans, but very few, if any Brits. Quite sad really.

Next stop was the mortuary temple of Seti I. Another site that is not on the usual tourist trail and to be fair, I had been to Luxor twice before and hadn't managed to see it until now.

Maybe not as remarkable as Seti's temple at Abydos, this was still fairly complete and well worth an hour wandering around. Made even more enjoyable by having the place to myself.

The temple is set away from many of the other mortuary temples in quite a picturesque palm grove.

It was severely damaged by floods in 1994 and has been extensively restored. The entrance is through a small door in the northeast corner of the reconstructed fortress-like enclosure wall. The first and second pylons and the court are in ruins. The pharaoh's palace has also gone, but recent excavations have revealed its foundations, just south of the court, and it is therefore the earliest-surviving example of a palace within a memorial temple; its plan is similar to the better-preserved palace at the memorial temple of Ramses III at Medinet Habu.

The walls of the columned portico at the west facade of the temple, and those of the hypostyle court beyond it, contain some superbly executed reliefs. Off the hypostyle are six shrines and to the south is a small chapel dedicated to Seti's father, Ramses I, who died before he could build his own mortuary temple.

My guide was angling for a lunch break at this point, but I wanted to carry on before the afternoon sun got really hot. It was only around 32 degrees at this point and in a few hours, it would be up to the high thirties. So, we set off for Deir El Medina, the workers village and tombs. These tombs are so different from the majestic tombs of the valley of the kings and show real, everyday life. Once again visiting involved climbing a very large hill, before scrambling down a number of shafts, steep steps and then back up again.

All the tombs are colourful, we saw about five in total, some having small pyramids built on top of their entrance. The worker's village was full of the best artisans in Egypt, who were brought to Luxor (Thebes) to spend their lives working on the tombs of the Pharaohs.

Some were artists, some were plasterers, some were chiselers, some were architects. What you do notice is that the tombs of the artists have wonderful paintwork but are maybe small tombs. The chiselers and architects have bigger tombs, with more chambers and statues, but the paintwork is a bit amateur. There were several highlights here.

The most beautifully decorated tomb was that belonging to Pashedu, who lived here during the reigns of Seti I and Ramses II. He had the title "Servant in the Place of Truth on the West of Thebes". He was a stone mason, responsible for cutting the corridors, chambers and pillared halls of the royal tombs in the Valley of the Kings.

At the bottom of the entrance stairs there is an entrance into the first burial chamber, behind which the second burial chamber lies. A short-vaulted passage leads into the third, innermost burial chamber. Two large reliefs of Anubis are painted on both sides of the passage walls. There is the god Ptah in the form of a falcon depicted within the vaulted area above the doorway. His elaborately painted wings stretch out below a wedjat-eye. The falcon sits in a boat. There are 15 lines of a hieroglyphic inscription. Pashedu's sons Menna and Kaha both kneel beside the boat worshipping the gods.

The rear wall of the innermost burial chamber shows the god Osiris, the ruler of the kingdom of the dead, on his throne with the mountain of the West behind him. Osiris wears a crown and holds a flail and sceptre. A seated god before him presents a bowl with burning tapers. The inscription written in columns of black hieroglyphs contains a spell for "lighting a lamp for Osiris". Behind the throne of Osiris, a small figure of Pashedu is depicted kneeling. Pashedu and his wife sit before an offering table in a small boat of the Abydos pilgrimage. One of their daughters sits at Nedjem-Behdet's feet. They both wear elegant, pleated costumes made of fine linen and have long and elaborately coiffed hair.

Unfortunately, whilst down here, the lights failed. And having climbed down steep steps. Crawled under a narrow opening and then descended a ladder, there wasn't much I could do, in the pitchest, of pitch blacks, other than wait. I did have a torch, but quite frankly, it didn't really help.

After someone put some more money in the meter, I scrambled out to find my guide asleep in the shade. He sort of moved and pointed towards another tomb, towards which I went.

This was the tomb of Irynefur, a necropolis workman during the early part of Ramesses II's reign. His title was the "Servant in the Place of Truth".

Just above the arch of the entrance to the chamber, depiction of green-skinned winged goddess Nut, her name indicated by the hieroglyphs shown above her head, is depicted. Nut is kneeling in front of Horus and Hesat.

The depiction on the southern wall, which lies towards the left side of the burial chamber, shows the mummification of the dead person, who rests on a bed with lion heads. Mummification is performed by Anubis, the jackal-headed god of the dead.

It was in one this tomb that one of the most embarrassing things I have ever heard come out of an American's mouth was uttered.

This middle-aged woman points at a painting of the God Anubis and shouts "oh cool, it's the mummy guy!" Even her fellow Americans were mortified. The guardian, who could barely speak English, was mortified. They really shouldn't be allowed to leave their country.

On the lower part of the eastern wall within the burial chamber we see Irynefur standing in the solar barque worshipping the phoenix, symbol of the sun god of Heliopolis. The phoenix in the form of a grey heron wears the solar disk, the image of Ra and assures Irynefur of his future rebirth.

Above, the Irynefur and his wife pray to a young bull-calf standing in between 2 sycamores, the sacred trees of Heliopolis, the calf being a prefiguration of the solar bull as it moves through the sky. Across the wall, the parents of Irynefur, their age indicated by their white hair, pay homage to Ptah, the patron deity of craftsmen. Irynefur himself kneels in the scene in front of Ptah's. throne and offers a figure of the goddess Ma'at.

The rear part of the eastern wall is divided into two reliefs. The upper is dominated by an extraordinary scene, showing the worshipped god Ptah standing in front of the enshrined black shadow of the deceased and two birds. One flies, the other sits in front of a black sun.

The lower register of the far side of the western wall shows Anubis leading Irynefur to Osiris seated on his throne. Next to the shrine there is a representation of Irynefur who worships Horus in the form of a falcon. Horus holds a flagellum, the sign of regeneration and rebirth, which gave the power to decide on entry into the afterlife.
I scrambled back to the daylight and my guide was now awake and marched me across a high ledge to the other side of the hill to another set of tombs.

There were two tombs together, the first belonging to Khaemteri. He too had the title Servant of The House of Truth under Ramses II. Although the quantity of reliefs in this tomb are maybe not as abundant as in other tombs, the rear wall has an amazing depiction of Khaemteri's mummy on a table with Anubis attending it.

The other tomb of note was that of Sennedjam. One of the earliest finds and most well-known tombs at Deir El Medina, but one I hadn't seen previously.

Sennedjam was another "Servant of The Place of Truth" who worked upon the tombs built in the Valley of the Kings, and Valley of the Queens under the reign of Seti I.

An entrance pit descends a short 4 metres down into the earth, with hand holes used by the ancient builders are still visible. At the bottom of the pit a narrow sloping passage led into an undecorated chamber, a pit from this room led into a second at the end of which lay the decorated burial chamber.

The burials had survived the years intact - in the burial chamber a total of eleven mummies were found. They consisted of: Sennedjam, Iyneferty (Sennedjam's wife), Khons and his wife Tamakhet (son and daughter-in-law of Sennedjam), the Lady Isis wife of Khabekhnet (second son of Sennedjam).

The final burial chamber is covered with scenes of Sennedjam and his family. Firstly, there are the usual funerary scenes where Anubis attends Sennedjem's mummy. Then Sennedjam and Iyneferty face tribunals of gods, pleading to be allowed admittance to the afterlife. Anubis appears again, this time he leads Sennedjam forward to be judged by Osiris who stands waiting underneath a canopy. Finally, scenes on the eastern walls of the tomb show Sennedjam and his family in the Beyond, ploughing fields and living for eternity.
This is one of my favourite places in Luxor, but after a quick look around the village and the simple temple there, the exhausting sun had taken its toll and we decided it was time for a cold beer and some lunch. We went back to the same restaurant we had eaten at the previous day which was fine. The food was good, and the beer was cold.

Lunch over, we went to our destination which was the tombs of the nobles at Sheikh Abd El Qurna. More steps and the mercury was now at 35 and climbing was becoming difficult. There were six tombs to see here, none of which I had seen before. They were fascinating but maybe not as colourful as the workers' tombs. Either that or even my interest was beginning to wane.
The most memorable were the tombs of Rekhmire, Rahmose and Menna.

Rekhmire was Governor of Thebes under Tuthmosis III. As you enter his tomb, on the left-hand wall, Rekhmire supervises the delivery of grain, wine, and cloth from the royal storehouses. He inspects carpenters, leatherworkers, metalworkers, and potters, who all come under his control. In the lower row is a record of the construction of an entrance portal to the temple of Amun at Karnak showing that Rekhmire supervised the manufacture of the bricks and each stage of the construction.

On the right-hand wall Rekhmire may be seen at a table, and there are scenes of offerings before statues of the deceased, the deceased in a boat on a pond being towed by men on the bank, and a banquet with musicians and singers.

What you notice here is that images almost come to life. Workers bend to mix mortar or squat to carve a statue. A man raises a bucket to his colleague's shoulder. Another is engrossed in carpentry. The elegant ladies of Rekhmire' s household prepare for a social function with young female attendants arranging their hair, anointing their limbs, or bringing them jewelry.

Ramose was also Governor of Thebes but under the reign of Akhenaten. As with all Amarna tombs, the artwork is very different. It is uncertain whether the deceased was ever buried in this tomb, or whether he followed Akhenaten to his new capital, Akhetaten, but no tomb has been found for Ramose there.

The plan of the tomb is a traditional T-shape but built on a very large scale with some of the most beautiful relief carvings of any Theban tomb. A wide stairway leads down to the courtyard in front of the tomb and the entrance leads into a large hall, its roof once supported by four rows of eight papyrus columns. Some of these have recently been restored. There has been a great deal of damage to the tomb, to the reliefs depicting Akhenaten, which isn't surprising in Thebes where he was public enemy number one. Damage was also caused because of a collapsed ceiling, although this probably contributed to the preservation of the remaining reliefs.

The wall on the left of the entrance shows Ramose, wearing the gown of a vizier consecrating offerings to Amun-Re, Re-Horakhty, Atum and Khepri and followed by his attendants. The scenes of the banquet on this wall are particularly beautiful, carved with very fine detail on limestone and left uncoloured except for the eyes of the figures. Each guest, some of them the relatives of the deceased, is named in the accompanying texts. These say that Ramose married his brother's daughter, Meryt-Ptah.

The end wall on the south side portrays the funeral procession in two long registers. This wall was not carved but its paintings show very good colour and detail of the funerary goods being transported to the tomb with the procession of mourners moving towards the Western Goddess. The canopic jars in their shrine are taken with the sarcophagus to the tomb on sleds.

The second register shows more of the procession with the tomb furnishings and burial goods being carried to the tomb. A group of mourning women dressed in white robes with their hair loose, are shown in a well-known scene at the centre of the procession. Further on nine kneeling women wail and cover their heads with ashes and bare-chested women dressed in yellow and red beat their breasts.

On the right of the entrance Ramose can be seen kneeling prostrated before Akhenaten and his queen Nefertiti, who are shown in the 'Window of Appearances' with the rays of the Aten showering down on them. This relief is executed in the new style of Amarna art and was defaced, presumably after Akhenaten's reign ended. Ramose is shown receiving the 'Gold of Honour' one of the highest awards in the land, and many courtiers and officials are bowing low before the royal couple. Beyond this scene the wall is unfinished. Drawings have been sketched in but were left uncarved. These show foreign delegates (four Nubians, three Asiatics and a Libyan) coming to pay homage and offer tribute to the king.
Menna was a 'Scribe in the fields of the Lord of the Two Lands of Upper and Lower Egypt' during the reign of Tuthmosis IV. His wife's name was Henuttawi, a Chantress of Amun.

Opposite the entrance to the inner tomb Menna and his wife are being offered a bouquet by a shaven-headed priest before an offering table heaped with produce. The rest of the wall shows guests at a banquet and men carrying offerings below.
The right-hand end wall of the hall is designed in the form of a stela, with double scenes depicting Anubis, Osiris, and the goddess of the West on the left and Re-Horakhty and Hathor on the right, with Menna and his wife.

A passage leads into the inner chapel and here Menna and his wife can be seen leaving the tomb to take part in the 'Beautiful Feast of the Valley'.

The left wall of the chapel depicts the funeral procession with traditional scenes of offering-bringers carrying food and burial equipment to the tomb. The sarcophagus is transported on the river in a barque which is towing another boat containing mourners, and later the sarcophagus can be seen dragged on a sledge towards the Western Goddess and Anubis.

The far end of the wall depicts a judgement scene, in which Menna must account for his earthly actions and have his heart weighed. Here it is Horus rather than Anubis who oversees the scales and Thoth, God of writing and wisdom, who records the verdict. Osiris, as usual presides over the scene.

The wall on the right-hand side, after the statue-niche contains two scenes of the deceased and his wife receiving offerings from relatives. Next comes some of the most beautiful paintings in the tomb which show Menna with his family in papyrus boats spearing fish and hunting birds with a throw-stick in the marshes. This beautiful scene depicts much of the wildlife in the river and papyrus thickets of Menna's time – including a crocodile which lurks beneath the boat, and a cat on the top of the thicket trying his luck.
It was around 4 o'clock when I finally got back to the hotel. I think I was asleep before my head hit the pillow and my hands had reached for a cold beer in the fridge.

I snoozed for an hour but awoke to see the sun go down. As I was preparing to go for dinner, my hotel room phone rang, and I was informed that somebody was waiting in reception for me. Somewhat bemused, I went down in the lift and saw that it was my driver in Luxor, who had asked his wife to bake me some homemade bread which was still warm. There is a lot said by people who know nothing, that tourists need to be wary of locals and the like. But I have always found the people of Egypt to be warm and very welcoming. I was quite touched by this and put thoughts about where the hell I was going to put the bread on my long trip to Cairo the following day, out of my mind.

The evening was a relaxing one. My feet were shouting due to the walking and my throat was dry. I went for the Radox and the cold beer.

8. The Goddess of Destruction

This was a very long day. It started with a view of balloons over the Nile in Luxor at 6.15 in the morning and ended in Cairo, in a posh room overlooking the Great Pyramid at nearly 11pm.

I woke up at 6.15 and saw a few balloons but decided to get another hour's sleep. I would have stayed in bed longer, but had I not gone to breakfast by 7.15, the French masses would have devoured the breakfast buffet.

I didn't have to meet the guide until 11.30, so I spent my last few hours in Luxor, watching Nile Steamers and sailing boats drifting down the river from the balcony.

Our first port of call today was a brief one at The Mummification Museum. It is nothing special, having just a few worthwhile exhibits. The main reason for going was really the fact that the last time I was here I searched high and low for it and never came close to finding it. At least that has been ticked off the list now.

The museum is located in the former visitor centre, a modern building on the banks of The Nile. Its main hall is divided into two parts, the first one is an ascended corridor through which the visitor could have a look on ten tablets which throw lights on the funeral journey from death to burial. The second part of the is on the lower level which has more than sixty pieces displayed in cases. Artefacts range from Sarcophagi, mummified animals, canopic jars, and other tools used during the process.

The serious sightseeing started at Karnak Temple. I had been here twice before, but this time I wanted the access all areas tour, which meant greasing a few palms. This isn't exactly possible when you are in a tour group, but when you are on your own, more doors open, if you can afford them too.

The main temple is spectacular, and my guide pointed out a few things I hadn't noticed before.

However, it was the temples within the temple I really wanted to see. Karnak had a holy trinity of Amun Ra, Mut and Khonsu, all three having temples, whilst there was also a further temple for Montu. The Khonsu temple is being restored and will officially open in a year or so. However, my guide knew the right guardian to bribe, and we sneaked in and even managed to climb to the top of one of the pylons and get to the roof which was cool.

The pylons were erected and decorated by Ptolemy III, however the main temple that stands today was constructed by Ramses III on the site of an older temple. on the site of an earlier temple.
The hypostyle hall was erected by Nectanebo I and is not of great size. Inside were found two baboons that were thought to have been carved in the time of Seti I. It is now believed that they belonged to the earlier building on the site.

Numerous blocks with unmatching and inverted decorations can be seen, showing the amount of reconstruction and reuse of material from the surrounding temple complexes, especially in Ptolemaic times.

The door in the middle of the rear wall leads into a larger hall, where the Sanctuary was designed to house the god's sacred boat. The reliefs on the outer walls depict the King (Ramses IV or XII) in the presence of various gods. Built into the walls are blocks bearing reliefs and cartouches of Tuthmosis III.

On each side of the Sanctuary are dark chambers with reliefs of Ramses IV, and to its rear, a doorway built by one of the Ptolemies gives access to a small chamber with four 16-sided columns and the reliefs, which show Ramses IV and to the right and left of the entrance the Emperor Augustus of Rome in the presence of the Theban gods. One of the few surviving Roman representations at any Egyptian Temple.

Adjoining the southwest side of the Temple of Khonsu is a small Temple of Osiris and Opet (the hippopotamus goddess of childbirth and mother of Osiris) built by Euergetes II. It stands on a three-meter-high base topped by a cavetto cornice, with the main entrance on the west side. On the upright side of the doorway, the king is depicted before Osiris and other deities.

Next was what is known as The Open-Air Museum, which is a collection of shrines and statues erected by various pharaohs over the years. Most of them have been reconstructed as over the years, Pharaohs demolished works carried out by the predecessors to construct their own memorials from the rubble.

Several small shrines have been restored to their former glory. The first we came across was The Alabaster Chapel of Amenhotep I, originally started between 1525 and 1504 BC by Amenhotep I and then continued by Hatshepsut between 1479 and 1458 BC.
It is a one roofed rectangular structure made of large blocks of calcite with access doors on its short sides. The interior reliefs are the oldest surviving depictions of the sacred barque of the statue of Amun Ra of Karnak.

The chapel was demolished by Tuthmosis III around 1525 BC and the rubble was found in the Third Pylon of the main temple. It was built to hold the sacred barque of Ra, but each Pharaoh, being a son of Ra, clearly had to have their own shrine for it. Hence these structures had a limited life expectancy.

The most famous of these structures is known as the Chapelle Rouge or The Red Chapel of Hatshepsut. Built by Hatshepsut between 1479 and 1458 BC, it is a unique red quartzite barque chapel. It has both a vestibule and a chapel and sits on a grey diorite platform. The beautifully carved relief decoration on the chapel's exterior sides includes scenes showing the raising of Hatshepsut's obelisks at Karnak and the Opet Festival processions. Once more it was Tuthmosis III who demolished it in order to build his new Pylon. He too has his own barque shrine here which fared as well as all the others.

The other complete shrine here is The White Chapel of Senusret I. A far older structure than the others, dating back to 1971 BC, another small limestone barque shrine, built by one of the earliest Kings to have added to Karnak. The shrine has four interior pillars and twelve pillars around the façade, its decoration commemorates the heb sed of Senusret I and some traces of yellow paint still exist. The Chapel may have functioned as a festival kiosk where the king could sit on a double throne. Holes in the floor, between the four central columns indicate the use of poles to hang banners, hiding the King from the public eyes.

It may not originally have been intended as a barque shrine, but Amenemhat III or Amenemhat IV converted it into one. The altar is of rose granite and probably dates to the restoration at this time.

There are also part remains of other shrines. The most remarkable being part of a wall erected by Amenhotep IV before he changed his name to Akhenaten. Most remains from his reign resulted in the priests defacing the Pharaoh, however as this was clearly before his heresy. It is Amenhotep (Akhenaton) who has defaced Ra.

The next part of the temple is definitely closed to the public and even my guide said he had only been there once. That is the ruins of the Temple of Montu. There isn't too much left apart from a statue of Amenhotep III and one of Sekhmet, the lion goddess. There is also an impressive entrance arch that was erected by Ptolemy IV, which in order to get to we had to go cross country. It was whilst traversing scrubland that my guide said, "watch out for snakes!" Not my favourite phrase.

'Cobras?" I replied.

" No, the really deadly ones" my guide replied.

What fun I had looking at my feet rather than the temple.

Montu was the God of War and an old local god of Thebes. It was originally built by Amenhophis III, but was several times altered and enlarged down to the period of the Ptolemies. The temple is so badly ruined that it is difficult to even make out the ground plan, but the older fragments of sculpture and architectural elements display a high standard of artistic skill. Outside the north entrance stood two obelisks of red granite, of which the bases and some fragments still remain.

This temple consisted of the traditional parts of an Egyptian temple with a pylon, court and rooms filled with columns. The ruins of the current temple date to the reign of Amenhotep III who rebuilt the sanctuary dating from the Middle Kingdom era and dedicated it to Montu-Re. Ramesses II increased the size of the temple by adding a forecourt and erecting the two obelisks there. A large court with gantry gave a hypostyle open on the court, characteristic of the buildings of the reign of Amenhotep I.

After a quick tour back round the highlights of Karnak, Hatshepsut's Obelisk, The Sacred Lake amongst others, we came to an archaeological dig. It has been discovered that Amenhotep III kept a zoo here. The dig is still quite recent, but to date they have found remains of baboons, wild cats, dogs and even an elephant.

At this point we decided it was time for lunch and the Guide took me to his favourite restaurant in Luxor. So that was chicken and chips again. Very nice chicken and chips. But nevertheless, chicken and chips.

Post lunch we went to the rarely visited Temple of Mut. Despite being no more than 500 yards from the Eastern Gate at Karnak, you feel that you are in the middle of nowhere. There was a small convenience shop, but apart from that, the only other living creatures in the immediate vicinity were a pack of rather menacing dogs who looked rather hungry. This was a very strange experience.

There isn't much left of the temple, and it is nowhere near the size of Karnak, yet they have unearthed over 70 statues of the goddess Sekhmet here that are all on display, taking over the entire Temple. In fact, it is estimated that there may have been over 570 of them originally. Sekhmet was prayed to in times of disaster, plague and when they felt the world was coming to an end. For this many statues all to be erected at roughly the same time, there must have been something seriously weird going on.

The dates 1450- 1500 BC tie in with the eruption of the Greek Island volcano at Santorini (Thera) which almost certainly is responsible for the science behind the myths of the Biblical ten plagues of Egypt. You must wonder whether this is related.

Surrounding the Mut Temple proper, on three sides, is a sacred lake called the Isheru.

Today, most of the compound is still destroyed, but it is currently being renovated. Surrounding the Mut Temple, is an enclosure wall made of mud brick dating to the 30th Dynasty. The Mut Temple proper was made of mediocre sandstone, and it is positioned north and south and is directly aligned with the Precinct of Amun. It was also called the "Temple of Millions of Years" and was dedicated to Ramses II and the god Amun-Ra. Within the temple are two stelae, one referring to Ramses II's work on the temple and the other telling of his marriage to a Hittite princess.

The goddess Mut is the wife and consort of the god Amun-Ra. She was also known as the Mother Goddess, Queen of the Goddesses, and Lady of Heaven. Mut was the Egyptian sky goddess, and her symbols were the vulture, lioness, and the crown of Uraeus (rearing cobra). She was the mother of Khonsu, the god of the moon. Amun-Ra, Mut, and Khonsu made up the Theban Triad.

Amenhotep III was originally thought to have been the first to build the Mut Temple, but now evidence tells us he contributed later to the site. The earliest dated cartouches are of Thutmose II and III of the 18th Dynasty.

During the 19th Dynasty, Ramses II worked broadly on the Temple, he placed two massive statues of himself (as per usual) and two alabaster stelae in the front of the temple's first pylon. During the 20th Dynasty, Ramses III built a small side Temple, it was used until the 25th Dynasty when it then became a quarry for renovations for the main Temple. During his reign, Kushite ruler Taharqa in the 25th Dynasty made major changes to the Mut Precinct. He built a new sandstone gateway in the northwest of the site that leads to the side Temple. He also renovated parts of the Mut Temple proper, erecting a columned porch facing the south. Ptolemy VI during the Ptolemaic period erected a small chapel inside the Temple too. Several stelae found on the site mention construction on the site by Roman emperors Augustus and Tiberius from the 1st century BC to the 1st century AD.

The site is most famous for the statues of Sekhmet. The statues are made of diorite or "black granite" and initially approximately 570 granodiorite statues were thought to have been at the Precinct of Mut at one time. Amenhotep III commissioned the many statues to be built as a "forest". Amenhotep III described Sekhmet as the terrible, mighty goddess of war and strife and her origins came from the earlier Memphite triad as the mother-goddess, and she eventually became recognized with the local Theban deity, Mut. The fact that these statues were built under Amenhotep III is bizarre as this is widely regarded as the most prosperous period of Egyptian history.

Amenhotep III was an excellent ruler who helped Egypt thrive. During his reign, he not only built magnificent palaces and statues, but also was a skilled diplomat. He made great connections with surrounding nations, not by trying to conquer them or forcing submission, but by giving them large gifts of gold, which put them in the debt of Egypt.

His focus was on maintaining Egypt as a lavish and peaceful kingdom and putting his effort into creating new buildings and sculptures.

Considering this, it makes absolutely no sense why he would build nearly 600 statues of the Goddess of destruction.

Some claim that the statues were built in the hope that Sekhmet would grant Amenhotep good health. Throughout his life, Amenhotep III had various health issues, particularly dental ones. As he got older, he also gained a significant amount of weight and struggled with obesity, as well as arthritis. It is unclear which of his ailments killed him, but when he was about 54, after a reign of more than 30 years, Amenhotep III died. More than likely, due to the lack of modern medicine, he had an abscessed tooth which led to an infection. If he built the statues for good health, you must wonder, given his physical state, why he kept bothering.

By now I was beginning to look at my watch, as I had a flight to catch to Cairo. For all his protestations about the pace of our sightseeing, I must give my guide in Luxor his due, he was determined to get everything in. So even though I had been to Luxor Temple twice before, off we set.

Luxor Temple is always impressive. The two towering statues of Ramses II that great you at the entrance are one of the most famous sights in all of Egypt. Having said that, I actually wanted to have a quick wander outside of the temple and see how the restoration work on The Avenue of The Sphinxes was going.

The Avenue once connected the Temples of Luxor and Karnak and was used for ceremonial processions during the Opet Festival. The plan is to completely restore the avenue to its former glory. The problem is that a number of residential buildings and the small matter of a main road now intersect it.

Around 40% of the avenue is now restored, which accounts for around 650 of the original 1350 sphinxes. The section from Luxor Temple now extends 350 metres, whilst a second section of 600 metres has been restored near the town library. The path was originally 2700 metre in length.

It was originally built during the reign of Hatshepsut around 1500 BC, and it is likely that it led to the Red Chapel that she erected at Karnak. What is visible today is a bit more modern as the avenue was renovated by Nectanebo I around 350 BC. Recent excavations have found many treasures including reliefs bearing the cartouche of Cleopatra VII who would have walked along the avenue during her Nile trip with Mark Anthony.

We walked briskly into the Temple to find an Italian film crew with an enormous drone that they were trying to get airborne without much success.

It was a whistle stop tour of the temple, but I did what to ensure I got to see the The Chapel of Alexander The Great, which isn't particularly spectacular but does have the only surviving relief of Alexander as Pharaoh of Egypt.

Alexander is depicted on the walls of the 'chapel of the barque', which he is credited with restoring. In a sequence of reliefs in the traditional Egyptian style, Alexander is depicted dressed as pharaoh, facing the god Amun-Ra. The accompanying texts identify him as 'King of Upper and Lower Egypt, Lord of the Two Lands, Beloved of Amun, Chosen of Ra, son of Ra, possessor of the crowns, Alexander'. This is the standard form of address for a pharaoh, and the inscribed texts note that he has carried out the work for his father Amun-Ra. The 'chapel of the barque' would have contained the cult image of the god, standing in a ceremonial boat. At major festivals the image would have been carried by the temple priests in procession in the boat.

As we came out of the chapel, back into the open courtyard, there was a great whirring noise and a cloud of dust, as the drone finally took off and threw half of the desert in everybody's face.

With this it was time to say goodbye to Luxor until the next time. I got back in the car and was whisked off to the airport, just in time to check in for the 6.20 flight to Cairo.

It was around 8.30 by the time I picked my suitcase up and the tour rep met me at the airport. 9.30 before Mohammad, who still wasn't getting any rest, got me to The Mena House Hotel.

I had planned for a restful day the following morning, just wandering across the road to the pyramids and Giza Plateau. No such luck.

Firstly, they had been unsuccessful in getting permission to get to Abu Sir and secondly there was a massive event in Alexandria two days later, so it was thought wise to go there the next morning. This would mean a 6am breakfast and on the road by 7.

Then to replace Abu Sir we made the decision to travel to Bubastis and Tanis in the Nile Delta, which would be a monumental day trip. No rest for the wicked.

9. A Town Called Alex

After about five hours sleep, it was time to get up again. I made a mental note to come back home for a holiday. I skipped breakfast and just about had time to have a quick cup of tea on my balcony whilst admiring the Great Pyramid.

I had been so exhausted by the time I reached the Mena House the previous night, that I took their offer of getting a golf cart from reception to my room. The property is quite large and full of lush, palm tree-filled gardens, interspersed with outside cafes and kiosks, as well as numerous identical blocks of rooms. Partly because it was dark and because I was so tired, I didn't take any notice of where I was going. As a result, I managed to leave my block by the wrong door and get completely lost, resulting in me being five minutes late to meet Sami and Mohammad who were twiddling their thumbs outside of reception fearing I hadn't woken up.

Nevertheless, it was good to get the gang back together and we embarked on the two-hour drive north to Alexandria, which was truncated a very welcome stop for a coffee at an Egyptian service station.

My first impressions of Alexandria were positive. It seemed a bit more relaxed and cosmopolitan, which is hardly surprising. Even in ancient times it was regarded as more Greek and European than African. Not as many women in hijabs or donkeys pulling the carts. I don't want to go too far. It was still pretty dirty, which is a shame as the city was voted one of the prettiest in the world in the 1950's.

Having said that, so was Cairo in the 1920's. You hate to say it, but ever since the British left, they do seem to have lowered their standards a bit. Tactfully, for once, I kept my thoughts to myself. Considering that I had been dealing with historic sites that dated back 4000 years, the fact that Alexandria was only founded in 330 BC, makes it almost modern history.

First stop was the ancient Greek and Roman catacombs at Kom El Shoqafa. The artwork was quite different from what I had seen over the past week. Whereas the Egyptian gods are still pictured, Horus, Thoth, Anubis etc., they are portrayed in Greek/Roman attire. The pharaohs from 330 BC through to Cleopatra, although embracing the Egyptian culture, were still Greek than Egyptian and then after Octavian invaded, Egypt became a Roman colony and Roman culture took its effect.

Throughout the day, our sightseeing was blighted by three coach loads of Chinese tourists, taking photos of each other and barging people out of the way. This proved especially annoying on the spiral staircase that descends to the catacombs.

I must admit I was unaware of the fact, but along with such notable sites such as The Great Wall of China. Stonehenge, Leaning Tower of Pisa and The Colosseum, these catacombs are included in the Seven Wonders of The Middle Ages. I am not quite sure why Stonehenge is included as it is older than most of the seven wonders of the ancient world. For the record, the other two structures were Hagia Sophia in Istanbul and The Porcelain Tower of Nanjing.

The necropolis consists of a series of Alexandrian tombs, statues, and archaeological objects of the Pharaonic funeral cult with Hellenistic and early Imperial Roman influences. Due to the time period, many of the features of the catacombs of Kom El Shoqafa merge Roman, Greek, and Egyptian cultural styles; some statues are Egyptian in style yet bear Roman clothes and hair style whilst other features are reversed. A circular staircase, which was often used to transport deceased bodies down the middle of it, leads down into the tombs that were tunneled into the bedrock during the age of the Antonine emperors (2nd century AD). The facility was then used as a burial chamber from the 2nd century to the 4th century, before being rediscovered in 1900 when a donkey accidentally fell into the access shaft.

Why there isn't a memorial to the poor donkey I do not know. But animal rights aren't exactly at the top of the agenda in this country.

To date, three sarcophagi have been found, along with other human and animal remains which were added later. It is believed that the catacombs were originally only intended for a single family, but it is unclear why the site was expanded in order to house numerous other individuals.

Another feature of the catacombs is the Hall of Caracalla, which contains the bones of horses which were the tombs created for the horses of the Emperor Caracalla in 215 AD.

The catacombs were named Kom El Shoqafa, which means Mound of Shards, because the area used to contain a mound of shards of terra cotta which mostly consisted of jars and objects made of clay. These objects were left by those visiting the tombs, who would bring food and wine for their consumption during the visit. However, they did not wish to carry these containers home from this place of death so they would break them. At the time of the discovery, heaps of these broken plates were found.

The catacombs consist of three levels cut through solid rock, the third level being now completely underwater. The catacombs have a six-pillared central shaft which opens off the vestibule. On the left is a triclinium, a funeral banquet hall where friends and family gathered on stone couches covered with cushions, both at the time of burial and also on future commemorative visits.

A stone staircase descends to the second level. In the lobby of the building two pillars are topped by the papyrus, lotus, and acanthus leaves of ancient Egypt and two falcons flanking a winged sun decorate the frieze. Figures of a man and a woman are carved into the wall. The man's body has a stiff hieratic pose typical of Ancient Egyptian sculpture, with the head carved in the lifelike manner of the classic Greek. The woman's figure is also rigidly posed but bears a Roman hairstyle.

There are three huge stone coffins with non-removable covers along the sides of the chamber. It's assumed that bodies were inserted in them from behind, using a passageway which runs around the outside of the funeral chamber. There is a hallway with 91-inch-deep walls in the central tomb chamber, with carved recesses, each providing burial space for three mummies.

By this stage The Chinese hordes were in front of us, but as we moved on and drove to The Serapeum and Pompey's Pillar, they were disembarking en masse.

We decided to give them ten minutes and stopped at a café for a coffee. It almost felt as though you were in a busy French town here, sitting at a table on the pavement, drinking coffee, watching the world go by. Trams, that must have been operating when the British were here, still trundle around the city, and all in all it was very pleasant, apart from the noise The Chinese were making.

They weren't going anywhere fast, so I left Sami and Mohammad to enjoy their coffee, crossed the road and went into the park where the remains of The Serapeum were.

The park is dominated by Pompey's pillar. The pillar has an interesting story. Pompey was Julius Caesar's rival for the throne of Rome. He had sailed across the Mediterranean to see Ptolemy 13th in order to shore up support prior to Caesar landing in Egypt.

Ptolemy knew that Caesar hated Pompey and had him beheaded. When Caesar arrived, Pompey's head was placed at his feet as a gift. Whereas this was in theory a good plan, what Ptolemy did not consider was that Caesar would lust after his sister, Cleopatra, and aid her claim for the throne of Egypt. The story goes that Pompey's head was then placed on the top of the pillar. This is of course rubbish. The pillar was actually erected in 297 AD, commemorating the victory of Roman emperor Diocletian over an Alexandrian revolt.

The pillar is still interesting though. It is the largest triumphal column constructed outside of Imperial Rome and the only one in Egypt. In 1326, a Muslim traveler Ibn Battuta visited Alexandria. He describes the pillar and recounts the tale of an archer who shot an arrow tied to a string over the column. This enabled him to pull a rope tied to the string over the pillar and secure it on the other side in order to climb over to the top of the pillar.

In early 1803, British commander John Shortland of HMS Pandour flew a kite over Pompey's Pillar. This enabled him to get ropes over it, and then a rope ladder. On February 2, he and John White, Pandour's Master, climbed it. When they got to the top they displayed the Union Jack, drank a toast to King George III, and gave three cheers. Four days later they climbed the pillar again, erected a staff, fixed a weathervane, ate a beef steak, and again toasted the king. I asked Sami if I could do the same. I could do with a decent steak. He glared at me.

Pompey's Pillar stands on top of the ruins of The Temple of Serapis or Serapeum. To the untrained eye, there is little more than a few foundations and piles of rubble, interspersed with a couple of restored sphinxes. But underneath the rubble are underground tunnels from both the Temple and from The Sanctuary, which was an overspill from The Great Library of Alexandria.

By all detailed accounts, the Serapeum was the largest and most magnificent of all temples in the Greek quarter of Alexandria. It was originally built by built by Ptolemy III around 230 BC and dedicated to Serapis, the protector of Alexandria, who was part Egyptian Apis Bull but owed just as much to the Greek and Minoan ancient Bull cults.

The inscription plaque made for that Ptolemy III has been found and was written in both Greek and Egyptian hieroglyphs and the subterranean galleries beneath the temple were most probably the site of the mysteries of Serapis. In 1895, a black diorite statue representing Serapis in his Apis bull incarnation with the sun-disk between his horns was found at the site; an inscription dates it to the reign of Hadrian. A replica of the statue still resides at the end of one of the tunnels.

What remains of The Sanctuary is a monument to the barbarity of the Christian Church. The main Library was burned down by accident after Julius Caesar set light to his Fleet in the Harbour. The Sanctuary housed the documents that could be saved and survived until 391 AD. Constantine had closed the Temple of Serapis in 325 AD but allowed the manuscripts to stay in the Sanctuary. By 391, the uneducated masses had been brainwashed into fearing their Pagan past and to believe only what their Roman rulers told them. A bit like the BBC today really. So, when Theophilus, Bishop of Alexandria preached to the masses, proclaiming that there was pagan literature in The Sanctuary and its mere existence threatened their very way of life. The mob was stirred up to such a degree that they looted, pillaged, and completely destroyed everything. And that was the last chance that humanity had to read about the true history of mankind. The Church would now set the narrative and still does. To make matters worse, the wave of destruction of non-Christian idols spread throughout Egypt in the following weeks with thousands of years of a glorious History obliterated and Temple after Temple destroyed. All because of a book that wasn't translated properly.

Without going off at too much of a tangent, this is very sad, because within no more than 300 years, the story of Jesus and the Christian or Nazarene movement had been blown out of all proportion.
It is my belief that Jesus was a historical figure and was in fact the Great Grandson of Julius Caesar and Cleopatra. As such he was the rightful heir to the throne of Egypt. Although we know that Caesar and Cleopatra had a son, Caesarean, we know he was killed by Octavian after Egypt fell to the Romans. There is evidence however that when Cleopatra fled Rome, after Caesar was killed by Brutus, she was pregnant and there are records in Cyprus, where she first fled, that she gave birth to a daughter, Thea Musa. Thea Musa was sold by Octavian to The King of Persia to be his Queen.

She had a daughter named Juliana and both, along with another son, were banished from Persia for plotting against the King. By this time, Juliana was pregnant and gave birth to a son whilst travelling through what is now Syria. The son became King of a region called Odessa, which is Southern Turkey today. His name was Izas Manu (Jesus Emmanuel?) and was one of the instigators of The Jewish Revolt in 68AD, and a contender to be Emperor of Rome after the fall of Nero. Technically he was a rightful heir to thrones of Egypt, Rome, and Persia, the three big Empires of the day. A King of Kings perhaps?

If you consider that Caesar declared himself God, and to The Romans, he was still a God, Izas was a son of God. If you consider that Cleopatra and all daughters of the Pharaoh are seen as Isis, the eternal virgin, reborn, Izas was born of a virgin. There are many other things that link him to the Biblical story. None more so than after his defeat by Vespasian in Jerusalem in 69AD, he was crucified, whilst his army was taken to Alexandria. The Roman historian, Josephus (Joseph of Arimathea?) had him taken down from the cross. He was then taken to Alexandria, where his troops truly believed he had risen from the dead. There are massive similarities between Josephus' book "The Jewish War" and The New Testament and it is distinctly possible that the whole thing was made up to keep the Jews under control after Jerusalem was raised to the ground and they were driven out of Israel.

So technically, Alexandria could be the spot where Jesus "arose from the dead!"

Seeing the sanctuary and where the scrolls were kept made me quite sad. You must wonder where humanity would be if the information here had never been lost. We truly are a species with amnesia who seek comfort from the first semi believable fairy story that we are told.

We moved on, thankfully without The Chinese tour buses for a quick visit to a roman amphitheatre.

The theatre has marble seating for seven to eight hundred people and is actually the largest Roman theatre in Africa. In Byzantine times, gladiatorial games were superseded by chariot races here. Along the northern side of the theatre's portico are thirteen auditoria that might have been part of Alexandria's ancient university, with an annual enrolment of five thousand students. It has been proven that the theatre was built in the 4th century AD and was used up until an earthquake hit Alexandria in the 7th century, encompassing the Roman, Byzantine, and Islamic eras.

To be honest, as pleasant as it was, I have seen far bigger and more impressive amphitheatres around the world, so I didn't hang around too long here.
We got back in the car and got to the shores of The Mediterranean. This was a pleasant respite from desert scenery and the beach here was quite rocky. There again, if most of your country is covered in sand, do you really need a sandy beach?

We got out of the car and wandered past children playing in the sea, men fishing, ice cream sellers and people just taking in the view. A seaside town is the same the world over. We were here to see what is now known as Fort Qaitby, which has an interesting, if not spectacular history. However, the base on which it is built is very important, as it is the original base for The Pharos Lighthouse, one of the original Wonders of The Ancient World.

The lighthouse still stood and functioned well into the 14th Century before succumbing to an earthquake.

The lighthouse was constructed in the 3rd century BC. After Alexander the Great died, Ptolemy I announced himself king in 305 BC, and commissioned its construction shortly thereafter. The building was finished during the reign of his son, Ptolemy II Philadelphius, and took twelve years to complete at a total cost of 800 talents of silver. The light was produced by a furnace at the top, and the tower was said to have been built mostly with solid blocks of limestone. Although, since the lighthouse was over 300 feet tall the use of limestone as the main material is doubtful due to the possibility of collapsing under its own weight. Rather, pink granite found nearby is more probable as it is much stronger and can withstand more weight.

Arab descriptions of the lighthouse are consistent despite it undergoing several repairs after earthquake damage. Given heights vary only fifteen percent from c. 103 to 118 m (338 to 387 ft), on a 30 by 30 m (98 by 98 ft) square base.

The lighthouse was partially cracked and damaged by earthquakes in 796 and 951, followed by structural collapse in the earthquake of 956, and then again in 1303 and 1323.

The Egyptian Sultan built the Citadel on the base of the lighthouse in 1477. It remained in use as a fort until the British bombarded it in 1882.
We had lunch, across the road, at a very nice seafood restaurant, which made a pleasant change from chicken, which seems to be the norm here.

After lunch we went to the new Alexandria Library or as it is technically known, the Bibliotheca Alexandrina. Whereas it is trying to be as near to the original Great Library as possible, nothing can replace what was lost. In order for it to be a true representation of what the original library stood for, all nations would need to get together and donate their greatest literary treasures to the library. That will never happen. It is certainly the greatest library in Africa, but in reality, that is all it can aim for.

The Great Library of Alexandria was the largest and most significant library of the ancient world. The library was part of a larger research institution called the Mouseion, which was dedicated to the Muses, the nine goddesses of the arts. The idea of a universal library in Alexandria may have been proposed by Demetrius of Phalerum, an exiled Athenian statesman living in Alexandria, to Ptolemy I, who may have established plans for the Library, but the Library itself was probably not built until the reign of his son Ptolemy II. The library quickly acquired many papyrus scrolls, due largely to the Ptolemaic kings' aggressive and well-funded policies for procuring texts. It is unknown precisely how many such scrolls were housed at any given time, but estimates range from 40,000 to 400,000 at its height.

Alexandria came to be regarded as the capital of knowledge and learning, in part because of the Great Library. Many important and influential scholars worked at the Library during the third and second centuries BC, including, among many others: Zenodotus of Ephesus, who worked towards standardizing the texts of the Homeric poems; Callimachus, who wrote the Pinakes, sometimes considered to be the world's first library catalogue; Apollonius of Rhodes, who composed the epic poem the Argonautica; Eratosthenes of Cyrene, who calculated the circumference of the earth within a few hundred kilometres of accuracy;
Aristophanes of Byzantium, who invented the system of Greek diacritics and was the first to divide poetic texts into lines; and Aristarchus of Samothrace, who produced the definitive texts of the Homeric poems as well as extensive commentaries on them.
The new Library was opened in 2002 and in 2010, the library received a donation of 500,000 books from The National Library of France. The gift makes the Bibliotheca Alexandrina the sixth-largest French library in the world.

The library has shelf space for eight million books, with the main reading room covering 20,000 square metres (220,000 sq. ft). The complex also houses a conference centre; specialized libraries for maps, multimedia, the blind and visually impaired, young people, and for children; four museums; four art galleries for temporary exhibitions; 15 permanent exhibitions; a planetarium; and a manuscript restoration laboratory.

There is a small museum downstairs which houses some mosaic floors of the original library, unfortunately all that remains after the fire.

Outside of the Library is a massive statue of Ptolemy II. Originally, I had thought this to be a poor relation to the many similar statues of earlier Pharaohs that I had been seeing over the previous week. However, Sami pointed out that it was only rescued from the sea in 1995 and had spent nearly 2000 years under water. Hence the erosion.

As we waited outside of The Library for Mohammad to bring the car to pick us up, I overheard an American family ask their Egyptian tour guide, where the best place was in Egypt to celebrate St Patrick's Day. I can safely say that I have never seen Guinness in Egypt and the last time I checked; saints weren't that highly regarded in Islamic countries. Having said that, you find Irish pubs in most parts of the world, so you never say never.

We got back to Cairo in time for me to enjoy a cup of tea on the balcony, watching the sun set behind the pyramid.

I finally got to try the restaurant at the hotel and must report that the dinner buffet was very fitting for a five-star hotel.

Then it was back to my room for an early night and a chance to catch up on some sleep.

10. Pyramids

For once I wasn't up at 6am and could enjoy breakfast in a relaxed manner. This is a 5-star hotel, and the food is as it should be. I probably gained a couple of pounds, but all of the exercise I was getting should keep it to that. Back on the diet when I get back.

Having said that I was hardly going mad. Loads of fresh fruit for breakfast and a freshly made omelette is hardly over the top. I will admit to having two strawberries coated in white chocolate though.

But as I said, it was a 5-star hotel, and you need to act accordingly. The first embarrassing American of the day was at breakfast, who asked the Muslim chef why they couldn't have pork sausages. They shouldn't be allowed out.

I met Sami and Mohammad at 11 o'clock and we simply crossed the road from the hotel to the Giza Plateau. We spent around three hours wandering around. I have seen the main two pyramids extensively, but this time wanted to explore the smaller pyramid of Menkaure and some of the other tombs and temples.

The other two occasions I had been to Giza were quite rushed and this time I just wanted to wander for a bit. Taking in the amazing quality of the surviving casing stones, the craftmanship that was needed to create the basalt pathway around the structure and just to gape at in awe. All sorts of things go through your mind when you stand in front of the two main pyramids, and you cannot really appreciate their sheer size without stepping back and taking it all in.

As we stared up at The Great Pyramid, we noticed that there was a man clambering up it. Over our shoulders we heard shouting and soldiers with machine guards were heading in our direction.
"Not again" I thought to myself. Surely, they weren't going to ask for money because I had paused for too long to take in the view.

It transpired that the man climbing, who had now sat down, about a third of the way up, had threatened to top himself by jumping off. He shouted at the soldiers and the soldiers pointed their guns at him, whilst the pyramid was sealed off. This provided entertainment for a good ten minutes, with a large crowd began to appear, shouting at the guy. As to whether they were telling him to jump I don't know, but if I had spent a load of money on hoping to enter the pyramid and some bloke was ruining it by threatening to jump, I would join in the chorus.

The baffling thing was the soldiers. The poor guy threatening to commit suicide may never have got the chance with these trigger-happy maniacs aiming their Kalashnikovs at him. Thankfully it all ended peacefully. I am guessing that the military managed to access the poor guy's bank account and realised he couldn't pay the bribe.

As you take your time and wander around, without being rushed between sites and then back to the tour bus, you not only notice the two massive necropolises here, full of mastaba tombs, but also shaft after shaft with massive black holes disappearing straight down through the sand. The network of tunnels and caves below Giza is truly astounding. It is alleged that these tunnels stretch all the way to Saqqara with some being natural and some probably less so.

Behind the Khafre Pyramid are a few smaller satellite pyramid tombs, supposedly for his Queens. I had the opportunity to go into one of them but declined having seen what it involved. Very steep, very deep, and very narrow. Basically, it would be on your hands and knees in reverse going down. And then I have absolutely no idea how I would have got back up again.

We explored a couple of mastabas in the necropolis which has tombs dating back over 4,500 years. The whole area being a complete minefield, as once you get off the beaten track there are hundreds of pits and endless shafts without warnings or covers. The whole area is a broken leg or neck waiting to happen.

Only open since 2012, the Tomb of Meresankh is an amazing structure, hidden away amongst the maze of locked mastabas in the Eastern Cemetery,

Meresankh III was the granddaughter of Khufu, supposed builder of the Great Pyramid, and wife of Khafre, supposed builder of the second pyramid. The nature of this queen's burial illustrates the importance of royal sons and daughters in Egypt in the IVth Dynasty, a period when the Old Kingdom was at its zenith, and a time when craftsmanship in sculpture and painting reached a high level of sophistication.

It is here that there are hieroglyphs stating that Khufu is the son of Ra. The first known mention of a Pharaoh being the son of God. The tomb was discovered on 23 April 1927. It consists of a surface mastaba, a stone-built chapel, and a funerary chamber.

This chapel is one of the better preserved, and certainly one of the most beautiful, in the necropolis of Giza. The technical achievement, and talent, of the sculptors and painters displays a high level of mastery. Moreover, and very rarely, two of the actual craftsmen are named in the monument.

There are sixteen statues — an unusually large number — built into the walls. Among these, ten statues of women on the north wall reveal the importance granted to women of the royal family.
The entrance stairway leads down into the large main chamber of the tomb, which contains two square pillars, and its walls are decorated with many beautiful and colourful reliefs of daily life in the Old Kingdom. Texts near the doorway give her name and titles with the date of her death and funeral.

On the left-hand side of the doorway, two sculptors whose names are given as Re' hay and Inkaf, carve and paint statues of the Queen, while below other men are shown carving the funerary sarcophagus and false door. Gold workers are also shown smelting gold and making a palanquin. On the southern wall, three niches contain six statues of men who are not identified but are thought to be scribes or priests. An incomplete false door stela on the western wall shows Meresankh seated at a table.

The walls of this chamber show many interesting scenes of various industries – fowling, mat-making, furniture-making and agricultural and hunting scenes. Meresankh is shown with her mother Hetepheres gathering lotus flowers and catching birds. On the pillars of the main hall, the deceased Meresankh is depicted facing into the tomb and dressed in an elegant white robe. Her two sons, Niussere (later pharaoh) and Duaenre stand at her feet. The northern wall is a rock-cut extension to the large chamber which contains a group of ten statues varying in size. They are unidentified but are thought to represent the deceased four times, her mother three times and three daughters.

The second chamber is smaller than the first and has two large openings leading into it. The left-hand wall is decorated with funerary scenes, offering lists and scribes bringing accounts of the estate. The small portion of wall between the doorways shows scenes of agriculture, and on the northern wall, food and wine is being prepared for the banquet, while musicians, singers and dancers entertain Meresankh who sits above holding a lotus flower and watching over the proceedings. These reliefs are unpainted. Two more niches on the western wall contain statues, probably of Meresankh and her mother with a false door between them.
In 1927, in the second chamber, archaeologists found a large burial shaft whose chamber contained Meresankh's black granite sarcophagus complete with the mummy of the queen.

The other mastaba which we managed to get into belonged to Qar. The limestone superstructure of the mastaba has now almost completely disappeared, and the remaining chambers are below ground. This official, also known as Meryre Nefer, was 'Overseer of the Pyramid Towns of Khufu and Menkaure', and 'Tenant of the Pyramid of Pepy I', probably during the Dynasty VI reign of Pepy I or II. His wife Gefi, a 'Prophetess of Hathor', is known from tomb inscriptions. It is generally assumed that Qar is the father of Idu but there are suggestions that the truth could in fact be the opposite.

The entrance to the tomb is down a flight of steps which lead into a passage which in turn opens into a hall with pillars supporting an architrave, richly worked in incised hieroglyphs. On the faces of the pillars the tomb-owner is shown in various stages of his life. The wall to the right of the entrance depicts the funerary rites, with Qar seated at a table to receive offerings. He is shown in a similar manner with his wife on the western wall, with offering lists and illustrations of the funeral procession – the purification tent and embalming-house are the focus of the ceremonies. On the southern wall of the open court, a niche contains statues of the deceased and his family, including his young son. Carved in high relief the row of six life-like standing statues is cut from the rock. Four of them have identical wigs and short narrow kilts, while the fifth is a naked young boy with a shaved head. The sixth and full-sized statue also had a shaved head or short wig and wears a longer flared and pleated kilt.

The worn inscription above the statues gives another of Qar's titles 'Overseer of all the Works'. There is another statue of Qar seated in a niche on the eastern wall, where there are more offerings.

An offering chamber is entered from the western wall and here there are more offering scenes and texts. In the doorway there are more reliefs of the deceased.

The false door of Qar is set into the western wall of the offering chamber with offerings and offering-bringers to either side. The tomb of Qar is thought to be an excellent example of later Old Kingdom art.

We wandered away from the Eastern cemetery and made our way to the Pyramid of Menkaure, the smallest of the three on the Plateau.

Supposedly built by Menkaure in the 26th Century BC, it is 61m high and made from limestone and granite. The lowest 12 layers of casing are made from rose granite whilst the upper levels are the more traditional Tura limestone. Interestingly, on close inspection of the lower casing stones you see that many have strangled lumps or bobbles projecting from their otherwise smooth surface. Yjese are identical to the bobbles found on pre-Incan stonework found in Peru and pre-Mayan stones in Mexico. It is hard to explain this, but clearly there was some sort of link here. I very much doubt the Inca, Maya and Egyptians were in any type of contact, however there is clearly a common technology that links them, maybe through a common ancestor we are not aware of. These stones really are proof of some sort of geo polymer or type of concrete that was used in ancient megalithic buildings. As previously stated, a mixture of sodium carbonate, water and crushed granite would have been made into a liquid form and then poured into wooden moulds or some sort of hemp cloth bags. The bobbles we find on certain stones would be where traces of the mixture seeped out.

The entrance is about 4m above ground and then descends underground. I did go in to this one and it was about sixty steps down, doubled up in two due to the low roof and then down another small shaft. There isn't much inside, there never is, but this pyramid was different because it had stone portcullises.

The official line is that it was designed to keep grave robbers out, which if it was a tomb clearly didn't work. The layout of the inner workings of the pyramid are similar to both The Great Pyramid subterranean chamber and the pit of Zawyet El Aryan. This leads to a conclusion, that maybe, before the structure was turned into a pyramid, its original height was just the height of the twelve granite casing stones, and it was some kind of reservoir or outlet for fresh water. The stone portcullises would then be able to control the flow of water and actually serve a purpose. The ruins of Abu Rawash are also 12 layers high which may not be just a coincidence.

The so-called burial chamber had a large black sarcophagus made of basalt, like the one found in the Kings Chamber in The Great Pyramid. This was lost at sea in 1838 by the British in an attempt to get it to the British Museum. We do know that when it was found, it was totally empty. A further shaft leading from here is sealed off. The official line is that it was unfinished, but this is very unlikely in a structure that is accurate to the very centimetre. This, along with the sealed off well shaft In the Great Pyramid, almost certainly leads to the ground water that seemingly flows from Lake Moeris.

The main problem here was that two coach loads of school kids were clamouring to enter the pyramid after me. I crawled down very slowly and there was only room for me. Sami was very good. He kept slipping the guard at the door a few hundred pounds every few minutes to hold back the masses. But before I could make my last ascent, about twenty kids broke the barrier and charged into the pyramid, screaming like a Mongolian horde. I had to wait about ten minutes for them all to come down and then when finally, there were no more coming, I started the climb back up, with the first of the kids already wanting to run back up.

As I huffed and puffed back to the surface, I caused a bit of a traffic jam and despite attempts, the kids were unable to overtake. There are times when having a big backside is useful as there was no way for them to get past that.

As we wandered around the base of the pyramid, there were three satellite pyramid tombs and the remains of an outer wall that once surrounded the structure which would originally been higher than the entrance to the structure. If this had been a moat, water would easily flow down into the structure. As flood waters would rise up the well, fill the moat and when the level reached the entrance it would flood the subterranean levels, fill the ante chamber, and rise back up, purified by charcoal into a reservoir. The portcullis system could be used to seal the flow of water off in times of overflow resulting in excess water flowing back to the Nile or Lake Moeris.

As with the other pyramids, I strongly believe that the Pharaoh traditionally believed to have built the structure, Menkaure, refurbished an older structure and erected the upper levels of the pyramid. He may well have buried himself in there too.

At the end of the twelfth century al-Malek al-Aziz Othman ben Yusuf, Saladin's son, and heir, attempted to demolish the pyramids in the name of Islam, starting with Menkaure's. The workmen whom Al-Aziz had recruited to demolish the pyramid stayed at their job for eight months but found it almost as expensive to destroy as it would have been to build. They could only remove one or two stones each day. Some used wedges and levers to move the stones, while others used ropes to pull them down. When a stone fell, it would bury itself in the sand, requiring extraordinary efforts to free it.

Wedges were used to split the stones into several pieces, and a cart was used to carry it to the foot of the escarpment, where it was left. Due to such conditions, they could only damage the pyramid by leaving a large vertical gash in its north face which is still visible. From here we walked through the desert to the famous viewpoint where you get an amazing vista of all three pyramids. It was here that I think Sami finally gave up with me. All the other tourists were gawking, understandably, at the amazing view. I, on the other hand, was looking in the opposite direction, trying to see where Zawyet El Aryan was.

The highlight of the day for me was visiting The Valley Temple next to the Sphinx. This was clearly built at the same time as The Osirion at Abydos and shows far greater building techniques than other structures at Giza. The monoliths are massive and in places the stones are even cut to go around corners, as if they were melted into place.

The Valley Temple was constructed with immense blocks of granite, surrounded by a wall of even larger blocks of limestone, the largest estimated to weigh approximately 200 tons.

The Valley Temple would have originally been connected to a dock on The Nile and a covered causeway led from there to the Mortuary Temple and finally the pyramid itself.

The reason the Valley Temple at Giza is so well preserved is that it was buried in sand for centuries. It is hard to know just how long it had been buried before excavations in the 1850's when it was uncovered.

There are two basic construction periods to the Valley Temple. An older limestone block layer, and then a newer granite layer over top. The limestone layer has blocks cut out of the Sphinx enclosure, presumably when that statue was being carved. They cut and moved the blocks intact for the temple building. And they are not small stones by any means, some over 150 tons, and placed high up in the wall. The ability to cut, transport, and raise such large blocks is a wonder in itself.

This original construction is claimed to be the work of the Pharaoh Khafre, to whom the second pyramid, sphinx and temples are attributed. Basically, the only "evidence" for this is a famous diorite statue of Khafre in the Cairo Museum that was found buried upside down in the Valley Temple.

Circumstantial evidence at best. This idea fits with the modern Egyptological timeline of the Old Kingdom but as with other buildings around here, it seems far more likely that Khafre simply renovated an older structure.

It appears that the limestone blocks became severely weathered and were covered over with Granite. No one is sure exactly when this addition happened, and this could have been the work done during the Old Kingdom. The covering stones are a marvel, laid similar to what can be called Inca masonry found in sites in Peru, where the stones are cut to multiple angles and placed against other stones with multiple angles. This is amazingly difficult work, especially given they are not core blocks of the wall, but a layer of stone placed against the original eroding limestone. The corners of the rooms are even more amazing, given that they do not in many cases create straight edges but rounded corners. The work that had to be done to carve blocks of granite to make a rounded corner joint is staggering and were likely not done with simple copper and stone tools of the day. This was also not some sort of whimsical laying of stone, but a very carefully orchestrated design feature. The exact placement of stone blocks on one side of a walkway or room, is matched with similar blocks shaped and placed exactly opposite. This mirroring technique of placement is known as harmonizing a structure to make each side of it resonate.

The most known feature of this temple is the 16-pillared room. Around them are space for 23 statues. The same layout as in The Osirion.
Regardless of what the original purpose would have been, Khafre would have placed 23 statues of himself in the alcoves, one of which is on show in The Cairo Museum. The 23 statues would have been illuminated only by sunlight coming through small slits in the roof, likely timed to strike certain statues only on specific days of the year.

Also, to note, there is not one hieroglyph or drawing on any of the walls of this temple, as found in later temples built around Luxor. This too is a clue to its age.

To the left of the pillared hall is a series of three small vestibules, on top of three similar vestibules making six. They are called storage chambers, though without proof objects were stored in here. To the other side of the hall is a ramp that leads out to the Sphinx and causeway.

The view from the temple, up the causeway to the Pyramid of Cheops is wonderful. As I wandered along it, I took a moment to admire The Sphinx.

The official line is that there is no entrance into it and there is nothing inside, but my guide admitted that he helped on the restoration of it 10 years ago and confirmed there is an entrance on top of the head that goes deep into a shaft. I found a second entrance too which is located at the rear end of the sphinx. Officially it doesn't exist, but if you look hard enough online, you can find pictures of people coming out of it. My guide dismissed it as a drain, but I am not convinced.

Just off the causeway is a fairly nondescript, locked gate with a large black void seemingly behind it. I would loved to have seen inside, but The Antiquities Department aren't very keen to let people in, no amount of bribery would suffice.

Officially it is known as Campbell's Tomb or more colloquially as The Osiris Shaft. It is one of 4 massive vertical shafts to the rear of The Sphinx. It descends, in three stages, some 125 feet below the ground to a chamber, where a sarcophagus in a subterranean chamber, flanked by four columns, sits on an island, surrounded by water.

Officially it is another Royal Tomb, but going back to the times of Herodotus, ancient Egyptian priests spoke of a long-held tradition of the creation of underground chambers by the original builders of ancient Memphis. In 1993, these stories were confirmed when these large cavities were discovered during a survey conducted at Giza, An article about the find stated: "…We have discovered a subway used by the ancient Egyptians of 5000 years ago. It passes beneath the causeway leading between the second Pyramid and the Sphinx.

It provides a means of passing under the causeway from the Great Pyramid to the Pyramid of Khafre. From this subway, we have unearthed a series of shafts leading down more than 125 feet, with roomy courts and side chambers…".

The Osiris Shaft, so called because some say it is the tomb of the God Osiris and is often inaccessible due to flooding. The problem is that the authorities claim they have no idea why this is occurring nor the source of the water. Recent tests have shown the water to be saltwater. This rules The Nile out as the source and the only possible answer is Lake Moeris, the Lake that was artificially made near The Hawara pyramid and Labyrinth. In ancient times this lake was a freshwater lake with an area of 656 miles, and with two pyramids sitting in the centre of it. Today, due to the lake receding to a mere 78 miles and what remains being below sea level, it has become a saltwater lake. This has happened due to the dam at Aswan and the annual Nile flood not taking place anymore.

In 1934, an Egyptian archaeologist tried to pump the water out of the shaft for four years continually. He failed and still today it fills up. If this isn't a smoking gun for the pyramid irrigation and water pump system, I don't know what is.

The Egyptian Government seem reluctant to allow archaeologists access to the shaft. Whether this is down to fears for their safety or fear for their own narrative which promotes tourism is another matter.

Perhaps the locations for all great pyramids around the world are based on a water need. In 2015, with the aid of Electric Tridimensional Tomography, scientists discovered a lake and caverns running underneath the Mayan Kukulkan Pyramid at Chichen Itza. This water source connected both east and west of the pyramid. All pyramids in the Yucatan area seem to have associated Cenotes, which are deep natural water holes.

Teotihuacan also has a water source, as does the Bosnian Pyramid, which also has an extensive underground tunnel network which runs for more than ten miles.

One day I may get the opportunity to explore down there, but for this day, the sightseeing was over.

I had asked to go to a papyrus shop to buy some artwork for my walls at home. Sami was more than happy to oblige as I am sure the shop he took me too gave him a healthy commission.
I was back in the hotel by 3.30 and have had a relaxing afternoon, a delicious dinner and found a tv channel that showed the Brighton Man Utd game albeit with Arabic commentary.

11.   A Day In The Delta

My last full day in Egypt was another early start with no time for breakfast. I had to meet Sami and Mohammad at 7am for the long drive Northwest to The Nile Delta.

It was a good two-hour drive to get to the outskirts of the modern Egyptian city of Zagazig. As we pulled off the highway, Sami's phone rang, and he spoke quite angrily to someone in Arabic. Mohammad pulled the car over to the side of the road and stopped.

Lo and behold, ten minutes later, a military jeep with four heavily armed soldiers turned up along with a local police car. There was a heated argument between Sami, the army and the police and the net result was that the police car went ahead of us with its blue lights flashing, and the armed guard took up the rear behind our car.

Once again I should point out that the locals have never been anything more than friendly towards me and at no time have I ever felt in danger in Egypt. This is simply a protection racket. In any case, if there were terrorist's hell bent on taking a pot shot at me, the last thing I wanted to do was draw attention to myself with blue lights flashing, a siren wailing and a battalion of The Egyptian Army. Travelling incognito would have been far more preferable.

This also meant that what was already going to be a long day, was now going to be an extremely long day, because as word got out, there would be more and more soldiers and policeman, suddenly coming on duty to get a slice of the pie.

Just beyond Zagazig, under the shadow of an extremely unpicturesque flyover, lie the red granite ruins of a city sacred to the followers of the cat goddess Bastet. She was worshipped for thousands of years in ancient Egypt, and her popularity peaked during the 22nd dynasty, whose pharaohs built her a magnificent temple in the city, then named Per-Bast.

This city is referenced in the Bible, sometimes by its Hebrew name of Pi-beseth. In chapter 30 of Ezekiel, it is mentioned, along with Heliopolis, as a pagan shrine that will be destroyed by the wrath of God, but it is better known today by its Greek name, Bubastis.

I don't think it was God, but there are ruins and then there is Bubastis. Literally all that was there was a massive area full of rubble. Some bits of column, maybe some bits of wall, but generally, piles of broken masonry for as far as the eye could see. I honestly think that if you spent a week here, simply sifting through the rubble, you could find some amazing things. Unfortunately, we only had an hour.

After declining and falling into ruin over the millennia, this mysterious city captured the imagination of 19th-century European scholars who flocked to the Nile Delta in search of it. Guided by intriguing hints from classical accounts, they wanted to find Bastet's city, unearth her glorious temple, and gain a clearer understanding of how the cat goddess played such an important role throughout the long history of ancient Egypt.

One of the most important sources about the city is found in the works of Herodotus. In his fifth-century B.C. tour of Egypt, the Greek historian provided a vivid description of Bubastis, the Temple of Bastet, and the fervour of her worship: "In this city there is a temple very well worthy of mention, for though there are other temples which are larger and build with more cost, none more than this is a pleasure to the eyes."

He described the city's beauty and the noisy revelers traveling in boats to Bubastis, "Barges and river craft of every description, filled with men and women, floated leisurely down the Nile. The men played on pipes of lotus. the women on cymbals and tambourines, and such as had no instruments accompanied the music with clapping of hands and dances, and other joyous gestures.

Thus, did they while on the river: but when they came to a town on its banks, the barges were made fast, and the pilgrims disembarked, and the women sang, playfully mocked the women of that town, and threw their clothes over their head. When they reached Bubastis, then held they a wondrously solemn feast: and more wine of the grape was drank in those days than in all the rest of the year."

Herodotus described the city and its temple as a wonderous sight to behold: - "Temples there are more spacious and costlier than that of Bubastis, but none so pleasant to behold. It is after the following fashion. Except at the entrance, it is surrounded by water: for two canals branch off from the river and run as far as the entrance to the temple: yet neither canal mingles with the other, but one runs on this side, and the other on that. Each canal is a hundred feet wide, and its banks are lined with trees.

The propylaea are sixty feet in height and are adorned with sculptures (probably intaglios in relief) nine feet high, and of excellent workmanship. The Temple, being in the middle of the city, is looked down upon from all sides as you walk around; and this comes from the city having been raised, whereas the temple itself has not been moved, but remains in its original place.

Right round the temple there goes a wall, adorned with sculptures. Within the enclosure is a grove of fair tall trees, planted around a large building in which is the effigy (of Bast). The form of that temple is square, each side being a stadium in length. In a line with the entrance is a road built of stone about three stadia long, leading eastwards through the public market. The road is about 400 feet (120 m) broad and is flanked by exceedingly tall trees. It leads to the temple of Hermes."

In the 18th century, European scholars began hunting for the places mentioned in ancient texts. To the French scholars who accompanied Napoleon on his 1798 expedition to Egypt, Herodotus's account served as an inspiration to locate it.

One of them, Étienne-Louis Malus, spotted features in the Nile Delta mentioned by Herodotus, and found ruins nearby that he declared to be Bubastis. Lying northeast of Cairo, this site, known as Tell Basta, became the accepted spot where Bastet's city once stood.

Most of the major finds from the site are in the museums in London, Paris, or New York. There is a small museum on the site which houses a small collection of statues and other smaller artefacts found in the ruins. Outside is an area where several larger statues and stones with hieroglyphs are displayed, but again these are mostly damaged. I have a vivid imagination but even I struggled to picture what this place looked like in its better days.

Bubastis became a royal residence after Shoshenq I, the first ruler and founder of the 22nd dynasty, became pharaoh in 943 BC. It declined after the conquest by Cambyses II of The Persian Empire in 525 BC.

After the Muslim conquest in the seventh century, Bubastis was abandoned, and the memory of its location was lost for centuries. At the Bubastis temple, some cats were found to have been mummified and buried, many next to their owners. More than 300,000 mummified cats were discovered when Bastet's temple was excavated. It has been suggested that the status of the cat was roughly equivalent to that of the cow in modern India. The death of a cat might leave a family in great mourning and those who could, would have them embalmed or buried it in cat cemeteries.

Still today, the odd stray cat wanders around the ruins as though they own the place. Maybe they do.

It would have been nice to grab some sort of refreshments here, but Bubastis, and for that matter, Zagazig, seemed devoid of anything, not even bottles of water.

As a result, we got back into the car and continued our journey. As we drove deeper into the Nile Delta, the landscape changed markedly from arid desert to lush farmland. Tributaries of the Nile abound, and the resulting greenery is a pleasant and welcome change.

The blue lights continued to flash, and sirens wailed when a car slowed us down. Curious onlookers seemed to be trying to peak through the window to see who this important dignitary was getting an armed guard. I prayed none of them were armed.

It was another two hours north to the ancient city of Tanis. We swapped soldiers and policemen a few times and were now running quite late.

There is no record of Tanis prior to the 19th Dynasty, 1292 BC. The earliest known Tanite buildings are datable to the 21st Dynasty. Although some monuments found at Tanis are datable earlier than this, most of these were in fact brought there from nearby cities, mainly from the previous capital of Pi-Ramesses, for reuse. In fact, it is highly likely that much of the materials for Pi Ramesses came from the abandoned city of Amarna, therefore some of the ruins here could come from Akhenaten's abandoned city. Furthermore, it was the last great city built in Egypt before Alexandria was built by Alexander the Great.

During the late New Kingdom, the royal residence of Pi-Ramesses was abandoned because of its branch of the Nile being silted up and its harbour consequently becoming unusable. After Pi-Ramesses' abandonment, Tanis became the seat of power of the pharaohs of the 21st Dynasty, and later of the 22nd Dynasty, along with Bubastis. The rulers of these two dynasties supported their legitimacy as rulers of Upper and Lower Egypt with traditional titles and building works, although they pale compared to those at the height of the New Kingdom. Many of these rulers were also buried at Tanis in a new royal necropolis, which replaced the one in the Theban Valley of the Kings.

In later times Tanis lost its status of royal residence, yet it remained populated until its abandonment in Roman times.

Today there are ruins of a number of temples, including the chief temple dedicated to Amun, and a very important royal necropolis of the Third Intermediate Period. Many of the stones used to build the various temples at Tanis came from the old Ramesside towns and many former generations of Egyptologists believed that Tanis was, in fact, Pi-Ramesses.

However, the burials of three pharaohs of the 21st and 22nd Dynasties — Psusennes I, Amenemope and Shoshenq II — survived the depredations of tomb robbers throughout antiquity. They were discovered intact in 1939 and 1940 by Pierre Montet and proved to contain a large catalogue of gold, jewelry, lapis lazuli and other precious stones, as well as the funerary masks of these kings. If it hadn't been for the outbreak of World War 2, these finds would have been more famous than that of Tutankhamun. The treasures they found, which I have seen in The Egyptian Museum are staggering. Yet who has heard of Psusennes I?
One thing that Tanis has in its favour is that there is more left of it than there is of Bubastis. There isn't much but there are some impressive statues, mostly of Ramses II and some broken sections of obelisks. You can still make out several important structures. The Temple of Amun, which has a fascinating Nilometer that was formed from two water wells, The Temple of Mut and The Temple of Khonsu. It is interesting that the 21st Dynasty Kings adopted the trinity of Gods from Ancient Thebes, maybe in order to give their new capital some more importance.

The major reason for coming to Tanis though was for the necropolis. In no way is this as remarkable as The Valley of The Kings, Saqqara or any of the workers tombs I had seen during the week. You must realise that Egypt by this period was in sharp decline and was invaded several times before The Greek Ptolemies restored some sort of order in the 4th Century BC.

These tombs were much smaller and much simpler. Yet they were the tombs of Pharaohs and as such amazing to see.

A couple of the Royal tombs are now open to the elements and can be seen by looking down into the open roofed chambers.

The first of these was for Psusennes I who ruled between 1047 and 1001 BC and was generally accepted as the architect behind the construction of Tanis. The tomb was discovered intact by French archaeologist, Pierre Montet in 1940. Despite the destruction of wooden artefacts within the tomb due to the moist Nile delta area, the king's magnificent funerary mask was recovered intact; it proved to be made of gold and lapis lazuli and held inlays of black and white glass for the eyes and eyebrows. Psusennes I's mask is considered to be "one of the masterpieces of the treasures of Tanis" and is currently housed in the Cairo Museum. The pharaoh's "fingers and toes had been encased in gold stalls, and he was buried with gold sandals on his feet. The finger stalls are the most elaborate ever found, with sculpted fingernails. Each finger wore an elaborate ring of gold and lapis lazuli or some other semiprecious stone."

Psusennes I's outer and middle sarcophagi had been recycled from previous burials in the Valley of the Kings through the state-sanctioned tomb-robbing that was common practice in the Third Intermediate Period. It is in fact thought that the story of King Solomon's mines relates to this, and that "Solomon" was in fact a Pharaoh from Tanis who looted gold from Thebes.

A cartouche on the red outer sarcophagus shows that it had originally been made for Pharaoh Merenptah. Psusennes I, himself, was interred in an "inner silver coffin" which was inlaid with gold. Since "silver was considerably rarer in Egypt than gold," Psusennes I's silver "coffin represents a sumptuous burial of great wealth during Egypt's declining years."

The tombs here are one room structures, unlike the mazes that twist underground in The Valley of The Kings. In both the tomb of Psusennes I and that of Shoshenq III, which lies adjacent to it, a large sarcophagus dominates the one room. The reliefs on the wall are carved into the rock and quite faded. Not much in the way of colour remains but this is hardly surprising as they are open to the elements. Not that Shoshenq particularly deserved a fantastic burial as he was the pharaoh who lost control of Upper Egypt to the Nubians and only ruled Lower Egypt.

I noticed Sami having a word with a guardian and slipping him some money. Suddenly, some keys came out and I was ushered over to a locked gate. The guardian unlocked the padlock and asked me to crawl through a narrow hole. I looked nervously at Sami, but he beckoned me in.

Then, before I know it, I am in a tomb and standing on a sarcophagus which belonged to the pharaoh Osorkon II. This generally isn't left open as the reliefs in the tomb are a lot more preserved. Osorkon II reigned from 872 BC to 837 BC and undid the damage that Shoshenq had done by uniting Egypt again.

This tomb was first discovered in 1939 by Montet. The sarcophagus, on which I was standing, was made from granite recycled from a massive statue of Ramses II. The tomb had been robbed in antiquity, but Montet still recovered fragments of a hawk-headed coffin and canopic jars. The jewelry that remained "was of such high quality that existing conceptions of the wealth of the northern Twenty-first and Twenty-second dynasties had to be revised." Although a lot cruder in quality than those in Luxor, the reliefs are still beautiful and showed the deceased King with the Gods Osiris and Isis and his preparation for the afterlife.

Ramesses II was a pharaoh who wanted to be remembered as the most influential Egyptian ruler. He adopted hundreds of monuments representing other pharaohs and ordered their names changed to his own. Therefore, many ancient statues identified previously as Ramesses II did not originally belong to him and come from different periods. With his reign comes the first information about a town in the area around Tanis, but a small settlement had been located there at least since the Old Kingdom period.

Today was certainly not one for the average tourist who may have struggled to get too much out of the piles of rubble. But I found it all quite fascinating.

Less enjoyable was the four and a half drive back to Cairo and still no sign of refreshment. In fact, we did finally manage to find an open shop for a packet of crisps and a can of coke, but that was it for the day.

By the time I got back to the hotel I was exhausted and passed out on the bed. I woke up several hours later freezing cold and shivering, despite the thirty-degree temperatures outside.

I decided against dinner and stayed under my bedclothes. In fact, I was still shivering the following morning and as I didn't need to check out of the hotel until midday, I remained covered up as long as I could.

My airport taxi picked me up on time and I was dropped off at Cairo International Airport for the afternoon flight back to Heathrow. I still felt rather unwell but managed to navigate everything successfully until I got to passport control. The problem was that I seemed to have lost a fair bit of weight and my trousers were in danger of falling around my ankles. Not something you particularly want to happen in front of an Egyptian Immigration Officer. Not that it should have been a problem, but when you have to hold your passport in one hand, your hand luggage in the other and there is no hand left to keep your trousers up, we nearly had a diplomatic incident.
I returned to Heathrow around eight o'clock to find snow covering the ground and temperatures below freezing. Having been shivering already and having got accustomed to temperatures in the mid-thirties, this was a bit of a shock to the system.

To make matters worse, I couldn't find the right car park either. Eventually I managed to get my act together and get back on the M25 that was that for another year.

CARTHAGE HAS BEEN DESTROYED

TUNISIA 2019

1. A Load of Old Ba'alocks — 214
2. Colditz — 225
3. The Troglodytes Of Bulla Regia — 232
4. The Colour Purple — 240
5. The Empire Strikes Back — 248
6. The Tunisian Flintstones — 256
7. Islam's Fourth Holiest Site — 263

One.

A Load of Old Ba'alocks

"Carthage must be destroyed!" So proclaimed Roman Senator Cato The Elder on numerous occasions as he pressed for a Third and final bloody war between Rome and Carthage starting in 149 BC.

Carthage was the major city in the Phoenician Empire, which stretched from the Iberian Peninsula to the west and as far as Lebanon in the Eastern Mediterranean. As was the Empire, Carthage was mainly involved in trade and had been flourishing since the 9th Century BC. In fact, it was the original "New Town" as that is what the direct translation of the word is in Phoenician.

The fact is, the modern world could have been very different, and a lot more peaceful in my opinion, had Carthage, under the leadership of Hannibal, the great General, still studied at Military colleges today for his ingenious battle tactics, conquered the fledgling Rome. With the resulting Rome concentrating on trade rather than military conquest. This was not to be though.

It is said that the Romans had cumbersome ships prior to the First Punic War, but by the time of the third War, the Roman Fleet had copied the faster and easily navigable vessels of Carthage, and vastly outnumbered them. As a result, after a long siege, Carthage fell in 146 BC and was raised to the ground. This breadbasket of Africa had salt thrown all over its fields and Rome did what Rome did, wiping out all traces of it.

Records were destroyed and its history was erased. In fact, it became the first real example of what is now known as "Fake News".

The official history was based on a poem by the Roman Virgil, who told of a mythical Phoenician Queen called Dido, cursing her Roman lover Aeneas, and setting sail, to found Carthage, where she ended up. This is complete fiction, but was taught as fact for many years, showing that Joseph Goebbels wasn't the first to come up with idea that if those in charge tell a lie, however massive, and keep repeating it, people will eventually believe it.

A system still well used today. Recall the lie America used to justify the First Iraq War, stating Iraqi soldiers were throwing Kuwaiti Babies out of incubators in hospitals. Totally fabricated, using the Kuwaiti Ambassadors daughter as a witness. Then of course there were "Weapons of Mass Destruction" and "The Gulf of Tonkin Incident" in Vietnam which were both fabricated but got the masses believing the lies. In fact, most wars start on the basis of lies. Notably those involving America these days!

But despite the propaganda, Carthage rose a second time. Even the Romans could see that the agricultural riches of North Africa could feed it's growing Empire, and so Carthago Nove (New Carthage) rose from the ashes and became one of the most important Roman cities in Africa and leaving some of the finest Roman remains in the world to explore.

This was my second attempt to get to Tunisia as I had previously planned to do so a few years ago, shortly prior to the terrorist attacks at The Bardo Museum in Tunis and on the beaches of Sousse. For once, these attacks happened early enough for me to reschedule and four years later, Tunisia was opening its doors to tourists again.

So why Tunisia? First and foremost, the aforementioned Roman remains, the best outside of Italy. The Bardo Museum has the finest mosaics to be found anywhere in the world. And then there is what was left of the original Carthage. The city that nearly brought Rome to its knees.

As my flight was on a Saturday afternoon, there was no rush hour on the M25, and I got to Heathrow and through check in procedures very smoothly. The Tunis Air flight even left on time. But that was when the horrors started. The flight was full of about twenty or thirty small children. Loud is not the word. Personally, I would throw a few toys in the hold and let them get on with it. There was everything from ear piercing screams to primordial grunts, non-stop for three hours. And to make it worse, there was no onboard tv screen with earphones to block out the noise. The highlight of the flight was dinner.

Not I hasten to add for the rather weird tuna and green bean salad which came with a slice of turkey ham, but for the fact that a child jettisoned his bread roll about five rows forward, hitting another brat on the back of the head. I was hoping for an all-out bun fight, but alas adults stepped in.

The most chilling part of the flight was the small child across the aisle and one row in front who stared at me for three hours. I swear his eyes were black and he was the spitting image of Damian from the first Omen film. If a big black dog had come bounding down the aisle, I would have locked myself in the loo for the rest of the flight.

We landed on time and most of the passengers broke out into a round of applause. I said to the woman next to me, don't flatter the pilot, he might take off again and want to do an encore.

There were about twenty people on the tour, quite a few more than I was used to. Probably because it was quite cheap. We are staying in the Gammarth area of Tunis, which is to the North of the city, amongst a group of beaches known locally as le Baies des Singes, which even with my rudimentary French, I could translate as the Bay of The Monkeys. But there are no baboons or gibbons, sunbathing or playing volleyball on the beaches here, the local fishermen dubbed the European sunbathers as monkeys in the 1950's, and the name stuck.

First impressions of Tunis were quite good. I was expecting something similar to Cairo, but it seemed worlds apart. Everything seemed clean for a start. Drivers seemed quite refined and even stopped at traffic lights. The architecture appeared quite unique in that you can see the Mediterranean influence, but there is also a lot of French aspects too. Not too surprising really.

Women seemed to be mostly in Western clothing, although that would likely change once away from Tunis. There also seem to be a fair few bars around which was promising. Having said that, this tour is full board, so there was little chance to go off piste. The Tunisian authorities were happy to invite tourists back to their country, however seemed to prefer they stayed in their hotels, rather than go and explore alone.

The El Mouradi hotel at first glimpse appeared adequate. Nothing more, nothing less. Daylight would prove to be the real test for this. As it was quite late, I declined the offer of a beer in the bar, and settled into my room for an early night, as sightseeing was due to commence at 8.30 the following morning.

For a hotel that boasts such a lavish reception, you would hope that the beds were not rock hard and the pillows lumpy. This unfortunately was the case. In fact, this would prove to be a theme throughout the tour. Hotels that had spectacular reception areas tended to have far from spectacular rooms.

One thing that I had failed to notice in the dark the previous night, and I really do not know how, was the twenty-foot tall, plastic penguin outside of my window. I have had many a room with a view, but this was quite unique.

Breakfast was OK. I steered clear of the big steaming bowl of cauliflower, and sort of hoped the rest of the group would too. There was nothing weird on the menu. Okra laced with turmeric was perhaps slightly weird. I don't particularly like either, but together they seemed slightly more edible. Tunisian dates are not in the same league as Egyptian ones and are not far away from what we get at home. There was a date cookie dipped in sesame seeds that was quite nice though.

The weirdest thing was that whilst eating breakfast, I noticed a man on the next table with a splint on their, obviously broken nose. Unfortunate you think, until you look behind you and see another man with a similar injury. Well, you think, at least if it was a fight, they came out equal. That is until you notice another and then another broken nose. Very strange I thought, and it turned out that the hotel was a hotbed of plastic surgery and the place to go in Tunisia for a nose job. Very bizarre in a hotel and quite unnerving for the tourist residents.

For a capital city, Tunis is very quiet. It has a weird layout, with the enormous seawater Lake Tunis right in the middle of it. Therefore, the only way to get from east to west is to head north and take the one road that crosses the lake from north to south and then continue the journey. As a result, it feels like five or six small towns all linked together with a 30-minute drive to get from one part to another.

We started the morning at Carthage, which was strewn across the northwestern part of Tunis. Much of the classic literature about Carthage portrays an impenetrable metropolis, clinging to the cliffs and numerous lagoons where the trading ships would sail in and out. Having been to a multitude of ancient sites, you get used to having an imagination that can attempt to picture what places looked like in antiquity.

Carthage seriously put my imagination to the test. There wasn't much left after the city was first of all sacked by the Vandals in 439 AD and then the Muslim hordes arrived in 698 AD. Much of the stone and building blocks were taken to build mosques and other monumental buildings.

Hence, our first stop, The Carthage Amphitheatre was little more than foundations and very little of what had been above ground was left. Thankfully, I could draw from my visits to Rome's Colosseum and at least work under the subterranean workings of the place. The site is now A UNESCO World Heritage Site and is one of the few amphitheatres in The Roman Empire where we actually have proof that Christians were put to death (almost none were put to death in Rome itself). Christianity was rife in North Africa during the second century and was seen as a means of escape from the clutches of Rome (this of course changed when Rome realised this, formed The Church, allowing Christians to join the Empire too!). in 180 AD, twelve Christians, stood trial at the amphitheatre, having gone on a rampage of destroying statues of Ba'al and other Gods throughout Carthage. The authorities had them executed for vandalism, after they refused to repent. Despite their executions being for anti-social behaviour and vandalism, the Christian Church today, still claims them to be Martyrs. I find it quite telling that after the death sentence was proclaimed by The Pro Consul of North Africa, the ringleader, named Speratus proclaimed "Thanks be to God" and the twelve convicts began to celebrate. For it is true that Christianity at this time had become a Death Cult and that many wanted to die and be resurrected by Jesus' side. Giving it rather similar parallels to modern day Islam in places. A large cross has been erected by the Church at one end of the ruins and there is a small chapel in the basement section, dedicated to two of the alleged martyrs.

Having said that, not all executions were simple beheadings. In 202 AD the "Martyr" Perpetua was trampled to death by a wild cow. There is a marble column for her, and in 258, St Cyprian became the first African bishop to lose his head. It is claimed that St Augustine of Hippo (and Canterbury) lectured here too.

The amphitheatre of Carthage was built at the end of the First century or the beginning of the Second century, to the west of the hill of Byrsa where the main Citadel sat. An inscription date certifies that it was in service from 133 - 139 AD. It expanded during the Third century.

We needed no more than 20 minutes at the amphitheatre before moving on to Byrsa Hill and the main citadel. Once again, the Islamic hordes had beaten us to it and there wasn't much left. Although this was the actual site of the original Phoenician Carthage, very little survives. The Romans burned it to the ground in 146 BC. Then Augustus Caesar levelled it and built a new temple here only for the Arabs to level it again. To cap it all off, the French built a cathedral on top of it in the 19th Century.

All that remains are a few foundations that have been excavated from the original city, a couple of Punic graves and a marble platform and a few pillars and stumps from the later Roman temple. On the face of it, not that impressive, however the view over the clear blue Mediterranean at least showed what a strategic and picturesque city it would have been.

So, on we went, looking for some sort of meaningful remains of this once great civilization. Next stop was a site known as The Tophet. According to the Roman Poem that rewrote the history of the city, this was the spot where the fictitious Phoenician Princess landed in Tunisia. In reality it was a religious sanctuary where the people worshipped the sun God Ba'al.
It was believed, well into the 20th Century, that this was a spot where the Barbarian Carthaginians would sacrifice small children by burning them alive. Archaeology has actually proved otherwise, as other burial sites have shown that the local funerary culture was one of cremation, and far from burning children alive, there was a high mortality rate, and deceased children were cremated here. This again, was almost certainly part of the Roman "Fake News" agenda which branded the people of Carthage as Barbaric savages who ate and sacrificed their own children. Unfortunately, this took over 2000 years to prove wrong.

The Tophet site was used as a centre for the worship of Ba'al right up until the Christian era. There are a number of underground tombs here too, that we explored, one of which was once believed to have been of the now fictitious princess. Another area has numerous pottery urns, which were believed to have been the remains of the sacrificed children. They are probably the ashes of children, but those that died of natural causes.

En route to The Roman Baths, we passed what remains on the original Punic Harbour which has two basins in which The Carthaginian fleet, the mightiest in the Mediterranean once laid anchor.

It's a sleepy, non-descript place now, but according to the ancient sources, the commercial harbour was in the shape of a rectangle measuring 456 meters by 356 meters, linked with the sea by a channel 20 meters wide. The naval harbour to the north, which was surrounded by a high wall, had a diameter of 325 meters. A channel giving it direct access to the sea was constructed only during the Third Punic War.

The naval harbour alone had moorings for some 220 vessels, both along the landward side and around the island.

A final stop in Carthage was the impressive Antonine Baths. This mammoth Roman bath complex, although in ruins, is similar in size to the great Baths of Caracalla in Rome. They date from the 2nd century AD, but only the foundations and some scattered columns remain, sprawling across the coast, overlooking the Mediterranean. The remnants allow you to imagine the original layout of this once grand complex and you can walk through the rooms – from the caldarium (hot room) to the central frigidarium (cold room) and palaestra (gymnasium) as Roman bathers once would have.
As much as I love wandering through ancient remains, even my imagination was struggling with the scant debris we were being shown, so it was with some relief that we moved on to something a little more modern.

Our next stop was Sidi Bou Said, which is a small enclave by the sea in Northern Tunis. Perched on top of a steep cliff and surrounded by breath taking Mediterranean views, it's the perfect antidote to the hustle and bustle of the Tunisian capital and a favoured getaway destination for locals and visitors alike. The town's cobbled streets are lined with art shops, souvenir stalls, and quaint cafés. Brilliant, blue-painted doors and trellises contrast beautifully with the pure white of Sidi Bou Said's Grecian buildings, and the air is scented with trailing bougainvillea.

The town is named after Abu Said Ibn Khalef Ibn Yahia El-Beji, a Muslim saint who spent much of his life studying and teaching at the Zitouna Mosque in Tunis.

After journeying through the Middle East on a pilgrimage to Mecca, he came home and sought the peace and quiet of a small village on the outskirts of Tunis named Jebel El-Manar.

The village's name meant "The Fire Mountain" and referred to the beacon that was lit up on the cliff in ancient times to guide ships navigating their way through the Gulf of Tunis. Abu Said spent the rest of his life meditating and praying in Jebel El-Manar, until his death in 1231.

His tomb became a pilgrimage site for devout Muslims, and over time, a town grew up around it. Eventually, it was named in his honour - Sidi Bou Said.
It wasn't until the early 1920s that the town adopted its striking blue and white colour scheme, however. It was inspired by the palace of Baron Rodolphe d 'Erlanger, a famous French painter, and musicologist known for his work in promoting Arab music, who lived in Sid Bou Said from 1909 until his death in 1932. Since then, the town has become synonymous with art and creativity, having provided a sanctuary for many famous painters, writers, and journalists.

By now it was approaching lunchtime and we headed back over Lake Tunis to the port area of the city, which looked a bit like Newhaven, for the local speciality, Fish and chips! OK, it wasn't battered, but it was still fish and chips, accompanied by a bit of rice and some carrots. Less said about that the better.

Post lunch we set off for the world famous Bardo Museum. It is one of the best archaeological museums in the world and has the best collection of mosaics in North Africa, and rivals anything in Rome itself.

The Bardo National Museum building was originally a 15th-century Hafsid palace, located in the suburbs of Tunis. The Bardo is one of the most important museums of the Mediterranean basin, and the second largest on the African continent after the Egyptian Museum.

It traces the history of Tunisia over several millennia and through many civilizations. The Bardo brings together one of the finest and largest collections of Roman mosaics in the world thanks to the excavations undertaken from the beginning of the 20th century on archaeological sites in the country including Carthage, Hadrumetum, Dougga, or Utica.

The mosaics represent a unique source for research on everyday life in Roman Africa. The museum also contains a rich collection of marble statues representing the gods and Roman emperors found on various sites including those of Carthage and Thuburbo Majus.

Apart from the amazing Roman mosaics and some treasures from Pre-Roman Carthage, including the enormous altar, it also had a collection of Byzantine mosaics. To see the two styles together was quite embarrassing really and goes to show how culture and craftsmanship nosedived after the onset of Christianity. Whereas the Roman gods and wild beasts are realistic, the Byzantine ones are no more than bad caricatures and cartoon like.

But the most striking monument in the Bardo is the memorial to those who lost their lives here in 2015. On 18 March 2015, 24 people were killed in a terrorist attack when three terrorists in civil uniform attacked the Bardo National Museum in the Tunisian capital city of Tunis and took hostages. Twenty-one people, mostly European tourists, were killed at the scene, while an additional victim died ten days later. Around fifty others were injured. This attack took place after the famous Charlie Hebdo attack in Paris where many journalists were killed Two of the gunmen, Tunisian citizens Yassine Labidi and Saber Khachnaoui, were killed by police, while the third attacker is currently at large. Police treated the event as a terrorist attack. It was the deadliest terrorist attack in Tunisian history.

A monument stands in the foyer with the names of the dead engraved and the flags of their nationalities draped over it. Two bullet holes have been left in the wall as a reminder.
This monument was quite poignant, and despite the spectacular mosaics, which are the best I have ever seen, this is the memory that will stay with me.

The final stop of the day was the Medina and centre of Tunis. We walked through the maze that is the Souk, thankfully the shops were shut on Sunday, and at least, within the confines of the city walls, Tunis felt a little more like Cairo or Istanbul and was dominated by the impressive tower of The Great El Zituna Mosque, built in 703 AD. But at the end of the day, if Cairo was London and Istanbul was Paris, Tunis would probably be Slough. It wants an identity, but it can't seem to find one.

One thing that was interesting in the Medina was the site of the former British Embassy which was one of the very first diplomatic embassies ever set up in Africa. In fact, it dates back to Charles the 2nd in 1662.

Two

Colditz

Having eaten too much at the dinner buffet the previous night, I decided to skip breakfast and head straight for the coach which left at 8am. I did notice however; a whole new bunch of broken noses had checked in to the hotel and hoped that this was not going to be the case in every hotel we visited in Tunisia.

Equally strange was the fact that Mohammad, our guide, was still wearing the thick, dark, long coat he had been wearing the previous day. It had been a bit breezy the day before and as a result, nobody really took any notice, but today was warm, very warm and he still wore the coat, even whilst sitting on the bus.

After the inevitable circum navigation of Lake Tunis, we hit the road west. Our destination? Well, anybody's guess was as good as each other, as this day was the filler day of all filler days. It was a Monday. All ancient sites shut on a Monday. And to top things off, it was Martyrs Day, Tunisian Bank Holiday, commemorating the events of 1952 and 1956 when Tunisian soldiers were killed liberating their country from French colonial rule.

As we left Tunis and drove in to the hilly, green countryside, there were numerous Roman remains, mostly part of the Zaghouan Aqueduct. Also known as the aqueduct of Hadrian, and built around 130 AD, the Zaghouan Aqueduct was constructed as a response to several years of drought which had hit the area.

The town of Zaghouan in northeastern Tunisia lies on the northern slope of Mount Zaghouan at an elevation of 4,249 feet. It was built on the ancient Roman site of Zigus. The Roman aqueduct and canal network built in the 2nd century BC under the emperor Hadrian was used to bring water more than 80 miles from Zaghouan to Carthage.

Zaghouan Aqueduct is one of the best-preserved Roman aqueducts among the hundreds built throughout Europe and North Africa. Over the centuries, the aqueducts endured attack and abandonment followed by restoration and revaluation. The two destructive attacks were that of the Vandals in the 5th century and that of the Hilalians in the 13th century.

The aqueduct continued to function until at least the end of the Vandals (536 AD). It is believed that during the Byzantine period, which was marked by frequent political unrest and insecurity in the rural areas, the aqueduct began to deteriorate, though without going completely out of service.

More than six centuries later, Sultan Hafsid, gave new life to the aqueduct by making the necessary refurbishment from 1250 to 1267, to link it with the new construction, at the Kasbah of Tunis which run through the gardens of Ras-al-Tabia, of Bardo and Rabta. The aqueduct was partially restored in the 19th century but today lies mostly in ruins. Some of the best remains can be found about 3km south of the village of Mohammedia.

I had my preconceptions of what Tunisia would be like, but the Northern part at least, is reminiscent of the South Downs. Lots of rolling green hills, sheep and cows grazing and crops in the fields. It seems a million miles away from Egypt. The roads are good, the streets are clean and there are no beggars or vagrants on the streets.

Our first stop of the day was the small town of Beja. Well actually it was at a Starbucks situated outside of the town, A welcome cup of coffee, but most of us agreed we would rather have stopped in the actual town and gone to a local café. This was about to get quite bizarre. We were only halfway through our coffees when Mohammad received a phone call and we were all bundled back on the bus and shipped to the Beja's main Square, le Place du 7th Novembre.

It started quite normally. We entered the Medina and walked through the open fruit market, watching the hustle and bustle of everyday life. As you do, I had read up a bit about the town before coming here and it had sounded remotely interesting. It boasted one of the oldest mosques in Tunisia, dating back to the 10th Century, and built atop of a Roman Temple. There were ruins of an Arabic Palace and on the outskirts of the town was a Commonwealth War Cemetery from World War Two. More than enough to keep us amused for an hour or so,

As we strolled through the fruit and veg, Mohammad received a phone call and a worried look descended upon his face. Out of nowhere, an armed policeman joined the tour, and we were marched away from the main street into a labyrinth of back alleys. Rightly so, the authorities are paranoid about tourists being here again, and there was a notable police presence everywhere we went. Credit where it was due, Mohammad didn't flinch and continued his tour as if nothing was wrong.

By this time, we had all concluded that he wore his coat all the time because he had a massive firearm hidden in the inside pocket. The problem for Mohammad was that the back streets of Beja are very boring and there was not much he could point out. The highlight was when we stumbled across some old woman making homemade bread and we were all piled in to watch as though this was something we would never see again. After receiving another phone call, we were marched back to the main Square, thrown back on the bus, and hot wheeled out of Beja, all scratching our heads as to what had actually just happened.

From here we continued driving west towards Tabarka, making a short stop at an Allied cemetery from World War 2. In May 1943, the war in North Africa came to an end in Tunisia with the defeat of the Axis powers by a combined Allied force.

On 8 November 1942, Commonwealth and American troops made a series of landings in Algeria and Morocco. The Germans responded immediately by sending a force from Sicily to northern Tunisia, which checked the Allied advance east in early December. Tabarka was just behind the limit of the advance that winter. Tabarka Ras Rajel War Cemetery contains 500 Commonwealth, mainly British, burials of the Second World War. The visit here was quite moving, and we spent a good half hour contemplating what had gone on here and the futility of it all.

In about an hour we rolled into the small seaside town of Tabarka. This was our lunch stop and once again we were promised a traditional Tunisian feast. Once again, we got fish and chips. This time however, it was accompanied by a brick. Or more properly spelled, a briq. The was effectively a runny fried egg, deep fried in batter that once you sank your teeth into it, exploded with molten oil and egg yolk down the front of your shirt. There were numerous accidents because of this.

Post lunch, we were given an hour to wander around the town. Not particularly because there was much to see, but basically because we couldn't check in to our hotel until later in the afternoon. In all fairness, Tabarka was quite pretty. It has a Genoese fort overlooking the harbour and its own version of the needles, like the Isle of Wight. We had an hour to wander around, which was probably 45 minutes too much.

The town was pretty much deserted. There was a small, tacky theme park based on Disney characters, a little marina, full of quite expensive yachts and more restaurants, presumably all selling fish and chips. The town seemed to have one supermarket and six ironmongers which a number of the tour party decided were interesting enough to investigate but having never been a connoisseur of ironmongery, I plumbed for a walk along the coast.

Tabarka had been a Roman Colony and served as a port where marble was shipped to build the monuments of Rome. A small rebellion against the Empire occurred here at the end of the 4th Century and apart from The Vandals building a monastery here, and the Genoese building the massive fortress, overlooking the bay, purely to protect their coral fishing interests, nothing of note has ever really happened here. Coral Fishing is still the major industry here, along with cork, which is obtained from the surrounding forests.

The fortress, dating back to 1541, was really impressive, but was a good 20-minute walk in either direction and nobody could actually guarantee whether it was open to the public. Therefore, we decided that it was best to simply admire the view from the harbour and move on.

The area known as Les Aiguilles is a group of spiky pinnacles of rock, vaguely similar to the Needles in the Isle of Wight. An undercliff walk, stretching four miles, has been cut through the formations, which made a pleasant stroll for thirty minutes, albeit it only really needed ten.

One slowly paced ice cream later we all rushed back to the bus only to find the driver sound asleep. I was quite annoyed that this option had not been available for the rest of us quite frankly.
With locals in swimsuits running around, Mohammad made his way back to the bus in his thick black coat and finally we were allowed to move on.

Our hotel for the night was in a small village called Hamman Bourguiba, a small village in the mountains that boasts natural thermal springs and was Roman Tunisia's answer to Bath in Roman Britain. Unfortunately, the Roman baths complex has never been excavated, therefore, as was the case for the rest of the day, there seemed little reason to go there.

As we snaked our way through the tree lined mountain switchbacks, a small side road appeared on the right-hand side. This was the border crossing with Algeria, a place that has been very heavily guarded for several years due to the terrorism issue and that Western Tourists are strongly advised to avoid.

As we reached the top of the hill we were driving up, we could see a rather large, Soviet style building, sitting atop a smaller hill ahead of us. It was almost Colditz like, but this was The El Mouradi Hamman Bourguiba, our hotel for the night.

Obviously on tours such as these, you know which hotels you are booked into and can read what other people had written about the place. The reviews of this hotel were, to say the least, not overly hopeful.

One not so happy camper had written "We felt as though we were in a sanatorium rather than a hotel. This is, without a doubt, the most bizarre hotel we've ever stayed in. We felt unwelcome and out of place in this institutional type of facility. It had the aura of a rehabilitation centre. The 'spa' pool was nothing more than a physical therapy pool. The food was dreadful. Do not stay here. *

Whilst another complained: - "Stayed with my wife for 1 night in November (yes, it's out of season) during a Voyages Jules Verne Tunisia tour. A/C didn't work. Told it was only 'on' in summer and turned off for the winter. Not good during a winter heatwave. Staff not very helpful. Restaurant buffet can only be described as diabolical. Again, to be fair, it was out of season. Very limited selection, unwashed fruit (grapes to be specific), overcooked turkey and lamb along with undercooked bloody chicken for dinner. No bread or tea for breakfast, just coffee (not hot) boiled eggs, cheese, liver sausage and dubious croissant and pastries was it.

Rooms tired and in need of refurbishment. Would plan to avoid this hotel if I ever go back to that region. Tunisia 4 stars rating wouldn't get any stars elsewhere in the world."

They were not far from the truth. From the outside it didn't look too bad. It was surrounded by sports facilities, I was informed that football teams had preseason camps here, and the entrance was quite impressive, albeit full of large Tunisian women walking very slowly.

The full horrors were to be revealed later. The basic room I had, had no duvet but a basic, grey, prison issue blanket and rather unclean sheets. There were electric plugs, but these had bare wires hanging out of the walls. For a hotel in the mountains covered in green forest, I had hoped for a better view than a brick wall, two feet outside of my window. It wasn't the brightest of rooms. I understand that this was not a one off case.

The buffet dinner was probably the most disgusting ever, but thankfully the hordes of old women and their accompanying families had seen most of this off before we could get close. I think dinner was a bowl of watery soup and a stale piece of French Bread.
To cap this off, a group of us endeavoured to retire to the lounge bar to have a beer, only to find that as it was Martyrs Day, the hotel had hired a local band, and the locals were dancing around and clapping, albeit very gingerly, the ensuing racket.

As was the case in Tunis, this was an El Mouradi hotel and it was fast becoming clear that El Mouradi was Tunisian for National Health service. Unlike the plastic surgery bonanza that we had unearthed in Tunis, Hamman Bourguiba was the place for overweight elderly ladies with mobility issues. All being sent to bathe in the Thermal springs.

I can report that traditional Tunisian music was not my cup of tea, nor was it very musical. But as it was Martyrs Day, I didn't want to complain in fear of adding any more martyrs to the list. So, it was back up to my room in the rickety old lift for a night shivering under my prison blanket. I could have warmed up by plugging in an appliance to the dangling electrical socket but decided that Tunisia must have more to offer than this and went to sleep.
Thankfully everything reopened the next day. I was hopeful we may even see something.

Three

The Troglodytes of Bulla Regia

The day didn't start too well as breakfast at Colditz was about as good as could be expected. I had been woken up a few times by a scratching sound and wasn't sure if it was mice or people digging a tunnel to escape. The breakfast buffet was limited to say the least. I put two stone cold poached eggs on my plate but gave up when I tried to dunk my rock hard baguette in the yolk and it literally bounced off. I think it was fair to say we were all glad to leave.

As we passed the Algerian border again, we drove through a small town called Ain Draham which is to the French Empire, what Shimla was to the British Raj. A hill station where the colonial rulers would escape the summer heat and move to the mountains for cooler air. Our guide implied that the French tried to recreate an Alpine village in Tunisia and that in Winter, it did actually snow here. That took a lot of imagination to see in the height of Summer.

A 2-hour drive got us to the ruins of the Roman town of Bulla Regia. Famed for its extraordinary underground villas, the Roman city of Bulla Regia offers a rare opportunity to walk into complete, superbly preserved Roman rooms rather than having to extrapolate how things once looked from waist-high walls. To escape the summer heat, locals retreated below the surface, building elegant homes complete with colonnaded courtyards and internal plumbing. Many of their fine mosaics remain in situ, though some of the best are now in the Bardo Museum in Tunis.

Bulla emerged in about the 5th century BC under Carthage. The 'Regia' (royal) was added later when it became the capital of one of the short-lived Numidian kingdoms tolerated by Rome following the destruction of Carthage.

Bulla Regia truly flourished under Roman rule, particularly in the 2nd and 3rd centuries AD, as its citizens grew rich on wheat; most of the site's buildings date from that era. In fact, it got a reputation for being quite a rowdy town as when Saint Augustine visited in 4th Century, he left in disgust due to the town being full of what he described as theatrical types and loose women.

The colossal Memmian Baths that overlook the entrance were named after Julia Memmia, wife of Emperor Septimius Severus. The most extensive of the site's above-ground structures, its rooms are surrounded by arched service areas – a reminder of the slaves who kept the waters hot and Roman backs scrubbed.

Walking northwards, following the signs to the Quartier des Maisons (villas quarter), takes you to the city's wealthiest residential neighbourhood. The villas – seven of which have been excavated – vary in their level of sophistication but are all built to the same basic plan, with a central courtyard open to the sky. As you descend into each, you'll feel a significant drop in temperature – just what the Romans intended.

The first home you come to is the small, subterranean House of Treasure (Maison du Trésor), named after a cache of Byzantine coins discovered here. The large dining room is decorated with a geometrically patterned mosaic; next door is a bedroom.

Continuing north, you pass two side-by-side, 6th-century Byzantine churches (basilique chrétienne), with some columns and a walk-in, cross-shaped baptismal font. North of here is the rather unloved-feeling, subterranean House of the Peacock, named after a mosaic, that's now in the Bardo.

Across the road is the truly impressive House of the Hunt (Maison de la Chasse), centred on an underground hall with eight ornate pillars; hexagonal holes at the top of each cleverly reduce the structure's weight.

Off the courtyard is a spacious mosaic-floored dining room, an indication of the lavish lifestyle once enjoyed here. Upstairs are some neat, side-by-side latrines, next to the building's private hammam – this place was state of the art.

Next door, an above-ground hunting mosaic has been left in situ at the House of the New Hunt (Maison de la Nouvelle Chasse). Large chunks are missing, but there's still plenty left to view, including an action-packed lion hunt. Underground is a five-column hall with a swirling geometric floor.

Taking the path east and then north to Bulla Regia's star attraction, the House of Amphitrite. The underground mosaic is exquisite – a perfectly preserved portrait of a nude Venus flanked by two centaurs, one shocked (having his hair tugged), the other quizzical. At the base are some lively cupids riding dolphins – one of them is checking himself out in a mirror at the same time. Leaping fish add to the vibrancy and balance of this masterpiece.

South of here is the spacious House of Fishing (Maison de la Pêche), the earliest of the villas. This place had a fountain in the basement; a small room contains a mosaic with a fishing theme.

Heading southeast, you pass on your left the spring that once supplied ancient Bulla Regia with water – and still delivers its cool waters to nearby Jendouba. There is a fine panorama from atop the nearby mound across the rolling hills.

Further on is the forum, surrounded by the ruins of two temples – the capitol, to the west; and, to the north, the Temple of Apollo, which yielded the truly godlike statue of Apollo now displayed at the Bardo.

Just south from here was the market, and a little further down is a small but beautifully preserved theatre with a large mosaic of a not-very-fierce bear, which Augustine would have stared at whilst chastising the locals. The front three tiers are extra wide and separated from the rest by the remains of a low wall – VIP seating.

Southwest are the remains of the small Temple of Isis, which honoured the Egyptian goddess, a fashionable addition to the Roman pantheon.

This really was a unique Roman site and well worth a couple of hours of our time, but as we had a lunch stop to get to, we were hoarded back on the coach and driven off. Another two-hour drive later we finally arrived for a somewhat late lunch!

We were promised another local delicacy. "It's going to be fish and chips again" we all thought. But for once it wasn't. We were promised wild boar. Now this was quite strange. Tunisia is an Islamic country and Muslims don't eat pork. As far as I was aware, a wild boar was still a pig. An undomesticated, hairy pig with tusks, but ultimately a pig. It turns out that in Northwest Tunisia, there is a bit of a problem with Boars, who eat farmers crops. As a result, the farmers shoot them and although wouldn't be seen dead eating it themselves, they are more than happy to feed them to the unclean tourists. Boar ragu with some rice sounded quite nice to me, but the reality was somewhat different. If Lidl did a boil in the bag boar dinner for one, this was it. Very bland and very tasteless.

Five minutes from our lunch stop was our second and main stop of the day. The Roman city of Dougga which is set against a stunning backdrop of lush green hills and fields full of livestock and crops. It could have been Wales.

Arguably the most magnificent Roman site in Africa, Dougga's ancient remains – a UNESCO World Heritage site since 1997 – are startlingly complete, giving a beguiling glimpse of how well-heeled Romans lived, flitting between bathhouses, the imposing Capitol, a 3500-seat theatre, and various temples. The city was built on the site of an ancient Numidian settlement called Thugga, which explains why the streets are so uncharacteristically tangled. The 2nd-century-BC Libyco-Punic Mausoleum is the country's finest pre-Roman monument.

A Roman city with a view, Dougga is set on an enchanting hillside surrounded by olive groves and overlooking fields of grain, with forested hills beyond. Built of yellowish-tan stone, its mellow tones meld harmoniously with the brown, tan, and dark-green landscape of the Kalled Valley and the Teboursouk Mountains.

Nestled into the hillside, the outstanding restored theatre, whose 19 tiers could accommodate an audience of 3500, was built in AD 168 by one of the city's wealthier residents, Marcius Quadratus. The nosebleed seats have spectacular views of the encircling valleys. Today, the theatre serves as a superb setting for listening to North African music during the month-long Dougga Festival, usually held in July or August.

North of the theatre, the ruins of the Vandal Church of Victoria are the only evidence of Christianity at Dougga. The church was built in the early 5th century using stone taken from the surrounding temples. The small crypt next door is packed with large stone sarcophagi.

A bit further north stands the Temple of Saturn, which must have been a magnificent sight after its completion in AD 195, but today only six stunted columns remain. Built on a platform facing east over the valley of Oued (River) Kalled, it dominated the ancient city's northern approach. The structure stands on the site of an earlier temple to Baal Hammon, the chief Punic deity, who was reinterpreted as Saturn in Roman times and was the favoured god of Roman Africa.

Nearby, the so-called Numidian Wall protected the city in pre-Roman days. At the wall's southern end, the reconstructed apse next to the Temple of Saturn is all that remains of the Sanctuary of Neptune. Dozens of primitive dolmen graves, the oldest structures at Dougga, dot the northwestern edge of the Numidian Wall.

From the Sanctuary of Neptune, a rough path takes you to the nine Cisterns of Ain Mizeb. The city's main water supply was fed by a spring some 200m to the west and remained in excellent condition.

A dirt route leads northwest where you can glimpse the underwhelming remains of the Temple of Minerva. Looking northwest from here, it's possible to discern the outline of the circus, once the staging grounds for chariot races and now an elongated wheat field filling a saddle between two hills.

A path runs south of the cisterns to the cavernous but not as well preserved Cisterns of Ain El Hammam, added during the reign of Commodus (AD 177–192) to meet the city's growing demand for water. They were supplied via an aqueduct, sections of which are visible among the olive trees west of the cisterns, fed by springs 12km to the southwest.

Immediately east is the Arch of Alexander Severus, dedicated to the emperor who ruled between AD 222 and 235. The arch was built around this time, and it marks the city's western entrance.

A path leads southwest from here through olive trees to the Temple of Juno-Caelestis (Heavenly Juno), dedicated to the Roman version of the Carthaginian god Tanit. Funded by a resident made a flamen (a Roman priest) in AD 222, it was adapted as a church in the 5th century. The pillar-surrounded sanctuary retains an impressive portico, reached via a flight of steps.

Passing under the Arch of Alexander Severus towards the town's most impressive feature, the imposing Capitol, built in AD 166. In remarkable condition, it has 10m-high walls and six mighty, one-piece fluted columns – each 8m high – supporting the portico. The massive walls are the finest known example of a construction technique called opus africanum, which uses large stones to strengthen walls built of small stones and rubble.

In the temple's inner sanctum are three large niches in the north wall, which once housed a giant statue of the Roman god Jupiter flanked by smaller statues of Juno and Minerva. The carved frieze shows the emperor Antonius Pius being carried off in an eagle's claws, with an inscription dedicating the temple to the three gods. The Byzantines were responsible for the fortifications that enclose the Capitol and the forum, built on the orders of General Solomon, and constructed using stones filched from surrounding buildings.

The nearby Square of the Winds is surrounded by temples and named after the large circular engraving listing the names of the 12 winds.

You can make out some of the names, including Africanus, the name of the south westerly hot desert air. The meagre remains of the Temple of Mercury are to the north of the square. To the east are four square pillars belonging to the tiny 2nd-century Temple of Augustine Piety.

Below the forum is a grand neighbourhood of homes and bathhouses. An unusual solid square doorframe marks the entrance to an unidentified temple referred to as Dar El Echab, after the family that once occupied the site. On the left, sandwiched between the ruins of two houses is the Temple of Tellus, where a once-colonnaded courtyard leads into a sanctuary with stone niches set into the back wall.

Following the road as it winds southeast you get to the 3rd-century Licinian Baths. Entering the complex through the vaulted passage originally built for the slaves who kept the baths operating, a reminder of how the good life enjoyed by the Roman elite was maintained. The walls of this extensive complex – an indication of the town's prosperity – remain largely intact, especially those surrounding the grand frigidarium (cold room). A small tepidarium (warm room) and caldarium (hot room) branch off from the frigidarium. The large room with columns was the palaestra, an area used as a gym.

Continuing along the road for another 75m and descending some steps, you come to the House of Trifolium, a huge complex that must have had seriously wealthy owners. It's now been incorrectly dubbed as the 'brothel of Dougga' because a relief of a phallus can be spotted in the street leading to the house, but these symbols were used to protect against bad luck, not to signpost the red-light district. In typical architecture of the region, a central courtyard is surrounded by several rooms, one of which has had its roof restored and is shaped like a clover leaf, giving the house its name.

Next door are the Baths of the Cyclops, named after the remarkable mosaic found here (now in the Dougga room at the Bardo Museum in Tunis). The baths themselves are in disrepair, except for the sociably horseshoe-shaped row of 12 latrines just inside the entrance.

Along the path to the west is the Nymphaeum, a huge, partly restored fountain, thought to have been supplied with water by an underground conduit from the Cisterns of Ain El Hammam. The Ain Doura Baths (also called the southern baths) are further along still. Some geometric floor mosaics remain in place, but the structure isn't as grand as the Licinian Baths.

Near the Baths of the Cyclops are the ruins of the Arch of Septimius Severus, which unfortunately no longer retains the shape in its name. It was built in AD 205 when the city was promoted to the status of municipe (a city in the Roman Empire that was allowed to govern itself and whose inhabitants benefited from Roman citizenship).

On the southerly path below the remains of the arch is the Libyco-Punic Mausoleum. This triple-tiered, obelisk-shaped monument, an amazing 21m high, is crowned by a small pyramid with a seated lion at the pinnacle.

It was built during the reign of Massinissa at the beginning of the 2nd century BC and is dedicated, according to a bilingual (Libyan and Punic) inscription, to 'Ateban, son of Ypmatat, son of Palu'. The inscription, which once occupied the vacant window at the base, was removed by the British consul to Tunis in 1842, who, as British consuls of the time were often seen to do, destroyed the whole monument in the process. The stone was taken to England (it's now in the British Museum in London), and the monument itself was rebuilt by French archaeologists in 1910.

It was late afternoon before we left Dougga and a good three hours to our hotel in the coastal resort of Hammamet, some 60km South of Tunis. In fact, we had to traverse Lake Tunis again, which sort of made some of us question as to why we had to travel all the way to Tabarka the previous day.

We were staying in Hammamet for a couple of nights and for once the hotel was not in the El Mouradi chain and was excellent. A wonderful buffet spread for dinner and a relaxing bar for a few beers afterwards, it's just a shame all they had was Heineken.

Four

The Colour Purple

The difference between the cold, rubbery fried eggs of Colditz to the expansive breakfast spread at our Hammamet hotel was as vast as it could possibly be. And despite enjoying it a little too much, I still managed for a quick wander down to the beach before it was time to board the coach for the day's sightseeing. Hammamet is one of several beach resorts, that prior to the terrorist attacks of 2015 were full of European tourists. Today the beaches were empty, but I hoped that one day the madness in the world would calm down enough for more people to return and give the country a much needed boost. The security around tourists here, although understandable, was pretty stifling. Although we were staying in a beach resort, my attempt to access the beach ended in me being turned away by a man with a large gun. It seemed extreme.

Today we were exploring the northwest corner of Tunisia which is known as Cape Bon. Pointing northwards towards Sicily, the Cap Bon region is a vast garden where orange and lemon trees put out their flowers in the middle of winter. Its beaches of fine sand are among the most beautiful in Tunisia. As we headed north, we could see hundreds of bright pink flamingos standing in the coastal wetlands.

Towns seemed very few and far between and the cape is almost a small wilderness of coastal sand dunes and inland lakes.
The main purpose of our trip to the northern tip of Tunisia was to visit Kerkouane. Set on a turquoise curve of prime coastal real estate, and atop a carpet of multi coloured wildflowers, the UNESCO-listed Punic settlement of Kerkouane is the world's best-preserved example of a Carthaginian city.

Abandoned during the First Punic War, the town was never reoccupied by the invading Romans, so its chequer-board network of streets, houses and workshops remains as it was around 250 BC. Kerkouane' s houses are best known for their pink-red baths where residents soaked in private, a major difference to the opulent Roman public baths found elsewhere around Tunisia.

Kerkouane was a well-planned town protected by double fortifications, but little is known of the settlement's history, not even its original name; Kerkouane was the surname of one of the French archaeologists who stumbled on the site in 1952. The oldest remains date to the early 6th century BC, but most are from the 4th to 3rd centuries BC.

The town was home to an urban, sea-view-loving elite of merchants and craftsmen. It had around 300 houses and 2000 inhabitants. Excavations have uncovered pottery workshops and kilns, though Kerkouane's main business was producing the Phoenicians' favourite colour: a dye known as Tyrian purple (named after their first capital, Tyre in modern-day Lebanon) that was extracted from sea snails. It is said that this was one of the main reasons for The Roman invasion. They industrialised the production of the purple dye and it became synonymous with the robes of the Roman Emperor and to this day, The Roman Pope.

There is a small museum, which has a collection of pottery, jewelry, statues and everyday objects from the site. Imported Greek, Italian and Egyptian artefacts indicate the residents' wealth and sophistication, as well as their overtly cosmopolitan tastes.
The houses are Kerkouane's main attraction, particularly those of the wealthy northeastern quarter, with some wonderful examples of opus signinum flooring (scatter-pattern pink-and-white mosaic).

A short walk into the site is the House of Tanit, which features a simple white Tanit sign (representing the Punic goddess) set into the floor, used as a protective symbol to ward off bad luck, similar to the hand-shaped hamsa seen on doors in Tunisia today.

Further along the street is the town's finest address: a house with a peristyle (colonnaded) courtyard and an impressive bath, with a seat and armrests, decorated with white mosaic – the bather possibly even had a sea view.

The town also had public baths, but unlike Roman bathhouses, these are small-scale and functional. They were probably used by local artisans, and are near the temple, so may have been used to wash up pre-worship.

The remains of the principal temple are west of the public baths and further along is the Priest's House. In its centre, protected within a small room, is a circular bread oven, like the tabounas still used in modern Tunisia that we had seen in use in Beja.

It was a fascinating site, but ultimately, there was little left and many of the group, not that fussed with archaeology, were getting a little restless.

The further north we drove, the worse the roads became. There had been bad floods in the area during the previous winter and the roads, although being repaired, were still washed away in places, which caused a few issues for a large coach.

From here we went to a restaurant on the beach which was quite pleasant, but it was back to fish and chips again with a slightly less runny brique than we had in Tabarka, before driving ten minutes to Ras ben Sakka, the most northerly point of the African continent. Rather underwhelming to be honest, with nothing more than a car park. John O'Groats is fairly bleak, but this made that look commercialised. A ten-minute photo stop here was far too long. If Mohammad didn't smoke, it would have been two or three minutes at most.

It was another three-hour bus ride back down the western side of the Cape, which was nowhere near as scenic nor as interesting as the Eastern side. As we had a bit of spare time, we stopped off in the town centre of Hammamet and spent some time wandering through the old medina, which was quite fascinating, with it having its original battlements dating back to the 9th Century.

Early planning constraints dictated that hotels should not overreach the height of a tree, meaning that Hammamet' s buildings sprawl horizontally, a far cry from the brutal high-rise developments that have scarred so many other Mediterranean coasts.

Hammamet is small-scale and suitably relaxed. The town's centre is packed with restaurants and shops, overlooked by its towering fort and medina walls.

The Medina is in the old town of Hammamet. It can make you believe that Hammamet is still a small fishing village rather that the tourist resort full of beach hotels that it has become. There are narrow, bustling alleyways, a hubbub of voices, time-honoured buildings, colourful markets smelling of spices and mint tea. Similar to what we had seen in Sidi Bou Said the buildings were blue and white. The Souk is an explosion of colour and smells. The contrast of turquoise ornaments, colourful flowers and overpowering spices. The prominent building within the medina is the Great Mosque of Hammamet. It was completed in the 15th century after centuries of construction and renovated in the 1970s. Just outside of the Medina walls is the Kasbah. For centuries, the Kasbah was the city fortress of today's Hammamet. The impressively thick fortress walls withstood many attacks, even from pirates. It completely encloses the medina and can be walked around. We had a coffee in a café on the Kasbah walls and took in the view of the sea and miles upon miles of sandy beach.

I had hoped that I could persuade Mohammad to take us to Hammamet's premier attraction, Carthageland. It is Tunisia's first, and maybe only, theme park, and according to the leaflets, you could recreate the Punic Wars in bumper cars. I couldn't understand why nobody else wanted to do that. I even offered to allow them to be the Romans. Most disappointing.

From here, it was back to the hotel for another amazing spread, a few more beers and a good night's sleep in the knowledge that we were back to El Mouradi hotels for the next few nights.

The following morning was an early start and a 500km drive South. Despite this, we still had to go North a circum navigate Lake Tunis again, before finding the road towards the Sahara region of the country. All in all, it was eight hours on a coach with only one stop, which was only one hour out of Tunis. But it was worth it. Surrounded by shimmering wheat fields and olive groves like those that made its fortune, Thuburbo Majus has a prosperous air even in its ruinous state. In the 2nd century, this Roman colony for war veterans had 10,000 inhabitants, the wealthiest of whom tried to outdo each other by donating public buildings and fine mosaics; many of the latter are now in Tunis' Bardo Museum. Its appealing Capitol, with four full-length fluted Corinthian columns, dominates the site.

It was tempting to make a dash straight for the grand Capital, but first we took a look at the Byzantine House of the Oil Press. In the cellar, you can clearly see a massive circular press made from stone that drained into what used to be a Roman-era bathing pool.

On a platform looming over the surrounding residential ruins is the unmissable Capital, with four giant reconstructed pillars of veined pink marble marking the entrance to the temple, which honours the Capitoline Triad: Jupiter, the king of the gods; Juno, his wife; and their daughter Minerva, the goddess of wisdom. Built in AD 168, it is reached by a wide flight of stairs leading up from the forum (AD 161–2), which is colonnaded on three sides. A giant sandaled foot and head of an enormous statue of Jupiter, estimated to have stood 7.5m high, were found here.

The Temple of Peace, northeast of the forum, holds a few stone bas-reliefs, including one of Pegasus.

On the southwestern side of the forum, the unusual Temple of Mercury, with a circular design, was dedicated to the god of merchants and overlooks the market. The market stalls can be discerned on three sides of the courtyard below the temple. Directly behind the market is a very un-Roman tangle of residential streets, obviously laid out before their arrival. Beyond is the spacious House of Neptune, with some impressive geometric-patterned mosaics.

To the east are the wonderful porticoes of the Palaestra of the Petronii, named after the family of Petronius Felix, who paid for the construction of this gymnasium complex in AD 225. It was surrounded by Corinthian columns made of an unusual, yellow-veined grey marble; one row remains standing (supported by scaffolding), still holding aloft a Latin inscription. In the southeastern corner, some letters are carved into the floor, part of a game used to learn the alphabet.

Conveniently placed next to the palaestra for a post-gym wash is the huge summer Baths complex, which covers 2800 sq. metres. Although larger, they aren't as well preserved as the Winter Baths, 150m to the east, which have a grand entrance flanked by pockmarked, veined marble columns.

Both were full of mosaics – the finest are now on display in the Bardo, though some geometric patterns can still be seen in situ. About 50m south of the Winter Baths, the Sanctuary of Baal is a small square temple that's easily identified by the two yellow-veined grey pillars atop its steps. It was dedicated to the Punic god Baal Hammon, whose cult survived (in Romanised form) long after the fall of Carthage.

The adjacent Sanctuary of Caelestis, reached through a freestanding yellow-stone arch, was for another adapted god – this time the Roman version of the Punic goddess Tanit, the wife of Baal Hammon. The temple was later converted into a Byzantine church, traces of which can still be seen.

A rough path leads southeast from the Sanctuary of Baal towards the ruins of massive, arched cisterns set into the hill that once supplied the town with water. The mound beyond the cisterns marks the site of a small amphitheatre, which has not been fully excavated. The Roman version of recycling is obvious here: stones with unrelated Latin inscriptions have been turned upside down to help shore up the base of the structure. Another rough path through prickly plants leads north from here to a low hill topped by the remains of the Temple of Saturn, though not much has been uncovered.

After an hour we were shuttled back on the bus for the rest of the long journey south. A couple of hours later, the rolling green hills were replaced by desert scrub. It was quite surreal how the landscape changed yesterday from green and fertile to desolation in under twenty miles. I was hoping that there were some scenic parts of the desert, as from what I saw out of the bus window, it was full of plastic bags, burnt out cars and old electrical appliances. Nobody seems to care about fly tipping here and nobody seems to be bothered to clear it up.

So, with the lack of things to admire out of the window, talk on the bus turned to our hotel in Tozeur and more shocking reviews had come to light.

The most worrying read as follows: - "These people should be prosecuted for claiming 4* rating for this hotel. It was a shambles.

The dining room - well I've never experienced anything so hideous in my decades of travelling, not even in full capacity ferries or cruise ships. The dining room was swarming and held hostage to a gang of very rude, badly behaved minors who were unsupervised and were pushing and shoving everyone and barging into queues. The staff did nothing whatsoever to try and direct guests, help older people with lots to carry etc., just the usual Tunisian damp squid expression and the propensity to blame everyone else, even the guests.

The whole thing was insane. To see/access the food selection you have to queue ALL the way so 48 minutes later I got to the end of the queue (remember constantly being shoved and having food dripped over me as others were grabbing mounds of food over people's heads) only to find a solitary table with no cover on it, a broken chair and not a single person around to bring a bottle of water.

So, I took the plate of disgusting, congealed food into the Director and asked if he'd like to eat it, explained the horrors of the dining room, and got the usual indifferent, sneery Tunisian hotel trade attitude if you dare to criticise. I just love the line "oh but we're very busy" YES that's what hotels are meant for - to be full of lots of people!!

The best moment was checking out. Don't go. It's awful.
Also, I've no idea what the hype about Tozeur was all about either... the town centre is dirty and has nothing there. Cafes are disgusting and toilet facilities enough to make you vomit. General landscape nothing special. "

Well, what could possibly go wrong?

We arrived late in the afternoon, and to be fair the hotel entrance was quite impressive. Having said that, the other Al Mouradi Hotels had impressive foyers. There were quite a few locals in swimming trunks or with bath robes floating around but they didn't look as unhealthy as the ones at Colditz.

To be fair, the room wasn't too bad, and the food was OK, nothing special, but OK. It seemed as though this was a spa centre and there were a team of masseurs working there. One of our group plucked up enough courage for a massage and supposedly it was quite relaxing. I preferred to relax over a cold beer.
I had read that Tozeur was infamous for an illicit date liquor that is sold in brown paper bags around the oasis. As we were supposed to go for a walk there the following morning, it would be wrong not to try it.

Five

The Empire Strikes Back

Tozeur is a world apart from coastal Tunisian resorts such as Sousse and Hammamet, with a medina (old town) full of unique brick-pattern architecture and a rambling palm grove that slices a sea of green through the desert sand.

The plan today was to explore the centre of Tozeur in the morning and then some of us had opted to take 4 x 4 vehicles out to the desert in the afternoon. Unfortunately, there had been an incident at The Oasis overnight and as a result, date wine was off the menu for the time being.

The first stop of the day was only a few hundred yards from the hotel and, for the life of me, I don't know why we needed to take the bus there. The authorities really are that paranoid. The Dar Chraiet Museum Housed in the Koubba of Sidi Bou Aissa is Tozeur's small Folk Museum (Musée des Arts et Traditions Populaires). It houses a series of exhibits and dioramas that explain the culture and day-to-day life of traditional Tozeur households. Some of the dioramas themselves are a tad scruffy, but the artisan work on display within them is finely crafted. There are also rather eclectic collections of Roman columns and fragments of statues on display, as well as local craft products, furnishings, coins, pottery, jewelry, wedding costumes, and Qur'anic inscriptions.

To be honest, the actual building was very pleasant and had many shady areas in the many courtyards that proved pleasant relief from the scorching Saharan sun. The Museum wasn't that fascinating, and the most memorable moment was the ice-cold drink that I managed to get from the gift shop.

We drove another four hundred yards before having to get out of the bus again. Mohammad, despite the temperatures being in the mid-thirties, still had his thick black coat on. We were now convinced he had a gun under there.

Tozeur's medina (old town) is the town's main point of interest. Known as Ouled Hadef, this is the most atmospheric part of Tozeur. Jumbles of higgledy-piggledy lanes ramble through the district, lined with traditional desert houses that sport beautiful decorative brick facades of intricate patterns.

The geometric brick designs of the houses are very similar to the age-old design motifs found on many Berber carpets. This Tozeur-style architecture is made from local kiln-fired clay or mud bricks and can also be found in neighbouring desert towns.

Frequently, the upper floors of the houses extend across the street to join with houses on the other side, forming covered-bridge passages between households and providing inhabitants with shelter from the harsh sun.

Tozeur must have been from time immemorial an important staging point on the caravan route from the Sahara to the northeastern Mediterranean coast. The town is first mentioned in Roman times under the name of Thuzuros as an important bastion in the defence of the southern frontier of the province of Africa. During the Christian period, Thuzuros continued to flourish. In the middle of the 7th century, the Arabs took the town after a long, hard struggle. Under Arab rule, Tozeur enjoyed a long period of peace during which, as the "gateway to the desert," it developed into a key staging point on the caravan routes. The town prospered and became an important point on the North African slave trade, with a large slave market here. Many of the town's present-day inhabitants are the descendants of these black slaves (the Haratin).

The heyday of the town was in the 14th century when it is believed to have had three times its present population. Its wealth, however, made it the target of increasingly frequent raids by the nomads and of oppressive taxation by the Ottoman authorities who then controlled Tunisia.

As a result, economic decline began in the 15th century, and in the following century, it was visited by a devastating epidemic of cholera during which half the population died. Thus, when the French took Tozeur in 1881 without a fight, it was an insignificant little oasis town. Thereafter, it was developed along modern, European lines, though retaining its traditional style of brick architecture.

Once inside the Medina walls, we headed straight for a gift shop, although the real reason we went in there was to go to the rooftop, where you could see across the whole Medina with its flat roofs interspersed with palm trees and to the new town and towering minaret of the mosque. It was quite fascinating and despite everything being a sandy brown colour, quite beautiful in its way.

I think one of the most enjoyable and unexpected moments of the whole trip was in Tozeur Medina. As we walked through the maze of alleyways, we stopped at a normal looking house with a courtyard and were invited to go to a small upstairs room which was full of Roman and Islamic artefacts. The woman who lived there was a keen amateur archaeologist and had dedicated three rooms in her home to become the unofficial archaeological museum of Tozeur. I thought this was a brilliant idea and she charged a small entrance fee and made a small income out of her hobby. It was certainly an improvement on the tacky gift shops or carpet and leather goods sellers.

Exiting out of the Medina, through an ornately decorated gatehouse, we found ourselves in modern day Tozeur. It was still full of carpet shops and leather goods but was worth twenty minutes walking up the main street. Dominating the street was the towering minaret of the great mosque built in 1030.

Some people in the group were complaining about the lack of European goods in the shops, so Mohammad took us to a large French supermarket on the outskirts of town. I hate to say that this was enjoyable, but I actually quite like going around foreign supermarkets to see what people actually eat. I also managed to buy a big bag of fresh harissa Chili to take home with me,
It was back to the hotel for lunch and then around half of the group were brave enough to venture out into the desert in 4 x 4 vehicles, which was a brilliant experience. As we drove out of Tozeur towards the desert you really could not experience the true bleakness of the desert landscape. After about twenty miles though we turned off the main road and what little green scrub there had been slowly began to disappear, to be replaced by sand dunes and what appeared to be tiny little jewels, glistening in the sand. These were of course salt granules and the further we drove along, the more of them there were, resulting in a shimmering salt lake.

We got out of the land rovers at a place called Ong Jamal, which is roughly translated as Camel's Neck. A large rock, protruding over the desert is claimed to look like a camel, but they must have a stronger imagination than I do. The salt lake named Chott El Gharsa, although not as large as the one we would cross the following day, shimmered as far as the eye could see and was backdropped by the imposing Atlas Mountains, which stretched all the way through Tunisia into Algeria and then on to Morocco.

It had come to my attention that in order to move on from here, the land rovers had to descend a sixty-foot sand dune. Not something I would try in my car, but nevertheless we all shut our eyes and prayed the brakes were working OK.

Another half a mile down the road we stopped at what at first appeared to be a small village. However, in the village square, there seemed to be strange antennas and weird electrical devices. It was in fact a film set that was used for The Phantom Menace, one of the Star Wars Films, and I was told that Darth Vader had been born in one of these huts. To be honest, most of this went over my head. My sister took me to see the first Star Wars film in 1978 and I wasn't that impressed. I haven't seen any of the subsequent ones.

The strange devices were just made of plastic and the huts, although realistic from the outside, were papier mâché on the inside. The whole film set is being reclaimed by the desert. The sands are encroaching at a rate of twelve to fifteen feet per year but in the meantime, the authorities are making money out of it.

There was a small market here which sold desert roses, which are intricate rose like formations of crystal cluster of gypsum or baryte mixed with sand. They occur naturally in desert environments giving the rock a rose like formation. They can grow up to 4 inches wide and are quite beautiful. Less attractive was the trade in camel skulls, which seemed to be quite popular and whole market stalls were devoted to them. Not sure I needed one of those to hang on my door.

On the way back to Tozeur, we stopped briefly in the Roman Spring town of Nefta, where the natural spring is an oasis. Known locally as La Corbeille (The basket), a deep, palm-filled gully that takes up much of the northern part of town and cuts the town in two. It measures almost 1km across at its widest point and is about 40m deep. Originally there were 152 natural springs feeding the oasis but since 1980, these have begun to dry up. We viewed it from above, and despite many of the springs having dried up, there is still what you would call a picture perfect oasis in the desert. Bright blue water, surrounded by green palm trees and there were some bright magenta flowers too.

There was a walk you could take to stroll down the crater and then around the lake, but time did not allow this. Having declined a camel skull at Ong Jamal, it didn't take much to refuse what was offer on sale here. A lone stall was selling live animals in plastic containers, ranging from desert foxes, which looked quite cute but sad, and sand vipers, which looked less so.

The following morning, we were told we could go to the oasis in Tozeur and hopefully date wine was back on the menu. Again, we had to drive four hundred yards to get dropped off at the caleche stop. Here we would catch horse drawn carriages around the area that spans ten square kilometres.

Despite being a serene and tranquil world, the oasis here is not as picture perfect as the one in Nefta. There is no central lake, instead below the shade of outstretched palms, a series of red-dirt paths winds through a wonderland of lush agricultural land. Approximately 400,000 date-palm trees grow here fed by underground springs and Tozeur alone produces 1000 tons of dates each year. The other main crops here are Pomegranates which fall from the trees and scattered on the ground with figs and apricots. It comes to something when you can grow better plants in the Sahara than on Seaford seafront.
Unfortunately, I didn't see anyone lurking behind the trees trying to sell alcohol, so it was back to the bus for the two-hour drive to our next port of call, Douz.

In order to get to Douz we had to cross the Chott El Djerid. With a surface area of more than 7,000 square kilometres, the Chott El Djerid is the Sahara's and Africa's largest salt lake. During winter when the rains have come, some of it must be navigated by boat, but in summer it nearly completely dries up leaving the salt crust with its bizarre patterns exposed, stretching on for miles to the horizon. Fata Morgana (mirages) are commonly sighted here.

The scenery was amazing and totally different to anything else. We stopped for photographs and there was a small stall selling souveniers. These once again consisted of camel skulls, dried out horned vipers and mounted scorpions. I declined. I did, however, buy a desert rose and some purple quartz which was very pretty.

It was quite cool to see the desert roses forming in the wild and they seemed to be everywhere. The salt lake itself was amazing.

Abandoned boats sat on it, awaiting the winter rain before they could move again, whilst temporary salt mines appeared everywhere to collect the precious minerals. The midday sun reflected so brightly off the salt that you needed sunglasses to admire it properly.

And so, it was on to Douz. And once again, our irate reviewer had left a scathing review of the hotel we were heading to, which read "Marginally better than the dire El Mouradi in Tozeur, but certainly not a place I'd ever want to go back to.

Seems they're having an economy drive on electricity as the place was generally very dark. We were met by an incredibly sour looking, miserable reception team who kept us hanging about for ages, and only then, after asking many times where the room keys were, told us the rooms weren't ready. Because of their incompetence, we then had to bolt down our insipid lunch to rush out again with the group.

The dining room was small, unwelcoming, dated and the food very boring. Hot dishes were cold and there was little choice and mostly what there was, was the worst of Tunisian food and too spicy. Not everyone likes spicy food or is content to just eat salad! At dinner I tried some soup that was congealed, cold and greasy. Meat was greasy and chewy, salads looked about two weeks old. All the bread was just white, dense cheap baguettes. Breakfast there was so much missing and impossible to find just a nice fresh croissant, decent ham and the cheese made me vomit. I had no idea what it was or that food could taste so bad.

Impossible to get most alcoholic drinks other than beer, no sugar free sodas, no decent coffee. Seriously, how can an alleged 4* hotel (ha ha) be incapable of making a cup of coffee?

The room was drab, dusty with an ancient tv, a fridge that didn't work, hard beds, old smelly army blankets, lumpy pillows, and yukky towels.

Like the Mouradi Tozeur ... the best bit was checking out."
One thing he had left out was, the once again, amazing foyer and the man who seemed to be polishing it on the same schedule as the painters of the Forth Bridge use. In other words, get to the end and then start again. The result was that the foyer, which was in fact the size of an ice rink, could actually be used as one, even in rubber soled shoes.

To be fair, the food wasn't quite as bad as made out and it is the only place I have managed to eat pigeon and a camel burger, but the rooms, considering the grandeur of reception, were pretty basic. There isn't much to do in Douz. It is billed as the curtain to the Sahara and driving through the compact, narrow streets of the town centre, you had to wonder what all the hype was about. The ferocity of the midday sun meant that much of the town was deserted. We were reliably informed that the town came to life after dark descended, but that wasn't much use to us as we were under a curfew.

We went to a small museum that promotes the lifestyle of the people of the Sahara. Not many people live there and there was little to see. A one room museum with a male and female robe, and a stuffed camel.

Then we went to the local racetrack, supposedly the Royal Ascot of the Sahara, where they stage camel racing. The Festival of The Sahara dates back to 1910.

It was called the camel festival because it was originally just about camel races, but it evolved and became concerned with horse racing, equestrian and hunting with saluki dogs. It is also a cultural festival for the Bedouin people who celebrate with poetry and song. There were a few camels training today, but I didn't see anything worth having a flutter on.

There was a rather shifty looking man offering rides in his microlite over the Sahara, but I think we all agreed that this was a bad idea, Instead, I did walk about 500 metres into the desert, and you have to think that I could have carried on through most of Algeria and Niger before getting back to greenery.

And then it was back to the hotel. We had seen Douz!

I spent the rest of the day chilling out in the hotel. Conversation in the bar turned to the hotel and as all of the other El Mouradi hotels seemed to offer some sort of medical treatment, what did this one offer. To be honest we were at a loss for quite some time. A couple were sitting at the bar. A middle-aged woman, who we were pretty sure was Dutch and a younger Tunisian man who were bickering over a beer. Nothing particularly strange here. Tunisia is quite well known for middle aged European women seeking younger Arabic men.

Halfway through the evening, a rather fat man wearing a red suit with white trims and a big bushy beard walks in and sits in the corner of the bar. The beard was black, and not white, but yes, we made the analogy. In turn, the man and woman at the bar went over to the man in the red suit, gave him some money and sat with him. This was all quite bizarre. We decided that this hotel was offering marriage guidance counselling and although we sort of guessed that the guy in the suit was some sort of Islamic cleric, we couldn't help wondering whether this was what Santa Claus does to pay the bills in the summer months.

Six

Tunisian Flintstones

It was another long 4 and a half hour drive back to the Northeast of the country today, with three stops along the way. Firstly, we east through the Sahara to the Berber region of the country. The Berbers have a long history and are what the Romans first referred to as Barbarians. As was the case with much of Rome's propaganda, they weren't really savages at all, they simply held different beliefs. Even when the Phoenicians established Carthage around 1000 BC, the Berbers already inhabited these lands. Invaders have come and gone, from Rome through to Muslims and the French. All leaving their mark on the country, but none erasing the original Berber culture. Notably, since the 2011 colour revolution in Tunisia, the culture and traditions of the area's indigenous inhabitants have increasingly been in the spotlight thanks to the proliferation of Berber organisations working to promote their social and cultural heritage.

These groups have helped spark an earnest interest in Tamazight, the language of the Berbers (who call themselves Amazigh), as well as their unique cuisine, intricate handicrafts and fascinating architecture.

Centuries-old Berber villages can be found along the length and breadth of Tunisia. As a strategy to defend themselves from invaders, Berber settlements were either built on fortified mountaintops or dug into the ground in the form of troglodyte dwellings hidden in the rockface. Today the age-old stone buildings of many of these villages and towns are largely abandoned as their inhabitants have moved to newly built satellite towns of modern buildings.

Southwest of the coastal city of Gabes lies Matmata, perched on the edge of the Sahara Desert at 600m and overlooking the Dahar Mountains. Matmata is famous for its troglodyte homes dug into the rock in a series of large pits interconnected with hidden passageways and open-air courtyards.

This unique Berber building method protected its inhabitants from the scorching sun while retaining heat in the winter. A few Berber families open their homes to visitors (for a small donation), and it was here that we stopped to learn more about this culture. To be honest I had made my mind up fairly early on. Mohammad made a phone call and a woman in traditional costume scurried out of a large house, which sat on the road and was not in the slightest bit underground, had a satellite dish and a large new car in the drive. She descended into the troglodyte house that was a couple of hundred feet away and we were told that she had lived there all her life. No TV in sight, so why the satellite dish? Anyway, the house was interesting, and she offered us some homemade bread and honey which was very pleasant. But this almost certainly came out of the fridge in the big house too. To be fair, I could see people using these underground dwellings in the Summer in order to escape the heat but if the woman can afford a new car and satellite TV, she can probably afford air conditioning.

Troglodyte houses have existed for millennia. This system has enabled inhabitants since Phoenician times to protect themselves from the recurrent severe heat waves that rage in the region. They are generally established around a large circular open-air well allowing daylight to be captured. The temperature rises from 15°C in winter to 25°C in summer.

In this region of Djebel Dahar, dotted with palm trees and olive groves, this type of dwelling makes it possible to keep the interior cool during the summer heat waves and to resist the winds and cold of winter.

Despite the modernization and civilization experienced by the country since its independence, despite the construction of new towns and despite the fairly significant rural exodus, these dwellings have resisted and their occupants have insisted on remaining there either out of love for the land and the roots, or for lack of means to afford a new life.

Thus, many families of this Berber community have preferred to stay in these ancestral troglodyte dwellings.

These houses are made up of rooms measuring four to five meters deep by two meters high, carved directly into the rock. A corridor, called a skifa, provides access to a circular courtyard dug into the ground.

Social life takes place in this courtyard: the laundry is washed there, the dishes are washed, we eat there, we welcome visitors, we carry out commercial transactions, In the courtyard emerge the ghorfas, cells used as attics.

I got the impression that there were more authentic Berber dwellings than this one and it had crossed my mind that this was actually Mohammad's mother who was in on the deal. We were asked to leave a substantial tip and allowed back on the bus.

After a pleasant surprise for lunch where we got chicken and chips rather than fish for once, we started venturing up the East Coast. We stopped at the town of El Jem, some 200km south of Tunis. The amphitheatre here rivals the Colosseum in Rome for both size and importance. Known as Thysdrus in Roman times, the city rivalled Sousse as the second most important Roman city in North Africa after Carthage.

The Amphitheatre of El Djem is a free-standing monument and is built entirely of stone blocks without foundations. It is said that in these respects, it is modelled after the Colosseum in Rome. Whilst the Colosseum holds the title of being the largest Roman amphitheatre, the Amphitheatre of El Djem is not too far behind. The larger axis of the Amphitheatre of El Djem measures at 148 m, whilst its smaller axis measures at 122 m. In addition, the rows of seats rose to a height of 36 m. It has been estimated that the amphitheatre would have been capable of holding up to 35,000 spectators at any one time. Given the grandness of this structure, it would only be natural to be under the impression that the amphitheatre was built when the Roman Empire was experiencing a period of prosperity and peace. Yet, this is not the case.

Whilst the exact date of the amphitheatre's construction is uncertain, it has been speculated that work began in A.D. 238. This year is also known as the 'Year of the Six Emperors', as there were six people recognised as emperors of Rome during this year. The amphitheatre may have been commissioned by one of these emperors, Gordian I, or his grandson (also one of the six emperors), Gordian III. The year A.D. 238 was not exactly a peaceful year for the Roman Empire, and it was an uprising in the Roman-ruled areas of Africa that made Gordian I, who incidentally was nearly 80 years old at that time, the emperor of Rome.

The uprising was sparked by dissatisfaction with the emperor Maximinus Thrax. In order to pay for the expenses of his campaign on the Danubian frontier, Maximinus was compelled to extract more and more revenue from the Roman aristocrats and landowners. To meet the demands of the emperor, some unscrupulous procurators were willing to make false judgments to issue fines and confiscate property. One such procurator in the province of Africa was assassinated in El Djem and led to the proclamation of Gordian I as emperor. This was also acknowledged by the Roman Senate several days later, as they had no love for Maximinus.

Gordian I's reign, however, lasted less than a month, as the governor of the neighbouring province of Numidia, Capellanus, marched his troops against him. Whilst Capellanus had a formidable army at his command, Gordian I could only muster a mob from amongst the residents of Carthage, where he was now residing. Capellanus is said to have been involved in a lawsuit against Gordian I in the past, which could indicate that the governor bore a grudge against the new emperor. Additionally, Gordian I had sent someone to replace Capellanus as governor as he was a loyal supporter of Maximinus. Gordian I's forces, led by his son, Gordian II, were easily defeated, and the emperor is said to have committed suicide within this very amphitheatre. Later in the year, Gordian III became emperor.

Another sign that the amphitheatre was not built during a period when Rome was prosperous is that the structure seems to have not been completed. This may be attributed to the lack of funds and the political turmoil within the Empire. Thus, although Gordian I intended to bestow a grand amphitheatre on his birthplace, or that Gordian III intended to honour the memory of his grandfather with this monument, it might not have materialized. Nevertheless, the Amphitheatre of El Djem, completed or not, is still an impressive tourist attraction today, and its historical importance was recognized in 1979 when it was inscribed as a World Heritage Site.

After Roman times, the colosseum later doubled as a last line of defence. The Berber princess Al Kahina was besieged here by Arab forces at the end of the 7th century. According to legend, the colosseum was linked by tunnel to the coastal town of Salakta, enabling Al Kahina to torment her besiegers by waving fresh fish from the top of the walls.

In light of this fact, I thought Mohammad could have got another of his relatives to have a fish stall on the top tier so that willing tourists could recreate this vital piece of Tunisian history.

When you enter the colosseum for the first time, you are struck by the indulgent grandeur of the Roman vision. The south side of the amphitheatre is the most intact, allowing a sense of how the seats swept down from the upper tiers to the marble-walled arena, beneath which ran arched corridors.

You can still climb to the upper seating levels and gaze down on the arena. It's also possible to explore the two long underground passageways that were used to hold animals, gladiators, and other unfortunates in their last moments before they were thrust into the arena to provide entertainment for the masses. It was here that many spent their final lonely minutes, listening to 35,000 people baying for their blood. I tried to imagine the smell, but then wished I hadn't.

The amphitheatre remained all but intact until the 17th Century when much of it was demolished to obtain building materials and by the 18th Century it was being used as a place to manufacture saltpeter.

We still had one more place to visit, so it was back on the bus to drive a mile across town to what has become known as The Africa House or The House of Africa.

This museum showcases an exceptional collection of Roman mosaics which, in my eye, were more spectacular than those in The Bardo Museum. All are richly coloured, in excellent condition and sensitively displayed. Highlights include a gory array of scenes from the colosseum and multiple images of a drunken Dionysus. At the rear of the museum is the House of Africa, an AD 170 Roman villa from the heart of El Jem that was excavated in the 1990s and transferred here for display.

The House of Africa owes its name to an impressive medallion mosaic depicting the Goddess Africa, a moody-looking young woman symbolising the Roman province of Africa (by the hide and two elephant tusks she wears as headgear). Others believe that the villa was named after Scipio Africanus, the Roman General from the Punic Wars, who played a vital role in the defeat of Carthage. In fact, the only man in human history to have an entire continent named after him.

One of the specialties of the region of Thysdrus was making mosaics. Its artists were renowned: they made pictures surrounded with very sophisticated frames based on complex geometric patterns and vegetal arabesques.

But the most interesting thing is that the mosaics from Thysdrus often depict the brutal shows of the Roman amphitheatre. Wild animals were thrown in the arena so that spectators could see the predators chase their prey and devour it.

That is the reason why rich inhabitants of Thysdrus decorated their houses with mosaics depicting scenes of wild animals.

Behind the House of Africa is an area where Roman villas have been excavated – you can wander around the remains, which feature some mosaics in situ and around a garden that has been planted with shrubs and plants that would have grown at the time.

I could have spent hours here admiring the mosaics, but it was nearing 5 o'clock and the curator seemed to be getting anxious as he clearly had somewhere better to be. Now most of us managed to get back to the bus on time, however one bright spark decided he needed to have one last look at something. The curator was already locking the front door, when Mohammad realised we were a man down and what transpired nearly became a diplomatic incident. Technically once the door to the museum was locked, anyone inside should have been arrested for trespass and thrown into a Tunisian prison cell. A long heated argument between Mohammad and the curator ensued, before the curator reluctantly went back in and hauled out our rather sheepishly looking travel mate.

It was another two hours to travel to Sousse, where our hotel was. As we travelled north, the harsh landscape transformed into fields upon fields of olive trees and then as we approached Sousse itself, into a resort town full of hotels, most of which were shut, it has to be said.

Having said that, The Movenpick Sousse was on a par with our hotel in Hammamet, the food was excellent, the room had a view over the sea and the bar had plenty of cold beer. Some of us even managed to walk down to the sandy beach without getting stopped by a man with a gun.

Seven

Islam's Fourth Holiest Site

An interesting last day of the tour saw us drive an hour inland to the holy city of Kairouan. It is the fourth most important city in Islam, after Mecca, Medina and Jerusalem and they have a sort of loyalty card pilgrimage there, where four visits are equal to one visit to Mecca.

Historical records relate that in 670 AD the Arab conqueror, Uqba ibn Nafi crossed the deserts of Egypt and began the first Muslim conquest of the Maghreb region of North Africa. Establishing military posts at regular intervals along his route, Uqba ibn Nafi came to the site of present day Kairouan and there decided to encamp his soldiers for some days (Kairouan, also spelled Qayrawan, means "camp" in Arabic).

Old chronicles describe the region as completely deserted, covered with impenetrable thickets, and being distant from trade routes. Apparently inhospitable as a long term settlement site, why then did this temporary military camp soon become the greatest Muslim city in North Africa and the 4th holiest city of Islam.

Legend tells of a warrior's horse that stumbled on a golden goblet buried in the sands. This goblet was recognized as one that had mysteriously disappeared from Mecca some years before. When the goblet was dug from the desert sand, a spring miraculously appeared, and the waters of this spring were said to issue from the same source that supplies the sacred Zamzam well in Mecca. The power of these three miracles - the mysteriously lost and then found Meccan goblet, the miraculous gushing forth of the spring, and the source of that spring - exercised a magnetic effect upon the early North African Islamic people and thereby established the site of Kairouan as a pilgrimage destination for ages to come.

By 698, following several more military campaigns in the Maghreb, the Arabs had driven the Byzantines from their garrisons in Carthage and become masters of the provinces of North Africa, called by them Ifriqiya. The town of Kairouan became the capital of this vast province. Governors were appointed to the province by the Ommayyad and Abassid caliphs (ruling from Damascus and Baghdad), and they exercised their rule from Kairouan. This tradition was continued over the centuries by the Aghlabid emirs (9th century), the Fatamid caliphs (10th century), and the Zirid emirs (11th century). During these centuries, the city became one of the most important cultural centres in the Arab world, witnessing a flowering of sciences, literature and the arts. Agriculture was favoured by the execution of sizable irrigation projects and an active increase in trade with the surrounding regions added to the general prosperity. Kairouan grew in size and beauty and nowhere was this more evident than in the construction and continuing elaboration of its Great Mosque.

We started our tour outside of the main walls at the local tourist information centre. A bit strange we all thought and wondered whether Mohammad had gone in for a few leaflets to see what was there. It turns out that if you climb to the roof of the building, via several flights of stairs, you get the best view of the Aghlabid Basins. These cisterns, built by the Aghlabids in the 9th century, are more impressive because of their engineering sophistication than as sights in themselves. Water was delivered by aqueduct from the hills 36km west of Kairouan into a smaller settling basin and then into an enormous main holding basin, which was 5m deep and 128m in diameter.

In the centre of the main pool was a pavilion where the rulers could come to relax on summer evenings. It does make you question the fact that if Allah had provided the natural spring in order to provide water for the first inhabitants, why the faithful then had to go 36km to find another water source. But then again who am I to question Allah.

From here we drove about another half a mile before reaching the outside of the walled medina which meant we were on foot from now on.

Just outside of the walls was the Zaouia of Sidi Sahab. The complex is notable for its magnificent tile decoration, much of which dates only from the 19th century. You enter through a forecourt, on the left of which are the imam's lodgings, guestrooms, and ablution fountains. Opposite the entrance is the minaret. The forecourt also gives access to the madrassa, laid out around a small courtyard; the prayer hall beyond it; and (by way of a passage adjoining the minaret) another colonnaded courtyard, off which opens the tomb of Abu Zama El Belaoui (Sidi Sahab), one of the Prophet's companions. Legend has it that he always carried three hairs from the Prophet's beard with him, hence the zaouia's informal name, the Barber's Mosque. We could enter the courtyards, but only Muslims could enter the mosque, and the tomb was closed to the public. Kairouan's medina feels like it ebbs and flows to a different rhythm to modern Tunisia. Long protected by its monumental walls and babs (gates), most of it is given over to quiet residential streets that have changed little over the centuries, with modest houses sporting arches and shutters painted in bright blue and greens. Unlike the modernised Medina of Hammamet, this is probably the most authentic in Tunisia.

The first walls of the medina were built towards the end of the 8th century, but those you see today date mainly from the 18th century. Of the numerous gates, the oldest is Bab El Khoukha, which features a horseshoe arch supported by columns. It was built in 1706.

It's possible to wander much of the medina without being confronted by a single souvenir-buying opportunity, as virtually all the commerce is restricted to Ave 7 Novembre and the covered Souq. The medina's best-known building is the 9th-century Great Mosque, one of the most important religious buildings in the Islamic world. Also known as Sidi Okba Mosque, after the founder of Kairouan who built the first mosque on this site in AD 670, this is North Africa's holiest Islamic site. The original mosque was completely destroyed, and most of what stands today was built by the Aghlabids in the 9th century. Its minaret is the oldest in the Maghreb, and its magnificent prayer hall has 414 pillars supporting horseshoe arches; non-Muslims may peek into this from the internal courtyard but can't enter.

The exterior, with its buttressed walls, has a typically unadorned Aghlabid design. Impressions change once you step into the huge, marble-paved courtyard, surrounded by an arched colonnade. The courtyard was designed for water catchment, and the paving slopes towards an intricately decorated central drainage hole that delivers the collected rainwater into the 9th-century cisterns below. The decorations were designed to filter dust from the water. The marble rims of the two wells both have deep rope-grooves worn by centuries of hauling water up from the depths.

The northwestern end of the courtyard is dominated by the square three-tiered minaret. The lowest level was built in AD 728. At its base, two Roman slabs (one upside down) bear a Latin inscription.

The prayer hall is at the southern end of the courtyard. The enormous, studded wooden doors here date from 1829; the carved panels above them are particularly fine. The pillars were, like those of the colonnade, originally Roman or Byzantine, salvaged from Carthage and Hadrumètum (Sousse), and no two are the same. At the far end of the hall, it's just possible to make out the precious 9th-century tiles behind the mihrab (niche showing the direction of Mecca) between two red marble columns. The tiles were imported from Baghdad along with the wood for the richly adorned minbar (pulpit) next to them. The ribbed dome in front of the mihrab has epigraphic and floral decoration and is generally acknowledged to be an Aghlabid masterpiece.

The rugs covering every inch of the prayer hall floor were made by local female artisans, who donate their work as a gift to Allah. Visitors must be appropriately dressed; robes and we all had to wear robes which were available for free at the entrance. Women had to cover their hair too.

Supposedly, here, more than anywhere else in Tunisia, the town becomes eerily deserted during Friday afternoon prayers. Sundays and evenings are also very quiet.

The most bizarre sight in the Medina was still to come. The Bir Barouta is where a blinkered camel walks in a circle, drawing water from a 17th-century holy well that legend says is connected to the Zamzam spring in Mecca. It's very odd, slightly disturbing, and certainly cruel for the camel, keeping it in such close and dark quarters. But the well forms a large part of the city's foundation story and is also an important spiritual ritual for many.

Having left the Medina via another great gatehouse, we still had time to explore the Makhroud bazaar. It is dedicated to Kairouan's much-loved makhroud (a date-filled semolina pastries soaked in honey). Expert pastry chefs produce them most days and are happy for tourists or potential buyers to watch them working. They were very nice, but also molten hot.

We had time to enjoy a cup of coffee in the square outside of the Medina walls, before going back to what Mohammad had promised would be a special lunch. The restaurant was on the outskirts of Sousse and to be honest didn't look that special. There was no menu as such and after a few minutes a group of men went on to the pavement a lit a large fire. The chef then came out of the kitchen with a freshly slaughtered lamb and proceeded to barbecue it on a pavement next to a dual carriageway. To be honest, the resultant lamb dinner was delicious but maybe had slightly smoky overtones due to the diesel fumes.

After lunch we headed into central Sousse which for once we were trusted to walk around on our own. Most of us spent some time in and around the medina, which is dominated by the medieval Kasbah or fortress. Built in AD 859 on the site of an earlier Byzantine fortress, the Kasbah is one of Sousse's grandest monuments. Its 30-meter Khalaf al Fata tower (named after its builder) is one of the oldest towers still standing in North Africa. The Kasbah's topmost platform is 50 meters above that of the Ribat, making it the best place to get medina views. After its construction, the Kasbah took over the military role of the Ribat and the Khalaf al Fata tower is still used as a lighthouse.

We wandered through the Medina's souk which runs past the Great Mosque to the medina's west side. Partially covered stalls full of tourists and bustling locals with stores selling everything from tacky tourist tat, through to metalworkers and woodworkers selling their wares.

We had to meet up at The Ribat. The ribat at Sousse is both the oldest and most typical surviving example of the ribat typology as it existed in medieval North Africa. A series of small fortifications known as "ribats" were constructed along the North African coastline during the ninth and tenth centuries to accommodate both military and religious functions. Small garrisons of devout Muslim soldiers lived within the ribats and provided protection for their cities from maritime attacks. During times of peace, these volunteer warriors devoted themselves to their faith and served as religious teachers to the community. Ribats were typically simple in design and mostly unadorned, due to their principal function as a military fortification. The design of ribats such as the one at Sousse strongly influenced later madrasa design in the region, prefiguring the arrangement of multiple levels of small cells surrounding a central courtyard.

The height of ribat construction was limited to the first centuries of Muslim rule in the region. Though initially established by an Abbasid governor in 796 CE, the ribat at Sousse was demolished and fully reconstructed by Aghlabid caliph Ziyadat Allah I in 821 CE/AH 206. It is this ninth century structure that survives today, restored but largely unaltered.

The watchtower was inspired by similar Abbasid minarets that were constructed during the late eighth century throughout Ifriqiya, the coastal region comprising modern day Tunisia, western Libya, and eastern Algeria. The tower rises to a height of approximately thirty-five meters, with the balcony located thirty-one meters above the ground.

The entire structure of the ribat was constructed in stone, primarily in a coursed ashlar pattern. The ceilings of the small cells on the ground level are composed of stone rubble. The exterior walls are topped by one-meter-high defensive stone merlons with central arrow slits and semi-circular profiles.

The exteriors of the southern wall and adjacent towers feature a continuous cornice of scalloped corbelling just below the merlons, as well as arrow slits accessible from the first level prayer hall. One notable structural feature is the small freestone dome located above the entrance porch. The circular dome rises from an octagonal base supported by squinches. This dome is the oldest of its kind in existence, and a precursor to the dome of the nearby Great Mosque of Kairouan (817-838, 856-863).

Though the ribat features extremely limited ornamentation, there is a commemorative inscription located above the door that provides access to the watchtower. This carved inscription is the oldest in Tunisia, listing the date of reconstruction of the ribat as 821 AD and its patron as Ziyadet Allah I.

During the centuries after its construction, the ribat was used variously as a military base or as a caravanserai for religious pilgrims, depending on the political climate of the era. The ribat at Sousse was damaged during the 1943 shelling of the city during the North African campaign of the Second World War. It was subsequently restored between 1951 and 1953. Though no longer in use as a military centre, the ribat is frequented today by pilgrims, architectural historians, and tourists.

It was the first Islamic city built in North Africa and the arabs conquered the rest of the area, plus southern Spain from there.

We had thirty minutes to explore the building which was unlike any other fortress or castle I had ever come across, before being shuttled into large room where we had a ninety minute lecture on the history of the Tunisian people. I, and a select few others found all of this fascinating, finding out how many times the Berber people had been conquered yet had still survived, but I think the majority of the group got itchy bums after half an hour and by the time 90 minutes were up, at least one woman had taken three ten-minute toilet breaks. I don't think it was the lamb.

So back to the hotel for a night enjoying the amazing buffet spread and the cold beers in the bar. The following morning, we would board the coach for one last drive. Travel across Lake Tunis for one last time in order to get to the Airport and a lunchtime flight back to London.

Little did we know that this would be the last holiday for a long time due to the COVID nonsense.

THE RAIN IN SPAIN DRAINS MAINLY THROUGH MY UNDERPANTS

ANDALUCIA, SPAIN 2022/2023

1. Y Viva Espana — 274
2. Drenched — 281
3. Feria — 288
4. Plan B — 295
5. Europe's Most Beautiful Building — 303
6. Winding Down — 315
7. Return To Seville — 318
8. Flamenco Loco — 328

ONE

Y Viva Espana

If you had told me five years ago that I would be heading for a week in Torremolinos or The Costa Del Sol, I would have scowled and said that not even a lobotomy would get me to go there and mix with a load of English oiks, drinking lager and eating all day breakfasts. But my brain was still intact and here I was heading for Gatwick for the early morning flight to Malaga.

The problem being that in 2022, the world was still in a state of overhyped panic due to Covid, and this would be my first venture abroad for over two years. And to be fair, the choice of destinations was not that extensive. If Spain had not been that reliant on British tourism, the chances are that I would have needed to wait even longer to get away and there was also the fear that the whole thing could kick off gain at any moment, and we would all be locked in again.

In truth, there are a few interesting excursions that I could make from Torremolinos and combined with a couple of days of rest and relaxation, something I rarely do, should have worked out to be a pretty good trip.

Having said all of that, having gotten to Gatwick at 3.30am and found the check-in queue already snaking around the terminal, the realities of post Covid travel were about to hit me with a jolt. Only two fit members of ground staff meant that check-in took nearly two hours, leaving me with only an hour to get through security and to the gate. That was breakfast down the toilet.

I walked God knows how many miles to get to the gate, only to find out that the flight was delayed 90 minutes as they could not find enough ground crew.

It was at this point that my initial fears became somewhat of a reality as the queue was made up out of what seemed to be extras out of Eastenders. The finest specimens from Kent and Essex were not happy. One was counting off the pints of Stella he wouldn't have that afternoon, another was furious because he was going to miss watching Chelsea on the telly in the pub, whilst one quite frighteningly ignorant woman kept complaining that she had left her sixth glass of prosecco in the lounge in order to get to the gate. I concluded that these people didn't travel for the culture.

The poor staff, who hadn't tested positive for Covid, mostly Asian or West Indian in origin, were getting dogs abuse from the baying crowd. One bloke even shouted out "Is this Uganda Airlines?" I don't think that really helped the situation.

Just when you think things can't get worse, all the abundant racism and drunken women paled into insignificance with three uncontrollable brats who were louder than air raid sirens and totally out of control. I felt sorry for Spain at this point as no country deserved to let this crowd into their country. I spent most of the flight drafting a letter to the airline recommending that children should be treated as baggage and kept in the hold or preferably thrown out midair. The rest of my time was spent trying to come up with a collective noun for screaming children. The best I could come up with was barbarianism. I prayed like never before that they weren't staying in my hotel.

We arrived in Malaga some two hours late and despite having no issues with immigration, my bag was last off the plane as per usual. As a result, I had to run, with my suitcase, to find the coach which was taking me to my hotel. Not that I needed to bother, as some chav decided to go AWOL and have a beer and a fag before looking for the coach. It was now 2pm and originally, I had planned to be in a bar with a cold beer by 12.30.

Thankfully, when we did finally get underway, the airport was less than three miles from Torremolinos, and my hotel was the second on the list of stops. I was on the eighth floor with a view over the concrete jungle, despite the hotel being on the seafront. There was, what estate agents would call, an oblique sea view from the balcony and the room was of a decent standard.

No hanging around though and it was a quick change into a t shirt and some shorts before heading into the town to find a Mexican café I had pinpointed for lunch. The temperature was in the mid-twenties, and this made traversing the streets of Torremolinos slightly more challenging, as most of it was uphill or steep steps. By the time I made it to the café I was somewhat thirsty, partly down to the fact I had gone ten hours without water having not had time at Gatwick and then nothing offered on the flight and partly down to climbing God knows how many steps.

As a result, two bottles of ice-cold Negra Modelo (a very nice Mexican beer) and a litre of iced water were downed long before any food appeared. When it did turn up, the food was excellent. A couple of authentic tacos and a torta, which is basically a Mexican sandwich. I sat at a table on the pavement watching the world go by, people watching, and it soon became apparent that Spanish women take the term "mutton dressed as lamb" to a whole new level. I think I saw more Mature women in miniskirts and high heels in that hour than you would in a lifetime in Seaford. Not that I was complaining in the slightest, more power to their elbow and all that, but there were one or two with Norah Batty legs who should maybe retire the stilettos.

I wandered back, downhill, through the shopping centre of Torremolinos. It was a Sunday and as a result many of the shops were shut. In a way it reminded me a bit of Amalfi or Positano in that the shops cling to the hillside as you climb up and down hills that seemingly get steeper and steeper, but it was a slightly cheaper version it has to be said.

I strolled back to the hotel, flopped on the bed and passed out for three hours. It had been a long day, having left home around 2.30am. By the time I woke up it was time to go and investigate the buffet at the hotel. I had booked breakfast and an evening meal each day, but fully intended to eat out on a few occasions.

After a few minutes I regretted this decision. God the food was awful. The salads were laced with vinegar, I actually spat the main course of beef out, it was that bad, but thankfully there was lots of fresh fruit to fill up on. So, dinner this week will probably be based around melon, strawberries, plums, and pineapple.

After dinner, I wandered past the pool area at the front of the hotel and out to the beachfront road which was bustling with tourists of numerous nationalities. I bought myself an ice cream and wandered down to the sun loungers, which were free after 5pm. I presume this is when The Germans get up and take their towels home. It was quite pleasant watching the sun go down on a deserted beach, only really inhabited by the odd fisherman and people walking their dogs.

I had planned to try the hotel bar for a pint before turning in but on hearing a load of drunk English people singing Viva Espana and Una Paloma Blanca, I thought it more prudent to have a can in my room, a shower, and an early night.

With the knowledge that I would need to be up early for the rest of the week due to trips I had planned, I made sure that I didn't get up for breakfast before 9 o'clock. After the rather unappetizing fayre on offer the previous evening, the breakfast buffet surpassed the evening one by a clear distance. A decent omelette with grilled tomatoes and then plenty of fruit. Rather unsurprisingly, most of the inhabitants were going for the full English of course. Some even going for their first beer of the day!

By mid-morning I was ready to venture out into the sunshine and take a stroll along the seafront in the direction of Malaga. The beach at Torremolinos stretches for around five miles with my hotel about four miles away from the Malaga end and another mile of hotels and bars stretching in the other direction. To be fair it was quite pleasant and not full of the English bars, bawdy nightclubs, and characterless, concrete buildings that I had envisaged. Palm trees shrouded the Mediterranean side of the road, whilst the street side was a mish mash of small bars, touristy shops, restaurants, and hotels. I walked about a mile and a half, perusing the odd gift shop and stopping for the occasional cold drink as temperatures were in the high twenties.
The sun loungers were full of Germans who had probably been there since 5 a.m. the cafes were full of English people having bacon and eggs and the footpaths were full of French people standing around, getting in the way.

By midday it was time for a serious drink, so it was off under a palm tree at an alfresco bar to sip a couple of Mojitos. People watching is scary here. The worst sight here was an extremely fat woman in a skimpy thong that had disappeared way up where no man would ever dare go. I took another sip and looked the other way.

Conversing with the locals and menus were slightly challenging. Whereas in France or Italy, I can sort of scrape by, I only know ten words in Spanish. Si (yes), por favor (please), adios (goodbye), ola (hello), cerveza (beer), jamon (ham), queso (cheese), gracias (thankyou), pollo (chicken) and bendejo (an obscure Mexican insult roughly translated as bum Hair). I was quite proud that I had managed to use the first nine within 24 hours of arriving. The last one was being saved for emergencies.

Just as I was enjoying my second drink, the chef lit an alfresco barbecue that began wafting smoke in my direction. I was contemplating having some lunch there, but due to choking, I decided to wander a bit further back towards the hotel to find an alternative lunch stop. The seafront was full of seafood restaurants, all boasting locally caught fish. In the evenings, you can see loads of little boats going out to catch the next day's menu. I had an amazing T Bone sized swordfish steak with chips and then retired back to the hotel for a siesta. When in Spain and all that.

Around 3pm I got up and decided to wander back into the town centre of Torremolinos. Thankfully, due to a little bit of research, I discovered that there was in fact a public lift that for a small charge, negated the need to climb all those steps. I had missed it the day before as it is hidden away down a dingy alleyway, probably so that the locals can laugh at the fat foreigners struggling to get to the top. The little square where the lift took you to was actually a fairly good viewpoint over the concrete jungle and the beach. Cruise ships and oil tankers sat on the horizon and a multitude of fishing vessels hunted for their catch nearer to the shore. The town itself was still not that busy. Despite being a Monday, it was a Spanish bank Holiday and as a result, many of the shops were still shut.

The town centre was pretty soulless to be honest. Most of the interesting buildings were amongst the myriad of staircases that wound their way back down to terra ferma. There were a couple of pretty little churches, one amazing house that was perched upon a sheer rockface and needed stilts to keep it from toppling down on to the bemused tourists below and a Moorish tower which was more akin to the local Andalusian history.

The tower is only about 12 metres in height and dates back to around 1300 when a Muslim dynasty named The Nazries governed the Malaga area between the 13th and 15th Centuries. It was originally designed as a lookout tower, scouring the horizon for invading ships. The name Torremolinos means The Mill Towers and it was during the Islamic period that these water mills were introduced, one of which still exists on the outskirts of the town.

After the fall of the Islamic caliphate in Granada, to the invading Christian armies, Torremolinos fell into disrepair and became a constant target for North African pirates. It was all but destroyed during the War of Spanish Succession when an Anglo Dutch fleet, under the command of on George Rooke bombarded it. It always seems to be the British who destroy these places. In fact, a census from 1769 states that the town's population was a mere 106. Despite an attempt during the early 20th century to reopen the mills, from the 1930's onwards, the town has promoted itself as a holiday resort. These days it has a population of over 70,000 and is the sixth largest city in Andalucía.

There was a list of famous inhabitants of Torremolinos but the only one I had heard of was Danny La Rue. Am not sure if that was a big selling point for the town.

Strolling back down the hill I came across a sweet shop. I had been asked by a friend to find a packet of Conguitos. The sweets themselves were irrelevant, merely chocolate covered peanuts, but it was all about the packaging, which was based on caricatures of rather stereotypical African bushmen with spears and big lips. There was a sign outside, albeit slightly toned down from what I had seen during my research, but unfortunately, this turned out to be a pick and mix shop, and a brown paper bag would not suffice.

They do seem to have had a bit of a rebrand though and I'm not sure they are quite as racist as before. You can probably blame the EU for that. The search will continue and should be easier once the Bank Holiday is over. I was pretty certain I could find them in Seville or Granada.

I stopped at a bar that claimed to be a Craft Beer bar but only had Budweiser on top of the local firewater, Cruz Campo. I still stopped for a cold pint before continuing down the hill, towards the beach. I really should walk along the beach more at home, however it just seemed more pleasant here. Palm trees, no cold wind, miles of sand rather than pebbles somehow make a beach somewhat more attractive. I strolled back along the beach, back to the hotel for a quick shower before dinner.

Having had a big lunch, I didn't really bother too much about the buffet this evening, although the lure of the plums, strawberries and watermelon was enough to make me go for a big bowl of fruit if nothing else. Once again, I followed dinner with an al fresco ice cream, laying on a sun lounger on the beach. The airport is only a few miles away and you can watch planes circling over the sea before making their final approach. This was quite relaxing for an hour, and I could quite happily see myself as a midnight beach bum for a week.

As the temperature began to drop, I made my way back to the hotel, determined to try the bar this time. The choruses of Sweet Caroline and Yippie, Yippie Eye Aye, once again meant heading back to my room for a cold can from the fridge. I will try the bar one night.

TWO

Drenched

It should have been a long but good day today and everything seemed to be going smoothly when my tour bus picked me up at 9.15 on time.

As far as everyone was aware, we were going for an 8-kilometre hike through a gorge in the morning and then going to a typical Spanish village in the afternoon for lunch. It all sounded great in the brochure. Unfortunately, this had changed, and we now had tickets to start our hike at 2pm. This would not have been an issue normally, however due to the rather dreadful weather forecast, this was somewhat alarming. I had hoped to get through the gorge without the threat of rain but no, due to some administrative cock up, we were now in the hands of the weather gods.

Things were looking quite pleasant when our coach parked up at eleven o'clock, just outside of the village of Ardales. We were all marched off the bus and informed that we had an hour and a half to explore the town before meeting up at a hotel in the main square, where we would be treated to a local delicacy.

There was a castle, perched atop a rather steep hill, which we were told was about three kilometres away, but we were welcome to go and see it. It looked interesting, but three kilometres there and three kilometres back, prior to an eight-kilometre hike, seemed a little excessive, so I decided to take a slow walk, up a slightly less steep hill to the village centre.

Ardales was actually quite important in the History of Spain as it was the centre of the Christian resistance to the Moorish occupation. But there are remains at the castle that go back to Phoenician times which seemed to have been added to in Roman times.
The name Ardales dates back to Moorish times when it was known as Ard Allah, changing to Ardales after the Christian conquest. During the 9th and 10th Centuries there were many bloody battles between the Moors and Christians, and the town changed hands many times. In fact, it wasn't until 1453 that the Moors were finally driven out.

Today, Ardales is a typical pueblo white village, surrounded by reservoirs and olive groves. Crossing a Roman bridge from where the coach parked, over the River Turon, you climb a rather steep hill flanked by typically whitewashed terrace houses. There are a couple of pretty plazas, one of which boasts a small convent with colourful garden full of lemon trees.

A few shops and bars surround The Plaza de la constitution, but nothing that would really entice you to go into any of them. So, with nothing else to do for an hour, I found a bench, outside of a launderette and acted like a tramp for an hour before heading for the local wine tasting.

In hindsight, another half hour on the bench might have been preferable. I think what they served us was supposed to be sherry. But you can add as much sugar to paint stripper as you like, it just becomes very sweet paint stripper. I'm not sure the person trying to flog the stuff was that impressed when I got up, went to the bar next door, and ordered a beer.

By 12.30 we assembled at the allotted spot and got picked up a whisked off to what we thought would be Carmonito Del Ray, where we were going for a hike. No such like as it happens. It turns out that the car park for the hike is a further two kilometres away, circumnavigating a very picturesque dam named Embalse Guadalhorce. The Gorge that the dam water ends up in is called The Desfiladero de los Gaitanes, roughly translated as the Gorge of the Bagpipers.

Finally, we came to a ticket office and a long queue. The queue was for the toilets as this was a one-way walk, no turning back, no facilities, so in effect the last toilet for eight kilometres.
Entry is strictly controlled and only 660 tickets can be sold on any given day, with entry strictly controlled at half hour intervals. We were told we would have to wait to be given crash helmets. It was explained that this was necessary due to recent rock falls. To be honest this was the least of my concerns. Carmonito del ray, which means The Kings Little pathway, was only reopened in 2015. The walkway hangs some 100 metres above the gorge and due to the state of disrepair, five people fell to their deaths between 1999 and 2000, earning it the rather ominous title of The World's most dangerous footpath.

The walkway was built to provide workers at the hydroelectric power plants at Chorro Falls and Gaitanejo Falls with a means to cross between them, to provide for transport of materials, and to help facilitate inspection and maintenance of the channel. The construction began in 1901 and was finished in 1905. King Alfonso XIII crossed the walkway in 1921 for the inauguration of the dam Conde del Guadalhorce, and it became known by its present name. The walkway is 1 metre (3 ft) in width and rises over 100 metres (330 ft) above the river below.

The original path was constructed of concrete and rested on steel rails supported by stanchions built at approximately 45 degrees into the rock face. It deteriorated over the years, and there were numerous sections where part, or all of the concrete top had collapsed. The result was large open-air gaps bridged only by narrow steel beams or other supports. Few of the original handrails existed, although a safety wire ran the length of the path. Several people lost their lives on the walkway and, after two fatal accidents in 1999 and 2000, the local government closed both entrances. Even so, in the four years leading up to 2013, four people died attempting to climb the gorge.

Finally, we set off through the gorge which was spectacular. It clings to the rockface around 100 metres in the air and crosses the ravine on narrow wire bridges. The scenery was quite spectacular, however the black clouds appearing over the mountains and the rumbles of thunder were getting rather alarming.

I was fast discovering that all Spanish adults are no better than toddlers. They all love to play and have a good time, but as is generally the case with toddlers, something goes wrong, and the toys fly out of the pram. One Spanish brat had a strop on the walk and decided he was frightened of heights. The problem being this was a one way walk and the walkway was so narrow, that all of us behind the bugger had to wait 20 minutes for him to calm the hell down. I would have happily tossed him one hundred metres down the gorge but sadly I did not have a say.

The guide said we should look out for mountain goats, lizards, and water snakes. No such luck, but I did see a vulture circling overhead, hoping that I might follow through with my threat to toss the Spanish brat overboard.

Across the other side of the river, cave houses can be seen in the Parda Mountains. These were not particularly ancient cave dwellings unfortunately but homes for the workers of the hydroelectric complex powered by the dam.

The old Chorro Dam can also be seen near the entrance to the Gorge. This is where the 1904 power station was located before it was replaced by the Gaitanejo Dam Power Station.

The boardwalk at this point was quite narrow and made of quite polished wooden planks. I couldn't help thinking that should the heavens open, this could get quite precarious.

The path clings to the upper part of the gorge where the walls are only a few metres apart. You can clearly see how the rock has been worn away over the years by the water. As the gorge widens out, a series of steps and ramps zig zag their way down to where an aqueduct canal was built.

There was an alternative path that followed the walls of the canal, but our guide insisted we stayed to the rickety one that winds itself around the rock buttress.

Looking across to the other side of the valley you can see the railway line supported on large stone structures between the tunnels bored through the rock. It is amazing to think that the Cordoba to Malaga railway line was constructed between 1860 and 1866 and was used by all express trains to and from Malaga until 2007.

There is a stone bridge here and remarkably there used to be a railway halt on the other side of the valley, built especially for the workers on the dam. Currently it looks like a rickety stone bridge that could give way any moment, but allegedly it did have a basic handrail back in the day. I was just thankful we did not have to cross here.

A little further on after walking around a large rock buttress and descending some steps we climbed a few steps leaving the gorge section of the path behind. There was a small rest area, an information board about the fauna and meeting where we waited, for some considerable time, for some stragglers to catch up.

The clouds at the far end of the Gorge, behind us, were now very black and although I was trying to ignore it, there were definitely rumbles of thunder.

For the next kilometre, the path followed a gentle winding route through some woods. Supposedly, this was the area where some groups stopped and had a picnic, and normally this would have been idyllic. The encroaching Armageddon, however, meant that picnics were the last thing on our minds.

The inevitable rain began to fall. Lightning began to flash, and thunder roared. We were four kilometres in, and four kilometres from the coach. There was no escape. Well, that's not entirely true as there was a tunnel that cut off a corner, however it was pitch black and full of bats. I think we all decided to brave the elements. There was a little bit of shelter, before we crossed the ravine on a Perspex bridge. We took the opportunity to look back along the Gorge for the last time before we headed to the next part of the walk. One by one we braved the elements which were getting worse by the minute. Now I know I had a go at The Spanish earlier, but my pet peeve is still the French. These two French girls in front of me stopped on the bridge to take photos of each other. Complete disregard for the poor buggers, including me, who had to wait getting drenched as there was no way past them. Totally bloody oblivious.

The path soon doubled back on itself in a sharp u bend. Ironically, you could actually see the old, condemned footpath about ten metres below the one we were walking on. That would not have been fun.

It could not really have been much worse. We were about two miles from any sort of shelter in either direction when the heavens opened. And the rain was biblical in its deluge.

I don't think I have ever been so wet. The rain was cascading from my crash helmet, down the back of my shirt and forming a puddle in my underpants. This in turn was spilling like a waterfall down my leg, straining through my socks and forming a foot bath in my shoes. We had to walk an hour in this. My shirt and shorts were so wet they stuck to me.

On a normal day, the fern trees along this section of the walk would have provided welcome shade and shelter from the afternoon sun, however the leaves just made the drips larger that were bouncing off me in all directions.

By this point we just wanted to get to the finish line. There was another hanging bridge to cross and then an uphill walk through what was at first mud and then by the end was a river cascading down the hill at us. I am sure the views were lovely, but the lack of windscreen wipers on my glasses meant I didn't see too much more.

We finally reached a small kiosk where we had to give up our crash helmets. I was beyond caring at this point and was resigned to the top of my head getting drenched too. There was a toilet here, but they were small, and many people were sheltering from the elements. I just put my head down and walked the last 500 metres to where the coach was parked.

We all eventually made it back to the bus and had to sit in our wet clothes for another hour and a half before we got back to the hotel. It would have been an hour, but another French kid decided he was travel sick and his parents demanded that we stopped the bus. Thankfully the Spanish driver threw a strop along with the toys out of his pram and said no, it's my bus and refused. Mind you he has some vomit to clean up later.

The journey back was cold and uncomfortable. Back in Torremolinos, the weather was still dry and sunny which probably earned me a few strange looks when I poured myself off the bus and waddled back to my room. Thankfully there was a hair dryer in the bathroom, and I just used it on me rather than my clothes which went straight on to the balcony to dry in what was left of the days sun. Then it was straight into a hot shower followed by a hot coffee. Thankfully I packed two pairs of shoes as I couldn't see anything I wore today being dry for at least 72 hours.

Not quite what I had planned over here. I had planned to head quite a way along the beach to a restaurant I fancied trying, but quite frankly I couldn't be bothered. Thankfully there was a beef stew on the menu at the buffet and a rather tasty paella which hit the mark.

I also decided that it was time to hit some local bars. Well, it was just the one, but the three pints I had were well earned. Albeit a mistake, as I had to get up at 7.15 the following morning and was up all night going to the loo.

THREE

Feria

The bad news today was that it tipped down with rain all day in Torremolinos, so much so that my shorts from yesterday, which were drying on the balcony, were actually wetter when I came back from when I left in the morning.

The good news was that I went to Seville which was far enough west for the sun to be out for 98% of the day. There were a few spots in the afternoon but nothing more.

It was a good 3-hour drive to Seville and after being picked up at 7.45, it was gone eleven before we got there.

We parked on a leafy street and wandered into a park where we were confronted by an enormous square. The overwhelming Plaza de Espana is the most famous square in Seville. Several buildings were designed for the Ibero-American exhibition of 1929 in and around the Maria-Luisa Park. Anibal González designed this Spanish square, which is in Spanish Renaissance style with a diameter of 200 metres. Spain's goal with the exhibition was to make symbolic peace with its former American colonies.

The shape of Plaza de Espana is a semi-circle, surrounded by a row of buildings that today are, for the most part, used as government institutions. There are two tall towers on the flanks of the square. 52 benches and mosaics of tiles are located at the foot of the building as it curves its way around. There is one fresco for each of Spain's 52 provinces. The tiles are typical of Andalusia, known locally as azulejos.

A large fountain is in the middle and a small canal, which you punt a boat around, under a few cute bridges, encircles the whole plaza.

It was here that I realized the annual Feria was on where the locals dress up in traditional Andalucian outfits. The women in traditional, flowing flamenco dresses known as traje de gitano, literally translated as gypsy suit, whilst the men dressed in the traje corto, or short suit consisting of fitted trousers and a short, fitted jacket with wide-brimmed hat.

This year's fiesta was in full swing, and the streets were full of flamenco dancers in traditional dresses and castanets, with men wailing in the background. There a plenty of impromptu dancing and singing, which was a wonderful introduction to Seville. Everybody who wanted to be noticed was dressed up in their finest outfits and parading around. Many taking decorated, horse drawn carriages to parade around the city. Although I did not come across it, there are a number of casetas, which are large striped tents, that fill up with locals from early afternoon until the small hours of the morning. Tapas is eaten, rioja is drunk and there is lots of dancing to traditional Andalusian folk music. I tried to picture an English version of this but the nearest we would manage is a mixed Morris dancing Festival with plenty of ale and a few sausage rolls. Preferable to rioja and tapas personally.

We only got 30 minutes here, before crossing a roundabout and entering a smaller park, which was probably more of a garden to be fair. In the middle of it stood a tall monument that was dedicated to Christopher Columbus, who set sail from here to find America. Well, he didn't really do that unbeknownst to the vast majority of Americans who celebrate Columbus Day every year. He only made it to the Dominican Republic. Nevertheless this 75-foot monument is quite striking. Roughly halfway up the stone columns there is a bronze structure that resembles a ship, and it incorporates the two columns. It is in fact the bows, front of two caravel ships. This was the type of ship used during the 15th and 16th centuries, during the Age of Discovery.

The two bows are connected by two ornate plaques, one on each side of the vessel. The plaques bear the name of Isabel on one side and Fernando on the other. This pays homage to Queen Isabella I of Castile and King Ferdinand II of Aragon, King and Queen of Spain who sponsored Columbus's expeditions and voyages.

The two columns are topped with a narrow stone plinth on top of which there is the statue of a lion resting his paw on a ball. Underneath this, carved in the stone is the name of Cristobal Colón (Christopher Columbus is just an anglified version of the name) and the date 1492, the date Columbus set sail. I found it amusing that in effect the Americans were celebrating Colon Day.

Our guide whisked us through the historic maze of medieval streets, and we came to a small square, surrounded by a ring of fully ripe orange trees which was a picture. There was a chance for a toilet break here and a cup of coffee, however I had noticed what I thought was a church in the corner of the square. It turned out not to be a church, but was in fact the Hospital de los Venerables Sacerdotes, a former hospice for priests which is now a shrine, not quite big enough for a museum, to the local artist Velazquez. It's not a big collection, but each work is a masterpiece of its genre and even I recognized Velázquez' Santa Rufina and his Inmaculada Concepción.

The Hospital's ornately decorated chapel was very beautiful and there was also a delightful patio, encompassing a classic composition of porticoes, ceramic tiles and orange trees arranged around a sunken fountain.

Once everybody had queued up for the toilet, we continued through the maze, finally emerging at The Plaza Triunfo and the enormous and extremely impressive cathedral that is the icon of Seville.
It is the largest Gothic cathedral in the world, and third largest cathedral in all, behind St Peters in Rome and St Paul's in London. It was originally a mosque, and the bell tower, known as the Giralda was originally a minaret. Only this and the courtyard remain from the mosque, whilst inside is a rather tasteless collection of gold, stolen from Mexico and the New World. The alter was extremely hideous and dripping in South American blood.

The cathedral's construction lasted over a century, from 1401 to 1506. It is said that when the plans were drawn up, church elders stated, "Hagamos una iglesia tan hermosa y tan grandiosa que los que la vieren labrada nos tengan por locos." (Let us build a church so beautiful and so magnificent that those who see it finished will think we are mad).

The basilica occupies the site of the great Aljama mosque, built in the late 12th century by the Almohads, the ruling Moorish dynasty, of which the only remaining parts are the Patio de Naranjas, the Puerta del Perdon, and the Giralda (formerly the minaret, now the belltower).

Its central nave rises to an awe-inspiring 42 metres and even the 80 side chapels each seem tall enough to contain an ordinary church. Sheer size and grandeur are, inevitably, the chief characteristics of the Cathedral, although two other qualities stand out with equal force - the rhythmic balance and interplay between the parts, and an impressive overall simplicity and restraint in decoration. All successive ages have left monuments of their own wealth and style, but these have been restricted to the two rows of side chapels. In the main body of the cathedral only the great box-like structure of the coro (choir) stands out, filling the central portion of the nave. This opens onto the Capilla Mayor (Great Chapel), dominated by a vast Gothic retablo (altar piece) comprised of 45 carved scenes from the life of Christ, as well as Santa Maria de la Sede, the cathedral's patron saint. The lifetime's work of a single craftsman, Pierre Dancart, this is the ultimate masterpiece of the cathedral - the largest and richest altarpiece in the world and one of the finest examples of Gothic woodcarving anywhere. There is a staggering amount of gold involved.

Through the antechamber, you reach the Capitular (Chapter House) with its magnificent domed ceiling mirrored in the marble decoration of the floor.

There are several paintings by Murillo here, the finest of which, a flowing Conception, occupies the place of honour.
Alongside this room is the grandiose Sacrista Mayor (Great Sacristy) which houses the treasury. Amid a confused collection of silver reliquaries and monstrances are the keys presented to Fernando by the Moorish and Jewish communities on the surrender of the city, sculpted into the latter in stylized Arabic script are the words 'May Allah render eternal the dominion of Islam in the city.'

The highlight was the grave of Columbus and the chapel where Magellan prayed before being the first to circum navigate the globe. They claim that some of Columbus's bones are buried here, but he was not very lucky in life, having set off for India and ending up in The Dominican Republic, whilst in death he has been dug up five times. Having been buried in Seville three times, Dominican Republic once and Cuba once. The tomb itself is more recent, dating from 1892, and has four bearers presenting the kingdoms of Castile, Leon, Aragon and Navarra.

The most bizarre item here is a stuffed crocodile known as El Lagarto. It was a gift from the Sultan of Egypt to King Alfonso X, for asking for the hand in marriage of his daughter Berenguela. Although the Sultan did not wed the princess in the end, the crocodile stayed, and was stuffed on its demise. Now it is one of the cathedral's quirkier relics but who on earth would give their potential Father-in-Law a crocodile?

We had the option to climb the bell tower which was very tall. There are no steps as the original cardinal insisted on being able to ride his horse to the top, however as the only equine option was Shank's Pony, I passed and decided to take my time wandering around the city.

You exit the cathedral through the Patio De los Naranjos (Oranges). This patio dates back to Moorish times when worshippers would wash their hands and feet in the fountains here - under the orange trees - before their five daily prayer sessions. As leave the Patio, you pass through the Puerta del Perdon (Gate of Forgiveness), a stucco engraved horse-shoe shaped masterpiece, also dating from the original Almohad mosque.

It was nice to wander on my own after this, albeit not that successfully. Firstly, I wanted to see the Record of The India's, which has all the ships logs and accounts for all of the plunder that came back from The New World to Spain, from Columbus to Cortes. This unfortunately shut at 1pm and I was too late.

From here I wandered down the main street with an ice cream, avoiding the silent trams that seemed to creep up from nowhere. I came across a modern bar that claimed that it brewed its own beer. Having had three days of Cruz Campo, I decided this was an offer I could not refuse. Two glasses later, I was ready to hit the road again.

Next, I wanted to tour the bull ring, but that was closed as there are bull fights every night during the Feria. As much as I detest the idea of bull fighting, The Bull Ring itself was amazing and must be the nearest modern day arena to The Colosseum in Rome. It is one of the oldest and most important Bull Rings in the world and is known locally as the Cathedral del Toreo.

The building, with its impressive Baroque façade, dates from 1762 - 1881 (under a succession of architects) and was immortalized in Bizet's Carmen (March of The Toreadors). The arena accommodates 14,000 and, despite its size, the acoustics allow you to hear everything wherever you're sitting.

The main entrance is the Puerta del Príncipe (the Prince's Gate) with beautiful 16th-century iron gates, originally from a convent, made by Pedro Roldán. After an outstanding performance the torero (bullfighter) will be carried out through these gates on the audience's shoulders. One thing I did read was that there is a slight slope in the arena; it's higher in the centre than near the stalls to give the bullfighter an advantage - he can sprint downhill to get behind the barricade, while the bull has to come to a stop to avoid crashing into it.

One cute touch around this area was that during Feria, the pedestrian crossing lights had a green matador for crossing and a red flamenco dancer for don't cross.

Not having much luck with my planned sightseeing, I next tried to see the castle where the Spanish Inquisition was based. Only to read on their website that they hadn't reopened since covid.

At this point I said "To Hell" with sightseeing and headed for a bar I had looked up. Only to find it did not open until 6pm and we had to be back on the bus by 4pm. So, I gave up and found a traditional tapas bar for lunch. For around ten euros, you can still get three small dishes of food and a third of a pint of beer. And yes, it was Cruz Campo again. But I had patatas bravas (roast potatoes with spicy mayonnaise), a beef stew with four chips and a slice of Spanish omelette, which filled a hole and was nice to sit in a traditional Spanish Bodega for half an hour or so.

Before heading back to the bus, I headed for the Torre del Oro (Tower of Gold) which dominates the banks of the river Guadalquivir. It is a remnant of the Moorish fortified walls which originally enclosed the city, with 166 towers and 15 gates. A watchtower designed to protect the docks, its iconic shape makes it one of Seville's best-known monuments, after the Giralda which was built just a few years earlier.
The tower dates from 1220; the 12-sided lower part was built in stone by the Almohades (a Moorish dynasty) and was originally decorated with golden tiles, while the upper brick mini-tower was added in the 18th century.

During the invasion of the Americas, stories say that the tower was used to house gold plundered from the Mayans and Incas; some say this is where its name originates, rather than from the tiles which covered its outside and flashed in the sun, looking like gold.
I did a lot of walking today and a couple of hours sitting down on the coach, driving back to Torremolinos was quite welcome.

I had dinner at the hotel again tonight. After walking all day, I did not fancy going out again. Especially in the rain. The buffet is pretty dire and caters for the pizza, chips, chicken nuggets and dry beef burger brigade. The pasta is just a bowl of spaghetti and a large vat of tomato sauce. Thankfully the paella is edible and there is generally something along the lines of beef bourguignon or chicken chasseur to help things along. There were also zucchini (courgette) fries tonight which made a pleasant change.
Once again, I avoided the hotel bar and decided to chill out in my room and watch TV with a Cruz Campo.

FOUR

Plan B

I was really looking forward to today as Cordoba was the one place I really wanted to go to IN Spain. According to my ticket from the tour company, I was getting picked up around 8 o clock, so I managed to get a bit of breakfast in before heading outside to wait for the coach to turn up. Forty-five minutes later, with still no sign of any coach, I went back to my room to call the company. Only to be told that the bus had shown up and even asked for me at reception. This could not have been the case I thought, as I was ten minutes early.

To cut a long story short, the company that booked the tour for me online had screwed up and not forwarded an e mail stating that the departure would be half an hour earlier. The bus did turn up, but at 7.35 and was long gone before I went out there. They were most apologetic, and I got my money back without any fuss.

Even so, I really wanted to get to Cordoba, so I frantically booked some train tickets online and dived into a taxi, from the rank opposite the hotel, to take me to Malaga Railway Station. Had this happened on the days I was visiting Seville or Granada, it may not have been possible, but there was a train from Malaga at 10.30 that only took 54 minutes, non-stop.

In fact, I was probably in Cordoba before the bus and despite the station being nearly 2km out of town, it actually was quite pleasant to explore at my pace and go where I wanted to.

At first sight, Cordoba seemed a bit of a concrete jungle with no character. The station was so far out of town that I had to walk through what seemed to be a mile of non-descript office blocks and houses. There were a few parks to walk through, with some exotic flora that sheltered my head from the very hot sun but nothing to make you stop for a second to have a second look.

The old city centre of Cordoba did not let me down though. The centre of the city is a maze of tiny little alleys. with white painted houses, all with window baskets cascading the brightest flowers from the upstairs windows. The smell was amazing. This was the old Jewish quarter of the city which consists of a fascinating network of narrow lanes, more atmospheric and less commercialized than in Seville although souvenir shops have emerged.

At the centre of the quarter is the Synagogue in Calle de los Judios. one of only three originals remaining in Spain. A Mudejar construction dating from 1315. It was converted to a church in the 16th century and then held the Guild of Shoemakers until it was rediscovered in the 19th Century. The interior includes a gallery for women and plaster work with inscriptions from Hebrew psalms and others with plant motifs on the upper part.

Its main beautifully restored wall has a semi-circular arch where a chest with the Holy Scrolls of Law used to be kept.

Outside is a statue of Maimonides, a Sephardic Jewish Philosopher and Astronomer who was born in Cordoba in 1135 or 1138. Moshe ben Maimon, (his name in Hebrew) became one of the most prolific and influential Torah scholars and physicians of the Middle Ages. After Cordoba was conquered by the Almohads (Berber dynasty) in 1148 Maimonides moved about present-day Andalucía for the next ten years, residing in Fez (Morocco) before settling in Fustat (Egypt) in 1168. He died in Egypt in 1204. and was buried in Tiberias (Galilee, Israel).

Next to it is a Sephardic house which has been restored to how it would have been in the 14th century, before the Spanish Jews (known as Sephardi) were expelled from Spain by the Catholic Kings.

I didn't have time to go in, but it was an interesting five-minute stop and rest for my feet. Moving on I headed for the Plaza Del Potro, which is a long, rectangular square which slopes down towards the nearby Guadalquivir River to the south.

It is named after the 16th-century fountain in the plaza (1577), an octagonal structure which features a small, prancing horse balanced atop a vase; the square used to host a livestock market dealing in equestrian.

The medieval Posada del Potro, on the south side of the square, was a known haunt of adventurers and a favourite of Cervantes – he mentions it in Don Quixote. The writer lived in Cordoba as a child – his family moved there in 1553 from Valladolid, and stayed until 1557, living in a street called Calle Sillerias, now called Romero Barros. He probably also stayed at the Posada.

The city centre is dominated by The Mesquita, a 10th Century Mosque that was converted into the current day Cathedral. It was the reason I had wanted to come here, and the outside of the building did not disappoint. Originally constructed by Abd ar-Rahman III, one of the great rulers of Islamic history. During his reign Córdoba was one of the largest, most prosperous cities of Europe, outshining Byzantium and Baghdad in science, culture, and the arts. The development of the Great Mosque paralleled these new heights of splendour.

I wandered around the outside of the building first and took in the three main decorated gates dating back to Moorish construction. All three decorated in the traditional red and white stripes around the top of the arch.

To the South of the Mesquita is the River Guadalquivir and spanning it is a well-maintained Roman Bridge. On the Northern bank is the Puerto del Puente or Bridge Gate. It was completed in the days of Philip II.

The present triumphal arch is the work of Hernan Ruiz III and replaces what was first a Roman gate mentioned at the time of Julius Cesar and later a Moorish gate. A documented restoration took place in 720 AD. Today it is a traffic island.

Alongside is the most ostentatious of the statues erected in honour of St Raphael. It was finished by Miguel Verdiguier, a Frenchman who settled in Cordoba in the 18th century and is responsible for the distinctive Rococo style.

You can walk over the Roman bridge in either direction. According to the Arab geographer, Al-drisi this 'surpasses all other bridges in beauty and solidity', but reflects little of its Roman roots, owing to frequent reconstruction over many decades. In the centre of the eastern side's stone handrails there is a little shrine to St Raphael, at whose feet the devout burn candles.
It is, of course, unlikely that much of the original structure stands. The present structure is a medieval reconstruction, though the 19th-century cobbled paving does give a Roman feel. There is an irregular pattern to the 16 arches in size and abutment protections. There are good views of the bridge and the river from the south bank. Coach tours park to the south of the bridge, and wave upon wave of tour guides were shepherding their flocks over the bridge towards the Mesquita.

On the southern end of the bridge is the Torre de la Calahorra. It is a fortified gate originally built by the Moors (Almohads) and extensively restored by King Enrique II of Castile in 1369 to defend the city from attack by his brother Pedro I the Cruel from the South. It was originally an arched gate between two towers. Enrique II added a third cylindrical shaped tower connecting the outer two. In the 18th century it served as a prison and in the 19th century it was a girls' school. The tower was declared a national monument in 1931. The restoration of the tower and the Romain bridge and the surrounding area in 2007 was awarded the EU prize for cultural heritage "Europa Nostra" in 2014.

I had bought a ticket online to enter the Mesquita and had to be there for one o'clock. You enter through the Southern gate and enter the Patio de Los Naranjos, which was almost identical to the one in Seville and a hark back to the times where Islamic worshippers would clean themselves before entering the mosque. The smell of orange blossoms was almost overpowering here. When the mosque was used for Moslem prayer, all nineteen naves were open to this courtyard allowing the rows of interior columns to appear like an extension of the tree with brilliant shafts of sunlight filtering through.

The Mesquita must be one of the most stunning buildings I have ever seen. Towering above is the bell tower, formerly the mosques minaret, and perfectly aligned around the walls are red and white striped arches. The minaret or the Torre de Alminar is 93m high and was built on the site of the original minaret. It is possible to climb the steps to the very top for superb views of Cordoba. I passed; it was too hot.

The history of the site is quite remarkable. First, the Romans built a pagan temple on the site. After the fall of the Roman Empire, the new Germanic masters of Spain (the Visigoths) replaced it with the Christian church of Saint Vincent. When the Arabs conquered the peninsula in the early 8th century, they tore down the church and began building their great mosque, which - commensurate with Cordoba's importance as the centre of Muslim power in Spain - became the largest mosque in all of Islam after that of Kaaba, in Arabia.

When the Christians re-conquered Cordoba in 1236, they did with the mosque what they did in all the cities of Andalucía - instead of bothering to build a new church, they simply "converted" the building to Christianity and set up an altar in the middle. In the 16th century, this modest gothic insert was enlarged and given its current Renaissance - and later, baroque - styles, resulting in the strange hybrid which we now see, with its ornately carved altar and pews. The original mosque was permeated all around with open arches, so that the sunlight could flood in, leading the worshipper to the shadows of the central area, to represent his mystical journey towards Allah; but the Christians, being less inclined towards letting in the natural elements, plugged up most of the openings so that they could be used as a backdrop for chapels dedicated to the various saints. The minaret was left standing in the middle of the west wall, but did not fare as well as Seville's Giralda, which was simply capped with a belltower: it was used as the central core of a new baroque sheath (as you climb up inside it, you see the sealed-up arches and windows of the Moorish original- a tower within a tower).

Inside the Mesquita your breath is taken away by the rows upon rows of coloured granite jasper and marble arches. There are 856 of these red and white archways and the effect is amazing. It was unlike anything I have ever seen. Normally the Church would do what the Church does and demolish the mosque and build a gawdy church on top, like the one in Seville. But here they simply added a choir and a few chapels, maintaining the Islamic space. Sunlight streams in from windows in the four cupolas creating interesting effects combined with artificial light from the thousands of small oil lights.

The original Mihrab is still in place from the original mosque. This traditionally had two functions in Islamic worship, first it indicated the direction of Mecca (therefore prayer), and it also amplified the words of the Imam, the prayer leader. At Cordoba it is particularly magnificent. The shell-shaped ceiling is carved from a single block of marble and the chambers on either side are decorated with exquisite Byzantine mosaics of gold. The worn flagstones indicate where pilgrims crouched on their knees. The Cordoba Mosque Mihrab looks south in the same way as the Damascus Mosque and not southeast in the direction of Mecca. This was because originally, Muslims faced Jerusalem to pray, politics soon changed that.

In the centre of the mosque squats a Renaissance cathedral which dates back to the early sixteenth century while, to the left is the Capilla de Villaviciosa built by Moorish craftsmen in 1371.
The Mosque was consecrated as a Christian Cathedral in the same year that Cordoba was re-conquered (1236). Alfonso X built the Villaviciosa Chapel with stunning multi lobed arches. The Capilla Real (Royal Chapel) was also built as a pantheon for Christian Kings.

In the 14th century Enrique II rebuilt the royal chapel in Mudejar style. In 1523 with the support of King Carlos V the church built a huge nave inside the mosque. The cathedral was elaborated on over the years by many of the country´s leading architects and artists. Architect Hernan Ruiz continued working transforming the Cathedral into Gothic style.

Visiting here will stay with me for an exceptionally long time and it really was one of the most beautiful buildings I have ever come across. In fact, the whole old city centre of Cordoba was beautiful. I left the Mesquita and wandered up the Callejon De Las Flores, which is a small but well-known street and is the most photographed street in Cordoba.

A typical narrow, cobbled alley between whitewashed houses, its balconies and walls are decked out with flowers in terracotta pots, in characteristically vivid colours, such as brilliant pink, purple and red geraniums.

Looking back towards the Mesquita, you get a perfectly framed view of the Mesquita's tower framed by flower-covered white walls. An image you will see on many postcards around town.

I wanted to head somewhere for lunch but wanted a typical tapas bar rather than a restaurant. I firstly headed for the Plaza de la Corredera, which boasted several restaurants, all a bit touristy for my liking, but I did sit down for a cold Cruz Campo to take in the view. In Roman times, the area was used for chariot racing, but it is now a grand 17th-century square and has an elaborate history as a site of public spectacles, including bullfights and Inquisition burnings. Nowadays it is ringed by balconied apartments which would have given front row views to the burnings.

Suitably refreshed, I moved on towards what was left of a Roman Temple. The sheer size of the building is remarkable: it was dedicated to the cult of the Emperor, and along with the Circus Maximus, formed part of the Provincial Forum. It originally stood on a raised podium and had six free-standing Corinthian columns in the entrance. In front of this was the ara or altar. The present structure is a reconstruction and has left Cordoba yet another reminder of the splendour of the city in Roman times.

I stopped at a tapas bar across the street and ordered what I thought was squid and chips. It was not. It was just a plateful of baby squid which was a bit rubbery. Quite tasty, but it would have taken more than just another beer to get it all down.

From here it was about a mile back to the Railway station to catch the train back to Malaga. I am glad that I made the decision to do this trip myself, rather than sulk and be angry all day about the failures of the tour company.

Prior to catching a cab, I went into a supermarket at Malaga Railway Station for a cold can of Coke and finally came across a modern-day packet of Conguistos. They were very disappointing and the woke police had been out in full force, The once proud, head hunting chocolate peanuts with big lips and spears, were now nothing more than a multi-cultural Malteser with eyes and legs. Is nothing sacred! They will be banning bull fighting next.
I spent the evening lying on a sun lounger on the beach watching nine fishermen catch absolutely nothing. Clearly fishing is as exciting here as it is in Seaford. Mind you, we get excited at home to see one fishing boat, there were about 40 out fishing off the coast this evening here.

FIVE

Europe's "Most Beautiful Building"

After yesterday's debacle, I was suitably paranoid about missing the coach this morning. In fact, I almost camped outside all night. I was outside of the hotel at 7.25 for a 7.35 pickup. At 7.55 and still no coach I was reaching for my phone to give the tour company another mouthful when the bus finally turned up.

Today's trip was to Granada and The Alhambra, which some have described as the most perfect building in the World, but most would just claim it to be the most perfect in Europe.

Granada was first settled by native tribes in the prehistoric period and was known as Ilbyr. When the Romans colonized southern Spain, they built their own city here and called it Illibris. The Arabs, invading the peninsula in the 8th century, gave it its current name of Granada. It was the last Muslim city to fall to the Christians in 1492, at the hands of Queen Isabel of Castile and her husband Ferdinand of Aragon.

It wasn't that far to Granada, and we were there by 10.30. Our tickets for The Alhambra weren't until 2.30, so we had some free time, about 2 and a half hours to explore on our own. It was quite clear that if the bus had not shown up, Granada by train would not have been viable. The historic centre, or at least what little there is of it, is a good four miles from The Alhambra, the main attraction. The railway station was somewhere in between.

Much of the "Historic" Centre has been modernized and Granada had the feel of a more modern metropolis than Seville or Cordoba did. We were walked from the coach to The Plaza Isabel La Catolica. The Square is dominated by a statue of Queen Isabel giving Columbus her permission to make his journey and was sculpted in Rome for the Fourth Centennial of the Discovery of America in 1892.

The official name is Plaza Isabel la Catolica, but the grandiose amusingly call it La Plaza de Colon- Columbus Square - since there's no doubt in their minds that the real hero was the sailor and not the Queen, who merely signed the cheque entitling him to obtain the ships and supplies.

This in turn leads to the Plaza Nueva where Queen Isabel's stern confessor, the Muslim-hating Cardinal Cisneros, burnt some 80,000 books from the Muslim University, many of which were Arabic translations of Greek philosophers and science and mathematics tomes, claiming that they were all Korans. I am afraid book burning never ends well, but it does lower the IQ of the masses so that they blindly do what they are told.

The centre is dominated by The Cathedral, which is nothing like the partly Islamic ones in Seville and Cordoba. As in Mexico, beggars sat outside of a church, that was full of gold, silver, and priceless works of art. It was all a bit distasteful.

The Cathedral is in the centre of the Muslim area and dates back to 1523. It has a nave and four aisles, a crossing, and a circular apse. Alonso Cano built the main façade with sculptures by Duque Cornejo, Risueño and Verdiguier while the only tower of the two planned ended up half finished. On the northern side, there is La Puerta del Perdón, a magnificent work of Diego de Siloé who also built La Puerta de San Jerónimo. The chancel is not only stunning, but includes skillful architectural solutions provided by Siloé. Its circular plan and great height contain semi-circular arches upon which a double series of balconies rest.

The glass windows of the upper part add light and colour to the whole. Medrano and Mena sculpted the statues of the Catholic Monarchs and Alonso Cano the busts of Adam and Eve. The side chapels contain marvelous works of art. In the sacristy, there is a figure of Christ by Martinez Montañes, an Annunciation and a valued image of the Virgin Mary by Alonso Cano, together with other valuable objects in the Cathedral Museum.

It was worth exploring, but the juxtaposition of solid gold altars and solid silver Virgin Mary's compared to the poor buggers outside scraping an existence, left a bad taste in the mouth.

The Capilla Real (Royal Chapel) had a separate entrance and was not free like the Cathedral. The Catholic Monarchs founded the Royal Chapel for their own tombs. They chose to be buried in Granada because they saw its conquest as the crowning achievement of their reign. It was started in 1505 following a design by Enrique Egas and was completed in 1521. The northern facade is by Garcia Pradas and provides access to the interior; a plan in the shape of a Latin cross with four side chapels.

The crossing with the royal mausoleums is separated from the rest of the nave by a wrought iron screen, a real work of art by Master Bartolomé. The tomb of the catholic monarchs on the right was built by Domenico Fancelli, and on the left by Bartolomé Ordoñez using carrar marble. The chapel has a museum in the sacristy with paintings by Memling, van der Weyden, Botticelli, and Beriguete. The paintings belonged to the collection of Queen Isabella, whose crown and sceptre, together with King Fernando´s sword are kept here.

Isabel of Castille was at heart a woman of the Middle Ages, as demonstrated by her precious collection of Flemish masters on view in the Sacristy. She wanted a small, humble mausoleum for her and all her descendants, befitting the follower of Saint Francis who she was. But she died before the chapel could be built, and, in the company of Ferdinand, spent some twenty years in a provisional tomb inside the Alhambra walls, where a Franciscan monastery had been installed in the shell of the palace mosque.

The architects made the chapel-mausoleum larger and more luxurious than planned, with the result that it is neither humble nor truly grand; in any case, her successor and grandson Carlos V - the master of the new Empire which she had founded - judged it too modest for the masters of a reign on which the sun never set, and the Royal Pantheon for all subsequent monarchs was eventually moved to the blockbuster Escorial Monastery outside Madrid, built by his son Felipe II, who knew how to do things on the right scale! Despite the lack of historical sights, Granada did have by far the best selection of interesting shops, which seemed almost like Istanbul. The Islamic influence is still there and there are streets full of spices which, combined with the overpowering smell of Orange Blossom was full on for the senses.

The Alcaicería, home of the Great Bazaar of Granada, was originally a series of streets between Plaza Nueva and Plaza Bib-Rambla, bursting with stalls selling Arabic silks, spices, and other precious goods. Nowadays the only remaining section is Calle Alcaiceria, beginning just off the Calle Reyes Catolicos, and extending back as far as the Cathedral. It is an area rich in history and local culture, still packed with interesting, exotic things to buy. Alcaicería is a name which was used all over Moorish Spain and parts of the Middle East. The Bazaar was one of few Moorish traditions to survive the Christian conquest; Bazaars existed not only in Granada but across the Christian realm. The name Alcaicería, surprisingly, has Roman origins: the Arabic al-Kaysar-ia means "the place of Caesar", to thank the Byzantine Emperor Justinian, after he granted the Arabs the exclusive right to manufacture and sell silk in the sixth century. From then on, all Arabic bazaars were named in the same way.

The original Alcaicería of Granada was built in the 15th century, and survived until the 19th century, when a fire sadly destroyed it - caused, ironically, by a workshop selling Granada's first cardboard matches, which itself caught fire. A replica was built, but the result was more pastiche - the new Alcaicería was less than half of its original size, and was a cheaper, modern version of the Moorish style - neo-Moorish. As a result, after a comparatively short time, it is already looking the worse for wear.

Unlike the current Alcaicería, the original was home to more than 200 shops squeezed into a labyrinth of streets and alleyways. Each was very small and had a red ochre coloured door, which was tilted upwards to open (much like a garage door); when opened the door sat above the stall, providing an awning to protect the silks in the event of rain. The streets of the Alcaiceria were sealed by iron gates, to prevent guards and noblemen from entering on horseback, and were locked overnight to protect the precious goods and artefacts on sale inside.

I picked up a few souveniers here and spent half an hour wandering around before heading off for some lunch. There seemed to be a lack of traditional eateries in Granada and the fayre was more Torremolinos than Seville. I had a local delicacy for lunch. Croquette Potatoes! Four different flavours, potato and onion, blue cheese and spinach, ox tail and blood pudding. The beer washed them down. But as it was Cruz Campo, only just.
By one o'clock, I headed back to the coach to head for The Alhambra. The name Alhambra comes from an Arabic root which means "red or crimson castle", perhaps due to the hue of the towers and walls that surround the entire hill of La Sabica which by starlight is silver but by sunlight is transformed into gold.

But there is another more poetic version, evoked by the Moslem analysts who speak of the construction of the Alhambra fortress "by the light of torches", the reflections of which gave the walls their particular coloration. Created originally for military purposes, the Alhambra was an "alcazaba" (fortress), an "alcázar" (palace) and a small "medina" (city), all in one. This triple character helps to explain many distinctive features of the monument.

There is no reference to the Alhambra as being a residence of kings until the 13th century, even though the fortress had existed since the 9th century. The first kings of Granada, the Zirites, had their castles and palaces on the hill of the Albaicin, and nothing remains of them. The Nasrites were probably the emirs who built the Alhambra, starting in 1238.

The Alhambra became a Christian court in 1492 when the Catholic Monarchs (Ferdinand and Isabel) conquered the city of Granada. Later, various structures were built for prominent civilians, also military garrisons, a church, and a Franciscan monastery.

Emperor Charles V, who spent several months in Granada, began the construction of the palace which bears his name and made some alterations to the interior buildings. These measures were to cause interminable controversy often motivated by political agendas. The remaining Austrian kings did not forget the monument and have left their own more discreet impressions on it.
The Christian Kings deserted the Palace during the Inquisition. It was slightly awkward to be burning Muslims when the King had an Islamic palace.

There is only 35% of the buildings left or restored, it was once an entire gated community, Evidently Napoleon used some of the buildings as arms dumps in the early 19th Century and the British blew them up and took 1000 year of history with it. Is it me or is it always us who destroy things?
Our tour started in the Alcazaba. The Alcazaba, or fortress, is the oldest part of the Alhambra. It was built in the mid-13th century by the Sultan Alhamar, the founder of the Nasrid dynasty, after he fled from northern Andalucía and established what was to be the last Moorish stronghold against the Christian crusaders.

The largest tower of the fortress is the Torre de la Vela, so called for the great bell which hangs above it. When the Catholic Monarchs took Granada, they brought with them from Castile a bell called La Vela, "the sentinel", to ring the victory chimes from the Moorish castle. In the struggle between the creeds, the bell had become the symbol of Christianity, as the lamps of the mosques were the symbol of Islam.

La Vela has always been rung on great occasions of state, as well as to commemorate the Día de la Toma, the day of the conquest ("the taking") of the city, every January 2.

The grandiose have always called it the Palacio de Carlos Quinto, but its real name is the Casa Real de la Alhambra - the Royal Manor of the Alhambra. It is, well... big, and solidly built, much bigger and more solid than the earlier Moorish palaces which it was set down among. The 16th-century palace has the distinction of being one of the first Renaissance buildings created outside of Italy, modelled on Florence's equally massive Palazzo Pitti, and its architect, Pedro Machuca, was a student of Michelangelo in Rome. It is mainly distinguished by its circular courtyard, in the majestic Roman tradition.

The Palace was built for Charles I of Spain, He was the grandson of Isabel and Ferdinand. The young King married his cousin Isabel of Portugal, in Seville, and then brought her, with a huge following of courtesans and dignitaries, to Granada for their honeymoon in 1526.

Charles fell in love with the city, which still resembled the Arab medina it had been before the conquest and decided to have a great palace built for himself, next to the bucolic patios and gardens of the Moorish kings, which he planned to use as a recreational area for outdoor events.

But he wanted his palace to have the modern European comfort befitting a man of the Renaissance, with amenities such as doors, windows, and fireplaces, for those winter nights when the wind blows down from the Sierra. This was quite understandable, since the Moorish palaces, if one considers them as everyday living places, are more similar to desert tents than effective shelters in a region which for half the year, at least at night, is quite cold. To finance the construction, which required the importation of architects and craftsmen, the King decided to levy yet another tax on the city's beleaguered Moriscos, who agreed to pay rather than face further repression.

During the otherwise idyllic summer the Monarchs spent in Granada, there was an earthquake which frightened Isabel so badly that she could not later be persuaded to return. And once the work began, the tribute of the Moriscos soon proved to be insufficient to finance a building of that scale, as a result of which the pace of the work had to be geared to the collection of the tax. The construction ended up taking no less than 110 years.

It was restored and completed under the Franco dictatorship in the 1950's, not as a palace but a national museum. In fact, no king of Spain ever lived there at all.

The highlight of the tour are the Nasrid Palaces dating back to Moorish occupation. The casa Real Vieja dates back to the 14th century and is the work of two great kings: Yusuf I and Muhammed V.

The Alhambra contains the three divisions usually found in a Muslim palace, including a reception salon and the royal apartments Chamber of the Lions. This spectacular chamber is the work of Muhammed V and illustrates the most beautiful possibilities of Granada Moslem art. Throughout this chamber a subtle air of femininity and daintiness is sensed, in keeping with the function of these private apartments, devoted to the placid enjoyment of home and family life.

The Court of the Lions is characterized by its profound originality, a harmonious merging of East and West. It has been compared to a grove of 124 palm trees, most with double columns, around the oasis of the central fountain with its twelve lions. The twelve-sided marble fountain rests upon the backs of the lions. Water, so essential as a decorative element, acquires here an exceptional importance. It ascends and spills from the basin, which has been compared with the 'sea of bronze' of Solomon's Temple, to the mouths of the lions, from which it is distributed throughout the courtyard. A lovely "qasida" (ode) by Ibn Zamrak circles the rim of the basin.

Four large halls border the courtyard. The first, entering from the Court of the Myrtles, is the "Sala de los Mozárabes", whose name is perhaps derived from the three stalactite arches which form the entrance to the Court of the Lions. To the south is the "Sala de Abencerrajes", famous in legend for having a gateway decorated with "lazo" (ornamental knots). Light penetrates the hall through 16 graceful fretwork windows. On the east side is the "Sala de los Reyes" which is unusual and resembles a theatrical set, divided into three sections which correspond to three lovely porticos, separated by double arches of "mozárabes" (stalactites).

North of the Court of the Lions is the "Sala de las Dos Hermanas", so called because of the two large marble flagstones flanking the central fountain and spout. The adjoining hall is the "Sala de los Ajimeces" with two balconies overlooking the Garden of Daraxa. Between these two balconies is the "Mirador de Daraxa", dressing room and bedroom of the Sultana and a delightful retreat in this secluded section of the palace, in the style of a bay window or mirador.

The Courtyard of the Lions represents the Garden of Paradise, a desert oasis of leafy palms surrounding a bubbling fountain. The rectangles between the marble walkways were, under the Moors, sunken gardens overflowing with flowers and aromatic bushes. When the Christians arrived on the scene, they were amazed at the splendour of the Alhambra, which, by comparison with the harsh medieval fortresses in which their own monarchs lived, seemed incredibly luxurious. They called the most elegant part of it the "Room of the Lions", because of the curious fountain in its center - although its name for the Moors was the Palace of Mohammed V.

Although it is not known precisely where the lions came from, the Moors themselves could not have made them because the Koran forbade the representation of living creatures, to prevent a return of the idolatry which it was the Prophet's first mission to stamp out. They were probably made by Christian or Jewish artists, and as such, they - and the portraits of the Nasrid Kings in an adjacent hall - are proof of the fact that by the 14th century the grandiose had become irreversibly Westernized in their habits and tastes.

Four halls surround the courtyard, the largest of which is the Hall of the Two Sisters. This name refers to the massive twin slabs of marble which lie on either side of the central fountain, compared to two sisters in an Arabic poem. This hall was the reception room for the throne room, which lies just beyond it in an exquisitely decorated alcove.

Nowhere else in the Alhambra is there such a display of mocárabes, the encrustations with which the Moors coated archways and ceilings. These were pre-moulded in plaster and fitted ingeniously together to create the effect of stalactites in a grotto.

The Throne Room, similar to the one in the Tower of Comares, was set in a niche-like balcony, so that the light from behind would surround the Sultan in an aura. But romantic legend once more takes precedence: this enchanting place is known to all as the Mirador de Lindaraja - "lookout place of the queen" - for the wife of Sultan Muley Hacen who is said to have lived here. The balcony's windows overlooked the Albaicin on the other side of the valley, until the Christians built the rooms intended to accommodate Carlos Quinto on his visits to Granada, thus cutting off the splendid view forever.

Here, as everywhere in the Alhambra, the walls are covered with tapestry-like plaster relief, in a seemingly endless variety of geometrical and abstract patterns. The panels are framed by holy texts from the Koran, carved by the Moorish masters in contrasting calligraphical styles which dazzle the viewer with their intricacy and elegance.

To stave off the final defeat, the Nasrids reluctantly agreed to be the vassals of the King of Castile, at the beginning of their reign in the early 13th century. Everywhere on the richly decorated walls of the palace we see the shield symbolically given to them by the Christians, which, defiantly, they inscribed with the Arabic words "The only conqueror is Allah".

The two great Nasrid palaces which have come down to us intact are popularly known as the Tower of Comares and the Courtyard of the Lions. But the Moors knew them for the father and son who built them: respectively, Yusuf I and Mohammed V, whose reigns roughly correspond to the first and second halves of the 14th century.

The name Comares comes from the Arabic word camariyya, which means stained glass, for the coloured panes which once adorned its windows but were blown out by an explosion in a powder-house. The greatest of the many marvels of this unique room is, undoubtedly, the domed ceiling, with its wooden inlay representation of the Islamic universe. The Moors were masters of this kind of encrustation.

If the palace is amazing in its beauty, the gardens here are even more stunning. One courtyard, known as El Partal, is especially stunning for its symmetry and perfection.

El Partal comes from an Arabic word meaning "the portico", and is the name given to the remains of the residence of Sultan Yusuf III, the northernmost of the Nasrid Palaces. The stately Moorish homes which once filled this part of the Alhambra Hill were allowed to fall into ruin because they were not close enough to the new Christian palace to be conveniently used, by its intended inhabitants, as recreational areas, and decorated gardens, of the type so popular during the Renaissance. All that is left now are the archaeological excavations of several of these homes visible among the terraced gardens (planted in the 20th century) - and the picturesque arcade, tower, and pond of El Partal.

Near the pond stands a small mosque, one of the most charming buildings of the Alhambra.

It was built atop the ramparts and is barely wide enough for three or four people to kneel side by side. The "Mesquita del Partal" is the only free-standing mosque conserved in the city.

The higher part of the garden, at the foot of the church of Santa María, was the site of the palace cemetery or rawda, situated next to the Great Mosque. Here we have an external view of the star-shaped "lantern" of the Room of the Abencerrajes.

The Generalife Gardens are an attraction in their own right. The word "Generalife" has been translated as "garden of paradise", "orchard" or "garden of feasts". A Summer Palace for the Sultans once stood here and there is a hunting lodge where the rulers, accompanied by their wives, could escape the turmoil of the palace. The Moors, like today's Andalucians, did not combat the heat by seeking the open air, but rather by withdrawing into shady, secluded patios and rooms.

The gardens, built by the Moors, were self-watering. A spring at the top of the gardens ran into small channels that ran at a slight downward slope, filling ponds and watering the flower beds. Far too ingenious for The Christians. They probably burnt the instruction manual.

Despite obvious changes made by Christian monarchs, the gardens retain some of the Islamic symmetry and are very pleasant to stroll through.

So, the question is, is the Alhambra the most beautiful building in the world? I would say not. Having seen some of the ornate palaces in India and the sultans Palace in Istanbul, this really fails to hit those heights. Having said that, I don't think I have seen anything quite so exquisite in Europe. Some of the Renaissance palaces of Italy come close, but they do not quite equal what is here.

To be honest, I could have spent another hour or so at The Alhambra, but we had to curtail things and head back to Torremolinos, arriving back at 4.30.

Back in my room, I finally decided that my shorts had dried out from the drenching they received earlier in the week, and I could finally wear them again.

I couldn't face the hotel food tonight, so I walked to the next town along the beach, for a Vietnamese meal which was really nice. There was a Belgian beer bar next to it that I had penciled in for after's, but it had shut down by the time I had finished my meal. As a result, I took a slow walk back to the hotel and finally frequented the downstairs bar. I couldn't face another Cruz campo, so ordered a couple of Mojitos. Unfortunately, there was a Flamenco stage show going on which was a bit off putting. Lots of stomping around and pouting and from the wailing sounds, stomping on each other's feet.

SIX

Winding Down

It had been a full on week of sightseeing and for my last day in Torremolinos I decided to take it easier. No getting up before nine o'clock, a relaxed breakfast, not checking my watch every thirty seconds in case I missed a bus, and a short stroll to the shop outside of the hotel gates that sold The Daily Mail (Spanish Edition) which was read, enjoying the sun on my balcony. A pleasant, relaxing, Saturday morning.

I had contemplated a stroll along to the Eastern end of the beach where there were remains of a Roman seaside villa, dating back to the 1st Century BC and a Roman industrial centre which was used for preparing salted fish and Garum, the Roman ketchup, that was made of fish guts. It was too warm, even after 2,000 years, the thought of the smell of rotting fish guts on a balmy thirty-degree day, was too much to contemplate.

Around midday, I decided to take a leisurely stroll into the town centre. I used the back entrance to the hotel for a change as it cut off a few hundred yards, a wandered down a pedestrian street in the direction of the shops. On a slope, on the right hand side of the road stood a rather impressive mansion house. It is known locally as the Casa de los Navajas and is one of the few large houses built here in the 1920's that survived, firstly the depression and secondly The Spanish Civil War. At the start of the 1920's, several wealthy families chose to build second homes in Torremolinos. This was the home to the Navajos family, who made their fortune in the sugar cane industry, which at that time flourished in the estuary of The Guadalhorce River, lying to the east of Malaga.

It was too hot to climb the steps, so I joined the ample queue for the elevator. My aim was to find a café that I had read about on Trip Advisor, that claimed to make the best Cuban Sandwich, outside of Havana have never been to Cuba, but the Cuban sandwiches I had in New York were still memorable and this would have been worth it had they been half as good.

The post COVID world was beginning to sink in. As was the case with many such establishments, the shutting down of Europe's economies decimated so much and although finding the café I was looking for, it was boarded up and had never reopened.

Despite searching, in vain, for somewhere else to have lunch, the centre of Torremolinos is pretty soulless. I had thought about going back to the Mexican Taco restaurant I went to on my first day, and even walked there, but by that point, plan b had come to fruition. I walked past the taco Restaurant and continued into a residential part of town that seemed to include blocks of well maintained, upmarket apartments, and secluded, white painted mansions. For once it felt like I was in Spain rather than Essex.

In a leafy street I came to the top of a modern staircase that went down and down and down, in a windy route to ground level. I certainly approached this from the right direction. There seemed to be more steps here than there were at my end of town, and there were no places to stop for a drink to break the journey here.
The beach was only around one hundred metres away and lo and behold, as I turned on to the Promenade, there was the Belgian Beer bar that had shut on me the previous evening. Thank you, Google Maps.

After a couple of cold, and certainly tasty, beers I had a look at the food menu. The choice was aa bit limited. Moules Frites which could have been a disaster. I had a white shirt on and tip half of my food down my shirt at the best of times. I didn't fancy promenading along the beach with everyone else showing off their tanned bodies, whilst I was covered in a fishy broth. The second option was Flemish rabbit stew. Now I had that on a freezing cold day in Bruges once and it was absolutely delicious. But rabbit stew in 30 degrees wasn't really what I was looking for. As a result, I ordered another beer, before wandering back towards my hotel.

The beach here was known as La Carihuela and is separated from the main beach, El Bajondillo, by a rocky outcrop called La Punta de Torremolinos, into which a pathway has been carved. Once around the headland you are back to the gawdy bars and cocktails of the English tourists.

I looked for somewhere to eat, but places were either too full or too boring and as I quickly ran out of possibilities, sadly I ended up in the Burger King next door to my hotel for a burger and onion rings that I had on my balcony.

I relaxed for the rest of the afternoon before finally joining the rest of the Brits and going to a bar to watch football. Brighton were playing Manchester United and, in a way, I was dreading having to sit in a bar with a load of Man United fans thinking they were better than everyone else. It's funny that sometimes, despite all the history and culture, a trip can be remembered for something completely different. I went to Bratislava a few years ago, and I am sure there was lots of history there, but it will always be remembered for watching Brighton beat great rivals Crystal palace in an Irish pub. And now Torremolinos will be remembered as the place where I sat and watched Brighton beat Manchester United four nil, alongside a load of angry Mancunians. Who cares about the Alhambra!! Somewhat happy and a few German beers later, certainly better than the Cruz Campo, I staggered back to the remnants of the dinner buffet in the hotel. Cold chips and the last scraps of paella were all that was left but whatever. I even had another bottle of Cruz Campo to wash it down.

The coach picked me up at seven o'clock the following morning and Malaga airport was a breeze to get through. In total contrast to the chaos at Gatwick.

I was home by one o'clock in time to go to Mum's for a roast dinner. It's amazing how quickly you get back into a routine!

SEVEN

Return To Seville

Three months later, I was visiting some friends who said that they would be visiting Seville for a short break the following February, and asked if I would I like to join them. There was certainly a lot more of Seville that I hadn't seen and more importantly, the thought of escaping a cold February in Seaford to go to the balmy twenty degrees plus of Seville was too much to turn down.

Thankfully, this time we flew directly to Seville with no delays at Gatwick. Seville, although a major city in Spain, has a relatively quiet airport. All the sun seekers head for Malaga and get to their chosen resorts from there. When we landed, there was only one other plane at the terminal and as a result we were through immigration and on to a bus within thirty minutes.

The airport was a few miles outside of the city, so it was a further forty minutes before we were dropped off on the banks of the River Guadalquivir, opposite the Torre del Oro. I roughly knew where we were and it was a two hundred metre walk to the Bull Ring, where we turned right, and the hotel was a further few hundred metres on the left. The Hotel Adriano was, despite the rooms being a bit dark, very comfortable, and more importantly, central.

It was around 2pm at this point and we decided to take a stroll out for a tapas lunch and a drink. It was still Cruz Campo, but the tapas was OK. The whole idea of tapas is great. If you want a main meal, you can order what is known as a plate, where you get the full portion. But if you order the tapas size, it is about a quarter of the main meal, therefore you can have four mini meals and try more from the menu. All well and good, but if you are a vegetarian, like Amanda, it gets a little limited. There are only so many plates of sliced tomatoes that anybody can eat.

After lunch we wandered down towards the park and The Plaza De Espana, which I had seen the previous year, but Steve and Amanda had not.

On the way to the park, we passed a massive building, which today houses the University of Seville. In its prime, this was The Royal Tobacco Factory.
The Tobacco Factory today still resembles the many palaces that are scattered around Seville with a magnificent Baroque entrance. An impressive piece of 18th-century industrial architecture, which takes up an entire city block, this was the second-largest building at the time (El Escorial near Madrid was the biggest); measuring 185m by 147m, it is still one of Spain's largest industrial buildings.

At its height it produced 75% of all the cigarettes sold in Europe. Tobacco was one of the first discoveries that Columbus brought back to Seville and the city enjoyed a monopoly on the tobacco trade for many centuries. There is a stone carving of Conquistador, Hernan Cortes, renowned for massacring and plundering Mexico and Central America, but remembered here as Europe's first smoker. I am not quite sure which legacy is the most favourable. Supposedly, the factory had its own prison for workers who were caught nicking the occasional fag.

The factory that stands today, was not actually constructed until the early eighteenth century and is probably more renowned these days, as the setting for Bizet's opera "Carmen". It shut its doors in 2007 and subsequently became the University of Seville.

We finally arrived at the park which was colourful and full of ripe oranges. Despite warnings from both myself and Steve that these were almost certainly bitter, marmalade oranges, Amanda insisted on trying one of them. She then proceeded to spit it out and complain about it for quite a while.

In the evening we wandered to the Plaza del Triunfu where the cathedral and walls of the Alcazar were illuminated, making it an amazing spectacle. We chose to eat in the Barrio Santa Cruz, a fairly touristy district that runs off the Central Plaza. Originally the city's Jewish neighbourhood, it is the colourful, characterful centre of old Seville, and although it's always packed with tourists, it hasn't lost the small-town ambiance that has defined it for centuries.

Again, we had a few tapas dishes followed by a decent meal. Steve had steak and chips and I had some sort of pork schnitzel in a cheesy sauce. Amanda had aubergines cooked in honey and then proceeded to send a picture of it to their daughter Alice, who was working in Brazil. She then complained for the rest of the evening that she had not got a response. I'm not sure what I would have done in my twenties if my Mum had sent a picture of every dinner she ate for me to look at. A picture of Mum's stew and dumplings turning up every so often would have been quite cruel and made me very homesick. Not sure a picture of aubergines was having that effect though.

A couple of drinks later we wandered back to the hotel, quite tired having had to be up at four to get to the airport.

The following morning, after a quick breakfast, we headed back to the centre of Seville as we had tickets for the cathedral and to climb the bell tower, or Giralda. Something I did not have time for on my previous fleeting visit.

At 103 metres in height, the Giralda is the icon of Seville and has been its tallest structure for over 800 years. Originally built in 1195 as the minaret of the Aljama mosque, it is now the belltower of the cathedral, and is recognised as World Heritage by UNESCO. The minaret was the culmination of Almohad architecture and served as a model for those at the dynasty's imperial capitals of Rabat and Marrakesh. It was used both for calling the faithful to prayer (the traditional function of a minaret) and as an observatory.

The Giralda was highly venerated by the Moorish rulers, who wanted to destroy the minaret before the Christian conquest of the city in 1248, rather than have it used for a religion other than Islam but were prevented by the threat of King Alfonso X that "if they removed a single stone, they would all be put the sword".
There are no steps, but a series of 35 ramps wind their way upwards. Originally designed so that the Muezzin, who called the faithful to prayer, could ride up on a donkey or horse. By the 15th ramp I was wishing that there were still donkeys for hire at the bottom, but the sheer number of tourists wheezing their way to the top would not make that practical. And then when you finally make it up to the summit, there are so many people that you can't really enjoy the views.

After that climb it was definitely beer o'clock and we stopped for a couple of drinks and some more tapas. Amanda had yet another plate of tomatoes and I had some sort of local fishcakes and spicy potatoes.

After lunch we explored the maze of medieval streets that run to the north of The Plaza del Triunfu. It is a labyrinth of touristy shops and restaurants which leads to the Plaza Nueva which is the tree lined heart of Seville. A ring of shady palm and orange trees surround the Plaza, which one side hosts the monumental, Ayuntamiento, or Town hall in English. In its original form, the building dates to the 16th century, but a major 19th-century makeover saw the addition of an imposing neo-classical façade. Some Renaissance carvings still survive on its eastern walls.

The Plaza seemed full of people sitting, sipping glasses of wine, and generally enjoying the sunshine. In Spain, officially, people work in the mornings, before having a lunchbreak and a siesta. They are supposed to start work again, but not many seem to.

Taking pride of place in the centre of the square is a statue of King Fernando III, also known as San Fernando, who reconquered the city from the Moors in 1248.

The maze of shops continues to the north of the plaza, but the shops become a little less touristy, offering traditional Flamenco fayre and fairly high-end goods.

Eventually the maze comes to an end, and you find yourself on a modern main road. To the right of us was one of Seville's more modern attractions, The Metropol Parasol.

Intended as a Guggenheim Bilbao-type landmark, to put Seville on the contemporary architecture map, this extraordinary, flowing structure (known locally as Las Setas, the mushrooms) consists of six huge, linked parasols made of waffle-type crisscrossed wooden beams - it is said to be the world's largest timber-framed structure.

Metropol Parasol's trademark amorphous shape can be seen reflected in every detail of the development, from the curvy benches to the sinuous flowerbeds. The parasols, which measure 150x70m in total, took six years to build, and cost a reported 123 million euros.
The building serves a number of purposes: an archaeological museum in the basement, Antiquarium, with Roman and Moorish ruins discovered when area was being excavated to build a car park; a food market and restaurants on the ground floor; an open-air shaded concert space on the first floor; and a walkway and more restaurants on the second and third floors. The last feature is the best, offering views of the city from 30 metres up, including a large mirador, viewing area, at the very top of the building. It has been open since 2011.

Having walked up the Giralda, which was 103 metres, the thought of paying more than twenty euros to see the city from thirty metres didn't seem that great a deal. More importantly, Seville's most famous cake shop was opposite, and we stopped for afternoon tea. In the evening I had planned an evening in a different area of town known as the Alameda de Hercules. This is basically a square Flanked by bars, cafes, and restaurants, that I had read was bursting with energy and people. There were also a few interesting bars in the area that served proper beer!

So having walked half an hour, we found out that most bars shut in Seville on a Monday night and most people stay in. We sat outside one bar, which at least had an American IPA rather than just Cruz Campo on its menu and watched a whole lot of nothing. This was a shame as the square was quite a historic place and there been people, quite cool. It was originally laid out in the late 16th century and became a fashionable promenade during the city's 17th-century Golden Age. There are two Roman columns at its southern end which are 2000-year-old originals, topped by statues of Hercules and Julius Caesar.

So, it was back to the Santa Cruz district for more tapas, the obligatory plate of tomatoes, Cruz campo and a rather tasty swordfish steak. From here we did find a decent bar that sold rather strong Belgian beer. Which was a good remedy for my aching feet.

The following morning, we took the train to Cadiz, which was about 90 minutes south of Seville, and although attached to the mainland, stuck out like an island in the Atlantic Ocean, a few miles before it turns into the Mediterranean at the Straits of Gibraltar.

Cadiz is believed to be the oldest city still standing in Europe. Its history is marked by its strategic military and commercial location on the Atlantic Ocean and at the entrance to a large, sheltered bay. The settlement was founded by Phoenicians from Tyre (modern day Lebanon) following the Trojan War in 1.104 BC.

The fortifications that surround the city were started in the 16th century as a direct result of raiders. In addition, the Spanish built the Baluarte de la Candelaria, a fortress guarding the sea passage into the port of Cádiz situated on the northern point of the 'star'. Again, it is massively built, not something even Nelson would have liked to challenge.

On the southern tips of the star, at either end of the Playa de la Caleta, guarding the sea approaches to the city there are two more solid castles, the Castillo de Santa Catalina built in 1598 after the sacking of Cádiz and the Castillo de San Sebastian built in 1706. Amongst its claims to fame is the Barca family. The father, Hamilcar, was a successful Carthaginian commander during the First Punic War 264 to 241BC; there is a street in Cádiz bearing his name. The son, Hannibal based his army, including the elephants, at Cádiz during the Second Punic War, 218 to 201BC, before marching the whole lot into Italy where he put the fear of God into the Romans.

Much later Columbus travelled the other way, west. His second and fourth voyages to the Americas set off from Cádiz. The port itself became the home of the Spanish treasure fleet and, when the Rio Guadalquivir started to silt up in the 18th century, Cádiz replaced Seville as the centre of trade with the colonies. Unfortunately for Cádiz, its wealth made it a target for passing raiders. The sixteenth century saw many attacks by the Barbary Pirates.

A legacy of Columbus's discoveries are the fig trees brought back from the Americas as saplings and planted on the promenades. They have grown into massive, magnificent specimens.

In 1587 Francis Drake occupied the city for three days capturing six ships and a great deal of booty and destroying a further thirty-one ships. The event became known as 'The singeing of the King of Spain's beard.' Drake was by no means the only person to be attracted by the lure of gold. The Earl of Essex and Lord Howard sacked part of the town in 1596, the Duke of Buckingham had a go in 1625 and, during the Anglo-Spanish War, the British blockaded the port from 1655 to 1657. In 1702, during the War of the Spanish Succession, the English returned but, on this occasion, they were beaten back.

Undeterred the British came back in 1797 to blockade and lay siege to Cádiz. It was a costly failure. Two years later Nelson, nursing a wounded arm after his defeat at Santa Cruz, in a fit of pique and with no military objective, bombarded the city as he sailed north on his way back to England.

When we arrived, the city was preparing for the annual Cádiz Carnival. It was influenced more by the carnival at Venice, with whom merchants from Cadiz traded with, rather than the local Seville Feria. It is known as the premier carnival in Spain, mainly because it can last anything up to three weeks. It was still the rehearsal stage of the Carnival when we were there, but if we had been there a week later, the streets would have been full of bands, people dressed in all sorts of costumes and people generally having fun. In fact, the Cadiz Carnival is the only one that Franco failed to ban!

Walking about half a mile in from the railway station, we first came to a large square, at the end of which stood Cadiz cathedral which took over 130 years to build. Starting in Baroque style and completed in Neo-classical style, the dome and the towers are much smaller than originally intended.

It is claimed that Cadiz cathedral is the perfect blend of Spanish Moorish roots and Italian baroque. This may explain why it all appeared to be a bit of a mish mash. In fact, I was finding the whole of Cadiz to be slightly disappointing, and all a bit run down. There was a Roman Amphitheatre, but that was locked behind a metal gate. But the prize goes to what I believe used to be an archaeological museum. I say this because there were two Phoenician sarcophagi lying alone in the window. I question this because a few metres behind these ancient relics were a group of tents and sleeping bags where homeless people were living. I think the sarcophagus would have been warmer than some of the tents, but thankfully nobody had prized it open yet. The British museum it was not.

We walked along the rather blustery seafront and eventually arrived at one of the castles that perch on each corner of Cadiz's sea defences. The Castillo de Santa Catalina is the oldest of the castles, built in 1598.

King Felipe II decided to reinforce the Playa de Cádiz, leading to the Castillo de Santa Catalina project by Cristóbal de Rojas to reinforce Santa Catalina cove on the city's seafront. Five months after the building works started in 1598, Felipe II died. The castle was completed exactly 23 years later, in September 1621, at the end of Felipe III's reign.

The castle's footprint is shaped like a three-pointed star, comprising two bastions and a moat. These regulated the water level, with sluice gates to protect the single entrance to the fort. The castle ramparts offer excellent views of the coast in all directions.
In 1769 Carlos III repurposed the castle as a military prison. Conscientious objectors, including 300 Jehovah's Witness who refused to undertake Spanish military national service, were held in the castle from 1965 until 1976. The castle continued to be a military prison until shortly before the Ministry of Defence handed the castle over to the city in 1991.

Inside one of the buildings there was a display telling the story of The Cadiz Explosion of 1947. This was a military accident when a storage depot at the local submarine base caught fire and 1737 sea mines, torpedoes and depth charges went up with it. 147 died and five thousand were injured. Buildings such as old folks' homes and an orphanage were blown sky high as was, more unfortunately, a well preserved Phoenician necropolis. This still one of Spain's most tragic peace time disasters and I would have learned more about it if a guard hadn't started shepherding everyone out of the castle, so that people could rehearse for the carnival.

We had lunch at the Mercado de Abastos. A remarkable and unique building that was built in 1830. The building was also originally conceived as a wide open plaza with a perimeter portico, however in 1928 this large central space was filled with two pavilions to expand the market. Nowadays in addition to the classic fish, fruit, or vegetable stalls, which are found in the large food market, there is an area for bars and cafes, where we took an alfresco seat. Steve and I shared a plate of deep fried squid, Amanda had yet another plate of tomatoes and once again this was washed down with a cold Cruz Campo.

After lunch we headed back to the coastal defences and walked through the Parque Genoves which is the largest green space in the city. Located on adjacent to the northern seafront promenade, Its origin dates back to the end of the eighteenth century. Today in the garden are more than 100 different species of tree and shrubs, including a New Zealand Iron Heart tree which is supposedly the best example of this in Europe. They all looked the same to me. This part of the walk around the city defences and sea walls was probably the most interesting and features a cobbled stone walkway, a stone balustrade, old sentry boxes, old cannons, and ornate lampposts.

We stopped for a warm cup of coffee as the sea breeze was getting quite chilly, and I think we all decided that Cadiz had seen better days. Admittedly it was February, but even so, I seriously doubt they would get the city back to its former glory in a few months. In any case, it would take that long to evict the homeless people from the museum.

We made our way back to the railway station and by the time our train arrived back in Seville, it had got dark. We dumped our bags back at the hotel and went straight out for dinner, once again in the Santa Cruz District.

I had a very nice paella tonight. Amanda had some more aubergines and once again took a photo of them, sending them to Alice, just in case the first picture never made it. We were still waiting for a response.

EIGHT

Flamenco Loco

I didn't get the chance to go to the Alcazar in Seville when I visited previously. Purely because the queue would have been too long and secondly, at that stage, I had not visited the Alhambra in Grenada, which is generally renowned to be better, although similar. Even this time we had to book in advance, and this gave us ample time to wander to the historic centre of the city from our hotel, enjoy a very cheap breakfast (two slices of toast and marmalade, orange juice and coffee for under 10 Euros) and be ready to look around at 10.30, still well before the tourist coaches arrive from the Costa Del Sol.

The word Alcazar means fortified palace, and this one is hidden behind castle walls on Plaza del Triunfu opposite the Cathedral.

The Alcazar of Seville is the oldest royal palace still in use in Europe – over 1,000 years of history, from Islamic Isbyllia through medieval Christian and Jewish Seville to present day.

The royal apartments, in the upper part of the palace, are the official residence in the city for the reigning Spanish monarch: the king's sister, Infanta Elena, held her wedding celebrations here. These rooms were not open to the public. You could say that this is Spain's Windsor. An ancient castle, still used by Royalty, which restricts public access.

The Alcazar started life in the 10th century as a fort for the Cordoban governors of Seville, but it was in the 11th century that it got its first major rebuild. Under the city's Abbadid rulers, the original fort was enlarged, and a palace known as Al-Muwarak (the Blessed) was built in what's now the western part of the complex.

Subsequently, the 12th-century Almohad rulers added another palace east of this, around what's now the Patio del Crucero. The Christian king Fernando III moved into the Alcazar when he captured Seville in 1248, and several later monarchs used it as their main residence.

A number of colourful and intriguing key historical figures of Spanish history lived at or visited the palace, from the Moorish poet-king Al-Mut amid, to King Pedro I, known as the Cruel (he killed his own brother); Christopher Columbus planned his second voyage here with Queen Isabella La Católica, and King Carlos V, the first Holy Roman Emperor, married Isabella of Portugal – a powerful union of two great royal houses.

Entry to the complex is through the Puerta del León (Lion Gate) on Plaza del Triunfu. Passing through the gateway, which is flanked by crenelated walls, you come to the Patio del León (Lion Patio), which was the garrison yard of the original Al-Muwarak palace. Off to the left before the arches is the Sala de la Justicia (Hall of Justice), with beautiful Mudéjar plasterwork and an artesonado (ceiling of interlaced beams with decorative insertions). This room was built in the 1340s by the Christian king Alfonso XI, who occasionally stayed here with one of his mistresses, Leonor de Guzmán, reputedly the most beautiful woman in Spain. It leads to the pretty Patio del Yeso, part of the 12th-century Almohad palace reconstructed in the 19th century.

Before seeing much of the palace's interior, we went to explore the impressively large gardens, full of orange trees, peacocks, and statues. Not at all like the gardens at the Alhambra which retain their Islamic symmetry and design, the gardens here are mix of ancient and modern, but still retain a certain charm.

One of the gardens' most arresting feature is the Galeria de Grutesco, a raised gallery with porticoes fashioned in the 16th century out of an old Islamic-era wall. There is also a fun hedge maze. A crowd was assembling around a musical water fountain that dated back to the 16th Century. The crowd, and I, braced ourselves for a spectacular display but a few mechanical pan pipes and some dribblesque squirts of water, were not quite what we had in mind.

Dominated by the facade of the Palacio de Don Pedro, the Patio de la Monteria owes its name (The Hunting Courtyard) to the fact that hunters would meet here before hunting with King Pedro. Rooms on the western side of the square were part of the Casa de la Contratación (Contracting House), founded in 1503 to control trade with Spain's American colonies. The Salón del Almirante (Admiral's Hall) houses 19th- and 20th-century paintings showing historical events and personages associated with Seville. The room off its northern end has an international collection of beautiful, elaborate fans. The Sala de Audiencias (Chapter House) is hung with tapestry representations of the shields of Spanish admirals and Alejo Fernández' celebrated 1530s painting Virgen de los mareantes (Madonna of the Seafarers).

This palace, also known as the Palacio Mudejar, is Seville's single most stunning architectural feature. King Pedro, though at odds with many of his fellow Christians, had a long-standing alliance with the Muslim emir of Granada, Mohammed V, the man responsible for much of the decoration at the Alhambra. So, when Pedro decided to build a new palace in the Alcazar in 1364, Mohammed sent many of his top artisans. These were joined by others from Seville and Toledo. Their work, drawing on the Islamic traditions of the Almohads and caliphal Córdoba, is a unique synthesis of Iberian Islamic art.

Inscriptions on the palace's facade encapsulate the collaborative nature of the enterprise. While one, in Spanish, announces that the building's creator was the 'highest, noblest and most powerful conqueror Don Pedro, by God's grace King of Castilla and León', another proclaims repeatedly in Arabic that 'there is no conqueror but Allah'.

At the heart of the palace is the sublime Patio de las Doncellas (Patio of the Maidens), surrounded by beautiful arches, plaster work and tiling. The sunken garden in the centre was uncovered by archaeologists in 2004 from beneath a 16th-century marble covering.

To the north of the patio, the Alcoba Real (Royal Quarters) feature stunningly beautiful ceilings and wonderful plaster and tile work. Its rear room was probably the monarch's summer bedroom.

The covered Patio de las Muñecas (Patio of the Dolls), the heart of the palace's private quarters, featuring delicate Granada-style decoration; indeed, plaster work was actually brought here from the Alhambra in the 19th century, when the mezzanine and top gallery were added for Queen Isabel II. The Cuarto del Príncipe (Prince's Suite), to its north, has an elaborate gold ceiling intended to recreate a starlit night sky.

The most spectacular room in the Palacio, and indeed the whole Alcazar, is the Salón de Embajadores (Hall of Ambassadors), south of the Patio de las Muñecas. This was originally Pedro I's throne room, although the fabulous wooden dome of multiple star patterns, symbolising the universe, was added later in 1427. The dome's shape gives the room its alternative name, Sala de la Media Naranja (Hall of the Half Orange).

On the western side of the Salón, the beautiful Arco de Pavones, named after its peacock motifs, leads onto the Salón del Techo de Felipe II, with a Renaissance ceiling (1589–91), and beyond, to the Jardin del Príncipe (Prince's Garden).

Reached via a staircase at the south-eastern corner of the Patio de las Doncellas is Alfonso X's much remodeled 13th-century Gothic palace. The echoing halls here were designed for the 16th-century Spanish king Carlos I and are now known as the Salones de Carlos V (after his second title as Holy Roman Emperor Charles V). Of the rooms, the most striking is the Salone de los Tapices, a vaulted hall with a series of vast tapestries.

As beautiful as it was, it just wasn't the Alhambra. The Alcazar has been remodeled so many times that it has lost its identity. Part Moorish, part Middle Ages, and part modern.

The three do not really mix. Yes, there are more decorative tapestries and priceless works of art here, but The Alhambra does not need those. It has enough character on its own merit.

We left the Alcazar, stopping for a welcome coffee, before heading towards the River and Puente de Isabel II which crosses to the Triana neighbourhood on the opposite bank. Triana started as a separate city in Roman times, but it was the Almohads who built the first bridge that linked it to the city, a bridge made of barges that stood where the Triana Bridge now stands. During the times of Columbus, The Triana district was the recruiting ground for crew members but from the 17th century onwards, the district became synonymous with pottery, especially decorative tiles. There are numerous shops selling artistic tiles of all colours and designs today, however this was not our reason for being there.

After my abortive attempt to see the Castillo de San Jorge, the home of The Spanish Inquisition, on my previous visit, I was really looking forward to this. Unfortunately, it still hadn't reopened since COVID and to really rub it in, it reopened the following Friday, the day after we went home.

Much of the castle was demolished in the early 19th century and a market was built over its ruins. We wandered through the market and there was a viewing area that you could look down through to see some of the castle's foundations. Most Spanish markets seem so much more full of food than their English counterparts. A multitude of Iberian hams hanging above store fronts and every fruit and vegetable you could imagine was twice the size of what you could buy at home.

The plan was to walk back along the river until we got to the next bridge in order to cross back over. To be fair, it looked a lot more scenic from the opposite bank, but we did stop for lunch, and I managed to order a sandwich that I will probably never come across again. Cod, avocado and orange. Sounds weird but it works.

Walking back along the river, you get a perfect view of the reconstructed Sant maria, Columbus' ship, which is moored by the Torre del Oro. It was a pleasant walk, but after four days of walking, it was more pleasant to get back to the hotel and put my feet up for a few hours before the evening's entertainment.

In the evening we went to a Flamenco show at the Tablao El Arenal, what The New York Times describes as "the best place in the world to feel the emotions of Flamenco Art." To be honest, dance and performing arts are not really my cup of tea, but the other two insisted on going, so I gave it a chance.

The evening started with a guy with a guitar, a woman in traditional dress and a bloke who was straight out of The Bee Gees singing a traditional song. I say sing with a slight question mark, if only because both singers had a rather nagging cough which interspersed their efforts at music. Twelve months earlier this would have been shut down as a COVID super spreader event.

A rather thin looking man, somewhat resemblant to Gomez Addams, appeared stage left and ran around like a maniac, flinging his arms all over the place. It appeared he was getting into a lather about something and building up quite a sweat before he exited. Next came the leading lady who quite frankly had a face that only a trout could love. It was a bit like watching Norah batty do Flamenco. Amazing dress, but wrinkled stockings underneath. After a couple of quick turns, she exited but seemingly returned moments later in a different dress. I am no expert in such matters but was quite impressed by the speed of the costume change. That was until Steve pointed out that this was in fact a completely different woman. Blimey, I thought to myself. This must be the Flamenco version of Cinderella and these two were the ugly sisters. They continued to pout, scowl, and stomp their way around the stage before the thin man re-joined the action and the whole event became a cacophony of dance, wailing, stamping, and coughing.

I sat and sipped my complimentary glass of sangria totally bemused at what I had just watched. Thankfully, I was not alone. After the event, Amanda went up to one of the performers and asked, "What was that all about?" I could not stop laughing at this point. These dancers and singers had performed what was probably a traditionally deep and meaningful tale of love and betrayal only for someone to come up and ask what the hell was that all about. It would be like someone approaching Shakespeare after watching Romeo and Juliet at The Globe and asking what was going on there?

As punishment, we took Amanda, a strict vegetarian, to a bar that boasted a number of severed bulls' heads. Trophies from the nearby Bullring. The menu here didn't even have tomatoes, but in any case, we had reserved a table at a Moroccan restaurant nearby. This made a pleasant change from tapas and after some amazing traditional starters, had a lovely lamb tagine that had apricots and plums in it.

One last drink in a local bar and it was back for our last night at the Adriano Hotel.

For our last trip out of Seville, we needed to walk to the local bus station. We should have caught a bus there as it was very hot and seemed to be miles away. We were catching the bus to Italica, or at least ruins of Italica, which was once the largest Roman settlement outside of Italy.

The ruins are nine kilometres north of Seville and thankfully the bus terminates there, so we knew when to get off.

Italica was the birthplace of three Roman emperors - Trajan, Hadrian, and possibly Theodosius. One of the earliest Roman settlements in Spain, it was founded in 206 BC by Publius Cornelius Scipius to house legionaries after the battle of Ilipa, which saw the Carthaginians (from North Africa) were defeated.

The town rose to high social and military status in the 1st and 2nd centuries AD, when Trajan and his nephew Hadrian were in power. Hadrian named the town, which had a population of 8,000, Colonia Aelia Augusta Italica. The area was a major producer of grain and olive oil, and some families with private farms became very wealthy exporting to Rome.

From the 3rd century AD, the town lost its affluence, possibly due to a problem with its port on the river Guadalquivir. Throughout the Middle Ages and until the last century, the ruins were used as a source of building materials - for the road from Merida to Seville in the 19th century, and for grand houses in Seville. Most marble columns in Seville, originated in Italica.

Fortunately, the 25,000-seater amphitheatre, which was one of the largest in the Roman Empire, has partly survived (two stories out of three). The central pit was used for animal cages (bears and wild boar) during gladiatorial combats.

Beyond this, on and around the wide main avenue or Cardus Maximus, about five large houses of prosperous families have been excavated, some with well-preserved, colourful mosaics, including floors with exquisite designs of birds, Neptune, and the planets. These mansions measured up to 15,000 square metres.

You can also see the remains of the Traianeum, temple of the Emperor Trajan, Termas Menores and Mayores (baths), and the sophisticated sewer system normally seen in larger cities. There were also a few remaining commercial buildings such as a bakery, which had its ovens intact and a shop that would have probably sold wine or olive oil, which had a large serving vat.

We spent a pleasant 90 minutes here before heading back for the bus back to the city centre. As we had an evening flight home, there was plenty of time for one further tapas lunch and a last glass or two of Cruz Campo.

We wandered back to the hotel, collected our luggage, and called a cab to take us back to the airport. Unfortunately, on arrival at the airport, we found out that French air traffic control were on strike and as a result our plane was going to be late, due to having fly around France. It was pretty late when we got back to Gatwick and even later back to Seaford.

But this was a good add on trip and I now feel that I have seen most of what Seville has to offer. There is still plenty of Spain to explore, but that will be a few years in the future at least.

THAT PLACE OVER THERE

SOUTH AFRICA 2022

1. Foreword — 338
2. My Great Trek Without Underpants — 339
3. Another Man Down — 348
4. On Safari — 356
5. What Do You Call An Elephant Posing As a Roundabout? — 366
6. How Many Cows To The Pound? — 375
7. Men Of Harlech (Or Not) — 383
8. Spionekop — 397

FOREWORD

There are always certain destinations on a person's bucket list and South Africa had been on mine for quite a while. Unlike most of the trips I undertake, there wasn't a great deal of ancient history to explore, but for once this was about our colonial past and the age of Empire. Whilst studying A level History, we covered the British Empire in a way that would not be allowed today. It was all very jingoistic and made you proud to British without learning about the slavery, the atrocities, and the utter contempt for the locals. None of this nonsense that they didn't want us there at all!

The two great heroic failures of The Empire were General Gordon, single handedly, trying to ward off The Mad Mahdi at Khartoum before being beheaded (Yes that's on the bucket list too) and Isandlwana, where 40,000 Zulus inflicted the heaviest Imperial defeat on the British Army, only for 200 men to ward of the heathen masses at Rorke's Drift and win 11 Victoria Crosses.

The two films that were made about these battles, "Zulu Dawn" and "Zulu" are two of my favourites and I have watched them on many occasions. To be able to visit these sites was something I have wanted to do for ages.

Oh, and there were a few animals too and some bloke called Nelson. Unfortunately, not Horatio though.

1. My Great Trek Without Underpants

When I first got my tickets and details that my flight left Heathrow at 9.45 in the evening, I was slightly concerned about traversing the M25 during the rush hour. I had to check in by 7pm, therefore I had to leave home around 5pm. I need not have worried though as the roads were quiet and at Terminal 5 everything is automated. The machines check you in, print your tickets and then take your baggage within minutes of arriving. There was a small queue at airport security, but by 7.30 I was through to the departure area with over two and a half hours to kill and no desire to spend any money. Terminal 5 is pretty big, and you have to take a train to the departure gates. So, I just took my time, got to the gate early and queued up to board the plane on time. So far so good.

I don't know if there were any Special Olympic type events on in South Africa at this time, but just as I was about three people away from getting on the plane, there must have been fifteen paraplegics who were pushed in front of me, being manhandled out of wheel chairs and on to some type of gurney, which looked straight out of death row, in order to get them on the plane. It must have been pretty degrading for them, and I know that Thunderbirds was ahead of its time, but surely, they can invent some kind of seat in the departure lounge, that they can sit in and get their seatbelts on, that can then be transported directly to the plane, directly to where they need to sit. OK, it may have to be a specialist disabled area, which may cause offence, but they would have been spared the trauma, and more importantly, we would not have had to wait and watch them being tossed around.

The flight was fine, although there was nothing worth watching as far as movies are concerned. It all started going downhill at dinner. Prior to this we got a menu, they gave me two cans of a Brewdog beer, only brewed for British Airways and there was a lamb shank on the menu with my name on it. Despite having upgraded my seat to Premium Economy, by the time they reached me, the choice of lamb chicken or pasta was chicken, chicken, or chicken. Chicken curry it was then. And it wasn't a particularly tasty one.

I had a window seat and whilst we were over the heart of Africa, Mali was my guess, there was an amazing lightning storm in the clouds below us which illuminated the entire sky. By the time the sun rose, conditions had improved, and we were flying over The Congo. There was a wonderful array of colours as the sun appeared over the horizon, but within minutes it was fully risen and then so blinding that I had to draw the blind.

Breakfast was not much better as they had run out of English breakfasts by the time they reached me. Thankfully my complaints did not fall on deaf ears, and they found one from somewhere.
We landed on time, and I made it to immigration fairly quickly. Not quickly enough though as the fifteen wheelchairs all jumped the queue and took ages.

Then of course there was my baggage. Whereas I made it to Johannesburg. My suitcase was still in London. Good old British Airways. So, whilst the rest of my tour group were through customs and meeting our tour guide, I had to find a British Airways Desk to report the problem and pray that the group didn't leave me behind. I was informed that my case would be on the flight that night and would be delivered to my hotel in Pretoria Later that day.

I took this news with a pinch of salt and was thankful that I always pack my pyjamas and a change of clothes in my hand luggage. It was 31 degrees in Johannesburg, very hot and sweaty and I only had one pair of underpants. No change of trousers and only one spare t shirt. I had no washing stuff, and all of my plug adaptors were in the case too. I hoped that the case would arrive as promised otherwise things could get smelly.

So, I was late meeting the group because I had to fill in a load of forms. So that was a delay but thankfully they had waited, and I didn't need to get a taxi to Pretoria. But just as I was united with the tour group, another guy pipes up that he had left his binoculars and camera in the baggage hall and needed to get back in. Our guide, Patrick, having already had to report the loss of my luggage to the tour company, now had to convince airport security to allow another one of our group, back through customs to reclaim his items. The rest of us all agreed that his binoculars were destined to be blown up as a potential bomb threat and that Patrick would be well on the way to a nervous breakdown before we had even left the airport. They reappeared an hour later, thankfully with the binoculars. I am unsure whether this would have been allowed at Heathrow.

We walked to our tour bus, which was overshadowed by an enormous statue of Oliver Tambo, after whom the airport is now named. Tambo and Mandela were among the founding members of the ANC Youth League, and the two opened the first black law practice in South Africa in 1952.

Tambo became the ANC's President in exile; he guided the movement from its low ebb in the 1960s through to its democratic victory in the 1990s. Although he did not live to see democracy in South Africa (he died a year before the 1994 elections), Tambo's democratic legacy endures in the Constitution and the Bill of Rights, both of which he helped to draw up.

So on to South Africa. Good news, the tour bus was comfortable, and the locals drove on the proper side of the road. The motorway between Johannesburg and Pretoria was well maintained. This one, along with all of the main highways here are privately owned toll roads, and as a result run very smoothly. Motorists just have an electronic pass on their windscreen and get billed on a monthly basis.

Our guide seemed very knowledgeable and came up with several pearls of wisdom, such as there is 34% unemployment here and there are rolling power cuts for up to 8 hours every day due to the mismanaging of the country. We hoped that the latter wouldn't affect us and that our hotels had their own generators.

Pretoria straddles the Apies River and extends eastward into the foothills of the Magaliesberg mountains. It has a reputation as an academic city and centre of research, being home to the University of South Africa (UNISA), the largest academic building in the continent.

The city was founded in 1855 by Marthinus Pretorius, a leader of the Voortrekkers, who named it after his father Andries Pretorius and chose a spot on the banks of the Apies River (Afrikaans for "Monkeys River") to be the new capital of the South African Republic (Dutch: Zuid Afrikaansche Republiek; ZAR). The elder Pretorius had become a national hero of the Voortrekkers after his victory over Dingane and the Zulus in the Battle of Blood River in 1838. The elder Pretorius also negotiated the Sand River Convention (1852), in which the United Kingdom acknowledged the independence of the Transvaal. It became the capital of the South African Republic on 1 May 1860.

My first impression of Pretoria was that it seemed to be a lovely city. It is known locally as Jacaranda City as it is full of 6000 jacaranda trees, all imported from Brazil, that were currently in full bloom. The whole city was awash with lilac and purple.

Our first stop was at The Voortrekker monument which commemorates the Boers deciding they didn't want to be ruled by the British and coming north to get rid of the Zulus. A somewhat simplistic view of The Great Trek I suppose.

The British had turned up at Cape Colony (Cape Town) in 1815 and declared that it was theirs. In most countries, the natives simply shrugged their shoulders and let the British get on with it, but here there was an established Dutch Colony that was not so keen to submit to British Rule.

By the 1830's several groups of Boers (a collective name for Dutch farmers and other colonists of varying descent, who wanted self-determination) left the Cape in their thousands and headed North, ultimately forming The Transvaal, Orange Free State and Natalia (modern day KwaZulu Natal).

Some settlers were successful, such as Pretorius in the Transvaal. Others less so, such as Hans Van Rensburg led a group of settles to their deaths in Mozambique, massacred by a local tribe who refused to give up their land, Hendrik Potgieter led 200 voortrekkers and was outnumbered 150 to 1 by Matabele warriors near the Zimbabwe border. Although a small core of the Boers survived here, the Matabele stole 50,000 sheep and 5000 cattle, resulting in starvation and poverty. Other expeditions ended in mass deaths due to fever.

Ultimately though, guns won over spears and the Boer Republics were formed, which ultimately led to the Republic of South Africa and the apartheid regime. On December 16th, 1838, at The Battle of Blood River, Pretorius and his men massacred over 3000 Zulu warriors, losing only 3 Boers. December 16th is still a national holiday for the Boers, much to the chagrin of the Zulu people. It was rebranded in 1995 as the Day of Reconciliation, but I don't think many see it that way. The Boers lost one of their early leaders, Piet Retief, but remembering him on the day thousands of Zulus were massacred and then ultimately became second class citizens in their own country for 150 years, doesn't seem that fair.

In the 1940s, Afrikaner nationalists used the Great Trek as a symbol to unite the Afrikaans people and promote cultural unity among them. This move was primarily responsible for the National Party winning the 1948 election and, later, imposing apartheid on the country.

Today, the Great Trek is remembered by the imposing, Art Deco, structure, known as The Voortrekker monument. It is perched over Pretoria, allowing expansive views over the city. On 16th December 1938, descendants of the Boer leaders laid the cornerstone when the building commences. Later on 16 December 1949, the monument was officially opened.

Every aspect of the monument symbolizes and honours the Voortrekkers who embarked on the treacherous journey. The twenty-seven marble friezes depict the history of the Great Trek and incorporate aspects of everyday life, work, beliefs, and culture of the Boers. The story culminates in the Battle of Blood River where a party of Voortrekkers under Andries Pretorius, overcame a Zulu army which greatly outnumbered them. The event is pivotal to the sense of Afrikaner nationalism and is recalled as a devotion to the vow made to God to honour the day should they be victorious. A copy of the Vow, the anthem "Die Stem" and of the land deal between Piet Retief and King Dingaan are buried under the foundation stone of the Monument.

There are many symbolic features of the monument including the cenotaph which honours the vow, the statue of a Voortrekker woman and two children honouring the strength and courage of the women, statues of Voortrekker leaders, and a depiction of the 64 ox-wagon laagers used at the Battle of Blood River.

The frieze of The Battle of Blood River was particularly interesting and in a perverse way was very similar to The Elgin Marbles. I did think that I had the perfect right to hack these down with a hammer and chisel and present them as a gift to The British Museum but decided against it.

Interestingly the monument has an open ceiling and whilst finalizing his design, the architect, Moerdijk, went to Karnak Temple in Luxor and allegedly the design here was supposed to mirror the open-air temples to the Sun (Aten) of the Akhenaten, Amarna period of Egyptian history, employing sun rays in the architecture, which can be seen in the friezes.

It was now getting increasingly hot, and everyone stopped for a cold drink. I was also getting quite concerned that my one and only t shirt was going to get quite hot and sweaty before the reinforcements were sent over from Blighty.

As we left the Voortrekker Monument, our guide pointed out a gnu, sitting under a tree. Most of us shrugged our shoulders, under the belief that we were going to Kruger National Park in 48 hours' time, and we would see loads of them. It turned out we didn't, and this was the sole gnu of the trip.

We drove at speed, through the heart of Pretoria, as it was deemed unsafe for us to wander around on our own. Our guide pointed out a few points of interest as they flashed past, namely, Church Square, The Kruger Museum, Jan Smuts House, and The Palace of Justice. It was too fast to get any photographs.

It was deemed safe enough to get off the bus at The Union Buildings which were atop another hill, named Meintjieskop, overlooking a park.

Although technically still the official seat of the South African government and the offices of the President, they have not been used since Nelson Mandela lay in state here in 2013.

The impressive horseshoe shaped buildings were designed by South Africa's most famous architect, Sir Herbert Baker, and the building was completed in 1913. Built from light sandstone, the Union Buildings are 285 metres (311 yards) long and their architectural design ranges from Neoclassical to Renaissance to Edwardian to Cape Dutch. It is considered an architectural masterpiece and was declared a National Heritage Site. I believe the buildings will still be used for future presidential inaugurations; however, the Parliament now sits in Johannesburg.

Somewhat bizarrely, just as The Voortrekker Monument had its roots in Ancient Egypt, The Union Buildings used inspiration from Ancient Greece. Inspired by ancient Greek architecture, the author of the project, British architect Howard Baker, wanted to build a modern Acropolis atop of the Meintjieskop hill - the highest point in Pretoria. The semi-circular shape of the Union Building with two wings on the sides has the same meaning. However, the side wings of the complex, built a century earlier, do not commemorate the reconciliation of whites and blacks, but the reconciliation of the British and the Boers after the fierce second Boer War. As well as two domes symbolizing two languages - English and Afrikaans.

The building is surrounded by beautifully terraced gardens of indigenous plants. In the park below the "acropolis" is an enormous statue of Mandela. Nelson's column I guess and certainly the pigeons treat Mandela exactly the same as they do poor old Horatio. Pigeon poo adorns his head and trickles down his face. Mandela is portrayed with open arms, and this is supposed to represent him welcoming all colours and nationalities. However, in my opinion, he looked more like Al Jolson performing Mammy.

A tented village has sprung up in the park and is a protest by the San people, initially known as Bushmen who are indigenous to the Northern parts of South Africa. Despite being renowned as being a Rainbow Nation of all colours, the Bushmen, unlike all other native tribes, did not have their rights written into and protected by the new constitution. This is an ongoing protest which is seemingly being ignored. Maybe because the government isn't here any longer. I didn't have the heart to tell them.

From here we drove back through the jacaranda-lined streets to our hotel which was in a fairly quiet neighbourhood. It seemed to be a very nice hotel; it would just have been nicer if I had had my luggage with me.

We had an hour or two to relax prior to dinner and I used these to contact British Airways to confirm that my suitcase was still en route. The fact that there was shower gel and other toiletries provided in the bathroom meant I could at least have a shower and feel slightly more human.

There was a special dinner this evening which involved a few mini courses and a different bottle of wine with each course. Personally, I would have preferred beer, but when in Rome and all that.

Well, we have all heard of Clarence the cross-eyed lion, but I never thought I would meet his long lost relative, Giveus, the cross-eyed sommelier. I know absolutely nothing about wine, but I can safely say that he knew less. Pearls of wisdom included "chenin Blanc" is a white wine and that Merlot (a red wine) went with fish. It was so bad it was funny, and we just went along with it, eating and drinking whatever was placed in front of us.

The food was actually quite nice and included something called Kudu which we all agreed was some kind of roadkill. Maybe the gnu we had seen earlier. There was a very nice duck dish and a delicious Thai salmon salad. But everything was surpassed by the 'fine collection of South African cheeses' which included a Dairylea triangle and a cube of Laughing Cow. This was of course served with a pinot grigio!!

2. Another Man Down

I didn't have the best night's sleep as I was subconsciously expecting a text from British Airways saying my suitcase had arrived. Unfortunately, this never came and at this point I still had no idea where it was. I had a case number, but each time I checked it, it just said they had no idea where it was. Not particularly reassuring.

Breakfast was an array of meat and sausages as far as the eye could see. There were some tomatoes and fruit juice to wash it down with. I had hoped for lots of fresh fruit, but this seemed limited to watermelon and papaya, locally referred to as paw paw.
It was a 9 o 'clock start for the 30 mile drive to Johannesburg. The first thing we noticed was that the tour bus had shrunk and was a lot smaller and less comfortable. This was supposedly due to the comfortable bus not having a permit to enter Swaziland. Suddenly, the six-hour drives looked a little less appetising.

It was back down the same motorway today and back to Johannesburg. As you approach the city, you see the mounds of dirt created by the copious amounts of gold and diamond mines around here. Johannesburg has a rather chequered history of white people making lots of money from gold and diamonds, and black people being paid a pittance to mine it for them. I would like to say things have changed and that black people now own all the wealth, but it is still the same people all over the world who do that. Letting black people govern themselves is one thing. Giving them the money? I don't think so.

The city was founded in 1886 when the first gold was found and from having 100,000 people in 1887, it now boasts 14 million inhabitants, is South Africa's largest city and home to all its financial institutions.

Our first stop was the suburb and one time township of Soweto. Soweto (an abbreviation of Southwestern Townships) was created in the 1930s when the White government started separating Blacks from Whites, creating black "townships". Blacks were moved away from Johannesburg to an area separated from White suburbs by a so-called cordon sanitaire (or sanitary corridor) which was usually a river, railway track, industrial area, or highway.
This was carried out using the infamous Urban Areas Act of 1923. This was rather a quandary for me. Everything I had ever heard about Soweto was bad. I had a mental image that conjured up extreme poverty, slums and lots of poor black people roaming around with nothing better to do. The reality was a bit different.

There are parts of Brighton that are more run down than parts of Soweto. There were still a few tin shacks, but I am not sure if they were just there for show. Many homes were newbuild, two-bedroom properties with running water, satellite dish and four by four car in the driveway. Many, it seems have grabbed the opportunities that the end of apartheid offered, but as with all walks of life, some people have no desire to better themselves. And generally, these are the ones that complain loudest.

Our first stop was The Hector Pietersen Museum. Pieterson was an 11-year-old schoolboy who was shot dead by white police after schoolkids in Soweto protested about schools teaching Afrikaans as the main language.

Soweto came to the world's attention on 16 June 1976 with the Soweto uprising, when mass protests erupted over the government's policy to enforce education in Afrikaans rather than their native language.

The police arrived and fired tear gas into the crowd in order to disperse them. There are conflicting accounts of who gave the first command to shoot, but soon children were turning and running in all directions, leaving some children lying wounded on the road.

Although the media often named as the first child to die that day, another boy, Hastings Ndlovu, was actually the first child to be shot. But in the case of Hastings, there were no photographers on the scene, and his name was not immediately known.

When Pieterson was shot, he fell on the corner of Moema and Vilakazi Streets. He was picked up by Mbuyisa Makhubo who, together with Pieterson's sister Antoinette (then 17 years old), ran towards Sam Nzima's car. They bundled him in, and journalist Sophie Tema drove him to a nearby clinic where he was pronounced dead. Mbuyisa and Nzima were harassed by the police after the incident, and both went into hiding. Mbuyisa's mother told the Truth and Reconciliation Commission that she received a letter from Mbuyisa in 1978 from Nigeria but she has not heard from him since. Pieterson and Hastings Ndlovu are buried at the Avalon Cemetery, Soweto. Ten people died as well and 250 people were injured.

The impact of the Soweto protests reverberated through the country and across the world. In their aftermath, economic and cultural sanctions were introduced from abroad. Political activists left the country to train for guerrilla resistance. Soweto and other townships became the stage for violent state repression. Since 1991, this date and the schoolchildren have been commemorated by the International Day of the African Child.

I think today we all can see how wrong apartheid was, but I think seeing this in Soweto, brought the reality home. Whereas the videos of the kids involved, talking in later life, was powerful, the most eye-opening part of the exhibition were the videos of news reports by the White South African media of the day.

They all but claimed that 11-year-old kids were dangerous and started throwing stones and virtually implied that they jumped in front of the bullets. A good lesson in that those who control the media control the narrative. Something a lot of people still don't see today. At the other end of the spectrum was a simple message from Peterson's elder sister, who wanted the chance to remember her brother as her sibling, rather than a martyr, which many seemed to promote him too for their own political ends.

We got back on to the bus, but only drove a few hundred yards before disembarking again. Around the corner from the museum was the house Nelson Mandela lived in when he was arrested and still owned on his release from prison. Outside in the road were Zulu warriors dancing and African male voice choirs singing the only song they knew, "The Lion Sleeps Tonight" for the tourists. The house is a single-story red-brick matchbox built in 1945. The house was small but not tiny. I commented that Mandela had the largest outside toilet I had ever seen but was corrected as the next door house had been commandeered and turned into toilets for the tourists. The one downside to the house would have been the coal stove which may have been a bit smoky.

Our guide was quite good and there were a few facts about Mandela that I was not aware of. Firstly, I did not know that it was the American CIA who found Mandela and told the South African authorities of his whereabouts. This was done purely because Mandela had met Fidel Castro in Cuba. Thus, giving the great champions of democracy had another great victory in imprisoning Nelson Mandela. Secondly, when the local police force were bored, they would drive down the street and open fire at Mandela's house with automatic guns. The bullet holes can still be seen.

As we were looking at Mandela's spare bedroom, there was a bit of a kerfuffle outside and we were told to stay where we were. Outside of the toilets, unbeknownst to us, one of our tour group had collapsed and fainted. I believe it was a diabetic problem and it was down to high sugar levels. In any case after a long delay, he was shipped off to a Soweto hospital with Patrick, our guide, and the rest of us were left to go on foot to a local restaurant which was a buffet and had lovely cold beer. The food here was good, bad, and downright weird. The good was the carrot and baked bean salad (don't knock it until you try it), the bad was what I believed to be beef stew that turned out to be tripe and onions and the weird was some sort of bone covered in very little meat that I have absolutely no idea what it actually was.

We sat in the restaurant for a few hours, awaiting news of our stricken traveler and concluding that we probably weren't going to get to either The Military Museum or Constitution Hill which had been on our itinerary. After a long delay, the guide returned to say that our fellow passenger was on a drip in hospital, but we could carry on the tour and see one of the two sights we had planned before picking him up later. We decided to go to Constitution Hill and set off through Johannesburg's Friday afternoon traffic. On the way, we passed Soccer City, the stadium built for the 2010 World Cup and where the memorial service for Mandela was held. We also passed the home stadium of The Orlando Pirates, one of Soweto's two football teams, the local derby against The Kaiser Chiefs was being played later that evening.

Whilst en route to Constitution Hill I checked my phone, and lo and behold, British Airways were now stating they had found my suitcase. Albeit no news of as and when I would be reunited with it. Constitution Hill is where the High Court of South Africa is situated.

But it has been built around a notorious prison where many black activists were held. The term activist is slightly vague, as many blacks were thrown into prison for simply looking a white man in the eyes. The conditions were horrific. Sixty prisoners were kept in dark cells designed for twenty people. All sharing one toilet. Even here there were cells for whites, coloureds, Indians, Chinese and blacks. It is strange that when the Japanese came on the scene, they were classified as white, which must have cheesed the Chinese off but shows how ridiculous the whole system was.

The prison was known as Number 4, and it was here that the students arrested at The Soweto Uprising were sent.

Blacks were strip searched every day, had batons inserted up their backsides, and their food bowls were only allowed to be washed every six months. Meanwhile, the white prisoners got cake for tea. One famous inmate here was Mahatma Gandhi. And it transpires that although he championed Indian rights, he still believed that the blacks were at the bottom of the pile and that the system worked. So, one bright spark asked the guide (and for once it wasn't me) whether Gandhi was a racist. The guide replied that he couldn't answer the question because he was on duty. But read into that what you will.

We didn't get too long here as we had to get back to the Soweto Clinic to pick up our stricken passenger from hospital. On discharge, he had to sign a waiver form, stating that if it happens again, he is on his own and the tour guide could leave him to his own devices. Better news came in at the hospital that my suitcase was now at Johannesburg Airport. But BA, being officious, claimed they couldn't send it to me thirty miles away tonight. Instead, they would I ship it 500 miles north to the safari park we were heading to the following day. Both the guide and I tried to reason with them that this was a stupid idea, but I was fast coming to terms with the fact that in Africa, everything runs on African time. Which is nowhere near as fast as European time. I will believe it when I see it, but whatever happened I was destined for another 24 hours in the same underpants.

What had struck me was that here I was, talking on my mobile phone, on a street corner in Soweto with the sun going down. And I felt completely safe.

It was dark when we got back to the hotel. South Africa only has one time zone, therefore when you are in the East, where I was, it gets dark around 6pm and light around 4am. If you go to Cape Town in the West, the evenings are light until 8pm but it doesn't get light until after 6am. I also noticed that from around 4pm, there is a prolonged dusk period.

After another fairly tasty dinner, which included the salmon salad with Thai dressing again, it was an early night for everyone. Apart from me, I sat up and suffered watching Brighton lose at Brentford and spent another night of tossing and turning.

Another bright morning saw us greeted by a different array of sausages for breakfast. Whereas in China they eat anything with legs, I was beginning to think that here it was anything with legs went into the mincing machine.

We had been told at dinner last night that our itinerary had changed today, but Patrick was being somewhat coy about why. Whatever the cause, we were now destined to be on the uncomfortable bus for a grueling day that started at 7am and would not end until 6pm. It gave me no great pleasure to know that my suitcase was making an identical journey.

Despite being sunny in Pretoria when we left, the further into the mountains we went, the cloudier it became.

We stopped after a few hours, mainly so that I could buy some T-shirts and underpants in case my suitcase never turned up again. But despite buying two garishly coloured t shirts and some wildebeest patterned boxer shorts, the highlight here was that I managed to buy a Bar Six Milkshake. I used to love a Bar Six.
At the back of the shops were some onyxes and a few buffalo. A couple more to tick off but I was hoping to see better in Kruger.
Finally, Patrick explained why our itinerary had to change today. Basically, the locals had shot a German recently, near to the Numbi Gate of Kruger National Park, where we had to enter. Maybe they misheard Deutsch for Dutch I thought. The Dutch aren't exactly popular here amongst certain circles. I tried to explain to our guide that we are happy shooting Germans too, so it shouldn't be an issue. But as a result, we had to make a five-hour detour on top of a six hour journey, just to get where we were going to anyway. So, we never got to the gold mining village we had planned to see nor the second biggest canyon in the world. Although we were promised a spectacular view of it at a viewpoint called Gods Window. Or at least it would have done if visibility hadn't been down to five feet and tipping down with rain.

So, this didn't happen and were taken to Graskop Gorge, if only for a toilet break. You could take a lift down into the gorge and do a circular walk. Sounds good but what they didn't tell us was that the path was on wooden boards which due to the rain were treacherous underfoot and there were also three rope bridges to cross. I think we all regretted this and spent the entire 600 metre circuit staring at our feet in case we slipped and broke something.

Six of us had taken the lift down to the Gorge. The others, more sensibly, had sat down for lunch. Our lunch was a sandwich on the go which was supposed to be the speedy option. But as we had found out, there is no such thing as a speedy option in South Africa. Of course, my sandwich was the last to be made, so I had to run back to the bus and try and consume a bacon and egg sandwich whilst our driver was doing 90mph around hairpin bends and over humpback bridges. It reminded me a bit of the scout troop who wrote to Jim'll Fix It so that they could eat their packed lunch on a rollercoaster.

So, we entered Kruger National Park around 2pm and had to get to the entrance where our hotel is by 6pm. We made it with fifteen minutes to spare. We did see quite a few animals, lots of elephants and antelopes, a few zebras, giraffes, and warthogs and one baby hyena. I got a few pics but as we were in the minibus it wasn't easy. We had an all day safari the following day in an open top land rover, so the pictures should be better.

The camp we were staying in was ok. The rooms were posh tents with electricity and a shower at the back with no roof. There were some very strange noises in the night, but I was not brave enough to venture out and find out what was making them.

The good news was that my suitcase finally turned up at 9pm this evening. Why they couldn't get it to Pretoria last night or even this morning is beyond me. That would have been a 45-minute drive. They drove it for 7 hours today! A new camera had been stolen but everything else was intact. I still had another camera and planned to claim for the missing one on my insurance. It must have been stolen in London as only Customs could get in. You need a special key to unlock the case.

3.   On Safari

Despite having been reunited with my luggage, there was no way I was going to take a shower at night as we were in a designated Malaria area and the shower was open roofed. The beds have mosquito nets, but that hasn't stopped them in the past.

I'm not sure what time I actually got up this morning, but it started with a 4 and I needed a daylight shower before breakfast at 5 and heading out on the Land Rover for an all-day safari by 6.

It was already light, and it seems that the east of the country has bright mornings and early sunset. There is only one time zone here and it is a big country. The east, where I was gets light early but dark early, whilst in Cape Town in the west, there is a 90-minute difference. But it is weird. Dusk seems to start around 3pm and then the sun drops at 6 to 6.30 and everything goes dark.

Kruger National Park is renowned as one of the best game reserves in the world. It covers an area of 7,576 square miles in the provinces of Limpopo and Mpumalanga in north-eastern South Africa and extends 220 miles from north to south and 40 miles from east to west. Areas of the park were first protected by the government of the South African Republic in 1898, and it became South Africa's first national park in 1926.

To the west and south of the Kruger National Park are the two South African provinces of Limpopo and Mpumalanga, respectively. To the north is Zimbabwe, and to the east is Mozambique. It is now part of the Great Limpopo Transfrontier Park, a peace park that links Kruger National Park with the Gonarezhou National Park in Zimbabwe, and with the Limpopo National Park in Mozambique. There are over 420 recorded archaeological sites in Kruger Park which attest to its occupation before modern times. Most sites however had relatively short occupation periods, as the presence of predators and the tsetse fly limited cattle husbandry. At Masorini hill, iron smelting was practiced up to the Mfecane era. The reconstructed Thulamela on a hilltop south of the Levuvhu River was occupied from the 13th to 16th centuries and had links with traders from the African east coast.

Before the Second Anglo-Boer War, the area now covered by the park was a remote section of the eastern South African Republic's last wild frontier. Paul Kruger, President of the South African Republic at the time, proclaimed the area, which was inhabited by the Tsonga people, a sanctuary for the protection of its wildlife.

James Stevenson Hamilton noted many cattle kraals along the Sabi River and also further north beyond the Letaba River, although the north was sparsely populated compared to the south. Many of the local natives were employed by railway companies for construction of rail connections, notably that between Pretoria and Lorenço Marques in Mozambique, during the end of the 19th century. Abel Chapman, one of the hunters who noted that the area was overhunted by the end of the 19th century, brought this fact to wider attention.

In 1895, Jakob Louis van Wyk introduced in the Volksraad of the old South African Republic a motion to create the game reserve. The area proposed extended from the Crocodile River to the Sabi River in the north. That motion, introduced together with another Volksraad member by the name of R. K. Loveday, and accepted for discussion in September 1895 by a majority of one vote, resulted in the proclamation by Paul Kruger, on 26 March 1898, of a "Government Wildlife Park." This park would later be known as the Sabi Game Reserve.

The park was initially created to control hunting, and to protect the diminished number of animals in the park.

James Stevenson-Hamilton became the first warden of the reserve in 1902. The reserve was located in the southern one-third of the modern park. Singwitsi Reserve, named after the Shingwedzi River and now in northern Kruger National Park, was proclaimed in 1903. During the following decades all the native tribes were removed from the reserve and during the 1960s the last were removed at Makuleke in the Pafuri triangle. In 1926, Sabie Game Reserve, the adjacent Shingwedzi Game Reserve, and farms were combined to create Kruger National Park.

During 1923, the first large groups of tourists started visiting the Sabie Game Reserve, but only as part of the South African Railways' popular "Round in Nine" tours. The tourist trains used the Selati railway line between Komatipoort on the Mozambican border and Tzaneen in Limpopo Province. The tour included an overnight stop at Sabie Bridge and a short walk, escorted by armed rangers, into the bush. It soon became a highlight of the tour, and it gave valuable support for the campaign to proclaim the Sabie Game Reserve as a national park.

After the proclamation of the Kruger National Park in 1918, the first three tourist cars entered the park in 1927, jumping to 180 cars in 1928 and 850 cars in 1929.

Warden James Stevenson-Hamilton retired on 30 April 1946, after 44 years as warden of the Kruger Park and its predecessor, the Sabi Sabi Game Reserve.

Stevenson-Hamilton was replaced as warden by Colonel J. A. B. Sandenbergh of the South African Air Force. During 1959, work commenced to completely fence the park's boundaries. Work started on the southern boundary along the Crocodile River and in 1960 the western and northern boundaries were fenced, followed by the eastern boundary with Mozambique. The purpose of the fence was to curb the spread of diseases, facilitate border patrolling and inhibit the movement of poachers.

The Makuleke area in the northern part of the park was forcibly taken from the Makuleke people by the government in 1969 and about 1500 of them were relocated to land to the south so that their original tribal areas could be integrated into the greater Kruger National Park.

In 1996 the Makuleke tribe submitted a land claim for 19,842 hectares, namely the Pafuri or Makuleke region in the northernmost part of the park.

The land was given back to the Makuleke people; however, they chose not to resettle on the land but to engage with the private sector to invest in tourism. This resulted in the building of several game lodges from which they earned royalties. On a positive note, at least they have built a load of casinos and cheap cigarette shops like the Native Americans have done with the land they were given in The United States.

Our game drive was excellent, and we saw virtually everything we wanted to. We didn't manage to tick off cheetahs, rhinos, or leopards. Neither did we see a hippopotamus out of water, but we had high hopes for the following day or for our other game drive later in the week. Have yet to see a leopard or a cheetah, a rhino, or a hippo out of water. Hoping to tick a couple of those off tomorrow but unlikely to see a rhino until later in the week.

Having said that, the biggest obstacle of the day was getting on board the Land Rover. They each held eight people, the driver and guide at the front, and then three rows of two, which were all slightly higher than the row in front. In order to get on board, there were steps on the side which were more like a ladder. As I was the youngest, it was decided I should get the back seat, which had the steepest steps.

I swear the first step was at least three feet off the ground, and getting into the vehicle was not pretty or elegant. Getting out of the vehicle was no easier, as you had to pirouette and come down backwards, leaping off the bottom step with enough faith that terra ferma isn't that far away.

You have to enter the park at the crack of dawn as that is when the main action is. Within minutes we came across a herd of buffalo ambling down the road but half a mile further along was one of their former herd members who had been killed by a big cat during the night. The cat had now left the scene of the crime, suitably fed, but there was an enormous feeding frenzy going on as hundreds of vultures were ripping the flesh off. Both the sights and smells left little to the imagination.

As the morning went on, we saw different species of antelope, giraffes, a male lion walking through the grass, a warthog, a 3-day old baby elephant with its mother, hippos submerged in the water and a zebra crossing a road.

The next kill was a giraffe that had been felled by a lion, who was still tucking in. It is easy to see the food chain here. As the lion tucked in, a hyena was sunning himself under a tree waiting for seconds, whilst the vultures hopped around expectantly. But none are brave enough to eat anything until the lion has had enough. Once the lion has left the area, the hyena would tuck into what's left and then the vultures would strip any surplus meat from the carcass.

Moving on we saw a pack of wild dogs, another female lion sitting on a rock, a pack of baboons with babies, the mother removing nits from the baby's head, more elephants, a crowned hornbill, yellow hornbill, and more zebras.

It was nice to see what a Kudu was, especially having eaten part of one on our first night and finally we got a real close up with an elephant.

Elephants in Kruger are becoming a bit of a problem. Ten years ago, there were fears for their numbers, due to the concerns over ivory poaching. Various government and park initiatives have curtailed this issue and now there are too many elephants.

In 2000, there were 7000 elephants in Kruger. The latest annual report claimed that this had risen to 31,527. That's 31,527 elephants that all have to eat. Elephants can eat for 20 hours a day; therefore, you need a lot of trees to keep them happy and Kruger has a finite number of fully grown trees.

Elephants have no real predators, apart from the odd baby one that a very brave lion might target, and since 2010, Rangers have not been able to kill them. Elephants generally stay within ten miles of their favourite source of water and although as natural as can be, Kruger has many artificial water sources which attract the animals. Therefore, within a ten-mile radius of each waterhole or source, you can find trees that have been bulldozed, stripped of leaves, or just completely destroyed by the hungry elephants. Leaving very little left for other herbivores such as giraffes.

Once again, the cause of the issue is down to human beings. Two hundred years ago, elephants could roam freely throughout much of Southern Africa, but by herding them all into Game Reserves, you have the same elephant population inhabiting only 17% of the land they used to wander through.

There are only three options open to Kruger. Firstly, go back to culling to maintain population numbers, something that hasn't been done since the 1980's. Secondly, they could relocate the elephants, but this is not good for the animals who are attached to their local environment more than most creatures. Or finally, some form of contraception, but any person willing to get a female elephant to take a morning after pill, with a randy elephant bull on the loose, is a braver man than I.

After a while you stop getting excited about seeing antelopes and buffalo as they are so common. We stopped for lunch at a designated tourist village and restaurant. I had high hopes for a giraffe on a spit roast or a hippo carvery, but the meal was pretty bland to be honest.

The highlight was the lime milkshake I managed to get afterwards. I have been on a quest to find a decent lime milkshake since a family holiday in 1975 when we visited a café called The Golden Egg most nights, that served the best milkshakes in town.

I also managed to buy my Mum some Marula marmalade. The fruit of the Marula fruit ferments when it falls from the trees and elephants and baboons eat them and tend to go on a drunken rampage, destroying trees. Adult supervision may be needed when I give it to her.

We returned to our camp around three o'clock which allowed me time to get reintroduced to my luggage and have a snooze before dinner. Firstly, I made a cup of coffee and sat down outside with my newly reunited laptop, uploading all the photos I had taken. All was well for half an hour and then there was some buzzing and a bee the size of a golf ball arrived and started to head towards the door. Having gone about being worried about Zulus and the British who repelled them at Rorke's Drift, one bee was enough for me to sound the retreat and go back to my room and hide. Thankfully it didn't find the alfresco shower and make a nest in the bathroom.

We had a group meal under the stars in the evening, which was supposedly a traditional African thing. The food was still a buffet, full of sausages and meat as far as the eye could see, which was brought to life by a rather potent local hot sauce that nobody else was brave enough to try. There is one girl on the tour who is vegetarian. Somebody asked yesterday if she still ate chicken. That's how bad it is.

All main courses seem to be accompanied by something called Pap, which is like a cornmeal porridge. I was not a fan. Desert seems limited to Malva Pudding and custard. Basically, a sponge pudding made with apricot jam and occasionally with currants. It was quite pleasant on the first evening, but this was now night four and we had been served this every night with no alternatives.

One thing I had hoped to see in Africa was the night sky, but I was especially disappointed here by the lack of visibility. It may well have been spectacular in the middle of the night after the camp lights had been shut off, but I wasn't venturing outside after the bee the size of a golf ball and any other animals that come out at night.

It wasn't such an early start the next day, as we had arranged to go on the eight o'clock bush walk rather than the six o'clock. In hindsight this may have been a mistake, as most of the wildlife are active early in the morning. Eight o'clock is mid-afternoon here!

We were slightly concerned that when two rangers turned up with rifles that our guide had had enough of our group's problems and we were being marched out into the bush, never to return. The guide was named Sunny Boy, not very fitting as he was the most dead pan person I have ever come across, although an excellent guide.

We came across a herd of impalas and came very close to a herd of buffalo. It was here that Sunny Boy was at his finest. He told us all to stop talking and not to scare the Buffalo who were protecting a baby. If they charged, he claimed, he only had twenty-two bullets and there were over thirty of them. Funnily enough we stopped talking.

But this walk was more about the plants and what could be seen on the ground. Mostly poo to be honest, but by the end of the walk we were able to recognize which poo came from which animal. Furthermore, the most interesting fact of the day was that Rhinos only ever use one toilet. They always return to the same spot to do their business. Not sure I could cope with that as if I got caught short here it would be a seven-hour drive, followed by a ten-hour flight and another two hour drive. My bladder isn't that sturdy these days.

Sunny Boy told us about the problems that Kruger is currently facing with Rhino poachers. The Chinese pay staggering amounts of money for rhino horn, which they use as an aphrodisiac. In 2020, the going rate was $82000 per kilogram.

Currently there are around 2500 rhinos in Kruger but there were 783 deaths in 2019/2020. At that rate the rhino population would be extinct in a few years.

Again, the problem is a human created one. Throughout history, the area has been full of poor and starving African people. The pandemic and AIDS has not helped the situation and the hunger and desperation leaves many into the hands of the poachers.

More than two million poor people live up against the park's border. In Bushbuckridge youth unemployment stands at a staggering 60%. With hungry bellies, their days are often about pure survival. Many are from Mozambique on the other side of Kruger which is sandwiched between the two countries.

So, when poachers roll in along potholed roads in their expensive new 4x4s with Rolexes on their wrists and money to spend on dishing out food or paying rental arrears, how could they not be seen as heroes? Bushbuckridge and the communities that span the length of the Kruger fence are fertile ground for the swaggering "middlemen" of the poaching syndicates.

International crime syndicates are targeting the park with up to seven poaching groups operating daily. In seven years from 2014 there were 19,154 logged poacher incursions, an average of 2,736 a year. You'd think that would demand greater ranger presence, but there are presently 82 unfilled ranger posts and poorly paid rangers are being lured by syndicate cash.

That's not difficult. Sophisticated, organised crime syndicates with deep pockets are able to coax information via a "drop-off" from some staff. Inside the park, it must be so hard for employees to resist the temptation of tip-off money.

Poaching rhino horn escalated in the 21st century, with 949 rhinos killed in Kruger in the first 12 years, and more than 520 in 2013 alone. A memorandum of agreement is seen as a necessary milestone in stemming the tide between South Africa and Vietnam, in addition to the one with China, while negotiations have not yet started with Thailand.

The amount of rhino horn held in storage is not publicly known. Since 2009, some Kruger rhinos have been fitted with invisible tracing devices in their bodies and horns which enable officials to locate their carcasses and to track the smuggled horns by satellite. South Africa's 22,000 white and black rhinos represent some 93% of these species' world population.

We also got a few survival tips and learned which plants, if mixed with water, could be used as soap and also which plant was the softest and could be used as toilet paper. You never know when you might need this.

The birdlife in and around the camp was amazing. Everything seems bright red, yellow or blue. It makes everything very colourful. We got back to camp around ten and thankfully Sunny Boy had not felt the need to discharge any bullets.

I had planned to spend a couple of hours on the balcony, relaxing, but the sun was so hot and there was no shade. Having spent the rest of the morning, fighting the pretty scarce internet in my tent, to get some pictures back home, it was back on the land rover at 2pm for another 4-hour game drive.

There were still no leopards, cheetahs, or rhinos, but we did get to see some hippos slightly out of the water. There were plenty of sightings of impala, zebra, elephant, buffalo, giraffe, and kudu, but the highlights were the hippos, a family of baboons climbing a rock to get shelter for the night and a family of hyenas, with lots of babies. We also got a fantastic close up with a giraffe.

The African scenery is beautiful. The greenery is interspersed with granite peaks and crystal blue lakes. The sunset tonight was stunning. It's a shame really, because as we headed back to the park gates as the sun went down, you could see that things were beginning to come back to life and many of the nocturnal animals were beginning to get active. I don't believe there are any tours of Kruger after 6pm, but it would be interesting, although very dark. Once again, the food for dinner was getting very boring with buffet roast dinners on the menu every night. I would really like to try some decent South African food that is different to home.

So that was Kruger National Park, which was an amazing adventure and wonderful to see all of these animals in their natural abode. The following morning, we were heading to Swaziland or Eswatini as they call it these days. But due to the local gate closure, we would still have another three-hour drive through The National Park.
My guide had assured me that the beer in Swaziland was the best on the trip. I was hopeful.

4. What Do You Call An Elephant Posing As a Roundabout?

Am not sure any day on this trip has passed smoothly as yet. This morning saw more delays and as a result the following day became somewhat challenging and a race against the clock.

Because we couldn't use the gate that we should have used to exit Kruger, due to the German being shot, we had a three hour detour through the National Park. To be honest, most of us at the time saw this as a good thing, as it was an extra game drive, albeit on our tour bus. We did manage to see some hippos out of water for once, some rhinos in the distance, a wildebeest, and a crocodile, on top of the multitude of zebras, impalas, and giraffes. We even came across a leopard under a tree, but it was hard to photograph. I have a picture with some spots in it. No head or tail, but I am reliably assured it was a leopard.

The main delay in the morning was an elephant having its breakfast and standing in the middle of the road whilst doing so. Our driver didn't think he could squeeze past without disturbing it, so we had to wait for it to strip the tree and move on. Imagine our driver's horror when the elephant had finished with the tree in question, turned around, crossed the road, and chose a tree on the other side. All in all, this was a good 45 minute delay which could have got worse, if another elephant hadn't carried on walking and decided against stopping at this roadside café.

Even an elephant has to admit he is full sometimes and after 45 minutes he finally moved on into the bush and we could finally continue along our way.

We stopped at a bridge over the Crocodile River, which was at the entrance to the park. From the bridge we could see quite a few crocodiles plus a few hippos sunbathing. There was also a great variety of birdlife which excited a number of them on the bus.

We were now well behind schedule and our driver was clearly putting his foot down and overtaking anything and everything in order to get to the border between South Africa and Swaziland which was a further hour along the road. We eventually got there, and all had to pile off the bus to go through South African customs. This was quite easy, but at this point our guide whisked us off to a very touristy cultural village where (supposedly) a tribe of locals live a traditional life and put on a song and dance show.

To be fair, the young female guide who escorted us around was very entertaining. We were told that this village belonged to a single family, and I am pretty sure the whole enterprise was a family affair. Supposedly the chief has two wives. The first wife has 15 children and the second one 9, and they all live together in this village, in no man's land, between South Africa and Swaziland. Hundreds of people and trucks laden with goods cross the border each day, yet we were supposed to believe these people were living just as their ancestors had done for millennia, oblivious to the 21st Century. Despite a few people on my tour believing this nonsense, I remained skeptical. One member piped up and asked whether they still worshipped their own Gods. Not that I was aware they worshipped Gods as such, and were more into ancestor worship, but I digress. The young guide, whilst keeping a straight face, replied that they no longer worship false idols and are now all Christian. I'm not sure the Church of England would allow 24 wives (24 choirboys maybe) and was quite stumped as to where the bit about multiple wives was in the Bible. Am guessing it must be in an apocryphal text. I concluded that they must be Roman Catholics as The Pope is generally fine with all of this nonsense as long as you say sorry every Sunday and slip a few notes in the collection tray. "I'm sorry your Holiness but I have taken another wife." "Don't worry my son, fifty Hail Mary's to keep the Virgin happy and just slip fifty rand in the tray and we'll say nothing more of it!" Morality at its finest.

We were told that the Chief slept alone, but when he decided to visit either wife a or wife b, he would go to their hut, lie in the corner, bang his knobkerrie (long wooden war club) on the ground, and said wife would have to crawl over to him and perform whatever he had in mind. He could repeat this as many times as he wished, but once satisfied, he had to go back to his own hut. I was hoping that this one had not been mentioned at confession.

Despite some of our group hanging on to every word as though it was a cultural exchange, it was clear to me that this was more entertainment rather than culture. And to be fair, the singing and dance performance at the end was very slick and quite tuneful. Albeit "The Lion Sleeps Tonight" and "Amazing Grace" were slipped in to keep the tourists happy. The more traditional songs and dance were quite good. We were all guilt tripped into buying their CD which will almost certainly be consigned to the outer limits of my record collection.

Our guide had also stated that she was unable to get married until a potential suitor paid her father her worth in cows. All very traditional, but I didn't see the point, as he owned a restaurant on the site that took credit cards. Far easier and quicker than cows.

The restaurant had what was referred to as a Swazi buffet. This involved a lot more meat and more Malva Pudding and custard. By the time we had finished lunch and then gone through the rather stern Swazi customs who wanted to see all documents multiple times, it was 2.30 in the afternoon, and we were supposed to go to the national museum of Swaziland in the capitol, Mbabene, which was 3 hours away and shut at 4. As a result, this was postponed to the following morning.

Our hotel was on the other side of Mbabene, so we were in for a long drive, which our driver tried to get over and done with as quickly as possible, but Swaziland is such a mountainous country, the roads are full of switchbacks and hair pin bends.

We did stop at a glass-blowing factory, which was shutting 15 minutes later, but that was it. It wasn't very exciting, but some people enjoyed the shop. I was most upset that a local liquor store next door had already shut, whilst others had similar feelings about a chocolate shop. Nobody was too bothered about the glass.

The scenery throughout Swaziland was beautiful. Rising mountains and crystal-clear lakes make it the perfect picture postcard setting. A bit like The Lake District with higher mountains.

We were staying in a colonial inn tonight which is very nice. Once you were inside, you could be in Lewes. There's was even a Harvey's Brewery poster above the bar. However, the local brew was nowhere near as good.

The Hotel was called The Foresters Arms and the name goes a long to explain why such a survivor of The British Empire was here. Forestry was always a major industry whilst Swaziland was a British protectorate, however after World War Two and the new South African Republic becoming independent of Britain, thousands of trees, mostly pine and eucalyptus, were planted to ensure that the country maintained its independence from South Africa. The lumber industry is still one of Swaziland's major sources of income. Somewhat alarmingly, asbestos is still it's major export, but the paper mills, supplied by the lumber mills of this area, provide much of the continent's paper.

The whole experience of the Foresters Arms was amazing from start to finish. From the cozy little bar which could have been in any country pub in England, to the period rooms that were a home from home.

The highlight though was dinner, which was an event in itself. The menu wasn't extensive, in fact there was a choice of three starters, five mains and a couple of desserts, all preceded by an all you can eat salad bar. The novelty here was that you could have as many dishes as you wanted.

If you wanted three starters, they would provide three starters. Five mains? Not a problem, and you got five mini main courses. And for once it wasn't impala sausages and chicken breast with pap followed by Malva Pudding.

Every course was amazing. Homemade pea soup and crusty roll was my only starter, but I did have two mains. I finally had a Cape Malay Curry which was quite fruity rather than spicy and also a sesame pork casserole with dumplings, which quite frankly I could have eaten for every other dinner on this tour, it was that good. Brioche Bread and Butter Pudding with custard for desert and I went to bed a very happy bunny. And as we were in the mountains, it was cool enough to snuggle under a blanket and have a good night's sleep, dreaming about what delights would be on the breakfast menu.

Probably the last thing I had expected to be on the breakfast menu in Swaziland were Arbroath Smokies, but there they were. Not that I partook, as I was too full from the previous evening. I managed some grapefruit and a poached egg on toast but others, namely those who didn't have two main courses the previous night, tucked into the smokies.

We knew today would be a long day, due to the delays on the previous day, but hadn't quite realised how long this day was going to be.

First stop in the morning was the National Museum of Swaziland, back in Mbabene. This proved to be an interesting hour and explained the fascinating history of the country.

The "Swazi" were one of the few tribes that fought back against the European or Boer expansion in the North of the country in the 19th Century. Although its borders were all but established in the mid-18th Century, the country takes its name from King Mswati II, who unified the country 100 years later. The name Swaziland is another example of The British not listening and hearing Swazi rather than Swati. Hence the name change to Eswatini after they were granted independence.

The European expansion would see clashes amongst the nearby African tribes as they struggled to find enough pasture for their cattle and sources of food for their people. A Bantu people, the Swazi were unfortunate enough to encounter the expanding Zulu. Under the leadership of Mswati II they were able to expand their territory to the Northwest and stabilize the southern frontier with the Zulus.

Mswati was to initiate the first contacts with the British in an attempt to get some kind of protection from the Zulus. It did not help that the Boer Trekkers had started off another round of realignments amongst their tribes. The Zulus themselves were feeling the pressure from Boers hungry from land and so would clash with the Swazi in turn. The creation of the Boer Republic of Transvaal would see the Swazi squeezed between the Boers to the north and the Zulus to the south.

A further strategic concern was the Portuguese port of Delagoa Bay to the immediate east of the Swazis. It was one of the finest natural ports in Africa and was eagerly sought after by many European powers although the Portuguese were firmly in control. There was a secondary port available to the south of Delagoa Bay at the mouth of the Kosi River. This was in Tongaland to the East of the Swazi, but the Boers were interested in acquiring a port of their own and this was the only one available and Swaziland lay between the port and the republic.

Boers would apply enormous pressure on the Swazi to gain access to this port. Bizarrely, Boer representatives were able to supply the Swazi king with plenty of alcohol and get him to sign a document making their President Kruger his heir.

Horrified by these developments, the British quickly repudiated the agreement and tried to create a joint administration over the Swazi territory.

This was in effect from 1889 to 1893 when the Transvaal Volksraad (parliament) repudiated the agreement. Transvaal was growing increasingly wealthy due to their huge gold deposits, and they were feeling more confident. They were also seeking closer diplomatic relations with the Germans at the expense of the British.
The British did not wish to be drawn into a war over Swaziland, especially with the Germans hovering in the wings. The Germans actually sent a fleet to Delagoa Bay in an unsubtle show of force. The British agreed to allow Swaziland to become a protectorate of Transvaal but only with stipulations and provisions safeguarding the rights of the Swazis. The Boers were notoriously racist and treated natives with contempt. In return, the British claimed control of the area north of the Transvaal which would become known as Rhodesia. The Boers reluctantly agreed.

The British sought to extend some protection to the Swazi population but were also happy to keep some diplomatic avenues open in the region. British officials in the Cape and back in London were already seeking ways of incorporating the rich goldfields of Transvaal into the British Empire. It was thought that the Boers would be unable to restrain themselves from poorly treating the Swazi and so provide a pretext for war or annexation of the Transvaal.

As events transpired, the Swazi were able to isolate themselves from the Boer War that did break out in 1899. Many Swazi did volunteer to work for the British even if they were prevented from fighting for them. With the destruction of the Transvaal state in 1902, Swaziland passed under full British protection.

Given its large population, the white framers of the Union of South Africa did not wish to add such a large black grouping to their new political entity.

Swaziland would therefore not join the Union in 1910. This was probably a blessing as the Swazi avoided the worst racist laws of South Africa. However, the Swazi could not isolate themselves fully from the South African regime as other blacks sought refuge in the Swazi lands and markets were opened and closed at the whim of the white regime.

Swaziland would gain its independence in 1968.

Next door to the museum is the Swazi Parliament, or the Libandla as it is known locally. It is probably the most pointless parliament in the entire world as Swaziland is one of the last surviving absolute monarchies and what the King Maswati III says, goes. Actually, that is not quite the case as the king must rule jointly with his mother, who is given the title "Ndlovukati" which literally translates as The Great She Elephant. It is actually a law here that should the people elect members of parliament that the King disagrees with, he is perfectly within his rights to appoint enough members who support him in order to gain a majority in the house.

Overlooking Mbabene are two identical peaks, known locally as Sheba's Breasts. On the other side of the Ezulwini Valley is a mountain that has a frightening sheer drop. It is known as Execution Rock and is very important to the local culture. Not only are all of the former Swazi Kings buried up there but before the British arrived, Swazi justice was two warriors marching anyone who had committed a serious crime, up this mountain, and making them jump off. If they survived, they were deemed innocent.

From here we went to a local shopping mall where I picked up a bottle of fiery African sauce called Bushman's Revenge and a few bits and pieces. It's always nice to see what supermarkets sell in different countries and it must be said that this one was as large and as impressive as our local Morrisons. Something I wasn't really expecting here.

Once again, a number of us fell foul to African timekeeping. We had twenty minutes before we had to be back on the road so ordered a coffee. Thirty minutes later when they turned up, we had to down them in one and run for the bus.

Our other stop today was The Miliwane Nature Reserve. It wasn't particularly impressive after Kruger. I think I saw one wildebeest, one warthog and a couple of impalas. There was a multi-coloured lizard too.

As we hung around the gift shop, a guy turned up on a motorbike and changed into a traditional costume in the toilets. He then came out and told us he was taking us to his village. After yesterday I was dreading another touristy fairground attraction where we supposed to believe that they all slept together in one mud hut but thankfully this was slightly more realistic, in that we walked through their village called Umphakatsi, but their houses were made of brick and there were signs of modern life.

There was an enclosed area (a kraal) where we met The Lady Chief who explained their customs. This then became a song and dance show before, to my horror we were all expected to join in. The women first, who seemed to enjoy it and then the men who were all mortified, apart from a Welsh guy who seems to enjoy singing hymns. Having said that, his version of Swazi dancing was more akin to the New Zealand Haka.

But whereas the first village had all been about CD sales, it was explained to us that many of the children who performed with the adults were from a local orphanage and that any proceeds went to their upkeep. This seemed far more acceptable and furthermore, we were taught to say hello in their language, which went something like "Yebo Nkosi."

We headed further into Miliwane for our lunch stop. A chicken tandoori ciabatta made a pleasant change. I would argue that Miliwane is not really a Game Reserve and more a Nature Reserve. There really aren't many animals there, but the beautiful lakes and crystal clear streams, backdropped by the mountains, makes it a very peaceful place. Imagine Lake Windermere with crocodiles in it and there you have it,

By the time we had eaten lunch it was nearly three o'clock and time to head south back to South Africa and KwaZulu Natal. There was plenty more pretty scenery and thankfully customs and immigration back into South Africa was not as lethargic as it had been entering Swaziland.

The hotel we were staying in was called The Ghost Mountain Inn in a town called Mkuze, which offered what were supposedly spectacular views. As it was nearly 7 when we got there it was already dark and the views would have to wait for another day.
By the time we had all eaten dinner, everyone retired to their rooms as we had to be up at 4 for another game drive.

5. How Many Cows To The Pound?

The room and the facilities at The Ghost Mountain Inn were by far the best we encountered on the entire tour. This made it a shame that we had to get up at 4 a.m. get handed breakfast to go in a paper bag and crawl half asleep back on to the bus.

The sunrise over Ghost Mountain was spectacular and its history is quite interesting. A section of the Ndwandwe tribe, headed by the Gaza family, had their home beneath Ghost Mountain until they were conquered by Shaka, the great Zulu warrior King in 1819 and the head of the family, Soshongane, fled with his followers into Mozambique, where he founded the Shangaan tribe.

From early times it had become customary to bury the bodies of Chiefs on Ghost Mountain. High on its slopes there is a taboo cave, used as a tomb by generations of the Gaza family. Soshongane and his descendants, although they lived many miles away in Mozambique, were carried back to the Ghost Mountain when they died.

Their bodies, mummified and wrapped in the black bull skins, had to be transported by bearers who travelled by night and hid during the day to avoid detection by the Zulus. After the Anglo Zulu War in 1879, when the British tried to rule Zululand by dividing it into 13 separately ruled states, there was a period of chaotic rivalry, feuding and fighting. The two principal rivals were Prince Dinuzulu, the son of the deposed Zulu King Cetshwayo, and his Usuthu warriors, and Zibhebhu, head of the powerful Mandlakazi section of the Zulu nation.

In a series of bloody fights, Zibhebhu gained the upper hand. Dinuzulu, in desperation, enlisted 600 Boers and Germans, led by Louis Botha (later General Louis Botha, who was also to become the first Prime Minister of The Union of South Africa), who were promised rewards of farms for their help. In June 1884 Dinuzulu's army of Zulus and Europeans invaded Zibhebhu's territory. Zibhebhu was a resolute leader and his Mandlakazi section was made up of the finest warriors, and although he also had a handful of white supporters, including the famous frontiersman, Johan Colenbrander, he had little chance against the opposition.

Zibhebhu made a fighting retreat to the Mkuze River Pass through the Lebombo, and on the 5th of June, in this rugged gorge beneath Ghost Mountain, there was a vicious struggle known as the Battle of Tshaneni. The Mandlakazi fought stubbornly, but heavy rifle fire from Dinuzulu's army mowed them down and they broke and fled into the dense forest country of Tongaland. The battlefield was littered with thousands of bodies, and of this the late Col. Reitz makes mention in his book "Trekking On", where he claims that in the early 1920's he journeyed through skeletons that were still strewn about on the slopes of the Ghost Mountain.

It was only a 45-minute drive to Hluhlowe Umfolozi Game Park where were booked on to an early morning game drive. We were in the jeeps by 6 and set off for a three hour drive. Unlike Kruger, which was flat apart from the odd granite mound, this reserve is set in the heart of the Limpopo Mountains. They spread down from Swaziland right through the state of Natal and are unlike any other mountains I have seen. They are well over 3000 metres tall, but there are few peaks, apart from Ghost Mountain. They are virtually flat on top, and the result is a 3000 metre wall spreading south. Against this backdrop, we saw plenty more animals including zebras, wildebeest, impalas, kudus, warthogs, buffalo, giraffe, and crocodile.

Hluhluwe–Imfolozi Park is the oldest proclaimed nature reserve in Africa. It consists of 960 km² of hilly topography and lies 170 miles north of Durban in central KwaZulu-Natal.

Throughout the park there are many signs of stone age settlements and iron smelting sites. The area is claimed to have been declared a royal hunting ground for the Zulu kingdom in the time of Shaka, the great Zulu King.
The park is famous for its rhinoceros population and we saw loads of rhinos up close. The southern white rhino, first identified by Western naturalist William John Burchell in 1812, was virtually eliminated during the 19th century by European hunters, and by 1895 was believed to be extinct. A population of between 20 and 100 was identified in South Africa and preserved by establishing the Umfolozi Junction Reserve and Hluhluwe Reserve, which are now parts of the Hluhluwe-Imfolozi Park.

Historically, tsetse flies carrying the nagana disease protected the area from colonial hunters. Later, as the Zululand area was settled by white farmers, wildlife in the reserves was blamed for the prevalence of the tsetse fly, and the reserves became experimental areas in the efforts to eradicate the fly. Farmers called for the slaughter of game and over 100,000 animals were killed in the reserves between 1919 and 1950, although the rhino population was spared. The introduction of DDT spraying in 1945 virtually eliminated the tsetse fly from the reserves, although subsequent outbreaks have occurred.

The park is the birthplace of rhino preservation, having been responsible for breeding the southern white rhinoceros back from near extinction in the first half of the 20th century. There are reportedly 1,600 white rhinos in the reserve these days.
The rhino population remains severely threatened by the increase in rhino poaching within the park and elsewhere, with 222 rhinos poached in the province in 2017, most of them in the park. On 6 March 2020 two of three suspected rhino poachers were killed in a shootout, after an infrared camera automatically alerted the operations centre, providing number of persons, grid reference and direction of the incursion. Hluhluwe–Imfolozi has implemented Smart Park which facilitates the integration of systems, including drone technology, for early detection and rapid response to target poachers.

We stopped at a picnic site in order to have our packed breakfast. I, along with most people on the bus had eaten most of it before we got there and subsequently left a few morsels on our seats for the return journey. In my case, I couldn't really eat a packet of salted peanuts and raisins at 6 in the morning and I'm not quite sure they were that palatable at 9 o'clock either.
One member of the group was meticulous though and had saved his breakfast for the designated time. He sat on a bench, laid all of his goodies on the table, and was then mortified when a couple of velvet monkeys bounded on the table and ran off with his banana and his blueberry muffin. To make matters worse, the monkey that stole the muffin, sat across from him, licking his fingers, and smacking his chops.

As good as it was to see the rhinos and other animals, it was a lovely morning and it was just pleasant to drive around with a breeze on your face, taking in the beautiful scenery. The animals were a bonus.

The next bonus was that the game drive finished at 9 and by 10.30 we were back at the hotel and finally had some time to relax, which was very welcome. So, after a quick cup of coffee in my room, it was back to bed for a couple of hours to make up for lost time. After a light lunch (Roast Chicken and Malva Pudding) we had another trip out to the local Zulu homesteads and villages. Originally, I had feared that this was going to be another tourist trap with staged dancing and everybody dressing up as extras from the film Zulu or Zulu Dawn. Thankfully this was not the case.
The hotel is surrounded by field upon field of sugar cane, which seems to be the local crop of choice. Enormous railway sidings seem to be every half a mile with massive trains getting filled with the raw cane. The sugar cane fields are occasionally interspersed with corn fields.

There are hundreds of villages, all on the top of the plateau of the mountains. So, you have to drive up 3000 metres and then everything springs to life. The views are stunning, and every turn seems to lead to another valley or pass with the soaring temperatures getting more bearable, the higher you climb.
We stopped in a village which, to be fair, was a little ramshackle. Certainly not the well-maintained homesteads we had seen in Soweto. We were met by a young female guide and another man who was going to tell us about modern day Zulu life.

Despite having to adapt to modern society, their way of life still hangs on too many traditions. The guy who was talking to us explained that he wanted to get married to his girlfriend but was unable to until he acquired 11 cows and so far, he only had 10. To make matters worse, he had got her pregnant twice and that had cost him 4 cows on each occasion, so now he still needed another nine. I think this could work at home and could be better than standard contraception. If you run the risk of being billed for four cows if you have an unplanned pregnancy, it may put you off the idea and be a bit of a dampener. An average cow in South Africa sells for 10,000 Rand which at the current rate is approximately £500. So that's £5,500 to get married, plus £2000 for each indiscretion. Once the bride's father gets the cows, they supply all the beer for the wedding. Not a bad deal I reckon. Cows are clearly quite expensive it would seem. But the whole society seems based on their value, which makes it very bizarre, but probably less volatile than the pound or the dollar.

To make matters worse for this man, he was now 47 and in Zulu terms, that is getting on a bit. He also had younger brothers who wanted to get married but under Zulu tradition, the oldest son has to marry before the younger ones. I fear there are not enough cows to go round or else there is an opening for some cattle rustling in these parts.

The "cow" system is called ilobolo. This term is particularly used by Zulu people when it comes to bride wealth. Every African ethnic group has different requirements when it comes to bride wealth. In pre-capitalist Zulu society, ilobolo was inextricably linked to the ownership of cattle. During that time, there was not a fixed number of cattle required for the wedding to happen; it could be paid before the marriage or during the marriage.

The groom takes the cattle from his father's herd in order to perpetuate the family heritage. Nonetheless, this ritual has changed during colonization because in 1869, Theophilus Shepstone, then Natal Secretary for Native Affairs, formalized the ilobolo payment to 10 cattle for commoners (plus the ingquthu cow for the mother), 15 for hereditary chief siblings and 20-plus for the daughters of a chief. They found it too lenient to let the groom give whatever amount he wants, so they decided to establish a specific number of cattle that would be needed before or at the start of the marriage. This has been accepted by Zulu men who were educated in mission schools, but according to more ritual people this became "untraditional". The payment of ilobolo can be difficult for some families, but as it is often considered a symbol of pride and respect, many are willing to maintain this tradition as long as possible.

The homestead itself was quite interesting. The family lived in one shack, the chickens in another and the goats just seemed to share both. There was an outside tin shack that was an outside toilet or The Zulu Loo as I christened it. Then there was a more traditional round building with a thatched roof that we were invited in to. Every Zulu homestead has a building for the spirits of their ancestors and this I think was quite a good idea. A quiet place where you can remember your loved ones who are no longer alive and maybe think what they would do in a current situation. Far better than a book of remembrance or a cold gravestone in a freezing cemetery.

Whole families seem to live together with goats and chickens, and whatever cows they can muster. Despite no running water, they do all seem to have satellite TV and cars. It was a fascinating insight into a totally alien culture.
I was almost waiting for the comment about them all being Christian now, and sure enough it was mentioned. Worshipping Serapis the Bull in Ptolemaic Egypt or even Minoan Bull Worship may have been a better route for these people to take. But Christianity? Really. Once again, I concluded they were Roman Catholic and shrugged my shoulders. Hopefully the local Priest doesn't expect a cow in the collection box each Sunday or this poor man will never get married if he can't keep his trousers on.

Traditional Zulu religion includes belief in a creator God (uNkulunkulu) who is above interacting in day-to-day human life, although this belief appears to have originated from efforts by early Christian missionaries to frame the idea of the Christian God in Zulu terms. Traditionally, the more strongly held Zulu belief was in ancestor spirits (amaThongo or amaDlozi), who had the power to intervene in people's lives, for good or ill. This belief continues to be widespread among the modern Zulu population, but don't tell the priests as there aren't enough cows to go around.

We continued along the plateau, with some schoolchildren waving and others shouting, "Give me money!", but with what we had just learned that cows are the ongoing currency, this was not practical. How they could expect us to keep a few spare cattle on a minibus is beyond me.

We stopped at a viewpoint overlooking Lake Jozini before descending the mountain. The sun had begun to set, and it was quite chilly, misty and the view could have been better. It looked quite small from 3000 metres in the air, but would no doubt seem bigger the following morning as we were cruising on it. So, we got back on the bus and headed back to the hotel.

The downside to the wind getting a bit brisk was that we were in open top land rovers and the roads were caked in dust. It was straight in the shower when I got back, and my shorts were consigned to the laundry bag.
Impala sausages were back on the menu that evening and after dinner there was a planned display of Zulu dancing. I'm guessing that these people were Zulu's, but dancers they were not. They were supposed to be demonstrating the noble art of Zulu stick fighting which is a celebration of manhood for Zulu men. These men can begin to learn this fighting art form as young as the age of five years old. There are multiple reasons why men learn how to stick fight. For example, men may want to learn so that they can set right any wrongs or insults made towards them.

Other reasons some men choose to learn are for sporting purposes, proving skills or manliness, and self-defence. The goal of stick fighting is to injure the opponent and sometimes even kill. There are rules of etiquette that must be abided by when stick fighting. The men can only fight a man the same age as them. One cannot hit the opponent when they lose their stick. Only sticks are allowed when fighting. This all seemed fair, but these were clearly amateurs. Every time they jumped, they ended up on their backsides and every time they hit an opponent's stick, it seemed fly out of their hands, and we had to wait for them to recover it.

I left at the interval and didn't come back for part two.
The following morning was quite grey and overcast. We set off for Lake Jozini at around 8 a.m. and it was actually quite chilly.
The lake is actually the Pongolapoort Dam and to be honest I wasn't that hopeful of seeing much. The brochure mentioned there might be elephants, but even before we got there, the guide let us know that all the elephants had packed their trunks and cleared off towards Swaziland.

The dam and its surrounds support over 350 bird species which includes rarities such as African broadbill, saddle-billed and yellow-billed storks, African finfoot, Pel's fishing owl and Narina trogon. The dam also supports a breeding colony of pink-backed and great white pelicans. Additionally, the dam supports a stable population of Nile crocodiles.

The dam is also home to the southernmost population of tigerfish. Other fish species include catfish and kurper.
It was a pleasant couple of hours sailing around. In the end we saw some hippos and some ostriches which we hadn't seen on the trip. The highlight was the birdlife which was bountiful and very colourful. This kept the Twitchers on board very happy as they ticked off various permutations of starlings and warblers.

By 10.30 we had to return to the hotel and board the tour bus to Dundee and the next leg of the trip.

6.   Men Of Harlech (Or Not)

By 11 we were heading south to Dundee which took just over three hours and included a lunch break at a large Spa supermarket where I bought two pieces of fried chicken, and something called Russian Chips. Firstly, whereas Colonel Sanders may use 11 herbs and spices and his fried chicken, this place only used one, salt. Whilst the Russian chips were chips with lumps of hot dog mixed in. I am still at a loss as to what this has to do with Russia.

Our driver kept a good speed and by 2.30 we reached the town of Dundee and The Talana Museum which is built upon the site of the Battle of Talana, which was the first major clash of The Second Anglo Boer War 20th October 1899. Our local guide walked us around the battlefield and talked us through what was not exactly The British Army's finest hour.

Part of the Boer plan at the start of the war was for the army under Commandant-General Piet Joubert to invade Natal, defeat the only British field army in South Africa, probably near Dundee or Ladysmith, and then march to the coast at Durban. That British army was under the command of Lieutenant General George White, who had taken up his new post just six days before the start of the war. He had decided to make a stand at Ladysmith, but under political pressure had been persuaded to leave a 4,000 strong brigade at Dundee, forty miles further along the railway to the Transvaal.

That detachment was commanded by Major General Sir William Penn Symons, White's immediate predecessor in command in Natal. He was supremely confident in the ability of the British regular soldier to deal with the Boers, who he saw as a band of farmers. His position at Dundee was not strong.

The town was surrounded by flat topped hills, the most important of which was Impati, to the north of the town, the source of Dundee's fresh water. Two more hills, Talana and Lennox, overlooked the town from the east. Astonishingly, Penn Symons left these crucial locations unguarded. It was not to be his only mistake.

On 19 October a force of 4,000 Boers was approaching Dundee. Early the next day they discovered the British pickets and forced them back. Penn Symons received news of this clash but dismissed it as a simple Boer raid. No preparations were made to meet any possible attack.

Accordingly, the first most of Penn Symons's men knew of the Boer presence was when they were spotted on top of Talana and Lennox hills, just moments before the Boer artillery opened fire on Dundee. The Boer force had split into two. Two commandos, with 1,500 men, were on Talana Hill, three more occupied Lennox Hill while another 4,000 men occupied Impati Hill. Their plan was simple – they would use their artillery to wake up the British, and then wait for them to attack their strong hilltop positions.

Penn Symons was perfectly happy to cooperate with that plan and decided to attack Talana Hill. Unlike many later British commanders, he committed much of his command to the attack. The British artillery was very soon returning the Boer fire, with some effect. The Boer artillery was quickly silenced, while a number of the Boers, coming under artillery fire for the first time, fled. However, the real battle would begin when the British infantry attempted to climb up the hills in the face of accurate Boer rifle fire.

First, the British had to reach the base of the hill. Here they were aided by the presence of a small forest of blue gum trees at the base of the hill. Despite a brief expose to accurate Boer rifle fire the British infantry were soon in place at the base of the hill.

However, while the shelter of the trees had encouraged the British advance so far, now it brought it to a halt, as the troops were understandably unwilling to leave the relative safety of the trees. Penn Symons rode to the front line in an attempt to speed up the attack, and at the edge of the trees was mortally wounded.

His second in command, Brigadier General James Yule, took over, and got the attack moving. The advance was generally successful, although the British troops did then come under fire from their own artillery, apparently unaware that any of the distant figures near the top of Talana Hill were actually British. The artillery fire did serve to push the Boers off the top of hill, and once it stopped the British were able to occupy Talana Hill in relative safety.

With the Boer army retreating slowly east, the artillery had a chance to make up for their earlier mistakes. Yule sent them to Smith's Nek, the pass between Talana Hill and Lennox Hill. Once there, the artillery commander, Lieutenant Colonel Edwin Pickwoad, found himself in an ideal position to bombard the Boers, potentially turning their orderly retreat into a rout. Instead, he sent a message to Yule asking for orders. In a war that would be plagued by missed chances, the first battle provided the first missed chance.

It also provided the first example of gallant stupidity. A small cavalry detachment, under the command of Lieutenant Colonel Bernhard Drysdale Möller, had been sent out on a sweep around the north of Talana Hill. This force now found itself in the path of the entire Boer army. Möller decided to make a stand. Not surprisingly his tiny force was swept aside. Möller now led the survivors in the wrong direction, ending up behind Impati Hill, where he was quickly captured.

Talana Hill was in many ways a British victory. Penn Symons's force drove off a Boer force at least twice its size, and one that had taken up just the sort of strong defensive position that would cause the British so many problems later in the war. However, it came at a high cost. Ten officers (including Penn Symons) and 31 other ranks were killed, 185 men were wounded, and 220 men captured or missing (many from Möller's cavalry). Boer losses were reported at on 23 dead, 66 wounded and 20 missing. Soon after the battle, General White called all of his detachments back into Ladysmith, where he would soon be besieged. The battle of Talana hill may well have been a British victory, but it had little or no impact on the course of the war in Natal.

Apart from its military history, the museum reflects on the industrial history of the area. The fact is that Dundee, where funnily enough many Scottish emigrants had moved to, was one of the most important towns in the Empire. In the 1880's an enormous seam of coal had been found and the town was known throughout the Empire as Coalopolis. It was so successful that the Verdant Coal Works here, was listed on The London Stock Exchange. Times have changed and the pits are now closed, but The Talana Museum reflects on that very well. It is rather a diverse place, incorporating a museum of coal mining, with all its horrors brought to life as you walk through a reconstruction of a 19th Century mine. I was somewhat underwhelmed by the exhibition of 19th Century Ladies underwear.

Our hotel for the next couple of nights was a twenty-minute drive from the museum and on first impressions it looked a bit grim. I think it was either a hospital, barracks, or a prison in earlier life. The air conditioning was broken in every room and the chorus of frogs outside was so loud it was deafening.

I didn't have to worry about the fact that there were no towels in my room as we had to head straight back out. We had been invited to the local MOTH Hall for a braai, which is basically a South African barbecue. At the beginning of the tour, I had been quite excited about this, but considering the amount of meat that had been thrown our way, this was now quite a daunting thought.

MOTH stands for the Memorable Order of Tin Hats, and it is basically The South African version of The British Legion. A place for ex-servicemen to grab a few cheap beers and socialise. The Dundee MOTH Hall is quite special, as its curator is also the curator of The Talana Museum and she has created an impressive collection of military memorabilia here, picked up by South African servicemen across the globe, dating from the Zulu Wars through to The Gulf War.

Not that we could see much or eat much when we arrived. It was dark outside and there was a power cut inside which meant food was delayed. Thank God the beer fridge seemed to have its own generator. Pray and you shall receive!

The lights were due to be switched on at seven and on cue, everything came back on, revealing a rather large Nazi flag at the end of the room. We were reassured that this had been captured in Berlin by a local and didn't ask any further questions.

The braai, as feared, was meat hell. Five types of sausage, six plates of steak, chicken thighs and pride of place went to some Warthog chops, which was another animal I had eaten to tick of the list. It can't be fun for vegetarians. A South African lettuce is no different to a British one, but warthog! Now we were talking. Apart from the meat, there was some potato salad, but by God, this took a lot of eating and copious bottles of beer to get it down with.
We headed back to the hotel around ten o'clock, where the frog chorus was so loud you couldn't hear what anybody was saying.

There were still no towels in my room and supposedly reception was about a mile away through a field with wildebeest in, so I had an early night.

The following morning was certainly a first for me as I have never drawn back my curtains and been stared at by an ostrich. Evidently the hotel we are staying at employs ostriches rather than guard dogs as they are more effective in chasing people off the property. It's a shame that there haven't been any intruders whilst we have been here as I would love to see them chased away by an ostrich. Maybe I should get an ostrich to fetch me a towel, as the locals don't seem that interested.

More worryingly this morning was the weather. After having warm sunshine every day so far, this morning was cold (17 degrees) and wet with clouds shrouding the mountains. The forecast said 90% chance of heavy downpours.

We set off after breakfast at around 8am with a new guide who has been brought in to tell us about the battlefields. We were still in the same minibus but were travelling over the original dirt roads which have barely changed since the Anglo Zulu wars in the 1870's. Oh how we wished we had the Land Rover back. Then again, the Land Rover had no windows and with the driving rain would have been rather wet.

Our first port of call was Isandlwana. Zulus didn't really have place names or towns. They just built their houses where they wanted to, generally where they could see where their cows were. But the British, being British asked what the name of the mountain was, and the natives replied Ilsandlwana, roughly translated as "that place over there."

Our first view of the iconic mountain that overlooks the battlefield was somewhat limited as much of it was enveloped in cloud. Thankfully the cloud and drizzle lifted, but there was still a biting wind.

In mid-December 1878, envoys of the British crown delivered an ultimatum to 11 chiefs representing the then-current king of the Zulu empire, Cetshwayo. Under the British terms delivered to the Zulu, Cetshwayo would have been required to disband his army and accept British sovereignty.

At eleven o'clock in the morning of January the 22nd 1879, a troop of British scouts chased a group of Zulus into the valley of Ngwebeni in Zululand. The scouts stopped dead in their tracks when they saw what the valley contained. Sitting on the ground in total silence were 20,000 Zulu warriors. It must have been an astonishing sight.

The battle that followed this remarkable discovery was a disaster. It wasn't meant to be this way. When the High Commissioner for Southern Africa, Sir Henry Bartle Frere, came up with the flawed idea of annexing the British-friendly kingdom of Zululand into a greater South African Confederation by force of arms, he presumed Zulus armed with spears, clubs and shields would be no match for the mighty British Army.

Without bothering to seek the permission of the British government, Frere issued the order to attack the lands ruled over by King Cetshwayo, a reasonable, thoughtful ruler who had regarded the British as his friends until Frere cynically engineered him into a position of being unable to accept Frere's unreasonable demands.

When Cetshwayo failed to agree to Frere's ultimatum to disband his army, Frere grasped his chance to invade. Chosen to lead the invasion was Frederic Thesiger, the 2nd Baron Chelmsford. Lord Chelmsford massively underestimated how many men he would need to take into Cetshwayo's territory. So confident was Chelmsford of an easy victory that he took with him a mere 7,800 troops. His plan was to invade Zululand with three columns of infantry, artillery, and native cavalry, with each column heading off through different sections of Zululand to engage Cetshwayo's army.

The ultimate goal was the capture of Ulundi - Cetshwayo's village. The central invasion column was under the direct command of Chelmsford. It headed out from the mission station of Rorke's Drift in the British-held territory of Natal on the 11th of January, crossing the Buffalo River into Zululand. By the 20th of January, all three columns had progressed into the kingdom unopposed, with Chelmsford's central column reaching the hill of Isandlwana, where the fateful decision was taken to make camp.

Against official military policy, Chelmsford did not order the camp to be 'laagered' - the practice of circling the column's support wagons to create a makeshift fort behind which troops could form a defensive position should an attack occur. Instead, on the morning of the 22nd, Chelmsford left just 1,300 troops guarding the camp as he took a sizable number of his men off to attack what he thought was the main Zulu army. In reality, the small numbers of Zulu warriors Chelmsford's scouts had spotted and reported back to the general were a ruse devised by Cetshwayo's commanders to draw out Chelmsford and then attack his forces from behind with the bulk of the main Zulu army. The ruse worked, and the overconfident aristocrat marched 2,800 soldiers away from the camp, splitting his forces in two.

While Chelmsford was off chasing an imaginary Zulu army, the real one moved to the valley of Ngwebeni. Back at the British camp, Lieutenant-Colonel Henry Pulleine was in charge of the camp's defence. Pulleine was an administrator, not a soldier, and it was his inexperience that contributed to the disaster that was about to unfold.

Pulleine could have been replaced at 10:30 that morning when Colonel Anthony Durnford arrived from Rorke's Drift with five troops of the Natal Native cavalry and a battery of rockets, bringing the camp's fighting strength up to 1,700 men. Durnford, a seasoned soldier, was Pulleine's senior, and tradition in the army dictated that he should have taken command. He chose not to do so, leaving a much less experienced man in charge.

When the attack came, it came quickly. The minute the encampment at Ngwebeni was discovered by British scouts, the entire Zulu army sprang into action. The plan was instantly changed from attacking Chelmsford's rear to attacking the camp at Isandlwana. Word reached Pulleine that a large Zulu force was approaching fast and in huge numbers. As the warriors began to arrive over the horizon, they started to muster into an 'impi' – the traditional Zulu formation of three infantry columns that together represented the chest and horns of a buffalo. The central column of the impi headed directly for the camp, while the two 'horns' of the left and right columns fanned out on either side of the camp to encircle the British.

Pulleine sent all six companies of the 24th Foot out to engage the central Zulu column head-on. At first, the extended British firing line held the attack off with considerable ease with help from the two mountain guns of the Royal Artillery. The legendary Martini-Henry breech-loading rifle was more than a match for an attacking force armed with spears and clubs, and with a firing rate of twelve rounds per minute, the experienced soldiers of the 24th Foot were able to hold the central column of the Impi at bay, inflicting heavy casualties on the Zulu side, forcing many to retreat behind Isandlwana hill to shelter from the hail of shells and bullets.

Unfortunately for the soldiers holding the line against the Zulu central column, the horns of the impi began to make headway against less experienced opposition. Durnford, defending the British right flank, had already lost his rocket battery, and was now haemorrhaging troops. Unlike the regular soldiers of the 24th Foot, Durnford's forces consisted of African troops who were not fully armed with Martini-Henry rifles. Only one in ten of Durnford's rank and file troops bore firearms, and even then, they were armed with inferior muzzle-loading rifles. Faced with certain death or escape, Durnford's men began to leave the battlefield before they could be fully encircled and cut off by the impi.

Durnford's troop numbers diminishing fast, so their rate of fire began to drop. This drop in fire meant more Zulus were able to press against Durnford's defensive line, pushing it back towards the 24th Foot who were still holding the central column of the impi at bay. As Durnford's men retreated back against the left horn of the impi, the 24th Foot's right flank, which up until this time had been protected by Durnford, was now dangerously exposed. Realising he could no longer hold the line against the central and left-hand columns of the impi, Pulleine ordered a fighting retreat to camp. This was done in an orderly fashion by the stout regulars of the 24th. Unfortunately, Durnford's retreat was anything but orderly, completely exposing the flank of the 24th's G Company, which was quickly overrun and butchered by Zulu warriors.

As the remaining troops fell back to the camp, the skies above them darkened. A solar eclipse occurred at 2:29 that day, turning the skies black for several minutes. When the sun returned, not one tent was left standing in the camp and the area was now a killing round. The final stand was a brutal affair. British soldiers stood back-to-back, furiously stabbing away with their bayonets as wave upon wave of Zulu warriors thrust at them with their spears and battered them with clubs. Screams rang out across the camp as soldiers were stabbed and clubbed to death where they stood.

Durnford and a valiant band of native infantrymen and regulars of the 24th Foot had managed to keep the two horns of the impi from joining up by defending a wagon park on the edge of the camp. They could only hold on so long, however, and as their ammunition ran out, they resorted to hand-to-hand combat until they were overwhelmed. Durnford's body was later found surrounded by his men, all stabbed and beaten to death.

Pulleine fared no better than Durnford. His body was never formally identified, and he is said to have either died early in the fighting after the retreat to the camp, or in one of the desperate last stands that took place before the end of the battle where the remaining soldiers fought on until they were overwhelmed and killed.

Isandlwana was a humiliating defeat for a British government that hadn't even ordered the attack on Zululand in the first place.
As the remnants of the camp began to flee, no quarter was given to the remaining British and native soldiers. Those attempting to flee were cut down as they ran, while those lying wounded on the ground were stabbed and clubbed to death. The trail of butchered British soldiers reached right back to the Buffalo River – the very same river where Chelmsford's men had so confidently crossed into Zululand a mere eleven days before.

As the enemy melted away, taking rifles, ammunition, artillery and supplies with them, the extent of the massacre became clear. Of the 1,700 men tasked with defending the camp, 52 British officers, 806 rank and file soldiers and 471 African troops had been killed. On the Zulu side, an estimated 2,000 lay dead. The Battle of Isandlwana was - and remains to this day - the worst defeat ever inflicted by a native force on the British Army.

Our guide drove us around the battlefield bringing the whole battle to life. It is an eerie place. Loads of white cairns, piles of white stones, mark the spot of the dead who were buried 20 to a grave.

Scattered amongst the cairns are memorials to the regiments involved. Most of the men belonged to the 24th Regiment. An officer tried to flee in order to save the Queen's colours, but both he and the flag perished trying to cross The Buffalo River. To this day the 24th Regiment have a ball and chain on their insignia because they are the only regiment to ever lose their colours.

There is also a monument to the Zulu warriors which was opened in 2005 at a cost of 1.4 million rand. On being invited to it's opening, the Zulu King of the time took one look and stormed off in a huff. Supposedly the only memorial the Zulu accept is a certain type of tree being planted. The King only returned after such a tree was found.

Rorke's Drift is 17km away and over the Buffalo River which was swelled due to the overnight rain.

We stopped for lunch at The Rorke's Drift Hotel which was lovely if not a little difficult to get to. There are no paved roads here, so the minibus had to traverse a dirt track full of potholes and then a 1 in 2 slope. Once we parked up, a large pack of Irish wolfhounds ran barking out the hotel. I think I would have preferred screaming Zulus.
Funnily enough, nobody was too keen to get off the bus first but once they had coaxed us off with claims that the dogs were actually friendly, lunch was amazing. The hotel was empty, but then again, nobody in their right mind would attempt to get there.

One cultural faux pas was narrowly avoided here. I ordered a beer and the rather buxom barmaid responded, or at least this is what I heard, "Would you like some arse with that?" I thought that was a strange offer, especially as it was only midday and said no. She then pointed to the ice bucket, and I felt like a fool. Very strange accent the South African one.

After lunch we went to the site of Rorke's Drift, where a record 11 Victoria crosses were awarded and 142 British soldiers held off 4000 Zulus, still high after the massacre at Isandlwana a few hours earlier.

The site is pretty much as it was at the time. The church is still a church, and the field hospital is now a museum. Having watched the film Zulu many times. to actually stand in that building was quite moving. The Battle of Rorke's Drift, alongside General Gordon's defence of Khartoum in the Sudan, are probably the two most iconic Battles of the British Empire. British spirit fighting against all odds to overcome the heathen hordes. Although it must be said that Gordon's defence was a heroic failure.

As the Zulus left the battlefield of Isandlwana in triumph or spent a happy evening polishing off the regimental grog, 4,000 of them, who had been held back as reserves split from the main army and headed for the mission station at Rorke's Drift.

During the afternoon a message was brought to the Drift that the Zulus were approaching the Mission Station. It was realized by Lieutenant Chard and Lieutenant Gonville Bromhead, commanding a company of 2/24th left as a garrison that, with some thirty injured or sick soldiers in the hospital, they could not escape. Assisted by Commissary Dalton, they began to prepare the position for defence by stacking heavy sacks of mealie corn and biscuit boxes around the position. Helping them were three hundred natives under the command of Captain Stevenson. This officer fled with his NCOs and workforce as the Zulus approached and did not take part in the battle.
One of the fleeing NCOs, Corporal Anderson, was shot in the back by a 24th defender; Anderson is buried in the cemetery along with the other soldiers killed in the action. The defended area included the hospital and the store; the defenders were now reduced to 139 men, including the Reverend Smith and Surgeon Reynolds with his 35 patients.

The first Zulu appeared in force at about 4 p.m. and repeatedly attacked in successive waves until after dark. This was in fact the Zulu downfall. Rather than amass 4,000 troops and attack together, they had all run the 17km and arrived in small groups, the fastest and fittest first. The hospitals thatched roof was set ablaze and during the following hours the soldiers occupying the hospital were forced, room-by-room, through the building until they reached the high window facing the British position. One by one, the wounded were lowered to the ground, under constant fire from the Zulus. Corporal Allen and Private Hitch, both already wounded, nevertheless successfully ferried the wounded to safety. The hospital was then abandoned to the Zulus.

By firing the thatch, the Zulus inadvertently illuminated the area for the defenders who were able to keep them at bay until dawn; by then the British had fired 20,000 Martini-Henry rounds and repelled numerous hand-to-hand assaults with the bayonet. The Zulus withdrew at dawn when they saw Chelmsford's force approaching the drift. The battle of Rorke's Drift is famous, not only for the ferocious action taken by the defending officers and men, but for the recognition of their bravery by the award of eleven Victoria Crosses, seven of which went to the 24th Regiment, the most ever awarded to one regiment for a single action.

Isandlwana was a humiliating defeat for a British government that hadn't even ordered the attack on Zululand in the first place. When news reached home both of the massacre and the valiant defence of Rorke's Drift, the British public was baying for blood. The government duly obliged their vengeful subjects and in just under six months, an enlarged invasion force armed with gatling machine guns conquered Zululand. The kingdom would remain a British protectorate for the next eighteen years until it was annexed and absorbed into Natal in 1897.

And what of Cetshwayo, the courageous king who stood up to the might of the British Empire and won the day? He was captured following the Battle of Ulundi on the 4th of July 1879. The fact is that the British press demanded that the Zulu capital was captured and destroyed, and here is one of the many myths that exist about this period. The Zulus didn't have a capital, but the British press invented one for them. The final battle at Ulundi just happened to be where Cetshwayo was at the time.

In fact, the British press were probably more responsible for the 11 Victoria Crosses at Rorke's Drift than those defending it. In order to downplay and cover up as much of the humiliation of Isandlwana, Rorke's Drift was over hyped as a famous victory so that they only had to print a few paragraphs at the bottom of the page about the worst defeat in Imperial history. The British press printed propaganda back then as much as they do today.

One final general misunderstanding about Rorke's Drift is the role the Welsh played. If you watch the film starring Michael Caine, the Welsh soldiers sing "Men of Harlech" in the face of the Zulu hordes. In fact, a Welsh guy on the tour had printed the words out for the entire group to sing at the battlefield. It turns out that the 24th Regiment only became the Welsh Regiment two years later and that although there were a couple of Welsh soldiers in the regiment, the majority came from the West Midlands, namely Wolverhampton and Leamington Spa.

It was still a very moving place with memorials to both the British and Zulu dead. The Zulu memorial being accompanied by the correct tree this time.

Our battlefields guide at this point got a little confused and started to refer to the Zulus as fuzzy wuzzies. Now, I always thought that the fuzzy wuzzies were the North Africans who with The Mad Mahdi fought Gordon. The Zulus were called something else entirely. I would have brought this up, but I feared I would end up sounding like The Major out of Fawlty Towers.

We got back to the hotel around 5.30 and because I was kept awake for most of last night thanks to the frog chorus, I did manage to get a couple of hours sleep before dinner. Thankfully I also had a towel in the room so could have a shower.
Another meal of meat, meat and more meat and I had to feel sorry for the vegetarian woman who was promised an omelette just as we were collecting our first course, only for it to arrive 90 minutes later when the rest of us were in the bar. They won't hurry for anything here.

7.   Spionekop

Better weather greeted us for our final day of sightseeing with clear skies and temperatures in the mid-twenties. After a relaxed we returned to our rooms, left our suitcases outside for the porters and a few of us tried to find reception. I thought it had been a joke when we had checked in 48 hours previously, that reception was a mile away through a field of wildebeest. They weren't wrong. We got so far, and the signs were still pointing out into the fields, where it wasn't the wildebeest, I was worried about, it was the psychopathic ostriches which were guarding the property. So rather than check out at reception, we decided to take our keys back to the rooms and leave them in the locks.

Clearly this was a two-way arrangement as reception had still not sent any porters to pick up our luggage and we were forced to do so ourselves. We're British, we shouldn't have to do this sort of thing. I think I would have fitted in quite well to the Empire.

Our battlefield guide was back again this morning as we headed from Dundee to the town of Ladysmith. We were back to The Boer War today and the aftermath of the Battle of Talana which we had learned about a couple of days earlier.

Lieutenant General Sir George White deployed his forces around the garrison town of Ladysmith, with a detachment even further forward at Dundee. The entire British force could concentrate only after fighting two battles at Talana Hill and Elandslaagte. As the Boers surrounded Ladysmith, White ordered a sortie by his entire force to capture the Boer artillery. The result was the disastrous Battle of Ladysmith, in which the British were driven back into the town having lost 1,200 men killed, wounded, or captured.

The Boers then proceeded to surround Ladysmith and cut the railway link to Durban. Major General John French and his chief of staff, Major Douglas Haig escaped on the last train to leave, which was riddled with bullets.

Ladysmith was then besieged for 118 days. White knew that large reinforcements were arriving and could communicate with British units south of the Tugela River by searchlight and heliograph. He expected relief soon. Meanwhile, his troops carried out several raids and sorties to sabotage Boer artillery.

Louis Botha commanded the Boer detachment which first raided Southern Natal, and then dug in north of the Tugela to hold off the relief force. On 15 December 1899, the first relief attempt was defeated at the Battle of Colenso. Temporarily unnerved, the relief force commander, General Redvers Henry Buller, suggested that White either break out or destroy his stores and ammunition and surrender. White could not break out because his horses and draught animals were weak from lack of grazing and forage, but also refused to surrender.

On Christmas Day 1899, the Boers fired into Ladysmith a carrier shell without fuse, which contained a Christmas pudding, two Union Flags and the message "compliments of the season". The shell is still kept in the museum at Ladysmith.

The British made several attempts to end the siege, and we were off to the battlefield of another of these heroic failures, Spionekop, which was about 18 miles outside of Ladysmith.

Whereas the main roads in South Africa seem perfectly fine, once you turn off, you take your life in to your own hands. Spionekop is a national monument but is a very steep hill. In order to climb the hill, our driver had to unattach the trailer that was holding all our luggage. We would not have made it up the hill with that still attached.

Spionekop was another military disaster for the British and a pattern was beginning to develop here. Talana, Isandlwana and now Spionekop. I did think of pointing out to the battlefields guide that the British won both Boer Wars and the Zulu one, so why were we only going to the battles that we lost.

Unfortunately, most of what I learned about the battle came in the following days from reading various articles. This was due to the guide marching us through scrubland on which he kept banging his Zulu war club (knobkerrie). When asked why he was doing this he replied that it was due to snakes, and we should keep our eyes open. And then to make matters worse, he was asked what type of snakes and his response was "all of them, mambas, cobras, vipers." I am afraid that was enough for me, and I spent the rest of the tour staring at my feet and everything the guide said went in one ear and out of the other.

Things were not helped by the swarms of flies that were getting everywhere. Mouth, ears, everywhere. It would have been a very interesting site had it not been for the wildlife. Our guide also pointed out the toilets, should anyone feel the need. They were down a grassy path, behind a bush and had a wonderful view of the new Spionekop Dam. If he thought I was dropping my trousers with Black mambas on the loose he was wildly mistaken, I didn't notice any other takers either.

Recalling the battle of Spionekop, the Boer commander, Denys Reitz, wrote, 'There cannot have been many battlefields where there was such an accumulation of horrors within so small a compass.' A century later, it is hard to imagine that it was on this quiet, sunlit hill that Boer and Brit fought one another in the bloodiest battle of the Anglo-Boer War.

At the turn of the century the Boers had occupied much of Natal and were ranged along the Tugela in preparation for an onslaught into the Natal heartland. They whipped the British on several fronts, the most humiliating British defeat being the Battle of Colenso where the toll of over a thousand British casualties to only eight Boers was a severe blow to British national pride.

In January 1900, the commander of the British forces, General Sir Redvers Buller (who had done little to distinguish himself since being sent to rout the invading Boers) crossed the Tugela and, together with General Sir Charles Warren, planned a two-pronged attack to outflank the Boers and advance on Ladysmith - which, although held by the British, was besieged by the Boers.

Boer forces in the area numbered only five or six hundred men, so the armies had to advance without delay if they were to succeed. However, Warren procrastinated for several days, during which time the Boers reinforced their numbers.

Buller eventually lost patience and gave Warren an ultimatum - move on Ladysmith or retreat across the Tugela. Warren's decision was to take and hold Spionekop, the commanding hill which seemed to be the key to relieving Ladysmith. On the night of 23 January 1900, he sent about 1,700 men to storm Spionekop under cover of darkness. The men began the long climb up the southwestern ridge of Spionekop in a steady drizzle. When they reached an open slope below the summit five hours later, they were ordered to fix their bayonets. Just metres away in the darkness a slumbering Boer party of men were woken to the chilling clatter of hundreds of bayonets fixing into their sockets. Firing wildly, all but one of the Boers escaped into the darkness.

At 2am both Boer and British camps 400m below heard the troops cheer as they crested the summit. But the British triumph was misplaced. One advantage the Boers had was their familiarity with the area's topography and terrain. Warren had ordered the attack on Spionekop without any prior reconnaissance - and did not realise that, viewed from the north, Spionekop was not the bastion it appeared to be from the south. The Boers moved seven pieces of artillery onto the surrounding hills and prepared for battle.

On the summit of Spionekop the British began to dig a trench but soon struck rock below the surface and could manage only a shallow ditch less than half a metre deep. At dawn a thick mist shrouded the summit and when it began to lift at around 7 am, the full horror of their situation became clear - the summit was totally exposed to the surrounding hills.

An hour later, when the mist finally lifted, Boer forces engaged the British in ferocious hand-to-hand battle. This was followed in the afternoon by a relentless shelling of British reinforcements arriving on the scene. Boer shells rained down with deadly accuracy, sometimes at a rate of seven a minute, turning the summit into a hell of splintering rock, flying metal and shattered bodies.

Winston Churchill, as a war correspondent witnessing the battle, wrote: 'Many of the wounds were of a horrible nature. The splinters and fragments of the shells had torn and mutilated in the most ghastly manner.' The British finally succeeded in breaching the Boer lines by evening, and to secure the hill they had only to bring in more reinforcements.

However, a combination of official incompetence and poor communication produced an order for a British withdrawal from the summit. Ironically, the Boers simultaneously retreated down their side of the hill, believing they had lost the battle.

By the following morning the British had withdrawn to the banks of the Tugela. When several Boers cautiously climbed the northern slope of Spionekop looking for wounded comrades, they found to their utter amazement that, apart from those killed or wounded, the summit was deserted. The British had gone.

In a bizarre incident on 25th January as the victors were collecting Lee-Enfield rifles from British bodies, one Boer failed to notice that a Lancashire Fusilier's finger had been stiffened by rigor mortis and was still hooked around the trigger of his elevated rifle. When the Boer gave it a tug, it fired a bullet into his chest, killing him instantly. It is the only known incident of a dead Englishman killing a Boer.

While Buller made repeated attempts to fight his way across the Tugela, the defenders of Ladysmith suffered increasingly from shortage of food and other supplies, and from disease, mainly enteric fever, or typhoid, which claimed among many others, the life of noted war correspondent G.W. Steevens. The Boers had long before captured Ladysmith's water supply, and the defenders could use only the muddy Klip River.

Towards the end of the siege, the garrison and townsfolk were living largely on their remaining draught oxen and horses (mainly in the form of "chevril", a meat paste named after the commercial beef extract "Bovril").

Eventually, Buller broke through the Boer positions on 27 February. Following their succession of reverses, his troops had developed effective tactics based on close cooperation between the infantry and artillery. After the protracted struggle, the morale of Botha's men at last broke and they and the besiegers retreated, covered by another huge thunderstorm. Buller did not pursue, and White's men were too weak to do so.

The first party of the relief column, under Major Hubert Gough and accompanied by war correspondent Winston Churchill, rode in on the evening of 28 February. White reportedly greeted them saying, "Thank God we kept the flag flying".
The peak of Spionekop is littered with monuments to the fallen and probably the most poignant are the filled in shallow trenches that the British built that are now used as mass graves.

As we headed back to the minibus, two cyclists somehow had struggled their way up. No mean feat when you consider the bus barely made it. One of them asked where the toilet was, and somebody sheepishly pointed to the grass track. Nobody mentioned the black mambas though.

We finished here around midday and after reconnecting the luggage at the foot of the hill, it was a two-hour drive to our hotel which is in the heart of The Drakensberg Mountains.

Once again, we stopped at a service station for lunch, and I managed to end up with a stone cold cheeseburger. It did cross my mind to go back and ask them to microwave it for a few seconds but as 30 seconds is akin to 3 hours here, I decided against it.

The Drakensberg Mountain range stretches for more than 600 miles from the Eastern Cape Province in the South, then successively forms, in order from south to north, the border between Lesotho and the Eastern Cape and the border between Lesotho and KwaZulu-Natal Province. Thereafter it forms the border between KwaZulu-Natal and the Free State, and next as the border between KwaZulu-Natal and Mpumalanga Province.

Unlike the Limpopo Mountains that just seemed like an enormous wall, these actually had rugged peaks which was a stark and stunning contrast.

We had been led to believe in our tour brochure that we would have time to relax at our hotel in The Drakensbergs. There were walks through the countryside of varying lengths, a spa and I had rather been looking forward to a round at the nine-hole golf course on the Monday morning. As we approached the hotel, Patrick, our guide, informed us that rather than leaving at 1 p.m. the following day, it would now be 10 a.m. due to one person in the group booking the wrong flight. Johannesburg Airport was a good five to six hour drive away and we all had to travel together. I often say that I don't go on holiday to relax, so I guess it was a case of practicing what you preach.
The Cathedral Peak Hotel was an amazing place. The hotels in Swaziland and Mkuze had been really good 4-star hotels, but this was without doubt a really good 5-star property set in the valley below Cathedral Ridge.

Cathedral Peak Mountain is part of The Cathedral Ridge and towers 9860 feet high. The Afrikaans or Boer Settlers decided that it looked like a cathedral, yet the local Amangwane people had always called it The Little Horn. Here we go again with the clash between cows and the church.

Rather than individual rooms, we were allocated our own little cottage which was nice and mine had a nice little area outside which overlooked the golf course and the river that was rushing through the valley. There was a pretty little chapel a few yards away which blended in perfectly with the backdrop of Cathedral Peak.

I am used to hotel rooms with limited television channels around the world and to be honest, I rarely turn the TV on in most places. But here there was one channel and it just showed cricket for 24 hours a day. Not everyone's cup of tea, but I was happy with it.

The hotel bar seemed very colonial with lots of black waiters waiting on the whims of the white residents. I did partake in a cold beer during the afternoon but then decided to go back to my cottage and get a couple of hours sleep before dinner.

By the time I woke up the weather had completely changed and it was pouring with rain. The restaurant was a good two-minute walk away and there was no shelter, hence there were some very soggy people around the table.

The food was what you would expect from a five-star hotel. It was still a buffet of sorts but there were salads, roasts, stir-fries, pasta, and a whole cornucopia of desserts. You could eat as much as you like. Which I did and as a result it was a four-minute walk back to the room in what was now a fully fledged lightning storm.

The weather the following morning was dry, but you could still feel the moisture in the air amongst the mountains. The clouds were still enveloping Cathedral Peak and as it happens, I would not have been able to play golf due to the flooding caused by the overnight downpour.
Breakfast was as much of a feast as the previous night, fruit, porridge, cheese, salad, muesli, and every type of egg under the sun. I stuck to a simple English breakfast as I was still weighed down by the previous night's dinner.

We left at ten and this time there were no issues about porters not turning up. The journey back was fairly boring. Once out of The Drakensberg Range you enter The Free State (formerly Orange Free State) which is unremarkable. Our guide likened it to Kansas in America with miles upon miles of flat corn fields and farmland.

Highlight or lowlight was lunch at another service station. Wimpy are still a thing over here and you don't really see MacDonalds or Burger King. Another guy and I had been reminiscing about them and had decided that should the opportunity arrive, we would have a Wimpy burger for old times' sake, if only to see if they had improved. Well, the opportunity arose, and our scientific research concluded that they were still as bloody awful as they always were.

We got back to Oliver Tambo Airport despite the Johannesburg traffic, around 3.30. Patrick, our guide, seemed to run off very quickly, clearly glad to see the back of us. One passenger ran for their imminent flight and the rest of us had six hours to kill.

By the time it was due to board the plane, around 8.30 p.m. the most apocalyptic electric storm had descended upon Johannesburg. Forks of lightning were attacking the ground in packs of three and the rain was so hard you could hardly see it. The only positive was that the rain was hitting the terminal roof so hard, it was drowning out the thunder. It did cross my mind that I was about to undertake a live Faraday cage experiment, once aboard the plane!

Regardless of all of this, we took off on time and as per usual I was sat across the aisle from the plane nutter. During take-off, whilst strapped in, he attempted to change his contact lenses. Funnily enough, he spent most of the remaining flight, on his hands and knees, looking for his lens which had fallen under his seat. He was still there when dinner was served an hour and a half later. As to why he did not change his lenses whilst in the terminal in one of the numerous spotless toilets, I will never know.
We arrived back around 7 a.m., and so did my suitcase this time. Another holiday over and as per usual I arrived back feeling I needed a rest.

OY GEVALT!

OR

JESUS CHRIST, MY PART IN HIS DOWNFALL

ISRAEL AND PALESTINE 2023

1. Foreword — 408
2. My Take On The History Of Abrahamic Religions — 409
3. Holy Breast Milk And Catholic Business Models — 432
4. Crowdfunding Jesus — 444
5. Once In Royal David's Khazi — 456
6. The Dead Sea And Other Low Points — 467
7. "There Is No Such Thing As a Palestinian" — 478
8. The Scar Of Bethlehem — 488
9. Holy Fish — 499
10. Epilogue — 512

FOREWORD

The fact that there is so much archaeology in Israel has meant that it has always had some sort of interest for me. But to be honest, the social and political history of the current Israeli state, has always kept me away.

Over the past few years, I have studied religions and the stories behind them. And it really had reached the stage where the only way to discover what has substance and what is pure make believe was to visit the sites where they are said to have taken place.
At first, I tried to find a group tour that I could join, but this proved to be fruitless. There were the grand Christian tours, full of loud Americans and where every breakfast would be met with a Bible verse. Up to forty Americans shouting "Jesus" and being as brain dead as they generally are when confronted with a reasonable counter argument would only end up with me being arrested at gun point by The Israeli Defence Force. Or there were the secular tours, that seemed to spend three days floating in The Dead Sea and visiting wineries in The Golan Heights before running the gauntlet and spending the last night in Jerusalem. The tour run by the company I generally use didn't even visit Bethlehem.

So, I was faced with organising my own hotels. Guides and transport. And whilst this allows you the freedom to do what you want, there is always the nagging doubt that something might go pear shaped and you will be stranded somewhere.

The compromise was organising tours with different guides, but rather than travel around the country, use a hotel in Jerusalem as a base. I think I came up with a pretty good itinerary, taking in both the religious and historical heritage of the country, whilst also exploring the political situation.

The trip itself was amazing, but before we get to that, I have written a shortish essay, outlining my beliefs revolving around the central characters in The Bible. To do this justice, it should really be a lot longer and more detailed, however, it does cover some of the points that will be touched upon during my travels.

MY TAKE ON THE HISTORICITY OF THE ABRAHAMIC RELIGIONS

Blind faith can be a very toxic belief system. Over the span of time, an inordinate amount of people have lost their lives based on belief systems which lack physical evidence. Governments and regimes around the world have ruled people's lives based on texts written. thousands of years ago, most of which contain allegorical points of reference, at best. The Bible, The Talmud and The Koran have all been used to instil control and fear over the centuries. The followers of these texts, which are considered theologically sacred, insist that people meekly accept and embrace their divinity. With the inception of social media, it could be argued that we are in a similar situation today akin to George Orwell's 1984.

For the past ten years, I've been having weekly debates with a friend about the existence of a God. The debates have included the relevant passages of The Bible. and their historical correctness, the role that the Church and all other organised religious organisations play, as well as the suppression and control of the masses. My friend and debating partner started this journey as a fully-fledged elder in The Jehovah's Witnesses who believed every word in the Bible, or at least the Bible that the Witnesses have re written to forward their ideology. He decided to leave the organisation after acquiring the clarity to truly observe the hypocrisy of the movement and their intransigence towards questions. Although the final straw may have been when one of the fire and brimstone Governing Body JW members was caught red handed on camera, buying nearly £500 worth of 25-year-old Scotch in his local liquor store, when he should have been at his local Kingdom Hall preaching. My friend is still a devout Christian, but is now searching for his own answers, reinterpreting some of the Biblical tales and realigning them in their historical context.

I began this journey at the other end of the spectrum, having travelled through Egypt and The Middle East where most religions began. Some of the religious murals, whether they be Christian or Egyptian were hard to comprehend, and I believed that a more in-depth knowledge of the Bible and other religious works would help me understand the history of the region.

The whole concept of religion has always fascinated me, and several of my close associates who identify as being well educated, well informed and capable of debating on most rational subjects, become totally irrational when it comes to religion. Many in society hold a blind faith, believing what is quite clearly, mythological at best. I have never been an active participant in any religion but was exposed to Christianity in childhood. The state sponsored education system in England does not allow the questioning of Darwin or the Big Bang theory. If you want the relevant gold star or pass mark in an exam, you need to embrace these as fact. However, the truth is in the title. Both are theories that society have embraced, just as Constantine, the Roman Emperor embraced Christianity in the 4th Century.

These so called "facts" are taught with a religious fervour, not unlike those implemented by The Church and the leaders of the Inquisition. Anybody who questions Darwin or the Big Bang faces state ridicule, their books banned on Amazon and their Twitter accounts shut down. Lately, the cassock seems to have been replaced with white lab coats. In the Middle Ages, people listened to their Priests because they thought they knew what they were talking about and today it is the same with Scientists. Just because someone has spent thousands on a university education and acquired three PhD's, their knowledge or "expertise" should not be construed as a singular truth. In order to obtain a PhD, students simply end up reciting the same opinions as other PhD's in order to pass. Academia is all too often a clique with theories passed off as fact. In the field of archaeology, if you write a book that challenges the consensus, even though you can prove it to be true, you will be ridiculed and called a pseudo archaeologist. Mainstream academia and its' consensus will always win because they have the monopoly on publishing deals and earn their living by regurgitating the same findings and discrediting conflicting points of view. Any new facts that threaten the narrative of general consensus are censored or ridiculed as soon as possible by "scholars" and publishers.

This is nothing new. Just look at the imprisonment of Galileo or the Papacy's refusal to accept the first Egyptian discoveries that predated their Biblical timeline. The Book comes first, even though there was evidence to the contrary.

Today we have discoveries that date back to 10,500 BC that have been carbon dated. There are claims that some man-made buildings in Indonesia go back to 25,000 BC, yet the academic Archaeology book club, still insist that a small group of hunter gatherers, decided to start farming, somewhere between modern Turkey and Iran, 6,500 years ago. Many have closed minds and open bank accounts. As is the case in many areas, the truth is the enemy of the story being spun. As Nazi spin doctor Josef Goebbels rightly stated, "If you tell a lie big enough and keep repeating it, people will eventually come to believe it. The lie can be maintained only for such time as the State can shield the people from the political, economic and/or military consequences of the lie."

In the past, when few people were educated or literate, this was hardly an issue. Debates and changes to long held theories were welcomed. Now we have mass education, and the fear that somebody may prove something other than the prescribed narrative as dictated by the state is far too high. If the state and academia are not telling the truth about history, what else could they be lying about. That could be another 28 volumes.

This still leaves the issue that there is absolutely zero hard evidence for the existence of many of the characters in The Bible. The Church claims that faith in their existence is enough, but surely if these characters are so pivotal in our shared history. Shouldn't there be some sort of record somewhere? Abraham, Joseph, Moses, David, Solomon, Mary and even Jesus himself are nowhere to be found outside of the Biblical pages.

How could humanities' collective consciousness be duped by something that has no more proof than a fairy tale? Surely these characters must appear somewhere in the historical record. I believe they are, just not where the Church allows you to look.

Christianity, Islam and Judaism would have you believe that Abraham, the patriarch of all three religions, was a humble shepherd from Mesopotamia who after consulting with his God, fled a famine in Canaan and went to Egypt, where the Pharaoh gave him even more sheep.
Yes, it may be true that pastoral nomads grazed their sheep over the borders of Canaan and Egypt. Much of Canaan was under Egyptian rule in any case. Despite this, it appears that not one of these characters was important enough to interest a Pharoah. That is of course unless, as was the case with Abraham, they crossed the border with tens of thousands of armed men.

We are left then with the issue that either sheep rustling was at an industrial scale and Abraham needed these troops to protect his sheep or that Abraham was not a shepherd. This theory is in fact more important.

If you watch historical or archaeological programmes on mainstream television Channels, you get the impression that Egypt was a united country from the day that Narmer united Upper and Lower Egypt around 3100 BC, right up to the fall of Cleopatra in 30BC. This was not the case and apart from the first six dynasties 3100BC to 2181BC and the New Kingdom from Ahmose in 1550BC to Ramses III in 1155BC, Egypt was rife with Civil War, invaders, and religious intolerance. Pharoah's of Upper Egypt ruled concurrently with Pharaohs in Lower Egypt.

To understand this better, it becomes necessary to go back to the beginning, prior to the unification of the country. Upper Egypt, which rather confusingly is the Southern part of the country, seems to have had a number of animal based religious cults which evolved in Nubia and further South. In Lower Egypt, in the North, the beliefs seem to have centred around what would become the great Temple of Heliopolis, albeit that was the Greek name, the Egyptian or Khmetian name being Iunu, or the Biblical Temple of On or Anu. Note the similarity to the all-powerful God of Sumeria, Anu. It's also true, that throughout the entire history of Egypt, the God of Heliopolis was Atum. The letters T and D are interchangeable in ancient Egyptian language, thus the pronunciation, was Adum. This may be a coincidence, as the other main God of Heliopolis was Set (Seth being the son of Adam in the Bible that all men were descended from). Whilst many creation myths differ greatly from the Sumerian, myths from other cultures around the world always tend to end up at the same starting point.

If I indicated that biblical Abraham was a pharaoh of Egypt, would it appear to be an utterly absurd figment of a deranged mind? Initially that may seem so, but this is only because we have grown so used to the orthodox ecclesiastical creed that we have forgotten that the Biblical Abraham was in fact a very powerful man. Josephus, the first century Jewish historian says of Abraham:

"Pharaoh Necho, king of Egypt at the time, descended on this land with an immense army and seized Sarah the Princess, mother of our nation. And what did our forefather Abraham do? Did he avenge the insult by force of arms? Yet he had three hundred and eighteen officers under him, with unlimited manpower at his disposal!"

Three hundred and eighteen officers, not men, under his command, and it was obviously quite a sizable army that Abraham had at his disposal - possibly running into the tens of thousands. In this case, the image I have portrayed above is not quite so absurd. At most, it is just an embellishment on what the texts say, for they do not explain from what lands and over what peoples Abraham was such a leader. Yet how many options do we really have? How many nations in this era would have such a powerful army? It is somehow explained to us by theological clergy that the whole of the Western world was suddenly transfixed by the philosophy of a family of nomadic sheepherders wandering around the Negev desert. A family who had held their traditions through thousands of years, and at a time when most such individuals were illiterate.

But if the biblical family were pharaohs of Egypt, should we not see them in the historical record? Indeed so, but first the precise era to study needs to be decided and the clue to this comes from the Bible. The patriarchs in the Bible are known as being shepherds, as I have just indicated. In fact, the Bible is quite specific about this point. Joseph's family are asked by pharaoh:

   "What is your occupation? And they said ... Thy servants are shepherds, both we, and also our fathers."

This point is not just interesting, but it is fundamental for understanding what the Bible is trying to tell us. For it just so happens that a whole dynasty of pharaohs were known as shepherds!
These were the Hyksos pharaohs who, in the historical record, had 'invaded' northern Egypt during the 14th to 16th dynasties. Hyksos is a term which translates as 'Shepherd King'. Clearly, we have a very obvious and very strong link here. In fact, it is amazing that so little has been said about this "coincidence". There is a great deal of synergy here, and the Bible mentions a very special family lineage of Shepherds of which it says the "Kings will come out of you" and likewise the historical record tells us that some of the pharaohs of northern Egypt were called Shepherd Kings.

At the centre of this conundrum is the term shepherd. Why should an Egyptian pharaoh wish to be known as a shepherd? The answers lay in the Egyptian records and their fascination with astrology. The Hyksos pharaohs were being compared to the constellation of Aries. With this concept firmly in the back of the mind, the Bible suddenly starts to release its' long-hidden secrets: for there are numerous references to sheep and cattle in the Bible. Although the subject matter coincides with the quaint pastoral image being plied by the clergy, none of them made any literal sense. But once suitably translated, with the sheep becoming the constellation of Aries (or their followers) and the cattle as Taurus (and their followers), everything fits into place.

The era of Taurus lasted until about 1800 BC, when Aries came into ascendance. This date is not only very close to both the era of the first Hyksos pharaohs and the arrival of Abraham in the Bible, but I would also suggest that this change in the constellations caused a social rift between the Apis Bull worshippers in Egyptian Thebes (the Taureans) and the Hyksos Shepherd pharaohs in the north (the Arians). The country was divided, and just as the historical records indicate, these events happened during this exact period of time.

The Bible has direct evidence that shows this to be true. In addition, the following quote seems to be a verbatim conversation that has been preserved for some 3,500 years. The scene is set by the 3rd century BC Egyptian historian Manetho, who indicates (as does the Bible) that there were actually two exoduses from Egypt. The first being a major migration, and the second being a much smaller exodus of priests. After the first exodus, the patriarch Joseph (He with the coat of many colours, i.e., a priests' stole) goes back to Egypt and rises to become the most powerful man in Egypt, save from the pharaoh himself. Joseph asks his family to join him in Egypt, but he has a warning for them.

    (Paraphrased) You are shepherds as you know, and your duty is to feed
    the cattle... And it shall come to pass that pharaoh will call
    you, and shall say what is your occupation. You must say in return that your
    trade has been cattle from our youth even until now, both we and also our

fathers. Otherwise you will not be allowed to stay in the land of Egypt,
for we shepherds are an abomination to the Egyptians. Genesis 46:32

What could Joseph possibly mean by this statement? The Egyptians had no prohibitions on the eating of sheep meat, so why was the pharaoh so interested in the occupation of the brothers, and why was the lowly but honourable profession of shepherd so despised? The solution is simple, a couple of words have been altered by the scribes to give the conversation an agricultural bias, but in truth they were discussing the most important topic in Egypt - religion. Replacing the words with their original astrological counterparts, the full import of the statement becomes dramatically clear.

(Paraphrased) You are Hyksos/Arians as you know, and your duty is to
convert the followers of Taurus ... And it shall come to pass that pharaoh will call
you, and shall say what is your religion. You must say in return that your
religion has been Taurean from our youth even until now, both we and also our
fathers. Otherwise, you will not be allowed to stay in the land of Egypt,for we Hyksos/Arians are an abomination to the Egyptians.

Suddenly it becomes dramatically obvious why the Egyptians thought that shepherds were an abomination. This was not a reference to a profession, but to a religion and an entire nation - the Hyksos. Egypt had just been through a bitter and bloody civil war with these peoples, a war between southern and northern Egypt which resulted in the Exodus of the Hyksos peoples and the destruction of much of the northern delta lands. Of course, the 'shepherds' were an abomination to the (southern) Egyptians - they were the Hyksos Shepherds!

Further evidence that this is the correct interpretation to be placed upon the Old Testament writings is provided by the later works in the New Testament. Jesus, who was descended from the same family as the patriarchs, was born as a Lamb of God. In other words, he was a young Shepherd (Hyksos) prince in exile, he was just a lamb for the time being. As Jesus matured to become a Shepherd, another momentous astronomical event was happening in the skies above. At just this precise era, the constellation of Aries started to wane in the heavens and Pisces came into the ascendance. Accordingly, Jesus changed his title according to the age-old tradition, the young shepherd became a Fisher of Men, a king of Pisces.

As for the historical record. Mayebre Sheshi, is recorded as the first Hyksos king of Egypt and founder of the 15th dynasty. Is there a massive difference between the name Mayebre and Abraham? The Pharoah Yaqub Har (Jacob) also falls within this Dynasty.

If we have deduced that the Biblical patriarchs were The Hyksos "Shepherd Kings", then that should aid us in finding evidence for the exodus out of Egypt. The North and South of Egypt were once again reunited under the rule of Ahmose I, who came to the throne in 1549 BC. It was also Ahmose who drove the Hyksos out of Egypt towards Syria and Canaan, thus creating the first great Exodus.

There are many arguments as to when and where The Exodus started, and there is very little evidence of the event. Finding the Pharoah of The Exodus has been likened to asking who was Prime Minister of the UK during Peter Pan's adventure to Never Land. As with the Romans, military defeats and heresies were not dwelled upon. People were written out of history, - their faces removed from monuments and within a few generations, the illiterate population would have forgotten all about them. If you are looking for a charismatic Egyptian Prince called Moses, who led his people to a promised land, you are never going to find him in any of the official records.

However, there is still some irrefutable evidence that points to a large exodus of people out of Egypt in the late 16th Century BC.

Roman Historian Josephus, quoting the earlier words of Egyptian Historian Manetho mentions the expulsion of The Hyksos from Egypt.
"After the conclusion of the treaty they left with their families and chattels, not fewer than two hundred and forty thousand people, and crossed the desert into Syria. Fearing the Assyrians, who dominated over Asia at that time, they built a city in the country which we now call Judea. It was large enough to contain this great number of men and was called Jerusalem."

Thirty years ago, a Stele, from the time of Ahmose I was uncovered and the translation of part of it is uncannily similar to the texts of The Torah, Bible and Koran. The Tempest stele, as it has become to be known, was erected by the pharaoh Ahmose I at the beginning of the eighteenth dynasty of Egypt, which equates to about 1550 BC. The stele derives its dramatic title from the great storms that it details, which evidently struck Egypt during the reign of Ahmose I. Climatically speaking, southern, or Upper Egypt can be thought of as being in the midst of the Sahara Desert, and although the occasional desert thunderstorm will create a flash flood every decade or so, the area is otherwise arid and dry. Ahmose's account of a raging nationwide tempest of rain continuing without cessation and being louder than a waterfall at Aswan, can therefore be considered to be highly unusual in this region.

"... now then ... the gods declared their discontent. The gods [caused] the sky to come in a tempest of r[ain], with darkness in the western region and the sky being unleashed without [cessation, louder than] the cries of the masses, more powerful than [...], [while the rain raged] on the mountains louder than the noise of the cataract which is at Elephantine."

This was certainly a notable occurrence. It was not only worthy of an Egyptian stele being created to record these events, but was it also worthy of a sacred scroll being written too? Was the Israelite equivalent of the stele the second book of the Torah - Exodus?

This would certainly coincide, The Exodus with the eruption of the Thera Volcano, which would have caused meteorological mayhem throughout the Mediterranean region. Black skies, rivers running red, plagues of locusts and cattle dying; all for no apparent reason. These types of catastrophes would have happened after such a cataclysmic event.

The biblical plagues have a similar theme to that which has been translated from the Tempest Stele:

"... a thick darkness, without the least light, spread itself over the Egyptians; whereby their sight being obstructed, and their breathing hindered by the thickness of the air ... under a terror least they be swallowed up by the dark cloud ... Hail was sent down from heaven, and such hail it was, as the climate of Egypt had never suffered before ... the hail broke down their boughs laden with fruit."

This brings us to the rather interesting translation of the Tempest Stele, which accords so well with the biblical account. Indeed, it appears to be a direct quotation from the Bible. There are several biblical quotations and similarities inscribed on the Tempest Stele and one of them reads as follows:

Then his Majesty began ... to provide them with silver, with gold, with copper, with oil, and of every bolt [of cloth] that could be desired. Then his majesty made himself comfortable inside the palace.

In the Bible, an exact equivalent of the description above is to be found. During the exodus the Bible says:

This is the offering which ye shall take of them; gold, silver, and brass [copper]. And cloth of blue, and purple, and scarlet, and fine linen ... oil for the light, spices for anointing oil and for sweet incense ... and let them make a [palace] sanctuary that I may dwell among them.

The Book of Exodus ties in very well with the Egyptian writings of the time and that a massive Exodus of people left Northern Egypt for an area around Jerusalem. It also confirms the extreme weather recorded in The Tempest Stele, explained by the eruption of Thera, it seems we have proof of an Exodus.

However, was this really the Exodus of Moses? I do not believe so, but this exodus did fill the lands of Canaan and the Northern Sinai, with what would become Israelites and Jews. What was missing was a leader, an organised religion, and a cause.
Moving forward to the mid fourteenth century BC, Egypt had once more fallen foul of religious divides and greedy priests. Popular Egyptology will claim that Akhenaten was a religious heretic who abolished all the Theban Gods in favour of his preferred monotheistic God, The Aten. But this was not really the case. Changes had begun to be made during the reign of Amenhotep III, and his Royal wife Tye, who was clearly of Semitic descent, as was her Father, Yuya. All three were buried in a Royal Tomb in The Valley Of The Kings. Some believe that Yuya was the Biblical Joseph (I do not), and clearly both he and Tye had a major role in the upbringing of Akhenaten and his brother Tuthmosis. Both Royal princes became priests at Heliopolis and studied the old religion of Egypt. It is my belief that rather than being a heretic, Akhenaten was trying to restore the original religion of the North and that of the Hyksos. A religion that worshipped an unseen, all powerful creator God, and not the animal deities of The South and their idol worship.

The Temple of The Aten at Amarna, was virtually identical to the First Jewish Temple. Many of the current Jewish beliefs and traditions, even most of the holidays, have roots in this period of Egyptian history. Some believe that Akhenaten and Moses were the same person. Again, I remain sceptical of this theory, and would veer more towards his brother or the High Priest, but the real proof of this comes in the line of priests that fled Amarna after the Theban Priests restored the Southern religions back to the country of Egypt.

In the Bible, the High Priests of The Jewish Temple are appointed by God and descend from the tribe of Levi. The first of these Levitical Priests is Phinehas. The Egyptian translation of this name is Panehsy and it just so happens that Chief Servitor Of The Aten in Amarna was called Panehsy. The meaning of the name is actually "Nubian", which would suggest that he was dark skinned and came from modern day Sudan. Something that modern Judaism deems dismissive and would have to be airbrushed out.

In the Tomb of Meryre, High Priest of The Aten at Amarna, a prayer is written on the wall. It is almost identical to Psalm 103. Furthermore, in the Bible we find a "Merari" whose descendants were responsible for The Tabernacle. I would suggest that they are one in the same person. Furthermore, when The Dead Sea Scrolls were found in 1947, a document written by The Essenes, the Nazarene Jews, was discovered. Their founder was known as Merkabah, a Hebrew version of the name Meryre.

It is highly likely that these exiled priests headed north and managed to firstly convert pastoral nomads to Atenism and finally converted the tribes of Hyksos, who had fled Egypt 200 years earlier, from their polytheistic religion based on The Temple of Heliopolis to a monotheistic version. Establishing the religion through the North-eastern Nile Delta, The Sinai and Canaan. This coincides with the first official recording of the nation of Israel, which came during the reign of The Pharoah, Merenptah, in the 19th Dynasty.

It is noteworthy that in Jewish religion, the name of God can no longer be uttered and is replaced by the word Adonai. Remembering that in Egyptian, the letters T and D are interchangeable, are the Jews still worshiping Yahweh, but referring to him as The Aten? This is quite conflicting, but very probable. Yahweh was a moon god, as well as a storm god. Both Judaism and Islam have lunar calendars and all mosques have a crescent moon on the minarets. Yet He is now being referred to as the Sun disk.

The Jewish Sabbath also has its roots in Atenism. It is based on the words "saba" (seven) and "Aten", when every seventh day the people pacified themselves and worshipped the Sun God.

The next major development comes two thousand years later with the building of the first Jewish Temple. One of the primary problems for Judaeo-Christian theologians is the disturbing reality that both King David and King Solomon, the most celebrated kings of Judaic history, cannot be found in the historical record.

Once again, Egypt found itself divided due to civil war. Israel had never really flourished and had become tribal once more. That was until the mythical King David unites them under one monarchy and has a son named Solomon who ultimately builds the greatest temple ever seen. However, not a single piece of archaeology has been found in Jerusalem to support this. There are plenty of ancient buildings named after the two Kings in Jerusalem, but the fact is nothing can be dated later than around 800 BC.

But if we use the same method as used for finding Abraham, we start to get some surprising results. There are two main claims to fame for King David. Phrases and imagery that have come down to us through the centuries and the millennia, and which are probably as familiar to us now as they were nearly three thousand years ago during the reign of this famous king - the ' "Star of David" and the "City of David".

There was an Egyptian pharaoh of the twenty-first dynasty whose name in the hieroglyphic spelling encompassed both the star and the city glyphs, and his throne name was Pa-seba-kha-en-nuit, or Psusennes II. The dates for the reigns of both King David and the Pharoah Psusennes are all but identical. But how do we get the name David from Pa-seba-kha-en-nuit? The simple answer to this - the name David is a greatly shortened nickname, based upon the star glyph. The common pronunciation for this glyph is seba, as can be seen from the name Pa-seba-kha-en-nuit. However, seba is not the only word in Egyptian that can be used to describe a star, and the one that the scribes were thinking about when they made the Judaic translation of this name was actually djuat. The Hebrew form of the name 'David' is pronounced Daveed and even in this translation it is not difficult to see how this name was derived from the Egyptian original of djuat or djuait.

Further proof comes from the fact that Psusennes had a daughter known as Maakhare Mu-Tamhat. Surprising as it may seem, King David had a daughter who bore a strikingly similar name; she was called Maakhah Tamar. The only appreciable difference between the names of these two royal princesses is that the Judaean lady has dropped the 'Mu' from her second name - in the Hebrew texts, the Egyptian name Maakhare Mu-Tamhat has become Maakhare Tamhat, or Maakhah Tamar.

The chief army commander of King David, is said to have been called Joab. Surprisingly enough, the chief army commander of Psusennes II was called Un-tchoab-endjed, or Joab for short. Surprisingly enough, the biblical and historical accounts give the same name for this army commander, a fact that serves to strengthen the links between Psusennes II and King David.

There is also an interesting reference to the chief architects of this era. The Bible indicates that the chief architect of King David and King Solomon was called Hiram Abi, who is the same individual as is it mentioned and revered in the masonic world as Hiram Abif. Meanwhile, if we search though the historical record, it can be seen that the chief architect of the pharaoh Psusennes II was called Herum Atif.

So, if David was really Psusennes II, that would make his son Solomon, the Pharoah Sheshonq. At this period, Northern, or Lower Egypt was far more powerful than the South. There are records of Sheshonq demanding untold riches as tribute from his poorer neighbours. This theory at this point, seems to indicate that state sponsored grave robbing in the Valley of The Kings is feasible. Perhaps this alludes to the mythical / allegorical origins for the legendary gold mines of Solomon?

Sheshonq built the great temple at Tanis and also added to The Temple of Heliopolis. It is not beyond the realms of belief he also built one at Jerusalem, but there is absolutely no evidence for this. Tanis, as it is known today, was known as Zoan at the time. As the Great Temple of the Jews was built at Zion, you cannot fail to see the connection here.

There is no real record of a temple or royalty in the city of Jerusalem for another two hundred years. By this time, the 22nd Dynasty pharaohs had been driven out of Egypt and there is every chance they headed for The Levant and maybe even Jerusalem.

There are no records of a first temple in Jerusalem or Mount Zion. The first records we have are from after the Jews return to Israel after the Babylonian exile in 538 BC. There are, however, records of a magnificent temple at the city of Zoan which seems identical in construction.

The second Temple at Jerusalem, although constructed around 516 BC, was never the same. By the time of Jesus, it had been remodelled by Herod and even had a large gold Roman eagle on it.

There were a small group of Jews who wanted nothing to do with this and refused to worship anywhere that had anything non-Jewish in its sanctuary. In the first century BC, the Maccabee Kings of Israel had abolished the rule that all priests at the temple had to come from the Levitical line. There was a radical movement that wanted to overthrow Roman rule and once more purify the temple.

This brings us on to Jesus. Many have searched for the historical Jesus, born in a manger at the turn of the new millennium and crucified in 32 AD. Nobody has ever found him in the historical record, and this is because everybody has been blinkered in to looking for what the Bible claims to be true. The problem is that we are now into the realms of The New Testament, which unlike The Old Testament, is not historically accurate, unless you want to know where Paul travelled to, and what he thought about the locals. But if we can look outside of the constraints of the Bible, we can find a family that fits the bill of Virgin birth, son of God and crucifixion.

In 44 BC, Julius Caesar had returned to Rome, victorious after his Iberian campaign, and his lover, Cleopatra, Pharoah of Egypt. She waited for him with their son, Caesarion. Within days of his return, Caesar was assassinated by Brutus and Cleopatra was forced to flee Rome. The Roman writer Cicero, records that Cleopatra was pregnant and an heir to the Roman throne would be born. But we hear no more of this from Rome. Cleopatra flees to Cyprus which was an Egyptian colony at the time. There are images of her with two children. Caesarion and an infant girl. This girl was named Thea Musa Aurania. Cleopatra eventually returns to Egypt and makes an alliance with Marcus Antonious, mothering three more children, two boys and another girl named Cleopatra Selene.

In 33 BC, Egypt was invaded by Augustus and falls under Roman rule. Cleopatra commits suicide and her children are taken and paraded through the streets of Rome. The three boys, once they reached the age of 16, were executed, but the girls were given as gifts to foreign rulers. Cleopatra Selene was gifted to the King of Mauretania, whist Thea Musa Aurania was gifted to The King of Parthia, modern day Persia.

Thea Musa has a son, Phraatacees, whom she marries (a typical Egyptian Royal move to maintain the bloodline) when he reaches his teens, and then attempts a coup against the ruling King. She installs herself and her son as monarchs, but within a few months, the Kings' supporters rise, and force her to leave Parthia. She leaves with her Royal Household, along with Phraatacees and her daughter Helena Julianna, who is heavily pregnant. They leave Parthia and head towards Syria and Northern Judaea, but en route, Helena goes into labour and gives birth to a son. They are visited by magi's, wise men of The Parthian court, who still believe Thea Musa to be the rightful Queen. And here we have the origin of the Nativity.

But what about the Virgin Birth and Son of God claims? This requires assessing Cleopatras' family tree. All female descendants of Cleopatra were considered to be reincarnations of Isis, the eternal Virgin, whilst Julius Caesar was regarded as a God by this point in Rome. This was a Prince who could claim to be The King of Kings as he had rightful claims on the thrones of Egypt, Rome, and Parthia. His name was Izates Manu (Jesus Emmanuel).

There is no evidence to suggest this happened in Bethlehem, but 4 AD would seem to be right as the possible date, which ties in with the Bible.

Egypt would be the obvious place for the Royal Family to head, and interestingly enough, there is a well, next to the site of The Temple of Heliopolis, that is supposedly where The Virgin Mary (Muse) rested and got water for the Baby Jesus. This is probably myth and legend, however where else would a young Prince and heir to the Egyptian throne be safer, than learning the sacred rights and laws of Egypt at Heliopolis, as did Akhenaten and The Shepherd Kings before him?

We know that by the time he had reached his twenties, Izates had returned with his family to Syria and had claimed his own Kingdom of Edessa, which is modern day Sanliurfa in Turkey. His Mother Helena however, had converted to Judaism and was the richest benefactor in Jerusalem during the 1st Century.

The one thing the New Testament does possibly get right is that Izates spent much of his time in Capernaum and The Galilee. This area was a devolved state of Judea at the time and was the epicentre of revolutionaries and so-called miracle workers. It is possibly here that Izates learned of The Essenes and their Nazarene Judaism. The Essenes were based in Qumran, south of Jerusalem and are attributed to being the creators of the Dead Sea Scrolls. However, it was the Essenes who devised the end of days, Messianic form of Judaism. They believed that the Temple in Jerusalem was polluted, and that Romans and all other Gentiles needed to be driven out and the Levitical Priesthood restored. We know that John The Baptist was heavily linked with the Essenes, and it seems that Izates was as well. The incident of Jesus and the money changers is clearly explained by this. Not only were the priests of the temple conducting business at the temple, but they were using Roman coins, items that should never have been allowed, within the walls of the Temple.

Also, what a lot of scholars fail to mention when talking of The Dead Sea Scrolls, is what non-Biblical scrolls were also found. Notably the Copper Scroll, which is today in a museum in Jordan. This scroll is effectively a treasure map and is inscribed with the name of the Pharoah, Akhenaten. Many have claimed that this is the map to find the hidden treasures of The Jewish Temple, but these were taken by Rome and there are images on The Arch of Titus, showing them being paraded through the streets. More likely, these are the treasures from the Temple of The Aten in Amarna. It's essential to question why a group of Jews, who have rejected the current form of Judaism, would have a scroll with the name of a 1500-year-old Egyptian Pharoah. Furthermore, there is a claim within the scroll, that the first Jewish temple was based on the design of The Aten Temple in Amarna. Anyone can observe this if they go to Amman and visit the Jordan Museum.

The issue with this theory is that it does not end with Pontius Pilate crucifying Jesus in 32 AD. We have no other source or record for this other than the Bible. For this story to end, we need to move forward a further 30 years to 68 AD. It is here that we have somebody called Jesus, who was born of a virgin, crucified for trying to save the world.
In 68 AD Rome was in a mess. Nero had died and the void left behind was causing dissent throughout the Empire. Possible successors were positioning themselves to make their bid to become Emperor. The main contender was the Roman General Vespasian, but I believe that Izates Manu also saw himself as the rightful heir to the throne, being a direct descendant of Julius Caesar. Izates raised an army from the revolutionaries in Galilee and attempted to drive the Romans out of Jerusalem, in what has become known as the Great Jewish Revolt.

This is why Jesus can not have been The Messiah. There was no Christianity at this point, therefore the only Messiah had to be Jewish. The main stipulation was that the Messiah would lead an army and drive the invading forces from Israel, furthering the Jewish nation, which he failed to accomplish. In fact, within two years, as a direct result of his actions, the Jewish Temple was demolished brick by brick, the entire Jewish nation was in flames and the Jews were to be in exile for nearly 2,000 years. Hardly Messiah material. Simon Bar Kochba, another "Son of The Star", lead a further revolt in 135 AD, and got a lot further than Jesus, yet he is not regarded as the Messiah. I believe that this is because The Roman propaganda machine, lead by Josephus Flavius, did what they did best - rewrite history. The fact is that there were over 300 "Messiahs" in the 1st Century alone and the "miracles" of Jesus can all be explained. Galilee was awash with miracle workers and was to Jerusalem, what Harley Street is to London today. As a Messiah, he would not have stood out unless he was a charismatic leader, who led the Jews to believe that he was the one who could lead them to freedom from Roman rule.

First century Judaea was an oppressed place, and under the rule of Rome. Numerous revolts had resulted in a large military presence and to make matters worse, The Temple and the Pharisee and Sanhedrin Priests had been corrupted and Romanised. Izates was offering to drive out the Romans and because of his links with The Nazarene Essenes, reinstate the Levitical Priesthood to the Temple. He would have easily raised a powerful army to attack Jerusalem, but he failed. The Roman armies of Titus and Vespasian defeated the insurrection, laid siege to Jerusalem and then set fire to it, dismantling the Temple, brick by brick. All within two years.

It is reported that Izates was set for crucifixion and was nailed to the cross. However, he was taken down fairly quickly and sent to Alexandria to appear before Vespasian. According to numerous ancient Roman historians, Emperor Vespasian was widely believed to be able to perform holy miracles. Three ancient scholars—Tacitus, Suetonius, and Cassius Dio (the first two lived during the reign of Vespasian)—specifically mentioned two instances of miracle healings that Vespasian allegedly performed. The healings were both said to have occurred in Alexandria around June or July of the year 69. As the story goes, two debilitated men approached Emperor Vespasian together and threw themselves to the ground before him. One of the men was blind and the other had a paralyzed hand. Vespasian decided to let the supplicants speak. The result of their interaction would become one of the most talked-about events in the reign of the new emperor.

The pair announced that the god, Serapis, had appeared to them in a dream or vision and had proclaimed that Vespasian possessed the power to heal their disabilities. Serapis had apparently also given specific instructions on how the cures could be achieved. The blind man claimed that he would be healed if Vespasian spat into his eye and the man with the atrophied hand would be healed if the emperor stepped on it. Almost exactly what Jesus did at The Pool of Shiloam.

According to the tale, the emperor was bashful about attempting the healing, yet his advisors ultimately convinced him to try. Following the procedure provided by the god, Serapis, Vespasian spat into the blind man's eye, and, to everyone's amazement, the man exclaimed that he could see again. The emperor then stepped upon the other man's hand, which then immediately began to work perfectly. It is also true that Vespasian took on the mantle of The Jewish Messiah at this time and many ancient historians make this claim. He was Governor of Judaea and went on to rule the Roman World. This is effectively what the Messiah was supposed to do. The only problem being that he wasn't Jewish.

It is unlikely that Izates, was one of these men, but had been brought before Vespasian on a separate occasion to teach him how to "perform" these so called miracles. Most of Izates army would have been imprisoned in Alexandria and would have been shocked to see their leader had been crucified, and suddenly resurrected before them. By kneeling before Vespasian, Izates ultimately saved his own life and was exiled to the darkest corners of The Empire.

At this point the Roman propaganda machine created fantastical tales in an attempt to quell the Jewish rebellion. The majority of Jews in the First century, including Saul/Paul who composed the doctrines of the Church and transformed Izates from a warrior to the "Son of God", something Izates never claimed, believed that the apocalypse would happen in their lifetime.

Many knew that Izates hadn't died, therefore if you can convince the illiterate masses that one day, in the foreseeable future, he would return from exile and lead the Jews to freedom, if they "gave unto Caesar what belongs to Caesar" and become good Roman citizens. The Gospels all show a man with revolutionary ideas but with all the fight taken out of him.

The dates and names are changed, but the invention of the "Prince of Peace" is either fictional or based on Izates. Myths always have hidden truths hidden within them. So, the illiterate prayed for the return of their leader and the ultimate apocalyptical end to Roman rule which never happened. The church still uses the same document to disempower most of the world. Saul/Paul spun this into the doctrines of a Church, and all of a sudden Jesus was rejected by the Jews and was known as the saviour of the gentiles. The Jews were demonized because they were blamed for rejecting this newly invented God Man. Despite the fact that it was technically The Romans that killed Jesus. This engineered hatred continues even today, which ultimately leads to the Holocaust of the 20th century.

All for a man, who if he truly was a Nazarene Jew, would have refused to share a meal with a gentile. If you refer to the Bible, Jesus' Brother James, his family, and his disciples all continue the movement after the crucifixion, returning to pious prayer at The Jewish Temple. Even the resurrected Jesus prays at The Jewish Temple to the one true God, El, YHWH, Yahweh or as Jesus would have said in Aramaic, Elaha. Pronounced Allah (But that's another black hole of which I won't elaborate upon here).

The Jewish followers of Jesus, and for that matter, the Muslims at a later date, saw Jesus as The Jewish Messiah. But they still worshiped the original one true God. The Messiah was simply a great leader and a prophet of The Jews. It was only through the imagination of Saul/Paul that Jesus became Son of God and then ultimately Divine himself. The Roman State would never tolerate a religion that followed a mere mortal when the Emperor was Divine. If Jesus were ever to return, he would be horrified by the countless atrocities that have been done in his name. He ultimately failed in his Messianic duties; therefore, most Jews still await an actual Messiah who will restore their lands and rebuild the Temple.

"The Son of Man" as Jesus referred to himself, was transformed in to "The Son of God" and "Judaism Light" as Early Christianity was, was spread by Zealots throughout the Empire, totally unaware of its Egyptian, sun worshipping roots.

1. HOLY BREAST MILK AND OTHER CATHOLIC BUSINESS MODELS

It was a mid-afternoon flight from Gatwick, which thankfully meant no crack of dawn alarm or early morning queues to check in. In fact, it all went quite smoothly. The plane departed a few minutes late, but the time was caught up with a decent tailwind behind us.

The downside to all of this was the late arrival in Tel Aviv. The two-hour time difference and four and a half hour flight meant it was gone nine o'clock before we touched down. The pilot did seem to accelerate for the last half hour of the flight, and this may be because of a missile that had been fired from The Gaza Strip in the direction of Tel Aviv. I managed to smuggle in a bacon sandwich, as I knew I would not be able to get anything to eat when I arrived, and it did cross my mind that this missile could have been a porcine seeking missile, as they are not too keen on pork around here.
I had booked a driver to transfer me to Jerusalem, firstly due to the lateness of my arrival and secondly, it was still the sabbath, and half of Israel had laid down tools. He was waiting for me in the arrival's hall, and we were soon on the modern motorway to Jerusalem, some fifty miles away.

Everything was fine until we hit a massive traffic jam, which was traffic heading back from the airport after a massive protest rally. I was not sure as to whether this was down to my bacon sandwich arriving in Israel or Prime Minister Benjamin Netanyahu catching a flight out of the country. Regardless we were stuck in traffic for a good 30 minutes and went nowhere fast.

We finally made it to my hotel around 11.30 and it was far too late to explore. My first impressions from the car were that Jerusalem was remarkably like Brooklyn in New York. Lots of tall buildings, shops, and orthodox Jews. Inviting but unclean at the same time. We did not pass the historical centre, so it was hardly fair to pass judgement yet. I drew the curtains, ate my bacon sandwich before retiring to bed as I had an early start the following morning.

The weekend in Israel is Friday and Saturday, so Sunday is a working day. And they start early, not that I slept much as it was a first night in a new bed, but I could have done without the pneumatic drill starting off at 7 a.m. The room itself was fine and on the sixth floor, looking over Jaffa Street, one of Jerusalem's main shopping streets.

I was really hungry, heading for breakfast, having only had my illicit bacon sandwich the night before. I had hoped for some meat for breakfast but forgot that this was Israel, and everything has to be kosher. So, it's either meat or fish and dairy. They went for the fish and dairy here. To be honest I would have eaten anything this morning. There were eggs and some nice roasted vegetables and then I had a cheese bagel and a Danish pastry with some grapefruit juice and a coffee. I would have preferred bacon and sausages, but when in Rome and all that.

As I was leaving breakfast, I was approached by an old Rabbi (long beard, big hat) who asked where I was from. It turns out he is on a tour with other rabbis from Sussex and he was from Brighton. I declined the offer to join them. My beard isn't long enough, and it was too wet to wear a suit. But should I feel the need to read the Torah and eat gefilte fish, I know where to head when I get back home.

My guide picked me up on time at 8.30 and he was really cool. I wasn't going to talk religion or politics, but he started it, so I joined in. We were pretty much on the same hymn sheet. He was a Muslim and to be honest I think they are going to be far easier to get on with that any orthodox Jewish guides.

The weather was miserable with pretty solid rain falling for most of the morning. The locals were loving it, they needed the rain. But it was hardly sightseeing conditions. There is a ring road around the old walled city, which I got my first view of. The road was gridlocked, and Jerusalem traffic seems to be pretty dreadful.

Of course, despite being a Sunday, this was still the rush hour at 8.30 in the morning. But the issue is of course, Jesus, who all Christians have a day off for and worship on a Sunday, would be completely thrown by it. As a Jew, he would have considered the sabbath as being between sunset on Friday and sunset on Saturday. Under Jewish law, which he fought to uphold, those Christians who worship him on a Sunday but worked on a Friday and Saturday could be executed. This is the first of many points of order that I fear will be raised on this trip.

We have all seen the Christmas cards of Bethlehem. Some of us have been in nativity play (I was a sheep and thank God it wasn't the Welsh or New Zealand version), and all will of have seen the idyllic scenes of Mary and Joseph, with their baby with the donkey, the wise men, and the shepherds. The reality is somewhat stark and dystopian.

My first stop was The Tomb of Rachel. The Biblical wife of Jacob, Mother to a number of the twelve tribes of Israel who died giving birth to Benjamin in Bethlehem before reaching Hebron. The tomb was in Palestine, but in 2002, Israel annexed it and claimed it for themselves, much to the anger of the Muslims who regard Rachel equally as holy. The Christians should too in theory, but they don't seem to care anymore. Checkpoint 300, the main checkpoint to enter the West Bank at Bethlehem is 300 yards away. There are soldiers, armoured cars. Barbed wire, snipers, and a fifty-foot high and three foot thick wall keeping the Palestinians away.

Despite the short distance from the checkpoint and the adjacent bus stops, you are not allowed to walk along the road leading to the tomb. If you do, you will be shot. In fact, there is an hourly bulletproof bus that comes here, bringing worshippers.
You must drive down and park in the designated car park. My Muslim Guide had to stay in the car and was not allowed to enter the tomb for fear of being shot too. Once inside it was very weird.

What was happening on the inside of the building was a complete contrast to what was outside. It was one of those moments you enter a room, and it seems as though you are in an alternate reality. There were dozens of orthodox Jewish men, long beards, big hat, side locks of hair and big black coats, standing around a giant sarcophagus, which was covered in clear plastic, nodding their heads backwards and forwards in reverence, whilst mumbling texts from The Torah. They all seemed totally oblivious to the fact I was there taking pictures of what resembled a ZZ Top convention. There was a separate entrance for women, who seemingly had no access to the sarcophagus. I couldn't see if they had beards too.

Is this truly the Tomb of Rachel? Maybe. It is certainly a site that has been revered for over a thousand years. There are records of it from the Fifth Century, with a small dome covering it. This was added to, and the tomb enclosed in 1841. Anything dating back to around the 16th Century BC would be underground but is quite conceivable there is a grave there and it is Rachel's. Strict rules mean that it cannot be investigated by archaeologists, therefore it is a slight leap of "faith". But I will be kind and say this is possibly what it claims to be.

It was so surreal that as I exited the building and was confronted once more with pouring rain and machine gun nests, I almost felt like turning around and going back in, just to check it wasn't some sort of apparition.

Rather than entering The West Bank at Checkpoint 300, we went back to the main road and crossed a less severely armed border a few miles away. We headed some 30km south to the city of Hebron to the second holiest site in Judaism, The Cave of Machpelah, otherwise known as The Tombs of The Patriarchs.

Palestinian towns, despite being ringfenced by a large concrete wall, all seem to be fairly pleasant. Far nicer and modern than Egyptian towns of the same size. The problem is the ever-increasing illegal Jewish settlers who are bulldozing Palestinian houses to build their own properties. There have been a few violent incidents recently with these settlers, but the Israeli Government are spinning it to make The Palestinians look bad. Two Israeli settlers were shot In the West Bank today, nowhere near where |I was though. My guide, Yousef, said that the Government here are heading towards a Kristallnacht moment, where ordinary Israelis will turn on Palestinians due to the constant baiting on the television. The narrative and quite apparent belief amongst Israelis, that they are superior is ironically very similar to Germany in the 1930's. It will explode soon, and the rest of the world will do nothing as the Israelis kill the Palestinians. From the Berlinesque Wall, you can plainly see it is an apartheid state already. Palestinians need to apply for a pass to enter Jewish land and still get turned away for no reason. What makes it worse, is that the Israeli military, parading around with sub machine guns are nearly all teenage girls and boys doing National Service. Teenagers with MK 47s. What could possibly go wrong?

So on to Hebron. The Tombs of The Patriarchs is a strange building that holds the dubious title of being the only historical building in Israel never to have been destroyed or demolished. The current building was started by Herod at the turn of the 1st Century and has served as both a church, synagogue, and mosque. Since 1967 it has been split into two, part mosque and part synagogue. As my guide was a Muslim and I didn't tick any of the required boxes, we went to the Islamic side.

You cannot enter both and Jews are strictly forbidden from the mosque and vice versa. Of course, the difference is that the Jewish side has a marble staircase, greenery, and a pleasant façade whilst to enter the mosque, you must go through two iron gates in a back alley, pass soldiers with guns, show your passport, and hope the Israeli Defence Force soldier is in a good mood to let you in.

Both sides have access to the tomb of Abraham and the tomb of his wife Sarah. The Muslim side has the tombs of Isaac and his wife Rebecca, whilst Jacob and Leah are on the Jewish side. There are large sarcophagi for all of them, but the actual tombs are in a cave below the building. It's easy to dismiss this as religious nonsense, but it is conceivable, that if Abraham and his dynasty were part of the Hyksos regime in Egypt and returned to Canaan at a later date, that there could be some legitimacy in this, and it is a family tomb.

The Jewish side also claims to have the bodies of Adam and Eve! I think we can file this one as bullshit. Even the Jews admit there was a flood, and there are no records of Noah putting two corpses on board the Ark!

Within the mosque is what looks like a star shaped drain. 1967, after Israel had recaptured the West bank from Jordanian control, a 12-year-old girl was lowered down this hole in order to see what was actually below. It turns out that the cave below did have human remains and there is every chance that they belong to Abraham and his family. They certainly belong to somebody of note.

This is a holy site for Islam too, with Muslims believing that Mohammad visited here on his nocturnal journey from Mecca to Jerusalem to pay his respects. He encouraged Muslim pilgrimage here saying. "He who cannot visit me, let him visit the Tomb of Abraham" and "He who visits the Tomb of Abraham, Allah abolishes his sins."

Sins abolished, we headed for the old souq and market in Hebron. This too is being forced shut by illegal Israeli settlers. The Israelis have built houses above the market and have been pelting the Muslim stall holders with rocks and rotten fruit. There is now a net covering the market, but you could feel the hatred towards the Israelis there. A few bloody-minded stall holders continued to ply their trade, but the attacks have driven trade away, and it is inevitable that there will be more settlers and less store holders in the years to come.

As we left Hebron, we passed a butcher's shop which was clearly out of beef and lamb. A camel had been carved into parts and was hanging outside for all to see. How did I recognise it was camel? The head was hanging up too, still with the poor animal's last meal of a few blades of grass, hanging out of its mouth.

On the way to Bethlehem, we made a stop at The Herodium, King Herod's palace and fortress outside of Jerusalem. Everyone has a bad view of Herod because he supposedly, but almost certainly didn't, want to kill all the babies in Judaea. There is absolutely no evidence for this outside of The Bible, but throughout Israel, there is evidence for numerous amazing building projects he undertook, that were well before their time. I had already seen the Patriarchal structure at Hebron, but Herod also built numerous castles, Palaces, Fortresses, and municipal Projects throughout the country.
The towns of Caesarea and Sabastea were lavishly constructed during his reign and of course The Second Temple was completely transformed. He really does get a bad press. From Christians because of the fantasy infanticide and from Jews because he Romanised the Temple.

Despite having a Palace within the City Walls, The Herodium was really Herod's Jerusalem pad. A typical motte and bailey castle, with a lavish palace at its base. It was the only building named after Herod, although it has had different names over the centuries. The Crusaders called it the Mountain of Franks, the Palestinians refer to it as Jabal al Firdous (Mountain of Little Paradise) and when the British were here it was known as Frank's Mountain. We are just so imaginative.

The fortress was built after 40 BC when the Parthians invaded Syria and Herod feared they would advance into Judaea. The castle was built on an artificial hill with four great towers. One was Herod's palace, which supposedly had extravagant living quarters filled with frescos and mosaics. The other three were used as living quarters for staff and guests. At the foot of the hill was a large Roman Bath House plus extensive gardens and an amphitheatre.

We didn't have too much time here and in an ideal world I would have explored further, but things were a bit crowded as a coach load of nuns arrived and swamped the visitors' centre. The thought of exploring the castle whilst fifty odd nuns cursed Herod for trying to kill Jesus was something that should only happen in nightmares, so we hit the road again.

By the time we got back to Bethlehem, the sun had won its battle against the rain clouds, and we were able to walk around the city without getting drenched. Not that there is much there apart from gift shops selling some of the most hideous plastic Jesus figurines you could ever hope to see and Virgin Mary's in every conceivable shape and posture.

Manger Square and The Church of The Nativity were interesting, mostly for the ridiculous crying Americans who kept getting in the way praying. From the outside, The Church of The Nativity is not spectacular, in fact quite bland. The entrance was made tiny by The Crusaders, partly to keep enemies out, but also so that you are forced to bow your head when entering the Church.
Apart from the horrific queue full of Americans, waiting to see what they think is the manger, the first thing you notice on the inside of the church is that it is a mish mash of everything. This is hardly surprising as The Catholics, Armenians and Greek Orthodox have divided it into three parts as they can't quite get their stories straight.

There are parts of byzantine mosaics on the wall, Roman mosaics on the floor, pictures of Jesus with the sun around his head for the orthodox sun worshippers, silver figurines, and incense burners for the Armenians and lots of statues of Mary for the Catholics, who almost seem to forget about Jesus. I never quite understood this mother of God thing. If God created the universe out of nothing, was Mary living in a vacuum before she gave birth to him? Alternatively, if Jesus is to be seen as God, rather than son of God, are you honestly telling me, that the Almighty who keeps the universe intact, managed to do so whilst going through the terrible twos? Is it just me who asks these questions?

The fact is that this may not even be the actual Bethlehem. In order to make Jesus fit at least some of the requirements as the Jewish messiah, he had to come from the City of David. Pretty easily fixed I guess as there is no archaeological proof for david either, but Jews believe this to be the Bethlehem near Jerusalem. The other Bethlehem is near Galilee and they have found an old Byzantine Church that seemingly dates to around the second century AD, that was built over a cave, that seems to have been revered. The cave in question was bricked up a long time ago and the church demolished.

One wonders whether the Church did this to protect their side of the story. It would certainly make more sense as far the Biblical story goes.

If Mary and Joseph were going to Bethlehem because of a census, it would have had to have been the Quirinius Census of 6 AD. There are no others on record in Judaea. If the Holy Couple lived in Nazareth (I know they didn't but let's pretend), surely it would be cruel to make a heavily pregnant woman travel such a great distance on a donkey, especially when only the men had to report for the census. Secondly, if this was Joseph's family home, why couldn't he stay with family? Was he that unpopular? The other Bethlehem is a short donkey ride from Nazareth. If they had moved King David to the other Bethlehem, I could have believed that. But this makes no sense to me. In any case, I have already outlined who I believe "Mary" and "Joseph" to be, Parthian Royalty.

I just stood open mouthed at the Americans. Thankfully my Guide, Yousuf, managed to get me through the "Exit" to the birthplace and manger, so that I didn't have to queue. A silver star marks the spot where the baby popped out (according to the church) and on the opposite side of the chapel is a small cave in which we are supposed to believer that the happy parents, the baby, the donkey, shepherds, three wise men and an angel all squeezed into. Good job the Yanks weren't around at that time. One of the American women had to removed by an armed soldier as she had knelt down on the spot where Mary was said to have given birth and was then unable to get up again due to being overcome. No miracles there then! Although I think she was playing to her audience. I am baffled by Americans. Their economy is tanking, but they seem oblivious. They are drawing the entire planet into a third world war, but they don't seem to care. A small star on the ground and a cave in a church, and they burst out crying and lose the ability to walk.

As was the case with the cave of the Patriarchs, I cannot rule The Church of The Nativity out as not being the place where Jesus, or at least the person we now refer to as Jesus, was born. He had to be born somewhere. If I had to stick my neck out, I would still go for the other Bethlehem, but that is never going to get any recognition, as too many people and too many invested interests would stand to lose a lot of face and money if that was ever admitted.

From here we wandered to what is known as The Milk Grotto. I love these Catholic sites that are so blatantly money-making operations they don't even hide it. Here was where Mary, allegedly, first breast fed the Baby Jesus. She supposedly spilled a drop and the whole Church turned a milky white! The Catholic Church, to this day still sell holy milk powder at two shekels a packet. What nobody seems to notice here is the blatant neglect that Mary had for Jesus. If he was born a quarter of a mile away in the Church of The Nativity, why did she wait until she could walk over here to feed the poor bugger. Don't mention that in the Gospels do they. The authorities would have him taken away these days.

After a lunch of hummus and falafels I actually bought a couple of souveniers. A bottle of Nativity Pilsner and a bottle Of Shepherds Brewery IPA. My way of wetting the baby's head I suppose.

We wandered back to the car on what was now quite a pleasant afternoon and set off for Jericho, which was about an hour away. For all the bad press that Palestine gets, it must be said that the towns and cities, as well as the roads are a giant leap forward from neighbouring Egypt. Roads and pavements seem well maintained, shops seem less chaotic and the traffic sems to obey the rules of the road. There are some quirks that would only happen here though. Israeli cars have white number plates and Palestinian ones are green. Should a white number plate be behind a green one, you can guarantee it will tailgate and try to overtake as soon as possible. That arrogance and sense of superiority clearly extends to road etiquette.

Jericho was interesting with silly religious overtones. Our first port of call was what has been dubbed, The Mountain of Temptation. Clinging to its Southern face, is a Greek Orthodox Monastery that any monk would need crampons to reach. Currently there are three mountaineering monks there. Thankfully for tourists, there is a cable car, but the same group of Nuns from The Herodium were about to ascend. There is something about Nuns that scares me and the thought of an entire group of them cursing the devil at once was too much to take. I passed.

Somewhat unsurprisingly, the Monastery is known as The Monastery of Temptation, and is built above a cave that it is claimed that Jesus sat in for 40 days and 40 nights and was tempted by Satan. The site was "identified" by The Patron Saint of Archaeology, Augusta Helena, Mother of Constantine, The Roman Emperor. How this woman is regarded as a saint only the Church can justify, and her bizarre findings will be a regular theme this week. When Rome accepted Christianity as it's state religion, she was given an extensive shopping list and didn't come home empty handed. She found every Biblical site in her pilgrimage in 326 AD, the Church sanctified everything and now we are stuck with them. Evidence or not.

As a result, I am calling this one out as utter nonsense. No evidence, no Jesus, no temptation.
There was a gift shop, something I would normally avoid like the plague as it was full of Americans, but Yousuf insisted as it sold local produce. The dates from Jericho, and bananas for that matter, are regarded as the best in the country, so we bought a box each and left the Yanks to their plastic Jesus figurines.

More interesting was the old city of Jericho, Tell Es Sultan, which claims to be the oldest inhabited city in the world. To be fair there isn't too much left, but there is an interesting film you can watch about the history of the city for which I was the only taker.

Everybody else was too busy cursing Satan out of his cave or in the Gift Shop. The ruins are fairly extensive, and yes there are walls and yes, they were knocked down and quite possibly at the time of Joshua. But there is no real proof that they fell down because of a marauding group of Israelites with a magic box, blowing their trumpets made from goat horns. Interestingly though you can see clear burn marks in the rocks of the foundations that do date back to the 12th or 13th century BC. The story could well be real in the sense that the walls of Jericho were brought down by a nomadic army at the time the Bible claims they were. As a result, this story gets labelled plausible.

Yousef got me back to Jerusalem in time to watch Brighton win on the telly and then in the evening I went to a local barbecue restaurant which was OK. The only reason I went there was because it was bucketing down with rain again and it was opposite the hotel.

2. CROWDFUNDING JESUS

I woke around 7 a.m., drew back the curtains, and saw that the rain was still falling with Jaffa Street glistening through the wet. This was not a good sign as today I was supposed to be heading for Masada and The Dead Sea, which was not going to be much fun in the rain.

Before I had a chance to go to breakfast, my guide, Yazid, called and said that the road to Masada was underwater and that we would need to rearrange for another day. This was a slight issue as I had planned such a full itinerary, there wasn't much room for manoeuvre. The only real option I had was to reschedule Masada for Wednesday, which Yazid could do, switch my coach to tour to Galilee from Wednesday to Saturday and then cancel my guided tour of Jerusalem and try to get to as many of the sites on that tour today. I frantically looked online for any last-minute tours around Jerusalem and found and booked a tour of the sites of The Mount of Olives for the afternoon, which left a few other places to head to in the morning. I finally got to breakfast, and then planned my strategy for the morning.

It was still raining when I set off for the old city around 9 o'clock. It takes around 15 minutes to walk to the Jaffa Gate, the nearest entrance to the old city. The old city walls date back to Crusader and Islamic Rule, mostly from the 12th to 14th Century. It works quite well, with the modern city, public transport, and shopping malls outside of the walls in a typical modern city, whilst the old city is a maze of covered medieval shopping streets, interspersed with immense religious structures, all claiming to represent something from the life of Jesus.

The main thoroughfare, or The Cardo, dates to Roman times and Jesus would have walked these streets, full of stall holders selling fragrant spices and brightly coloured cloth. Today of course, these stalls are dominated with tacky gift shops, fake antiques, and souvenir t shirts, but you still have to barter, and the shop holders can sniff a tourist wallet from half a mile away.

It would be easy to get lost in this labyrinth and I was thankful for a mobile phone signal so that my sat nav worked and I could wind my way through without too many issues.

My first stop was the Church of The Holy Sepulchre, which the Church claim to be the site of the crucifixion and the tomb of Jesus. This is interesting as a Temple of Aphrodite stood here until the 4th Century. If anything, this was worse than The Church of The Nativity in Bethlehem. It was full of tourists from all over the world pushing each other out of the way to get a glimpse of what they have been told to believe in. The first thing that really hit me was that it was darned convenient that Jesus was crucified, laid out, buried, and resurrected, all within the one church, albeit a big church. Once again, we have the patron saint of archaeology, Constantine's Mother, to thank for this one. She found a nail and a wooden cross, immediately claiming it was the spot of the crucifixion and then subsequently found the slab and a cave tomb. At the end of the day, you could do the same at your local B and Q. The problem here though is that unlike Bethlehem, where you have The Catholics, The Greek Orthodox and The Armenians fighting over the manger, here you can throw The Russian Orthodox and The Ethiopians into the fold. All have their chapels, and all have their lumps of holy rock, claiming to be Golgotha, the site of The Crucifixion. It is so bad that avoid clashes, the keys are kept in the possession of the Nusseibeh family, thought to be the oldest Muslim family in Jerusalem. It is still their job today, to unlock the Church every morning and secure the doors at night because the Christians can't be trusted.

As you enter the church, you are confronted with a large stone slab on the ground, known as the Unction Stone, which it is claimed, was where Jesus was laid out and daubed with oils after he died.

Another of Helena of Constantinople's "discoveries", all denominations claim this to be genuine, and no doubt share in the takings as it is showered with dollar bills each day by the American tour groups. At the end of the day, it is a slab of rock found by a woman three hundred years after the event. In fact, it isn't even the stone Helena found. This one only dates back to 1810. And whereas you can't say that it isn't the rock Jesus was laid upon, but there is absolutely no way you can say it is. And that is how The Church sells the story. With much emphasis on the selling part.

I refused to queue for 30 minutes to be shuffled through The Aedicule, the "tomb" where Jesus woke up, peaked outside, and didn't see his shadow. This meant another three weeks of winter. Or am I getting Jesus and Punxsutawnay Phil mixed up? Ah yes, that's Groundhog Day. Easy mistake to make. The queue was enormous, and people were being shuffled along at gun point and getting a few seconds to see the "tomb" before being shepherded out. I am sure it was long enough to leave some money though.

The whole thing leaves a bad taste in the mouth and the fact is, that as a Jew, there is no way that even a criminal, as The Romans regarded him, would have been buried within the city walls, which this was. There is a far more likely setting for the tomb, outside of the walls, that I would be visiting later in the week.

As I walked around the Church, I became more and more aghast at the overreacting that was going on. As with most of these sites, the archaeology does not reflect the pious nonsense. There is a chapel for everything, and I thought it quite strange that there was one chapel for where he got nailed to the cross, yet another one, some 50 metres away for where he supposedly died. Quite an achievement if he was nailed to a cross and managed to walk somewhere else. The collection trays were brimming over for all denominations.

One other interesting fact was that in 638 A.D., when the Muslim Caliph, Omar invaded Jerusalem, he was invited to pray in the Church but declined. If he had done so, the Church would have had to be converted to a mosque and Omar claimed he had too much respect for the life of Jesus to do that. I doubt such respect would be shown today on either side.

Moving on from Christian nonsense I went to find some Jewish nonsense at The Western or Wailing Wall. It was a lot smaller than I had imagined and due to the rain, there weren't too many people praying there. Once again, the men had 80% of the wall and the women got their own 20% behind an enormous curtain. They are not allowed to pray together.

From an archaeological standpoint, the Western Wall is amazing. Some of the Herodian stones, dating back to the 1st Century BC are well in excess of 100 tons each and some of these monoliths are comparable to anything I have seen anywhere else. It is a shame that you cannot enjoy the entire Temple Mount and Walls today, but religion dictates otherwise. After the Jews were thrown out by the Romans in 70 A.D. and their temple burned to the ground. The temple mount has changed hands several times. For much of this time it has been under Islamic control and The Dome of the Rock and Al Aqsa Mosque are a testament to this. But many find it strange that when Israel captured Jerusalem from Jordanese control in 1967, they did not insist on control of Temple Mount. I am guessing this would have a step to far for The Arab World and would have resulted in an all-out war had they attempted to do so.

But one day they will try and there will still be an all-out war. It is just a matter of time.

I left the old city via The Dung Gate, which unfortunately is not named for the flinging of said substance from the battlements.

However, the name does arise from a similar tale. Supposedly the Essenes had a small congregation here that lived near the gate. They were so strict that they refused to defecate within the city walls, however on the outside of the walls or gate was fine. Hence the name.

I headed for Mount Zion, which was rather steep, where I visited King David's Tomb (Probably isn't) and The Room of The Last Supper (definitely isn't).

David's Tomb was a bit like The Tomb of Rachel but without the machine gun nests and bulletproof buses. It attracts the same ultra-orthodox Jews in their black coats with beards and side dreadlocks, wo rock back and forth muttering texts from The Torah. But whereas Rachel's Tomb had a possibility of historical substance, this really hasn't. No evidence for King David has ever been found, not even a mention in any documents dating to the time. If, as I believe is the case, that david was as actually Djuat, otherwise known as Psusennes, I have stood inside his tomb at Tanis (otherwise known as Zoan) in Egypt. But it is difficult to have a body for someone who you can't prove exists, therefore this tomb merely panders to the myth of David that the Jews want to believe in.
The myth that David is buried here only dates to the 9th century AD and in the time of Jesus and Herod, it was assumed that David's remains were in Bethlehem, in a family tomb with his Father, Jesse. The tomb here is possibly the last remains of The Hagia Zion, a 4th Century Byzantine Church that was destroyed by the Muslims. The fact is it is about 2,000 years younger than any tomb of David would have been, which is a very large margin for error, even for here. I think the final nail in this coffin is the fact that The Crusaders only noticed the tomb was there in the 12th Century.

And wouldn't you know it, upstairs from David's tomb, in the same building, is "The Room of The Last Supper," otherwise known as the "Upstairs Room" or the Cenacle. Pilgrims to Jerusalem report visiting a structure on Mount Zion commemorating the Last Supper since the 4th century AD. Here we go again. When did Helena turn up and make all these amazing "discoveries?" Ah yes, the 4th Century. In Christian tradition, the room was not only the site of the Last Supper, but the room in which the Holy Spirit alighted upon the twelve apostles and other believers gathered and praying together on Pentecost. Acts 1 - 2 tell us that Judas had been replaced by Matthias, and 120 followers of Jesus gathered in this room after His ascension.

Well, there were more than 120 American tourists in here today, but I fear they are all barking up the wrong tree. The Gothic architecture is a slight giveaway. Most scholars today regard it as a Crusader structure built slightly before 1187, when Saladin conquered the city.

Some will say the current structure is built on top of the place where the Last Supper was held but this cannot really be proved. The problem is that Mount Zion seems to be moveable. When King David invaded Jerusalem, Mount Zion was the eastern hill of the city. When the Temple was built on the Temple Mount, that became Mount Zion too, but also known as Mount Moriah. Today for reasons I do not know, Mount Zion is the Western Hill of Jerusalem because a mosque stands on The Temple Mount and a mosque can't stand on Mount Zion. Hence, there is no way that either of these sites, the room of the last supper or King David's tomb, can possibly be on Mount Zion, because mount Zion was elsewhere when these events happened.

Despite this, I swear the Americans were in the room of the last supper looking for service hatches and the kitchen. They certainly don't let the facts get in the way of their story.

Next door to these two sites stands the impressive Dormition Abbey. A Catholic Abbey celebrating the spot where Mary died and ascended to Heaven. I couldn't find the entrance, but I hope she found the exit, rather than bumping her head on the way out. It is quite heavily guarded due to the fact that some Jews have desecrated it in the past few years. It is a fairly modern structure and dates back to 1910. It was paid for by Kaiser Wilhelm and reflects the style favoured by Imperial Germany.

In October 2012 and in May and June 2013 the abbey was vandalized with anti-Christian graffiti and insults in Hebrew. The offensive words compared Christians to monkeys and called for revenge against Jesus. Two cars were also covered with graffiti and all the tyres were slashed. One of the gates of the nearby Greek Orthodox cemetery was also marked with graffiti. This was allegedly a "price tag" attack carried out by nationalist religious extremists for the dismantling of an illegal Jewish settlement. On 26 May 2014 a box of wooden crosses was set ablaze inside the Dormition Abbey.

It is believed that this was some sort of failed arson attempt. At the same time of the arson attempt, Pope Francis was conducting a service in the building next door in the Cenacle, The Room of The Last Supper. In January 2016, vandals wrote slogans on the walls of the Abbey such as "Death to the heathen Christians, the enemies of Israel" and "May his name (Jesus) be obliterated."

I don't understand why this Abbey has been singled out, but it would appear that Israeli intolerance extends a little further than just the Palestinians.

It was still damp, and I had a couple of hours before my afternoon tour, so I went back to the hotel to dry out and have a hot drink and an omelette sandwich with some rugelach (little chocolate pastries) from a local bakery. One day I will find a meat sandwich!
The afternoon tour to the Mount of Olives left from The Jaffa Gate, and we drove through the crazy traffic to the summit where we all had to get out and walk down, seeing the various sites on the way. Unfortunately, the tour was graced by several our Trans-Atlantic friends. One God fearing couple from Idaho stood out with their ridiculous questions. "Is that The Wailing Place?" as we passed The Western Wall, only to be trumped by the question of "why do Orthodox Jewish Men wear cowboy hats?" Thoughts turned to Alias Cohen and Goldberg, or maybe The Lone Rabbi but I was pretty sure that Rawhide wasn't Kosher.

The Mount of Olives is one of the holiest mountains of both Judaism and Christianity, our tour was to see the most important sites that have been built here.

Our first port of call was The Chapel of the Ascension. Although now part of a mosque, it is located on a site traditionally believed to be the earthly spot where Jesus ascended into Heaven after his Resurrection.

Funnily enough, this site was discovered some 300 years after Jesus' death by Helena of Constantinople. She immediately recognised a rock that had Jesus' footprints in it and declared it to be the spot where he lifted off to Heaven. The rock is in the middle of the chapel and try as I might, I couldn't see any footprint. If there was a footprint, I am guessing this was caused by the G Force during take-off. There were two footprints but only the right one remains. The rock was broken in half by Muslims in the 12th Century and the left footprint is now in the Al Aqsa Mosque on The Temple Mount.

Rather cleverly, the original construction here was a rotunda, with an open roof. Clever because according to Jewish belief the Messiah will descend here and for Christians, Jesus will return to the same place he ascended from. Above the rock is a large collection box. I took this to mean that they were crowdfunding his return flight. I just hope that he has considered that in the 7th Century a church with a roof was constructed over the rock and doesn't crash land when he comes back.

We wandered down the hill and came to the next stop on Helena's pilgrimage of 312 AD. The Pater Noster Church (Lord's Prayer Church) stands on the site of the Church of Eleona which was founded by Helena in the 4th century.
Within its walls is a cave that was supposedly mentioned in the Acts of John, written in the 2nd Century, which was associated with the teachings of Jesus. No Biblical texts claim that Jesus sat in a cave and came up with the Lord's Prayer here, this was totally added in the 4th Century by Helena. But the Church are always one for a good business plan and today, this Church, owned by a French Monastery, has hundreds of red, white and blue plaques, with the Lord's Prayer translated into every conceivable language. I found Mayan, Cherokee, Zulu, and Esperanto, to name just four. It was interesting to see the same text written in all of these languages, but at the end of the day, it was still as much nonsense as Jesus' launch pad.

The original byzantine Church lasted a couple of hundred years before the Persians destroyed it in 614. The Crusaders rebuilt the church in 1106, only for Saladin to destroy it again in 1187, after which it fell into ruin, eventually being rebuilt in 1851.

We went into the main Jewish Graveyard on The Mount of Olives, where you must be very, very rich to be buried. The reason for this is that firstly you get an amazing view of The Temple Mount and The Dome of The Rock and are serenaded by the Iman in The Al Aqsa Mosque calling the faithful to afternoon prayers every day.

Secondly, as The Messiah will arrive on the Mount of Olives, you will get resurrected first and see The Third Temple as you wake up. A small Jewish Memorial service was taking place here and it was interesting to see the various traditions and beliefs being carried out.

Continuing down the hill, we came to Dominus Flevit, which for once cannot be blamed on Helena. Dominus Flevit is roughly translated as The Lord Wept, and according to the Catholic Church, this is the place, referred to in Luke Chapter 19, Jesus, while riding toward the city of Jerusalem, becomes overwhelmed by the beauty of the Second Temple and predicting its future destruction, and the diaspora of the Jewish people, weeps openly. An original Church was built in Crusader times and there is no record of the place being venerated before this.

The Church was designed to look like a teardrop. It looked like a bell to me. The current Church was built between 1953 and 1955 by famous Italian architect Antonio Barluzzi.
Whilst the Americans were admiring another Church, I took it upon myself to investigate an old Canaanite tomb and an Ossuary that dated back to the 2nd century AD. An Ossuary being the poor people's way to get buried on the Mount of Olives. They were stone boxes in which a person's bones were interred and then kept with other ossuaries in a large cave. Far more exciting than another Church based on stories that can't be proven.

The other highlight here was the view across the valley to The Temple Mount. The sun was out now and was glistening off the golden Dome of The Rock, which looked stunning.

There were more golden domes to our right where the onion shaped domes of The Russian Orthodox Church of Mary Magdalene sat in and amongst the trees. I had really wanted to see this one, but alas this was not possible. Our guide explained that they only opened on a Thursday morning for anybody who could speak Russian or perversely, any day if you were a member of the British Royal Family. I wasn't sure I could pull that one off, so we had to walk past the locked gate. Evidently Princess Alice of Battenburg, the mother of Prince Phillip, Duke of Edinburgh, asked to be buried here and when she died at Buckingham Palace in 1969 her body was prepared for internment. Somehow it took until 1988 for her remains to be transferred to the crypt here, but she is there now. So, if Charles wants to see his granny, he must come over to Jerusalem, climb The Mount of Olives and knock on the door.

At the foot of the hill is The Garden of Gethsemane and it's adjoining Church of All the Nations. It was here that Jesus was arrested before his crucifixion and to be honest I was quite surprised that there wasn't a blue flashing light to mark the spot. Some of The Americans were asking whether any of the olive trees in the garden dated back to the times of Jesus. A 2,000-year-old olive tree maybe a little bit ambitious, but there were some very old trees that dated back as far as 1092.

When The Pope visits Jerusalem he always takes the time to stroll through the Garden. To feel at one with Jesus? No, the Vatican are the sole owners of the Olive trees here and sell the olive oil at extortionate prices.

The Church of All Nations was designed by the same Italian architect who built the bell-shaped Dominus Flevit. There is a very beautiful Byzantine style mosaic that adorns its façade, but the inside of the church is nothing special. Needless to say, an original church was constructed on the orders of Helena in the 4th Century, but that was flattened by an earthquake in 746 AD. The current basilica dates from 1922 but almost burned down in 2021 when an Orthodox Jew set fire to it in an arson attack.

During an archaeological dig here in 2020, a mikvah, a Jewish ritual bath, dating back to the 1st Century AD was found here. This is the first and only find here that dates to the time of Jesus and although I may be somewhat flippant with my comments about the Church, they are aimed solely at the Church, who have rewritten everything to suit their business model. The fact is, that Jesus, whoever he was and whatever he was, almost certainly spent a lot of time in and around The Mount of Olives. It may not have been exactly where these shrines and Churches have arisen, but the chances are that within about 300 metres, he was actually there.

So enough of Jesus for one day, but there was still one site to visit. To cap everything off, The Tomb of The Virgin Mary. It was old and was almost certainly a tomb dating back to the right period, but as with everything else, the tradition started in the 4th Century, when The Romans had to justify making all of this official. In any case, tradition has it she left with Peter for Ephesus and The Catholic Church recognise this by charging to enter a 4th century house. You can't have your cake and eat it! Here too there was a launch pad for Mary's lift off to heaven, and once again there was crowdfunding for her return. A little less tasteful than the donation box for Jesus, as the slab on top of the tomb was covered in dollar bills where Yanks had tossed their money away with no thought about the aesthetics of the place.

Once more there was a queue and a soldier at the end to push you in at gunpoint and another to drag you out if you took too long. I am afraid whereas the pious were crying, clutching beads, and muttering prayers, I just laughed. It is totally crazy. Don't get me wrong, the afternoon, in fact the whole day, had been fascinating and I had learned so much, but at this point I just had to laugh at the complete and utter nonsense that was around me.
The Mount of Olives is a bit like Disneyworld for Christians. Lots of attractions based on age old stories. I just think I could have designed it better. Maybe a runaway train through the graveyard, Dumbo flying over The Church of Mary Magdalene, so you get a good view and an Ascension simulator at The Temple of The Ascension. Disneyworld Jerusalem. You heard it here first.

It was another 35-minute walk back to the hotel and I did some of that along the Via Dolorosa, the street which has the stations of the cross. I felt quite envious of him to be honest. A cross would have been bloody useful in barging the American tour groups out of the way. And as I had now trudged well over 20,000 steps for the day, he probably was moving quicker than I was.

After resting my feet for an hour, I ventured out again to The Machaneh Yehuda market. This was amazing. The were over 250 stalls selling nuts, spices, fruit, cakes, bread, fish, halva, in fact anything you could think of. There were several craft beer bars too. I went to one called Beer Bazaar which had local brews which were really good. To cap it all off, I had the best pastrami and kimchi sandwich which was washed down with another pint of Israeli craft beer.

It had been a long day but thankfully, after the initial disaster, I salvaged my itinerary and saw some amazing places. Tomorrow would be no different.

3. ONCE IN ROYAL DAVID'S KHAZI

It was thankfully dry, albeit not very warm, when I met my guide today, Schmuel, at The Jaffa Gate at 8 a.m. I originally had three tours booked with him, but due to him having a family emergency, which I had been informed of a couple of weeks prior to leaving, he was now only available today. As a result, Sunday's tour to The Herodium had been cancelled, and Thursday's tour to The City of David was combined with The Temple Mount Tour today in what promised to be a marathon day and another assault on my poor old feet.

Our first stop was the Cardo, a Roman shopping street that was built right through the heart of Jerusalem, from one end to the other. There are still quite a few Roman remains and parts have been restored quite well. The cities of the Ancient Roman Empire had a special tradition of decorating main roads with spectacular stone columns. These streets were called "Cardo" and Jerusalem, just like any other Roman city, had a Cardo of its own. This ancient street originates at The Damascus Gate in the north, running southwards through the Old City, terminating at The Zion Gate.

The north side of the Cardo, from Damascus Gate to David Street, was built during the Roman period in Jerusalem. The south side, however, was built in the 6th century, during the times of the Byzantine Empire in Jerusalem, and it extends along the western side of the Jewish Quarter. Archaeologists have excavated and restored part of The Cardo, near to the Western Wall. You can clearly see that it consisted of a central open-air passage for animals and carriages, as well as footpaths for pedestrian use from both sides of the street. A few of the original stores located on the sidewalks were also found at several sections of the street.

A Byzantine level was discovered by archaeologists in the southern side of the Cardo. This level contained beautiful columns which have been restored. Today it is possible to walk along the Cardo, for about 200 metres, just like the ancient Jerusalemites did back in the 6th century. The Crusader's Bazaar, which was built in the 12th century, is now renovated with modern stores selling fake antiques and souvenir tat.

We also stopped outside the main synagogue of Jerusalem to see the enormous golden menorah. This has been made for when the third temple comes into being, but despite people always saying how canny the Jews are, they cocked up here. There are multiple inscriptions and descriptions of the original menorah from the Second temple period, and they obviously wanted an exact copy.

But the makers made a hexagonal base rather than a round one, and when you order a five-foot solid gold menorah, made of 94 lbs. of solid 24 karat gold, you can't afford to go back to the drawing board. To make matters worse, they got somebody in Rome to make it for them. Rome of all places, as they were the ones who melted down the last one, built an arch honouring Titus, that showed it being paraded through the city with the other Temple loot and built the Colosseum from the proceeds.

The morning part of the tour was to the top of The Temple Mount or as it should currently be called, Al Haram al-Sharif, which is roughly translated as "The Noble sanctuary." Non-Muslims can only access the site from 7.30 in the morning until 10.30 am, and from tomorrow, it will be shut to all non-Muslims for the entire month of Ramadan. So, it was today or never for me.

Non-Muslims must access The Temple Mount from The Western Wall Plaza, heading up a covered wooden ramp that is overloaded with soldiers and security checks. Once you get through all of this, you are confronted with a large open space. Despite being the size of 35 football pitches there is not too much on Temple Mount apart from The Dome of The Rock and The Al Aqsa Mosque, neither of which we are allowed into because we didn't have the correct invisible friend. In fact, I did try to look through the windows of the mosque and a rather irate looking woman drew the curtain. The mosque is nothing special from the outside but is the third holiest site in Islam. It is a functioning mosque and can accommodate up to 5000 worshippers at a time. The name Al Aqsa means 'farthest mosque', a reference to the journey Muhammad is believed to have made on his way to heaven to receive instructions from Allah.

Originally built by order of the Umayyad caliph Al Walid in 715, Al Aqsa stands on what the Crusaders thought to be the site of the First Temple and what others believe was a marketplace on the edge of the Temple. Some Christians revere it as the location where Jesus turned over the tables and drove out the moneychangers, but they have been known to make things up!

Rebuilt at least twice after earthquakes razed it, the mosque was converted into the residence of the kings of Jerusalem after the Crusaders took the city in 1099. On the death of Baldwin II in 1131, the building was handed over to a decade-old order of soldier-monks, whose members soon began referring to themselves as the Templars after their new headquarters. The order added several extensions, including the still-remaining refectory along the southern wall of the enclosure. The other Crusader structures were demolished by Saladin, the first of the Sunni Ayyubid dynasty, who added an intricately carved mihrab (prayer niche indicating the direction of Mecca) to the mosque.

Tragic events have repeatedly occurred at the mosque over the last century. King Abdullah of Jordan was assassinated in 1951 while attending Friday prayers here. He is now interred in a mausoleum on The Temple Mount. In 1969, an arson attack by an Australian visitor irreparably damaged priceless religious objects. Israeli metal detectors were temporarily installed at entrances to Al Aqsa in 2017 as a response to the shooting of two Israeli police officers this prompted bloody clashes and several deaths.

The mosques dome, which was supposedly extremely spectacular, was irreparably damaged during the 1967 Israel – Jordan conflict.

What we have today is a rather ugly concrete and lead dome that really doesn't do the building any justice. And as to how long the mosque will remain standing is another concern. Not just from Israeli plans to bulldoze the entire Temple Mount and build a Third temple, but from a rather frightening crack that has appeared in The Southern Wall directly below it. It is believed that if there is an earthquake, and they are not infrequent here, that the whole lot will crash to the ground.

Much of The Temple Mount, apart from the two major buildings, seems to be covered in rubble. The Temple Mount has been stormed several times over the years. The Jews built there Temple here around 3000 years ago, only for The Babylonians to destroy it some 400 years later. Then they built a second temple, only for The Romans to demolish it in 70 AD. Then came the Christians, only for the Muslims to take it in the eighth century. Next came the Crusaders, only to fall foul to the Muslims again around 1300, and then it stayed in Muslim hands until the British turned up and decided it was ours. We cleared off in 1948 and Jerusalem became part of Jordan until 1967, when Israel invaded and took it back.

The area between the Al Aqsa Mosque and The Dome of The Rock is full of fountains, trees, archways, and communal water stations, where Muslims can perform the Wudu, which is the ritual cleansing, before entering a holy site.

The Dome of The Rock itself is truly beautiful and is the enduring symbol of today's Jerusalem. As its name suggests, the dome covers a slab of stone sacred to both the Muslim and Jewish faiths. According to Jewish tradition, it was here that Abraham prepared to sacrifice his son, Isaac. Islamic tradition has the Prophet Muhammad ascending to heaven from this spot on his flying horse but claim he was told to kill his son Ishmael in Mecca. It's all a bit tit for tat really. We have some sort of historical NASA with Mohammad's lift off site in plain view of Jesus' launchpad on The Mount of Olives, literally across the valley, and then does it really matter which son and where God told Abraham to murder him? The fact that he did it should raise a few alarm bells surely. Jewish tradition also has it that this marks the centre of the world. Steps below the rock lead to a cave known as the Well of Souls, where according to medieval legends the voices of the dead are said to be heard falling into the river of paradise and on to eternity.

Once again, we were not allowed into the building as we had the wrong views but could admire it from the outside. The building was constructed between 688 and 691 CE under the patronage of the Umayyad caliph Abd Al Malik. His motives were shrewd as well as pious – the caliph wanted to instill a sense of pride in the local Muslim population and keep them loyal to Islam. He also wanted to make a statement to Jews and Christians: Islam was both righteous and all-powerful, so it could build a structure more splendid than any Christian church on a location that was the location of the Jewish Holy of Holies, thus superseding both religions.

Malik had his Byzantine architects take as their model the rotunda of the Holy Sepulchre. But instead of the dark, gloomy interiors or austere stone facades of the Christian structures, their mosque was covered inside and out with a bright confection of mosaics and scrolled verses from the Quran, while the crowning dome was covered in solid gold that shone as a beacon for Islam.

A plaque was laid inside honouring Malik and giving the date of construction. Two hundred years later the Abbasid caliph Al Mamun altered it to claim credit for himself, neglecting to amend the original date. Briefly repurposed as a church under the Crusaders, it promptly became an Islamic shrine again in the 12th century under Saladin. In 1545, Suleiman the Magnificent ordered that the much-weathered exterior mosaics be removed and replaced with tiles.

These were again replaced during a major restoration in the 20th century. The original gold dome also disappeared long ago, and the dome you see today is covered with 5000 gold plates donated by the late King Hussein of Jordan. The 80kg of gold cost the king US$8.2 million – he sold one of his homes in London to pay for it.

You leave the Temple Mount through a covered Palestinian Souq, that was selling a multitude of plastic crap that the faithful were gobbling up for Ramadan. At the entrance to The Temple Mount, from inside the market, two young, female, Israeli soldiers with painted nails and MK 47's were turning away Muslims who didn't have the right pass. This really is why the area shuts during Ramadan for non-Muslims, as the tensions will be high and loads of visitors will travel here without the relevant paperwork and get the hump when they are turned away at the barrel of a gun.

Having said all of this, I actually think this national service thing here works really well. You feel safe in Jerusalem, day and night, and I think this is because there are no gangs of teenagers hanging around as they are all in the army. Once they leave, they all seem to have mellowed out and are quite rounded human beings apart from the institutional racism that seems to be drilled into them.

After a quick coffee, we set out on part two of the day's itinerary. We left through the Dung gate and made our way to The City of David, which was about 400 yards away, on the opposite side of the road. As teeming with controversy as it is with ancient history, the City of David is one of Jerusalem's most active archaeological sites. The oldest part of Jerusalem, it was a settlement during the Canaanite period; David is said to have captured the city and to have brought the Ark of the Covenant here 3000 years ago. Excavations began in the 1850s and are ongoing, as are arguments over the development and expansion of the site which many consider to be on Palestinian lands.

There are buildings here dating back 3500 years to when a group of people known as The Jebusites lived here. Nothing is really known of their civilization, but they did have an amazing irrigation system of which more anon.

The city is built on a hill and over a natural water source known as The Gihon Spring. It lies to the south of the southern wall of the old city of Jerusalem. No evidence has been found here to show that either King David or Solomon were ever here but it is an ongoing archaeological dig, and they are hopeful of finding some evidence. You first come to what is known as The Royal Quarter, which was first constructed in the 10th century BCE, most likely as a fortification wall for a palace on the ridge. During the First Temple period an aristocrat's home (Achill's House) was built against the wall, but it was destroyed along with the Temple in 586 BCE.

Judean and Babylonian arrowheads were found in one of the chambers, called the Burnt Room because of its coating of ash, vivid reminders of the bloody battle waged here. Archaeologists have also located 51 royal seals (in ancient Hebrew script), including one thought to be that of the prophet Jeremiah's scribe, Gemaryahu Ben Shafan. The seals were all located in one chamber, indicating that the room once served as an office.

The house of Achill is actually quite important. It is a four bedroomed house that is mentioned in the Bible, as is the name achier. The name found on shards of pottery in the house, is exactly the same as the Biblical record. This alone gives the site some credence but calling it The City of David will remain dubious until they actually find anything. Some believe David didn't exist, others claim he was an Egyptian Pharoah (Psusennes III), and others claim he was nothing more than a nomadic bandit. But at least we can say with some certainty, that by 700 BC, this was the Jewish capital.

Schmuel pointed out a large stone that had a hole drilled through the centre of it. He announced it as King David's toilet and normally I would have been excited by this. It may well have been a toilet, but the chances of it being the Royal throne are somewhat slim. It looked a bit rough to me. Surely a King would have at least had his toilet polished.

They have found lots of evidence for the reign of King Hezekiah, who ruled around 700 BC, and remarkably, for once, the archaeology ties in with the Bible. Evidence has been found for most of the King's building projects mentioned in The Bible, especially the irrigation project, that is mentioned at length.

But to reach the tunnels dating back to Hezekiah, we had to descend the long, sloping Warren's Shaft which was named after Sir Charles Warren, the British engineer who rediscovered it in 1867.

The tunnel, which runs underneath the City of David to the Gihon Spring, allowed the Jebusites to obtain water without exposing themselves to danger in times of siege. It's just inside the city's defence wall and is possibly the tunnel described in 2 Samuel 5 as the means by which David's soldiers entered and captured the city. Modern archaeologists, however, tend to doubt this theory, suggesting the invaders used a different tunnel.

The irrigation system was amazing and was originally carved into the bedrock by The Jebusites. This would have been before the age of iron, which makes the achievement even more amazing. We walked down steps under the city and came to two massive cisterns that were filled by the natural spring. Jebusite and no doubt Jewish women later on, would walk down these steps to fill their pots with water.

At the end of Warren's Shaft, you come to the irrigation system installed by Hezekiah. This 500m-long underground watery passage ends at the Pool of Siloam, where it is said that a blind man was healed after Jesus told him to wash in it. However, this is not true. It turns out that this pool was built by The Byzantines, as they could not find the real one. It only dates to the 5th Century. The purpose of the tunnel was to channel water flowing from the Gihon Spring, a temperamental source that acts like a siphon, pouring out a large quantity of water for some 30 minutes before drying up for several hours.

Gihon means 'gushing', and the spring is the main reason the Canaanites settled in the valley rather than taking to the adjacent high ground. There is believed to be enough water to support a population of about 2500 people. The tunnel was constructed around 700 BCE by King Hezekiah to bring the water of the Gihon into the city and store it in the Pool of Siloam, thus preventing invaders, in particular the Assyrians, from locating the city's water supply and cutting it off.

Although the tunnel is narrow and low in parts, you can wade through it; the water is normally between 50cm and 1m deep. The tunnel is as little as 60cm wide at some points. There were two reasons why I declined to go wading through the tunnel here. Firstly, due to the rain we had in the previous 48 hours, the water was at least 1 metre deep and secondly there was a school trip of around 60 orthodox children who were screaming so loud it was reverberating throughout the entire cave system.

It also crossed my mind, that if what Schmuel had pointed out, really was David's toilet, God knows what would have floated down that tunnel. Thankfully, the local Tourist board have built a second, dry, tunnel that comes out in a similar place.

When we emerged back into daylight, the kids were soaking wet and splashing around in some very brown looking water which Helena of Constantinople constructed in the 4th century, claiming it to be the Pool of Siloam where Jesus healed a blind man.
As we looked back along The Kidron Valley, the Biblical Valley of Jehoshaphat, you could see a few monumental tombs on The Mount of Olives. The most famous of these is known as The Tomb of Absalom, who was supposedly King David's third and favourite son. The fact is that dates back only to the 1st century. Interestingly though, archaeologists now believe it may have belonged to Agrippa, Herod's son. However, the two I was interested in were The Tomb of Zechariah and The Tomb of The Egyptian Princess.

The latter refers to the wife of Solomon, who was an Egyptian Princess, but there is no evidence that the tomb was hers as it too dates to the 1st Century. Nor is the other tomb, the last resting place of the Biblical Prophet. What was fascinating was that they were identical to some of the tombs I had seen in Luxor in Egypt. Both having pyramids on the top of the tomb. Not that you are allowed to say there is any link between the Jews and the Ancient Egyptians.
If you head up the stairs and a few crumbling steps, you get to the real Pool, which is actually known as the Shiloach Pool. The pool, built during the Second Temple period and used for purification rituals, was rediscovered by a bit of 'good luck' after an underground sewage pipe burst during excavations in 2004. Archaeologists and historians have theorised that this is the actual pool where Jesus is said to have healed a blind man. You needed your imagination here a bit as it had been drained and there were bulldozers and archaeologists on an ongoing dig.

From the Shiloach Pool, you can head up the flight of wooden steps to the Eastern Stepped Street, an ancient flight of stone steps. The stair pattern – pairs of short steps with a long gap between them – is thought to have been designed for animals, so sacrifices could be led upwards with ease. A drainage ditch is located under the steps, and it was here that archaeologists found Roman-era coins and pottery, leading historians to believe that the ditch served as a hideout for Jews while the city was being sacked in 70 CE.

2000 years ago, the staircase would have gone all the way to the Temple. Only about thirty steps have been restored to date, but the work is ongoing.

Thankfully from here there was a minibus that took us back up the very steep hill, to the entrance of The City of David. But we still had one more tunnel to traverse. It is accessed through an ongoing archaeological dig, at what used to be the city's Givati Parking Lot. It's believed soldiers of the Roman X Legion were garrisoned here – roof tiles marked with their sign were found at the site. As recently as 2010, when a volunteer was digging around a niche above a doorway in the large Roman villa, 264 golden coins in mint condition tumbled out. Minted in Jerusalem in 613 with the portrait of Byzantine emperor Heraclius, which now reside in the Israel Museum.

The drainage tunnel which runs from The Temple Mount, right down to The Pool of Shiloach Is 650m-long and was recently discovered and opened to the public. Originally it channeled water out of the Temple Mount/Al Haram Ash Sharif area. You can access it through the Givati Archaeological dig, and it tunnels directly under a Herodian era road and comes back up in the Davidson or Southern Archaeological Park. The tunnel was generally wide enough, but we did have a few tight squeezes.

The tunnel resurfaces near Robinson's Arch which was a monumental archway where the staircase finished at The Southwestern corner of The Temple Mount. So named, as it was rediscovered by Biblical Scholar, Edward Robinson in 1838.

The most interesting sight in the archaeological park were the piles of enormous blocks of stone that would have been hurled down to the ground from The Temple Mount in 70AD by The Romans when they destroyed the Temple. Some being well over 100 tons. Schmuel left at this point, but I wanted to wander along the Southern Wall and get a decent view of The Al Aqsa Mosque from below and also the Southern Entrance to The Temple Mount, through which the Messiah is supposed to enter. Somewhat bizarrely, the Muslims bricked this entrance up. Now correct me if I'm wrong, but if any messiah can fly through time and space and land on the allotted rock on The Mount of Olives, then resurrect all the people buried there. Is a brick wall going to keep him out? Am not sure they thought that one through.

I somehow staggered back through The Western Wall Plaza, back down the Cardo, stopping for a few bottles of beer near the Jaffa Gate. On the way back to the hotel I stopped off to pick up what was undoubtably the most delicious salmon and cream cheese bagel I have ever had. It had everything in it! I just about managed to eat it before passing out for three hours on my bed.

When I woke up, the fact I had cleared nearly 60,000 steps in 3 days had taken its toll. My legs were refusing to play ball and rather than seek out a restaurant I had penciled in for the evening, I just about made it to a burger bar a few hundred yards from the hotel. The burger was excellent, as was the beer I had with it back in my room.

I prayed to every known Rain God for the skies to be clear the following day. As another 20,000 steps were never going to happen. I needed a day sitting in a car being driven around!

4.   THE DEAD SEA AND OTHER LOW POINTS

I was still a bit stiff when I woke up this morning, but I managed to haul myself down to breakfast in time. The breakfasts here really aren't doing it for me. There is a time for cheese and salad, but it is not 7.30 in the morning. The cooked offerings have become less appetising as the week progressed and all in all, I decided to skip breakfast for the rest of the week. A relaxed cup of tea in my room seemed quite sufficient.

My guide, Yazid, was waiting for me at 8.30, and gratefully, I plonked my backside down in his car and awaited to be chauffeured around for the day. Yazid was really nice, and we were soon chatting about various things before we hit the topic of football and it just so happened, he was a huge fan of English football and had actually heard of Brighton and could name quite a few players. It certainly passed the time as we crawled through Jerusalem's rush hour traffic.

Today we were heading south from Jerusalem to the Dead Sea area, and I was sort of hoping that there would not be quite as many tourists as there had been in Jerusalem. We stopped briefly on the main road near Jericho where there is a sign that you have reached sea level. It was only going to be downhill from here.

Our first port of call today was Masada, which was about 90 minutes south of Jerusalem. Herod the Great's fortified complex at Masada was a winter retreat but also an insurance against a feared rebellion of his Jewish subjects or an attack from Rome. Luxurious palaces, barracks, well-stocked storerooms, bathhouses, water cisterns sat on a plateau 400m above the Dead Sea and desert floor. Herod's personal quarters in the Northern Palace contained lavish mosaics and frescoes.

But by the time the Jews revolted against the Romans, Herod had been dead for seven decades. After the temple in Jerusalem was destroyed, the surviving zealots fled to Masada, under the command of Eleazer Ben Yair. Around 960 men, women and children holed up in the desert fortress as 8,000 Roman legionnaires laid siege from below.

Using Jewish slave labour, the Romans built a gigantic ramp with which they could reach the fortress and capture the rebels. On 15 April 73AD, Ben Yair gathered his people and told them the time had come to "prefer death before slavery". Using a lottery system, the men killed their wives and children, then each other, until the last survivor killed himself, according to historian Flavius Josephus's account.

The Romans advanced but found only "an awful solitude, and flames within and silence, they were at a loss to conjecture what had happened Here encountering the mass of slain, instead of exulting as over enemies, they admired the nobility of their resolve". Josephus recorded that two women and three children survived to tell the tale.

After the declaration of the state of Israel in 1948, Masada took on a new significance, symbolising heroism, and sacrifice. Newly enlisted soldiers were taken to the desert fortress to swear their oath of allegiance, including the shout: "Masada will not fall again!" I have seen t shirts in Jerusalem that read "Masada – Death Before Slavery" with the Star of David imprinted on them. Of all the many stories that have sprung from this very small piece of land, if you ask any Israeli to define what personifies them as a nation, the answer will almost certainly be Masada.

But some have cast doubt on the "myth of Masada", saying it was either exaggerated or the suicide story was simply wrong. In all likelihood, The Romans simply massacred everybody.

My hopes of not having to confront any Christian tour buses today was short lived. As we entered the visitor centre there was a guide preaching to his American group that whilst at Masada, they should contemplate whether suicide can ever be forgiven. You just shake your head sometimes. Unless you believe that Jesus was instrumental in The Jewish Revolt of 68 AD, there should be absolutely no link between Masada and Christianity. It is certainly not mentioned in The Bible. Yet here they are, praying and getting in everybody's way.

Before ascending the hill, you get an eight-minute film, starring Peter O'Toole, explaining the historical significance. From here you start to queue for the cable car that takes you to the summit, which is only forty metres above sea level, but some 490 metres above the Dead Sea. Some brave souls decided to walk up a winding track known as Snake Path. I would have done, but Yazid insisted we took the cable car.

The plateau atop Masada measures 550 metres by 270 metres. The Northern Palace here was Herod's most adventurous building project. On the summit of the hill was built a massive fortress with enormous storerooms which could keep enough food for months on end. Cascading down the side of the cliff were three circular terraces that held opulent living quarters. The upper terrace of the Northern Palace included living quarters for the king and a semi-circular portico to provide a view of the Dead Sea area. A stairway on the west side led down to the middle terrace that was a decorative circular reception hall whilst the lower terrace was also for receptions and banquets. It was enclosed on all four sides with porticos and included a Roman bathhouse, including a pool from which the King could take in the views. It must have been amazing.

There is also a Western Palace, which was slightly more functional and had a throne room where the King could conduct matters of state. There were living quarters here, but these would have been used mainly for guests and there was another swimming pool.

The most amazing site here are the remains of eight roman camps that can be seen from above and also the remains of the actual siege ramp used to storm the castle. The Romans were a great military machine but storming a castle. One thousand feet in the air caused them a few issues. They laid siege to the castle, yet it took them over six months to build massive ramps that they could wheel battering rams and other military hardware up. Finally, they got close enough and set fire to much of the castle. This was late in the day, so the Romans decided that they would return the next morning to finish things off.

And it is here that the story here takes a twist as the zealots were all killed by their own swords, the last man falling on his own weapon. When the Romans entered the castle the next day, everybody was dead. This is a massive date in Jewish History and the term Death not Slavery, stems from this. Or so the story goes. There is every chance that the Romans did what they were good at, and simply slaughtered everybody.

Our next stop was for me the highlight of the trip. Many people will have heard of Qumran as being the place where The Dead Sea Scrolls were found, but people who created them, The Essenes were a fascinating group who I have studied fairly extensively.

Excavations started here in 1949 and it is believed that the site dates to the Iron Age city of Secacah, which is mentioned in The Bible, in Joshua 15. The archaeological remains are not that extensive. There is a lookout tower, some ritual baths, a cistern, a kitchen, and a refectory. A couple of other rooms have been daubed as scriptoriums, but there is no real proof of this.

Once again, the tour buses were here en mass and I can guarantee that 99% of them took a picture of the cave where most of The Scrolls were found and left, thinking this was just the place where they wrote down the scrolls and then hid them so they could be found in 1948, thus legitimizing their beliefs. Many, I fear never got out of the supermarket sized gift shop. Although I do have some empathy there as it took me five minutes to find the exit.

There was a visitors' centre with another brief film, which did not really enlighten anyone and was more concerned with the shepherd boy who found the scrolls. To understand a book or any type of writing, you need to know about the people who wrote it. The "Communist Manifesto" would just be words on a page if you knew nothing of Karl Marx and the same goes for Chaucer and The Canterbury Tales. The texts are not enough therefore most people leave here thinking that there were people here who wrote scripts from the Bible. End of.

But even a short study of who The Essenes were and what they believed in, shows that they were instrumental in the foundation of Christianity, albeit unwittingly, and had their own messiah at least a century before the arrival of Jesus.

The Essenes valued holiness and purity to such a degree that many of them felt the need to cut themselves off from the outside world. According to some sources, they believed that the material body was temporary and would fade away while the soul was eternal. Their beliefs regarding the resurrection of the body differed from other Jewish sects and it is suggested by some sources that they did not believe in the resurrection at all.

But this should not be a surprise, as these are remarkably similar to the beliefs held by the Atenists who came out of Egypt and effectively established their religion during the First Temple Period. Some historians have claimed that the Essenes were actually sun worshippers, but if you look at any of the mosaics that were recovered from Qumran, they show a sun disk with outstretching rays of light and not a sun god such as Ra or Helios. Exactly as the Aten was portrayed in Akhenaten's Amarna.

Josephus wrote about the Essenes and stated that "before sun-rising they speak not a word about profane matters but put up certain prayers which they have received from their forefathers, as if they made a supplication for its rising…. that they may not affront the Divine rays of light."

They were not deifying the sun and giving it human form, but worshipping a divine existence that gave life to the universe. As did the Atenists, who were the priests who fled Egypt and established the Jewish religion in The Levant. The changes that had been made to Judaism during the exile in Babylon and the subsequent changes by The Maccabean Kings and The Romans, were abhorrent and they wanted to restore the values and covenant from Tabernacle and The First temple Period.

So where does Christianity fit in to all of this? The Essenes were a messianistic group. They referred to the first High Priest of the First temple, as the Teacher of Righteousness would return and purify Israel from foreign corruption. The Teacher in the text is said to have had an in-depth understanding of the Torah and was also qualified in accurate instruction. It is said that he was the one with whom God was willing to reveal the hidden things of Israel to the Jewish community. The Teacher of Righteousness depicted in the Dead Sea scrolls belonged to the House of Israel. As per the Dead

Sea scrolls, he was born without a father. The time of his birth was the era when Christianity was about to begin. There is no proof that Jesus was the Teacher of Righteousness, but they certainly preached along the same lines of poverty, humility, repentance, and love of innocence.

The Essenes believed that the end was nigh, and that God would act to free Israel from its invaders and return the promised land to the "sons of righteousness. But for this to happen, the world would face an apocalyptical future. One Scroll, Titled The "Messianic Apocalypse" states "The Sons of Righteousness shall shine to all ends of the world continuing to shine forth until end of the appointed seasons of darkness. Then at the time appointed by God, His great excellence shall shine for all the times of eternity for peace and blessing, glory and joy, and long life for all Sons of Light." That not like Revelation at all is it!

The Essenes knew they were in the Last Days, but they did not know precisely when the momentous event would happen. At the start of the gospels, John the Baptist and Jesus knew they were in the Last Days and urged people to repent, but they also did not know precisely when the occasion would be. Jesus himself explains it in Mark 13. For reasons that are not clear, Jesus comes to think that the Last Days really are at hand. In other words, they were literally down to days, not years.

Both Essene and Christian texts speak of a messianic personality in very human terms. But unlike the Christian belief that the messiah would bring salvation, or damnation, the Essenes avoided this definition, envisioning, rather, a final clash between the forces of good and evil. In that sense, perhaps, they saw themselves as social revolutionaries, who, by their example, would create a new world order. So, could this mean that they were the driving force behind the Jewish Revolt of which I believe Jesus was a leader? Their apocalypse was the final war that drove The Romans out of Israel. Which unfortunately for them never happened and it was they and not the Romans who disappeared after 70 AD.

The scroll continues to speak of a single messianic figure and describes the resurrection of the dead. It is almost word for word an exact parallel with the Gospels of Matthew and Luke. (In contrast, Jews believe that God, not the Messiah, will resurrect the dead. The Bible does not refer to a messiah raising the dead.)

This is the earliest evidence we have of a shift from nationalism, and a belief that a group of people can fight for their own survival to a belief that things are going to be so bad, that only a God like, Messiah can solve your problems. But the Essenes had their leader to lead the fight against The Romans. They may have deified him, but he was flesh and blood. What Paul and The Church did was use The Essenes flesh and blood leader, and turn him into some mythical superman, who could come back and fix anything. I remember praying once to Jesus for Brighton to win the FA Cup. They did not. He still has a 100% failure rate from what I can see.

The Jewish concept of the Messiah is first described by the Hebrew prophets, particularly the prophet Isaiah. In general, it was believed that the Messiah would be a descendant of David. It was also believed that he would restore Israel as a sovereign nation, gather the Jews who had been scattered across the earth, restore full observance of the Torah, and finally bring peace throughout the entire world. Something that the Biblical Jesus failed on all counts. Christianity had to complete reinvent the requirements for Jesus to be a Messiah and somehow make the Jewish saviour, the salvation of everybody else.

The fact is, that there would probably be no question that Jesus was an Essene, had he not been given a complete makeover by Paul and his subsequent Church, meaning that the majority of people see Jesus as the Son of God, which he clearly was not, and never said he was. He always referred to himself as the Son of Man, a phrase that appears quite often in Essene literature. There are numerous ways in which Jesus and the Essenes were similar:

- They were in the same small country, Judaea, about as big as Devon
- They were Jews
- They were seriously religious

- They were deeply conservative, basing their beliefs on ancient scriptures not the world as it was
- They disliked non-Jews
- They resented the temple priesthood, the Sadducees
- They disliked another Jewish sect, the Pharisees, but saw some good in some of them
- They expected God to change the world and destroy the wicked soon—they were apocalyptic and eschalogical
- They were disliked by the Romans and Jesus and many Essenes were killed by them

For Christians, If Jesus is to be God's revelation, he has to be unique. But he clearly was not. The Essenes had been preaching the same message for over a hundred years prior to his birth.

Messianism is both inspiring and dangerous. It offers the possibility of the highest achievements that are humanly possible, and, as well, devastating corruption. It can raise the human spirit or bury it in sinkholes of blood and confusion. It can encourage a deeper appreciation of one's spirituality and legitimize destruction and desecration – in the name of God.

It also seems pretty clear that John the Baptist spent some time with or was even trained by the Essenes. The traditional Baptismal spot for John is only a few miles from Qumran. Christian baptism is related to forgiveness and spiritual rebirth. The baptism of John was primarily related to repentance and preparation for a coming judgement. John also did not believe that his baptism was the ultimate. It was instead a preparation for a coming baptism that would be administered by a much greater being than himself.

John taught a basic moral message of living a life of justice and righteousness, just as per the code of The Essenes. In one instance, several Pharisees and Sadducees came to listen to one of John's sermons and he condemns them as a "brood of vipers," denouncing their hypocrisy. It is interesting that both John and

Jesus are critical of the Pharisees and Sadducees, but not of The Essenes. Which is probably because they were Essene!

Jesus, John, and The Essenes played a key role in the formation of Christianity, but it was unwittingly. Although the Essenes would have fought alongside other Jews in the Great Revolt of 70 AD, believing it to be a war against the soldiers of darkness. But after the Roman victory, Essenes would never have joined The Christian movement as it was largely a Gentile Church. Had Jesus survived, he would of have joined it either.

Yet the letters of Paul, draw on the apocalyptic Essenes vision, and start the belief that only if the Jesus, now promoted to Son of God, returns, will the world be saved. It is quite bizarre really. It is a bit like the English praying for King Harold to return so we would be free of French influence. But the newly formed Christian movement, although preaching Essenes ideology, could not be associated with a rebel faction or such a militant sect. Jesus was desperately trying to convert the sinners of Israel, expecting ha-Megiddo at any minute. What has come to us of his attempt has come from some of those converts. He was a professional Essene recruiting an army to fight The Romans. But preaching to the masses. He did not try to explain to them the finer points of theology. His object was to have them repent and be ritually purified by baptism, ready to fight and be ready for God's Appointed Time. The Jewish God's appointed time.

As I have stated, one of the major rules of The Essenes was cleanliness before God and this meant that they were not allowed to defecate within the town itself. I mentioned whilst in Jerusalem about the origins of The Dung Gate, where Essenes went to the toilet outside of the city walls. In Qumran, this seems to have taken a stage further and members of the community could not go to the toilet in the sight of any other person. Archaeologists have been baffled by the fact that no facilities have been found here. That was until a couple of years ago when one of the scrolls was translated and it explained that the lavatories were forty cubits outside of the settlement. Lo and behold, archaeologists found a rock, forty cubits from the settlement and behind it was the outline of two cubicles. It had to be there somewhere.

From here we headed to The Dead Sea and Kalia private beach. Yazid normally gets a break from guiding here and allows people a couple of hours to float in the water and chill out by the Beach. But due to my allergy to salt water, the former was a nonstarter and sitting looking at women in bikinis for two hours would probably get me arrested, so we did not stay that long. Unlike English resorts that have donkey rides, there were camel rides here. But as I have stated in many a book. I don't get on very well with camels.

I did allow Yazid a thirty-minute snooze whilst I sat and had a pint in what they claimed to be the World's lowest bar, 420 metres below sea level, which was quite pleasant. The view over the Dead Sea was very nice and across the water, in Jordan, were several beach resort hotels, one of which I will be staying in next year when I visit that country. I decided that rather than have a paddle here, I would wait until next year, when I had a hotel room to go back to and wash the salt of my feet.

In any case, what was billed as The Dead Sea's most beautiful beach, was not that stunning. This probably had to do with the thick mud you had to wade through to get into the water. It may have wonderful medicinal and rejuvenating qualities, but I wasn't walking through it to have a paddle.

As we still had some spare time, due to me not having a float, we managed to fit in a few extra places of interest. Firstly, the Baptism Site of John the Baptist on The Jordan River. I had always imagined it to be quite wide, but there was a Jordanian soldier, staring at us across the water, no more than thirty feet away. The reeds here must be fifteen feet high and if you disregard the armed soldiers, you can imagine it has not changed much since the times of John the Baptist.

But as with most places in Israel, there is controversy here. Prior to 1967, Jordan owned both sides of the river and promoted the site accordingly. During the war, land mines were placed throughout the area, which, in my opinion, would have made the present-day baptisms more exciting to watch. But they insisted on clearing them and reopened the site in 2002. But much to the chagrin of the Jordanians, Israel opened their own Baptism site, fifteen feet away on the other side of the riverbank, claiming that John the Baptist dunked people on their side.

Here we go again. Christianity and the need to make money from tourists. To be fair to the Church, they still recognise the Jordanian side which has the Churches and the museums. Not much was happening on the Jordanian side, but the money making was happening on the Israeli side. Baptism itself is free, but robes cost a few hundred shekels to rent, changing rooms are not free and the Baptiser does not come free either. These things do not seem to happen in Judaism or Islam.

I am not sure that Yazid saw the funny side of my suggestion of installing a bungy jump in order to get more customers went down too well. You could still baptise them as they hit the water. Or maybe a ducking stool. If you want customers, you need to think outside of the box.

The funniest moment of the day came at our last stop. The Inn of The Good Samaritan which was on the site of the Biblical Inn where Jesus stopped to help a stricken traveller and dress his wounds. We pulled into the car park and some guy came out of his hut and told us to clear off. Not sure he saw the irony, but I thought it was funny.

I got back to the hotel around 4 o'clock and had a couple of hours to relax before heading out for the evening. I decided to head back to the Mahane Yehuda Market, which seemed to have numerous opportunities to eat and drink. I had planned to go to a brewpub for dinner tonight, but it was full, and no tables were free. So instead, I went to another place I had pencilled in for later in the week called Hatzot. It is a traditional Jewish Chophouse and I had what was their signature dish called The Jerusalem Mixed Grill, mostly chicken and lamb in a slightly spicy mix which was delicious, and it came with bread and about thirty types of dips and pickles, plus a rather nice pint of beer.

After dinner I had another wander around the market, marvelling at the sheer diversity of produce and taking in the aromas of baked goods and smoked meats.

After a slow wander back to the hotel, it was nice to flop on the bed knowing that for once I did not have to get up at the crack of dawn.

5.   "THERE IS NO SUCH THING AS A PALESTINIAN"

It was nice to relax for a few hours after breakfast as things had all been quite hectic for the past few days. There was no guide today, but I did have tickets to visit an archaeological site known as The Tombs of The Kings between 11 and 1 o'clock. The main reason for going here was that the tomb of Helene of Adiabene was there who was the daughter of Queen Thea Musa Aurania of Parthia and daughter of Cleopatra. If my research is correct, she was the mother of Jesus.

Queen Helene converted to Nazarene Judaism at an early age and during the 1st Century she was Jerusalem's greatest benefactor, which included a golden plate and candlestick given to the Temple. Her palace is believed to have been found under the Givati Parking Lot Archaeological dig that I had seen on Tuesday. Jesus of course was also a Nazarene otherwise known as Essene Jew. Her tomb was remarkable. It was shaped like a pyramid, honouring her Egyptian roots, whilst the doors to the tomb were designed by the famed Hero of Alexandria, the 1st Century's answer to Leonardo Da Vinci. The Ancient Greek geographer, Pausanias, declared the tomb to be one of the wonders of the world. He wrote "The Hebrews have a tomb, that of Helena, a local woman, in the city of Jerusalem which the Roman emperor razed to the ground. There is a contrivance in the tomb whereby the door, which like the entire tomb is made of stone, does not open until the year brings back the same day and the same hour. Then the mechanism, unaided, opens the door, which, after a short interval, closes itself again. It happens at the same time, but if you try at any other time to open the door, you will not be able to do so; Power will not open it but will only break it."

You have to ask why nobody has heard of this Queen. She has clearly been airbrushed out of history and the only conceivable reason for this was that she was the mother of Izates Manu, the Jesus Emmanuel from the Jewish revolt who was catapulted to be the chosen one by the newly formed Church. They could hardly have The Virgin Mary lavishing gold candlesticks on the Jewish Temple and shipping in food from Alexandria to feed the poor during a famine that hit in 45 AD.

I called a taxi from the hotel, and he took me to where his sat nav thought the site was, and to be fair, I was following on Google Maps and that said it was there too. I got out of the cab which drove off. I walked up and down the street a couple of times but to no avail. It clearly wasn't there, despite Google and the taxi driver insisting it was. Later, I would discover that they were a good two miles in the opposite direction. This could explain why it is one of Jerusalem's less visited attractions.

The plan had been to wander around the tombs and then head to the Israel Museum. So, I decided to try and call for a cab once again to come and pick me up. All seemed good and the fare was accepted. My taxi was a few minutes away and then it got cancelled. I tried again and suddenly; no fares were being accepted anywhere in the vicinity. Unbeknownst to me, for the past three months, Thursdays have been a day of protest across Israel and especially in Jerusalem and Tel Aviv and today the protests caused Jerusalem to grind to a standstill, as the central thoroughfares were awash with protestors waving Israeli flags.

At first, I believed that they were protesting about the comments made by the Israeli Finance Minister, Bezalel Smotrich, the previous evening when he had denied the existence of the Palestinian people and stating their villages should be erased from the face of the earth. His claim was that the idea of Palestinian nationhood had been invented (Unlike the Israeli one that was first mentioned in a book!).

"Who was the first Palestinian king? What language do the Palestinians have? Was there ever a Palestinian currency? Is there a Palestinian history or culture? Nothing. There is no such thing as a Palestinian people," Smotrich said at a speech in Paris. Completely racist, and yes, The United Nations have given a verbal warning, but ultimately nothing will be done, because it is Israel and The United States will veto and UN action against them. But he current bunch of politicians in The Knesset are more right wing than ever before and one day they will go too far, and the entire Arab world will kick their arse.

It's not the first horrific thing the Israeli Government have committed. The plight of the Ethiopian Jews is perhaps even worse than the Palestinians. The fact is that these Jews probably originated from Nubian Egypt and have far more right to be in Israel than the majority of East European Jews who only adopted Judaism way after the Romans had destroyed the Second Temple. You do not see any black people in Jerusalem. This is because the Ethiopians are kept apart from the Israeli Jews and their women are forcibly sterilized. Since 2013, any Ethiopian Jew wanting to stay in Israel, must report is forcibly injected with contraceptives. There was an outcry across the civilized world, and Israel promised to make changes. They have not done so, and the practice continues. Is this any different to what Mengele did in Auschwitz? I don't think so.

My hopes that the demonstrators were protesting against racism towards the Palestinians soon faded when I realized the actual reason. The current politicians in Israel, especially Benjamin Netanyahu, the Prime minister, are so corrupt that they believe themselves above the law. They have introduced Judicial Reforms that would ultimately allow the Government to overturn judicial decisions, which has been seen by the public, as Netanyahu trying to preempt any conviction for fraud, with the power to overturn it.

The demonstrations had been growing since January 7th and it was just my luck that today was the day that Jerusalem got brought to a complete halt with hundreds of thousands of people blocking the main roads.

To make matters worse, today was also the first day of Ramadan, and thousands of Muslims from Palestine were trying to get into Jerusalem and the Al Aqsa Mosque. Everything seemed fairly good humoured so far on that front.

So here I was, in the middle of nowhere and without a clue as to where I was going. I had planned to go to the Israel Museum afterwards, but that was a further 30 minutes on foot and uphill. So, I used the local taxi app, which had worked the first time, to try and get a cab. Everything seemed fine, the cab driver was on his way, and then he got stuck. And stayed that way for a good ten minutes before cancelling. He had run into the protests and couldn't get through.

So, half an hour uphill, through a somewhat seedy park, it was. I didn't really care about what was on display at the museum at this point, as I headed straight to the shop to buy water.

After having a five-minute breather on the loo, I dropped my bag off and began to wander around what was a surprisingly large museum. The centrepiece is in a well-designed garden that has a few exhibits interspersed with trees. The Shrine of The Book is a dome shaped structure that reminded me a bit of a tagine pot lid. Quite weird and out of place really.

Its white dome is meant to symbolize the lids of the jars in which the first scrolls were found. The contrast between its white dome and the black wall alongside it refers to the tension in the scrolls between the spiritual world of the "Sons of Light" (as the Essenes called themselves) and the "Sons of Darkness" (the sect's enemies). The corridor leading into the shrine is meant to evoke the atmosphere of a cave, recalling the site where the ancient manuscripts were discovered. I'm not sure it did to be honest, but the exhibits were interesting, nevertheless.

The exhibit does a good job of explaining the significance of the manuscripts, the story of their creation, and the saga of how they were discovered.

The Dead Sea Scrolls are the oldest Biblical manuscripts in the world, found in 1947 by a Bedouin shepherd in search of a lost goat in the caves at Qumran, bordering the Dead Sea. Thousands of scroll fragments were uncovered in eleven caves, from which scholars have identified about 800 different manuscripts. All date from the period between 250 B.C. and 100 A.D., the time after the Hebrew Bible was formed but before the formation of Christianity and rabbinical Judaism.

At the center of the underground shrine is a facsimile of arguably the most important manuscript found: a complete version of the book of Isaiah, the oldest complete manuscript of a Hebrew scripture yet discovered and dating to before 100 B.C. (the original is too fragile and valuable to have on display).

There are also documents that relate to the daily life of The Essenes. One such document, named by researchers as the "Community Rule," details the conduct and beliefs held by the Essenes between about 150 B.C. and 70 A.D. Scholars regard the Dead Sea Scrolls as providing an invaluable window into an exceedingly complex and important time in Jewish history.

The upper galleries of the shrine feature the story of the sectarians living at Qumran and describe the manuscripts hidden for many centuries. Its lower galleries are devoted to the tenth-century Aleppo Codex, the oldest known complete manuscript of the Hebrew Bible. The Codex was written in Tiberias in the early tenth century, looted and transferred to Egypt at the end of the eleventh century, and deposited with the Jewish community of Aleppo in Syria at the end of the fourteenth century. The rabbis and elders of the community guarded it zealously for some six hundred years. During the riots against Jews and Jewish property in Aleppo in December 1947, the community's ancient synagogue was put to the torch and the Codex, which was kept in the synagogue's "Cave of Elijah," suffered damage, so that no more than 295 of the original 487 leaves survived. In January 1958 the Aleppo Codex was brought to Jerusalem, where it remains until today.

Also, in the gardens is what has become known as the Second Temple Model. It is a 2,000-square-metre (21,520-square-foot) model of Jerusalem in the Second Temple period. The model was built to a 1:50 scale using many of the construction materials of the time, including steel, Jerusalem stone and marble. Echoing historic times, the model's focal point is the reproduction of the Temple itself, which gives a real sense of the feat achieved by King Herod and his builders. For 40 years the model stood on the grounds of the Holyland Hotel in the Bayit Vagan neighborhood of Jerusalem, the brainchild of the hotel's then-proprietor Hans Kroch. It was based on the writings of Josephus and other sources. More recently, the model was renovated and corrected for archaeological inaccuracies and in 2006, it was transferred in its entirety to the Museum. I thought about playing Godzilla here and stomping through the whole thing, but there were too many armed guards.

From here I wandered to the archaeology wing of the museum, which was quite intensive and took at least two hours to take in. There were too many interesting artefacts to list them, so I will describe just a few of them.

As you enter the archaeology wing, you are greeted by en enormous sarcophagi that were found at Deir El Balah, which today is in The Gaza Strip. Made from clay pottery, they were found in a cave near the sea, which had been protected by large sand dunes. What was fascinating was the clear Egyptian influence on these sarcophagi which to me shows undeniable evidence of the origins of the peoples here.

In a way I was quite surprised to see prehistoric findings here as the whole society here relies on the texts of The Bible for acceptance. The oldest relic is a carved stone from an area of the Golan Heights that dates back around 233,000 years. They claim that this is the oldest piece of art found anywhere in the world and have done microscopic analysis that shows that it was carved by human hands, albeit an extinct form of human. Which must have been created before Adam, thus blowing the whole book out of the water!

There was also a skull dating back to the Lower Paleolithic period (250,000 years) which has been dubbed Galilee Man, as that was where it was found. One wonders whether he wore a big hat, a black coat and had a payot (Jewish Orthodox dreadlock) just like the Egyptian priests used to have! The text all but claimed it was the ancestor of modern Israel, but in reality, they would have been Canaanite or modern day Palestinian.

A couple of small figurines caught my eye. Firstly, one of Yahweh, the Canaanite Storm God from around the 15th Century BC. It shows that Yahweh was in existence at the time but was very much part of a Canaanite pantheon of Gods. A similar bronze figurine of El (God) and his wife Asherah was next to it, also dating from a similar period. Yahweh's promotion to sole God came within a few centuries but his wife stuck around quite a bit longer and it was only really the Christians who insisted that God could not have a wife. This was rather flippant of them as he had been married for well over 1500 years. I'm not sure what wedding anniversary that is. There are further inscriptions from the First temple Period, that also mention both Yahweh and Asherah.

There was a further clay figurine of Asherah which showed her with two unborn children in her womb. According to Canaanite belief, Yahweh and Asherah had twins named Shahar and Shalem. Clearly Yahweh was siring children long before Jesus.

The most bizarre display was a couple of Canaanite, basalt statues that were shaped like Weebles. In that they had a rounded bottom, and you couldn't tip them over. Nobody actually thinks that these could be fun items. The Archaeologists have decided these are Canaanite Gods that will always rise again having fallen over and wait for it, "a metaphor for the rise and fall of religious and cultural ideas, as well as the construction and decline of city states throughout history." Wow! All of that from two giant weebles. One wonders what archaeologists in 1000 years will make of the phrase "Weebles wobble but they won't fall down." I suppose it makes a change from the normal archaeologists cop out of "it is a ceremonial artefact."

There are several inscriptions that refer to characters mentioned in The Bible. There is an epitaph for King Uzziah, who ruled in the 8th century BCE, and was famous for his building projects. When he died, he could not be buried in the royal tombs, because he was a leper. Some 700 years after his death, in the Second Temple period, Jerusalem expanded, and Uzziah's tomb had to be moved outside the new city limits. This Aramaic epitaph was erected to mark the king's new burial place.

One of the more striking exhibits is a massive wall relief, taken from the walls of the Palace of Sennachherib in Nineveh, portraying his victory at Lachish in Northern Israel. It shows the Assyrian army attacking the city using a siege ramp and battering ram, whilst the Judahites shoot arrows and fire rocks back at them.

One interesting fact was that the earliest mention of Jerusalem in Hebrew comes in a stone script from the 6th Century. It reads "YHWH is the God of the whole earth; mountains of Judah belong to him, to the God of Jerusalem." If this is the earliest mention of the city in Hebrew, one must wonder whether it was really that important prior to this and as to whether the temple was elsewhere.

The sole surviving piece of the second temple has the inscription "The Place of Trumpeting." It was from the Southern corner of the Temple Mount, and it is believed that it would have been from here that priests would have blown their shofars (trumpets) to herald in the sabbath.

There are a couple of interesting ossuaries (bone boxes) on display. One for a man who was simply known as "The Builder of The Temple." It heralds from the time of Herod, therefore probably belongs to a man who was a skilled craftsman who worked on the restoration of the temple. Another is for the son of High Priest of the Temple, Caiaphas, who was High Priest between 15 and 36 AD. Caiaphas being the High Priest that Jesus was hauled before in the New Testament.

The final ossuary has caused a bit of a storm. It is a 1st Century Ossuary for Jesus, son of joseph. People got very excited about this, but at the end of the day, Jesus and Joseph were two of the most common names in 1st Century Judea. It could be anyone, and more importantly, it could be a well-made fake.

On the wall opposite is the only remaining evidence of crucifixion in this part of The Roman Empire. The remains of a heel bone with a very large nail hammered through it, is displayed as though it is the actual heel bone of Jesus. And that seems to be the problem here. They are so determined to show that the history written in their book is correct, they will show any old piece of rock to back it up and in the past have been known to display forgeries that promote their narrative. You feel that if they found a dead king on a throne, buried in Jerusalem but holding a sign saying he was king of Palestine, it would be removed and destroyed quite quicky. But any old piece of rock with the letters D.V.D on it will be seen as proof that there was a King David, and his palace was here, and his son built the first Temple!

The real archaeology was amazing though, especially the remains of Herod's great palaces. There were frescos from Masada which were truly beautiful and having seen the setting of where they were, his palace there would have been out of this world. As was his grand sarcophagus which was found in the past ten years at The Herodium near Bethlehem.

The galleries continued into Roman Times and then Islamic and Crusader periods. All of which had their fascinating moments and beautiful artifacts. By this time my feet were complaining, so I wandered back to a café at the entrance for a cold drink.

It was pretty hot by midafternoon, so I certainly didn't fancy walking back to the hotel which would have would have taken nearly an hour and was uphill. By chance, there was a taxi outside and I managed to call him and get a lift, albeit diverted around half of Jerusalem to avoid the protests and road closures. This cost me an arm and a leg. Well both arms and both legs actually.

I grabbed a burger for lunch and took it back to my room to chill out for a few hours. Around 6.30 I went back out again and took a slow wander back to the Jaffa Gate and the Old City. This was quite pleasant as I had not seen the old city at night and lit up. Hundreds of protestors with Israeli flags were still amassed by the gate, but everything seemed quite chilled and friendly. One woman was mouthing off on a megaphone, but there's always one.

I had dinner in the Armenian Quarter. It does seem quite strange that there is an Armenian quarter. You can understand the Jewish, Christian, and Muslim quarters, but supposedly the Armenians were granted their share as they were the first nation, as a whole, to accept Christianity. I had dinner at an Armenian Restaurant, called The Armenian Tavern. which was very tasty but set in a cave full of religious icons and a large grey parrot perched at the end of the bar. Am not sure if that was considered as poultry. The meal was very interesting and the main was beef in a tahini (sesame) sauce.

The reason I was in the old city at night was because I had tickets for the King David Spectacular. A light show that is held on weekdays at The Tower of David, just inside The Jaffa gate. It's not really a tower and it has nothing to do with King David either as it was a citadel built during Crusader times. They believe that the remains of Herod's Jerusalem Palace, and where Pilate would have stayed whilst in Jerusalem, are buried beneath here. This I thought was interesting as, having seen the Scala Santa in Rome, the giant staircase that nuns ascend on their knees, as they believe it was the stairs that Jesus was condemned on. It is quite clear that the beautifully polished stairs did not originate from here. Methinks Helena of Constantinople strikes again.

The light show was entertaining, and they used images of famous works of art depicting King David, to tell his life story, with the walls of the citadel as the backdrop. It only lasted 30 minutes but it was certainly worth seeing. And I would have seen more if the coachload of Mexicans hadn't spent thirty minutes deciding where to sit, only for the show to end five minutes after they sat down.

It was all a bit strange tonight, as the clocks changed for summertime. Weird because it was a Thursday, the Israelis wanted an extra hour of daylight on the sabbath, and weird because in Palestine, where I was going the following morning, the clocks didn't change at all. This meant I had to get a bus at 9.30 from Jerusalem Bus station to get to Bethlehem an hour earlier. Very weird.

6. THE SCAR OF BETHLEHEM

There are days in everyone's life that will stay with you forever and change your outlook on the world completely. Today was one of those. Although being very aware of the Palestinian Israeli issues throughout the week I had been here, today they reared their ugly side and things changed markedly.

But let's start at the beginning. I didn't get much sleep due to some sort of rave going on nearby that didn't end until around 4 a.m. And the fact that the clocks went forward meant I only had a few hours after the music stopped before the alarm went off.

Things weren't helped by the fact that the last thing I read before going to sleep the previous night was that The Garden Tomb, which I had planned to visit on Sunday, wasn't open on Sunday, therefore the only opportunity I would have to go there was first thing this morning, before catching a bus to Bethlehem, where I was meeting my guide for the day.

So, there was no time for breakfast, and I had to hotfoot it to near The Damascus Gate, where the Garden Tomb is located. This is the other "tomb" that people believe could be the tomb of Jesus. It certainly looks the part, in a serene garden, that thankfully only had one tour group in it. I spent a few minutes in the tomb before any other tourists arrived but it didn't feel right. There is also what many think is Skull Rock or Golgotha, where the crucifixion was supposed to have taken place. It fits the description from the gospel of John perfectly. Again, it does look the part. But then you read the blurb and find out who was its leading advocate. None other than General Gordon, hero of the British Empire, forever immortalized for the glorious failure of his defence of Khartoum. As with many of the self-righteous and pompous individuals who set sail from Britain in these days, their arguments tended to me more fanciful and theological, rather than scientific. This particular tomb also has a stone groove running along the ground outside it, which Gordon argued to be a slot that once housed a stone, corresponding to the biblical account of a stone being rolled over the tomb entrance to close it. Funnily enough, a large stone has now appeared a few feet outside of the tomb.

Many Evangelicals and Protestants consider this to be the tomb of Jesus. But it isn't and it is nothing more than another attraction of the Christian Disneyland that Jerusalem promotes. To confound matters, the Church or at least the Catholics, have declared that Golgotha is the burial site of Adam. And that Jesus was crucified on the exact spot. That was very considerate of The Romans wasn't it. To be fair there is a possibility that Golgotha could be a place where crucifixions took place in the 1st Century. It is outside of the city walls and high enough for public crucifixions to be seen by passersby. So, we won't rule this one out completely.

The tomb, however, does have a few fatal flaws. Archaeologists have dated the tomb to around the 8th Century BC and was part of a wider necropolis that the Church has now removed. The groove outside of the door was a water trough built by the Crusaders to allow their donkeys to drink and the next-door cistern also dates to crusader times.

Suitably convinced I had debunked this one, I bypassed the collection box and headed for the nearby bus station to catch the number 231 bus to Bethlehem.

In hindsight, this probably wasn't the best day to go to the West Bank. It was the first official day of Ramadan and hordes of Palestinians were bussing into Jerusalem to go to The Al Aqsa Mosque. Outside of the bus station was a roundabout, in the middle of which, eight very twitchy soldiers were standing, pointing their MK 47s at the bustling crowd. Hordes of Muslims were coming into the city to pray, and all had to have their papers checked. Nobody under 40 was allowed today, therefore the majority were getting turned back, put on a bus at gun point and getting angry.

I found my bus stop and waited. Only for someone to come over and say that this bus wasn't running today because they wanted everybody to come through the Bethlehem checkpoint. Fortunately, there was another bus to the checkpoint that I managed to find, but this one stopped on the Israeli side so I would have to pass through the notorious Bethlehem 300 Checkpoint.

At the time, I thought to myself that it was a good thing I was heading in the direction out of the city as the checkpoint was swamped with Palestinians trying, mostly in vain, to get out of their prison camp to go and pray.
Things were beginning to feel a lot more real and seeing women and children being threatened at gun point for just wanting to go and pray was pretty disgusting. I think that the fact that South Africa has christened Israel an apartheid state says it all. Nd the Israelis seem to be taking things a stage further.

I felt quite embarrassed that my British passport allowed me to traverse the barbed wire, turnstiles, and security checks relatively quickly. No guns pointed in my direction and no sniffer dogs snarling at my backpack. Another hundred yards across no man land, one more turnstile and I was in Palestine, where I was met by a barrage of taxi drivers looking for a fare.

My guide, Salah, was running a bit late as he had been waiting for me in the centre of Bethlehem, where the original bus was supposed to go. Thankfully, mobile phones allow you to circum navigate these kinds of issues these days.

The sheer number of people trying to head to the Temple Mount was bewildering and Salah was adamant that the majority wouldn't get further than the checkpoint. He was in his 30's and is only allowed to leave Palestine if he applies for a special pass. You cannot just turn up at the gate and say that you want to come in. Unless you have a foreign passport.

It was a relief to get away from the chaos as we walked along the Separation Wall. The Israelis put up the wall in 2002 and it stretches for 700 kilometres, annexing Palestinian Land. Around the big cities of Ramallah and Bethlehem the concrete wall is about sixty feet high, covered in barbed wire and most frighteningly has both actual manned machine gun towers, but also Guns operated by Artificial Intelligence that works on facial recognition. Basically, any Palestinian who breaks the law, in Israeli eyes, and escapes "justice", has their face programmed into these guns and if they are spotted, they are taken out. You wouldn't want to be an identical twin!

The Israelis claim that the wall is necessary to maintain security, but it seems to have two main uses. Firstly, it keeps the Palestinians locked into the west bank and secondly, whereas the city centre's have 60-foot-high concrete walls and machine gun nests, more rural parts of Palestine just get a fence. A moveable fence which illegal Israeli settlers move in order to claim more and more land. Despite the United Nations and most of the civilized world (I do not include America in this) condemning the structure, Israel ignores the criticism. In the knowledge that if push comes to shove, the USA will always back them.

The walls are covered in Graffiti, portraits of Donald Trump, Larry David, and Shireen Abu Akleh, the Palestinian Journalist for Al Jazeera, who was murdered by The Israeli Army whilst reporting live on TV.

And the most famous graffiti artist of them all, Banksy, has what I can honestly say, is the best tourist attraction I have ever been to here. The Walled Off Hotel is a functioning hotel. It has nine rooms, all of which look directly onto the Separation Wall. Its selling point is that it claims to have "the worst view of any hotel in the world. "The hotel lobby also serves as a bar and a breakfast room but is full of some amazing pieces of artwork by Banksy. Room number 3, which we were not allowed in to, supposedly has an original Banksy on the wall portraying a Palestinian and an Israeli having a pillow fight.

Pride of place in the Piano bar goes to a piece entitled The Scar of Bethlehem, which is a model of part of the wall, with the biblical family in a traditional nativity scene at its foot. A large bullet hole penetrates the wall above the scene, replacing the traditional star. Other pieces include several CCTV cameras mounted as hunting trophies, a bust of a Greek God choking on tear gas and a painting of one of the wall's guard towers being used as a giant carousel. Some may see all of this as flippant, but it does serve to bring the Palestinian story to a wider audience.

Britain got its hands on Palestine in 1917 and the piano bar is themed as a colonial outpost from those heady days. It is equipped with languid ceiling fans, leather bound couches and an air of undeserved authority.

There is a museum that tells the story of The Palestinian conflict in an adjoining room. You like to think that you know what's going on in the world, but this really brought home the craziness of the situation. As in keeping with the general tone of the Hotel, the exhibits are described as military pornography. Various displays that it was British arrogance in the drafting of the Balfour Agreement that is the root of the problem. It may as well have been the same document that split up India. You can't have an external power acting as God for people they have little regard for. It was quite difficult to see stories of Palestinians who have been subjected to abuse, torture, and death by the Israeli army.

My guide, Salah, was a passionate Palestinian who has been on many marches and demonstrations, and it sank in quite quickly that the Palestinians here are treated far worse than the blacks ever were in South Africa. I think the scariest thing I saw today, and there were many, was the automatic machine gun, perched on the wall, that uses face recognition software. If it sees somebody whom the Israeli forces deem as a criminal, it shoots to kill. Regardless of who is nearby. In the museum there were recordings of Israeli military phone calls to Palestinian households, whose land was being reclaimed by the illegal Jewish settlers. Basically, the Palestinians get a phone call or a text stating that a missile has been fired at their house. The first missile is not that big and if they survive that, they have a few minutes to run before a much larger missile is fired to demolish the house. This is followed by the two-story bulldozer and before you know it. There are new Jewish homes.

There was also a film entitled "Five Broken Cameras." The film, directed by Emad Burnat, shows the realities of life in the West Bank. When Burnat's fourth son, Gibreel, is born in 2005, the self-taught cameraman, a Palestinian villager, gets his first camera. At the same time in his village of Bil'in, the Israelis begin bulldozing village olive groves to build a barrier to separate Bil'in from the Jewish settlement Modi'in Illit. The barrier's route cuts off 60% of Bil'in farmland and the villagers resist this seizure of more of their land by the settlers.

During the next year, Burnat films this struggle, which is led by two of his best friends including his brother Iyad. At the same time, Burnat uses the camera to record the growth of his son. Very soon, these events begin to affect his family and his own life. Burnat films the army and police beating and arresting villagers and activists who come to support them. Settlers destroy Palestinian olive trees and attack Burnat when he tries to film them. The army raids the village in the middle of the night to arrest children. He, his friends, and brothers are arrested or shot; some are killed. Each camera used to document these events is shot or smashed. All five destroyed cameras are in the movie theatre.

Salah insisted that we go to the Church of the Nativity, even though I had already been. Some tour guides feel they must include everything on their itinerary, I guess. It was still full of Americans. The queue was ridiculous to see the birthplace, but Salah did point out some cool Crusader graffiti on some of the columns.

Salah also told me how petty the Church has been over the years. In 1847, the 14-pointed star, which marks the alleged spot of the birth of Jesus, was stolen. At the time, The Roman Catholics, Armenian and Greek Orthodox Churches were in residence, and all blamed each other for its loss. None of them were prepared to pay for a new one and things got so bad that the entire Church was divided between the three, foot by foot and areas are defended resolutely. Even in the grotto they all must have the same number of lanterns to prevent arguments. It really has got nothing to do with Jesus. If he did return, he would be mortified.

Unlike Sunday, The Milk Grotto was open, so I got to see that. There was a big statue of Mary on a donkey on the stairs as you entered and I suggested that they should automate it, and for 50 shekels, little kids could ride with the Baby Jesus. They clearly don't know a good business idea when it kicks them in the face here.

I don't think Salah saw it either. The Grotto is all very silly. The Catholics claim that the walls turned white when Mary breast fed Jesus and a drop fell on the floor. But as with all sour milk, it turns yellow when it goes off and the walls needed a bit of touch up. Still at least we got to see the magic milk powder for sale in the gift shop. The Church claims that if you add chalk powder and Pray to Our Lady of The Milk (I am not making this up) it will increase a woman's milk and enable them to get pregnant. Personally, I would stick to the fertility clinic, but there are rows upon rows of letters from Mothers around the world who have claimed it worked. As to whether these are genuine, I am not so sure.

We stopped to see a couple of more Banksy paintings, both of which are quite well known. One of an Israeli soldier throwing flowers rather than a tear gas grenade and another of a white dove in a bullet proof vest with an olive branch in its beak.

Our last stop in Bethlehem, well actually it was in a small village on the outskirts called Beit Sahur, was what is known as The Shepherds Fields. I remember getting in to trouble at school for singing about whilst shepherds washed their socks by night, but regardless I wanted to see where they did it. To be honest I was disappointed. There was a large font in the middle of the Church and to be honest, I had secretly been hoping for a washing machine. There was a fountain though, so maybe that was where they washed them. No sign of any sheep though.

One thing that was interesting here were the remains of some houses dating back to the second and first century BC. There was not much left overground, but all had caves underneath where families would keep their livestock. This might partly explain the nativity. In that, the chances are that there was no inn, but if most houses had these underground living facilities, it is not inconceivable that people could have been put up there.

It was quite a long drive to the next stop, and I had asked Salah to come here especially, if we had the time. In 1982, Nadim Khoury started making beer in his dorm room at Boston University. In the summer, he would return to Palestine and bring home brew kits for his father. In 1994, Nadim and his brother David returned permanently to Palestine and along with their father, began constructing a brewery next to his house in the village of Taybeh, with the blessing of the then President, Yasser Arafat. Taybeh Gold was launched in 1994 and was the Middle East's first craft beer.

By 1997, Taybeh Brewing had a franchise in Germany which allowed them to export around the world. Something they could not do from Palestine. More and more beers were added to the range and by 2005, the brewery was well known amongst craft beer connoisseurs. So much so, that they were able to hold an annual Oktoberfest, which is ongoing. It may seem strange for a brewery to be a success in an Arab country, but Taybeh is a Christian Village and by 2023, Taybeh not only have a very successful brewery, but make their own wine and have a hotel so that you don't have to drive home after sampling the wares.

I did partake in a few the brews and bought a few bottles for later. Their shop also promoted local produce such as Honey and Olive Oil. In a country that is so downtrodden, it is wonderful to see a real success story.

Unfortunately for Salah, Israel had shut the main road between Taybeh and Ramallah for reasons only known to themselves. This meant we had a rather long detour to get to the Palestinian capitol. As was the case in Bethlehem, the city was surrounded by a large concrete wall and snipers and machine gunners watched our every move. We walked along a stretch of the wall and saw empty Molotov cocktails burned out on the ground. The black marks on the wall showed where they had landed. Very few tourists get to Ramallah. My Israeli guide from Tuesday said I was insane to come here, but I don't see it that way. Most Israeli's view Palestine as a dangerous ghetto, which it most certainly isn't. But this is what is portrayed in their media, so they believe it. As I have said before, I felt a lot safer here than I did walking around parts of Egypt. And when you consider how many people are shot in America and what some of their cities have become, whilst on this day, Paris was on fire due to riots. That's where I wouldn't feel safe.

We got back in the car and drove through the Qaddura refugee camp. We often hear the term "Palestinian refugee camps" casually thrown around in any discussion of the Israeli/Palestinian situation… To me a "camp" is a temporary place with tents. And these refugee camps once did have tents fifty years ago. But these camps are no longer camps in the traditional sense. The Palestinian refugee camps are, for the most part, indistinguishable from a typical neighborhood in the areas where they are found. The "camps" have been in place for decades in most instances. They have multi-story permanent structures now along with paved streets, electricity and running water. But these people were forcibly removed from their homes when Israel was divided in 1948 and nobody has ever tried to rehouse them. In many cases, refugees can see their former homes and land being farmed by illegal Israeli settlers, over the partition wall. There is nothing they can do about it. They are not allowed passports to go anywhere else, so they have to live in these shanty towns.

Some of the Palestinian refugee camps have foreign sponsors that paid for the construction of the buildings and the paving of the streets. Down the road from the Qaddura is a camp that was sponsored by the late Saddam Hussein. A large marble block engraved with his image rests at the entrance of the camp and Saddam Hussein murals abound. Many Palestinians, not just those down the road, actually have quite fond memories of Saddam for having launched Scud missiles at Tel Aviv during the 1991 Gulf War.

On the edge of Qaddura Camp is Raffaele Ciriello Street. The street is named for a freelance Italian photographer, killed on March 13th, 2002, after being shot six times in the torso by the machine gun of an Israeli tank while he was covering the Israeli invasion of Ramallah during the Second Intifada.

To be honest, there are parts of Ramallah that are quite pleasant. We went to the Yasser Arafat Mausoleum and Museum which was very educational and moving. It is criminal that in the UK, you can't even discuss this without being shouted down as an anti semite or holocaust denier by people who have never been here.

The mausoleum is in a glass building surrounded by fountains, in front of the museum. Because Israel opposed Arafat's wish to be buried in Jerusalem, the Mausoleum was built on water to express its impermanence and is meant to be moved in the future to fulfill his wish. The museum was Arafat's headquarters when The Israeli Army stormed it in 2002. A siege continued for two years during which time the Israeli military fired artillery bombs and destroyed most of the compound, which houses the security institutions of the Palestinian Authority. The displays include his old office and bedroom. Arafat's life is portrayed in a moving way with exhibits including, his Nobel peace prize, his famous headscarf and the toxicology reports from Paris that showed he was poisoned before his death in 2004.

Unfortunately for Palestine, Arafat's successor Mahammad Abbas, seems to bow down to Israeli pressure far too easily and is seen by many, including Salah, my guide, as an Israeli asset.

There was one last stop in Ramallah which was a world-famous ice cream factory. It was a hot day, so why not. Rukabs has been making ice cream for 80 years and was founded by Sarah Rukab in the 1930's, when things were a little more pleasant here.

Supposedly people flock from all over Palestine to come to Rukabs which is still a family business. I was confronted with well over 100 flavours and quite frankly it was too much. I plumped for a dollop of Mars bar flavour and must report it was quite tasty.
The plan from here was to drive back to Bethlehem, which was about 90 minutes away, and I would catch the bus or get a taxi back to Jerusalem on the other side of Checkpoint 300. We got back to Bethlehem around 5.30 and the number of people returning from Jerusalem was in the hundreds, if not the thousands. Salah and I walked to the gate but were turned back by an Israeli soldier wielding a gun. The gate was shut, and nobody could leave Bethlehem regardless of whether you were a tourist or a local.

There was a possibility that they might have opened it at eight o'clock if the crowds had subsided. Not that it would, because there would be four hours' worth of people wanting to get back to Israel. The soldiers didn't care, in fact they seemed to be enjoying the misery they were causing. Salah offered to put me up for the night, but I explained that I had to get back as I had a tour to pick me up at 5.30 a.m. the following morning. He couldn't drive me back as he would get stopped at any of the other checkpoints and didn't have a pass to go to Jerusalem. The 231 bus was still not going anywhere and the taxi drivers in Bethlehem can't travel outside of Palestine.

And to make matters worse, the sun was going down on the Sabbath, which meant Jewish taxi drivers stopped working for 24 hours and any Muslim ones would be heading for their Ramadan Iftar meal, having fasted all day. Salah made several phone calls and seemed to get turned down by everybody. Finally, he phoned a friend who had the right pass to enter Israel and for a rather hefty sum of cash, I managed to get a lift back to the hotel. If the taxi ride from the museum on the previous day had cost two arms and two legs, this one included kidneys too.

Back in Jerusalem, everything was shut for the Sabbath, but I did find one bar that did a decent steak and chips and had beer. But it was back for an early night at night as my last full day tomorrow and I had to be up before dawn. Thankfully this time I was staying in Israel and there would be no checkpoints.

7. HOLY FISH

No rest for the wicked, as after yesterday's shenanigans, I had to up before dawn to go and catch a coach tour to Nazareth and the Sea of Galilee. I'm not sure which I was dreading more. Getting up before five in the morning or having to sit on a bus all day with a load of loud American Christians.

As my hotel wasn't accessible by a big coach and down an alleyway, I had to walk five minutes, in the rain, to The David Boutique Hotel. I noticed a sign whilst walking to the coach stop that advertised the Museum of Taxes. Who on earth would want to go there! I won't be rushing there tomorrow that's for sure. There were a few others waiting and naturally the bus was half an hour late. When we were finally picked up, a minibus rather than a full-blown coach turned up and I rather stupidly thought that there wouldn't be as many Americans as I had dreaded. Unfortunately, this was just a shuttle bus to another hotel, where a bigger bus, full of hallelujah shouting Yanks were already getting worked up. To make matters worse, we were rendezvousing with another bus that was leaving Tel Aviv with even more of them, at a service station further down the road.

I found a seat shut my eyes and went to sleep, hoping that when I woke up our trans-Atlantic friends had calmed down a bit. Our guide woke everybody up at a truck stop, just north of Tel Aviv where we could go and get a cup of coffee and a croissant. It was all change here again, as the two coaches were now split between those who spoke English and those who preferred Spanish. Thankfully I could stay on the same bus and sat back and watched the chaos unfold with about fifty Americans unable to follow instructions and getting lost. There were two buses. How difficult could it be? Greatest nation in the world? I think not.

We left the truck stop and continued North. Our Guide pointed out a small, green mound to the left of the bus. Evidently this was The Valley of Megiddo. There were a few sheep grazing there, totally unaware of what their future has in store for them if The Christians, have got it right and this really is the site for Armageddon. I always find it strange that there was a major battle here in 1918, where the British finally routed The Ottoman Empire. But maybe they blinked and missed that.

As we approached Nazareth, our Guide pointed out two hills, although he declared them to be mountains. To the right of the bus was a dome-like hill that was known as Mount Tabor. It is only 420 metres high (200 metres lower than Jerusalem!) and that in my mind does qualify as a mountain. It is less than a third of Ben Nevis! According to our guide, it has throughout history been a place of mystique and atmosphere, where humanity has sought contact with the divine. Which basically when you break it down means that because it looks like a large breast, people have always been drawn to it.

Tradition has it that this was the place where the divine incarnation of Christ appeared to his disciples. The Bible does not actually name the place this happened, but good old Helena on her tour, decided this was the spot and the Church have stuck doggedly to the story and built a Church with collection boxes on the summit. The problem is that, even if you follow the New Testament stories, the disciples were nowhere near here at this time and to make matters worse, in the 1st Century, there was a Hasmonean Fort built on the summit. These days there is a Church up there that dates to the 17th Century.

The other hill, on the left side of the bus, is known as Mount Precipice and is even less of a mountain than Mount tabor, coming in at a measly 395 metres. According to the Gospel of Luke, the people of Nazareth, not accepting Jesus as the Messiah tried to push him from the mountain, but "he passed through the midst of them and went away." As per usual, there was no record of this place before the 4th century when suddenly it became the place where Jesus was almost executed. In 2009 The Pope held a sermon here but unfortunately nobody tried to throw him over the edge.

Finally, we arrived in Nazareth and surprise, surprise, we were taken straight into a gift shop for half an hour. This is the big problem with these large coach tours, they do deals with various outlets and bring customers to the shops. I did take advantage of the lavatory, but that was about the extent of it. But loads of the God botherers were buying crosses and other things that they were told would be blessed when we finally got to The Church of The Annunciation.

Today, Nazareth is the largest Arab city in Israel, but there is no evidence it even existed at the alleged time of Jesus. Nazareth is not mentioned in The Old Testament or The Jewish Talmud. Josephus Flavius who wrote an extensive First Century History of the Jews, mentions 63 towns in the Galilee area, but does not mention Nazareth and there is no evidence that early Christians even tried to find it, unlike other towns in the area. You would have thought that the town where Jesus was brought up and home to Mary and Joseph, would be high up on the list of pilgrimage spots, but there is absolutely no evidence for this. The archaeological evidence seems to suggest that it was first inhabited at some point between the Jewish Revolt in 66 AD and the Bar Kochba Rebellion of 132 AD.

So why would this be? I have already touched on this in that Jesus was known as A Nazarene or a Nazorite. This had absolutely nothing to do with Nazareth. As with most issues with The New Testament, the problems are in the translation. The Nazorites were a revolutionary Jewish sect, closely aligned to The Essenes of Qumran, hell bent on driving foreigners out of Judea and restoring the rule of The First Temple. The failure of the 68 AD Jewish Revolt and the subsequent airbrushing of the details from the Roman History books meant that by the time of the Third and Fourth Century, Helena and her travelling band of God Botherers translated Jesus the Nazarene as to meaning Jesus of Nazareth, which by now was an established city.

This is not to say that Jesus was not in Galilee area. He almost certainly was. Just not in Nazareth. In the 1st Century, the whole area of Galilee was independent from Judea and ruled by Herod's son, Agrippa. As a result, it attracted a great swathe of revolutionaries, militants and supposed miracle workers, of which more anon. It was the ideal place to gather an army for an uprising, which was why Jesus was almost likely to have been here. Eventually, our guide managed to extract all the group out of the gift shop, clutching their cheap crappy crosses, so that hopefully some bloke in a cassock would cross for them for a hefty donation.

The lamp shade shaped dome of The Church of The Annunciation towered down from the end of the street. It was a five-minute walk to the entrance and as we arrived, there seemed to be a lot of people fussing around and singing. Pretty normal for a church I suppose but it was actually Annunciation Day. I am surprised that Women's Rights movements have never had an issue with this. If any other woman woke up and was told they were pregnant, they would call the police and charge someone with assault. But it seems fine as it was God? Not much of an example to set really. More importantly, it meant it was exactly nine months to Christmas, because Jesus had to have the perfect nine-month pregnancy!

For once, Helena of Constantinople is not responsible for this Church. She founded a different church which is a few hundred yards away. The Greek Orthodox church still recognize Helena's original construction, which is very similar in structure to The Church of The Nativity in Bethlehem.

The Catholics however jumped ship and built their own Church over what they claimed were the remains of Mary's house. But it can't have been because Nazareth didn't exist at the time. But anyway, I digress. The current church is very modern and dates from only 1969. The Upper Basilica is modern, but the sunken area has a dimly lit grotto which is claimed to be the house of Mary. Believers file past, crossing themselves and crying, but if they only read the sign on the wall, all they were bowing to were the remains of a 4th Century Byzantine Church. It states this clearly on the wall. It's all a bit tasteless really. Would you really want to see where you were conceived? The Catholics were in full operation here. There were confessions available in any language, for the right price and for those wanting their cheap crappy crosses blessed, there was a cheap crappy priest who was doing so for money in what was a production line.

Don't get me wrong, I have no problem with people making money and The Roman Catholic Church have been doing so for years. They found a good business venture in the 4th century and are still milking it dry. But I think the sheer front of it all left a bit of a sour taste in the mouth here.

The Israeli Antiquities Authority found, what they claim to be, a 1st Century house here in 2009 and of course, the Church not being able to turn down such a golden egg, immediately said it was the house Jesus grew up in. Mary obviously moved a few yards from the house she conceived the baby in.

But as previously explained, the house dates to the latter part of the 1st century and goes against the story they are trying to sell. Just when you think things can't get any sillier, we went to the adjacent Church, which is called The Basilica of Saint Joseph, dedicated to the man who stopped Mary being stoned to death by marrying an unmarried Mother. The Church insists that Joseph's carpentry workshop was next door to where Mary got pregnant. The church is also known as the church of the Nutrition and somewhat creatively, The Church of Joseph's Workshop. When it was built in 1914, on top of an old Crusader era church, its tall tower would have stood out, but today it is rather overshadowed by The Church of The Annunciation.

A stairway in the church descends to a crypt where caverns can be seen through a grille in the floor. Seven further steps lead to a 2-metre square basin or pit with a black-and-white mosaic floor. This is believed to have been a pre-Constantinian Christian baptistry, perhaps used as early as the 1st century.

Beside the basin, a flight of rough steps leads down to a narrow passage which, after turning 180 degrees, opens into an underground chamber 2 metres high. This, the Church claims, are the remains of Joseph's workshop. Unfortunately for the Church, archaeologists did a dig here and did not discover evidence of badly made wooden chairs, rather that in fact it did date to the 1st Century but was in fact the remains of a sewer. Therefore, anything of Joseph's that was ever here but would have been of a more organic nature than made of wood.

The Americans seemed quite impressed by all of this and were more than happy to see the name of a building and ignore everything that has been written about it. The God Botherers were happy and quoting verses from the Bible and staring skywards. I looked down, shook my head in disbelief and walked back to the bus.

Our next stop was Magdala, the alleged home of Mary Magdalene, however this was purely a lunch stop rather than a sightseeing one. We had four choices for lunch, chicken, beef kebab, sea bass fillet, or a whole Tilapia, freshly caught from The Sea of Galilee. This was sold as the fish that Saint Peter would have caught in the day, which got the masses interested. I ordered the whole fish, which with the free side salad was quite pleasant.

However, one Japanese guy got over excited. The waiters brought out the chicken and the beef first. Then he brought out the sea bass fillets. But the Jap couldn't contain himself and started shouting "Hory Fish, Hory Fish" The waiter handed him the sea bass and the Jap shouted, "This not Hory Fish" "Where Hory Fish." Finally, he got his Tilapia, and he hated it.

After lunch, we passed The Mount of Beatitudes, where Jesus supposedly preached his sermon on the mount. But we didn't go there because the afternoon was all about miracles.

We stopped in Tabgha at The Church of The Multiplication, where Jesus is said to have fed the five thousand with two loaves and four fishes. Once again, we have a modern Church built on top of a 4th Century one that was founded by Helena of Constantinople. Some of the original Byzantine mosaics are quite beautiful and naturally have a fishy theme. But the floor is covered with images of peacocks, cranes, cormorants, herons, doves, geese, ducks, a flamingo and a swan, as well as snakes, lotus flowers and oleanders. By the altar is a mosaic of two "Hory Fish" and four loaves. Under the alter is the rock on which it is believed Jesus placed the loaves and fish when he blessed them.

Illegal Jewish Settlers attempted to burn down the adjacent monastery in 2015 and as a result security here is quite tight.
So, did the miracles of Jesus really happen? Probably not in the literal sense. I can be pedantic here and state that "miracle" is a post enlightenment word, therefore nobody in the time of Jesus would have seen it as such. A miracle is a violation of the physical laws governing the universe. Since no one in the first century, including Jesus, could conceive of physical laws governing the universe, how could anyone, Jesus included, imagine violations of those laws? They couldn't.

One of the major problems with this one is that Tabgha is very tiny. 5000 people would struggle to assemble here today. In the first Century, the population would have been no more than 1500. In fact, in 2019, Israeli archaeologists unearthed another Byzantine Church at the village of Hippos, on the Southeastern Shore of the Sea of Galilee, and many are now saying that there is far more evidence that Jesus was there rather than in Tabgha.

The problem we have is that for nearly four hundred years, nobody really cared about any of this. The Western Roman Empire had adopted Christianity, but had Constantine not decided to jump camps when he did and make Christianity the religion of The Eastern Empire too, the whole thing would have probably fizzled out with a whimper. But when you turn up 350 years later and pretend to find everything that is referred to in a book, science goes out of the window and your whole story is filled with cracks and holes. There is no way that anyone can claim that Jesus was in Tabgha. There is no physical evidence and certainly not 5000 fish skeletons. In my view, this was an attempt by the Bible writers to make Jesus perform a feeding miracle, like the prophets Moses, Elisha, and Elijah. Other miracles are far easier to debunk. In the gift shop earlier, I had seen bottles of wine from Cana, where Jesus is said to have tuned water into wine. In the 4th Century, this may have seemed a miracle, but in the first century it was a common party trick at well to do weddings. I have already mentioned the remarkable 1st Century inventor, Hero of Alexandria, who had created the amazing tomb of Helena of Adiabene.

In my view, the mother of Jesus. He invented an amazing trick jug that could serve wine, water, or watered-down wine. His original drawings for these are easily found on Google. My guess is that Jesus picked one of these up in Alexandria, or even had Hero bring one over to Judea.

My favourite miracle is the so-called miracle of the swine, where Jesus casts demons out of a man into a herd of 2000 pigs who then turn full lemming and jump off a cliff into the sea and drowning.

According to the Gospel of Mark, this took place in the town of Gadara, which is an actual place. Unfortunately, it is 7 miles from The Sea of Galilee and at an elevation of 1200 feet. To reach the sea, the pigs would have had to descend into the ravine of the Yarmuk River, cross the major tributary of The Jordan River and scale The Golan Heights. How many people cursed Jesus that day when 2000 demonic pigs stampeded through their land.

The fact is that Galilee was awash with Healers and Miracle Workers, some more famous than Jesus. One of the most famous was a man called Hanina Ben Dosa, who still has worshippers in the Jewish world today and was claimed to be immortal amongst the mystics during the 1st Century. Unlike Jesus, many of Ben Dosa's miracles are recorded in The Talmud and Jewish children still read books about his life. His healing power was legendary and was even called upon by Gamaliel to heal his son. Other miracles include making a candle full of vinegar burn all night and turning a table leg into solid gold. He too multiplied bread for the poor.

The other famous 1st century miracle worker from Galilee was Honi the Circle Maker. Again, unlike Jesus, he is mentioned in The Talmud. Honi's specialty was controlling the weather. He would draw a circle in the sand and pray to God for rain, telling the Almighty he would not budge from the circle until it started to get wet. On one occasion he drew his circle and prayed, and within minutes torrential rain was lashing down so much that Jerusalem flooded, and the people had to climb The Temple Mount to get away from it. But Honi drew another circle and the rain stopped.

Now I am not saying that the miracles of Ben Dosa and Honi are any more believable than those of Jesus. But both are mentioned in Historical documents, unlike Jesus. And what it does show I that as much as The Church would like to portray Jesus as being unique and exceptional. This was far from the case and others were "performing" miracles that were just as believable.

I felt that I was on a roll with my business ideas out here and for Tabgha it seemed quite obvious that they needed a Fish and Chip Shop outside the church. But not any old chip shop, this one should have a wheel that customers could spin with the chance of winning unlimited fish for their entire group. If they ever do a Biblical Dragons Den, I'll be there in a shot.

Now I have probably been quite unfair to Jesus in this book. It is not really him that I have an issue with, it is the people who came a few hundred years later and transformed him into something he wasn't. Jesus was certainly in the Galilee region during the First Century, and almost certainly lived in Capernaum, our final stop, for a short period.

Capernaum is on the banks of Galilee, which to be fair should be referred to as Lake Tiberias as it is no bigger than Lake Windermere. The Sea/Lake was very pretty, with The Golan Heights as a backdrop and there were some first century remains, including a synagogue that Jesus would have frequented if he did live here and the alleged House of Peter, which is a first century fisherman's house, that now has a church on top of it. For once I will put my neck out and say that finally, I had found somewhere where the real Jesus had frequented.

Whether he delivered sermons or argued with rabbis in the synagogue is irrelevant. As is Peter's house. It is definitely a 1st century fisherman's house. There is absolutely no way of confirming whether it belonged to peter or as to whether Jesus ever slept there. But it is almost certain that he would have walked on the very cobbles that I was walking on and had a similar view over Lake Tiberias (Sea of Galilee) that I had on this afternoon.

This was quite a moving moment in a way, albeit maybe not as moving as it was for the God botherers. I sat by the water, watching a fishing boat cast its nets, and felt that after a week of seeing some of the most contrived sites and listening to unbelievable myths, I had found the real Jesus in Capernaum. The most misunderstood man in history who wanted to free his country from Roman Rule, only to unwittingly become the figurehead of the Holy Roman Empire for the next 2000 years. I sat and pondered as to whether he had sat in this very spot, wondering what life had in store for him.

I could have sat pondering for a while longer, but the Americans had had their pictures taken in Peter's House and in the Synagogue, so it was back to the bus. The final stop of the day was another baptism site on The Jordan River, but unlike the one I had seen near Qumran, this was a commercialized one. There is no proof that John the Baptist or Jesus ever set foot in Yardenit. But that has never stopped them in the past.

This was just so blatant that it was fleecing people. There were charges for being Baptised, charges for robes, charges for showers, it was a total money-making machine, including the world's largest Christian Gift Shop. A couple of people took the plunge, but I really wasn't interested, and sat with an ice lolly until I could get back on the bus.

And that was when the real fun started. There were two tours. One in English and one in Spanish. But after the baptisms, one bus would return to Jerusalem and the other to Tel Aviv. It was very simple. The destinations were written on the front of the bus, and you needed to get on the right one. All the English-speaking people seemed to be fine, but the Latin Americans were an absolute nightmare. Walking on and off both buses with no idea what was going on. Six of them were over half an hour late and a seventh is still there as far as I know. Two and a half hours in a cab back to Jerusalem would be expensive, but all they had to do was tell the time and get on the right bus. It got that chaotic that I thought next time, if there is an option to book a tour with cats and dogs, I will go for that because they are better behaved than the Hispanics. Two Italian girls on our bus had arranged to be dropped off at The Jordanian Border and had transport from there. Unfortunately, due to the delays caused by the Spanish speaking contingent, the border had shut for the night by the time we got there. The Italians then started yelling at the Spanish and vice versa. The two Italians now had to arrange a further nights' accommodation in Jerusalem and hope to get to Jordan tomorrow.

It was well after 7 when I was dropped off and most of The Spanish were still onboard, clueless as to where they should disembark. They are probably still wandering aimlessly around Jerusalem. The weekends here are weird. Everything is shut. No restaurants, no buses, no trams, no shops. One or two places are open, and I managed to find somewhere to buy a pizza tonight and bring it back to my room. Not quite the last night in Jerusalem meal I had envisaged.

The following morning, I woke up around eight and had a couple of hours to potter around, pack my case and then leave my luggage downstairs for a few hours, as my flight home was not until around 10 p.m.

It was a pleasant stroll back to the old city and the Jaffa Gate. In fact, it was nice to see people and public transport again after they had disappeared for a day and a half. I wandered through the maze of markets and went back to The Western Wall Plaza.

I had booked a couple of tours here which I had been looking forward to. Firstly, there was a virtual reality experience called "A Look In The Past." You walk down a dank alley, into a dark room and I began to hope that this wasn't it. I have always been slightly wary of virtual reality experiences as when there was the 3D cinema phase, they never quite got it right for people with glasses. I remember at Universal Studios in Los Angeles, there was a Hitchcock 3D experience. Everybody donned their special glasses and were terrified as birds seemingly came through the screen and started attacking them. It was a little less terrifying when all you see is a 3D blur.

I sat in a rather comfy leather chair and a man approached me with a large headset. I was told to keep my glasses on and put the headset on over the top. Great, I thought, they have finally solved the problem for glasses wearers.

You are then transported back 2000 years to the days of The Second Temple. Starting outside on the steps, before moving all the way through to the Holy of Holies. It was remarkable. You could move your head and even look behind you and you got a full 360-degree experience with lifelike people and sounds within the temple. I was really enjoying it before the mist started to descend. They may well have rectified the issues from the 3D days, but fully enclosing your glasses in a warm environment tends only to have one result. They mist up. You can't take them off as they are enclosed within the headset, so as a result things got foggier and foggier until we had a real pea souper in the Holy of Holies. Back to the drawing board then!

The second tour I had booked was through the tunnels that are below the current Western Wall. Much of what you see would have been above ground 2,000 years ago, and the tour stretches for about 300 metres along the Northeastern Wall. As you walk through the Western Wall Tunnel, what is known as the master course of stones can be seen. These are some of the first rows of cut stones that support the Temple Mount Western Wall. The largest stone found in the Western Wall measures 44 ft. in length (longer than a bus). It's almost 12 ft. high and its width is 14 ft. It weighs over 600 tons (equivalent to 200 elephants, or ten tanks, or two 747 jumbo jets, including the people and their luggage). There is no machine big enough today to lift it. It was carved outside the city and then placed here. The stones were carved and placed with such precision that not even a credit card will fit between the joints. By comparison, the largest stones in the Egyptian Pyramids are 15 tons. I have seen some giant monoliths around the world, but this one is by far the biggest. It defies logic as to how it could have been positioned.

About halfway along you come to what is called Warren's Gate. This is the closest place along the Western Wall to where the temple used to be. It is, therefore, according to the Jews, the holiest place in the Western Wall. Just 200 ft. towards the east is where the temple was originally located.

The bedrock of the Western Wall of the Temple Mount can be seen as well. The masons who laid the great stones to build the Western Wall chiseled the bedrock of the mountain to make them look like they were stones, but in reality, they are the bedrock of the mountain upon which the Western Wall rests.

You walk along a 2000-year-old street with its original tiles and reach a Hasmonean aqueduct built over 2,200 years ago. The walk ends at The Struthion Pool, where water was stored for use in the city of Jerusalem. Well, I say the tour ends. The reality is that you have to turn around and retrace your steps to exit in the same place as you came in.

After a quick coffee, I started to stroll back along The Cardo in the direction of The Jaffa Gate. From here it was back down Jaffa Street and past my hotel, finally ending up at the Mahane Yehuda Market.

After one last beer at Beer Bazaar, the best bar in Jerusalem, I strolled around the market for an hour and then sat down at the Tsar David Smokehouse for a smoked beef brisket sandwich and onion rings, which was delicious.

I got back to the hotel lobby around 4 o'clock and within an hour my pre-booked taxi had turned up to take me back to Ben Gurion Airport in Tel Aviv. The airport and check-in procedure seemed extremely chaotic. Especially boarding where the clerks at the gate couldn't seem to handle more than one person at a time. If a group of three or perish the thought, five, turned up there was confusion and chaos, mixing up passports and being unable to match them to the relevant boarding pass. By the time we got on the plane, things were already running late and were about to get worse.

One Brazilian woman refused to board through the front door of the plane, the only one that was open, as her seat was near the back. Then a group of orthodox Jews got on and couldn't find anywhere to put their luggage as they had left boarding to the last minute. They kept wandering up and down the aisle checking overhead lockers for space, seemingly expecting God to part the other hand luggage so that they could get theirs in. The cabin crew were getting angrier and angrier, trying to explain to these people that if we didn't take off in the next 15 minutes, we would lose our air traffic control spot and be forced to sit on the ground for a further 3 hours. It got so bad that the captain had to speak over the intercom, ordering them to sit down or else he would have them thrown off the plane.

Finally, we got away and what was a four-hour inbound flight was a five-hour return flight due to headwinds. It was well past 2 in the morning when we got back to Gatwick, which meant that it was empty and easy to get through passport control. Unfortunately, it was so empty that when my luggage never showed up (again!) There was nobody from the airline or baggage company working, so I could not file a missing luggage report. I always feel that I leave part of me behind in the countries I travel to and in this instance I did. My suitcase had an extra three weeks break in Poland and Turkey before coming home!

EPILOGUE

This trip was a bit like my visits to Egypt, in that I had read so much about the history, the myths and geography of Israel and Palestine that I would never be happy if I hadn't seen things for my own eyes.

I am not sure what I was hoping to find. My friend who I have weekly theological discussions with is so adamant that Jesus exists and will come and save us all from ourselves, that maybe I wanted to see if I could find any trace of fact in the Biblical tales. Maybe then I could find a safe place to snuggle up in and let the fools who run the world get on with it, in the knowledge that it would be fine in the end. But I didn't.

I realized that The Church and religion are not on the same page years ago. I am fine with religion; it is a personal choice, and everybody should be entitled to that. But once you are told what to believe in by someone preaching at you, it becomes control. If God gave us freedom of choice, he would never condone stoning, burning, shunning, torturing or beheading people who think differently.

Jerusalem and The Holy Land is the very beating heart of all three Abrahamic religions. I went to Holy Sites from all three of them and the contrast between the three is quite stark. I feel a lot more respect for Judaism than I previously did. Do I think that God really promised the area to The Israelites? No. But most of their prophets and even miracle workers and Holy men from thousands of years ago, can be proven to have existed. There is a grey area with the time of David and Moses, and I think the Egyptian influence here is maybe a little more than they would care to admit, but the stories pan out. But they stick to the story and the Torah and Talmud have not changed for millennia.

As for the Muslims, the fact they ultimately believe in the same God as the Jews (El, Allah) certainly helps their cause. I would go as far as to say that their current form of worship is as near as possible that we could get in the modern world to the Atenism and First temple Judaism. Mohammad was certainly a real person. They regard Jesus as a great warrior and prophet rather than the Son of God and they too have not amended the Quran since the 4th century.

There are of course the nagging rumours, that the Western Roman Empire, were behind the rise of Mohammad and that it was all a ploy to destroy the power of Constantinople which was trying to establish its own Orthodox version of Christianity. Maybe a conspiracy theory too far, but it does sort of make sense. Unlike the miraculous stories of Mohammad in the Quran.

Then there is Christianity. Somehow, through the brilliance of Saul/Paul and the Evangelists of the first couple of centuries, completely reinvented Jesus from the "Son of Man" into "The Son of God". And perhaps most remarkable of all, completely ditched the God that Jesus devoutly followed and wanted to restore to Judea and promoting Jesus himself into being God himself. Unlike the other two main religions, the Christian Bible can be rewritten at will. If the world goes gay, we can have gay priests, if you like a bacon sandwich, you can eat pork again, you don't want to be circumcised, not a problem. Come one, come all and please give generously.

The problem was compounded in the Fourth century when Constantine wanted to convert The Roman Empire. The real issue here was that as a Roman Emperor, he was seen as a God. He could not bow down to a mere human, therefore Jesus needed to be promoted, whether it made sense or not. And when The Temple of Ephesus started complaining that they would not be able to sell little statues of the Goddess Artemis, the Virgin Mary was promoted too and the statue makers could continue to sell idols, giving a tithe to Rome. This is the crux of the matter. Neither Judaism nor Islam allowed idol worship. The Roman World was full of it and there were too many people making money out of it.

This is the same position that Akhenaten found himself in in Egypt with The Priests of Thebes who were more concerned about money making and inventing more Gods, rather than praying to God.

In a way this was the ultimate victory for The Theban Priests. Despite the Atenists leaving Egypt and establishing a state where the worship of God was paramount, in the end they, with a little help from Rome, invented the ultimate idol worshipping religion.

So, when Helena of Constantinople was sent to Judea by Constantine to find these "Holy Sites", authenticity was not really an issue and as a result, 1600 year later, we have what is a Christian Disneyland, attracting worshippers from around the globe, to spend a load of money and buy trinkets that makes them feel they are closer to their chosen God man.

I find it sad that the real story is probably more heroic than the fictional one. Here was a man, heir to the throne of three great Empires, raising a rebellion against the greatest Empire the world has ever known that could have resulted in the peaceful coexistence of the then known world. But he lost, his cause was misconstrued, and he was transformed into something he never was or would have wanted to be.

The world is truly mad, and seemingly has been for a very long time.

Within weeks of my return, The Israeli Army had stormed the Al Aqsa Mosque during Ramadan and arrested Orthodox Christians at The Church of the Holy Sepulchre during Easter Celebrations.

The other major lesson I learned on this trip was that Jews and Israelis are not the same thing. The Jewish faith is perfectly fine and peaceful. In fact, it is probably the most "laissez faire" religion of them all. The problem is that the current group of people occupying the land are arrogant and dangerous. The tribes of Israel are long dead and only a very tiny minority of the current inhabitants could trace their DNA back to Biblical times. 80% of the current population are Ashkenazi Jews. These originated from Northern and Eastern Europe and scientists have shown that they are descendants of Iranian and Greek people who converted to Judaism rather than convert to Islam in the 4th Century.

At the end of the day, murder is murder and what happened to Jewish people, regardless of when they converted in Pogroms or Holocausts is horrific. But these people are as far removed from the children of Israel as I am.

It is the arrogant self-belief of these people that is causing the issues in Israel. Despite their genetics, they still believe that they are chosen by God and can do what they want to any other group because "God" says it is fine. And the fact that most of their racist bile is aimed at Muslims, who share the same God, makes it worse.

Jerusalem was a very safe city to walk around and is perfectly fine if you keep the blinkers on. But when you notice that there are no black people because those who came here were sterilized, that Muslims have been made homeless and are imprisoned behind a 60 foot wall with facial recognition sniper guns aimed at them and now even Christian Churches are being attacked, you have to conclude that the State of Israel has become a pariah and no amount of shouting anti semite at people who criticize it, is going to change the hard facts.

But the abiding feeling I have after this trip is not for any particular religion or country, but for the one man named Jesus. We will never know what he would have been like as a King or as to whether the world would have been a better place, had he defeated the power of Rome. In a way, I do put him up there with Moses as a prophet. There is no coincidence that there is a well, that still stands today in Egypt, next to what was The Temple of Heliopolis, dedicated to The Holy Family. It is likely that Jesus learned the ancient secrets and rituals of Egypt there.

And whereas Pharoah Akhenaten tried to restore the monotheistic religion to Egypt in the 14th Century BC, because of the excesses of The Theban Cults and Priests, leading to the Exodus of the Israelites, was Jesus not doing exactly the same?

Roman Judea was a mix of Roman and Greek Gods, plus a form of Judaism that was very different to what had come out of Egypt. Whilst in Babylon, the Jews had picked many Mesopotamian influences and once again, human interference had tainted the true nature of God as he saw it.

At the end of the day, if you believe that a book is the word of God. Why do lesser men need to keep changing it for their own benefit. If your God didn't get the book right in the first place, he is fallible.

The fact that he lost his battle and as a result things got worse is maybe not that relevant. But maybe what we should all learn from this is that every 1500 years or so religion needs a reset and a reality check, before things get totally out of control.

We are overdue!

BIBLIOGRAPHY

Due to some of the claims I have made in this book, I think it is only right to add a brief bibliography to back up my findings.

- Amen Maat Ra	The Roman Illusion Vols 1-3 2014
- Joseph Atwell	Caesars Messiah 2005
- Riaan Booysen	Thera and Exodus 2012
- Bart Ehrman	Jesus Interrupted 2010
- Alvar Ellegard	Jesus One Hundred Years Before Christ 1999
- Ralph Ellis	Jesus Last Of The Pharaohs 1998
- Ralph Ellis	Tempest and Exodus 2000
- Ralph Ellis	Solomon Pharaoh Of Egypt 2002
- Ralph Ellis	From Cleopatra to Christ 2006
- Ralph Ellis	King Jesus 2008
- Robert Feather	The Copper Scroll Decoded 1999
- Robert Feather	The Mystery Of The Copper Scroll Of Qumran 2003
- Robert Feather	The Secret Initiation of Jesus at Qumran 2005
- Kersey Graves	The Worlds 16 Crucified Saviours 1875
- Gary Greenberg	The Moses Mystery 2008
- Erik Hornung	Akhenaten and The Religion of Light 1999
- Kenneth Humphreys	Jesus Never Existed 2005
- Simcha Jocobovic The Naked Archaeologist TV Series 2005-2010
- Johanne Joan	The Ancient Gospel Of The Essenes And Its Falsification 2020
- Derek Lambert	Mythvision Podcast YouTube 2019-
- Ted Loukes	Moses and Akhenaten Brothers In Alms 2015
- Ahmed Osman	The Hebrew Pharaohs of Egypt 1987
- Ahmed Osman	Moses and Akhenaten 2002
- Ahmed Osman	The Egyptian Origins of King David 2019
- John Parsons	Our Sun God 2007
- Jonathon Perrin	The Pharaoh Behind The Festivals 2020
- Graham Phillips	Atlantis and The Plagues of Egypt 1998
- Graham Phillips	The Moses Legacy 2003
- Donald Redford	Egypt, Canaan and Israel In Ancient Times 1992
- Charles River	Heliopolis 2015
- Dirk Scroeder	Amarna And The Biblical Exodus 2016
- Francesca Stavrakopoulou God An Anatomy 2022
- James Valliant	Creating Christ 2018
- Michael Wise	The First Messiah 1999

RIDING THE DIRTY DOG

UNITED STATES OF AMERICA AND CANADA 1991

1. Foreword   520
2. Burgess Hill   521
3. New York   522
4. Toronto   531
5. Bel Air (Baltimore)   536
6. Orlando   545
7. Saint Petersburg   561
8. Memphis   566
9. Denver   573
10. Santa Fe   581
11. Flagstaff   585
12. Las Vegas   592
13. Beatty   600
14. Yerington   604
15. San Francisco   606

FOREWORD

In 1991, having decided that work was not for me, I decided to join a friend of mine, Steve, and go backpacking across The United States, stay and work in Sydney, travel throughout Australia and then come back home via South East Asia.

This was a brave decision for someone whose sole experience of overseas travel had been a day trip to Boulogne.

As I travelled around, I kept several diaries. Having recently cleared out my parents' cupboards and shed, I have been reunited with two of these diaries. All but the last couple of pages have survived of the first diary, which traces our journey across America. The other partly surviving diary, my travels around Australia, will be written up in due course.

What struck me, whilst writing this up in 2020, was how the world was different in 1991. We were only used to four stations on the TV, there was no internet, no mobile phones and in my case, no money. I have tried not to filter out too many views on the world that I wrote down at the time. But they were made through the eyes of someone who had never left Britain and had gone through an education system that still taught that The British Empire was a good thing.

Suddenly, here we were in America, during the first Gulf War, and despite having watched loads of American TV shows, the whole country seemed rather alien.

Wednesday February 6th   Burgess Hill

The big day finally arrived and here I am still stuck on the sofa at my uncle's, sharing the lounge with my Mum and Dad.

The bad tidings were finally relayed last night, and it appears that Virgin Atlantic cancelled their evening flight due to bad weather and all the passengers ended up on the midday service, which we had hoped to catch.

To further complicate matters, the accommodation we had booked was not as good as first presumed. Whereas we had thought we were heading for a youth hostel, it turned out to be a hostel for down and outs. The description we found described it as "run down and in a largely homeless area."

Hence, we now have a new flight and a new place to head for. If things go to plan (and I am still not convinced) we should leave Gatwick at 5.00pm tomorrow and be safely in the YMCA on 3rd Avenue in New York by 9.00pm local time.

Another factor to consider is that Southern England has now seen its worst snow for four years. Having joked about how cold it was going to be in Toronto for the past few weeks, it might be quite nice to get there now in order to warm up. (If we ever get there of course!)

It still hasn't sunk in yet and probably won't until we hit New York, but somehow it just doesn't seem that I should be away from this country for so long. It's not so much the looking forward to seeing all of these new places and meeting new people around the world, it's more looking forward to the relief that financial worries and almost endless organising and packing was over.

After sleeping on a sofa for four nights (with my Father snoring next to me and my nephew waking me up at seven in the morning) the chance of suffering from jetlag in a quiet hostel room is a God send. I may not have been working for the past couple of weeks, but I really do need a break!

Thursday February 7th   New York

We finally arrived late last night, but not without incident. After snow and ice took a grip at Gatwick, it was not surprising that there would be delays and after our five o'clock flight, finally took off at ten to eight, I would not be too shocked to learn that Gatwick actually shut down afterwards.

It also appears that we may have taken off ahead of the scheduled midday flight to Newark. Rather ominous messages for a Mr. Hussain travelling to New York, who had loaded his suitcase, but hadn't got on the plane, were keeping it well and truly on terra ferma. In fact, I was quite surprised by the lack of checks by customs at both ends. Nobody seemed to care what you had in your luggage.

The flight itself was long and quite uneventful, apart from the idiot who sat in front of us and spent most of the journey annoying the air hostesses. Can't complain about the service on board. A four-course lunch, endless drink, ice cream during the main movie and afternoon tea. The latter having been scheduled for 5pm but served nearer 9. The in-flight movie was "Ghost" starring Patrick Swayze. I managed to watch half of it. That was the left half, because some 6-foot giant was blocking the other half of the screen.

We touched down around 10.15pm local time, and once we had passed George Bush's smiling face, welcoming us to the land of the free, things started to get expensive. We sailed through customs and entered into what was to us a completely alien land.

Taxi drivers were intermingling with the bewildered tourists in the arrivals lounge, touting for business. One guy offered us a ride to Manhattan for $47 plus taxes, however when you know there is a bus outside which costs $9.50, you appreciate what a rip off it all was. In fact, this turned out to be a bit of a bargain, as two guys who turned up at our hostel later that evening, were charged $197 for the same journey.

Our bus journey was certainly an eye opener with our driver doubling up as a salesman, having to join the taxi drivers on the pavement to ply for trade. No contest really if all the other passengers were as skint as we were.

This seemed totally alien to me and was certainly not something you would see a bus driver doing at Tooting Broadway. Nor are you likely to be charged $2.50 to go through a tunnel at home. Charging £1 to cross The Severn Bridge is bad enough, but at least it's a nice view.

The bus dropped us off at Grand Central Station and launched us into a hostile environment. First impressions of New York were not particularly positive. It was sleazy and probably what I had imagined it to be. Not so much an American dream but more of a nightmare.

Although the YMCA was only a couple of blocks from Grand Central, we decided to get a cab and I'm sure the driver still managed to rip us off.

Our room was small, dingy and had no sink, but thankfully no cockroaches either. It was also red hot due to the rather loud and primitive radiator hissing in the corner.

The major source of humour that evening was the diabolical standard of American television. We had access to about forty stations, and we still couldn't find anything that would make it to the BBC, or even ITV for that matter. This was our first exposure to the Home Shopping Channels, and as two budding, but ultimately unsuccessful entrepreneurs, we were intrigued by the ability to sell everything you never wanted to the gullible American public.

If this was bad, it was surpassed by the diabolical quality of everything else. Channel 35 caused some amusement. In a country known for its strict laws on alcohol, possessing more than its fair share of Christian zealots and on its immigration forms, weeds out anyone with dodgy political or immoral beliefs, it was an eye opener to see two naked men having sex followed by advertisements for local prostitutes of all shape, persuasion and gender. We hoped New York had slightly more to offer.

After this immoral viewing, we turned over to watch The Reverend Larry Lea, praying for the salvation of the troops in The Gulf. Unfortunately, all gifts and donations to his Church were liable to tax, so we decided against it.

Friday February 8th New York

Oh, my head! We finally found some bars last night and celebrated Friday night the US way. More of that anon.

Our day started at about 9 am as we went to Grand Central Station to book our train to Toronto. This maybe wasn't the best time to go to the station as it was very intimidating with hundreds of commuters who all seemed to know where they were going, whereas we hadn't got a clue. The actual building is enormous and built on a much grander scale than its counterparts in London. However, what it does have in common is a large number of dropouts and homeless people and neither of us fancied hanging around for too long.

With our ticket booked, we headed down Fifth Avenue to take in the sights. The street system of numbering each road and splitting the city into east and west is potentially a very simple one. I must be honest though; I am totally confused by it all.

The streets of New York, especially Fifth Avenue, tend to remind me of The Holborn area of London. Not that exciting, but full of promise for something better. Unfortunately, there doesn't seem to be an Oxford Street at the end of this Holborn.

Our first major sightseeing experience was a trip up the Empire State Building. The observation deck at 1250 feet was maybe not as high as I had imagined, nevertheless, the view of the city, down to The Twin Towers of The World Trade Centre and north to Central Park was amazing. I'm not sure what I had imagined, maybe some amazing art deco masterpiece, but the actual building seemed a lot more modern than I thought it would be. The nearby Chrysler Building seemed much more spectacular. We had planned to go up The World Trade Centre too, but having done this, we decided against it. It would just have been the same view from a different angle.

After an iced coffee in the lobby café, we continued along Fifth Avenue as far down as The Financial District and Wall Street. New York's financial District is no different to London really.

Endless office blocks and parades of men in suits. In fact, the only noteworthy experiences here were a rather tasty hamburger for lunch and the comedy of watching Steve trying to make an international phone call from a phone box. The American phone system seems totally confusing and neither of us could work out how to make a call back to the UK.

After lunch we took the 50 cents round ferry trip to Staten Island. The island itself is not worth visiting and we headed straight back on the same ferry, but it is the cheapest way to see The Statue of Liberty. The statue itself would appear to have seen better days and as with The Empire State Building, it seemed much smaller than I had imagined. Clearly, I had believed the hype that everything was bigger in America.

Both of us were feeling a little intimidated by the big city and after this we returned to the hostel to rest our feet for a few hours. Steve has decided that he doesn't want to go to New Orleans or Texas due to safety concerns. He is pushing to replace them with Reno in Nevada, Wichita in Kansas, and Mobile in Alabama. None of these are exactly on the standard backpacker route and may never have even seen a tourist before. We agreed to keep the itinerary flexible and see where it took us. If we got to San Francisco in plenty of time, it didn't really matter how we got there.

Back in the room, the shopping channel continued to be a major source of amusement with Steve threatening to stay in all day on Sunday to watch The Bargathon. The sale of a 6.8 carat topaz ring was unreal. They sold over a thousand of them in a few minutes, thanks to Barbara from Ohio phoning in to say she had one and it had been valued at $300. They even scrapped the commercials to keep on selling. Are these people gullible or what?

In the evening we met up with a couple of guys who were the sons of one of Steve's Father's associates and went to a few bars. The first was called O'Henrys on East 88th Street and 1st Avenue. I've heard of Happy Hours before, but free drink for an hour was a first and seemed too good to miss.

Unfortunately, what seems too good to be true is generally a disappointment. Customers grabbed a plastic cup and the barman just kept on pouring as you fought to get your cup under the tap. Had this been one of my favourite pubs at home I would have fought, kicked, and punched my way to the front of the queue for the hour, but free refills of Bud Light were not worth fighting for. In fact, after an hour of drinking this sickly sad excuse for a beer, I had drunk quite enough. My bladder needed attention, but drunk I was not.

We returned to their apartment for a phone in pizza, which was supposedly the best in the world. No better than Tesco's in my opinion. Then we headed to the Delta Club on 8th and 88th Street. We both had far too much to drink. The reason for this was the weak beer, Normally I wouldn't touch anything else, but because the beer was watery, we moved on to Jägermeister shots and vodka jellies. It was the first time I had tried Jägermeister and it was sort of alcoholic Benilyn.

I think someone got us a cab back, but we did wake up in our room at the hostel.

Saturday February 9th   New York

We started the day with the great American breakfast (ugghh!). Bacon (too crispy), eggs (scrambled), sausage, ham, tomato sauce (so far so good), fluffy pancakes (what?) and maple syrup. All on one plate.

Feeling a little queasy, after this we made our way up 5th Avenue in the direction of The Rockefeller Centre. The indoor shopping arcade wasn't particularly impressive, but the outside ice rink, on which it seemed a number of OAPs were trying out their Torvill and Dean impersonations, was certainly something London could learn from. We also visited The Radio City Music Hall which was around the corner and seemed to be a pretty good music venue.

Next stop was St Patrick's Cathedral. A Catholic church which seemed pretty similar to the cathedral near Victoria in London. But the architecture, as was the case with the rest of New York, obviously fails to reach the historical heights of Britain.

Further up 5th Avenue we came across a small hi tech, excuse for a museum, called Infoquest. On entering we were given a plastic card similar to a credit card. Personally, I found all of this very ominous, as most credit cards I have been given tend to be swallowed up by machines. The museum highlighted several electronic gadgets and had screen shows showing the advancements in electronic communication. We did get the chance to produce our own music video and there was an electronic cab ride that takes you anywhere in New York and more importantly, doesn't rip you off.

After my concerns about my card, it was amusing to see that Steve had a dud one instead. All in all, a very technical show portraying a very Orwellian future for us all.

Wandering down any street in New York you are sure to see clouds of steam billowing out of drains on the roadside. This was caused by the subway supposedly. I asked Steve if they still used steam trains down there, but he shrugged his shoulders. Can't see this would be allowed to happen in London.

We were aiming for Central Park, but on the way, we popped into Bloomingdales, New York's famous department store. OK, it was big, had a live fashion show on the second floor and we spent ages trying to find the toy department in vain, but Harrods it isn't.

As we left the store, a taxi driver was being booked by a cop, but we didn't hang around as the argument ensued. Just before we got to Central Park, we popped into The Trump Tower which was full of exclusive boutiques way out of our price range. Money may be able to buy you a lot of things, class isn't one of them.

Central Park was a pleasant relief to the sprawling buildings. Although it was certainly totally different to the great parks in London. Young kids were breakdancing, and horse drawn carriages were ripping off tourists more than the taxi drivers. An authentic park in the middle of an urban sprawl is never easy to create, but somehow this seemed very artificial.

After lunch at a café near the Park, we went back to the hostel to rest our feet and prepare for another evening out. We got back around 3pm, and I finally plucked up the courage to use the hostel toilet. Steve is still holding out. This was a surreal experience as the dividing walls between cubicles were so low you could stare out the bloke in the next stool. Meanwhile the water level is so high that if you fire too hard, you flood the floor.

As I came back to the room, Steve was getting very excited about a video rewinding machine in the shape of a car on the Home Shopping Channel. I swear if he had been able to work out how to make a phone call, he would have bought one. Unfortunately, the well-manicured hand that was demonstrating the item seemed to break it whilst pulling a cassette out and the item was quickly taken off air.

As if to prove my point, Steve tried to make another phone call from a call box, this time to Canada to arrange our accommodation there. He put the money in the phone, phoned the number, spoke to Toronto, put the phone down and walked away. So far so good. At this point the phone starts to ring and stupidly he picks it up again, only to find the operator demanding more money. In no way would we use this call box ever again, we would never meet the person demanding money on the phone, yet for some unknown reason he coughed up the extra 75 cents and put it into the machine. It seemed like a waste of good beer money to me.

There seemed to be a distinct lack of decent places to eat near the hostel apart from burger bars, but we eventually tracked down Houlihan's on East 37th Street which did half decent food, substandard beer and had good music on.

We sat by the window eating our meal watching the streets of New York. A policeman was called to see a couple of people who had reported something. Unfortunately, there was to be no Starsky and Hutch style screeching of cars and a rather embarrassed officer trundled up in something akin to an elongated Reliant Robin. I will never be able to watch an American cop show again.

An enjoyable evening was somewhat spoilt by our trip back to the hostel. We hailed what we thought was a cab, but on getting in we soon realised this was not the case. Firstly, the guy driving had no registration or ID on him, nor did he have a meter and when we asked him to go to East 47th he sped off in completely the wrong direction. It did get a bit hairy, and we got as far as East 15th before we managed to persuade him to turn around and go back the other way. It could have been a lot worse but dodging and weaving through the traffic on 5th Avenue on a Saturday night at 60mph was not my idea of a good time.

Sunday February 10th   New York

After the rather worrying end to the previous day, we decided that a quiet schedule was probably the best approach to our last day in New York. We finally went out around 9.30 and wandered towards Grand Central Station in the vain hope that there might be an English newspaper with the football results in it. No such luck I am afraid. And we ended up in The Grand Central Café for a coffee and a fried egg roll which was nice but a tad expensive.

After breakfast we headed for an area we hadn't investigated yet, 6th and 7th Avenues. The area around Madison Square Gardens, where Sugar Ray Leonard had ended his boxing career the night before, was exceptionally seedy. So much so that we didn't think it wise to take our cameras out. In the area's defence, it must be said that there aren't too many major sporting venues in particularly nice areas in Britain.

Wembley and Hampden Park come to mind. It was a shame really, as on Friday we had found a garden in Maddison Square, just off 5th Avenue and hunted high and low to find the arena. This would have been a far more civilized venue.

From here we wandered along Broadway, through the Theatre District to Times Square. Once again, we found this quite seedy, and you can't help comparing it to Leicester Square and The West End in London which is a little bit classier. The amount of strip shows, and porn cinemas were noticeable. Clearly that's where the money is.

After an hour and a half of walking, we found a café by Central Park. New Yorkers seem to live on a diet of stodge. If it's not hot dogs, they are eating pretzels, if not muffins it's burgers. We had two exceptionally heavy Danish pastries and a large coffee. It struck me as strange as to why we were still presented with a bowl of dill pickles to go with our pain aux raisins.

We walked back to the hostel along 3rd Avenue and took in The United Nations Building en route. Not that exciting on a Sunday as it was shut. Whether it's any more exciting on a weekday is arguable.

Back in our room, in our attempt to find some football, we had a minor success when we managed to watch a goalless draw between Juventus and Atalanta with a Spanish commentary. Still no English results though. And what was more worrying than not knowing how Brighton had got on over the weekend was the forecast on The Weather Channel which was far from promising for the North of New York State and Southern Canada.

We found a bar and bought a couple of newspapers to read. If you think The Sun is biased in its reporting, you should see how the American press is reporting on the war in The Gulf.

Statistics of how many tanks and soldiers have been lost by either side are paraded like football scores, whilst there was a major article on a joke shop in New York that has installed its own electric chair, where for $10 a throw, you can zap an effigy of Saddam Hussein. A lot of the bookshops and other stores seem to have hundreds of different types of war merchandise, ranging from maps of Kuwait to T shirts of George Bush saying, "Up yours Saddam!" God help us if they ever pick on anyone their own size.

An enjoyable evening was spent at O'Lonnies on 2nd Avenue. A friendly bar that actually sold pints of dark beer! Shame about some of the measures though. The bar staff were friendly and one Irish barman bought us a pint. We tried the trivia machine, but unfortunately, our knowledge of American trivia wasn't that hot. For the last time, we headed back to our room, fairly happy about the fact, to be honest. We fell asleep to Channel 35 and a phone in show that left little to the imagination.

Monday February 11th   New York to Toronto

After a final glance at The Home Shopping Channel, we headed for Grand Central Station to catch the 8.35 "Maple Leaf" train to Toronto. Neither of us were particularly sorry to see the back of New York but it would be wrong to judge an entire country on just one city.

The rail journey, however, did little to change my image of America. Despite the splendid scenery of The Hudson River, carving its way northwards beside the line on one side, the view from the other told a different story. I would say that everything, but the kitchen sink could be seen dumped along the track, but as I saw a couple of those too, I can't do that. There were hundreds of burned out cars, buildings being left to fall down and lots of junk. This seemed to be the story throughout New York State.

Of the places we passed through, Albany and Buffalo seemed quite attractive, however the severe blizzards that were falling through much of the state did hinder views of places such as Rochester and Syracuse.

The train was very slow, which was surprising as it was the only train on the route, and I am prepared to take everything back I have ever said about British Rail. Not only was it slow, but the announcer faded out on every second word, and somehow the snow managed to get through the door of the train, so much so that by the time we arrived in Toronto somebody had to find a shovel to dig us out.

Canadian customs at Niagara proved to be a long arduous affair. The official seemed to want to know our life story before grudgingly granting us a week in Canada. It took 90 minutes to clear customs, but once through, the difference was amazing. The sides of the track became clean, the snow began to disappear and even the guard's uniform was smarter.

When we were finally dug out of the train, we soon realised why it wasn't snowing in Toronto. It was far too cold.

We were met at Toronto station and from leaving the train to entering our flat we hardly had to bear the brunt of the city's climate.

Joe, our host, was in the middle of a surprise birthday party full of retired Bavarians, all of whom seemed to arrive in Canada late in 1945. Joe, it transpired, was a retired U Boat captain. We made a mental note to not mention the war.

The Bavarian salad was delicious, and the German beer was a God send after what we had to drink in America. We were both forced into some initiation ceremony which involved downing a large measure of schnapps in one. Steve mentioned that we had drunk Jägermeister a couple of nights previously and this was met with much derision and all and sundry said it was nothing more than a cough mixture. This only confirmed my suspicions at the time that it was alcoholic Benilyn.

Having not had the dubious pleasure of meeting any cockroaches in New York, we were somewhat alarmed when Joe's partner produced a live one from a match box. It had a jewel fitted on its back and was extremely bizarre, especially as it was allowed to crawl through the remains of Joe's birthday cake.

We retired to our flat early and sampled Canadian television, only to find four weather channels, an even more boring MTV channel and sadly no Home Shopping Club.

Tuesday February 12th   Toronto

Having your own flat or staying in someone else's can have its drawbacks. Namely you are almost certainly going to break something. It didn't take Steve that long, I fear as Joe's nice shower fitting shattered in his hands and to make matters worse, went down the plughole.

After a breakfast of bacon and eggs, whilst being yapped at by a manic shiatzu, we braved the cold and headed for downtown Toronto. The number 37 bus went from the end of the road and took us to Islington subway station, which was one stop from the end of the line. It's useful that the ticket you bought for the bus was also valid on the subway train. The stations seem very clean, more so than in London, but having said that, it was no surprise that after a few stops we got stuck at a station due to a train breaking down further up the line. Some things seem to be the same all over the world.

Mind you, the public announcements left The Northern line Information Service standing in both frequency and usefulness.

Disembarking at Bay Station, one stop too early, we were thrown into the heart of downtown Toronto. At first, we were surprised to see so few people walking around, especially when you consider that Toronto is Canada's major financial and commercial centre.

After a few minutes we began to realise why. It was absolutely freezing. The centre is very reminiscent of some of the smaller cities or larger towns at home. It was also a relief not to see steam coming out of the pavement and overall, it seemed remarkably clean.

We had a few things to arrange such as bus tickets and buying stamps, and once this had been done, there wasn't too much of the day left as we had arranged to be back by six.

We passed another open-air ice rink, and due to the extreme cold, it seemed a little more fitting than the one we saw in New York. It also seemed more popular. A large number of schoolkids were there for what I presume was their lunch break. Admittedly there was one guy who was probably around 50, wearing a suit, skating around, but unlike the rink at the Rockefeller Centre, it wasn't full of older people.

The major attraction in Toronto is the CN Tower, the world's largest free-standing building. The complex also boasts the Sky dome, the world's largest indoor sports arena, a space simulator, and a revolving restaurant at the top. We turned up intending to see most of the attractions but after being charged $10.75, just to get to the first observation deck, we decided against going any further. The view from the tower, although not as spectacular as that from The Empire State Building, was still a breath-taking one. There are fine views across the city and over Lake Ontario. We took these in whilst enjoying a cold beer and some nachos in the revolving restaurant.

Much of the rest of the afternoon was spent going around the shopping mall at Yonge Street. Not because we liked shopping, but because it was underground and heated, unlike outside where temperatures seemed to be dipping even further. We bought some chocolate from Marks and Spencer and spent about an hour trying to work out how to withdraw money from a Canadian cashpoint. One place of note was The Cockney Pub which sold Pie and Chips, Sausage and Mash, Steak and Kidney Pud and fizzy lager. Something put me off, can't think what.

In the evening we were taken out to what Joe called "a great pizza place." This turned out to be a Pizza Hut. An advert in the restaurant said that they were giving away free basketball sets at their Buffalo store. Weird, because Buffalo was all but 100 miles away and a shame because a mini basketball set could have killed time on a Greyhound bus.

Back at the flat it was my turn to try and wreck the joint. Joe presented us with some Bavarian Weiss beer, and we were told it was the expected thing and a great skill to pour the beer in its special glass in one go. Steve, being sensible, declined the challenge. Most of my beer ended up on the living room carpet.

We checked the TV before going to bed and all four weather channels were pretty ominous and forecasting a "Polar Blast for the following night. Temperatures were expected to fall to -24 degrees centigrade. Ouch!

Wednesday February 13th Toronto

A reasonably late start today as Joe and Lorraine were going to take us to Niagara Falls and Joe had appointments until 10am.

We went in Joe's Lincoln, an amazing computer operated limo, and headed south along the highway. The roads here, and even those around New York, seem a lot clearer and a lot wider, making for a smoother journey. There are probably issues during rush hour, but overall, I would imagine that it is far easier to get from a to b here than at home. The only drawback being the speed limit of 55mph. It may only be 15mph, but you certainly notice it and with the Police being very strict, nobody seems to go above the limit.

Coming out of Toronto, through towns such as Grimsby and Hamilton, which were just as unattractive as their namesakes, you can see Lake Ontario and the industrial area on its shores.
On several occasions, the road arches high over the lake in order that large ships, full of iron ore, Canada's largest export, can pass through on the way to Detroit in the States or further afield.
We forked off the highway just before the customs point and into Niagara National Park. The actual gorge that separates Canada and America is spectacular. Made even more so by the fact that in places, the river was frozen. No mean achievement considering how fast the water runs.

We passed a floral clock and went through a nature reserve, where all intelligent animals would be hibernating, and came to one of many vantage points. It seems to me that the whole Niagara experience is one that builds up. By this stage we had seen many smaller waterfalls, whirlpools, and rapids, we began to wonder where the main attraction was.

Before you get to the main falls, you reach the town of Niagara, where we were going to stop for some food. If it was not for this great gift from nature, I fear Niagara would not exist. On a freezing February day, Niagara was a ghost town. Souvenir Shops were shut. Fast food joints weren't reopening until the spring and there we were looking for something to eat. Eventually we found a hotel, with an unattended, presumably self-service gift shop and a bar that sold bowls of chili and Pints of Molson.

With most of the major attractions closed, we plumped for a close-up view of the falls. The spray and mist that are generated is astounding and the view of the crescent shaped falls is certainly worthwhile. Whether it deserves the tag of being one of the seven natural wonders of the world is perhaps debatable.

The major souvenir shop next to the falls was open and we bought a few postcards in case our photographs didn't come out. The one thing the has annoyed me about Canada is their sales tax.

Not the fact that there is one, but the fact that prices are displayed without it and unless your mental arithmetic is on the ball, you have no idea what the final cost of anything will be.

We headed back mid afternoon in order to make arrangements for our stay in Baltimore. Once again Steve called from a public call box, once again the operator called him back and once again, he put more money in the slot.

It appears that we have been bought some tickets for an ice hockey game on Friday night and in order to get there in time, we will need to leave Toronto slightly earlier than planned.

We were taken out for dinner this evening to a very nice Chinese restaurant. It was outside of downtown Toronto in an area very reminiscent of the High Road between Balham and Clapham in London. It was an area that attracted immigrants and as in London, there was a selection of ethnic cuisine on offer, notably West Indian which is surprisingly scarce at home.

The Chinese food here is Schezuan rather than Cantonese, whilst the presence of Barbecued Chicken Wings on the menu, owes mort to North America than China, I fear.

Although it was very cold tonight there is still no sign of the snow and polar blast that we were promised. Perhaps the forecasts here are as inaccurate as the ones at home.

Thursday February 14th   Toronto to Bel Air

We woke up this morning to find Toronto covered in a blanket of snow. Not quite as bad as predicted, but bad enough to cause a few problems on the road. From what we could deduce from the four weather channels on the TV, Montreal had got it far worse.

We didn't have time to do any sightseeing today, as we had brought our bus departure forward, had to pack and then meet Joe for lunch.

Hence much of the morning was taken up by watching TV. Overall, Canadian TV is fairly boring in comparison to what we saw in New York. We did manage to find a few highlights though. Whereas Steve was obsessed with the Home Shopping Club, I was getting equally enthralled by the TV Evangelists. I find it fascinating that a bloke can shout at a large audience, wave his arms about, shed a few tears and yell Jesus a few times and then get people to give him money because he has told them they are all sinners. Only tax-deductible donations to God can get their salvation. This really is the logical progression of the Catholic Church. Maybe they need to start accepting MasterCard.

Steve insisted that I turned the TV over, so we watched a programme about women's problems and unlucky enough to catch an episode discussing the problems three women had with their ginormous breasts and how they weren't being taken seriously in the workplace. Steve seemed rather too interested in this. I wasn't aware that he had a view on women's employment rights.

We met Joe for lunch at The Alpine Chicken Bar B Q in Albion Street. It did fine German food (I had schnitzel) and more importantly sold cold German beer. Something we were extremely thankful for as we were about to reenter the land of Budweiser and Miller Lite again. Unfortunately, due to the extreme weather outside, the restaurant was in the grip of a power cut, however, Joe knew the chef, who turned out to be the brother of Razor Ruddick, who was due to fight Mike Tyson next week, and he managed to throw something together. He must have had a primus stove out the back. After visiting Joe's office, which thankfully wasn't a submarine, we had to head back to the flat to collect our gear in order to get to the bus station.

We caught the bus to Islington once again, thankfully only after a short wait in the bitter conditions. The subway was also prompt and it wasn't until yours truly suggested we got out at Bay Station again and walked to the bus terminal, instead of changing trains, that the problems started.

For a start we managed to leave the station via a different exit which threw us a bit. The fact that it was snowing hard and getting colder by the minute didn't help either. After about twenty minutes off getting wet and Steve saying "I knew we should have taken the subway" we found a road we recognised and actually got to the bus station in plenty of time.

We strolled up to the ticket desk and promptly produced our Greyhound Bus pass for the clerk, who immediately looked at his colleague. Evidently as of last month, Greyhound Ameripass is no longer valid in Canada, and we had to cough up the fare as far as Buffalo.
Adverse weather conditions and rush hour traffic meant that our journey out of Toronto was a slow one. The onboard film was called "Night Crossing" and was about two guys escaping over the border of East and West Germany in a balloon. This was slightly ironic, as at this stage neither of us were sure whether Canadian customs should have taken our American landing cards from our passports and were not convinced, they would let us back in. A balloon may have been a better option.

Instead of going back through Niagara Falls, the bus took what seemed to be a longer route via Fat Erie. We didn't expect to be held up at customs for too long, assuming that, as was the case on the train, the officials would come on board and clear everything up whilst you were sitting down.

It seemed rather excessive when we were told to disembark, collect all our belongings, and walk into America. All a bit unnecessary. And then when it was my turn, I got the customs officer who wanted to grill me and ask twenty questions. Some of them were quite bizarre. He asked me if I could tell him where Dundee was. Thankfully I simply replied on the East Coast, but there was part of me that wanted to say a few miles south of Carnoustie and north of the Kingdom of Fife.

Due to the late running of the bus, we had very little time to wait in Buffalo for our connection. However, there was one slightly alarming moment when the ticket clerk informed us that we were travelling via a Trailways bus, and our tickets were not valid. I was beginning to wonder what the travel agent in London had sold us at this point, but thankfully we ironed out the problem.

So, after buying a couple of cans of coke for the journey, we set off from Buffalo around 9.30pm. What I hadn't considered was that because of the extreme cold, the coke in my can was frozen solid and when I opened it, liquid sprayed the aisle of the entire bus, making everybody entering or disembarking stick to the floor. I don't think this made me very popular and I got bugger all to drink too.

Friday 15th February   **Bel Air**

The brochure we received with our Greyhound bus pass invited us to lay back, take in the views and take pictures of the great scenery America has to offer. Unfortunately, by the time we had reached Baltimore, a thick film of grime had covered the window and visibility was down to zero.

Once again, we are staying with some associates of Steve's Dad, although this is the last of these until we reach San Francisco, so it's hostels for the rest of the way. We were met at the bus station around 9.45am and were whisked away for refreshments. After sitting in the same bus for over twelve hours I was more concerned that my knees were still moving and the walk across the road to the car park proved very refreshing.

We are staying in a town called Bel Air, a smallish town some twenty miles outside of Baltimore. Baltimore itself seems very pleasant. A mid-sized commercial district with its tall office blocks, centred around a natural harbour and its affiliated industries.

A welcome food break came at Chilis in Bel Air. A fairly upmarket burger bar which sold massive and very tasty hamburgers and chips (sorry fries) at a reasonable cost. The Hickory Burger was very nice but not as welcome as the endless cups of coffee and iced water which made up for the fact that my drink from the previous night was still stuck to the floor of the bus.

A rather strange incident occurred after leaving Chilis. Cynthia, our host, concluded that the locks on her car had frozen. I thought this rather strange as it was cool but nowhere near as cold as it had been in Toronto. Nevertheless, we both shielded her from the breeze as she lit some matches in order to heat up the lock. After a couple of minutes, I pointed out to Steve that our baggage wasn't actually in the car we were trying to get into. Steve in turn then realised that there was an identical car parked opposite. At this point we all cringed and sheepishly got into the correct car and made a quick getaway.

Back at base, it was nice to have our own rooms for a few nights. Any home comforts greatly accepted, and we both made the most of this by sleeping all afternoon.

We woke up in time to be taken to another "great pizza place." Once again this turned out to be Pizza Hut.

In the evening we had been bought tickets for The American Hockey League fixture between the Baltimore Skipjacks and The Halifax Citadels. I can't say I'd heard of either of them before, it was probably like taking an American to watch Leyton Orient.

This was my first experience of Ice Hockey live and I have to say it was a truly enlightening experience. The Baltimore Arena, not nationally renowned for its size, was still virtually as large as The Wembley Arena. Public stadiums here seem far better than those at home and if you can mentally block out the constant advertising that attacks you from all angles it was a very entertaining evening. High tech scoreboards show animations of every play, including fouls, everybody gets a seat, and you can drink beer too. We have a lot to learn from this. For the record, Halifax won 4-3 in overtime, not bad not bad considering they were a goal down with ten seconds left of normal time.

All in all, this was very enjoyable. Especially in view of the strange regulations that state if you fight back after being whacked around the head with a hockey stick, the referee was more likely to be lenient. The Baltimore Coach was actually sent off for fighting the Halifax players. It's probably as close to watching Gladiatorial Games in the Colosseum as I will ever get.

The final goal in overtime was greeted by silence by the home supporters who just politely stood up and filed out. For a crowd who was getting so worked up when the players were taking lumps out of each other, it was quite bizarre that when something actually happened in the game, they weren't that bothered. To make matters worse, the away supporters were just as silent. If I had travelled 2000 miles south, through Polar conditions to see Brighton score a last-minute winner, I wouldn't be quite so calm.

Thrown back outside into what was fast becoming an exceptionally cold night, we headed for a local bar called Walkers Exchange. It seemed a very nice place, in fact it was the nearest we had come to a proper pub. I did notice some bottles of Bass behind the bar, but decided it was too early to feel that homesick. Back to the Budweiser it was.

Saturday 16th February   Bel Air

This morning's breakfast was eaten whilst watching what American's call wrestling. I fear it has little to do with the wrestling that was on World of Sport on a Saturday afternoon.

We went to Washington DC today by car. It was about an hour and a half through fairly boring scenery. The outskirts of the capital are grim and there is a high percentage of African Americans there. Despite the bad press that Washington gets, the city centre was very nice indeed.

We parked behind Grand Union Station, the city's major railroad station, which was a world away from Grand Central in New York, It was clean, wasn't intimidating and there were quite a few nice shops to wander around.

As we only had a few hours in the city, we took a guided bus tour. For $11, the Trolley Bus Tour of the city was excellent value and covered the major sites in just over 90 minutes.

The tour starts outside of the station, in the shadow of the impressive dome of The Capital Building and next to a replica of The Liberty Bell. Heading through the area around Pennsylvania Avenue, dominated by the Federal and Government Buildings, it was striking that they were all white and almost identical. A stark contrast to Whitehall and I'm sure very confusing. Winding through the streets, passing the theatre where Abraham Lincoln was shot and the house where he died. We finally caught a glimpse of The White House. Totally unimpressive, very small and impossible to see properly due to an anti-war demonstration outside.

It wasn't just the American Government getting complained at, as we passed the Soviet Embassy, a pro Latvian independence movement were protesting equally as loud.

The tour continued past the Washington Hilton, where there was an unsuccessful attempt on the life of President Ronald Reagan. It was interesting to see how security conscious these people are, as they built a new garage, especially for the president, away from the main car park, so that he could leave his car and not have to meet the public at all.
The outskirts of Washington hosts the zoo and, on a hill, the Washington Cathedral which seemed very reminiscent of Guildford Cathedral, in that it overlooks the city surprisingly, its architecture is also very British as opposed to other churches which seem slightly different.

Coming back down from the cathedral, we went through the embassy district. Most of the embassies seemed very nice, period buildings, proudly flying their flags. I also noticed the Iraqi flag outside of The National Muslim Centre, which I thought was quite brave, considering the current state of public opinion, which was epitomised by a sign in a passing cab that wanted America to nuke Iraq. The British Embassy was very fitting, an office block and not a flag in sight.

The Georgetown district was interesting. Almost Georgian England and a bit like Brighton in fact. The main street had a number of what appeared to be fairly interesting shops and it was all set in a pleasant parkland area.

The trip back to the station took us back over the Potomac River, which cuts through the city, back past The Watergate Hotel, Lincoln Memorial and Washington Monument.

All in all, a very enjoyable afternoon. From here, Steve and I split up from our hosts and went to buy them a gift. Despite Steve wanting to buy them a model of Thomas The Tank Engine, we finally settled on an aerial view of The British Isles. We could have bought a satellite view of Kuwait or a map outlining Desert Storm, but we decided against this.

For the evening, we returned to the area of Baltimore known as Little Italy. We ate at a very pleasant restaurant and consumed a large helping of spaghetti and meatballs. We also managed to convince the staff that it was Steve's birthday, so he got a complimentary cake and plenty of embarrassment too.

On leaving the restaurant, an ominous black maria pulled away. I was concerned that the Nat West had tracked me down.

Sunday 17th February **Bel Air**

A minor triumph this morning when we found Saturday's football results in The Baltimore Sun. It's just a shame that Brighton didn't have a game and Tooting's game was postponed.

We went to the site of The Battle of Gettysburg today, setting off at about 9.30. It was a pleasant change to travel through the Maryland and Pennsylvania countryside, rather than on the highway which gets fairly tedious. There were lots of fields, lots of sheep, cows, and horses, all very rural but not spectacular in the slightest. The buildings, again pleasant, and straight out of "The Walton's" were totally different to farmhouses at home.

We stopped in a small town at a hotel for lunch. For $12, we could eat as much as we wanted whilst there was food left on the table. On a trip like this, such an invitation should be taken seriously and at least five plates should have been consumed. However, as we were in polite company, decorum was the order of the day, and we kept things down to a minimum.

After lunch, we headed firstly to New Oxford, where we spent an hour looking around antique shops. The word antique is somewhat subjective. For a nation that has very little history, what you put in the bin yesterday is today's antique.

The sad thing is that there is a long native history to this country, but we aren't allowed to mention that. They were all savages supposedly.

We finally arrived at Gettysburg around 2pm and went into the main museum which held the largest collection of American Civil War memorabilia in the country. This was quite fascinating and worth an hour before heading off for the battlefield which is the main experience here.

As it is America, you do not need to see the battlefield on foot. An American without his car is like a train without tracks, going nowhere. There was of course a cassette available which you could listen to as you drove around the site.
Although the numerous monuments and the site of General Robert E Lee's greatest defeat was interesting in itself, it was the way in which we toured it and how it was portrayed that I found most fascinating. Numerous cars, listening to the same cassette, driving around the site in a slow procession, all stopping at the viewing areas when told and reversing when they realised that they had been going too fast for the commentary.

Evidently this type of tour is available at sites throughout the world, including at home, but I've never come across it. The thought of roads being built through the site of The Battle of Hastings and cars solemnly driving up Senlac Hill would ruin any sense of history that the place still has.

It took a couple pf hours to complete the tour, by which time most of us had seen enough.

We took a different route back to Bel Air and got lost. By the time we reached base it was dark and time for tea. After this, we phoned Orlando to book our accommodation, however the hostel was far from full, and reservations weren't necessary.

The evening was spent in front of the TV watching the previous weeks Prime Ministers Questions from parliament. It was good to catch up with some news from home at least. America is extremely insular, and they really don't seem to care about any other country unless they are at war with it. Hence getting news from home will be difficult unless they decide to invade London.

It seems that unemployment has risen again. We thought it was too soon for the pair of us to have appeared in the statistics. More alarming was the drastic change in the hair colour of John Selwyn Gummer. We felt this was also unlikely to make the papers here.

Monday February 18th   Bel Air to Orlando

A relatively early start today in order to get packed and still have a bit of time to see something of Baltimore before had to catch the bus to Orlando. We arrived into the centre of the city at about 10am and prepared to take in the sights before our bus was due to leave at midday.
Due to what seems to be an American obsession with shopping, our tour consisted of a couple of malls, which didn't exactly leave a lasting impression of the city. There was only one shop that seemed worth visiting, called The Sharper Image. A store in which locals can experiment with new gadgets, such as running machines, exercise bikes or massage chairs. Quite a sight, but it's a shame nobody wanted to test drive the $3000 motorised bicycle or put on the complete set of medieval armour.

We did manage to get a quick glimpse of the SS Constellation, which resides in The Inner Harbour and the National Aquarium building. The harbour area is very pleasant and reminiscent of some of the new dockside developments at home such as Swansea or Bristol.

Baltimore looked interesting and it was a shame we didn't have enough time to see it properly.

The journey from Baltimore to Orlando proved to be a memorable one, not so much for the scenery as it was dark for much of the journey, but for the drivers. On the first leg we had a black guy who started preaching to his gathered congregation and then there was Jonesy. Jonesy took us on the overnight stretch of the journey from Fayetteville, North Carolina to Jacksonville in Florida.

As the clock rapidly approached midnight and most of the passengers attempted the impossible, to sleep on board a Greyhound Bus, Jonesy (he wouldn't tell us his friends called him) went into overdrive. The opening routine was a fairly predictable one, with classics such as "If this is your first time on a Greyhound Bus, we've got something in common." This was followed by a more original set of Greyhound Bus driver jokes which were probably very funny, if you were a Greyhound bus driver and it wasn't in the middle of the night. Jonesy's timing was perfect, he allowed a couple of minutes between each gag, just enough time for you to think he'd finally shut up and you could go back to sleep. The routine petered out at about 1 am and most passengers managed to get some kip.

At 2 am, we heard Jonesy's voice telling us to get up as it was time for breakfast. I've only ever had breakfast at 2 am once before and it must be stated that I was very drunk and hadn't actually gone to bed yet. Trucker Joe's was a pleasant roadside diner and maybe worth a stop. But at 2 am?

Everyone was marched off the bus and all but brainwashed into eating. Being patriotic, we both plumped for The British Brunch. We had hoped for bacon and eggs, but this was not the case. In fact, what we had served to us had very little to do with British cuisine. Notably the melon to start as you don't see many of them in British allotments.

Back on the bus, and after another quick fifteen-minute routine, we were allowed a few hours' sleep. At 6 am it was "Wakey Wakey you sleepy heads." No, we hadn't arrived in Orlando, this was just to let us know we had crossed state lines and were now in Florida.

We got rid of Jonesy at Jacksonville around 7 am. This gave us around three hours to recover before arriving in Orlando.

Tuesday February 19th   **Orlando**

We arrived in Orlando around 10 am., looking extremely silly in our coats and clutching scarves, and gloves as the temperatures touched 80 degrees. Amazingly, our luggage survived the five changes of bus from Washington, and we got away from the bus station relatively quickly.

We took a cab to the hostel and after New York, it actually felt safe to do so. Having said that, as we drove along, and on realising we were British, our "Irish" American cab driver suddenly blurts out, "So why don't you guys let Ireland look after itself?" I don't think he was very happy when I turned it back on him and pointed out if Americans stopped giving money to the IRA, they wouldn't be causing so much trouble. The fact is, that the guy says he is Irish and has probably never even left Florida. The Americans are very strange. Thankfully it was a fairly short ride, and we didn't get on to Nicaragua or Grenada.

Orlando seemed much more easy going and had a slower pace of life. The guy on the front desk at the hostel was so laid back he should have been lying down. It turns out he came from Watford. It's just a shame Steve mistook his accent as Australian, and it got a bit embarrassing. Thankfully I kept quiet. I thought he was South African.

The hostel rooms sleep 8 and have some of the tallest bunk beds I've ever seen. First priority was a shower and a change of clothes into something more fitting for the local conditions. After this, we wandered down to see what downtown Orlando had to offer.
The hostel is fairly central, overlooking the impressive Lake Eola. We walked around the lake on our way to the shops, where we planned to get our photographs developed, get something to eat and in my case, buy a hat before getting too sunburned.

First of all, we dropped off our films and then hit Mulvaney's Irish Pub in Church Street. The sign showing draught Guinness shone out like a beacon, so much so that I didn't see the bottles of Newcastle Brown Ale in the fridge. It sold good traditional food too. I had a steak and kidney pie, and Steve had a shepherd's pie and made a nuisance of himself with a Liverpudlian barmaid. Almost civilization.

The afternoon was spent around Church Street, which has been transformed into a 24-hour celebration of The Wild West. Not bad for a state that was under the control of The Spanish and was more Zorro than Jesse James.

You can buy anything from ten-gallon hats to authentic saddles for your horse, should you have brought it in on holiday with you. We decided against buying anything and instead plumped for the amusement arcade which had an interesting array of games which gave tokens for the amount of bonus points you could score. We found a suitable way of cheating at basketball; Steve was relatively successful on the golf simulator whilst I had some success on the baseball pitching. Most enjoyable was the Whacky Gator game in which five masochistic alligators attack you and you defend yourself with a large mallet. Between us we amassed 70 tokens which didn't quite reach the target desired. You needed around 3,000 for a portable telephone. We completed our good deed for the day by giving the tokens to a toddler who didn't have enough to get what she wanted.

Church Street has a saloon with swing doors, just like the Wild West. We would have loved to go there but a cover charge of $15 before you even start drinking was rather extortionate. On the way back to the hostel I finally bought the hat I had been looking for all week and also plumped for a pair of tartan shorts. Unfortunately, on returning to our room, I discovered they were in fact boxer shorts and maybe a little too risqué for the beaches of Florida.

I'm finally glad to report that the steak and kidney pie did the trick. After a couple of weeks of not performing to schedule, my digestive system is back to working regularly. Steve still has a long way to go on that front.

There is a 7 – 11 shop around the corner from the hostel and we thought it would be nice to get a cold drink and sit by the lake for a while. Steve got his drinks at the second attempt as the first one ended up all over the shop floor, as he forgot to put his cup under the tap.

In the evening we teamed up with Claude, a French guy who'd arrived from Miami earlier in the day. After deciding that Church Street Station was too expensive, it was back to Mulvaney's for that bottle of Newcastle Brown I had spotted earlier. Not only was it good beer, but the music was good too. Alarmingly, I also spotted that Watney's Red Barrel was on tap. It was taken out of British pubs over ten years ago (by public demand) and it is now seemingly, exported to the Americans and sold at twice the price.

After an enjoyable evening we strolled back through Orlando which was full of street entertainers, notably some marionettes of Kate Bush, Ray Charles, and other singers. Very touristy, but very secure and pleasantly warm at night.

Wednesday February 20th   Orlando

A fairly early start today as the bus from the hostel to Disneyworld left at 8.30 in the morning. We seem to be stuck with Claude now and in any case he's a nice bloke and some his attempts at English translations are quite amusing.

Considering the time of year, it was quite amazing to see how many people were already in the queue to get in. It's amazing how one attraction can draw so many people from so many places on such a regular basis.

There are three major attractions at Disney. The Magic Kingdom (home of Mickey Mouse), The Epcot Centre (a celebration of science, nature, and the countries of the world) and MGM Studios (self-explanatory). There are various passes allowing you to get into the park for different lengths of time, but as we were pressed for time and did not really fancy MGM studios, believing Universal to be better, we decided to get two one day passes.

Although the bus dropped us outside of Epcot, we wanted to see The Magic Kingdom first. To get there, we had to first catch the monorail. Disneyworld is no different to the rest of this country I fear, as after having waited ten minutes to get our tickets to get in now had to go back to the same booth to get a separate travel pass. The monorail took us most of the way, but we disembarked and caught a paddle steamer across the lake to finish our trip. Very pleasant with the breeze bringing welcome relief to what was already becoming a very hot day.

Walking through the throng of people that was Main Street USA, we decided to have some breakfast. This proved to be a hot dog, no trimmings whatsoever and exceedingly expensive.
The biggest shock of the week here was that Steve actually forgot to collect his change. It must be the heat. But he did go on about it all day.

The Magic Kingdom is divided into different areas. The first of them is Adventure Land which boasts The Swiss Family Robinson Tree House. This was actually shut which I was not too upset about as I never liked climbing trees. There were still a couple of major rides in this area. First thing in the morning we went on The Pirates of The Caribbean ride which was an amusing, underground ride in which you sail through pirate waters, get caught in the crossfire of two galleons and then back through the pirates' home port where they are having a jolly good time. One thing that proved annoying was the pathetic West Country accent adopted by the voice coming over the public announcement system.
We managed to get on Adventure Land's other major attraction, The Jungle Cruise, later in the day as there were massive queues in the morning. Quite frankly, I've never seen queues like it and what makes it extraordinary is that Americans can actually stand and wait their turn. The only drawback is that if you are stuck in a queue with them, you have to listen to their inane drivel.

The cruise was worth the wait and ranks as one of the best rides in the park. The boat disappears through the mist and steam and is confronted by numerous jungle hazards such as hippos, rising out of the water, surprise attacks by cannibals, going under a waterfall and then going through a herd of friendly elephants who like to spray water at you.

The next area was Frontier Land where we went to two attractions. The Big Thunder Mountain Railroad was probably the highlight. A good old rollercoaster based on the plot of the runaway train. The Country Bear Jamboree was a brilliant, animated figure show, starring a group of musical bears having a hoe down. The sort of thing you would expect from Disney and great entertainment.

Liberty Square was next and the first ride we went on was called Mike Finks' Keelboats, which proved to be little more than a trip around a lake, promoting other more exciting rides. The Haunted Mansion was next and ranks as one of the best, if not the best, ghost train you are likely to go on. Slightly more technical than the one on the end of The Palace Pier in Brighton, it used a clever mixture of animation and holograms showing various ghostly figures and strange goings on, culminating in you passing a mirror to see a decomposing skeleton sitting next to you.

Before exploring Fantasy Land, we stopped at Pinocchio's Café for another expensive meal. Fantasy Land seems to be the most popular area in The Magic Kingdom, which is not that surprising as it is where the rides relate to the classic characters.

The queue for The Peter Pan Ride was far too long, so we decided to join Captain nemo and go 20,000 Leagues Under the Sea. We boarded The Nautilus and went deep into the ocean, passing hundreds of fish, squid, shipwrecks and even mermaids, before arriving at the lost city of Atlantis. A very enjoyable ride and my first trip in a submarine too!
Mr. Toad's Wild Ride wasn't that wild and a bit of a waste of time. It consisted of a two-minute ride through a group of large cardboard cutouts, which were supposed to represent Edwardian London. After this, we were a little concerned about the quality of some of the rides on fantasy Land. We had already noted the rather poor quality of The Dumbo and Cinderella experiences, which were little more than glorified fairground attractions. The Snow White Adventure was a slight improvement as we fled from The Wicked Witch, through the forest and down a mine with The Seven Dwarves.

From here we caught the Skyway, a cable car, across the park to Tomorrow Land, where we had hoped to travel on The Space Mountain, supposedly the best ride in the park. This was unfortunately shut for refurbishment, so we headed for The Grand Prix Raceway instead. This, in theory, is a good idea with four lane racing, and you are in sole control of your racing car over the relatively long circuit.

That's the good news. The bad news is that due to its popularity, any dreams you may have of taking a Grand Prix circuit by storm are soon quashed and your ride starts to resemble the M25 during the rush hour.

The rest of Tomorrow Land proved to be a disappointment. The Dream Flight through the history of aviation was a bit boring whilst The Mission to Mars failed to get off the ground at all.

On to Mickey's Star Land where Mickey Mouse and all his friends live. It is set in the heart of Duckville, and we came across a few interesting characters. Goofy and Donald Duck were signing autographs outside of Mickey's house. We went into the house, but he wasn't in. As we walked along the street, The Sheriff of Nottingham accosted us, asking for money. I guess it makes a change from the normal beggars, but I am afraid he got the same response.

We caught the tram back to Adventure Land from here and then spent the rest of the evening looking around the various gift shops before the minibus back to the hostel left at 9.30.
Our new roommates all seem to be Japanese. It's hard enough trying to communicate with Claude, let alone this lot. In fact, at one stage this evening, Claude was acting as a translator between the Japanese and British. On working out that they had a car and were planning to head to The Kennedy Space Centre, I tried to bridge the language barrier. I fear this was a fruitless exercise.

Thursday February 21st   Orlando

Taking a day off from Disneyworld, we decided to head for Universal Studios today. A slightly cheaper exercise as we didn't have to pay the hostel $10 to get us there, just 75 cents to a local bus driver. Not exactly a direct route, but it did show us what the real Orlando looked like, away from the tourist orientated downtown area, it also proved quite amusing as en route we stopped outside a school to pick up twenty African American kids, aged around six, for a trip to the local library.

Today seemed even hotter than yesterday and to be confronted with queues, even longer than those at Disney, was not too comforting. It was made slightly more bearable, as we met a family from Haywards Heath who recognised my Brighton shirt.

That was the good news. The bad news was that they told me we had lost to Crystal Palace on Monday which ruined my day. I'd been trying to get the result for days and even bought Tuesday's copy of "The Times" for an extortionate $2.25, only to find it was the early edition and printed before the football finished. It's bad enough to do that outside of Victoria Station, getting the last train home, but in Florida!

About an hour later, another guy from Brighton approached me and asked if I knew the score. So, I ruined his day too. No wonder attendances are down this year, everyone's over here.

The rides at Universal proved to be some of the most fantastic I've ever seen and were ten times better than anything Disney had to offer. If only it wasn't for the waiting to get on them.

There are various sets throughout the studios depicting areas of the United States. You can move from Beverley Hills to Amity Bay (Jaws) to San Francisco and then to New York kin a leisurely ten-minute stroll/ No need for a Greyhound Pass here.

The sets are interesting, but the rides are brilliant. Our first adventure was with E.T. and immediately it became clear that Universal is more advanced than Disney. Whereas at Disney you are thrown straight into the ride, here you get a short film explaining what is going on. Before the ET adventure, Stephen Spielberg gives a five-minute talk. The object of the exercise is to get your dirt bike, along with ET and other friends to ride through the forest, avoiding the army and police, whose cars keep screeching out in front of you, and then after riding up a steep hill, there is no turning back and you take off, high over the city, before warping off to ET's home planet to meet his family.

Next, we had a sneak preview of the new "Back To The Future" ride which was being tested. The plot here is that a villain has stolen Doc Brown's De Lorean time machine and travelled back to the 1950's. The Doc has just built a new eight-seater time machine and you have to try it out to chase the rogue car. You accelerate to 88mph and are then launched into an amazingly simulated roller coaster ride. Back in the Fifties, you chase the other car over small buildings, down main roads and climb steeply over skyscrapers before both vehicles go further back in time to the age of the dinosaurs. Careering through a volcano, you see the other car falling foul of a tyrannosaurus rex and then it's your turn as you fly through its jaws. Just in time, the Doc manages to get both cars back. Probably the best ride I've ever seen.

After lunch at Finnegan's Irish Pub in "New York", we went into The Ghostbusters Fiore Station. Outside there had been a Blues Brothers Show and we had also seen a scene being filmed for a forthcoming movie, with stuntmen doing an SAS style raid on a third floor flat.
The Ghostbusters set is based on the end of the first film, on top of a New York skyscraper. A girl is showing off some special effects with Slimer, the friendly ghost, when an evil ghost sets free hundreds of evil spirits. Time for the Ghostbusters to appear on the scene and to zap the offending ghouls and save the day. As in the film, the scene ends with Mr. Stay Puft, the marshmallow man being destroyed. Brilliant special effects but not as exhilarating as the rides.

Next to the Alfred Hitchcock showcase where we were told we were going to see previously unreleased 3D footage of one of his films and one member of the audience was selected to play the lead in the shower scene from Psycho. The footage of the Best of Hitchcock was interrupted shortly after we put on our 3D glasses. The screen seemingly began to tear, and hundreds of crazed birds seemed to fly out and attack us in what was a quite frighteningly realistic couple of minutes.

From here, we moved on to The Psycho scene and more Hitchcock Trivia.

Next was The Hanna Barbara Show, which was fun waiting for as they showed various cartoons as you waited. Inside, we were watching a demonstration of the art of animation, when Dick Dastardly and Muttley kidnapped the Jetson's son and shot off. It was time for us all to board a rocket ship with Yogi Bear and Boo Boo to try and catch them. The simulated chase takes you through scenes from The Flintstones, The Jetsons and Scooby Doo before you finally catch the wicked Dastardly. Great fun!

Unfortunately, King Kong was having a few technical issues, so we went to The Earthquake simulator. The first half of this show is fairly mundane with a few special effects being shown off. Then, after boarding a San Francisco subway train and travelling to the next station, the real fun begins. First a minor tremor, the lights flicker, but not much else. Then a full-scale quake, lights failing, pavement and cars falling through the ceiling, electrical wires and fittings fizzing around and gallons of water gushing down the stairs. Very realistic and can't wait to get to San Francisco.
After more expensive food in the authentic fifties' diner, which wasn't as good as the one in London, it was time for the finale of the evening. This was a Miami Vice based show on the lagoon with three speedboats chasing and shooting at each other, before blowing up a large tug in the middle of the lake. An action-packed end to a great day.

Afterwards we went to The Hard Rock Café which was next door. A little bit expensive but still great fun, good food and good music. It was far better than the one in London which seemed to be showing a film on Jewish fundamentalism on the night we went there.

As the last bus went at 7.30, we had to get a cab back to the hostel, which was affordable. It was an interesting ride with the driver verifying most of the things we already thought about the locals and going on about how America needed to "Kick Saddam's butt." We were diplomatic and kept quiet.

Friday February 22nd   Orlando

It was a bit cooler today, which was a pleasant relief from yesterday's heat. Not that it was cold, just, a pleasant seventy degrees. It was back to Disneyworld again to see The Epcot Centre, which we had been told was the best site there.

The day proved to be a long one, not helped by the fact that the exhibits and rides were a massive letdown, especially after yesterday's excitement.

The giant golf ball, also known as Spaceship Earth, dominates the first half of Epcot. The displays are all based around science and technology and to be perfectly honest, most of it is getting a bit dated.

The highlights here were The Journey into The Imagination, which had a reasonable ride, with quite good animations, despite an infuriatingly infectious tune that kept getting played. The Universe of Energy wasn't too bad, with a voyage through the land of the dinosaurs, although the moving dinosaurs at The National History Museum in London are far better and more lifelike.
The biggest waste of time here was the Epcot poll. First you could vote for the person of the century. You had five choices, so I entered Lenin, in order to annoy the locals and to see if they would arrest me for being a communist, then Peter Ward (Brighton and Hove Albion 1976 – 83) and for my third choice I tried to enter my mate, Nigel. At this point the machine had a fit and seemed to seize up. Maybe the CIA had seen my first answer.

There was another poll that was supposedly going to be used in the US press later in the week. Strange then, that this cross section of American life consisted of about 75% foreigners and that the subject was about the forthcoming Oscar nominations, with half of the films not having been released outside of America. I don't know about anyone else, but if any of the five choices were British, or failing that, that I'd actually heard of them, they got my vote. Not an ideal survey, I fear.

The low points of Epcot, and there were many, were The Journey to The Land, a boat trip through a large greenhouse where we could look at Walt's onions and fish farming techniques. In fact, these seemed quite cruel, and we seriously considered reporting Disney to the RSPCA. Horizons was a look at life in the 21st Century, which I'm sorry to say seemed even more mundane than life in the 20th Century.

To be fair, The Body Wars ride in The Wonders of Life, would have been quite exciting if we hadn't been to Universal first, but to be perfectly honest, there is no comparison.

The World Showcase was a slight improvement, especially when the first two countries, Mexico, and Norway, had entertaining rides. Norway actually sold its own beer in a little kiosk which was a pleasant change from American rubbish. The Mexican display didn't have beer but did have an entertaining music section which killed a few minutes.

The Chinese display, along with the French and Canadian presentations, consisted of a 360-degree cinema and a film showing the highlights each of them had to offer the American tourist. All very artificial, but at least the French display had a wine tasting shop which we had to investigate thoroughly.

The German, Italian and Japanese shows were pretty boring and consisted of places to eat or buy souvenirs.

And then we arrived at "The Magical Adventure of The United States." This proved to be the most biased and inaccurately sweeping historical accounts I have ever had to endure. It totally ignored the puritanical regimes of the first settlers, (or the original Taliban as I prefer to call them), Showed one old Native American surrendering, without showing all of his mates being massacred as the white man plundered the natural resources, did not show the persecution of slaves and continued struggle of the African Americans, failed to mention they were late for two World Wars, didn't mention Watergate, Irangate or Vietnam, I could go on. It2 did, to be fair, in its American Hall of Fame, credit Albert Einstein, a fine German brain.

For a country with little in the way of history, this attempt to clutch at an identity brought almost a standing ovation from the crowd. We remained unmoved.

The Moroccan show was notable only because of the guys with American accents, wearing a fez and a sheet. I fear Disney couldn't find any authentic Moroccans to come out here.

At last, the British display. And how does Disney represent us Brits? A castle perhaps, to commemorate our centuries of history? A display about royalty? No. It was The Rose and Crown, "Traditional Cockney Pub." Perhaps it's not such a bad view of British life, but it was one of the worst pubs I've ever been in. The beer, Harp, Guinness, or Bass was expensive. They didn't sell crisps. And worst of all, they kept ringing the bell for last orders every five minutes. This may have seemed like a quaint English tradition to The Yanks, but it only succeeded in making me paranoid. Every time the bell rang, I had a knee jerk reaction to get up and rush to the bar to get one last pint.

To make matters worse, I managed to insult the bar staff. Personally, I thought that a Viz t-shirt, was a prime example of modern British humour, and quite frankly, the word "Bo****ks" summed up my feelings towards the place. However, the locals found it offensive, and I had to cover it up.
The British souvenir shop was good for a laugh. Union Jack dart flights, plastic dinosaurs (???), postcards of The Queen and hundreds of postcards of Fergie. In fact, Fergie's new book, that she has plagiarised was getting a big sales push here.

The most insulting gift was the set of English beer mats, which had the flag of the Royal Family (German) and The Union Jack (British), rather than the flag of St George. It seems as though gifts here have to play along with the ignorance of the locals who persist in calling Britain, England.

The most bizarre gift was the set of English cars, which included a London Bus, a black London cab and a New York Taxi!
The evening's entertainment concluded with a firework display over the lake. I've seen better and don't know what all the fuss was about.

We caught the Youth Hostel bus at 10.30, which is more than can be said for one of the Japanese guys in our room, who got left behind. We met a couple of English girls on the bus who were doing the same sort of trip that we were. When we got back to the hostel I was shattered and went straight to bed, Steve for some reason had woken up again and was off to sniff out the two girls.

Saturday 23rd February   Orlando

I got woken up by Steve early this morning who informed me it was 8.30 and time for breakfast. This I found surprising, firstly as I was under the impression that we weren't going anywhere until about ten and secondly, we had a hostel breakfast on Thursday and as far as I was concerned, Steve thought that doughnuts were just as palatable at this hour in the morning as I did.

It transpired that somehow Steve had managed to talk the two girls we had met on the minibus last night, into coming to SeaWorld with us. It was the first I had heard about going to SeaWorld, but hey ho, just go with it. Furthermore, we were to meet them for doughnuts at nine o'clock.

Sue and Sarah turned out to be good fun anyway and it seems as though we may bump into them again, somewhere along the route. And I'm sure we will if Steve can arrange it. I will keep my ears open for further early breakfasts, as that seems to be a sign.

Sea World, as with Universal Studios, can be reached by bus, with a similar journey time of around an hour.

As was the case with Epcot, the grand build up that Sea World got in the advertising blurb proved to be an exaggeration. There were several medium sized tanks that housed stingrays, sea lions and dolphins. The latter two could be fed for $1, which gave you five raw fish. After the expensive and ropey pizza, I had for lunch, I wished I had held on to the fish for myself.

The favourite display for the locals were groups of sailors from the US Navy walking around in groups of three. They seemed to get a round of applause for doing anything. I'm sure I even heard cheering in the toilet.

Apart from the tanks, there were a few set shows, the most entertaining being Seymour and Clyde, the sea lions, in their 10 million BC show. The killer whale show was good, but nothing different to what you will have seen on TV. The sharks had a big build up, but that was all, whilst the penguins didn't even get a build-up.

Highlight of the day was going to be The Cap'n Kids area, but unfortunately, we were all too tall for this.
I was beginning to think that it may have been more fun to stay in bed this morning to be honest.

In the evening we got some more photographs developed and rather than listen to the bagpipe band in Church Street, we went back to the hostel and got some snacks from 7-11 around the corner.

One of the Japanese guys left tonight, which proved fairly comical. He wished us all "Good Ruck" and then said he was off to Miami. He then got into a taxi! I hope he realised Miami was over 200 miles away.

Sunday 24th February — Orlando to St Petersburg

As we had decided against going to New Orleans and Texas, today marked the first real change to our original plans. As we were enjoying the warmth in Florida, we decided to head from Orlando on the East Coast to St Petersburg on the West Coast for a few more days in the sun.

With the coach not leaving until after ten in the morning, we had a civilized start to the day. Breakfast at Orlando Coach Station was perhaps not quite so civilized.

The Greyhound Bus drivers Hall of Fame continued today with "Gator." His opening speech included the immortal line "Don't call me oi driver! Oi you up there, fatso or baldy. I like to be known as Gator, not alligator, Gator."

So off we went down "the super slabs" with Gator, all the way to St Petersburg. Every stop on the route seemed to be the winter camp of a major league baseball team. Gator let us know which one, and then rated their chances for the upcoming season.

There was bad traffic jam between Tampa and St Petersburg which resulted in us getting there an hour late. Our first impressions were not that good but got worse.

Our "Let's Go USA" guide, said that the hostel we were staying at, picked people up from the coach station, but after phoning them up, we were informed this was not the case on a Sunday. Once again, we had to get a cab, although, as it happened, we could have gone on foot.

The Detroit International Hostel is certainly very interesting. It reminds me a lot of The Addams Family House. The mano on the front desk with his half set of teeth and psychopathic stare, makes an ideal Lurch substitute, whilst within minutes of Steve going to find some change for the lockers, he came back with a strange tale about a very ill looking man that he had seen in the lift.

Our room has four comfortable looking beds in it, but unfortunately that's where it ends. The bathroom is condemned and if you seriously need a bath, an advanced course in levitation might be in order.

Always the optimists, we went out to investigate. In the lift we came across the very ill man and kept well away. It would appear that St Petersburg closes down on a Sunday, apart from the pier. It's not quite in the same league as the piers at home and didn't have any arcades. It did have a few shops, an aquarium, which wasn't anywhere near the size of SeaWorld, and a café on the top floor. Outside there was a crazy golf course which we tried out, but I messed up. Two up at the turn and then threw it away.

At about six o'clock we went back to the hostel in order to change before going out for something to eat. After asking where the best place to go was, we decided we didn't need to change as the only place open was the café we had just been to on the pier. And to make matters worse, they shut at eight.

Preparing ourselves for a fun night at Cha Cha Coconuts, well until eight at least, we retraced our steps back to the pier. As it turned out, the food was reasonable in price, as was the beer and must rank as one of the better meals we have had. It was nice to sit and eat, overlooking the bay, with storks flying low across the water and light aircraft coming into the nearby airfield that's runway stretched into the sea. The service was good too and the waitress did her best to suggest things we could do the following day.

On the way back to the hostel we popped into The Pelican Bar for a quick drink, but I wish we hadn't. It was dire.

We returned for another early night only to find that a thrash metal band were playing directly below us. I wonder if they know "We've Got to Get Out Of This Place?"

Monday February 25th   St Petersburg

After a night sleeping in my sleeping sheet, rather than the bed clothes (I didn't trust them) we headed off into the town for breakfast.

St Petersburg seems full of pensioners, a sort of elephants' graveyard. Perhaps comparable with Eastbourne and Bexhill with a better climate, but not as nice in other ways.

The ill man was still in the lift this morning, and seemed to be riding it up and down with a small Latino in a baseball cap. We didn't ask. We had breakfast at South Gate Coffee Shop on 3rd Street. The waitresses all looked ill, the food wasn't good, and the cutlery and plates weren't washed properly. It may have been cheap, but I'm sure many a hospital bill has arisen from this place.

The object of the morning was to send parcels back home and to buy a new pair of jeans to replace the ones that zip had self-destructed on me in Orlando.

Both missions were successfully completed, so we came back to the hostel. A new person, a woman, was on the front desk. "You must be Reynolds and Scott" she said. God this place gives me the creeps. They've worked out who we are. We ordered the lift. The ill man got out. We got off on the second floor, his mate with the baseball hat was waiting for us as we got out of the lift. What a place.

Back in what we thought was the sanctuary of our room, we prepared to go out sightseeing for the afternoon. My bed had been stripped of all its bedding, and my belongings tossed on to the next bed. I just thought that the cleaners were halfway through their job and thought nothing of it. A few minutes later, the very ill man and his mate in the hat walk in and it transpires that they are actually the cleaners. It looks like another night in my sleeping sheet.

Once we thought the coast was clear we left, only to see the man in the hat by the lift. "See you later guys" he said. "Not if we see you first" we both thought to ourselves. We got in the lift. Pressed the button to go down to the lobby, we went to the top floor. By the time we got to the lobby, needless to say, the man with the hat was there again. By this stage we were beginning to expect it.

The shops in St Petersburg do not exactly warrant too much time. There is a new shopping mall, but at this stage, only four shops had opened. There was one street that had nothing but junk shops and not particularly nice ones at that.

To be honest, apart from the beach, there is very little to do in St Petersburg. The two major attractions, if not the only attractions, are situated next to each other, just a short walk from downtown.
The Salvador Dali Museum hosts what is boasted as the largest collection of the artists' works in America. This proved an interesting way to kill a couple of hours and was also quite enlightening, in that the guide pointed out segments of certain paintings that you were unlikely to discover by yourself.

Over the road is Great Explorations, yet another scientific and electronically based museum, primarily aimed at kids. There are numerous displays which test your strength, agility, and fitness. Obviously, we were both well below average on all counts. Somewhat disappointing I fear, and I didn't need to part with $4 to be told I was a physical wreck.

For lunch it was back to Cha Cha Coconuts and their happy hour which consisted of beers for 75 cents, cheap shrimps, chicken wings and tortilla chips, of which we had copious amounts. We sat on the balcony again, watching a number of F16 US Airforce planes flying back to their base in Tampa and the seagulls flying across the bay, one of which took a large dump straight into a woman's dinner on the adjacent table. Look on the bright side I thought, it could have been a stork.

We returned to the hostel around 5.30. There were a few old men watching the TV in the lounge, so we called the lift. The guy in the hat came out, we pushed the button for the second floor and ended up on the third again.

We hadn't planned to go out again until 7.30, so we sought sanctuary in our room. A German guy, who was sharing the room, was there and we were lazing around talking when the door began to open. Not the man in the hat again, we thought. Enter a man in full bright red motorcycle leathers, still wearing his crash helmet, carrying something under his arm that looked like a gun case.

Thankfully, first impressions are not always correct, and the guy's name was Paul, he was Canadian and was travelling across the USA on his motorbike.

The four of us went out for the evening to the two bars next to the hostel. The first of these was a rather seedy affair. Steve got collared by a Yugoslavian refugee and I got lumbered next to a strange man who had seemingly travelled the world, but was deaf in one ear, hence a rather one-way conversation. There was also a Christian Scientologist who carved sticks and had a sever hand infection which he believed God was going to cure. It looked as though he had been on God's waiting list for some time by the colour of the wound. Then there was the Greek gentleman who told a joke about a black woman and a bowling ball. All in all, I guess you could say it was a mixed crowd.

Not before time, we headed to the next bar. This one had a pool table, and you could escape the locals. After a couple of games, we retired to the main bar where there were a couple of other people from the hostel. Firstly, two Austrian girls, one of whom had a striking resemblance to Goebbels (I didn't tell her that). I fear both had drunk far too much, but this did not deter them from having any more. They had a fine grasp of the English language but seemed to favour set phrases such as "Oh Really" and "Are you serious?". Not too stimulating. The other person there was a Brit who left home a couple of years ago to work as a mechanic in Bermuda. An interesting decision to make.

There were also a couple of guys from home at the hostel. One was working as a pilot at the local airfield whilst the other had run out of money and was working for the hostel. Enough to live on, but no chance of saving enough to get home. Supposedly he was getting some money wired out to him. I would hope so for his own sanity, as being stuck indefinitely at The Detroit Hostel doesn't bear thinking about.

By the time we got back to our room, the entertainment downstairs was finishing. Slightly better tonight as it was Richard Thompson from Fairport Convention. Thankfully we could get some sleep before our long trip north in the morning.

Tuesday February 26th   St Petersburg to Memphis

Somewhat relieved, we checked out of the hostel at 8.30, without any further encounters with the cleaners. I bought a couple of postcards as souvenirs, but it must be said that the choice was a bit limited.
Before walking back to the bus station, we made another abortive attempt to buy a British newspaper to get the football results.

Evidently, they are delivered by Greyhound Bus. This explains a lot. In fact, greyhound continued to cock things up. Not that they haven't got us and our luggage from a to b each time, it's just that they don't exactly make it easy for themselves. Steve and I both had our tickets validated to Memphis, both had entirely different routes, neither of which were correct.

Our driver from St Petersburg as far as Tallahassee, although not as talkative as some of his predecessors, was still notable, mainly for his excessive use of the brakes. He'd nearly caused one accident before we got to Tampa and continued to terrorize other road users throughout Florida.

The bus stations in the north of the state were not much to write home about. The towns that we stopped in were minimal in size and the facilities reflected this. Most of them were located in garages, however there was one in a town called Perry, that seemed to have its bus station in a junk shop.

At every conceivable stop, about half of the passengers on the bus get off for a cigarette. This doesn't seem to matter whether it is for one quick drag, they still seem to do it. Unfortunately, at one remote stop, one guy took one drag too many and got left behind. Rather fittingly, this was very close to The Suwannee River, which he was now well and truly down.

Once again there proved to be plenty of weird people on the overnight leg of the journey. A less than peaceful night was not helped by a Japanese man who had the loudest nasal snore I've ever heard, and he was backed up by a local woman who insisted on clearing her throat every hour and spitting out the remains in the bus.

Around midnight, we changed buses in Birmingham, Alabama. I've had a few scary moments in my life, but I can honestly say, Birmingham Alabama bus station ranks pretty high on the list. Even worse than Birmingham, West Midlands.

Wednesday February 27th   Memphis

We arrived very tired, at seven o'clock in the morning. The outskirts of the city didn't exactly look memorable, however there must be something to see here.

First priority was to phone the hostel, as we had forgotten to do so from S t Petersburg. At 7.30 in the morning, the last thing you want to hear is that the hostel will be shut until 5.30 in the evening. This was far too long, so we decided to go upmarket for a couple of nights and checked in at The Days Inn Hotel, opposite the bus station in Grand Union Street. It only worked out to be about an extra $20 each for the two nights. By the time we would have paid for a taxi to and from the hostel, and subsequent rips into the city, the savings would be minimal anyway. In any case, it was nice to have a comfortable bed and more importantly, an ensuite toilet and a television, which always seems to be good for a laugh over here. Having said that, MTV are still playing the same records over and over (i.e., Wilson Phillips, Chris Isaak, London Beat and Billy Idol). After changing and cleaning up, we went out in search of some food as we hadn't eaten properly on the journey. We didn't really get the chance as our only prolonged stop was at Birmingham, Alabama, and we were too busy hiding from the locals to be brave enough to search for something to eat.

The first thing that struck me about Memphis is that there isn't anybody here. For what is supposed to be America's 15th largest city, it seemed strange that there was never any more than about ten people in sight at any given time. Perhaps they hibernate. I don't know, but it seemed very weird.

Breakfast at The Whizzy Q Lunchette did not prove to be the highlight of the day. In fact, it was so disgusting we left most of it behind. Notably the coffee with lumpy milk. Being British, we didn't complain.

Continuing through the deserted streets, we wandered down to The Mississippi River, which cuts through the centre of town. The best view is evidently from Mud Island, a complex set in the heart of the river, however this was shut, and we had to make do with what we could see from the bank. We also fancied a trip on a paddle steamer, but these were out of bounds too.
Along by the docks are a few remaining cotton factors, remnants of an age when the city and the river flourished, due to the transportation of cotton upriver from the plantations. Opposite the boatyard is a small, photographic display, outlining the role Memphis played in the industry, which is very interesting, but fails to do justice to what is an important part of the areas, and country's historical development.

On to Beale Street, birthplace of The Blues, and to a place we had hoped would be a bit livelier. Admittedly there was a large black woman in a red coat who shouted something that sounded like "Rabbi" at us, but that was about it. I've been called a lot of things in my life, but I must admit, never a rabbi.

There are several bars along Beale Street, but first we went into the local Police Museum, which was also in fact the Police Station. Quite an interesting museum and worth 30 minutes of our time. It was full of memorabilia, including photographs of a number of suspects from the thirties, most of whom would have been stopped and searched by The Metropolitan Police.

Next door to the Police Museum is Schwab's Store, which boasts to be the oldest in Memphis. I wouldn't be surprised if Abe Schwab was there when it opened about a hundred years ago as he tends to blend in quite well. We wandered around by ourselves for a while, looking at the goods on sale, most of which probably belonged in the museum on the second floor. To put it plainly, the clothes were not that fashionable and quite frankly, if you wanted something in particular, you wouldn't shop here. But if there was something you couldn't find anywhere else; I'm sure Abe would have it in stock.
It is unlikely that anyone can leave without Abe accosting them, getting them to sign the visitors' book and presenting them with a Schwab's gift pack.

By this time, we were thirsty, so we tried to sniff out a decent bar. Alfred's on Beale Street looked just the place, until a strange black man, who must have been about eighty, came out wearing an olive green, leather jump suit and asked us to come in.
We decided against this and proceeded to the next bar. Sitting outside was a fat, middle aged black gentleman with a large T Shirt stall and a ghetto blaster, playing the blues. He gave us so much grief, we went back to Alfred's. It wasn't too bad, a standard American bar that had live music in the evening. The strange man in the green suit introduced himself as "Pops." Evidently, we Brits are full of lurve, and the world needs more people like us. Hear, hear.
Before our afternoon itinerary began, we headed for a travel agent to bring the date of our flight from San Francisco forward. Money seems to be going a bit too quickly at present and fortunately, flights to Australia don't seem too booked up.

After we had sorted this out, we headed up 3rd Street to go to Sun Studios. For $4, the tour is not exactly long. You get about 15 minutes with a producer who tells you the story of how Elvis, Jerry Lee Lewis, Roy Orbison, Carl Perkins, and Johnny Cash started their recording careers there. Then he showed off a few bits of memorabilia. If it wasn't for its historical significance, Sun Studios would be small and a waste of time. But as it was where Rock and Roll was conceived, it will always remain a place of pilgrimage, in any case, if it's good enough for U2 to visit, it was good enough for us.

We went back to the hotel after this and lazed around in front of the TV for an hour or so, before heading out in the evening for something to eat.

In Downtown Alley, next to our hotel, there is The Rendezvous, supposedly a Memphis legend, whose barbecued ribs are evidently available via mail order. Seriously? If our local kebab shop offered that service, I can only imagine the congealed mess that the postman would have to post through your letterbox. It was cheap, it was close, so we gave it a try. I found The Rendezvous memorable for one major reason. From the moment we left our hotel, walked to the restaurant, ordered, had dinner, drank a pitcher of beer, settled the bill, and went back again, took only forty minutes. Truly amazing service. And the food? Bland and tasteless. I can hear my Postman sighing with relief from here.

Thursday 28th February   Memphis

Having fallen asleep at 8.30 the night before, it was perhaps a reflection on how tiring, travelling by bus is, when we awoke twelve hours later. Having said that, I'm sure we needed it.

The morning started with breakfast and after yesterday's disaster at Whizzy Q, we decided to go for the café at The Greyhound Bus Station over the road, as it couldn't be any worse. In fact, it wasn't bad at all, and two fried eggs, toast and coffee proved very reasonable.

We had booked a tour to Graceland at 10 am, which was to pick us up at our hotel. Blues City Tours run several different excursions and they are based within The Days Inn, where we were staying. The trip cost $22 and included a return trip to Graceland, which was about six miles from the city centre, admission to the house and grounds, a tour of "The Lisa Marie" Elvis' personal Aeroplane and a small museum called Elvis Close Up. We didn't get admission to the car museum but quite frankly, enough is enough.

I found the tour very interesting and although I have never been a fan of Elvis and never owned a single record of his, I left with a certain admiration and respect for the man.

You cannot deny that he had a great voice and was fortunate enough to sing some very good songs, however it was the personal side to the story that was most interesting. Here was a man who could have done, or had whatever he wanted, but still remained faithful to his own community where he was raised and didn't shirk his responsibilities, by doing National Service. The fact that he gave $50,000 per year to the city of Memphis is not that wonderful when you consider the amount of money available to the man, it is only when you consider that he refused to claim it back as tax relief that it becomes admirable.

Charity, unfortunately seemed to die with Elvis and a number of locals seem to be out to make a quick buck by opening tacky souvenir shops all along Elvis Pressley Boulevard, which leads to Graceland.
The tour of Graceland costs $11, which at first may seem steep to those not paying homage to a lifetime idol. Admittedly, a tour of an early twentieth century house with trashy sixties and outlandish seventies décor is not quite in the same league as Hampton Court, however, I personally found it worthwhile. The $4.75 for two minutes on an aeroplane, the $2 for three glass cabinets with nick knacks and probably the car museum, seemed excessively overpriced.

There was somebody on our tour who visited Graceland on a regular basis and as long as there are die-hard fans prepared to do this, there will be far more people happy to relieve them of their money.

My one regret here was that we were unable to buy a peanut butter and banana sandwich fried in bacon grease, the sandwich he was eating when he was found dead on the toilet. As the toilets were open to visitors, I thought this would have been a fitting tribute to the man. Maybe I should head back to Memphis after this trip and open a stall selling them. It's no worse than some of the other tack being sold around here.

The trip to Graceland was made even more worthwhile when we bought a copy of USA Today and it had the football results in.

On the bus back to the hotel we met a couple of middle-aged women from Las Vegas. They invited us to stay with them when we got there but I don't think we will as they are out of Steve's preferred age range.

Back at base, it was time for lunch, and we headed up Union Street to the corner of 3rd, to Sleep Out Louie's, an interesting bar that had an extensive selection of beers. I had a couple of bottles of Red Stripe along with an interesting salad. The main portion of the salad was a tuna and mayonnaise mixture. It was on a base of lettuce, melon, orange, and apple. On the side of the plate was a slice of chocolate cake/. Weird, but very tasty.

The afternoon was spent, firstly, in The Museum of Southern Folklore in Beale Street, which was just a display of local crafts, including a stuffed ninja turtle. I'm not sure I would recommend the place to other tourists.
The plan after this was to head to The Peabody Hotel, where at 5pm, the hotel's ducks are marched from the foyer fountain, across the red carpet and into the lift (the opposite happens at 11 am). As to whether the ducks have their own five-star rooms that they go back to each night is a mystery.

This plan changed, however. We left in plenty of time as we wanted to try and get a picture of "Pops" outside of Alfred's. He was sitting on the opposite side of the road by a shed. At first, we walked past and then on the way back we went to say hello, to see if he remembered us. This he did and invited us both to have our pictures taken with him. Then he marched us off into a local café to see his scrapbook. It transpires that Pops Davis is a local celebrity and has been hanging around Beale Street for years (around sixty at a rough guess). A few years earlier, Alfred's threw an 80th Birthday party for him and even President Reagan sent him a telegram. This along with hundreds of photographs are in his scrapbook. Which he is rightly proud of and we were both honoured to see. We offered to buy him a drink, but in the end, we ended up giving him some money, which he asked for. To "keep up appearances" was his excuse, but he probably saw us coming.

After going back to our room, having missed the ducks, we sat through a dreadful edition of Family Feud (Family Fortunes) before heading out for the evening.

The Rum Boogie Café is probably the most touristy venue on Beale Street. The food was reasonable; however, the service was slightly strange. The waitress seemed more obsessed with our accents rather than serving us any food or drink. The music, provided by The Rum Boogie Band was good and on top of just playing Blues, they also did requests, which made them popular with the crowd.

Unfortunately, I had managed to get a headache and wanted to return to the hotel for an early night, leaving Steve in front of The Home Shopping Club, which was having a baseball card sale, which attracted some complete anoraks to phone in.

Friday 1st March   Memphis to Denver

We checked out of the hotel at about ten o'clock and headed back to the bus station for some breakfast, prior to what was going to be our longest bus journey of the trip. Departing Memphis at 11.15 in the morning, we were due to arrive in Denver at 1 pm the following afternoon. We also lost an hour, crossing from Eastern Standard Time to Mountain Time too.

We had a couple of early morning calls overnight. Firstly at 3 am and then at 7 am we received wake up calls from reception, which were intended for other rooms.

Not only was this trip the longest, it was also one of the more eventful ones. The weather was pretty miserable as we left Memphis, in fact it was so wet that the rain was coming through the windows of the bus.

Our first nightmare occurred at Osceola in Arkansas. A pretty standard stop we all thought. A small town, nobody was waiting to get on, but the driver got off to check anyway. Five minutes elapsed and then there was a loud banging sound. Nobody moved as everyone is fairly apathetic on a Greyhound Bus. The banging continued until one lady got up and realised that it was the driver who had somehow managed to lock himself out. Five minutes ensued whilst the woman tried to work out how to open the doors and let the driver back onboard.

Far from being thankful to the poor woman, the driver almost left the next bus station without her. We had in fact travelled a few hundred yards down the road and stopped at a light, before the woman, who wasn't exactly young, caught us up and started banging on the door.

The inability of the American Greyhound Bus traveler to control the urge to smoke is amazing. At every stop, for whatever length of time, be it 30 seconds or 30 minutes, a procession of people leave the bus, light up, stub it out again and march back on. It's all quite sad really.

The nightmare continued, when at Festus, Missouri we picked up two black girls who started to sing very badly. The singing went on and on and set off a baby who was sitting in front of us.
There was then an unscheduled stop, when one guy got caught smoking in the toilet for a second time and was ejected from the bus.

The road to St Louis was incredibly straight and not exactly stimulating. In fact, perversely, the road started to bend at Herculaneum. Caesar and other Roman road builders would be turning in their graves. These Yanks get everything wrong.

On to St Louis, where we had to make a connection to another bus, heading to Kansas City and then on to Denver. If the trip to St Louis was bad, the trip west was ten times worse. For starters there were too many people and they had to lay on an extra bus.

The occupants of the second bus were as follows. Steve and I, a couple of locals going to Denver, a businessman going from The East Coast to Omaha on a bus for a bet, two single girls (Steve managed to sit behind one and across from the other), a group of eight black youths who spent the whole journey to Kansas City composing a rap song and a hillbilly who clearly hadn't washed for about a month and was on crutches. This man, despite the fact that he smelled, was the unfortunate victim of ridicule from everyone on board, including the driver, who on seeing him, told him that he should go back to the subway. On the presentation of a valid ticket, this poor guy was forced to struggle to the back of the bus, running the gauntlet of insults. The fact that he was just as entitled to board the bus as anyone else but got treated as a second or even third-class passenger was pretty bad. Unfortunately, it seems that if you aren't perfect in this country, you are not acceptable.

As far as I was concerned, our arrival in Kansas City didn't come soon enough. The bus station was relatively empty, apart from two Buddhist monks who seemed to be chain smoking and listening to their Walkman's. This is a bizarre place.

The ensuing journey overnight was very long, very boring, and very tiring.

Saturday 2nd March Denver

We didn't get to Denver until 2pm. The journey was not exactly helped by the Kansas scenery, which couldn't have been flatter and a driver whose incoherent mumblings resulted in nobody quite knowing where they were. Most notable stop being Aurora, which our driver pronounced as "Arrrrrr".

The glittering, mirrored skyscrapers, all too familiar from the opening credits of "Dynasty" are presumably what most people expect to see from downtown Denver. The reality is slightly different, Whereas the small area where most of these buildings are housed is very attractive, the most striking thing I found about the city were the vast areas of urban wasteland, just across the road.

The hostel was situated in such an area. A wide-open car park faced the building, whilst the adjoining roads housed such wonderful establishments as The Salvation Army hostel, not exactly renowned for its upstanding pillars of society. It's also a little disconcerting when you check into somewhere, where the warden, who worked in the launderette downstairs, informs you that whereas it is safe to go anywhere in the blocks towards the city centre, you should not venture more than a block back the other way.

This dwindled into incognisance as it soon transpired, we had bigger problems. We were given the keys to room 210. We were the first people to be given these keys for some time. The room had in fact been thoroughly fumigated four times since the last residents left, minus their bed bugs. Despite the reassurances from the warden, "If you have any problems with them, let us know. We couldn't help but draw the conclusion we were guinea pigs.

If we didn't have any severe problems with bugs, we were soon making sure that someone else opened the room door due to the severe blue flashes of static electricity that flew each time either of us touched it. Overall, The Melbourne Hotel is a good hostel, in that it is friendly, communal, provides free coffee and there are fridges in each room. The bedbugs and electric shocks were purely incidental.

After freshening up, we wandered back to the city centre and looked around the shops on 16th Street Mall. Not exactly Oxford Street, in fact there was hardly anybody around. Having said that, the shops were not exactly worth writing home about. The highlight, as expected, was a bar we found. The Mall Street Exchange Bar had a wide selection of imported bottled beers. I managed a bottle of Moosehead and a giant bottle of New Zealand Steinlager. Steve, being more adventurous, plumped for something called Sharps. This turned out to be a non-alcoholic version of Miller Lite (Ouch!) Considering supermarkets were spawned in this country, our inability to find one has been quite astounding. In fact, we considered it a major triumph to find a Japanese store on our way back to the hostel. Steve finally managed to buy some nuts, to relieve his complaint. Whilst we both splashed out 75 cents on a pot noodle. Disgusting, but cheap.

In the evening we went to The Mercury Café, which was a few yards from the hostel. The food, although slightly expensive ($8 for a salad and turkey stroganoff) was excellent. It's nice to eat properly every so often!

The café turned out to be one of Denver's trendiest eating and drinking establishments. Tonight, there was a play in the downstairs theatre and a band upstairs. This I fear turned out to be quite insignificant on the discovery of several bottles of Theakston's Old Peculiar in a fridge behind the bar. Some culture at last.

We actually went out with an American girl named Judy who we attempted to educate throughout the course of the evening. She seemed quite persistent in getting us to go to Boulder, a city about thirty miles north from here. The fact that we aren't going tends to suggest one thing. Steve wasn't interested in her.

Sunday March 3rd   Denver

A rather uneventful morning in that we did our washing in the adjacent launderette and found a Safeway, where we bought some food to eat at the hostel. A fruit salad for breakfast proved to be a pleasant change from the normal fat ridden American start to the day.

In the afternoon we headed back to the city centre to see if anything was open. If Saturday in Denver appears dull, Sunday seemed ten times worse. Our attempts to find something to do and somewhere to have lunch were epitomised by our break in McDonalds. We finally had to do it!

The only place that was open, apart from McDonald's, was The Denver Art Museum, a prison like citadel, blotting the otherwise pleasant part of town. We stayed for a couple of hours, both making full use of the exceptionally clean toilets. I must point out that they were not as scenic as the ones in the hostel, which had clear windows and gave amazing views of the city when you looked out. Slightly less enjoyable views looking in I would guess. As long as you can get your trousers down without anyone outside noticing, it proved very therapeutic.

The museum was on six floors, each devoted to a separate mode of art. Various exhibits from Mexican artists on the ground floor, of which, those used for political expression seemed the most interesting. Other floors included Native American art, an unimpressive American artist's section, some nondescript European art, and the top floor was for modern art. This consisted of a video screen showing somebody digging a hole. It went over my head.

The highlight of the visit, apart from the clean toilets, would have been the roof where the scenery over The Rocky Mountains was said to be spectacular, especially as today was a very clear day.

This was not to be though as somebody decided to jump off a few years ago and it was sealed off due to security concerns.
After leaving the museum, we tried to book up a trip to the mountains, Gray Line offer tours and there was one that left at 2pm in the afternoon going to Red Rocks Canyon, Buffalo Bills grave and The Coors Brewery which would give me a chance to tell the head brewer what I actually think about the garbage he produces. They have said that they need five people to run the tour and so far, we are the only two. We live in hope.

If finding some Old Peculiar last night was a major discovery, we surpassed it this afternoon. The Wynkoop Brewing Company, opposite the Railway Station, is a pub along the lines of the English Firkin pubs and brews its own ales. Its ESB was exceptionally tasty, and the porter was nice too. There was also an IPA and a stout which we didn't have time to sample, but it was very nice to come across a pub in our own tradition, rather than a typically naff American bar, serving cold fizzy, watery beer.

Feeling a lot happier with the world, we made our way back to base to discover a new guinea pig in room 210, As the Brits hadn't complained about the alleged bugs in the room, an Australian was now thrown into the den. In fact, he had not been informed of our privileged status and was somewhat alarmed to find out.

The three of us went out for dinner to The Old Spaghetti Factory, which was on the corner of 18th Street and Larimar. A fairly extensive pasta-based menu and most courses priced under $6. Not only cheap, but very filling.

We decided to call back into The Mercury Café on our way back but were mortified to discover that their supply of Old Peculiar had been exhausted. Not a happy end to the day.

Monday March 4thDenver

Horror of horrors, I woke up this morning fearing the worst. There seemed to be a strange itching sensation in certain areas but thankfully this would appear to have been psychological as it seemed to disappear by mid-morning.

There was more life in the city this morning, proving that people do actually live in Denver. Having said that, we still ended up in McDonalds for breakfast again.

First stop today was the US Mint, where you can get a free tour, which proved to be pretty tedious. You get to see a group of workers operating large machines, endlessly producing piles and piles of money to sustain the US economy. The only major point of interest was the search we had to endure on entering the building. A strange electronic device was used to see if we had anything dangerous on our persons and whereas I emptied my pockets, my bottom was still setting off an alarm. I was going to explain that I had been to McDonalds and that has a certain effect on my insides, but the security guard seemed to lack a sense of humour. This was not helped when my backpack set the alarm off too. Another full search ensued, thankfully not a full body one.

Our cheap day continued with a second free tour, this time around the Capital Building. To be honest, it is little more than a glorified town hall with a gold-plated dome, but the guide gave an interesting lecture as he walked us around. We also got to see the mountains too, as we scaled the stairs to the dome, from where you get some amazing views.

Unfortunately, though, this was as close to the mountains as we were going to get, as we phoned Gray Line Tours from here and they hadn't found anybody else who wanted to go on the afternoon tour.

It was in the Capital Building that Steve either showed his amazing multilingual abilities or American culture shot itself in the foot again. There were two Swiss girls on the tour and our guide tried to share his expert knowledge with us all. He had been to Switzerland and had enjoyed a mysterious Nerktal cheese. The Swiss girls shrugged their shoulders, but Steve managed to fathom out that he actually meant Neuchatel and saved any further embarrassment.

With no conceivable trips available to the mountains, it was back to the bedbugs and electric shocks of the hostel, and a look through our guidebook to see if Denver could offer anything at all. In the end, we plumped for The Colorado History Museum which proved to be fairly interesting and took a couple of hours to wander around. The sections relating to the early settlements were far more interesting as I have never found 20th Century history particularly fascinating. Having said that, there isn't much else in this country. Or at least anything they admit to.

The most fascinating part was that relating to how the Native American was pushed aside by the settlers. There was a picture of a Chief, negotiating with local officials, but only after his tribe had been wiped out. It has to be said American Foreign Policy hasn't changed much. It is all too familiar really. The Indians were rehoused in reservations and became second class citizens in their own country. And even then, lo and behold, there are records of oil being found on one reservation and the land that was given back to them was immediately stripped away again. One wonders whether in a hundred years' time, when the American influence over the world has declined and they don't control the narrative, whether a more truthful history will be written showing how it was all driven by greed and a contempt of human life.

Over the road from the museum was the library, where at last we found some football results. Brighton one's at least. Tooting results are proving a bit more difficult.

Wandering back down the Mall, passing a female version of Pops on the way, we ended up in Finnegan's, Denver's Irish pub. Not such a bad pit stop. I had a Samuel Adams, a beer from Boston which wasn't too bad, and, in the end, an American businessman paid our bill for us (four beers and some chips). The fact that we had both been slagging off his country might have been the reason and we took this gesture as a small apology on behalf of the American people.

Back at the hostel, we cooked the food we had bought the day before and discovered how everybody else had a wonderful time in New Orleans and had been skiing in the mountains. We kept quiet about the US Mint.

Tuesday March 5th   Denver to Santa Fe

We had to make an early start from the hostel at 6.30 am, but thankfully, once we had boarded the bus, there were not many people on board. In fact, after about ten minutes there were even fewer people on the bus as one guy, who was destined for Pueblo, decided to get off, claiming it was too claustrophobic. I suppose it beats being left behind. To make matters worse, he got off at a railway crossing just as a giant freight train was passing through and had to stand by the bus for five minutes.

Heading south towards Colorado Springs, we finally hit the mountains. Admittedly it wasn't quite the same way that the majority of travelers had got there, but nevertheless it was nice to sit back and take in the scenery.

The views, travelling through Pueblo and down towards Raton in New Mexico were in stark contrast to what we had seen before and was a refreshing change. Mind you, the towns of Raton, Wagon Mound and Las Vegas, New Mexico were hardly places I would ever want to end up in.

Las Vegas being especially noteworthy because it bears no resemblance whatsoever to its more illustrious namesake in Nevada, and secondly, because our driver managed to meet his long-lost sister. Hence a delay of at least ten minutes.

Rather ominously, we passed through a torrential rainstorm in the mountains to the north of Santa Fe. Thankfully it had stopped by the time we reached the bus station. But that was the least of our problems.

We had read about Santa Fe and had got the impression of a historical town, built in old Mexican adobe style. The reality appeared to be a little different. An adobe Greyhound Station? No chance! Another grotty building in an area that didn't have too much to say for itself architecturally. Our opinions were not helped by a mile-long hike, through some dodgy areas to the hostel. Not that this was a major issue, but it was a world away from some of the glitzier cities we had been in.

The hostel was hardly a welcoming sight for weary travelers. It consisted of two one story buildings, constructed out of baked mud in a suitable shade of brown. To be fair they did try and make us welcome here. There was free coffee and free Bounty Bars and then for $1 you could dig into the communal stew. This looked pretty revolting and to make matters worse, you were still expected to do a chore every day. Mind you the dormitories could have done with a clean and the toilets were hardly going to help Steve with his condition. The other person in our dorm was a strange guy with a beard who insisted on strumming nondescript tunes on his guitar. We made a quick exit and headed for The Plaza, where we had been told there were a few bars and places to eat. This proved to be another long walk and this time it did rain and quite hard too. The fat that we were soaking wet hardly helped the fact that these bars were either shut, too expensive or didn't even exist.

Before admitting the ultimate defeat and going to McDonalds, or heaven forbid, back for the communal stew, we decided to go to Pizza Hut. Knowing a bargain when we see one, the offer of buy one medium pizza and get a second for $4 seemed great. That is until you realise that a medium pizza is designed for two and when you are suddenly confronted with the second one, it becomes a bit of a struggle. Steve insisted that our second pizza, a local speciality called a "roadrunner" was put in a doggy bag, I really didn't care if I ever saw a pizza again. The rain was still teeming down and halfway back, the sodden doggy bag was discarded in a hedge.

Back in our room, there were an alarming number of hillbillies with an average age of around 40, which was probably a lot higher than there average IQ. Someone mentioned that it was likely to snow in the next few days. God, I hope not. I don't fancy being stuck here for a week.

We hung our soaking clothes up to dry and had another early night.

Wednesday March 6th   Santa Fe

Although we didn't get up until 9 o clock, there were still a few chores left to be done in the hostel. So, before we could escape, we had to clean the dorms. Outside of the hostel, the hillbillies were actually carrying out repairs to the building. It seems that they have come here to work. I can think of a few better places.

We finally escaped and headed for The Tecolate café, about 500 yards further down the road from the hostel. The breakfast here was probably the best we have had so far. The burrito was very filling, very hot and very reasonable in price. The only annoying thing was the service, which as per usual was frequent and in your face. Black Bear Records across the road was to prove too much of a temptation for Steve and he proudly walked out with a cheap CD and a Mexican Queen single.

Before we went sightseeing, we hit the library in our continuing search for English football results and finally a Sunday paper from Dallas came up trumps. Shame we lost at home to Oldham.

The town looked a little more appealing this morning. For a start it wasn't raining and secondly, the shops were actually open. Rather than the dull impression from the previous night, the town square looked fairly pleasant. All the shops, even Woolworths, were built in adobe style and a dull shade of brown. Woolies even had its own chili take away for sale, something that would never have caught on in the Bracknell branch.

The Palace of Governors proved to be a very interesting building. Outside there were lots of Native Americans, sitting on the ground, selling their own crafts and jewelry. This was, in a way, good to see that their traditions continued, but I am sure the white man makes them pay handsomely for their prime pitch outside of the palace. Inside was a museum outlining the history of New Mexico and plenty more evidence of how the white man trod all over the natives.

The prettiest building in Santa Fe was The Museum of Fine Art, which had some nice pieces on display and some less nice modern art.

The one thing we did ascertain the previous evening was the lack of decent bars, or at least affordable ones. When we did have lunch, it was fairly decadent in that we both had a Banana Cream Pie as solace for not being able to afford the beer.

To walk this off, we headed off down the old Santa Fe Trail and needless to say, got lost. We stopped at St Francis' Cathedral which was very modern and seemed out of place in such a historic town. In fact, there were other churches along the trail that seemed slightly more interesting, notably one that had a tale of a mysterious carpenter, who appeared out if nowhere, had very few tools but erected a spiral staircase in a small chapel, without the use of scaffolding. Then disappeared never to be seen again. They really are gullible aren't they.

Back at the hostel, we took advantage of the free coffee and Bounty Bars but left the communal stew to bubble away. We started speaking to a girl who was travelling by Greyhound bus too. Clearly, we weren't the only nutters doing it. As we left in the evening, the girl turned left, and so did Steve. I had to point out that beer and food were completely in the opposite direction.

We planned to bite the bullet tonight and pay for a decent meal. We couldn't go to Pizza Hut again, so we ended up in Vicki Lee's Southern BBQ. The food was cheap, albeit a little greasy, not that Steve minded as he was gawking at Melissa, the barmaid all night. I had other fish to fry, as a group of amateur Americans had ordered, what they thought was a glass of beer, only to get a large pitcher. We happily drank the rest for them.

The evening ended up with us taking on the proprietors' sons at darts, albeit with strange rules and no doubles. The final score was England 1 USA 1 (I lost), but we had a really good evening.
That was until we got back to the hostel, and we were informed that as we wanted to leave early the following morning, we would need to clean the toilets tonight.

Thursday March 7th   Santa Fe to Flagstaff

It was still dark when we got up and only just getting light as we walked back down the railway line to the Greyhound Bus Station, which was deserted when we got there.

By the time the bus was due, a few people had appeared, notably one guy who looked like he was straight from the set of The Magnificent Seven. Large moustache, a scar on one cheek, cheap cigarette dangling from his lip and dressed like a Mexican bandit.

In fact, it was quite revealing to get on a bus at 7 am, just to see the state of the passengers who had travelled overnight. The first stint of the journey was only a ninety-minute drive to Albuquerque, but the mountain scenery was very pretty, and it was a pleasant ride. Unfortunately, our connecting bus was full, so we had to wait for a second bus to be made ready. When we finally got away, it was quite relaxing to sit back and watch the Arizona countryside pass by. We also read the local paper and the major news story was about a twelve-year-old boy who had been taken to court by a sports memorabilia shop. Allegedly, the boy had been sold a $12,000 baseball card for only $12 and the shop owner was trying to get his money back. To be honest, if you're stupid enough to sell something at the wrong price, surely you should be liable. But clearly not in this lawyer happy country. To make matters worse. The boy swapped the $12,000 card for a different one and its current whereabouts were a mystery.

Instead of service stations along the roadside, we started to see Native American reservations and their affiliated art and craft shops, which to be fair are little more than tourist traps. The impressive sounding Indian City consisted of nothing more than a couple of tacky shops, whilst other reservations had gigantic tepees and in one case plastic mountain goats. This may have been twinned with Milton Keynes.

Our food stop was at the impressive Fort Courage, home of the infamous F Troop in the 1960's comedy series. These days the fort houses a post office and a gift shop, whilst the connecting café sells Navajo Burgers, which turned out to be an interesting cross between a hamburger and a kebab. At least it made a change from McDonalds.

The Eastern borders of New Mexico, next to Texas had been sweltering under temperatures in the nineties for the past few days, but the further west we went, the more snow became visible on the mountain peaks.

As we reached Flagstaff, the depth of the snow became quite alarming and on getting off the bus there was a noticeable drop in temperature. The fact that there was about two inches of slush everywhere, didn't exactly do my shoes any good. It looks like I might have to clean them before trying to get a job in Australia. I asked the porter at the bus station for the directions to the hostel and we set off in completely the wrong direction. I don't think that Steve was too impressed.

Walking back in the direction of Albuquerque, was not a good move and probably finished off my shoes completely. Going back past the bus station, we headed into the small-town centre. Not too much to write home about, but I've seen worse.

Our first port of call was the Tourist Information Centre where we booked a car for the following day's trip to The Grand Canyon. There were a few problems due to the short notice, but we did get a reasonable deal. It was hoped that we would find a couple of other people heading in the same direction. In any case, what else is there to do in Flagstaff? There were bus trips, but they left before the sun sets, which is one of the major attractions there.
We arrived at the hostel to find it unattended, hence we could not check in. Unfortunately, or fortunately, depending on which way you look at it, there was a bar directly below. Well, we didn't exactly feel like carrying our rucksacks any further, so Steve had a couple of cokes as he had to pick the car up, and I spotted some bottles of Sam Smiths on the shelf. Suddenly, America seemed OK again. It was about an hour before the hostel opened, so we had a couple of drinks and a few games of pool.

The hostel rooms were not too bad and actually had an en suite bathroom. Almost inevitably, I ended up in the top bunk which seemed about two feet wide at most. It's a good job I'm not a restless sleeper really. There was supposedly free coffee here, but on every occasion, I went to get some, somebody had just had the last cup.

We are sharing a room with a group of Americans and Olaf, a Swiss guy, basically doing what we are doing. He seems nice enough and wants to come with us in the car tomorrow. Steve also met an Australian guy called Simon, who will come along too. It should prove to be a fairly cheap day.

Despite the tropical conditions a hundred miles or so to the South, it was exceptionally cold this evening. We went to look for something to eat at about seven and temperatures had started to plummet. What bars there were got vetoed because Steve thought they were too rough. No worse than The Junction Tavern in Raynes Park as far as I was concerned, but whatever. Most of the places to eat were shut, whilst those that were open were too expensive or unappetising. Whereas earlier, we had ended up in the bar below the hostel, this time we ended up in its affiliated restaurant called Charly's. The food wasn't expensive, and the Chicken teriyaki Salad was extremely nice. As was the Anchor Steam Bitter which for once was sold by the pint.

By about 10 pm, we decided to call it a night and prepare for our trip to The Grand Canyon in the morning.

Friday March 8th   Flagstaff

A trip to The Grand Canyon is always going to be a highlight of a holiday in America. To say that this was memorable would be an understatement.

It was a fairly tame start to the day. We picked up our packed lunches from the hostel reception that we had ordered the previous night. These weren't great value for money but were probably cheaper than anything you can buy at the Canyon.

The four of us sat downstairs and waited for our car to arrive. A fairly modern vehicle turned up and quite an attractive young lady got out and whisked Steve off to the parking lot to pick up our car.

Five minutes passed, then ten and then fifteen before he came back. Naturally he had got lost between the parking lot and the hostel. It was not the cleanest car I've ever seen and as it was supposedly white, it stood out a bit from everyone else's.

The other problem was that the previous driver had not exactly filled up the tank with petrol. We presumed this wouldn't be too difficult to rectify and we would be able to fill up on the highway after we got out of Flagstaff. We took Route 180, which was supposedly more scenic than the main highway, as it went through the heart of Kaibab National Forest.

It was very pretty indeed, unfortunately there weren't too many petrol stations though. In fact, there weren't any buildings, full stop. After about an hour of travelling on fumes alone, hoping that the petrol gauge was faulty and only having Chris Isaak or Wilson Phillips on the radio for comfort, we finally came to Bedrock Junction. So called because of the giant cardboard cut-outs of Fred Flintstone and Barney Rubble that adorned the playground (which was incidentally shut) opposite.

Thankfully we managed to fill up with petrol and headed on to the entrance of The National Park, which was about thirty miles further down the road.
At the entrance to the park is the airfield and helipad where you can take expensive flights around the area. There is also what appears to be an unimpressive copy of Spaceship Earth from the Epcot Centre in Orlando, which houses a film show about The Canyon. Can't say I saw anyone go in there or hear of anyone doing so either. Why watch a film when the real thing is a few yards away? There is really no indication as to what lies behind the trees as you drive through the woodland, that shrouds the abyss. You get the occasional glimpse of the far rim, but nothing to suggest how vast it really is.

We parked the car in the car park at The Visitors Centre and rather embarrassed by the state of it, began to walk off. That is Olaf, Simon and I walked off. Unfortunately for Steve, he couldn't get the key out of the ignition. Luckily, before we all had to draw lots to see who stayed with the car, I came up with some divine inspiration, and pointed out that it might help if the automatic gear box was put in neutral. Brilliant! Not bad seeing I'd never driven an automatic before.

The visitor's centre was well worth a visit and had not just an interesting museum, but also a free newspaper which had some useful directions to viewpoints and what time the sun was going to set.

Our aim was to walk down as far as we could in the time available and then find a good spot to watch the sun go down, So much for plans!

We walked off in the direction of The Bright Angel Lodge, where the trail begins. The initial view of The Canyon is something that is likely to remain in my memory forever. You cannot envisage how vast it really is, and no pictures nor descriptions could ever do it justice. The US President, who on seeing the sight for the first time and exclaiming "My this truly is a Grand Canyon" cannot have been one of the greatest orators to hold that position. Most people we saw were more forthright. Mind you, the "F*** me it's bloody massive canyon, doesn't quite have the same ring to it I suppose.
Whereas much of what we've come across in America has been totally tourist friendly and everything that can possibly be done to make your stay more pleasant or interesting, normally to the extent of annoyance, is carried out, I was pleasantly surprised that this was not the case here. The Canyon doesn't need such superficial distractions as the views are so spectacular.

The weather was not exactly warm, but the sky was clear and the air crisp. In fact, conditions were perfect for a long walk. There was only one problem. The recent snowfalls and freezing temperatures had resulted in the first three to four hundred yards of the descent being transformed into an ice rink. Unless you had the correct footwear or were plain suicidal, there was no way you could safely go down. Steve and I, both sporting old pairs of trainers, with little in the way of grip, managed to get about three quarters of the way to the end of the ice, but were then faced with a corner of what looked like black ice. Many people were turning back at this stage and only those who came prepared looked comfortable in circum navigating the problem. Having said that, those who were coming up from the bottom couldn't care less, as they were hardly going to turn back.

The fact that there was nothing between you and the 12 second tour to the bottom, was enough for us. A few idiots tried and slipped over, clinging frantically to the rock at the side of the path. Some used their rucksacks as sleds and one man was just standing there frozen in fear, too scared to go any further and having realised what he had already walked over, too scared to go back up again.

Simon and Olaf had the right footwear and carried on. Steve, being the good Samaritan that he is, said to the man who couldn't move that we'd give him a hand. He then proceeded to head back up the bath and take photographs of me carrying the guy's rucksack, I don't think I have ever seen anyone as frightened as he was at that moment and hope I never get to that stage myself.

Continuing up the hill, passing a squirrel which seemed oblivious to the conditions, we came across a couple from New Zealand who had taken a coach trip over from California to see the canyon.

They were taking a leisurely stroll back to the bus stop when it was pointed out to them that Arizona was in a different time zone and instead of them having an hour to get back, they had about 30 seconds and around a hundred yards of ice to run over before they got left behind.

We were quite thankful that we had a car at this point as if we had come by bus, it would have been a total disaster. First things first, we had our packed lunch. Around a minute later we set off again!

On the way back to the car park, we investigated the railway station. This has been restored and there is now a steam train that runs daily between The Grand Canyon and Williams, Nevada. If we had been on a better budget, this would have been a good option, but if you wanted to walk to the bottom, you would have to be prepared to stay overnight. Still, it was better than Amtrak I suppose, and I have to say, I saw more trains in one day in Flagstaff than I've seen in four weeks in America.

Back in the car, we stopped at most of the major viewpoints, which all tend to be similar. The exception being at The Eastern end of The Canyon where you can see out to The Painted Desert and Wilson Mountain, which seemed like a giant flat mound.

We met the others around 4pm who confirmed that once you had got across the corner of ice, it was plain sailing to the bottom of the Canyon. We drove to Hopi Point, in order to see the sunset. Along with Ayers Rock in Australia, I suppose this has to be one of the places in the world to watch the sun go down. The expected changes of colour were not that spectacular, in fact I was more impressed by the view of The Colorado River, carving its way through the foot of the Canyon. At the bottom it is 40 metres wide, but from here it looked like a stream. My abiding memory of the sunset at The Grand Canyon was how cold it was. We were all rather glad to get back in the car again.

If only to prove how much we love to live dangerously, we had another exciting journey back to Flagstaff. We actually thought little of the fact that the petrol gauge was getting precariously low again, as we knew that Bedrock Junction was only a few miles away. Panic set in when the petrol station was shut! We knew that there was nothing on the road we came along in the morning, so we had no other option but to go back another way. Once more we were travelling on a wing and a prayer, and on borrowed time by the time we finally came across a petrol station. The following scene warrants a detailed description.

For starters it was dark and there was a distinct lack of street lighting. The garage was on the opposite side of the road and to be fair, none of us could actually see how to get into it. Steve aimed for what looked like a possible entrance, only to find that we were travelling over grass instead of road. This rather rude entrance must have caught the eye of the owner. Steve got out of the car and firstly seemed to have trouble with the petrol cap. Then he couldn't get the pump to work and stood there bemused. As though from a scene out of "The Great Escape", floodlights came on and a loud voice boomed over the p.a. system, asking what exactly he was trying to do. A rather exasperated voice gave directions on how to fill the car up with petrol, and eventually we were back on our way. Well, we tried. We couldn't find the exit either and left the same way that we came in across the guy's garden.

Back at the hostel, we went to Charly's again for dinner, this time bringing Olaf to try the Anchor Steam Beer.

Saturday March 9th   Flagstaff to Las Vegas

Our bus didn't leave until late afternoon, but as the car had to be back by 9.30, we decided to save a bit of energy by taking our luggage to the bus station and checking it in.

Steve got visibly excited as we left the hostel as there were two girls struggling with their luggage. Before he could offer them a lift, they had got into their own car and driven off. Instead, we were followed by a rather large Alsatian dog, which probably summed matters up. The dog seemed to think it was coming with us and was rather difficult to get rid of, but by the time we got out of the car lot, it had adopted somebody else.

After getting rid of the car, we went for breakfast at Ernesto's, which was about fifty yards from the bus station. A very nice fried breakfast spent reading the paper and as with most food here, it seemed good value and quality.

To be honest, there isn't much to do in Flagstaff itself. The Museum of Arizona was shut, so I'm afraid it was the shops. Yes, Steve did find a record shop and picked up some bargains. A couple of Fairport Convention promos spring readily to mind, as does the hitherto unknown Bruce Springsteen single he found. His face was a picture when it was pointed out it was actually by Bruce Springstone and taken from The Flintstones movie.

With nothing better to do and especially after a rather disgusting hamburger on the outskirts of town, it was back to the hostel bar, the pool table, and the Sam Smiths. This bar had the only gents' toilet where the queue was as long as the ladies toilet. This was due to the urinals being in full view of the entire bar, therefore everybody had to go to the one cubicle.

Back to the bus station, where we first met Simon and then Olaf, both of whom had come to similar conclusions about Flagstaff. Simon was heading north to Colorado, but Olaf was heading in our direction, and it looked like a big night out at the casinos was on the cards.

The characters on the bus once more proved to be a complete cross section of the lowest echelons of US society. Pride of place went to two Native Americans, both rather the worse for drink. One did us all a favour and passed out; his comrade, however, was less thoughtful.

He insisted on trying to tell everyone that he was a marine on his way back from The Gulf., which surprised me on several counts. Firstly, the conflict had only ended a couple of days earlier and it seemed unlikely that he could have got back so quickly.

Secondly, his shoulder length hair seemed to suggest that standards must have fallen appreciably in the US Marines. I don't think the war hero bit impressed many people, there were no great whoops of delight for this GI, nor was there a ticker tape parade down the aisle of the bus during his frequent trips to the toilet, sorry, restroom. Soon he began to pick on someone his own mental age and started to recite the ABC with a child, sitting across the aisle. This was followed by a thousand (at least it seemed that many) renditions of Twinkle, Twinkle Little Star. It came as a great relief when he finally passed out too.

Route 66 clearly had this effect on quite a few people, and I certainly wasn't getting any kicks out of it.

The scenery along the way was interesting, being the first time I had experienced a desert. It was very arid and strangely beautiful. It's a shame our bus was so late leaving Flagstaff, as it was dark too early, and we missed a lot of stunning scenery I am sure.

Before Las Vegas, you hit the town of Laughlin. I say hit as there is really no other way to describe it. One minute you are travelling through some of the most barren terrain on the continent and then there it is. A palace of lights, an oasis of water and a collection of extremely high-class hotels and casinos. I couldn't help comparing this to the country as a whole. One minute there is nothing and before you know it, there is this brash, colourful land. Las Vegas appears in a very similar manner, however due to some outskirts to the city, it isn't so instant. With Laughlin you're just there.

It was 9.30 pm before we arrived in Las Vegas and by the time we had phoned the hostel and caught a cab there, it was almost ten o'clock. The hostel was clearly a cheap motel in its former life and a far cry from most hotels in the area. Still Vegas is a night place, and you don't really come here to sleep.

Our main priority was to find some decent food and we were going to leave the serious gambling until the next day. However, there were plenty of special offers available at the hostel, with books of vouchers that gave you about $20 free play at certain casinos.

These offers seemed too good to miss, but needless to say, we didn't win anything. The five free spins on the one arm bandits had to be on certain machines and I fear it is very easy to be skeptical in these places as to whether you could ever possibly win.

We started off at Vegas World, a newly opened casino. The whole scene was visually vulgar really, but on the other hand, strangely compelling. The clientele of most of these places seem to be drawn from a large cross section. At the top of the scale are the big-time gamblers who throw money around with apparent ease, then the couples drawn from the middle classes or those on business trips, here to enjoy a playboy lifestyle for a couple of days and then there are the rows upon rows of ordinary Americans, sitting in machine like fashion, feeding the hungry fruit machines. Some may come away with a profit, one or two may strike it lucky but most will squander away money they can ill afford to. I could not live in Vegas; the temptation is there 24 hours a day and there is little else to do but throw your money away. Enough of my morals, if you can't enjoy yourself here you probably can't anywhere.

In a couple of casinos, we came across newlywed couples who had made use of the number of 24-hour wedding chapels that are situated along the strip.

It was noticeable that most of the brides seemed to be very young and most of the grooms seemed to be close to retirement age. Obviously, the men had great personalities. I doubt whether our $20 maximum spend, over two days, was going to impress many girls here.

There are too many places to mention along the strip and it was getting extremely late. Probably the most impressive casino we saw tonight was Circus Circus, which actually had circus acts inside. Outside, a giant neon clown beckons you towards the illuminated big top. Once inside, it is a standard casino, except if you look up, there are trapeze artists and other acrobats.

There is little you can do to change the interior of a casino. The successful ones just seem to have certain gimmicks. The book of vouchers for Circus Circus gave you money off a large hot dog, which we accepted somewhat ravenously. As with most American hot dogs, it was quite vile.

We finally got what we were looking for at The Sahara casino. A steak dinner for $4. The prices here are just unreal. We missed most of the casino's food tonight, but tomorrow was going to be a different story.

Whereas the punters can be classified, the casino staff too are all very similar. The blackjack dealers all seem to be oriental and seem mortally offended if you take any money from them. The cocktail waitresses are all middle aged (that's polite) and made up to look as attractive as possible. In some cases, I fear they run out of Polyfilla.

By the time we had finished, it was 3 am and we made our way back to the hostel. We passed a record shop which was still open. The temptation was too much for Steve although nothing was acquired.

We left the shop and walked past a strange youth with long greasy hair with headphones on, shouting about death and destruction. This I presume is normal in Las Vegas.

Sunday March 10th   Las Vegas

What we had hoped would be a reasonable lie in this morning was somewhat ruined by a group of locals who we were sharing the room with. I try not to categorize people but why are there so many arrogant Americans, whose mouth is as big as their head. Most of these guys were in their early twenties and persisted in talking about what a wonderful life they were having in Vegas. Evidently, they were working, or at least trying to work as dealers in the casinos and this apparently resulted in them being invited to countless parties. One guy, always trying to go one step further than the last, was bragging how a forty-year-old woman took him to a party the previous night and she just happened to be filthy rich. This he saw as a career move. I would say pathetic, but I have to wonder what I would have done in a similar situation. In any case, what we didn't need were the graphic details of what she did to him. This guy was also the one who attempted to break the cultural barrier. No mean feat after we had only managed four hours sleep.

Steve and Olaf were fortunate in that their beds were not directly in the firing line, unfortunately I caught both barrels of crap. Evidently, it's very cool to come from Britain (or England as they persist in calling it), something I couldn't deny. He was also interested in "the land down under" as he had a little side-line going in precious stones. Evidently his idea of a good time was a holiday in Coober Pedy. I have to agree here, as my idea of a good time, at that moment, was seeing him under the ground! His parting shot was that he wanted to go to Europe next year and see The Parthenon in Rome. Good luck with that one, he may be looking for some time. After they had gone, we got up, spent about 30 seconds each in the shower, due to the infestation of cockroaches, and set off into town.

The Las Vegas shopping centre is probably unique. There aren't too many supermarkets here, but pawn brokers and gun shops seem to be quite popular. Bail shops also seem prevalent and it is clear that you can sell anything, in order to get out of any financial mess you may have found yourself in. The car lots offer some of the most amazing cars at the most unbelievable prices. Sports cars or enormous Cadillacs for ridiculously low prices. Clearly when things go wrong, some people have gambled their cars and, in many cases, things seem to have got worse. For travelers wanting to drive from the West Coast to the East Coast, it is often the case that people make their way to Vegas and pick up their vehicle from here. The only expensive things here are the fruit machines.

On past more wedding chapels, one with a sign outside boasting that Jon Bon Jovi had recently got married there, and then past the cheap hotels with neon signs stating their hourly rather daily rate, we arrived at more casinos.

Before the gambling started, we decided to have some breakfast. The choice is amazing. You pay a minimal set fee and then eat and eat and eat until you can't eat any more. Fruit salad to start and then a cooked meal and a dessert. Of course, the waitresses brought around complimentary champagne too. Steve must have felt guilty when they offered him a second glass as he said no. Unfortunately, he had elected himself spokesman for all three of us.

The rest of the morning and afternoon was spent exploring the casinos in the centre of town, away from the strip. Without exception, there were fairly unattractive women outside each one, trying to entice people in. The offers at this end of town were not as good as those on the strip. A free $10 on the slots or the chance of winning a glove for the one arm bandits was not that tempting. We took the free $10, and between the three of us, left with a $5 profit, which they weren't happy about.

We did have a go on the Blackjack tables. I was brave and went for the ones with a $2 stake. Steve stuck to the $1 table and then went back to putting his quarters in the slot machines. Somehow, I actually made a $25 profit.

One thing we didn't quite work out the previous night was the knack of getting free drinks. The fruit machines were clearly not good enough, but if you timed your run correctly, you could sit down at a card table, play one hand of cards, and get a free bottle of beer. As the day progressed, we got braver and started ordering brandies too.

We went back to the hostel before heading out in the evening, but as the room was pretty dire, we decided that the less time we spent there the better.

We started the evening off in Vegas World again, mainly because you could get your photograph taken alongside one million dollars. This seemed to be a good souvenir and was not only the only chance we'll ever have to get close to that amount of cash, but also the only thing we left the casino with. Yet another book of vouchers which seemed to disappear extremely quickly with no sign of a win. We were going to the larger casinos at the end of the strip tonight, but first of all, just in case we missed out, it was off to The Sahara for a buffet. I must inform you that once again, Olaf and I managed to consume an unthinkable amount of food. Steve actually left us in disgust, but I'm not sure whether that was due to the second main course or the third dessert. But for $5 for as much as you can eat, I was making up for lost time. Having said that, both Olaf and I found it difficult to walk back down the stairs and needed to sit down at a card table for a free beer to wash it all down.

We wandered (slowly) along the strip, past several smaller casinos. We stopped at The Morocco Café where Ron Hertzel was Elvis every night. We were tempted, but then discovered that "every night" did not include Sundays.

So, we marched into Stardust, the next big casino, where we lost more money and I lost quite a lot of my dinner, which I was now regretting.

On past the biggest gift shop in the world, which was suitably filled with the world's biggest pile of plastic junk, continuing past Showboat, a casino, illuminated to look like a gigantic paddle steamer, we finally came to Caesars Palace. A structure so totally out of this world that it all but defies description. A moving walkway transports you through a sea of fountains and marble statuettes, whilst Charlton Heston's voice welcomes you to the Palace. When you finally emerge into the main hall it is utterly stunning. There are still rows upon rows of card tables and slot machines, but the décor is totally over the top. There are two thrones overlooking the entrance, and Caesar and Cleopatra oversee proceedings from here when they are not taking a leisurely stroll around the casino. I actually met Caesar as he used the adjacent urinal in the loos. I am definitely on an upward curve. Having previously urinated next to Jonathan Ross at The Astoria Theatre and Mr. Wimpy at Wimpy in Piccadilly Circus, I decided that Caesar was a far more salubrious person to stand in a toilet next to.

Everything here was just so much bigger, including the stakes. There was one table where the minimum bet was $100, with punters not blinking an eyelid as their money went in the same way as everyone else's.

If you try and find a comparison to all of this in London, there really isn't anything that comes close. I suppose The Festival Hall lights up at night and there are a few neon lights around Soho and Leicester Square, but quite frankly, this place makes them look like a village hall.

Suitably impressed, but annoyed that there were no card tables with a minimum bet in our league, we moved on.

Next door is The Mirage, which actually manages to surpass Caesars Palace. After passing a cascading waterfall, you enter what could be described as Las Vegas' very own nature reserve. Here is a casino that has now taken away the prestigious boxing title fights from Caesars Palace, that boasts a dolphinarium, a pair of Siberian White Tigers and most amazing of all, a tropical rainforest that you can walk through if you get bored of gambling. As with Caesars Palace, it was well out of our league, but to actually witness such a monstrosity of bad taste had to be done.

In any other city, this would be seen as the ultimate in bad taste, but in Vegas, something will out do it within a year and then another and another.

We were now around two miles away from the hostel and it was well past 1 am. We decided that enough was enough and headed back. To be honest, we did call into another establishment on the way back to rest our feet and for a free beer.

It was 3 am when we got back again, and we had a car being delivered at 9 am. There are days I am glad I don't drive as Steve has to wake up and drive a couple of hundred miles through Death Valley tomorrow.

Monday March 11th   Las Vegas to Beatty

Budget Rent a Car arrived on time this morning in a minibus. A little worrying at first, I don't think Steve fancied driving a bus through the desert, however things were about to get worse for him.

We had to say goodbye to Olaf this morning, which was a shame, as he was a genuinely nice guy, He was off to San Diego and then LA before going back to Switzerland.

We had booked an economy car. It was a brilliant deal really. $30 per day and unlimited mileage, Basically, Budget had to get the car to Reno, and we had 48 hours to get it there for them.

When we were presented with our vehicle, Steve's face was a picture. "I'm not driving that" was the initial reaction and to be honest, I wasn't totally convinced he was capable of driving something more akin to a chieftain tank than his old car at home. Here was a top of the range town car, all mod cons and about ten feet long. Steve has enough trouble in car parks at home, this promised to be amusing.

One wonders how the Budget staff must have felt with Steve virtually going from right to left across the dashboard, asking what everything did and then culminating in asking where the ignition was. They insisted that they had nothing smaller, so off we went, with me trying to concentrate on the map as it meant I didn't have to look out of the window.

Once Steve had got the hang of things it was fairly luxurious. Set on cruise control, you hardly had to touch the controls and you could play with the built in computers which gave you the temperature both inside and outside of the car, the distance you had travelled and the distance to your destination plus, most importantly after the Grand Canyon debacle, how long until we ran out of petrol.

Leaving Las Vegas, you come to Red Rocks Canyon, a barren wasteland typical of Nevada. I'm glad we arrived in Vegas at night, but equally glad we left in daylight. It makes you wonder how a city can survive in such a void of emptiness. It truly is amazing.

The rest of Southern Nevada is really one big wasteland. We stopped at the only town of any significance, a rather small place named Pahrump, which personally reminded me more of the sound emitted after eating a large plate of baked beans. To be fair, Pahrump, despite the large sign proclaiming that Jesus is Lord over Pahrump, is about as welcoming as a wet fart.

We went for breakfast at Archie's, a pretty grotty burger joint that's only claim to fame was that it offered a Pahrump Burger on its menu. For fear of cracking up when ordering it I ordered a cheeseburger. But then we delved into the possibilities of what could actually be in a Pahrump burger. I think the combination of baked beans, sprouts, spinach, and Quorn won the day.

There was nothing to see in Pahrump, in fact I found it quite worrying that people actually chose to live there. So, we headed off in the direction of Death Valley. Before we got there though there was one important stop. The petrol station, where we not only filled the car up but stocked up on bottled water and more importantly, sweets.

Admittedly, it was quite cool burning up a few hillbillies in their trucks as we flew along in our mean machine. Once into the valley and away from other cars, we stopped and got out. Well, I'll admit I made Steve get out first to check for rattlesnakes. It was totally eerie. High mountains on either side and miles upon miles of nothing. No life and no sound. Total peace but hardly tranquil.

As you get into the heart of the valley, the rocks and the sand on the surface make way for salt flats. A totally arid phenomenon. Close at hand, the rough forms are peculiarly striking, but bloody uncomfortable to walk on. From a distance, the area appeared to be a hazy sea of white. It's easy to see how early settlers struggling through the desert would mistake these salt flats for water. You can't imagine how distressing that must have felt.

At the lowest point, Badwater, there is a very small lake. A saltwater lake, even more disheartening.

The really remarkable thing here is that lifeforms, unique to the area, live in the water. Only small insect like creatures, but these are possibly the closest living organisms to what was the first life on earth. Further along at Salt Creek, there is a school of pupfish, again, unique to the region.

The Visitor Centre at Furnace Creek, where we had to pay, had some fascinating displays on the area. The history of the early settlers who made it, or failed to make it, across the valley and also a display of the wildlife native to the area. At least I now knew, or more importantly, Steve knew, what sidewinder tracks looked like. Again, it surprised me that people actually lived in such a place. I always thought that Americans were a bit mental, but who in their right mind could possibly want to live in a hellish place such as Furnace Creek?

Other places of note in the Valley were Artists Palette, an area of rock that is covered by various natural mineral deposits, giving a multi colourful display that I have never seen anywhere else in the world. The Devil's Golf Course is a vast salt flat that you can walk across, but how anyone could possibly conceive a resemblance to a golf course is quite beyond me. We didn't get to Dante's View, but you can easily see the possibilities Dante may have come up with if he had his vision of Hell from here.

We drove out through Mud Canyon, which was fairly unimpressive in comparison and before dusk managed to get to Rhyolite, a ghost town, deserted at the start of the 20th Century. Not quite what my mental image of a ghost town was, which in my mind harkened back to the days of The Wild West. The presence of streetlights, a petrol station and concrete footpaths shattered my illusions. Personally, I hope of sudden of wave of common sense hit the area and the citizens of Rhyolite realised that there was nothing there and their life would be better in LA or San Francisco.

A couple of miles away is the small town of Beatty, which boasts three casinos, a few houses, a motel, and a Post Office. After a long day at the wheel, Steve decided that we should stop and stay the night at The Beatty Motel.

A little more expensive than what we would normally have gone for, but there wasn't exactly a lot of choice. It certainly looked cool, turning up in our limo. I'm sure the locals were impressed until they saw us get out of the car. They were probably less impressed by our inability to open our room door, despite having the correct key. We both tried and failed, but naturally the woman on the front desk had no problem whatsoever.

We ended up in all three casinos and needless to say I managed to lose in each of them. We had a reasonably priced 3 course meal in the casino next to the motel, called The Exchange Club. It was also a bonus to be given free beer on the 25 cents one arm bandits. The casinos here were in a different league, with dealers twiddling their thumbs, looking for enough punters and no bright lights outside. Just a dark road with large dark shadows from the mountains gracing the ground and the distant howling of coyotes. Strangely peaceful.

We went back to our room and made up for lost time by catching up on The Home Shopping Club on the television.

Tuesday March 12th   Beatty to Yerington

The plan today was to set off by ten o'clock and take our time driving to Reno, for one last night in the casinos and possibly taking in Lake Tahoe on the way.

Unfortunately, the distractions of watching The Home Shopping Club from the comfort of our beds resulted in a slightly later start and it was nearer eleven before we hit the road. As there was nowhere in Beatty for breakfast, we decided to stop at the first place we came across.

Two hours later, by which time it was lunchtime, we were still looking for somewhere. The mining towns that grace the mid Nevada region are not the most welcoming places I have ever seen, and, in the end, we just said we would stop in the next town, come what may.

That honour went to the town of Goldfield, which quite frankly had no more to offer than any of the other places we had driven through. The shops, well at least the ones that hadn't shut down, seemed to mostly comprise of what Americans seem to refer to as antique shops, but what most Brits would probably regard as junk shops. I can honestly say, I have never seen such a pile of old tat anywhere in the world.

We decided to eat at The Mozart Club. Not because it looked inviting, not because of the skeleton painted on the outside wall but because there wasn't anywhere else. We plumped for a Mozart Burger, which although very tasty, does not take the silly burger title away from The Pahrump burger. I defy anyone to beat that.

The waitress managed to continue the butcherism of the English language and poor old Amadeus would be turning in his grave if he had heard her pronunciation of Mozart. We stuck to our guns and pronounced it as per The Oxford English Dictionary, only to get blank stares from the waitress. In the end we pointed rather than stoop to their level.

We managed to avoid the temptation of the poker machines in the corner, where locals were squandering their money. Not that there seemed anything else to squander it on in Goldfield.

The afternoon consisted of trying to find the quickest route to Reno, passing through Mina, Coaldale, and Luning, three of the most disgusting, downtrodden hell holes I have ever seen. Well, that was the plan.

In the middle of nowhere, on top of a hill and in what happened to be a military base during The Gulf War, Steve started to pull over to the side of the road. Disaster had struck and the wonderful car with so many modern gadgets, had apparently short circuited itself. At first, I thought he was messing about. However, five minutes later, when we were still there, any sound that the car was making sounded very sick and an extremely low naval helicopter had skimmed the road, I decided that this was not the case.

Unfortunately, my knowledge of cars doesn't even extend to being able to drive one, whilst Steve had his car for over a year before he realised, he had a spare tire and his tool kit only ever consisted of a hammer. Not that we even had a hammer, but somehow, I don't think Budget would take too kindly to us knocking the engine about. To make matters worse, I was now suffering from a severe headache.

This road was not exactly the M1, and it was quite some time before we saw any other form of life. They drove straight past.
Despite us having the bonnet up and both of us standing around at least trying to look as though we knew what we were doing.

The last town we had passed was about twenty miles back down the road and it seemed pointless in backtracking, Thankfully, before we started walking off into the desert, a Ranger passed in the opposite direction and pulled over. Attempts to stimulate our vehicle were pointless as it was as dead as the proverbial dodo. There was nothing else to do but abandon ship and get a lift to Yerington, another Nevada town with a couple of casinos and a motel.

The ranger dropped us off and Steve went into one of the casinos to phone Budget in Las Vegas. I stayed with the luggage and finally got the chance to take something for my headache. Unfortunately, the staff at Budget were not exactly helpful and seemed more concerned that they had heard reports from the police that their car had been abandoned in the middle of nowhere. It took some time to persuade them that we were not prepared to settle in Yerington and would like a replacement car. In fact, we had to arrange all of this via the reno office, which took even longer.

Eventually we checked in at The Casino West Motel and while we were enjoying dinner at the casino and a few drinks at the bar (and yes, we lost some money on the blackjack tables), Budget deposited a new car outside of our room and presumably picked up the other car from where we had left it.

In fact, we had a fair bit to drink that night and were quite drunk as we headed to our room. The highlight of the evening was discovering that our new vehicle, which was much more our size, had automatic seatbelts that trapped you when you shut the door. Frightening at first (especially when you are drunk), but quite a good laugh when you're used to them.

After playing with these for about ten minutes, we went inside and tried the TV, only to find we had the limited choice of a documentary on Led Zeppelin or an early episode of Star Trek. No contest. Steve went to sleep, and I boldly went where no man has gone before.

Wednesday March 13th   **Yerington to San Francisco**

Things were always going to be a bit rushed this morning. We had envisaged that we would be in Reno already and there would be no problem in catching the 1pm bus. We still had a good three hours of driving ahead of us and had to drop the car off too.

Things were not helped by the fact that I was holding the map the wrong way and we headed out of Yerington via the scenic route. The mountains were very pretty, and the snow made them quite spectacular, but I don't think Steve appreciated the fact.

The highlight of the journey, apart from breakfast at McDonalds again, was our vain attempt to spot The Ponderosa Ranch, famed from the days of The High Chaparral. Despite signs along the road of Hoss and the boys, we failed miserably. We did spot Bonanza Street and Virginian Road, but that was it.

We actually arrived in Reno in plenty of time, found the car lot straight away and got a free lift to the bus station. We had an hour to kill before our bus left, so we went to a casino for a change.

Reno seems to be a smaller version of Las Vegas with branches of Circus Circus and other Vegas casinos. It is a shame we didn't get here the previous night as planned, as it looked a lot more fun than Yerington.

Rather than lose any more money, we just had something to eat. A very nice plateful of liver and onions for $3 and I beer that we had to pay for. Clearly, they weren't as generous here as they were in Vegas.

Back to the bus station and our bus to San Francisco. Enter the next contender for The Greyhound Bus Hall of fame. "Good afternoon, I'm Igor and I will be taking you in to the snow zone." A novel introduction, and true enough, once we got into the mountains, the snow was pretty bad, but the warnings, especially the one concerning children's ears popping at altitude, were a little excessive, if not theatrical. In fact, the journey was so frightening I slept through much of it.

The only passengers of note were an elderly British couple who insisted on transporting their extremely large suitcase inside the bus, rather than down below, with everybody else's. In fact, the gentleman was lucky to leave Reno in one piece after attempting to put the case in the rack above the seats. There was no way that this was going to fit, and the rest of the passengers were wincing, expecting him to be crushed at any moment. It finally sunk in, and he was forced to leave it in the aisle for the entire trip to San Francisco. This gave birth to much merriment as people tried to circumnavigate the large object in order to get to the restroom.

The other highlight of the trip was passing through customs on the Californian border. Evidently it is an offence to take fruit and vegetables over state lines. An interesting concept but I can't see us stopping the Welsh at The Severn Bridge and frisking them for leeks.

First impressions of San Francisco from the bus were good. The bay looks very spectacular, and this was enhanced as we arrived by the sun beginning to set.

Before reaching San Francisco, you pass through Oakland which was still rebuilding from the earthquake in 1989. Going over The Oakland Bridge you get some breath-taking views of the bay.

We were met at the bus station by Rod, another of Steve's Father's associates. He picked us up and drove us back to his house in The Castro Region of town. This area is renowned as the gay area of San Francisco, and to be fair, there were some pretty colourful individuals hanging around. Steve decided he felt safer in our room. Rod seems very easy going and basically, we can do what we want and are not expected for meals. It was nice being looked after in Toronto and Bel Air, but this seems a far better arrangement as we can do what we want, when we want.

It was too late to go anywhere this evening, and to be honest, I'm not sure Steve thought it was safe to go out here after dark in case some guy fancied him. So, we ordered pizza to be delivered and watched some TV, before falling asleep.

Thursday March 14th   San Francisco

Travelling seems to be taking its toll and once again, neither of us could be bothered to get up and go sightseeing at the crack of dawn. I eventually got up around 9.30 and went to do my washing, only to be confronted by George the dog and Alice the cat. George, I fear is in for a hard time as both Steve and I seem to be doing Zippy from Rainbow impersonations in front of him.

We went out around eleven and wandered down to the nearest subway station. We passed several somewhat colourful characters on the way and outside of the station was a man with a large moustache, wearing a very tight pair of leather shorts. Forgetting what had happened the last time we were on a San Francisco tram at the Earthquake ride at Universal Studios, we hurried down the stairs.

We got off at the Bay area of town and after dodging the waves of joggers hurtling along the footpath, we began to make our way along the road. We were looking for somewhere to have lunch, but one of us always seemed to veto the others' choice. We finally stopped at a sandwich bar, which once again had some strange looking people in it.

We went to Alcatraz this afternoon. Red and White Tours run several trips each day to the island prison, and we went for the audio tour which cost a couple of dollars extra but allowed you to have a Walkman and listen to a tape of ex-cons tell you what life was like when the prison was still in use.

The actual crossing was memorable in itself in that it was not the calmest of days. Being brave, we sat outside, but the force ten gale and severity of the wavers put most of the other passengers off this idea. You actually get some good views of the city, plus The Oakland and Golden Gate Bridges from the ferry and today you also got some fairly interesting angles.

One strange point to note was a Japanese gentleman going mad with his camera beside the boat before we got onboard. Either he was a tourist who's completely flipped, or he was up to something. The tour of the cells and the stories of Al Capone, Machine Gun Kelly and the infamous Birdman of Alcatraz, Robert Stroud, were fascinating and it was much better listening to the tape rather than using a guidebook.

You get to see most of the prison, including the cells, dining area, showers, hospital, and recreation area, all of which have their own tale to tell. The views across to the city were very pleasant. This, I am sure, made it ten times worse for the inmates and despite its reputation for being impossible to escape from, it is perhaps surprising that only 36 tried.

Of those, 31 failed and the other 5 have never been heard of since. The audio and the visual presentation of the escape attempts were brilliant, as was the riot scenario. One wonders if somewhere like Broadmoor ever shuts down, whether the British Government would have the nerve to open it up to the public and declare it a National Park. I'm not convinced that they would.

There was also a slideshow that you can watch, which outlines the takeover of Alcatraz Island by Native Americans, who claimed it back as their own. The whole presentation of Alcatraz was very impressive, and I'm pleased to report that the waters were a bit calmer on the way back.

Lo and behold, when we got off the boat, there was the strange Japanese gentleman with a photograph of everyone who went over to the island. A perfect souvenir? Well, if sales are anything to go by, clearly not.

We had a browse around some of the gift shops around the wharf before making our way back to the city. As with most American cities, San Francisco is divided up into various ethnic areas. We walked through the Italian district, where we stopped for coffee and an expensive piece of chocolate cake in a trendy café, before heading to Chinatown. San Francisco's Chinatown is a little different from the excuse of one we have backing on to Leicester Square. In comparison it covers a vast area, and the shops and restaurants are all much more interesting. Admittedly, there is a Chinese community in London, but it's not as exclusively Chinese as this one. It is vastly different.

Cutting across California Street, we caught our first glimpse of the famous San Francisco cable cars, which seem very popular, due to the intense gradients of the hills here. Being real men, and tight, we walked up.

The financial district is similar to many US cities in that it is graced by numerous skyscrapers. The one building that San Francisco can boast is different is The Trans America Pyramid. A strange, triangular structure that towers above the rest and culminates in, as its name suggests, a pointed summit. Not quite The Giza Plateau, but still quite impressive.

We were heading for a bar recommended by our guidebook, which supposedly had cheap food and a good beer selection. That was until I suddenly had a vision from God! There we were, miles from home, and there was a pub with a Fullers sign on it. I now know what those pioneers must have felt like after days in the desert without water and finally coming across an oasis.

Steve picked me up off the floor and then had to run after me as I headed for this divine vision.

The Edinburgh Castle, at 950 Geary Street, despite having a Fullers sign (i.e., from Chiswick) is in fact a Scottish pub. This was getting better by the minute, and it was almost the best of both worlds as they had Fullers ESB and McEwan's extra on draught. I even excused them for spelling McEwan's with a K. This was a truly wonderful place, even though there wasn't a Scotsman in sight. It sold fish and chips wrapped in newspaper at a reasonable price and the jukebox had a vast selection of Scottish songs. Strangely, nobody seemed to be using it, but we couldn't resist. Steve, rather bravely for this city, put The Gay Gordons on whilst I had a burst of The Band of The Black Watch and Andy Stewart singing The Muckin O' Georgie's Byre, which I can guarantee nobody else knew the words to.

Steve had to forcibly remove me, kicking, and screaming from here, as we still had to get to Tommy's Joint, the bar recommended in our guidebook.

It was just down the road at 1101 Geary Street and despite its horrendously painted façade, was actually quite pleasant. My impressions of this city are improving by the minute, as following pints of ESB in the last pub, we now had bottles of Old Peculiar and Sam Smiths here. If this wasn't America, I could live here.

As a matter of fact, there were beers available from such wild and wonderful places as Peru and Papua New Guinea, however I knew my limitations and guessed they didn't extend that far.

The food was cheap too! The buffalo stew was delicious, a bit like strewing steak, but I did think that buffalo was an endangered species.

As we had entered the bar, there were two black guys begging for money. About 30 minutes later, one of them was sitting down to a steak dinner, far bigger than ours. I guess that's the American dream.

Friday March 15th   San Francisco

Yet another lie in this morning. Steve decided to do his washing whilst I stayed in bed watching The Home Shopping Club.
When we did finally go out, we wandered along Market Street, as opposed to catching the subway. Once again, the sidewalks were full of colourful individuals that Steve and I had no intention of going near.

As if by magic, we found another record shop and due to the amount of bargains Steve found, it looks as though I might be carrying some of his stock through customs in Australia. To be fair, he should make some money on most of these.

In fact, Steve was on a roll this morning as we popped into a library, and he actually found some Tooting football results that he had been looking for since we left the UK.

It was mid afternoon before we actually got to a tourist attraction. The cable car museum is no more than a terminus for The California Street Cars and there are a few displays and films you can watch around the main mechanics of the building. It is well presented and as it was free, so it was all good. It also served as a place to rest as you climb the impossibly steep hills around here. Still, we can't complain, we're only walking up because we are too tight to pay for a cable car. I suppose if we were looking for another reason as to why we were trying to kill ourselves on these hills, the views were amazing. From most side streets, the views over the bay and towards Alcatraz and The Golden Gate Bridge were quite stunning in places.

After reaching the summit, we turned towards the Bay and wandered back past Lombard Street, which is famous for its switchbacks. This would serve as a perfect instrument for traffic control at home, maybe I should contact The Met Police when we get back. The state of the road, however, did not stop a continual queue of traffic from proceeding along it, snaking through its twists and turns. Whether these drivers were tourists or just another group of irrational Americans I cannot say.

As we were taking photographs here, we were approached by an elderly American gentleman who persisted in telling us how he spent a week stationed in Britain during the last war. As with quite a number of locals, I found this person to be a bit odd. We told him that it was still foggy in London and made our excuses to leave. We made our way to Fisherman's Wharf for the second time. The first time having been in Universal Studios. Somehow the real thing didn't look as convincing.

There were a few rather tourist-oriented shops and eateries and also a sea lion in the water. The certainly didn't have a live seal at Universal Studios and it was drawing a rather large crowd and also making rather a lot of noise. The fact that all that could be seen was its head, didn't seem to deter anyone from taking photographs, but I fear there will be some rather boring snaps being developed over the next few days. Ours included.

Before the excitement really got to us, we decided to head off in the general direction of Columbus, to see if there were any good bars there. It must be said that San Francisco is rivalling Denver as the beer capital of America. After last night's treasure trove of a Fullers pub, today we found The San Francisco Brewing Company. A pub in the style of the Firkin pubs at home and it had a suitably fitting brew called Rambock. Although not as lethal as Firkin's Dogbolter or Draught Excluder, it was still somewhat more potent than what we have become accustomed to in the past few weeks.

Unfortunately, the waiter service was so diabolical, we had to approach the bar just like at home in order to get served. Because of this, we left after one pint, but I wouldn't write the place off, as with a decent waiter it could be quite good.

Food was next on our agenda and after actually finding somewhere decent in our guidebook the previous night, we tried again. Surprisingly it was another success with The Hunan Restaurant in Sansome Street. This was a relatively cheap Chinese restaurant and extremely tasty. It did take a bit of getting used to as in Britain we are used to Cantonese food, whilst in America they tend to have the much spicier Szechuan style of cooking. Due to the number of chilies in the food, we drank copious amounts of beer to cool us down.

Before spending too much on drink we headed back via the subway. The advertising down there left little to the imagination and left you in no doubt as to which group of people were being targeted. The aids prevention posters, proclaiming "Be a rubber man" with a rather well-built bloke dressed in skimpy rubber clothing is probably you wouldn't see on the London Underground.
In fact, our subway journey was a bit of a catastrophe, as we got on the wrong train and shot off down the wrong line. In searching for a correct station to board a train that would get us back to Castro, we ended…………………..

And that is where it ends. The last couple of the pages have not survived the 25 years since the trip and whereas I can't exactly remember how we got home that night, we clearly did.
The following day, Rod took us to Golden Gate Park and to some amazing viewpoints, overlooking The Golden Gate Bridge and the Pacific Ocean. We had a wonderful meal at a seafood restaurant and were then taken to the airport, where we checked in for the grueling transpacific flight to Sydney via Honolulu.

Printed in Great Britain
by Amazon